1987-88

THE
BEST PUBS
OF
GREAT
BRITAIN

FOURTEENTH EDITION

Edited by Neil Hanson

The East Woods Press
Charlotte, North Carolina

Contents

2

Editor: Neil Hanson. **Production Editor:** Jill Adam. **Breweries Section Editor:** Brian Glover. **Additional Research & Editorial:** Danny Blyth, Iain Dobson, Graham Lees, Denis Palmer, Les Pollard, Roger Protz, Jim Scanlon, Tim Webb. **Production Assistance:** Jo Bates, Sally Bennell, Carol Couch, Malcolm Harding. **Marketing:** John Dixon. **Cartoons & Illustrations:** Hector Breeze, Ken Pyne, Posy Simmonds (reprinted by permission of AD Peters & Co Ltd), Bill Tidy. **Maps:** Reginald & Marjorie Piggott. **Cover Design:** Cindy Kerr.

The editor gratefully acknowledges the help of several thousand CAMRA members in the compiling of the Good Beer Guide.

Library of Congress Number 86-46167
ISBN 0-88742-104-0

AMERICAN visitors to Britain who have not been deterred by the unlikely perils of Libyan terrorism have an additional peril to face—British beer! The image most Americans have of our national drink is that it is weak, warm, flat as last week's bathwater ... and just about as inviting. The strange thing is that once you have given our beer a fair chance, you tend to come away rather liking it.

You can't generalise too much about our beer, because wherever you are in Britain, there are different ones to try. Though, like the USA, we have a handful of giant companies trying to dominate the market, we also have a host of smaller companies ranging from breweries supplying 100 or so pubs, down to pubs brewing their own beer on the premises. As a result, British beers, like British pubs, are as different and full of character as the people who drink them.

It is true that our beer tends to be served warmer and flatter than beer in the US. This is partly because of custom, partly because of our not-always-excellent weather and partly because excessive cooling and carbonation kill the flavour and character of beer. If you're old enough to remember Britain during the Second World War, don't make the mistake of thinking that the weak, watery stuff that passed for beer then was typical.

While you're in Britain, you probably will hear a good deal of talk about "real ale" and you may wonder what on earth that is. Real ale is traditional British beer, brewed only from pure natural ingredients—malted barley, hops, yeast and pure water—and cask-conditioned (it continues to mature and improve in flavour in the pub cellar until the moment it is served, either straight from the cask or through the traditional hand-pump).

Our other type of beer we call "keg" or brewery-conditioned beer. It may be made from the same ingredients, but it usually has

PLEASE DO
NOT ASK
FOR SERVICE
AS A
REFUSAL
OFTEN OFFENDS

Ken Pyne

cheaper adjuncts replacing part of the barley malt and often has several chemical additives included. They are there to improve the eye appeal or shelf life of the product, but they do nothing for its taste. Before the beer leaves the brewery, it is chilled, filtered and pasteurised. It is kept under a blanket of carbon dioxide and served under CO_2 pressure. The result is beer that keeps well, but is cold, gassy and tasteless . . . just like a lot of American beer, in fact!

At its best, British beer has a character and flavour that compares with any in the world. If you want to try proper British beer— the real thing—avoid our keg beers and our fake "foreign" lagers (all brewed in Britain and about as foreign as fish and chips) and stick to real ale. Its flavour will shock you first, surprise you second, and may well finish up by delighting you. Wherever you go in Britain, you'll find new beers to enjoy. Each region has its own brewers and its own outstanding ales, but let me influence you a little.

Though there are well over 1000 different beers, there are four basic beer styles—mild, bitter, strong ale and stout. Mild refers to the flavour. Mild beers have less hops in them than the other styles so they are less bitter-tasting, although also usually weaker. While mild drinking is declining in Britain, it is still strong in the heartlands of the Midlands and the North West. Try a pint (or even two) of Thwaites rich, dark mild or Ansells or Banks's, frequent winners of the Best Mild award at the Campaign for Real Ale's annual Great British Beer Festival.

Bitter is the typical British beer, a bit stronger than mild, with the extra hop bitterness that gives the style its name. Every region has its own superb variations. Try to sample as many as you can of Adnams's, Bateman's, Brain's, Brakspear's, Donnington's, Fuller's, Holt's, Home's, Hook Norton's, Robinson's, Shepherd Neame's, Taylor's, Tetley's and Young's, and you'll be well on the way to understanding why the normally placid British can be roused to fury at threats to their traditional ales.

Further up the strength scale, although too potent for all-night sessions, are the best bitters. These include some of the finest British beers. Marstons Pedigree and my nominee as the best British beer of all, Timothy Taylors Landlord, are two that no serious student should miss.

At the top of the scale are the strong ales, brewed to mind-boggling alcoholic strength, often with a delicious flavour to match. Theakston's rich, dark Old Peculier (with its peculiar spelling) and Fuller's pale, hoppy ESB are the two leading examples of the genre, but nearly every small brewery has its own variant, often with outlandish, descriptive names such as Dogbolter or Moonraker. Silly young men often try to prove their manhood by drinking several pints of these strong ales; unless you, too, want to end your evening in the horizontal position, approach with care!

The last of the great beer styles is stout, synonymous to most British people with Guinness, black as night, bitter as a Chicago winter and one of the world's great beers. "Proper" Guinness is available only on draught in Ireland. British drinkers consume an imitation of the real stuff. Either stick to bottled (bottle-conditioned) Guinness or try two of the refreshing British alternatives, Timothy Taylor's Porter or Strathalbyn's superlative Beardmore Stout.

This quick tour of the beers of the British Isles should be enough to get you started. The true joy is in making your own discoveries . . . round every bend in the road there could be another superb pub with a range of distinctive local beers to offer. If you're not sure what to try, ask the landlord. If his pub is in this book, it means he takes a pride in his beer and should be pleased to offer some advice.

Delicious as our beer can be, it wouldn't be half the drink without our pubs in which to drink it. British pubs have evolved over thousands of years, and they have always been at the heart of our

"THE GUIDE SAYS THAT IT'S 'A QUIET UNSPOILT GEM OFF THE BEATEN TRACK'"

social life. No one can define what makes a good British pub something special, while anywhere else, it might be just a bar. There's a wealth of tradition, a character and an atmosphere in a good pub that can't be pinned down—it should just be enjoyed!

One warning before I leave you: Britain's licensing magistrates have not yet discovered that the First World War has ended. As a result, pubs in England and Wales are still controlled by laws introduced in 1915 to stop munitions workers spending too much time in the pub. Scotland and Ireland are relatively civilised, but in England and Wales, all pubs close for at least two hours in the afternoon, and evening closing time is either 10:30 or 11. Once the landlord has called "Time" you are allowed ten minutes to finish your drink. Luckily, not all licensees enforce this law with the energy our magistrates would no doubt like to see, especially in country areas.

In the following pages you'll find well over 5000 examples of the Great British pub. If you don't manage to fit them all in this year, don't worry, you can always come back next year to visit the rest! Cheers and good hunting!

Neil Hanson

Not Waving . . .

IN the late 1930s George Orwell described for readers of the London Evening Standard his perfect pub. It was called the Moon Under Water. It was easy to get to but sufficiently off the beaten track to deter casual drunks. Regulars went to the Moon Under Water to enjoy its comfort, conviviality and good conversation. It had no fake inglenooks but in the years BF (Before Feminism) it boasted a barmaid of generously ample mien.

As his readers searched the piece for the location of the pub, Orwell doused their fervour with a pail of literary cold water. The Moon Under Water did not exist; probably, given Orwell's increasing pessimism about life in general, could not exist.

The search for the perfect pub remains, nonetheless, a popular pastime, one that is likely to remain as long as the pub itself. How often have you been seduced by an overheard conversation in the saloon bar: 'Found this fabulous pub on Sunday . . . just off the A6 . . . by the duckpond', followed by the directions with the aid of route map and torch and ended up in a brewer's recreation of a London Underground station in the rush hour?

It is an experience that suggests that no two drinkers will ever agree about what consti-tutes the perfect pub. The imperfect pub, however, is easier to pin down. Every big town or city has at least one barn-like building where the few regulars huddle forbiddingly at the bar, forming a human barrier to the unwary intruder. The guv'nor, an expired roll-up in the corner of his mouth, slowly turns his attention from the intellectual rigours of The Sun, gives you a baleful stare and grunts 'Yeah?' Nervous inquiry discovers that the draught bitter is off, the pub hasn't sold mild for 15 years and the guv'nor has never heard of White Shield. You settle for a bottle of Guinness which, when poured, shows evident signs of having failed to renew its BUPA subscription.

The country pub, far from being a haven of cheer, can be as equally uninviting as a city boozer. That pleasant hum of conversation you heard as you approached the door ceases like a switched-off radio the moment you hover in the entrance. Every head turns in your direction and every eye strips you, monitors your bank balance and credit rating and scathingly notes your squeaky-clean green wellies. The word 'foreigner' hangs silently on every lip. You despatch your half of bitter with one gulp and leave. As the door crashes shut behind you that pleasant hum of conversation is instantly resumed.

The problem of the imperfect pub has been compounded in recent years by brewers engaging in what is known in the trade as the Instant Tart-up. Like a horde of locusts, carpenters and technicians descend on the quiet and unassuming local and within a few days have transformed it into the marketing department's notion of a modern pub that will attract extra 'traffic'. In the 1970s, tart-ups took the most hideous and bizarre forms. Pubs that had served their communities for decades with pleasure and lack of offence became, in the hands of brewery desperadoes, sputniks, pineapples, wild west saloons and even medieval torture chambers.

The extra traffic did not materialise. Now the emphasis is on 'tradition'. Fake beams, fake log fires and Orwell's detested fake inglenooks abound. Serving wenches leap on your empty glass while a bored-looking chef in traditional tall hat gives your meal a quick blast in a traditional, olde-English microwave.

The one item given scant attention is the traditional beer, overpriced, over-warm and over-age.

The mock-traditional revamp is popular with the big brewers. The regional companies that have the wherewithal to improve their houses tend to choose a style best described as Stripped Pine Modern. Spiky pot plants threaten to entangle you at every turn. Hanging baskets clunk the heads of the unwary and the over-tall. Lowered ceilings ensure that noxious nicotine fumes cause even greater distress to the hapless majority of non-smokers.

Even the exteriors of pubs are no longer sacrosanct. They are sprouting strange bulges and protuberances, added-on conservatories that may well be known in the trade as 'forecourts' if the aim is to attract that extra traffic.

A Watney pub called the Sirloin in Chingford, on the Essex–London boundary, has a canopied entrance to one bar with the legend 'OTTs' on the front. OTT is Yuppy-speak for 'over the top'. The title not only sums up the tasteless and unnecessary addition but is also doubly appropriate as the pub in question is in the constituency of Mr Norman Tebbit.

Pubs should be left alone. Attempts to turn them into ersatz night clubs, bier kellers and bistros always fail because the extra trade they hope to attract is transient and fickle by nature. The real trade, the genuine trade made up of pub goers and pub devotees, does not want to see decades and even centuries of authentic tradition destroyed by ill-considered refashioning that not only destroys that tradition

Flowers only occasionally, mainly week-ends, Bank and school holidays... ...and sometimes at Midnight Mass, Dec 24, & Easter Day....

Needs babysitters (£2·00 an hour)

Needs grass mown (£5·00 an hour...)

Needs mail forwarding, meters read, an eye kept on the place...£20 p.w. ...

Burst pipes dealt with... £10 an hour.

Pick 'em for all they're worth!

Not Waving . . .

but rapidly becomes tatty and tawdry.

The perfect pub may be unattainable because perfection is such a subjective judgement. But certain ground rules can be established that will attempt to ensure that pubs are at least pleasant and inviting. The first and most important rule is that pubs should not be tampered with. Paint them, re-carpet them, bring the toilets up to the most exacting standards, even in extremis knock two small bars into one, but on no account meddle with the essential character of a pub, a character that has often been indelibly stamped on the community the pub serves.

In spite of all the hard blows, external and internal, suffered by the pub in recent years, there are still more than 60,000 of them attempting to cater for all tastes. Some of those tastes are odd, to say the least, and perhaps it is best that the Moon Under Water was an invention, for I shudder to think what might have become of it.

A few weeks before this piece was written I happened to be in the Red Lion in Southwold, Suffolk, home not only of Adnams' brewery but also, as a plaque in the high street testifies, home to George Orwell for a few years. The Red Lion is an excel- lent, unspoilt pub a few yards from the sea, with its long bar, mass of prints of old Southwold and the harsh urban voices of visitors softened by the soft sing-song tones of the locals.

I had lunched on fresh crab and salad and wandered outside with my pint to enjoy the sun when a large estate car pulled up outside and disgorged three snap-pily dressed couples. One of the men went inside the pub, mutter-ing about looking at the menu. He returned a few minutes later and summoned his friends back to the car.

'Don't do chips,' he grated. 'Let's go back to that pub we saw on the main road. I bet they do chips – and they might have some beer on.'

As the Red Lion is quintessen-tially a beer house, serving Adnams' mild, bitter and new strong ale, I could only assume that what the driver meant by 'beer' was the carbonated chemi-cal pap manufactured by Bart & Felch or another of the brewing conglomerates. No doubt they found their Eldorado. I watched them go, then went back into the pub, bought another pint and raised my glass in tribute to the Red Lion, the pub without chips. That must be as near to perfec-tion as you can get.

Roger Protz

MOST OF THE WORLD'S beers are brought to maturity at the brewery, and this has been so since the lagering techniques of Munich, Pilsen and Vienna swept across an industrially burgeoning Continental Europe in the mid 1800s. Only we happily insular British have continued on any scale to condition our draught beers in the cask—and therefore finally to bring them to maturity in the pub.

The care of the pub as an institution is, therefore, essential to the health of top-fermented, cask-conditioned draught ale as our distinctive national drink.

Though the British are by no means the world's biggest consumers in volume of beer, it is around the serving of our national drink that we have created a unique social phenomenon in the form of the pub. In top-fermented, cask-conditioned draught ale, we have a distinctive national beverage; in the pub, we have a unique social focus; the two phenomena go hand in hand.

The British Pub

THE PUB we are apt sometimes to take for granted. It may require a guest from overseas to remind us what a singular institution it is.

Visitors want to see a pub not for its superb variety of architectural and social manners but for its singularity. It contrives to remain a pub whether it is a thatched house in Hampshire or Wiltshire; a half-timbered hotel in Gloucestershire or Worcestershire, Shropshire or Cheshire; a Victorian or Edwardian landmark in urban Liverpool or Manchester; or just a functional and bare boozer in the Pennines or on the Tyne.

There is nothing more English than a pub. It is not an American bar, trying still to escape from the long shadow of Prohibition; not a French cafe, outside which to sit and sip aperitifs; not a Bavarian beer-hall, full of swaying and noise. The Germans have names for five or six different types of drinking place; we have the pub, by whatever colloquialism we choose to call it.

To define the pub in negative terms is easy; we know what it isn't. To define it in a positive manner is harder; we don't know, or cannot all agree, what it is or should be. A pub always stocks beer, and usually spirits, but it may also serve wines, and even mixed drinks. A pub is always a drinking place, but it may also serve as a restaurant or hotel. A pub usually accommodates conversation, but it may also be a venue for organised meetings, sports, music, or other entertainments. Perhaps the critical requirement is that these sideshows do not take over. The inns which presented plays in Shakespeare's time eventually begat the theatre. The Victorian pubs which presented variety eventually spawned the music-hall.

The Good Pub

IN A GOOD PUB, the greatest attention is given to the drink, and in particular to the beer. Sociability, on both sides of the bar, comes a close second. A good pub encourages social intercourse, and is not dominated by cliques. A good pub has a caring, responsive landlord, not an uninterested time-server or an arrogant buffoon. In a good pub, whatever further services are offered, there is always one bar (and preferably two) to accommodate those people who simply want to drink and chat without the distraction or inhibition induced by overbearing decor, noisy entertainment, or intrusive dining.

Hence the sometimes paranoid proclivity among CAMRA members for pubs which may seem bare and utilitarian. As in restaurants, so in pubs, the patron obsessed with the decor and the ambience can easily forget what he is really there for. Excessive interior design is apt to be a warning sign because it suggests that appearance has been put before performance, and this often turns out to be the case. On the other hand, a publican who cares about the beer he serves frequently turns out to be equally conscientious in the matter of wine, food and conversation.

The Old Pub

THE QUALITIES of the English pub were not devised by designers, marketing men, or even customers. They were made not to a grand design but by a long and slow process of evolution. For that continuity we probably have once again to thank our island history. The pub grew as an English tribal artifact through centuries when other national cultures in Europe were being dragged hither and thither by political tugs of war which pulled less violently on our shores.

This is not to deny that the pub has benefitted along with the rest of our culture from what might be termed ethnic accretion.

The Roman taverna foreshadowed the pub sign by hanging out a vine or evergreen to advertise its wares. The Saxons "gathered in their ale-houses to govern and adjudicate," according to a writer of the time. The abbey hospice for pilgrims introduced ecclesiastical motifs like the Angel, the Salutation and the Mitre. After the Reformation, inns run by the lay gentry metamorphosed the Pope's Head into the King's Head, the King's Arms or whatever.

The post-houses of the coaching era, the "coffee" houses of the late 1600s, the Hogarthian gin "shops" which grew up in the 1700s after the right to distill had been granted, the much more commercially ambitious gin "palaces" which emerged a century later to counter the Duke of Wellington's beer legislation, the beer houses, penny gaffs and purpose-built "hotels" of the industrial 1800s are all threads which time has woven into the fabric of the English pub.

The Victorian Pub

THE NOTION of the family house opened to the public for refreshment and sociability had long thrived, and is still evidenced in some bar-less country pubs, but the terminology itself is surprisingly recent. The term "public house" does not seem to have achieved recognition until 1854, when it was used by a House of Commons Select Committee.

Several other familiar ideas were introduced in the same period. The characteristic island-shaped bar of the large city-centre pub was devised by Brunel, originally to facilitate the serving of a sudden trainful of customers in the station refreshment rooms of the new railways. From the central island, it was also possible to radiate partitions, creating saloon and public bars, smoke rooms and snugs, so that workers and bosses, philanderers and friends could do their drinking discreetly if they so wished.

Etched glass windows created privacy when pubs were illuminated by the new electric light, and mirrors enhanced the illumination inside. It was in this era of expensive and often speculative pub-building in the growing cities that the tied-house system finally locked tight its hold. Publicans had long borrowed from breweries to develop their premises, become debtors, mortgagees, and ultimately tenants.

During the first half of the twentieth century, the tied-house system was operated drastically to reduce customer choice, though the brewers are now making at least some gestures to right this wrong. Whether the system can ever be untied, and what would be the effect of that, is open to question. Many publicans of free houses seem to lack either the capital, the imagination or the will to utilise their liberty to the customer's advantage, and the prospect of pubs being controlled by the giants of the so-called leisure industry is enough to make even the toughest chicken turn in its basket.

As an institution, the pub requires care and attention, but it has developed through evolution, not atrophy.

Michael Jackson

Michael Jackson is the author of The English Pub (Collins, 1976), The World Guide to Beer (Mitchell Beazley, 1977/ 79) and other books.

BEFORE you read this, please pour yourself a pint of beer, raise your glass, drink deep and repeat after me, 'British Beer is best'.

We British take our beer very seriously. We have poems about porter, ballads to beer and we even Campaign to keep our ale real. But when it comes to the ingredients of our national drink we don't seem to give a damn.

On the other side of the Channel, the Germans, Dutch, French, Italians – and the rest – want, even demand, to know what their brews are made from. More importantly, they concern themselves closely with the additives that must not end up in the beer. Not surprisingly, they consider our lack of interest quaint, to say the least, and our beers are shunned and treated with grave suspicion in most European lands.

In theory I occupy my days by exporting, and selling, British beers in Europe. In practice I spend a large part of my time keeping up to date with volumes of law devoted to the purity of the European half litre.

Possibly the lowest point in my career arrived with the ringing of the telephone in the early hours of a Saturday morning. A slightly hysterical, and very Dutch, bar owner informed me that I was responsible for poisoning one of his customers who, at that very moment, was being sped by ambulance to the City hospital. 'It was that filthy flat English beer of yours – its worse than rat poison.' I assured him that it wasn't – crossing my fingers the while. The truth emerged that the injured party had consumed eight pints of England's strongest bitter to round off an evening spent sampling the alcoholic delights of Amsterdam. He recovered and so – just – did my reputation. The bar owner went bankrupt some two months later.

Skull & Crossbones

He wasn't the first, and I doubt if he'll be the last, to suggest that, as much of Britain's beer is stuffed full of all nameless additives and is sadly lacking in the vital ingredients (such as malt), every pint should carry a large skull and crossbones as warning to the unwary.

It is very difficult to convince the doubters. In light of the shelves of beer laws produced by our litigious EEC cousins, our own few pages of statutes concerning the drink seem very slim indeed. Not only do we seem to have problems in controlling what is added to beer – we are unable to produce a sensible definition of what beer is – even what it should be brewed from. Not so the Benelux countries. They demand that their beer must be brewed from a minimum 60% malt. Nor France or Italy – the present minimum malt levels here are 70 and 75% respectively.

Poison

Germany has the ultimate law – the Reinheitsgebot – under which beer must be brewed from malt, yeast, hops and water only. Not a hint of anything else, however seemingly innocuous, may even cross the brewery gates. Germans defend their law on the grounds that with an annual consumption per head of 300 pints per year, even tiny traces of the nasty bits (those that we seem to take for granted) would slowly poison the population. Seductive as this argument is it can take a bit of a battering when

you see a group of Germans washing down additive enriched Big Franzburgers with litres of ultra pure beer.

Bite

Other European lands don't attain quite such extremes, but they all keep a very careful eye on what ends up in the glass – and they bite very hard if you break the rules. Colouring? Forget it, unless it's caramel (and then not in Italy). A sniff of sulphur dioxide (a hundredth part of that allowed in headache inducing cheap wines), a drop of head stabiliser, a touch of natural acid for balance (or perhaps by accident) and a pinch of vitamin C – and that's about it – except, of course, for the malt, hops, yeast and water. Even in those countries where additives are permitted, the brewer is kindly requested to list them in full, ensuring an end product with all the appeal of a pack of instant pot noodles.

Drawbacks

Exporting beers from Britain, where some brewers have been known to consider potatoes and onions as suitable substitutes for malted barley, can have its drawbacks. A few of the larger brewers, wise to the business, will probably have a product for export only – one that doesn't contain dyes more suited to kippers or day-glo t-shirts. Thankfully, there are still some smaller concerns where the head brewer wouldn't recognise a flask of propylene glyco alginate if it walked in and introduced itself.

Nor, for the average European are the vague epithets of 'Best Bitter', 'Strong Ale', 'Supa Dupa Headbanger', or whatever, suitable names to describe beer. If it is beer (as defined by law) then you print that word on the label. If it's pils (Eurospeak for what lager should be) then the word pils is writ large.

Don't write off these strange practices as the products of

minds softened by years of real pilsner – or even as a means to prevent the hardworking importer introducing the best of British beers (though I sometimes allow myself a little doubt here). The simple fact is that when most people in Europe consume a glass of beer they know what it's brewed from and they are certain that it contains no dubious colourings, doubtful preservatives or dire additives. They are comfortable in the knowledge that the most harmful ingredient of their pure and natural brew is alcohol.

The price of this security can be heavy for British brewers trying to market their beers in Europe. Some years ago, I sent some cases of a famous dark ale to a British reception in West Germany. The beer never arrived. Many months later I received the cases back – now full of empty bottles – with a covering note from the German Customs authorities. I quote: 'Your English "beer" was analysed before being allowed to enter the country. It was found to be injurious to human health and we have, therefore, been forced to destroy it.'

Contemplate that as you enjoy your pint.

Denis Palmer

PROBABLY everyone associates hops with beer; an essential ingredient in the brewer's art. But what do hops do, exactly? Certainly, it has been recognised for centuries that they have a natural preservative effect, but it is their contribution to beer flavour for which there is no substitute. Hops bring two things to beer – the bitterness which is the hallmark of that refreshing drink, for which the lupulin or alpha acid is largely responsible; and secondly the aroma, the flavour topnote, derived from essential oils unique to each variety of hop.

Native culture

The decline in UK beer consumption during the 1980s, has been mirrored in nearly every other traditional beer consuming country. As a result, the English hop growing market is passing through a very difficult time. To make matters worse, the native culture of ale or 'bitter' is being submerged by the alien culture of lager. (Lager requires only two-thirds of the quantity of hops needed for brewing traditional British ale.) Lager is in fact the norm in virtually every country other than the UK, and when imported, it usually brings with it continental or other imported hops. The problem is compounded, because in some quarters it is believed that top quality lager can only be brewed by using foreign hops. It is simply not true. Brewing trials have produced no evidence to support such a view, and professional tasting panels have been unable to distinguish between comparable lagers, identical in every respect except that one contained an all-English hop grist, and the other top quality foreign hops.

English hops

In an attempt to redress the balance, English Hops Ltd. – the national co-operative of English hop growers – has undertaken an initiative to encourage the use of English hops wherever possible. Part of the promotional programme has centred on the introduction of the 'English Hop Mark' – as illustrated at the head of this article – as a seal or endorsement of quality for British beers brewed exclusively from English hops. Increasingly it is hoped that brewers will feel able to incorporate the Mark where appropriate, on beer containers and at the point of sale, to enable costumers to identify both lagers and ales brewed with English hops – hops with the finest pedigree.

ALLIED BREWERIES

Britain's biggest drinks group, formed in 1961 through the merger of Ind Coope, Ansells and Tetley-Walker, was given a nasty jolt late in 1985, when it received a £1.8 billion take-over bid from a company only a quarter of its size.

The cheeky predator is the Australian firm of Elders IXL, which includes Carlton United Breweries of Fosters lager fame. Chief Executive, John Elliott, is so determined to succeed that he even attended CAMRA's AGM in 1986 to explain his plans.

The surprise attack so shocked Allied-Lyons that it is trying to grow beyond Elliott's grasp by grabbing the international wines and spirits company, Hiram Walker, for 2.6 billion dollars. At the time of going to press, that deal is being challenged in the Canadian courts, while Elder's bid is being considered by the Office of Fair Trading.

A change of ownership at the top of a giant company might not be expected to filter down to the local pub, but already Allied have put more emphasis on the promotion of lager in a bid to prime their profits, while cutting back elsewhere. Their fine free-house chain in London, Nicholsons, soon felt the blast, having its 'independence' effectively stripped away.

Another major change in this eventful year has been the transfer of all Ind Coope's cask beer production from Romford to Burton-on-Trent early in 1986. The trading companies involved – Benskins, Friary Meux, Romford Brewery and Taylor-Walker – used the opportunity to fine tune their real ale recipes, while adding the word 'Best' to the beers' names.

Let's hope the new titles are justified. For the Romford brews were generally bland and often poor in quality. And with the move to Burton, delivery lines will be stretched even further. There is also the fear that recipes will be rationalised as Burton now brews a breath-taking ten real ales.

One of Allied's new 'Best' bitters – now brewed at Burton.

ALLOA Brewery, Whins Road, Alloa, Clackmannanshire, Scotland. ✆ 0259 723539. (Office: Orchard Brae House, 30 Queensferry Road, Edinburgh.)
Allied's Scottish arm which in 1980 became the third force north of the border with the purchase of 220 pubs from Vaux. Chiefly a lager brewery, with its own real ale in only 40 of the 239 pubs. Also sells Burton Ale.
Archibald Arrol's 70/- (1037) – hoppy ale.
Archibald Arrol's 80/- (1042) – new brew.

ANSELLS, PO Box 379, Tamebridge House, Aldridge Road, Perry Barr, Birmingham. ✆ 021 356 9177.
Allied's West Midlands and Wales company which lost its famous Birmingham brewery in 1981. Ansell's cask beers are now brewed in Burton, apart from Holt, Plant & Deakin. Altogether controls 1,441 pubs through six subsidiary companies (see below), 60 per cent of which serve real ale.
Ansell's Mild (1035.5) – dark and malty.
Ansell's Bitter (1037) – light and sweet.

Ansells Brewery, Blakesley House, Coventry Road, Yardley, Birmingham. ✆ 021 707 7311.
Runs 690 pubs from Wolverhampton to Coventry, of which over 380 serve real ale.

Ansells Burslem, Pitt East, Burslem, Stoke-on-Trent, Staffs. ✆ 0782 85731. Potteries company with real ale in 210 of 350 pubs.

Ansells Cambrian, Marshfield Road, Castleton, Cardiff. ✆ 0633 58422.
South Wales company with 174 pubs, 63 offering real ale. Sells **Buckley's Mild** (1032) as Ansell's Dark.

George's Haverfordwest, Withybush Road, Haverfordwest, Dyfed. ✆ 0437 5731.
West Wales wholesale company still run by the George family. Sole wholesaler of **Benfro Bitter** (1037) from **Pembrokeshire's Own Ales**, Llanteglos Brewery, Llanteg, nr Amroth, Dyfed. ✆ 083 483 677.

Holt, Plant & Deakin, 91 Station Road, Oldbury, W. Midlands. ✆ 021 552 1788.
Traditional Black Country company set up in 1984, now running 18 pubs, all serving real ale. The mild and bitter are brewed by Tetley-Walker in Warrington; Entire in its own small plant in Oldbury.
Holt's Mild (1036) – smooth and creamy.
Holt's Bitter (1036) – dry and hoppy.
Holt's Entire (1043) – full-bodied brew.

Lloyd & Trouncer, East Parade, Llandudno, Gwynedd. ✆ 0492 70933.
Runs 180 pubs in N. Wales, half of which serve real ale. Also runs the:
Minera Brewery, The City Arms, Minera, Wrexham, Clwyd. ✆ 0978 758890.
Minera Bitter (1037).
Serves 14 pubs in Shrewsbury, Llandudno and Wrexham. Malt extract.

Big Seven

AYLESBURY Brewery, Walton Street, Aylesbury, Bucks. ✆ 0296 20541.
Ceased brewing in 1935 and merged with Allied in 1972. Serves real ale in 185 of its 200 pubs. Beside Burton-brewed ABC Best Bitter, offers five other traditional beers: Draught Bass, Chiltern Beechwood, Everard's Tiger, Burton Ale and Morrell's Light. Fine example of an 'independent' company within a national giant.
ABC Best Bitter (1037) – well balanced.

HALLS, 34 Park End Street, Oxford. ✆ 0865 722433.
West Country company serving real ale in 243 of 296 pubs scattered from Cornwall to Berkshire. Main cask bitter, Harvest, is brewed at Burton, but in 1984 set up two local breweries near Bristol and Plymouth. However, the Bristol one (Jacobs) closed.
Harvest Bitter (1037) – light pleasant brew.

Plympton Brewery, Valley Road, Plympton, Plymouth. ✆ 0752 347171.
New brewery set up in Hall's Plympton depot in 1984. Real ale in 34 of 39 local tied houses.
Plympton Best (1039) – malty, darkish.
Plympton Pride (1045) – fuller-bodied.
Free trade from Plympton has, since early 1985, been run under the name of Furgusons, and three other beer wholesalers owned by Allied operate in Hall's wide trading area:

Coopers of Wessex, PO Box 130, Central Business Park, Bournemouth. ✆ 0202 295640.
Free trade wholesalers from Lyme Regis to Southampton, including the Isle of Wight.
Cooper's cask ale (1040) – brewed by Ringwood.

Tolchards, Woodlands Road, Torquay, Devon. ✆ 0803 64430.
Beer wholesalers in the Torbay area, offering Bass, Whitbread and Hall & Woodhouse cask beers besides Allied.

Treliske Cellar Supplies, Ind. Estate, Treliske, Truro. ✆ 0872 76181.
Allied's beer distributors in Cornwall.

IND COOPE, Allied House, 160 St. John Street, London EC1. ✆ 01 253 9911.
Allied's S. East and E. Midlands company based in Allied-Lyons head office, which in recent years has been split into six main operating companies, often under old brewery names. Early in 1986, cask beer production ceased at Romford, leaving the Burton brewery to produce 10 different real ales for Ind Coope companies, Ansells, Halls and ABC!

Allsopp, 119 Loughborough Road, Leicester. ✆ 0533 663663.
Runs 708 pubs from the E. Midlands down as far as Brentwood in Essex, offering the same beers as the Burton Brewery. Some 500 serve real ale. Ansells also available in the E. Midlands.

Burton Brewery, 107 Station Street, Burton-on-Trent, Staffs. ✆ 0283 31111.
Controls 41 pubs around the brewery, 39 serving real ale, though difficult to distinguish from Allsopp's houses.
Ind Coope Bitter (1037) – liquid mediocrity.
Burton Ale (1047.5) – full-bodied, fruity.

Benskins, PO Box 105, Station Road, Watford, Herts. ✆ 0923 28585.
Runs 601 pubs in the northern Home Counties, almost 90 per cent of which serve real ale. Also sells Burton Ale and Ind Coope Bitter.
Benskins Best (1037) – now less hoppy.

Friary Meux, Station Road, Godalming, Surrey. ✆ 04868 25955.
Around 560 of the 600 pubs in the southern Home Counties and on the South Coast serve real ale. Also sells Burton Ale and Ind Coope Bitter.
Friary Meux Best (1037) – improved bitter.

Romford Brewery, High Street, Romford, Essex. ✆ 0708 66088.
Controls 69 pubs around the brewery, some 59 serving real ale. All real ales now brewed at Burton.
Brewers Best (1037) – less distinctive.

Taylor-Walker, 77 Muswell Hill, London N10. ✆ 01 883 6431.
Ind Coope's Capital company operating 601 pubs in Greater London, 457 serving real ale. Also sells Burton Ale and Ind Coope Bitter.
Taylor-Walker Best (1037) – malty brew.

Nicholsons, Bald Hind, Hainault Road, Chigwell, Essex. ✆ 01 500 0261.
Allied's chain of 25 traditional free houses, chiefly in London, which also operated as beer wholesalers. However, in 1986 lost its 'independence', and range from non-Allied real ales now likely to be reduced.

JOSHUA TETLEY, PO Box 142, Hunslet Road, Leeds. ✆ 0532 435282.
Yorkshire's favourite brewing son, with real ale in an impressive 943 of the 1109 pubs, and an excellent record of pub conservation.
Tetley Mild (1032) – dark and malty.
Falstaff Best (1032) – local light mild.
Tetley Bitter (1035.5) – creamy and distinctive.

TETLEY WALKER, Dallam Lane, Warrington, Cheshire. ✆ 0925 31231.
Lags behind its brother across the Pennines, with real ale in only 361 of its 877 pubs in the N.West. Movement towards more real ale outlets disappointingly sluggish, though quality more reliable.
Tetley Mild (1032) – excellent ale.
Tetley Bitter (1035.5) – clean-tasting.

Peter Walker, 85–89 Duke Street, Liverpool. ✆ 051 708 5224.
Fine Merseyside-based chain of 84 traditional pubs, all serving their own Warrington-brewed range of real ales at popular prices.
Walker Mild (1031) – dark and fruity.
Walker Bitter (1033) – light and refreshing.
Walker Best Bitter (1035.5) – hoppier version of Tetley Bitter.
Walker Winter Warmer (1062) – dark seasonal ale.

WREXHAM Lager Brewery, 5 Central Road, Wrexham. ✆ 0978 355661.
No real ale. Concentrates on brewing 'foreign' lagers under licence.

BASS

'Great stuff this Bass' is a famous slogan from the past. CAMRA today would dispute that Draught Bass is quite the classic beer it once was, following the destruction of the Burton Union system of brewing, but Bass remains great – in size.

Britain's biggest brewers, with 7,400 pubs, also have the most breweries – 13 in all. And, unlike their national rivals, have commendably not closed a brewing site in over ten years. They have learnt the lesson that trunking vast amounts of near-water around the country is expensive.

In the City, they are regarded as the most efficient company in the industry, with profits of £255 million in 1985. They are the lager leaders with brands like Carling Black Label. They are the one to beat – except in variety of cask beer.

They offer too few real ales. The whole of S.East England has just one local cask beer – Charrington IPA. In Staffordshire only a battle by the local CAMRA branches stopped cask Springfield being withdrawn. In Scotland, Tennents barely bother to provide real ale at all.

And when Bass do venture out of their barrel, they soon retreat again. Highgate introduced two new real ales in recent years – Best Mild and Highgate Old. Both have now disappeared. The company admit that they only promote brands that are near-certain to succeed, and will not introduce new beers which might take sales from others, even if they add interest to the range.

It's time they **did** add a little interest. Without a more imaginative and positive approach to cask beer, the old red triangle will not attract discerning real ale drinkers in many parts of the country.

In a vain attempt to mask the modern, unacceptable face of brewing, Bass have changed the name of their vast chemical factory at Runcorn (left) to Preston Brook Brewery. Rumours had abounded that the troubled plant was due for closure because of poor industrial relations.

BASS BREWING, 137 Station Street, Burton-on-Trent, Staffs. ☎ 0283 45301. The original home of Bass, which has destroyed most of its traditional brewery buildings, including the famous Burton Unions. Concentrates on brewing national brands.
Draught Bass (1044) – elusively subtle bitter with unpronounced hoppiness.
Worthington White Shield (1052) – classic naturally-conditioned bottled pale ale.

BASS, MITCHELLS & BUTLERS,
Cape Hill Brewery, PO Box 27,
Birmingham 16. ☎ 021 558 1481.
Birmingham is dominated by M & B from its Cape Hill brewery, which completed modernisation in 1985. Bass's Midlands arm altogether runs three breweries, four trading companies and some 2,300 pubs, 70 per cent of which serve real ale.
M & B Mild (1036) – dark and pleasant.
Brew XI (1040) – sweet, uninspiring beer.

Highgate Brewery, Sandymount Road, Walsall, W.Midlands. ☎ 0922 23168. Unique mild-only brewery which supplies some 600 outlets. All the beer is cask, though pressurised in a few outlets. The winter brew, Highgate Old, was

discontinued in 1985.
Highgate Mild (1036) – rich and fruity.

Springfield Brewery (M & B West), Grimstone Street, Wolverhampton. ☎ 0902 54551.
M & B's Wolverhampton brewery, which also brews for Charrington.
Springfield Bitter (1036) – light and refreshing.

M & B Central, Newland House, 139 Hagley Road, Birmingham 16. ☎ 021 454 8421.
M & B East, 45 Spon End, Coventry. ☎ 0203 713321.
Bass Worthington, 328 Wetmore Road, Burton-on-Trent. ☎ 0283 41511.
Serves 620 pubs, 90% with real ale.

BASS NORTH, Headingley Office Park, 8 Victoria Road, Leeds. ☎ 0532 744444.
Runs around 2,200 pubs on either side of the Pennines, of which almost half serve one real ale. Operates through five trading companies, and is also responsible for four breweries at Runcorn, Sheffield (2) and Tadcaster.

Bass Runcorn, Aston Lane, Preston Brook, Runcorn, Cheshire. ☎ 0928 714141.
Modern keg brewery. No real ale.

Bass Tadcaster, Tower Brewery, Wetherby Road, Tadcaster, Yorks. ☎ 0937 832361.
The group's anonymous real ale brewery in the North.
Bass Mild XXXX (1031) – pleasant dark mild.
Bass Light (1031) – popular thin beer.
Bass Special Bitter (1036) – enjoyable if well kept.

Bass Lancashire, Talbot Road, Blackpool, Lancs. ☎ 0253 32131.
Trades from Liverpool to Cumbria. With Bass N.West runs 900 pubs, 365 serving real ale.

Bass N.East, Longlands Road, Middlesborough. ☎ 0642 246388.
Trades from N.Yorkshire to the Scottish border. Real ale in 127 of the 347 pubs.

Bass N.West, United House, Seymour Grove, Manchester. ☎ 061 872 5977.
Includes N.Wales and W.Derbyshire, besides Cheshire and Manchester.

Bass Yorkshire, Lockwood Park, Huddersfield. ☎ 0484 26361.
Chiefly handles W.Yorkshire and Humberside.

William Stones, Hope Brewery, Wadsley Bridge, Sheffield. ☎ 0742 349433.
Trading company for S.Yorkshire to Lincolnshire set in Bass's specialist bottled beer brewery, home of Jubilee Stout.
Stones Best Bitter is brewed at the neighbouring:
Canon Brewery, 43 Rutland Road, Sheffield. ☎ 0742 29331.
Famous bitter brewery since 1860.
Stones Best Bitter (1038) – fine, well-hopped pale beer.

BASS WALES & WEST, PO Box 116 NDO Maes-y-Coed Road, Cardiff. ☎ 0222 615831.
Covers a huge area from Hampshire to Cornwall and South Wales with real ale in the majority of the pubs. Operates through five regional trading companies, with all local real ales coming from Welsh Brewers in Cardiff, one of two breweries for which the region is responsible.

Bass Alton, Manor Park, Alton, Hants. ☎ 0420 87070.
Former Harp brewery bought by Bass. No real ale.

Welsh Brewers, Crawshay Street, Cardiff, South Glamorgan. ☎ 0222 33071.
Former Hancock's brewery taken over by Bass in 1968. Most of the 500 pubs in South Wales serve real ale.
Worthington Pale Ale (1033) – light, thin pale ale.
Hancock's PA (1033) – primed version of Worthington PA.
Worthington M (1033) – further primed version.
Worthington Dark (1034) – thin dark mild.
Hancock's HB (1037) – disappointing, characterless bitter.
Worthington BB (1037) – lightly hopped mediocre bitter.

Bass South, Temple Gate, Bristol. ☎ 0272 290436.
Bass West, Crabtree, Plymouth. ☎ 0752 29611.
Welsh Brewers East, The Brewery, Aberbeeg, Abertillery, Gwent. ☎ 0495 214141.
Welsh Brewers West, Fendrod Way, Llansamlet, Swansea. ☎ 0792 74701.

CHARRINGTON, Anchor House, 129 Mile End Road, London E1. ☎ 01 790 1860.
No longer brews, Charrington IPA being produced by M & B's Springfield Brewery in Wolverhampton. Three-quarters of the 1440 pubs sell real ale, including Draught Bass. Trades from Norfolk and Kent to Oxfordshire through four regional companies.
Charrington IPA (1039) – uninspiring beer.

Charrington Central, North Woolwich Road, Silvertown, London E16. ☎ 01 476 6911.
Charrington East, Josselin Road, Burnt Mills Ind. Estate, Basildon, Essex. ☎ 0268 27711.
Charrington South, Avis Way, Newhaven, Sussex. ☎ 0273 513255.
Charrington West, 36 Cumberland Avenue, Park Royal, London NW10. ☎ 01 965 0688.

TENNENT CALEDONIAN, 110 Bath Street, Glasgow. ☎ 941 552 6552.
Bass's Scottish arm with two breweries in Glasgow and Edinburgh and some 450 pubs plus extensive free trade. Predominantly lager brewers, with tiny commitment to real ale. Heriot Brewery 80/- renamed Tennents 80/- last year; and is much more widely available in keg.

Wellpark Brewery, Duke Street, Glasgow. No real ale.
Heriot Brewery, Roseburn Terrace, Edinburgh. ☎ 031 337 1361.
Tennent's 80/- (1042) – rare cask beer.

BASS IRELAND, Ulster Brewery, Glen Road, Belfast. ☎ 0232 611144.
No real ale. Chiefly free trade, with only 15 pubs.

COURAGE

The proud Courage cockerel is at present looking more like a chicken running round the farmyard after its head has been chopped off.

For in April, 1986, the brewing group acquired new owners when Hanson Trust took over Courage's parent company, the Imperial Group. And the move has left the old bird flapping in the air, fearful for its future.

Hanson has a reputation for shaking up companies, which often involves selling off parts of newly-acquired firms. Already the managed houses have been transferred from Imperial Leisure to Courage, amid much City speculation that the whole brewing group, or at least the northern arm of John Smiths, might be sold off. If Elders fail to take over Allied Breweries, they are seen as a likely buyer.

Meanwhile, down at the bar, following Watney's example with Webster's Yorkshire Bitter, cask John Smith's Bitter from Tadcaster is flooding into around 500 pubs in the S.East of England. It joins Courage Best, which the company now claims to be the top selling bitter in the South.

Plus something called Miller Lite, probably the thinnest lager ever launched, a sort of draught Perrier water with a touch of colour and the faintest taint of hops. It ain't heavy. It's the nearest thing to nothing in a glass.

Courage's rare Russian Stout – one of very few bottle-conditioned beers left in the country – has received new packaging, with the label more closely reflecting its origins when, 200 years ago, it was first brewed for Catherine the Great, Empress of all Russia. With an alcohol content of about 10.5 per cent, the powerful brew will continue to mature for up to five years. The 1985 brew will not be bottled until late 1986.

Following the takeover of its parent company, the Imperial Group, by Hanson Trust in 1986, an early reorganisation has seen the 1350 managed houses transferred from Imperial Leisure to Courage, bringing all 5,000 pubs under common management.

COURAGE Ltd, Anchor Terrace, Southwark Bridge, London SE1. ✆ 01 403 5000.
Responsible for the three breweries in Berkshire, Bristol and Tadcaster, plus managed houses, tenanted pubs and free trade, and wine and spirit merchants Saccone & Speed.

BREWERIES
Berkshire Brewery, Imperial Wqy, Reading, Berks. ✆ 0734 875393.
No real ale.

Bristol Brewery, Bath Street, Bristol. ✆ 0272 666944.
Courage's only real ale brewery in the South following the closure of traditional breweries in London, Plymouth and Reading. Now being expanded. If sales of the light Bitter Ale continue to fall at the present rate, this local West Country brew is likely to be discontinued within the next few years.
Bitter Ale (1030) – thin but flavoursome.
Best Bitter (1039) – malty, rounded brew.
Directors (1046) – full-bodied and distinctive.

John Smith's, Tadcaster Brewery, Tadcaster, N.Yorks. ✆ 0937 832091.
One of CAMRA's main campaigning targets for many years, which reintroduced cask John Smith's Bitter in 1984. Now in almost half the 1,120 tenanted pubs.
Bitter (1036) – good drinking beer.
*John Smiths also brew a powerful bottle-conditioned **Imperial Russian Stout** (1104) for Courage.

PUBS
The 3,660 tenanted pubs and 1,350 managed houses are now run through 12 areas, divided between John Smith (above) in the North (four) and Courage Simonds (below) in the South (eight).
Courage Simonds, 32 Bridge Street, Reading, Berks. ✆ 0734 55931.

Besides its 1700 pubs and four breweries, Greenall Whitley owns De Vere and GW Hotels, Treadway Inns in the USA, Cambrian soft drinks, Symonds cider, Drew and Cellar Five off-licences, and Gilbert and John Greenall, distillers of Vladivar, the 'vodka from Varrington'.

GREENALL WHITLEY, Wilderspool Brewery, PO Box 2, Warrington, Cheshire. ☎ 51234.
Although about half the 1,000 plus pubs serve real ale, the company has been heavily criticised by CAMRA because of its trend towards tank beer and chilled and filtered mild. Only one of its 50 houses in Cumbria serve real ale.
Mild (1033.7) – dark and sweet.
Local Bitter (1036.5) – pleasant ale.
Greenall's Original (1038.5) – fuller bodied beer.

DAVENPORTS, Bath Row, Birmingham. ☎ 021 643 5021.
Award-winning brewery which sold off its famous 'Beer at Home' service before being taken over by Greenall Whitley. Over 98 of its 123 scattered houses now use handpumps. Some pubs take Wem Special.
Mild (1034.8) – dark and smooth.
Bitter (1038.9) – well-balanced and hoppy.

SHIPSTONE, Star Brewery, New Basford, Nottingham. ☎ 0602 785074.
Taken over by Greenall Whitley in 1978, when the recipe of the distinctive bitter was modified and then restored to approaching its former character. Real ale in nearly all the 270 pubs, many now heavily modernised.
Mild (1034) – dark and well-hopped.
Bitter (1037) – popular and refreshing.

WEM Brewery, Noble Street, Wem, Shrewsbury, Shropshire. ☎ 0939 32415.
Largely untouched by the Greenall giant, serving real ale in all of its 215 houses, though has recently introduced keg beer, chiefly for the free trade. Wem Special voted best cask beer in Britain at the brewing industry international awards.
Pale Ale (1033) – pleasant, light bitter.
Mild (1035) – dark and creamy.
Best Bitter (1038) – full-bodied and distinctive.
Special Bitter (1042) – smooth but well-hopped.

GREENALL WHITLEY

With the takeover of Davenports of Birmingham early in 1986, Greenall Whitley of Warrington spread its shadow further across the land. The group already owned more pubs than Scottish & Newcastle.

From its solid N.West base, it has now stretched far across the Midlands from Wem in Shropshire to Shipstone in Nottingham. And two sporting gestures underline its national stance. First its Vladivar Vodka subsidiary backed the cricket streaker at Lords and then the brewery sponsored Newcastle United football club.

Now the ambitious company only look weak in the South of England. Independent breweries beware.

GUINNESS

Besides famous breweries in Dublin and London, runs eight other stout plants around the world in Nigeria (4), Ghana, Cameroun, Malaysia and Jamaica. There are also contracts to brew Guinness in 24 other countries.

In addition runs three ale breweries in Eire (Smithwicks, Cherrys and Macardle Moore) under the title Irish Ale Breweries, owned in conjunction with Ind Coope (Ireland).

Plus controls Harp Lager which it owns (70%) in conjunction with English regional brewers Greene King (20%) and Wolverhampton and Dudley (10%). Harp has its own brewery in Ireland at Dundalk, besides being brewed in London and under licence by Courage and Scottish & Newcastle.

SCOTTISH & NEWCASTLE
Breweries, Abbey Brewery, Holyrood Road, Edinburgh. ✆ 031 556 2591.
The smallest of the Big Seven with less than 1,500 pubs, most in the N.East of England and Scotland. Owes its national standing to the past penetration of its McEwan and Younger beers in the free trade. Operates three breweries and five regional trading companies. Also controls Thistle Hotels and Waverley Vintners.

Fountain Brewery, Fountainbridge, Edinburgh. ✆ 031 229 9377.
The beers are sold under either McEwan or Younger names depending on the area.
McEwan 70/- or **Younger's Scotch** (1036.5) – well-balanced, sweetish brew.
McEwan 80/- or **Younger's IPA** (1042) – heavy and full-flavoured.
Younger's No. 3 (1043) – a rich dark ale.

Royal Brewery, Moss Side, Manchester. ✆ 061 226 4371.
No real ale, but currently adding an ale brewing capability alongside the lager.

Tyne Brewery, Gallowgate, Newcastle. ✆ 0632 325091.
After a gap of 12 years, the Newcastle brewery introduced their own real ale again in 1984.
Cask Exhibition (1042) – pale and distinctive.

TRADING COMPANIES
Scottish Brewers, 7 South Gyle Broadway, Edinburgh. ✆ 031 334 0322.
Runs 558 pubs in Scotland, with managed houses under the Welcome Inns banner.

Newcastle Breweries, Gallowgate, Newcastle. ✆ 0632 325091.
Runs 650 pubs in the N.East of England, with real ale in around 250 outlets.

McEwan-Younger, Edinburgh House, Cowling Road, Chorley, Lancs. ✆ 02572 65544.
And Edinburgh House, Aberford Road, Garforth, Leeds, Yorks. ✆ 0532 863232.
Sells Younger's ales in Yorkshire, N.West England including Cumbria, and N.Wales, with real ale in over half their pubs.

William Younger, 53 Victoria Street, St. Albans, Herts. ✆ 0727 66277.
Markets Younger's ales in southern England and Wales.

SCOTTISH & NEWCASTLE

Will they, won't they? Scottish & Newcastle failed in 1985 to win control of major regional brewers, Matthew Brown of Blackburn, thanks to a spirited defence by the brewery backed by its customers and CAMRA.

But the Younger and McEwan men still hold nearly 30% of Matthew Brown shares, and all eyes are now fixed on December, when they could renew their bid. They failed by a whisker last time, so if they do enter the fray again, it will be another tight fight. They seem desperate to seize Brown's 500 pubs.

The likely fate of most of the Matthew Brown and Theakston breweries, if they do succeed, was underlined in 1986 when S&N ignored centuries of tradition and closed down their Holyrood Brewery in Edinburgh, the home of William Youngers for 237 years.

One move which could stop the Tartan army's advance on Brown, would be if S&N received a takeover bid themselves. In a year which has seen Courage change owners and Allied stalked by Australian predators, Elders, anything could happen. And probably will.

Also owns Taunton Cider in conjunction with Bass, Courage and Scottish & Newcastle.

Arthur Guinness, St. James's Gate, Dublin 8, Eire. ✆ 756701.
Main stout brewery, producing the famous bottle-conditioned brew, for Scotland and N.West England as well as Ireland besides the weaker Draught Guinness (1037.4) for Ireland. Unlike England, the draught is filtered but **not** pasteurised. Also produces a heavier Foreign Extra Stout (8% alcohol) for export.
Guinness Extra Stout (1042) – superb, bitter sweet beer, which provides a welcome friend in every bar – except in Scotland, where all bottled Guinness is now pasteurised. All non-returnable bottles and canned Guinness from supermarkets and off-licences are also pasteurised.

Arthur Guinness, Park Royal, London NW10. ✆ 01 965 7700.
Here Draught Guinness is all keg. Owns no pubs, but the overwhelming majority of British breweries stock Guinness.
Guinness Extra Stout (1042) – superb, bitter sweet beer.

Irish Ale Breweries, 107 James's Street, Dublin 8, Eire. ✆ 783911.
Parent company of Cherrys, Macardle Moore and Smithwicks. Each brewery produces a variety of keg brands, regularly brewing for each other.
Cherrys, Mary Street, Waterford, Eire. ✆ 74963.
No real ale. Also brews under the Perry's name. Main brand Phoenix.
Macardle Moore, Dundalk, Eire. ✆ 35441.
No real ale.
Smithwicks, St. Francis Abbey Brewery, Kilkenny, Eire. ✆ 21014.
No real ale.

Big Seven

WATNEY, MANN & TRUMAN, 91 Brick Lane, London E1. ✆ 01 377 0020.
The brewing arm of hotel and leisure group Grand Metropolitan, running five breweries and eight trading companies with 4,700 tenanted pubs. A further 1,500 managed houses are operated by the Host Group (see below). Webster's Yorkshire Bitter now available throughout England.

DRYBROUGH, Craigmillar, Edinburgh. ✆ 031 661 6161.
Watney's Scottish and N.East England company, running 190 pubs. Sadly, withdrew Pentland 70/- last year.
Drybrough's Eighty (1042) – dark and full-flavoured.

MANNS, Lodge Way, Harlestone Road, Northampton. ✆ 0604 52452.
Non-brewing Midlands company with 531 pubs. Following the closure of Wilson's brewery, Mann's Bitter now brewed by Ushers. Mann's IPA withdrawn last year. Also offer Wilson's Original Bitter and Usher's Founders Ale.
Mann's Bitter (1039) – sweetish brew.

NORWICH, Rouen Road, Norwich, Norfolk. ✆ 0603 660222.
Brewery closed in 1985 with the beers now brewed by Ushers. Real ale in 450 of the 730 pubs. Also offer Ruddles County.
S & P Best Bitter (1038) – unreliable brew.
Bullard's Old (1057) – winter ale.

PHOENIX, 1 Richmond Terrace, Brighton, Sussex. ✆ 0273 693500.
Non-brewing company on the south coast with 460 pubs, the great majority serving real ale including strong brews from independents Gales and King & Barnes. Tamplins Bitter withdrawn early in 1986.

USHERS, Parade House, Trowbridge, Wilts. ✆ 02214 63171.
West Country brewery whose trading area stretches to Cornwall and S.Wales. Around 500 of the 534 pubs serve real ale. Also brew for Manns and Norwich, with the Best Bitter sold by Phoenix.
Usher's PA (1031) – light amber ale.
Best Bitter (1038) – sweeter, rounded beer.
Founder's Ale (1045) – full-bodied and hoppy.

WATNEY COMBE REID & TRUMAN, 14 Mortlake High Street, London SW14. ✆ 01 876 3434.
The group's two London-based brewery companies merged in January, 1986, though their pubs remain under separate names and managements.

Truman, 91 Brick Lane, London E1. ✆ 01 377 0020.
London and S.East brewery with some 525 pubs, most serving real ale. Gradually losing its once 'independent' position within the group.
Bitter (1036) – well-balanced.
Best Bitter (1045) – hoppy and full bodied.
Sampson (1055) – distinctive strong ale.

Watney Combe Reid, Stag Brewery, London SW14. ✆ 01 876 3434.
Watney's 980 London pubs seem to be increasingly dominated by 'outside' beers, notably Webster's Yorkshire and Ruddle's County.
Combes Bitter (1038) – improved beer.
Stag Bitter (1044) – malty ale.

More choice – with Webster's new premium bitter, Choice. Less choice with the withdrawal of Pentland in Scotland.

SAMUEL WEBSTER & WILSONS, Newton Heath, Manchester.
Combined company of Websters in Yorkshire and Wilsons in the N.West, now with all beers brewed by Websters following the closure of Wilson's brewery in Manchester in the summer of 1986. Some 490 of the 700 pubs serve real ale.

Part of CAMRA's postcard campaign to save Wilson's beers.

WATNEY

A couple of years ago CAMRA predicted, based on inside information, that by the end of the Eighties, Watneys would be down to three breweries (two in London and one in the North) and a handful of national cask beer brands. Rubbish, laughed the Grand Metropolitan men. It will never happen.

Then, in 1985, Watneys closed down its Norwich Brewery. Four local real ales disappeared. Now, in 1986, another brewery has bitten the dust and a further four beers have vanished. This time it was Wilsons Brewery in Manchester which closed in August with all production transferred across the Pennines to Webster's Brewery in Halifax. The beers which went to the great tap-room in the sky were Webster's Dark Mild, Tamplin's Bitter, Mann's IPA and, saddest of all, Drybrough's Pentland in Scotland. At the same time, Webster's Yorkshire Bitter has become available throughout the country.

Who will be next to go? Drybrough's Brewery in Edinburgh in

1987? Or Ushers of Trowbridge? Which local beer will next be trampled underfoot in the rush to establish national beer brands?

Meanwhile, in London, Watney Combe Reid and Truman have merged to form a new joint company to manage all operations in the Capital and the Home Counties. This follows the formation in 1985 of a combined company in the North, Samuel Webster and Wilsons, to run their pubs on either side of the Pennines.

Watneys are thinking big again – and losing touch with local tastes and needs.

Webster, Fountain Head Brewery, Ovenden Wood, Halifax. ☎ 0422 57188. Increasingly used for lager production and heavily committed to the club trade. Dark milds rationalised when the brewing of Wilson's beers brought to Halifax. 230 pubs.
Green Label Best (1033) – bitter light mild.
Yorkshire Bittter (1036) – bland brew
Webster's Choice (1045) – new premium bitter.

Wilsons, Monsall Road, Newton Heath, Manchester. ☎ 061 205 2345.
Majority of the 475 pubs serve real ale – all now brewed by Websters.
Original Mild (1032) – malty brew.
Original Bitter (1036.5) – well-balanced.

BERNI & HOST GROUP, 106 Oxford Road, Uxbridge, Middx. ☎ (0895) 58233.
Runs approximately 1,700 pubs and branded restaurants through eight

operating companies, having merged with Berni Inns.
London Hosts, Westbourne House, 16 Westbourne Grove, London ☎ 01 727-5776.
Hamden Hosts, 71 The Avenue, Cliftonville, Northampton. ☎ (0604) 21631.
Anglia Hosts, Elizabeth House, 28 Baddow Road, Chelmsford, Essex. ☎ (0245) 260666.
Westward Hosts, Runnymede House, Heriot Road, Chertsey, Surrey. ☎ 09328 64933.
Pennine Hosts, Brook House, Oldham Road, Middleton, Manchester M24. ☎ 061 653-6868.
Gateway Hosts, Stoner House, London Road, Crawley, Sussex. ☎ (0293) 517617.
Special Operations, Queens Wharf, Queen Caroline Street, Hammersmith, London W6. ☎ 01 741-9416.
Branded Restaurants, (Berni Inns/Barnaby's Carvery) Elbry House, 59 High Street, Egham, Surrey. ☎ (0784) 36371.

WHITBREAD, Chiswell Street, London
EC1. ☎ 01 606 4455.
Whitbread, with 6,800 pubs and eight
breweries, has divided its activities into
five sections: Breweries, Trading (tenanted
pubs and free trade), Inns (managed
houses), Retail (restaurant and off-licence
chains) and Wines and Spirits.

BREWERIES

Whitbread Breweries, Park Street West,
Luton. ☎ 0582 424200.
Controls eight breweries, half the number
it ran in 1981, having heavily rationalised
its plants during the early Eighties,
including Luton itself.

CASTLE EDEN, PO Box 13, Castle Eden,
Hartlepool, Cleveland. ☎ 0429 836431.
N.East brewery whose ales are now sold
throughout the North and Midlands.
Durham Mild (1035) – mild for the
W.Midlands, sold as **Durham Ale** in a very
few outlets in the N.East.
Castle Eden Ale (1040) – rich sweetish
bitter.

CHELTENHAM, Monson Avenue,
Cheltenham, Glos. ☎ 0242 521401.
Now the only Whitbread traditional
brewery serving the S.West from
Hampshire to Cornwall and S.Wales,
following the closure of breweries in
Romsey, Cardiff, Tiverton and
Portsmouth.
West Country Pale Ale (1030) – light
session beer.
Flower's IPA (1036) – hoppy bitter.
Flower's Original (1044) – full-bodied and
well-hopped.
Strong Country Bitter (1037) – refreshing
brew for Wessex.
Pompey Royal (1043) – stronger bitter.

CHESTERS, PO Box 215, Cook Street,
Salford, Manchester. ☎ 061 832 8344.
Attractive Victorian brewery whose future
now seems more secure following growing
local trade.
Chester's Best Mild (1032) – thin and
dark.
Chester's Best Bitter (1033) – dry and pale.
Trophy (1036) – refreshing cask version of
well-known keg.

FREMLINS, Court Street, Faversham,
Kent. ☎ 0795 823311.
Whitbread's rival brewery to Shepherd
Neame in Kent, which now also brews
Flowers Original.
Fremlins Bitter (1035) – hoppy and well-
balanced.
Flowers Original (1044) – full-bodied ale.

MAGOR, Gwent, S.Wales. ☎ 0633
880661.
Major new keg brewery, producing no real
ale.

SAMLESBURY, Cuerdale Lane,
Samlesbury, Preston, Lancs. ☎ 0774
77681.
Second megakeggery. No Whitbread real
ale, though brews a cask bitter for
Everards of Leicester.

SHEFFIELD, Exchange Brewery, Sheffield,
S.Yorks. ☎ 0742 71101.
Whitbread's remaining Yorkshire brewery
following the loss of Leeds.
Trophy (1037) – cask version of the
common keg beer.

WHITBREAD

Whitbread seem to divide the drinking nation into two. Those in the
South who like real ale. And get it.
Those in the North who don't like
real ale. And if they do, don't get it
anyway.

In the South, breweries like Wethereds, Fremlins and Cheltenham produce a wide range of real ales. In the
South, the trading companies now
run schemes like the Traditional Beer
Club, introducing guest beers into
Whitbread houses. In the South they
have realised that cask beer is the
growth part of the ale market, and
are determined to exploit it.

But in the North, Whitbread seem
to be in another country, a land of
tank and keg beer. In areas like the
Wirral, drinkers pursue a popular
pastime called 'hunt the handpump',
normally arriving at a reported sight-
ing after the beer has gone but before
the promotional material (20 beer
mats) and the pumpclip turn up.

It's high time that Whitbread fol-

WETHERED, High Street, Marlow, Bucks.
☎ 06284 6969.
Fine traditional brewery, producing an
excellent range of real ales including a
new high-gravity bitter.
Wethered Bitter (1035) – well-balanced
brew, widely available in the S.East.
SPA (1040) – special fuller-bodied bitter.
Samuel Whitbread (1048) – new strong
ale.
Winter Royal (1055) – powerful dark ale.

PUBS

Whitbread Trading, 27 Britannia Street,
London WC1. ☎ 01 278 2491.
Whitbread runs its 4,489 tenanted pubs
and free trade accounts through 15
regions, which occasionally tie up with the
remaining breweries:

Blackburn, School Lane, Guide,
Blackburn, Lancs. ☎ 0254 661211.
Castle Eden – as brewery, above.
Chesters – as brewery, above.
With Delamere Inns runs 250 pubs, 100
serving real ale.
Flowers, Eastern Avenue, Barnwood, Glos.
☎ 0452 418551.

One of Whitbread's traditional breweries now receiving welcome investment – Wethereds in Marlow.

lowed a 'one-nation' policy, and gave their neglected northern drinkers a fair pull of the handpump.

Whitbread's spate of brewery closures (they shut down eight in three years in the early Eighties) appears to have ended, following the forced closure of Luton because of industrial problems in 1984. Welcome new investment is now being made in plants like Wethereds.

More worrying now are the activities of their sister company, Whitbread Investments, which with Whitbread has share stakes in at least ten breweries – Brakspear (27%), Buckleys (17%), Matthew Brown (8.8%), Boddingtons (22%), Devenish (26%), Fullers (10%), Hardy & Hanson (9%), Marston (36%), Morland (43%) and Vaux (2.2%), often with an accompanying seat on the board.

These stakes are worrying since Whitbread Investments, according to City sources, often plays a shadowy part in takeovers involving such companies, such as Marstons takeover of Border in 1984, Boddington's takeover of Higsons in 1985 and Greenall Whitley's seizure of Davenports.

On the beer front, the main concern centres around the march of Flowers Original throughout the South, squeezing sales of other premium bitters like Wethered's SPA and especially Pompey Royal.

There has also been a shabby trend towards serving bright and keg beers through handpumps, particularly in Wales involving keg Welsh Bitter. At national level, Whitbread have pledged that this deceptive practice will be brought to an end. Let's hope they keep their word.

With Severn Inns runs 680 pubs, most serving real ale.
Fremlins, Earl Street, Maidstone, Kent. ℰ 0622 58321.
Runs 551 tenanted pubs, the vast majority serving real ale.
London, 353 Kentish Town Road, London NW5. ℰ 01 485 5699. Out of 182 pubs, 96 serve real ale.
Merseyside, Kingsway Park, St. Anne Street, Liverpool. ℰ 051 207 3300.
Runs 135 tenanted pubs.
Northern Home Counties, Eastern Avenue, Dunstable, Beds. ℰ 0582 603188.
Scotland, 38 Southcroft Road, Rutherglen, Glasgow. ℰ 041 647 7164.
Wales, Ipswich Road, Cardiff. ℰ 0222 497211.
Around half of Whitbread's 500 pubs in Wales serve real ale.
Wessex, PO Box 8, Portsmouth, Hants. ℰ 0705 822281.
West Country, Howden, Tiverton, Devon. ℰ 0884 257777.
Runs 310 tenanted pubs, the majority serving real ale.
Wethered – as brewery, above. With the managed house company, Chiltern Inns, runs 206 pubs, all serving real ale.

Yarmouth, Brewery House, George Street, Great Yarmouth, Norfolk. ℰ 0493 842461.
Yorkshire – as Sheffield Brewery, above.

MANAGED HOUSES

Whitbread Inns, Park Street West, Luton, Beds. ℰ 0582 424200.
Runs 1,864 managed houses through ten regional companies, some from the same sites as the trading companies.

Bowland Inns – as Blackburn, above.
Britannia Inns, Hendon Ale & Wine House, Hendon Way, London NW4. ℰ 01 202 2411.
Chiltern – as Wethered, above.
Delamere – as Chesters, above. Runs 120 managed houses.
Hambleton, Bridge Road, Kirkstall, Leeds. ℰ 0532 744477.
Medway – as Fremlins, above.
Severn, Ellenborough House, Wellington Street, Cheltenham, Glos.
Sherwood, Bridge Street, Sheffield. ℰ 0742 730040.
Solent – as Wessex, above.
Westward, The Brewery, Romsey, Hants. ℰ 0794 512824.

ABERDEEN ALES, Scotland. See Devanha.

ADNAMS, Sole Bay Brewery, Southwold, Suffolk. ☎ 0502 722424.
E. Anglia's famous seaside brewery, with real ale in all 75 pubs and
1,900 free trade accounts in the S. East. Recently completed expansion of brewery and now looking to increase tied estate.
Mild (1034) – dark dry ale.
Bitter (1036) – well-hopped.
Extra (1044) – crisp and full-bodied.
Old (1042) – dark malty winter brew.

ALEXANDRA, Brighton. See Beckets.

ALICE Brewery, Harbour Road, Inverness. ☎ 0463 223825.
Ambitious project to serve the Scottish Highlands begun in 1983.
Alice Ale often pressurised in its 50 Highland outlets.
Alice Ale (1040) – refreshing brew.
Alice Sixty (1060) – winter ale.

ALLOA Brewery, Scotland. See Allied Breweries, pages 15–16.

ANN STREET Brewery, St. Helier, Jersey. ☎ 31561. No real ale.

ANSELLS, Birmingham. See Allied Breweries, pages 15–16.

ARCHERS, London Street, Swindon, Wilts. ☎ 0793 46789.
Successful new brewery set up in 1979, which in 1985 doubled its
brewing capacity. Services 100 free trade outlets from Oxford to
Bath plus two tied houses.
Village Bitter (1035) – light and refreshing.
Best Bitter (1040) – well-hopped bitter.
Special Brew (1048) – full-flavoured and smooth.
Headbanger (1065) – dark, strong and malty.

ARKELL, Kingsdown Brewery, Swindon, Wilts. ☎ 0793 823026.
Local family brewery with real ale in 57 of its 66 pubs and in two
off-licences. Now has widespread free trade in the Thames Valley.
John Arkell Bitter or **BB** (1033) – light and hoppy.
BBB (1038) – fuller-bodied, distinctive bitter.
Kingsdown Ale (1050) – stronger version of BBB.

ASHFORD, Kent. See Kentish Ales.

ASTON MANOR, 173 Thimblemill Lane, Aston, Birmingham. ☎ 021 328 4336.
No longer brews real ale, concentrating on bottling.

AYLESBURY Brewery Co. (ABC), Bucks. See Allied Breweries, pages 15–16.

AXE VALE, Cownhayne Lane, Colyton, Devon. ☎ 0297 53361.
Begun in 1983 and now supplying 25 outlets in East Devon and
into Somerset and Dorset.
Axe Bitter (1040) – nutty and smooth.
Battleaxe (1053) – mellow and well-hopped.
Conqueror (1066) – dark Christmas ale.

BALLARDS, Railway Inn, Elsted, Midhurst. W. Sussex. ☎ 073 081 4936.
Begun in 1980 at Cumbers Farm, Trotton, and in 1985 moved to
their first tied house, the Railway Inn, Elsted. Supplies some 45 free
trade outlets.
Best Bitter (1042) – well-balanced and nutty.
Wassail (1060) – strong, malty brew.

BANKS'S, Park Brewery, Lovatt Street, Wolverhampton. ☎ 0902 711811.
With Hanson's make up Wolverhampton and Dudley Breweries.
Famous for its mild and that most of the 800 tied houses serve cask
beer through metered dispense systems 'to guarantee a full pint'.
Paradoxically the new 'Hanson's Black Country Bitter' is brewed by
Banks's in Wolverhampton.
Banks's Mild (1035) – smooth and malty.
Hanson's Black Country Bitter (1035) – session beer.
Banks's Bitter (1038) – full-bodied and well-hopped.

BANKS & TAYLOR, The Brewery, Shefford, Bed. ☎ 0462 815080.
Set up in 1982 and now serving some 50 outlets including six tied houses. SOD often sold under house names.
Shefford Bitter (1038) – clean and hoppy.
Eastcote Ale or SPA (1041) – smooth, full-flavoured.
Shefford Old Strong (SOS) (1050) – full-bodied and fruity.
Shefford Old Dark (SOD) (1050) – rich brew.

BARKING, 6 Riverside Works, Hertford Road, Barking, Essex. ☎ 01 591 4404.
Set up in 1985 by brewery and pub equipment engineers, Ornawell, in their outer London premises. Not in production every week.
Essex Bitter (1036) – light session beer.
Alsatian Bitter (1040) – fuller-bodied and hoppy.
St. Bernard Ale (1050) – dark, bitter winter brew.

BARRON, Land Farm, Silverton, Devon. ☎ 0392 860406.
Farm brewery set up in 1984 supplying outlets around Exeter.
Barron's Draught (1040) – smooth and malty.
Exe Valley Bitter (1043) – full-bodied and well-hopped.

BASS, Burton-upon-Trent, Staffs. See pages 17–18.

BATEMAN, Salem Bridge Brewery, Wainfleet, Skegness, Lincs. ☎ 0754 880317.
One of Britain's true local breweries, maintaining close links with the community. Only one of their 92 pubs does not sell their 'Good Honest Ales' in traditional form. Presently up for sale.
Mild (1032) – smooth, creamy and dark.
XB (1036) – distinctive, well-hopped bitter.
XXXB (1048) – powerful, malty ale.

BATES, 4 Western Units, Pottery Road, Bovey Tracey, Devon. ☎ 0626 834024.
Begun in 1983 and now brewing for 35 outlets around Exeter.
Bates Bitter (1045) – full-bodied beer.
Blaster Bates (1066) – dark strong ale.

BATHAM, Delph Brewery, Brierley Hill, W. Midlands. ☎ 0384 77229.
Hidden behind one of the Black Country's most famous pubs, the "Bull and Bladder", this small family firm has managed to survive since 1877 brewing excellent beer for its eight pubs and an expanding free trade.
Mild (1036) – dark and tasty.
Bitter (1043) – distinctive and full-bodied.
Delph Strong Ale (1054) – a Christmas ale.

BEAMISH & CRAWFORD, South Main Street, Cork, Eire. ☎ 26841.
Subsidiary of Carling O'Keefe of Canada. No real ale. Keg and bottled **Beamish Stout** (1039) now also available in southern England through regional brewers led by Youngs of London.

BEARDS, Stella House, Diplocks Way, Hailsham, Sussex. ☎ 0323 847888.
No longer brews. Takes Harvey's range of ales under its own name for its 23 pubs and wholesales other beers, like King & Barnes.

BEARDS of SUSSEX

BECKETS, 19 North Street, Portslade, Brighton, Sussex. ☎ 0273 421066.
Ambitious brewery founded in 1982, originally under the Alexandra name. Owns five Becket's houses in the Brighton area.
Tudor Ale (1034) – amber mild.
Beckets Bitter (1036) – light and hoppy.
Beckets Best (1043) – well-hopped bitter.
Beckets Special (1047) – smooth and full-bodied.
Old Snowy (1054) – dark winter brew.

BELHAVEN Brewery, Dunbar, East Lothian, Scotland. ☎ 0368 62734.
Scotland's best-known independent brewery, which has had a turbulent but colourful history. Now linked to the Virani Group. Primarily free trade, with a third of its 600 accounts taking real ale. Owns 40 pubs and hotels, including some in London.
60/- Light (1031) – dark and malty.
70/- Heavy (1035) – light and hoppy.
80/- Export (1041) – heavy, full-bodied ale.
90/- Strong Ale (1070) – occasional rich brew.

Independent Breweries

28

BENSKINS, Watford, Herts. See Allied Breweries, pages 15–16.

BERKHAMSTED, Bourne End Lane, Bourne End, Herts. ✆ 04427 73781.
Brewery inside premises of Inn Brewing brewery equipment manu-
facturers. Beer chiefly sold "through the door". Varies between malt
extract and full mash.
Berkhamsted Best Bitter (1041) – a hoppy brew.

BERROW, Coast Road, Berrow, Burnham-on-Sea, Somerset. ✆ 027 875 345.
Begun in 1982 and now supplying about 20 pubs and clubs in
Somerset and Avon.
BBBB (1038) – full-tasting bitter.
Topsy Turvy (1055) – distinctive, pale strong ale.

BIG LAMP, Summerhill Street, Newcastle-upon-Tyne. ✆ 091 261 4227.
The only small independent brewery in the N. East, set up in 1982.
Now owns two tied houses.
Big Lamp Bitter (1038) – hoppy and distinctive.
Extra Special (1046) – full-bodied bitter.
Old Genie (1070) – powerful dark brew.

BIN HILL, Hill of Maude, by Buckie, Banffshire. ✆ 0542 35158.
Most northerly brewery on the British mainland. Started March,
1986, by Phil and Sue Gilbert, supplying six free trade pubs in
North-east Scotland and Aberdeen.
70/- (1036) – nicely rounded taste.
80/- or **Alba Ale** (1043) – darker heavy brew.

BISHOPS Brewery, c/o Fox Bros Ltd, Wellington, Somerset. ✆ 082 347 5335.
New brewery set up in 1983 by the founder of Cotleigh Brewery,
Ted Bishop, selling 12–15 barrels a week throughout the South.
Bishop's PA (1036) – light hoppy bitter.
Bishop's Best Bitter (1040) – fuller-bodied.

BLACKAWTON, Washbourne, Totnes, Devon. ✆ 080 423 339.
One of the earliest new small breweries, dating from 1977, and now
the oldest brewery in Devon! Serves 60 free trade outlets.
Blackawton Bitter (1037) – hoppy and well-rounded.
Forty-Four (1044) – premium, full-flavoured bitter.
Headstrong (1048) – like a strong mild.

BODDINGTONS, Strangeways Brewery, Manchester. ✆ 061 831 7881.
Manchester's most ambitious brewing son, which in 1982 swal-
lowed near-neighbours Oldham Brewery, followed by Higsons of
Liverpool in 1985. All 280 Boddingtons pubs serve real ale, but now
free trade accounts for over a quarter of the business.
Mild (1032) – dark and full-flavoured.
Bitter (1035) – popular straw-coloured bitter.

BORDER, Wrexham. See Marston.

BOSHAM, Walton Lane, Bosham, W. Sussex. ✆ 0243 573256.
Begun in 1984 and now supplies 14 local outlets with a range of
beers including two seasonal brews.
Harvest Pale (1036) – light summer bitter.
Old Bosham Bitter (1042) – hoppy brew.
Bosham Best Bitter (1048) – full-bodied beer.
Firkin Special or FSB (1060) – dark winter ale.

BOURNE VALLEY, Andover. See Hampshire.

BRAIN, Old Brewery, St. Mary Street, Cardiff. ✆ 0222 399022.
As much a part of Wales as Rugby Union. These good value, distinc-
tive beers are served traditionally in all their 126 pubs.
Dark (1034) – smooth and malty mild.
Bitter (1035) – light and well-flavoured.
SA (1042) – full-bodied, malty bitter.

BRAKSPEAR, The Brewery, Henley-on-Thames, Oxfordshire. ☎ 0491 573636.
Popular country brewery with many superb, unspoilt pubs, some of
which are now, sadly, under threat of closure. All but one of the 122
houses serve real ale.
Mild (1031) – thin but hoppy.
Bitter (1035) – distinctively flavoured.
Special (1043) – full-bodied premium bitter.
Old or **XXXX** (1043) – Special with caramel.

BRIGHTON, 35 Vine Street, Brighton, Sussex. ☎ 0273 690850.
Established in the late Seventies as Raven Brewery, the first small
brewery in Sussex. Renamed Brighton Brewery in June, 1986.
Owns one pub and serves 15–20 free trade outlets.
Brighton Bitter (1036) – light, well-balanced beer.
Best Bitter (1046) – full-bodied premium brew.
Old Master (1056) – heavy winter ale.

BROUGHTON Brewery, Broughton, Biggar, Lanarkshire. ☎ 08994 345.
One of the most significant new breweries set up in 1980 by former
S & N executive, David Younger, and now supplying some 150 out-
lets in Scotland, 100 of which take their widening range of real ales.
Greenmantle Ale (1038) – bitter-sweet beer.
Broughton Special (1038) – dry-hopped version of Greenmantle.
Merlin's Ale (1044) – magical golden brew.
Old Jock (1070) – bottled strong ale occasionally on draught.

MATTHEW BROWN, PO Box 5, Lion Brewery, Blackburn, Lancs. ☎ 0254 52471.
Large N. West brewery which, with the help of CAMRA, successfully
fought off an unwelcome takeover from Scottish & Newcastle Breweries. S & N still hold almost 30 per cent of Brown's shares and could
renew their bid from December, 1986. Also own Theakston's two
breweries in N. Yorkshire and Cumbria and converting selected Lion
pubs to Theakstons. Some 220 of the 550 houses serve real ale.
Lion Mild (1031) – dark and nutty.
Lion Bitter (1036) – well-balanced and malty.
John Peel (1040) – well-hopped, pale, dry bitter.

BUCKLEY, Gilbert Road, Llanelli, Dyfed. ☎ 0554 758441.
Wales's oldest brewery dating back to 1767, with cask beer in 155
of its 160 pubs in S. West Wales. Also has a major stake in Llanelli
neighbours Felinfoel. XXXX Mild sold as Ansell's Dark by Ansells.
XXXX Mild (1032) – dark and fruity.
XD Mild (1032) – extra dark mild for Swansea area.
Best Bitter (1036) – full-flavoured.

BUNCES, The Old Mill, Netheravon, Wilts. ☎ 0980 70631.
Set up in 1984 on the Wiltshire Avon, brewing a single premium
bitter for 30 free trade outlets in Wiltshire and surrounding area.
Best Bitter (1041) – full-bodied hoppy bitter.

BURT, High Street, Ventnor, Isle of Wight. ☎ 0983 852153.
One of Britain's most remarkable breweries which has managed to
survive, serving real ale in 8 of its 11 pubs, despite the lowest prices
in the South of England. Currently up for sale.
Bitter (1030) – rare light bitter.
Mild (1030) – dark nutty mild.
VPA (1040) – hoppy, distinctive bitter.
4X (1040) – winter old ale.

BURTON BRIDGE, Bridge Street, Burton-upon-Trent, Staffs. ☎ 0283 36596.
Begun in 1982 by former Ind Coope managers to demonstrate that
Burton is still the best place to brew beer. Over 35 outlets including
brewery tap.
XL Bitter (1040) – light hoppy beer.
Bridge Bitter (1042) – distinctive fruity beer.
Burton Porter (1045) – dark and bitter (also bottle-conditioned).
Burton Festival Ale (1055) – strong smooth ale.
Old Expensive or **OX** (1066) – dark winter warmer.

BURTONWOOD, Bold Lane, Burtonwood, Warrington, Cheshire. ☎ 09252 5131.
Family brewery with 290 scattered pubs including some in
N. Wales, 205 offering real ale. Beware of houses selling keg beer
(usually mild) through handpumps.
Dark Mild (1032) – pleasant, nutty flavour.
Bitter (1036.5) – light and creamy.
JBA Premium (1039.5) – new smooth, malty best bitter.

BUTCOMBE Brewery, Butcombe, Bristol BS18 6XQ. ☎ 027 587 2240.
One of the most successful new breweries, set up in 1978 by a former Courage Western managing director. Extensive penetration of
the free trade, particularly in Avon and Somerset. Owns two pubs.
Butcombe Bitter (1039) – dry, well-hopped and clean tasting.

CAMERON, Lion Brewery, Hartlepool, Cleveland. ☎ 0429 66666.
The N. East's major brewers of real ale, who narrowly escaped being
taken over by Scottish & Newcastle Breweries in 1984. In 1986
bought 80 pubs from Mansfield Brewery, particularly in Hull,
extending their estate as far south as Lincolnshire and Notts.
Lion Bitter (1036) – tasty, hoppy brew.
Strongarm (1040) – fine malty bitter.

CANTERBURY Brewery, 35 St. Margaret's Street, Canterbury, Kent. ☎ 0227 456057.
Non-brewing company with three pubs and two restaurants.
Draught beers brewed by Kentish Ales; bottled by Shepherd Neame.
Canterbury Ale (1037) – light, fruity bitter.
Buffs Bitter (1047) – strong pale ale.

CASTLETOWN, Victoria Road, Castletown, Isle of Man. ☎ 0624 822561.
One of the two independent breweries to satisfy the Manx thirst, pro-
ducing excellent 'Ale of Man' under the island's Pure Beer Act (only
malt, hops and sugar) for its 35 pubs.
Mild (1036) – dark version of the bitter. Rare in cask.
Bitter (1036) – fine, refreshing, fruity brew.

CHARRINGTON, London. See Bass, pages 17–18.

CHESTERS, Manchester. See Whitbread, pages 24–25.

CHILTERN, Nash Lee Road, Terrick, Aylesbury, Bucks. ☎ 029 661 3647.
Begun in 1980. Now supplying 30 widespread outlets including
some Aylesbury Brewery pubs and British Rail London stations.
Chiltern Ale (1036) – distinctive, light bitter.
Beechwood Bitter (1043) – full-bodied and nutty.

CIRENCESTER, The Workshops, Brewery Court, Cirencester, Glos. ☎ 0285 3144.
Founded in 1983 in old cellars, this small brewery changed hands in
1986 and gained a Roman accent. Serves 30 free trade outlets.
Fosse Ale (1036) – light, refreshing brew.
Best Bitter (1040) – full-bodied and well-balanced.
Centurion (1047) – dark and malty.

CLARK, Westgate Brewery, Wakefield, W. Yorks. ☎ 0924 373328.
Drinks wholesale company which began brewing again in 1982,
and now brews Clark's Traditional Bitter for 40 free trade accounts.
The other three beers are chiefly sold at their three 'Boon' pubs,
named after founder, Henry Boon Clark.
Clark's HB (1033) – light, refreshing bitter.
Traditional Bitter (1038) – well-hopped brew.
Wakefield Ale (1038) – darker version of bitter.
Hammerhead (1050) – rich, warming ale.

COTLEIGH, Ford Road, Wiveliscombe, Somerset. ☎ 0984 24086.
Begun in Devon in 1979 before moving to Wiveliscombe. In 1985
moved into new premises in renovated barn. Serves 50 outlets on
Devon/Somerset border.
Nutcracker (1036) – occasional dark mild.
Kingfisher Ale (1036) – light and refreshing.
Tawny Bitter (1040) – smooth and hoppy.
Old Buzzard (1048) – dark winter brew.

COURAGE. Brewing subsidiary of Hanson Trust. See page 19.

CROUCH VALE, Redhills Road, S. Woodham Ferrers, Chelmsford, Essex. ☎ 322744.
Begun in 1981 by CAMRA enthusiasts. Now supplying 50 free trade outlets in Essex and Great London.
Woodham Bitter (1035.5) – light bitter.
Best Bitter (1039) – distinctive and consistent.
Strong Anglian Special or **SAS** (1048) – deceptively powerful.
Willie Warmer (1060) – rude dark winter ale.

CROWN Brewery, Pontyclun, Mid Glamorgan. ☎ 0443 225453.
Former South Wales Clubs Brewery, specialising in the club trade where most of the beer is pressurised. Now also supplies some free trade pubs using traditional dispense. Also owns three pubs.
SBB (1036) – smooth and tasty bitter.
Black Prince (1036) – flavoursome dark mild.
Special (1041) – cask version of Great Western keg.

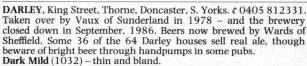

DARLEY, King Street, Thorne, Doncaster, S. Yorks. ☎ 0405 812331.
Taken over by Vaux of Sunderland in 1978 – and the brewery closed down in September, 1986. Beers now brewed by Wards of Sheffield. Some 36 of the 64 Darley houses sell real ale, though beware of bright beer through handpumps in some pubs.
Dark Mild (1032) – thin and bland.
Thorne Best Bitter (1038) – distinctive and full-bodied.

DAVENPORTS, Birmingham. See Greenall Whitley, page 20.

DEVANHA, Old Station Yard, Alford, Aberdeenshire. ☎ 0336 2393.
Small brewery set up in 1983 selling traditional draught beers through 40 outlets in N.E. Scotland. Under the name Aberdeen Ales, began selling bottled beer throughout Scotland in 1986.
XB (1037) – hoppy, bitter brew.
80/- (1042) – full-bodied pale ale.
XXX (1042) – dark and very malty.

DEVENISH, Redruth Brewery, Redruth, Cornwall. ☎ 0209 213591.
Head Office, 15 Trinity Street, Weymouth, Dorset. ☎ 0305 774511.
Waves of change have hit the S. West's major seaside brewers. Their old Dorset brewery in Weymouth closed at the end of 1985, with all production transferred to Redruth. Then Devenish were effectively taken over by leading free house chain, Inn Leisure, adding their 45 outlets throughout the South to Devenish's 300 pubs, the majority of which sell real ale. Devenish pubs now expected to operate more like free houses. Their own beer range has also changed.
John Devenish Bitter (1032) – pleasant light brew.
Cornish Original (1038) – new bitter.
Wessex Stud (1042) – fuller-bodied bitter.
Great British Heavy or **GBH** (1050) – new strong ale.

DILFORDS, 77 Allerton Road, Woolton, Liverpool. ☎ 051 428 7969.
Set up in 1985 in former surgical boot factory! Taken over by new owners in 1986.
Dilford's Bitter (1038) – hoppy session beer.

DONNINGTON Brewery, Stow-on-the-Wold, Glos. ☎ 0451 30603.
Britain's most picturesque brewery, set in an old mill alongside a lake. At its best the taste of the beer, served by handpump in their 16 Cotswold stone pubs, matches the beauty of the buildings.
XXX (1035) – rare dark mild.
BB (1036) – beautiful light bitter.
SBA (1042) – full-bodied bitter.

DRYBROUGH, Edinburgh. See Watneys, pages 22–23.

ELDRIDGE POPE, Dorchester Brewery, Dorchester, Dorset. ☎ 0305 64801.
Boasts Britain's strongest naturally-conditioned, bottled beer, **Thomas Hardy Ale** (1125). However, the award-winning draught beers are served using a caskbreather device in most 180 tied houses, resulting in a lack of Eldridge Pope pubs in the Guide.
Dorchester Bitter (1033) – light but well-balanced.
Dorset Original IPA (1041) – well-hopped beer.
Royal Oak (1048) – full-bodied malty brew.

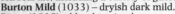

ELGOOD, North Brink Brewery, Wisbech, Cambs. ☎ 0945 583160.
Tucked-away brewery in the fenlands near the Wash, selling real
ale in around 30 of its 54 pubs. Beware of keg beer through handpumps in some houses.
Bitter (1036) – refreshing, well-regarded brew.

EVERARDS, Castle Acres, Narborough, Leicester. ☎ 0533 891010.
Everards now brew only Old Original themselves at their new brew-
ery in Leicester, with Mild and Tiger brewed at their old brewery in
Burton-upon-Trent by the Heritage Brewery. The undistinguished
bitter is produced under contract by Whitbread. 84 of the 140 pubs
sell real ale, including a variety of guest beers.
Burton Mild (1033) – dryish dark mild.
Bitter (1035) – bland session beer.
Tiger (1041) – tasty best bitter.
Old Original (1050) – malty, finely hopped ale.

FEDERATION, Wellington Road, Dunstan, Tyne & Wear. ☎ 0632 609023.
No real ale. Bright and keg beers only from the Northern Clubs
Federation Brewery. But now sells Morrell's real ale.

FELINFOEL Brewery, Felinfoel, Llanelli, Dyfed. ☎ 0554 773356.
Britain's champion brewers in the past, this famous Welsh brewery
serves its beers without pressure in 30 of its 76 pubs.
XXXX Mild (1031) – dark, nutty beer.
Bitter Ale (1034) – light, refreshing bitter.
Double Dragon (1040) – stronger, malty bitter.

FIVE TOWNS, Trent Trading Estate, Botteslow St. Hanley, Stoke.
☎ 0782 285262.
Potteries brewery established in 1982, now serving two tied houses
with its tasty, value-for-money beers.
Dark Mild (1035) – smooth and creamy.
Bursley Bitter (1039) – distinctive brew.
Bennett Ale (1057) – full-bodied and malty.

FLOWERS, Gloucester. See Whitbread, pages 24–25.

FRANKLINS, Bilton Lane, Harrogate, N. Yorks. ☎ 0423 74328.
Small brewery behind the Gardeners Arms, since 1980, now under
new management. Serves 25 outlets.
Franklin's Bitter (1038) – aromatic and fruity.

FREMLINS, Kent. See Whitbread, pages 24–25.

FRIARY MEUX, Surrey. See Allied Breweries, pages 15–16.

FULLER, Smith and Turner, Griffin Brewery, Chiswick, London W4. ☎ 01 994 3691.
One of only two independent brewers in the capital to survive the
takeovers of the Sixties. Now buying up pubs in and around London.
Has won more awards at CAMRA's Great British Beer Festival than
any other brewery. Real ale in 116 of the 136 houses.
Chiswick Bitter (1035.5) – pleasant, session beer.
London Pride (1041.5) – fruity, rounded best bitter.
ESB (1055.75) – Extra Special Bitter in every sense.

GALES, Horndean, Portsmouth, Hants. ☎ 0705 594050.
Traditional brewery with a fine range of cask beers in all but one of
its 96 pubs. HSB is also sold in some Watney and Whitbread houses.
Produces the only naturally-conditioned beer sold in a corked bottle
– **Prize Old Ale** (1095).
XXXL (1030) – light mild. **XXXD** (1031) – rare dark mild.
BBB (1037) – hoppy bitter, now named Butser Brew Bitter.
XXXXX (1044) – dark, sweet winter brew.
HSB (1051) Horndean's special, full-bodied bitter.

GIBBS MEW, Anchor Brewery, Milford Street, Salisbury, Wilts. ☎ 0722 29244.
Wiltshire family brewery since 1866 with 75 pubs and extensive
free trade, despite disposing of wholesalers, Robert Porter.
Wiltshire Traditional Bitter (1036) – light and hoppy.
Premium Bitter (1042) – malty brew linked with Best.
Salisbury Best (1042) – full-bodied hoppy bitter.
The Bishop's Tipple (1066) – distinctive barley wine.

GLENNY, Eagle Brewery, The Crofts, Witney, Oxon. ☎ 0993 2574.
New brewery set up in 1983 in part of Clinch's old brewery, supplying over 40 free trade outlets in Oxfordshire and London.
Witney Bitter (1037) – tasty session beer.
Wychwood Best (1044) – full-flavoured bitter.

GOACHER'S, Hayle Mill Cottages, Bockingford, Maidstone, Kent. ☎ 0622 682112.
Now supplying 25 free trade outlets since setting up in 1983.
Maidstone Light (1036) – light and hoppy.
Maidstone Ale (1040) – dark and malty.
1066 (1066) – a real conqueror.

GODSON CHUDLEY, Black Horse Brewery, Chisenhale Rd, London E3. ☎ 01 980 0604.
Company formed in 1984 by the merger of two of London's small independent breweries, Godson of Bow and Chudley of Maida Vale. Now all production in Bow. Serves 100 outlets.
Churdley Local Line (1038) – well-balanced bitter.
Lords Strong Ale (1048) – dry and pale.
Godson's Black Horse or **GBH** (1048) – dark and malty.
Draught Excluder (1066) – fully-fermented winter warmer.
Godson's Stock Ale (1087) – smooth, tawny ale.

GOLDEN HILL, Wiveliscombe, Somerset. ☎ 0984 23798.
Has the unique distinction of winning the Best Bitter award at CAMRA's Great British Beer Festival only months after starting in 1980. Larger plant installed last year to cope with increased demand. Now serves 100 outlets in the S. West.
Exmoor Ale (1039) – malty, well-balanced beer.
Exmoor Dark (1039) – darker, hoppier version.

GOOSE EYE, Turkey Mills, Goose Eye, Keighley, W. Yorks. ☎ 0535 605807.
Brewers since 1978, now chiefly for their bars in the mill.
Goose Eye Bitter (1038) – tangy, straw-coloured bitter.
Wharfdale Ale (1045) – darker, heavier beer.
Old Three Laps (1052) – dark, strong ale.
Pommie's Revenge (1058) – pale, fruity and dangerously drinkable.

GRAY, Rignals Lane, Galleywood, Chelmsford, Essex. ☎ 0245 75181.
No longer brews, but supplies its 50 largely unspoilt pubs with Greene King draught beers.

GREENALL WHITLEY, Warrington. See page 20.

GREENE KING, Westgate Brewery, Bury St. Edmunds, Suffolk. ☎ 0284 63222, and The Brewery, Biggleswade, Beds. ☎ 0767 313935.
East Anglia's largest regional brewery, brewing both in Suffolk and Bedfordshire. Also owns Rayments of Hertfordshire. Famous for its robust Abbot Ale, but cask beer dispensed by top pressure in half their 795 pubs. Now own six pubs in London.
KK (1031) – pleasant light mild (brewed only at Biggleswade).
XX (1031) – malty, dark mild (chiefly for Suffolk).
Simpsons Bitter (1033) – new light bitter.
IPA (1035) – dry, well-hopped bitter.
Abbot Ale (1048) – full-bodied and distinctive.
Christmas Ale (1052) – seasonal dark ale.

GUERNSEY Brewery, South Esplanade, St. Peter Port, Guernsey. ☎ 0481 20143.
One of two breweries on this Channel island, serving stronger than usual real ales in 20 of their 35 tied houses, owing to the excise duty uniquely being levied on quantity not strength. Trades under the name 'Pony Ales'.
LBA Mild (1037.7) – dark and sweet.
Draught Bitter (1045) – full-flavoured and hoppy.

GUINNESS, London and Dublin. See page 20.

HALLS, Oxford. See Allied Breweries, pages 15–16.

HANCOCKS. See Bass, Welsh Brewers, pages 17–18.

HALL & WOODHOUSE, Blandford Forum, Dorset. ☎ 0258 52141.
More usually known as 'Badger Beer', the brewery serves cask beer
in 150 of its 154 houses, though a quarter of the pubs use the cask
breather device on their Hector's and Tanglefoot beers.
Hector's Bitter (1034) – pleasant light bitter.
Badger Best Bitter (1041) – well-hopped and full-bodied.
Tanglefoot (1048) – lightish-coloured strong ale.

HANSON'S, High Street, Dudley, W. Midlands. ☎ 0384 57731.
The other half of Wolverhampton and Dudley Breweries (see
Banks's) which brews similar but separate beers to its Big Brother.
Now being given a more independent image within the company,
though the new **Hanson's Black Country Bitter** (1035) is brewed by
Bank's at Wolverhampton!
Mild (1035) – medium dark and malty.
Bitter (1038) – light but well-hopped.

HARDINGTON, St. James Street, S. Petherton, Somerset. ☎ 0460 40294.
Pub brewery begun in Hardington Mandeville in 1979 which
expanded into the free trade and in 1984 moved site to behind the
Brewers Arms, S. Petherton. 20 outlets in S. Somerset.
Hardington Bitter (1036.5) – light and fruity.
Somerset Best Bitter (1044) – full-bodied beer.

HARDYS & HANSONS, Kimberley Brewery, Nottingham. ☎ 0602 383611.
This brewery – the result of a merger in 1930 between two neigh-
bouring firms in Kimberley – serves cask beer in 183 of its 206
houses, but increasingly uses top-pressure dispense.
Best Mild (1035) – dark, malty brew.
Best Bitter (1039) – distinctive beer.

HARTLEYS, Old Brewery, Ulverston, Cumbria. ☎ 0229 53269.
Brewery famous for its 'Beers from the Wood', which was taken over
by Robinsons of Stockport in 1982. Still brewing for its 56 pubs.
Mild (1031) – smooth and dark.
Bitter (1031) – smooth and light.
XB (1040) – strong, well-flavoured bitter.

HARVEY, Bridge Wharf Brewery, Cliffe High Street, Lewes, E. Sussex. ☎ 0273 471222.
Traditional family brewery with real ale in all 29 pubs. New brew-
ing tower completed in 1985 to match the original Gothic design.
Also brew for Beards and a growing free trade from Surrey to Kent.
XX (1030) – pleasant dark mild.
Pale Ale (1033) – well-hopped light bitter.
BB (1040) – stronger, slightly sweet bitter.
XXXX (1043) – tasty, dark, winter brew.
Elizabethan (1090) – occasional draught barley wine.

HARVIESTOUN, Dollarfield Farm, Dollar, Clackmannanshire, Scotland,
☎ 02594 2141.
Small brewery in a former dairy at the foot of the Ochil Hills near
Stirling. Serves six outlets in Central Scotland.
Harviestoun 80/- (1040) – straw-coloured, full-bodied beer.

HAWTHORN, Steam Mills Road, Cinderford, Glos. ☎ 0594 25050
New brewery set up in 1985 producing keg beers and lager for three
tied houses and 30 free trade outlets around the Forest of Dean,
besides two real ales.
Dean Bitter (1032) – light session beer.
Hawthorn SA (1039) – darker full-bodied bitter.

HEAVITREE, Trood Lane, Matford, Exeter, Devon. ☎ 0392 58406.
Brewing ceased 1970 and 110 pubs supplied by Whitbread, Bass
and Eldridge Pope. In 1985 moved to new premises.

HERALD, Old Stables, Milburn Road, Coleraine, Co. Derry. ☎ 0265 57117.
Begun in 1983 as N. Ireland's second much-needed traditional
brewery. The cask beers are sometimes served under gas pressure,
often using pure nitrogen. Serves 35 outlets around Coleraine.
Herald Ale (1036) – amber, malty brew.
Old Faithful (1046) – dark, smooth porter.

HERITAGE, Anglesey Road, Burton-on-Trent, Staffs. ☎ 0283 63563. The brewing company of the new National Brewery Museum. (☎ 0283 69226) brewing beers under licence in the former Everard's Tiger Brewery. Primarily brews Burton Mild and Tiger for Everards.

HERMITAGE, Main Road, Hermitage, Emsworth, W. Sussex. ☎ 024 34 71533. Brewery attached to the confusingly-named Sussex Brewery pub.
Hermitage Mild (1034) – smooth and dark.
Hermitage Bitter (1039) – light and well-balanced.
Triple X (1044) – hoppy, flavoursome bitter.
Best Bitter (1048) – stronger, sweetish bitter.
Lumley Old Ale (1050) – dark, malty winter brew.

HIGHGATE, Walsall, W. Midlands. See Bass, Pages 17–18.

HIGSONS, 127 Dale Street, Liverpool. ☎ 051 236 1255. Merseyside's major remaining brewery, which in 1985 was taken over by Boddingtons of Manchester, chiefly for its lager-brewing capacity. However, Boddies have since given a long-term commitment to Higson's own cask ales, and are introducing real ale into an increasing number of the 156 pubs, including Boddingtons Bitter.
Mild (1033) – well-balanced dark ale. Good value.
Bitter (1038) – excellent hoppy bitter, back to its best.

HILDEN Brewery, Hilden House, Lisburn, Co. Antrim. ☎ 08462 3863. N. Ireland's brave new brewery, the first to brew traditional beer in Ulster for decades when it began in 1981. Hilden Ale also now naturally conditioned in bottle.
Hilden Ale (1040) – hoppy, straw-coloured bitter.
Special Reserve (1044) – a rich, tawny ale.

HOLDEN, George St., Woodsetton, Dudley, W. Midlands. ☎ 09073 2051. One of the long-established family breweries of the Black Country, producing a good range of real ales for their 17 tied houses.
Black Country Mild (1036) – dark and mellow.
Black Country Bitter (1038) – distinctive palate.
Special Bitter (1050) – full-bodied, sweetish ale.
Old Ale (1080) – powerful winter warmer.

HOLT, Derby Brewery, Empire St., Cheetham, Manchester 3. ☎ 061 834 3285. Traditional family firm, which brews one of Britain's true bitters of character. Real ale (including mild!) in all 92 tied houses, often delivered in huge hogsheads (54 gallon barrels) such is its enthusiastic following and amazingly low price.
Mild (1033) – dark, malty and bitter.
Bitter (1039) – famous bitter of distinction.

HOLT, PLANT & DEAKIN, Oldbury, W. Midlands. See Allied, pages 15–16.

HOME Brewery, Mansfield Road, Daybrook, Nottingham. ☎ 0602 269741. Another company famous for providing value for money in its 450 pubs throughout the E. Midlands upto S. Yorkshire. However, has recently embarked on a retrograde policy of converting pubs to tank beer. Real ale now in only 65 – 70 per cent of the pubs.
Mild (1036) – dark and malty.
Bitter (1038) – hoppy, refreshing beer.

HOOK NORTON Brewery, Hook Norton, Banbury, Oxon. ☎ 0608 737210. One of the most delightful traditional tower breweries in Britain, with all 35 country pubs serving real ale. Also extensive free trade.
Mild (1032) – light and fruity.
Best Bitter (1036) – distinctive and hoppy.
Old Hookey (1049) – genuine dark old ale.

HOSKINS, 133 Beaumanor Road, Leicester. ☎ 0533 661122. Old family concern which was taken over in 1983 and now has four tied houses, including the Tom Hoskins at the brewery.
Mild (1033) – smooth and dark.
Beaumanor Bitter (1039) – dry and hoppy.
Penn's Ale (1045) – stronger dark bitter.
Old Nigel (1060) – pale winter brew.

HOSKINS & OLDFIELD, North Mills, Frog Island, Leicester. ☎ 0533 532191.
Set up in 1984 by two brothers from the family who used to run Hoskins.
HOB Bitter (1041) – distinctive, hoppy brew.
Little Matty (1041) – darker version of HOB.
EXS Bitter (1051) – new, full-bodied beer.
Old Navigation (1071) – strong, dark and sweet.
Christmas Noggin (1100) – powerful festive brew.

HYDES Anvil Brewery, 46 Moss Lane West, Manchester M15. ☎ 061 226 1317.
The smallest of the long-established Manchester breweries, serving
real 'Anvil' ales in all 48 tied houses, largely in the south of the city.
The only Manchester brewery still producing two milds.
Mild (1032) – dark and malty.
Best Mild (1034) – light and hoppy.
Bitter (1036.6) – full-flavoured bitter.
Anvil Strong Ale (1080) – rich winter brew.

IND COOPE, Burton and Romford. See Allied Breweries, pages 15–16.

JENNINGS, Castle Brewery, Cockermouth, Cumbria. ☎ 0900 823214.
Traditional brewery in the far N. West whose real ales are not only
available in all 76 tied houses, but also in a number of Tetley houses.
Mild (1034) – dark and mellow.
Bitter (1034) – hoppier brew.
Marathon (1041) – new strong bitter.

KENTISH ALES, Grange Road, Rusthall, Tunbridge Wells, Kent. ☎ 0892 35832.
New owners have combined the former short-lived Ashford and
Royal Tunbridge Wells breweries to serve 40 outlets. Also brew for
Canterbury Brewery and act as beer wholesalers.
Kentish Gold (1037) – light, hoppy bitter.
Royal Sovereign (1039) – medium-coloured best bitter.
Old Gold (1047) – pale premium bitter.
Royal Porter (1053) – dark winter brew.

KING & BARNES, 18 Bishopric, Horsham, W. Sussex. ☎ 0403 69344.
Recently expanded Sussex family brewery which serves real ale in
all its 57 country houses. Runs a popular 'passport' scheme.
Sussex Mild (1034) – smooth, rare dark mild.
Sussex Bitter (1034) – well-hopped bitter.
Old Ale (1046) – malty winter ale.
Draught Festive (1050) – strong, full-flavoured bitter.

LEES, Greengate Brewery, Middleton Junction, Manchester. ☎ 061 643 2487.
One of Manchester's clutch of surviving family-owned independent
breweries, with 129 tied houses in the north of the city and in North
Wales, 121 of them serving real ale.
GB Mild (1032) – smooth, medium-dark mild.
Bitter (1038) – full-flavoured and malty.
Moonraker (1073) – rich, dark and sweet.

LIDDINGTON, 140 Wood Street, Rugby, Warwickshire. ☎ 0788 73751.
Litchborough Brewery was the pioneer of the new brewery revolu-
tion, founded in Northamptonshire in 1974. Taken over by beer
wholesalers, Liddingtons, in 1983 and moved to Rugby.
Liddington Bitter (1036) – malty bitter.
Tudor Ale (1044) – smooth, fruity brew.
Celebration Ale (1060) – heavy Christmas ale.

LLOYDS, Derbyshire. See John Thompson Inn, Home-Brew Pubs, pages 46–48.

LORIMER & CLARK, Caledonian Brewery, Slateford Rd, Edinburgh. ☎ 031 337 1286.
A subsidiary of Vaux of Sunderland with no tied houses of its own,
whose main business is supplying 70/- to Vaux pubs in N. East
England, where it is known as Lorimer's Best Scotch. Now Vaux
plan to close the Caledonian Brewery in Spring, 1987, and brew
Lorimer's beers in Sunderland.
70/- Ale (1036) – well-balanced brew; a true Scotch.
80/- Ale (1043) – full-bodied and flavoursome.
Caledonian (1080) – rich strong ale.

McEWAN, Edinburgh. See Scottish & Newcatle Breweries, page 21.

MACLAY, Thistle Brewery, Alloa, Scotland. ☎ 0259 723387.
One of Scotland's two remaining independent breweries after the takeover typhoon swept through the country, supplying real ale to 17 of its 27 houses and an appreciative free trade.
60/- Light (1030) – flavoursome dark beer.
70/- Heavy (1035) – well-hopped brew.
80/- Export (1040) – well-balanced beer.

McMULLEN, 26 Old Cross, Hertford. ☎ 0992 54911.
Hertfordshire family brewery which has recently built a second brewhouse. Serves the 'real McCoy' in 121 of its 161 pubs.
AK Mild (1033) – popular brew, more of a light bitter.
Country Bitter (1041) – fruity and distinctive.
Christmas Ale (1070) – seasonal warmer.

MAIDEN OAK, Ballymagroarty, Londonderry, N. Ireland. ☎ 0504 262114.
New brewery set up in Derry's enterprise zone in 1985. No real ale.

MALTON, Crown Hotel, Wheelgate, Malton, N. Yorks. ☎ 0653 7580.
New brewery set up in 1985 behind a pub by former Russells and Wrangham brewer, to revive Malton's proud brewing heritage.
Malton Pale Ale (1033.8) – light, session beer.
Double Chance (1037.8) – well-hopped bitter.
Owd Bob (1056) – dark, dry winter warmer.

MANNS, Northampton. See Watney, pages 22–23.

MANSFIELD Brewery, Littleworth, Mansfield, Notts. ☎ 0623 25691.
Took over North Country Breweries of Hull in 1985, and then sold off 80 of its enlarged estate of 400 houses to Camerons. Commitment to real ale limited; 4XXXX only being sold in some 70 pubs. Batemans also available in a few outlets.
4XXXX Bitter (1045) – well balanced creamy beer.

MARSTON, PO Box 26, Shobnall Road, Burton-upon-Trent, Staffs. ☎ 0283 31131.
One of Britain's great traditional breweries with real ale in most of their 857 pubs, stretching from Cumbria to Hampshire. The only brewery using the unique Burton Union system of brewing for their stronger ales. In 1984 took over Border Brewery of Wrexham. All Border beers are now brewed at Burton.
Capital (1030) – light mild.
Mercian Mild (1032) – dark and fruity.
Burton Bitter (1037) – well-balanced bitter.
Pedigree (1043) – full-bodied and smooth.
Merrie Monk (1043) – powerful, darker brew.
Owd Rodger (1080) – heavy, rich ale.

MARSTON BORDER, Holt Road, Wrexham, Clwyd.
The Border brewery was taken over by Marston of Burton-upon-Trent in 1984 and the brewery closed down. The three remaining 'Border' beers are now brewed at Burton. Real ale in a growing number of the 170 pubs, but with an increasing emphasis on Marston beers and the Marston name.
Mild (1030) – dark and malty.
Exhibition (1034) – a light mild.
Bitter (1034) – well-balanced and refreshing.

MARSTON MOOR, Ashley, Tockwith Road, Long Marston, York. ☎ 090 483 277.
Small brewery set up in 1984, brewing 7–8 barrels a week.
Cromwell Bitter (1037) – distinctive bitter beer.
Brewers Droop (1050) – strong ale.

MARTINS Ales, Martin Hall, Martin, Dover, Kent.
Set up in 1984 in an ancient brewhouse brewing **Johnsons Bitter** (1042) on an occasional basis.

MAULDON, 7 Addison Road, Chilton Ind. Estate, Sudbury, Suffolk. ☎ 0787 311055.
Head Brewer at Watney's Mortlake plant revived the name of his
former family brewery in 1982. Now supplying over 100 free trade
outlets in Suffolk, S. Norfolk and Essex.
Bitter (1037) – full-flavoured brew.
Special (1044) – premium, hoppy ale.
Christmas Reserve (1065) – festive beer.

MELBOURNS, Exton Park, Oakham, Rutland, Leics. ☎ 0572 813181.
The brewery in Stamford is now a non-brewing museum, but 32 of
the 34 pubs serve Samuel Smith's cask beer, and Marston's Pedigree
was also introduced in 1986 in some houses.

MILL Brewery, Unit 18C, Bradley Lane, Newton Abbot, Devon. ☎ 0626 63322.
Begun in 1983 to supply free trade in S. Devon and Torbay. The
Special is often sold under local pub names.
Janner's Ale (1038) – well-hopped bitter.
Devon Special (1045) – pale stronger ale.
Christmas Ale (1050) – winter brew.

MINERA, Wrexham. See Allied Breweries, pages 15–16.

MINERS ARMS, Brewery, Westbury-sub-Mendip, Somerset. ☎ 0749 870719.
The first new home-brew house in 1973 (in Priddy), producing
naturally-conditioned bottled beer, which in 1981 moved site and
switched to brewing draught beer for the free trade under the same
name. Now serves 25 outlets.
Own Ale (1040) – well-balanced beer.
Guvnor's Special Brew (1048) – stronger ale.

MITCHELLS, Moor Lane, Lancaster. ☎ 0524 63773.
The remaining Lancaster independent brewery after the takeover of
Yates & Jackson by Thwaites. Mitchells now brew in Y & J's former
brewery for their 50 pubs, 48 serving real ale.
Mild (1034.8) – dark and smooth.
Bitter (1036) – malty brew.
ESB (1044.8) – round and full-bodied.

MITCHELLS & BUTLERS, Birmingham. See Bass, pages 17–18.

MOLE'S, Merlin Way, Bowerhill, Melksham, Wilts. ☎ 0225 704734.
Established in 1982 by a former Usher's brewer. New serves around
40 outlets in the Wilts/Avon area. The brewery name came from his
nickname.
Mole's PA (1035) – tasty, lunchtime bitter.
Mole's Cask Bitter (1040) – light and well-hopped.
Mole's 97 (1050) – premium strong ale.

MONMOUTH, Queen's Head, St. James Street, Monmouth, Gwent. ☎ 0600 2767.
Home-brew pub which has now expanded into the free trade, serv-
ing 12 outlets in Monmouth and the Forest of Dean. Due to be sold.
Ten Thirty-Five (1035) – nutty bitter.
Piston Bitter (1045) – full-bodied brew.
Brain Damage (1080) – numbing strong ale.

MOORHOUSE'S Burnley Brewery, Moorhouse St., Burnley, Lancs. ☎ 0282 22864.
Long-established producer of hop bitters which in 1979 began
brewing beer. Has since had several new owners. Bitter gained silver
medal at Brewex in 1983 – a unique distinction for a small brewer.
Premier Bitter (1036) – smooth and full-flavoured.
Pendle Witches Brew (1050) – potent, malty bitter.

MORLAND, PO Box 5, Ock Street, Abingdon, Oxon. ☎ 0235 20770.
Thames Valley brewery with handpumps in more than half the 215
tied houses. But many of these use a cask breather. Also has a con-
siderable clubs trade.
Mild (1032) – refreshing dark ale.
Bitter (1035) – dry and bitter.
Best Bitter (1042) – full-flavoured and well-hopped.

MORRELLS, Lion Brewery, St. Thomas Street, Oxford. ☎ 0865 242013.
The famous university city's last surviving brewery produces one of
the widest ranges of real ales in the country for its 137 pubs, though
a few use blanket pressure. Free trade expanding to London, Bristol
and Coventry.

Light Ale (1032) – lightly hopped beer.
Dark Mild (1036) – rare malty ale.
Bitter (1036) – subtle well-balanced beer.
Varsity (1041) – full-bodied malty bitter.
Celebration (1066) – occasional strong pale brew.
College (1072) – sweeter, heavy ale.

MURPHY, Lady's Well Brewery, Cork, Eire. ☎ 503371.
Subsidiary of Heineken of Holland, now challenging Guinness with
its own keg and bottled stout not only in Ireland but also in Britain
and abroad. No real ale.

NETHERGATE, 11–13 High Street, Clare, Suffolk. ☎ 0787 277244.
New brewery set up by a microbiologist and two partners in a con-
verted garage early in 1986, supplying 35 outlets in the Suffolk–
Essex border area and in Cambridge, with just the one beer.

Nethergate Bitter (1039) – distinctive bitter brew.

NEWCASTLE, See Scottish & Newcastle Breweries, page 21.

NEW FOREST, Old Lyndhurst Road, Cadnam, Hants. ☎ 0703 812766.
Set up in 1979, the brewery concentrates on supplying keg beers to
the club trade in Hampshire and Bournemouth, but also produces
two real ales for 16 outlets.

New Forest Real Ale (1035) – well-balanced beer.
Kingswood Cask Bitter (1039) – fuller-bodied bitter.

NORTH COUNTRY, Hull. See Mansfield.

NORWICH Brewery. See Watney, pages 22–23.

OAK, Merseyton Road, Ellesmere Port, Cheshire. ☎ 051 356 0950.
Since 1982 has supplied W. Cheshire, the Wirral and Liverpool.

Oak Best Bitter (1038) – hoppy and light.
Old Oak Ale (1044) – Burton-style brew.
Double Dagger (1050) – special strong bitter.
Porter (1050) – dark winter brew.

OAKHILL, Old Brewery, High Street, Oakhill, Bath. ☎ 0749 840134.
Set up by a farmer in 1984 and now serves 60 outlets in Avon,
Dorset and Somerset. Oakhill Stout (1045) is only served under top
pressure through mini-handpumps.

Farmers Ale (1038) – all-malt bitter.

OKELL, Falcon Brewery, Douglas, Isle of Man. ☎ 0624 73034.
The larger of the two independent breweries in the Island, brewing
real ale under the unique Manx Pure Beer Act for virtually all its 71
tied houses. Has an impressive Victorian brewhouse.
Mild (1035.2) – dark and smooth.
Bitter (1035.9) – well-hopped, dryish brew.

OLDHAM Brewery, Coldhurst Street, Oldham, Manchester. ☎ 061 624 8305.
Taken over by neighbours Boddingtons in 1982 with the promise
that the brewery would survive for five years. Now that Boddies
have also taken over Higsons of Liverpool, the group looks to have
one too many production plants – with Oldham the most vulner-
able. Real ale in a third of the 87 pubs.
Mild (1031) – malty and dark.
Bitter (1037.2) – pale and full-flavoured.

OLD MILL, Mill Street, Snaith, Humberside. ☎ 0405 861813.
Professional new brewery set up in 1983 by a former Wilson's production director. Has had to expand the brewing plant.

Old Mill Traditional Bitter (1037) – distinctive hoppy brew.
Bullion Bitter (1044) – award-winning beer.

JAMES PAINE, Market Square, St. Neots, Cambs. ☎ 0480 216160.
Formerly owned by Paine's maltsters and millers, the brewing side
was taken over by new owners in 1982 and renamed James Paine.
Real ale in 7 of the 9 pub. In 1985 bought Robert Porters beer
wholesale company in London. Growing free trade.
XXX (1036) – smooth, medium bitter.
St. Neots Bitter (1041) – creamy and well-hopped.
EG (1047) – full-bodied and malty.

PALMER, West Bay Road, Bridport, Dorset. ☎ 0308 22396.
The only thatched brewery in the country, in a delightful seaside
setting. Now most of the 70 houses serve the beers without pressure.
BB (1030.4) – light, pleasant bitter.
IPA (1039.5) – well-balanced bitter.
Tally Ho (1046) – strong, nutty brew.

PARADISE Brewery, Paradise Park, Hayle, Cornwall. ☎ 0736 753365.
Unusual brewery set up in a bird park in 1981. The brewery is
behind the one tied house, the Bird in Hand.
Paradise Bitter (1040) – pleasant beer.
Artist Ale (1055) – smooth and full-bodied.

PEMBROKESHIRE OWN ALES. See Allied Breweries, pages 15–16.

PHILLIPS, Hundred House, Bridgnorth Road, Norton, Shrops. ☎ 095 271 353.
Set up behind the Greyhound pub in Marsh Gibbon, Bucks., in
1981, but closed in 1985 and moved to the Hundred House Inn in
Shropshire in 1986.
Heritage Bitter (1036) – fruity and well hopped.
Ailrics Old Ale (1045) – smooth, nutty brew.

PHOENIX, Brighton. See Watney, pages 22–23.

PILGRIM Brewery, West Street, Reigate, Surrey. ☎ 07372 22651.
Surrey's only free trade brewery, begun in 1982, which in 1985
moved from Woldingham to Reigate.
Surrey Bitter (1038) – hoppy, light bitter.
Progress (1042) – malty, dark beer
Talisman (1048) – strong ale.

PITFIELD, The Beer Shop, 8 Pitfield Street, London N1. ☎ 01 739 3701.
Britain's first new brewery, set up in an off-licence, set up in 1981 which
last year moved its brewery to a new site in Hoxton Square to cope
with increased demand. Serves 15 outlets in London.
Pitfield Bitter (1038) – dry and hoppy.
Hoxton Heavy (1048) – strong malty brew.
Dark Star (1050) – dark old ale (also bottled).

PLASSEY, Eyton, Wrexham, Clwyd. ☎ 0978 780 277.
Following the closure of Border Brewery in Wrexham, brewer Alan
Beresford set up his own brewery in an old dairy on a farm caravan
site, whose bars serve the beer.
Farmhouse Bitter (1038) – light, all-malt brew.

POOLE, 32 Sterte Avenue, Poole, Dorset. ☎ 0202 682345.
Dorset's only new brewery – it already has four established independent
companies – which in 1983 added a home-brew pub called the
Brewhouse in Poole High Street. Supplies 20 free trade outlets.
Dolphin Bitter (1038) – hoppy session brew.
Bosun Best (1046) – rich and smooth.

POWELL, Mochdre Ind. Estate, Newtown, Powys. ☎ 0686 28021.
Central Wales beer wholesale company which took over the plant
and premises of the neighbouring Powys Brewery in 1983 in order
to supply its own beer again. Serves 60 outlets.
Sam Powell Best Bitter (1036) – standard beer.
Samson (1050) – strong ale.

JOSHUA PRIVETT, Hants. See Pig & Whistle, Home-Brew pubs, pages 46–48.

RANDALL, Vauxlaurens Bry, St. Julians Av., St. Peter Port, Guernsey. ☎ 0481 20134.
Guernsey's smaller brewery, operating under the 'Bobby Ales' sign.
Seven of the 20 tied houses sell real ale.
Best Mild (1037) – dark, full-bodied brew.
Best Bitter (1047) – light and well flavoured.

RANDALL VAUTIER, PO Box 43, Clare Street, St. Helier, Jersey. ☎ 0534 73541.
No real ale. Some of the 18 houses stock Draught Bass.

RAVEN, Brighton. See Brighton Brewery.

RAYMENT, Furneux Pelham, Butingford, Herts. ☎ 027 978 671.
Small village brewery subsidiary of Greene King serving real ale in
23 of its 24 pubs in Hertfordshire and Essex. Plus expanding free
trade into London and East Anglia.
BBA (1036) – distinctive and refreshing.

REEPHAM, 1 Collers Way, Reepham, Norfolk. ☎ 0603 871091.
Set up in 1983 after owner was made redundant by a national
brewery. Now supplying 15 outlets in Norfolk.
Granary Bitter (1038) – hoppy and well-balanced.
Brewhouse Ale (1055) – full-bodied bitter.
Reepham Barley Wine (1078) – winter brew.

RIDLEY, Hartford End, Chelmsford, Essex. ☎ 0371 820316.
Essex's highly traditional brewery, selling real ale in all 65 houses,
chiefly from wooden casks, at the lowest prices in the S. East.
XXX (1034) – dark and distinctive mild.
PA (1034) – beautifully balanced bitter of character.
HE (1045) – fine full-flavoured bitter.
Bishops (1080) – strong Christmas barley wine.

RINGWOOD, 138 Christchurch Road, Ringwood, Hants. ☎ 0425 471177.
Begun by one of the fathers of the new brewery revolution, Peter
Austin, who has helped many others to start brewing. Moved to
new premises in 1985. Two tied houses and 80 free trade outlets.
Ringwood Best Bitter (1040) – hoppy and full-bodied.
Fortyniner (1049) – heavy, malty brew.
4X (1049) – tasty winter porter.
Old Thumper (1060) – well-hopped, strong bitter.

ROBINSON, Unicorn Brewery, Stockport, Cheshire. ☎ 061 480 6571.
Major family brewery with 320 houses serving real ale, which in
1982 took over Hartleys of Ulverston in Cumbria. Pubs concen-
trated in S. Manchester, Derbyshire, Cheshire and N. Wales.
Best Mild (1032) – sometimes darkened with extra caramel.
Bitter (1035) – well-balanced brew.
Best Bitter (1041) – full-bodied and well-hopped.
Old Tom (1080) – strong, smooth winter brew.

ROCKSIDE, Hornthwaite Hill Road, Thurlstone, Sheffield. ☎ 0226 764536.
Tiny new brewery set up in 1985 next to a bungalow brewing three
barrels a week.
Thurlstone Bitter (1042) – distinctive brew.
Thurlstone Bell (1050) – new strong ale.

ROMFORD Brewery, Romford. See Allied Breweries, pages 15–16.

ROYAL TUNBRIDGE WELLS. See Kentish Ales.

RUDDLES, Langham, Oakham, Rutland, Leics. ☎ 0572 56911.
Probably the most famous real ale brewery – with a far from tradi-
tional trade. It sold all its pubs to concentrate on supermarkets and
the free trade. Now also supplies Watney houses in London and
E. Anglia. Last year replaced draught Rutland Bitter with a stronger
Best Bitter.
Best Bitter (1037) – lighter version of full-flavoured County.
County (1050) – the only beer to have won Brewex twice.

Independent Breweries

St. AUSTELL, 63 Trevarthian Road, St. Austell, Cornwall. ☎ 0726 74444.
Popular 'holiday' brewery in Cornwall, which in recent years has
widened its range of real ales by adding two stronger brews. The
majority of the 132 houses now sell real ale.
BB (1031) – light bitter.
XXXX (1034) – rare dark mild.
Tinners Bitter (1038) – well-hopped malty bitter.
Hicks Special (1050) – a rich distinctive brew.

SELBY, 131 Millgate, Selby, N. Yorks. ☎ 0757 702826.
Old family brewery that began brewing again in 1972 after a gap of
18 years. Only a few free trade outlets and one tied house.
Best Bitter (1039) – a hoppy brew bottled as No. 1.

SEVENOAKS Brewery, Crown Point Inn, Seal Chart, Kent. ☎ 0732 810222.
Began as home-brew pub in 1981 but now supplying a few free
houses.
Sevenoaks Best Bitter (1038) and **Crown Point BB** (1038).

SHEPHERD NEAME, 17 Court Street, Faversham, Kent. ☎ 0795 532206.
The only survivor of the hop county's once-proud host of indepen-
dent breweries, serving real ale in most of its 250 houses. Has been
buying up pubs, notably in London.
Master Brew Mild (1031) – dark and sweet.
Master Brew Bitter (1036) – fine, hoppy brew.
Stock Ale (1036) – full dark ale.
Invicta (1044) – fruity premium bitter.
5X (1044) – rich dark winter ale.

SHIPSTONE, Nottingham. See Greenall Whitley, page 20.

SMILES, Colston Yard, 6–10 Upper Maudlin Street, Bristol. ☎ 0272 297350.
Avon's first new brewery, dating from 1977, now supplying over 50
free trade outlets and one tied house from its city centre site.
Best Bitter (1040) – full-bodied and hoppy.
Exhibition (1050) – dark, well-rounded bitter.

JOHN SMITH, Tadcaster, N. Yorks. See Courage, page 19.

SAMUEL SMITH, Old Brewery, Tadcaster, N. Yorks. ☎ 0937 832225.
Not to be confused with its larger neighbour, John Smith, which has
recently reintroduced real ale. Yorkshire's oldest brewery still produces 'beer from the wood' for the majority of its 300 scattered pubs
including 19 in London. Cask breathers used on Tadcaster Bitter in
some outlets.
Tadcaster Bitter (1035) – light and hoppy.
Old Brewery or **OBB** (1038.9) – full-bodied and malty.
Museum Ale (1047) – stronger brew.

SPRINGFIELD, Wolverhampton. See Bass, pages 17–18.

STALLION ALES, The Grange, Helland, Bodmin, Cornwall. ☎ 0208 2249.
Former Berkshire brewery attached to the Long Barn pub in Cippen-
ham, which moved to Cornwall in 1985. Now supplies around 15
free houses in North Cornwall.
Stallion (1040) – pure malt bitter.
Barnstormer (1060) – powerful ale.

STONES, Sheffield. See Bass, pages 17–18.

STRATHALBYN, 70 Beardmore Way, Clydebank Ind. Estate, Dalmuir. ☎ 041 941 2070.
Brave venture started in 1982 to challenge the keg stronghold of
Glasgow. Now in 30 free trade outlets. Owns two pubs. The highly-
praised porter was described as 'probably the most distinctive beer
brewed in Scotland this generation' at CAMRA's Scottish festival.
Strathalbyn Original (1039) – a premium bitter.
Strathalbyn II (1043) – traditional Scots Export.
Beardmore Porter (1043) – distinctive dark bitter beer.

SUMMERSKILLS, 15 Pomphlett Farm Ind. Estate, Plymouth. ☎ 0752 492841.
New brewery set up near Kingsbridge, Devon, in 1983 before moving to Plymouth in 1985. Owns two pubs.
Bigbury Best Bitter (1044) – full-bodied beer.
Whistle Belly Vengeance (1060) – real ail.

TATE, Kinford, Canon Pyon, Hereford. ☎ 043 271 328.
New brewery set up in 1985, named after the owner's cricketing grandfather, Maurice Tate, the Sussex and England paceman. Has now bowled into 45 local free trade outlets and into London.
LBW (1035) – light, session bitter.
Tate's Traditional (1040) – the original full-bodied beer.
Maiden Over (1051) – strong, dark and deceptive.
Hereford Hopper (1065) – notorious festival special.

TAYLOR, Knowle Spring Brewery, Keighley, W. Yorks. ☎ 0535 603139.
The fame of Timothy Taylor's quality ales – which have won a barrel full of Championship medals – stretches far beyond W. Yorkshire and their 29 pubs. One of the widest ranges of real ales, with Landlord the pride of the pack.
Golden Best or **Bitter Ale** (1033) – light and malty.
Mild (1033) – dark version of the Best.
Best Bitter (1037) – well-hopped bitter.
Landlord (1042) – distinctive, full-bodied bitter.
Porter (1043) – occasional rich brew.
Ram Tam (1043) – fruity dark winter ale.

TAYLOR-WALKER, London. See Allied Breweries, pages 15–16.

TENNENT-CALEDONIAN, Scotland. See Bass, pages 17–18.

JOSHUA TETLEY, Leeds. See Allied Breweries, pages 15–16.

TETLEY-WALKER, Warrington. See Allied Breweries, pages 15–16.

THEAKSTON, Wellgarth, Masham, Ripon, N. Yorks. ☎ 0765 89544.
And Bridge Street, Carlisle, Cumbria. ☎ 0228 24467.
Yorkshire Dales brewery renowned for its Old Peculier, which sprang to prominence with the real ale revival, and subsequently bought the former State brewery in Carlisle to meet free trade demand. In 1984 taken over by Matthew Brown, but both breweries kept open and some Brown pubs transferred to Theakstons. Now has over 40 tied houses. However, still threatened by Scottish & Newcastle's substantial share stake in Matthew Brown.
Best Bitter (1037) – light but distinctive. (Carlisle).
XB (1044) – strong, full-bodied bitter. (Masham).
Old Peculier (1057) – notorious, rich and heavy. (Both).

THOMPSONS, London Inn, 11 West Street, Ashburton, Devon. ☎ 0364 52478.
Begun in 1981 for just their own pub, but now supplying 18 outlets around Dartmoor and S. Devon. New brewery under construction.
Mild (1033) – dark and mellow.
Bitter (1040) – malty premium bitter.
IPA (1045) – strong and hoppy.

THWAITES, PO Box 50, Star Brewery, Blackburn, Lancs. ☎ 0254 54431.
Traditional Lancashire brewery, providing its award-winning real ales, including two fine milds, in 399 of its 413 houses. In 1984 took over Yates & Jackson's pubs in Lancaster, closing the brewery.
Mild (1032) – nutty and dark.
Best Mild (1034) – excellent malty brew.
Bitter (1036) – creamy and hoppy.

TITANIC, Travellers Rest, Newcastle St., Burslem, Stoke. ☎ 810418.
Eight-barrel plant set up in 1985 supplying the one tied house and 20 free trade outlets. Named after the Captain of the Titanic, who came from Stoke.
Titanic Best Bitter (1036) – hoppy and refreshing.
Titanic Premium (1042) – well-balanced and tasty.

TOLLY COBBOLD, Cliff Brewery, PO Box 5, Ipswich, Suffolk. ℰ 0473 56751. Ipswich brewery which has considerably improved the range of real ales in 300 of its 340 pubs. Like Camerons, owned by the Barclay Brothers hotel group.
Mild (1031) – sweet and malty.
Bitter (1034) – subtle and pleasantly dry.
Original (1037) – well-hopped, flavoursome bitter.
Old Strong (1046) – rich, fruity winter brew.
XXXX (1046) –new premium bitter.

TOOLEY St. Brewery, 52–54 Tooley Street, London SE1. ℰ 01 378 6721. Set up in 1984 chiefly to supply the Dicken's Inn, St. Katherine's Dock, on the other side of the Thames.
Dicken's Own (1036) – light malty bitter.
Dicken's Special (1045) – full-bodied, premium ale.

TRAQUAIR HOUSE, Innerleithen, Peeblesshire, Borders. ℰ 0896 830323. Eighteenth century Scottish brewery in an ancient fortified manor house revived by the Laird of Traquair in 1965. Previously known for his widely exported rich strong bottled beer, Peter Maxwell-Stuart introduced a draught beer for the free trade.
Bear Ale (1050) – strong draught ale.
House Ale (1075) – usually bottled but occasionally on draught.

TROUGH Brewery, Louisa Street, Idle, Bradford, W. Yorks. ℰ 0274 613450. Begun in 1981 brewing value-for-money beers for the club trade, but have since built up a tied estate of six houses. Currently malt extract, but new full mash plant being installed.
Trough Bitter (1035.5) – smooth, refreshing bitter.
Wild Boar Bitter (1039.5) – full-bodied and distinctive.

TRUMAN, London. See Watney, pages 22–23.

ULEY, Old Brewery, 31 The Street, Uley, Dursley, Glos. ℰ 0453 860120. New brewery set up in 1985 by former beer wholesaler to supply Gloucestershire free trade.
Uley Bitter (1040) – well-hopped and malty.
Old Spot (1050) – malty strong ale.

ULEY BITTER

USHER, Trowbridge, Wilts. See Watney, pages 22–23.

VAUX Breweries, Sunderland, Tyne & Wear. ℰ 0783 76277. Large regional brewing group which in 1986 announced that it was to close its Darley brewery in S. Yorkshire in September, 1986, and its Scottish brewery, Lorimer & Clark, in Spring, 1987. Brewing of Darley's beers would be transferred to its other brewery, Wards of Sheffield, with Lorimer's Scotch produced at Sunderland.
Sunderland Draught (1040) – thin session bitter.
Samson (1042.5) – flavoursome sharp bitter.
Regal (1044) – new darker brew.

WADWORTH, Northgate Brewery, Northgate, Devizes, Wilts. ℰ 0380 3361. Delightful market town brewery whose excellent 6X is popular in the free trade throughout the South. Solidly traditional, with all of the 149 houses selling real ale. Now opening new pubs in cities.
Devizes Bitter (1030) – a light bitter.
Henry Wadworth IPA (1034) – hoppier brew.
6X (1040) – a splendid, malty bitter.
Farmer's Glory (1046) – dark and distinctive.
Old Timer (1055) – heavy and fruity.

PETER WALKER, Liverpool. See Allied Breweries, pages 15–16.

WARD, Sheaf Brewery, Ecclesall Road, Sheffield S11. ℰ 0742 755155 South Yorkshire subsidiary of Vaux of Sunderland, with real ale in 63 of its 103 pubs, which since the closure of the neighbouring Thorne brewery in September, 1986, also produces Darley's beers.
Sheffield Best Bitter (1038) – malty bitter.

WATNEY, COMBE, REID, London. See Watney, pages 22–23.

WEBSTER, Halifax, W. Yorks. See Watney, pages 22–23.

WELLS Brewery, Havelock Street, Bedford. ☎ 0234 65100.
This regional company completely rebuilt its brewery on a new site and is now building up its tied estate, even in London. Some 190 of the 279 pubs serve cask beer without pressure. In 1984 opened a home-brew pub, the Ancient Druids, in Cambridge.
Eagle Bitter (1035) – a consistent bitter beer.
Bombardier (1042) – a full-bodied best bitter.

WELSH BREWERS, Cardiff. See Bass, pages 17–18.

WEM Brewery, Shropshire. See Greenall Whitley, page 20.

WETHEREDS, Marlow, Bucks. See Whitbread, pages 24–25.

WHITBREAD. See pages 24–25.

WILSONS, Manchester. See Watney, pages 22–23.

WILTSHIRE, The Old Brewery, Church St., Tisbury, Wilts. ☎ 0747 870666.
New brewery set up in 1985 in the premises of the defunct Tisbury Brewery. Owns two pubs and intends to have a further 10 by the end of 1986. Also wholesales for other breweries.
Regency Best (1038) – distinctive, pale bitter.
Regency Extra (1049) – smooth, rounded beer.
Old Devil (1060) – well-hopped strong ale.

WINKLE'S, Saxon Cross Brewery, Harpur Hill, Buxton, Derby. ☎ 0298 71720.
Begun in 1979 serving the local free trade and now concentrating on building up a chain of tied houses.
Mild (1037) – dark and malty. **Bitter** (1037) – well-hopped brew.
BVA (1037) – pale 'house' beer, known under various names.

WOOD, Wistanstow, Craven Arms, Shropshire. ☎ 05882 2523.
Begun in 1980 next to the Plough Inn. Supplies over 50 outlets.
Parish Bitter (1040) – refreshing, light bitter.
Wood's Special (1043) – full-flavoured, sweetish bitter.
Christmas Cracker (1060) – dark winter warmer.

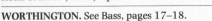

WOODFORDE, Spread Eagle Brewery, Erpingham, Norfolk. ☎ 0263 768152.
Begun in 1981 in Norwich, bringing much-needed choice to this Watney dominated region, before moving to the present site in 1983. Supplies 60 free trade outlets plus own pub at the brewery. Wide range of beers occasionally augmented by special brews.
Norfolk Pride (1036) – light but full-flavoured.
Wherry Best Bitter (1039) – pale and malty.
Norfolk Porter (1041) – distinctive, dark and hoppy.
Old Norfolk Ale (1043) – winter brew.
Phoenix XXX (1047) – full-bodied, malty bitter.
Head Cracker (1069) – pale winter ale.

WORTHINGTON. See Bass, pages 17–18.

WYE VALLEY, 69 St. Owens Street, Hereford. ☎ 0432 274 968.
Much-travelled brewery which started in Nottinghamshire as the Abbey Brewery, before moving to Canon Pyon in Herefordshire in 1985, and then moving again to its own pub in Hereford in 1986.
Hereford Bitter (1038) – clean, hoppy beer.
Hereford Supreme (1043) – malty, smooth ale.

YOUNG, Ram Brewery, High Street, Wandsworth, London SW18. ☎ 01 870 0141.
Last but not least is one of the most warmly regarded breweries in the country, which stood alone against the keg tide in the Capital in the early Seventies. All 145 houses offer real ale, some delivered by horse-drawn drays. Are currently buying pubs.
Bitter (1036) – light and bitter.
Special (1046) – full-flavoured and distinctive.
Winter Warmer (1055) – strong old ale.

YOUNGER, Edinburgh. See Scottish & Newcastle, page 25.

ABINGTON PARK,
Wellingborough Road,
Northampton. ☎ 0604 31240.
Cobblers Ale (1037)
Abington Extra (1047)
Abington Special (1055)
One of five Clifton Inns 'in-house breweries'; the other four are in London. Blanket pressure.

ALFORD ARMS, Frithsden
Herts. ☎ 044 27 4480.
Cherrypicker's Bitter (1036)
Pickled Squirrel (1044)
Rudolf's Revenge (1053)
Alexander the Great (1061)
Whitbread's first home-brew pub, founded in 1981. Malt extract.

ALL NATIONS (Mrs Lewis's),
Coalport Road, Madeley,
Shropshire. ☎ 0952 585747.
Pale Ale (1032)
One of four home-brew pubs left by the early Seventies before the new wave arrived. The others are the Blue Anchor, Old Swan and Three Tuns.

ANCIENT DRUIDS, Napier
Street, Cambridge. ☎ 0223 324514.
Kite Bitter (1035)
Druids Special (1044)
Charles Wells home-brew pub. Malt extract.

BAKERY & BREWHOUSE, 14
Gloucester Street, Oxford.
☎ 0865 727265.
Tapper (1038)
Best (1044)
Porter (1045)
Oxbow (1059)
Old Wrot (1072)
Hall's home-brew pub, uniquely linked with a bakery. Blanket pressure.

BATTERSEA Brewery (Prince
of Wales), 339 Battersea Park
Road, London SW11. ☎ 01
622 2112.
Battersea Bitter (1036)
Best Bitter (1040)
Nine Elms Mild (1040)
Power House (1050)

BEER ENGINE, Newton St.
Cyres, Exeter, Devon. ☎ 039
285 282
Rail Ale (1037)
Piston Bitter (1044)
Sleeper (1055)
'Rail' home-brew.

BLUE ANCHOR, Coinagehall
Street, Helston, Cornwall.
☎ 032 65 62821.
Mild (1040)
Medium (1050)
BB (1053)
Special (1066)
Extra Special (1070)
Historic thatched home brewery producing powerful ales.

BORVE HOUSE, Borve, Isle of
Lewis, Outer Hebrides,
Scotland. ☎ 0851 85 223.

The Stag & Hounds – Britain's smallest commercial brewery?

BOOM YEARS ARE OVER

The pint-size explosion of pubs brewing their own beer over the past decade has settled down. From 76 'in-house' plants last year, there are now only 72. But the good news is that while major companies are pulling the plug on the mini mash tun (Whitbread has recently closed three pub breweries in Cardiff, Southampton and Burgess Hill, Sussex), now that the novelty value has faded, more individual operations are appearing.

Probably the smallest commercial brewery in Britain surfaced last year when the Stag & Hounds, Burrough-on-the-Hill, Leicestershire, started brewing using home-made plant like a Baby Burco boiler and a cut-in-two barrel as a mash tun. The beer was excellent. While in Worcester, the Brewery Tap & Brewery was established as an old-fashioned private member's drinking club – with its own brewery.

Home-brew pubs are returning to what they should be – unique small-scale operations each with their own character – instead of chains of look-alike theme pubs where the latest gimmick just happens to be a brewery.

Heavy Ale (1040)
Extra Strong (1085)
Britain's most northerly brewery. Both beers also now bottled (unpasteurised).

BREWERY TAP & BREWERY,
50 Lowesmoor, Worcester.
☎ 21540.
Jolly Roger Quaff (1038)
Three Counties Best (1042)
Severn Bore Special (1048)
Old Lowesmoor (1058)
Worcester Winter Wobbler
(1086)
First private members' pub – with its own Jolly Roger ales.

BREWHOUSE, High Street,
Poole, Dorset.
Poole Bitter (1039)
Bosun Bitter (1048)
Purbeck Lager (1036)
Owned by Poole Brewery.
Blanket pressure.

BRIDGEWATER ARMS, Little
Gaddesden, Herts. ☎ 044 284
2408.
Triple BBB (1034)
BSB (1042)
Earl's Bitter (1048)
Old Santa (1066)
Blanket pressure.

BUSHY'S BREWPUB, Victoria
Street, Douglas, Isle of Man.
☎ 0624 75139.
Old Bushy Tail (1045)
Strongest draught Manx ale from the island's only pub brewery, established 1986.

DOG & PARROT, Waterloo
Street, Newcastle. ☎ 0632
616998.
Scotswood Ale (1036)
Wallop (1046)
Whitbread – malt extract.

DOWN ROYAL, Ballinderry
Road, Lisburn, Co. Antrim,
N. Ireland. ☎ 08462 82473.
Gold Cup (1035)
Export (1040)
Brewery since 1982.

FALCON & FIRKIN, 274
Victoria Park Road, London
E9. ☎ 01 985 0693.
Falcon Ale (1038)
Hackney Bitter (1045)
Dogbolter (1060)
David Bruce's eighth and latest 'Firkin' pub brewery.
Blanket pressure.

**FELLOWS, MORTON &
CLAYTON,** Canal St.,

Nottingham. ✆ 0602 506795.
Fellow's Bitter (1041)
Clayton's Original (1048)
Whitbread – malt extract.

FERRET & FIRKIN, 114 Lots
Road, London SW10. ✆ 01
352 6645.
Stoat Bitter (1038)
Ferret Ale (1045)
Dogbolter (1060)
Full name 'Ferret & Firkin in
the Balloon up the Creek' –
longest pub title in the world.
Blanket pressure.

FIRST IN LAST OUT, 14 High
Street, Hastings, Sussex.
✆ 0424 425079.
Old Crofters (1040)
Cardinal Sussex Ale (1048)
St. Clements Brewery
established 1985.

FLEECE & FIRKIN, 12 St.
Thomas Street, Bristol. ✆ 0272
277150.
Bootlace Bitter (1038)
Bristol Best (1043)
Coal Porter (1050)
Dogbolter (1060)
Black Sheep (1086)
Firkinstein Lager (1044)
Former Bruce's pub in old
wool market, now owned by
Halls. Blanket pressure.

FLOUNDER & FIRKIN, 54
Holloway Road, London N7.
✆ 01 609 9574.
Fish T'ale (1038)
Whale Ale (1045)
Dogbolter (1060)
Blanket pressure.

FOUR KEYS, Station Road,
Wadhurst, Sussex. ✆ 089 288
2252.
Mild (1035)
4K Bitter (1036)
Stallion (1050)
Malt extract beers. Mild on top
pressure.

FOX & FIRKIN, 316
Lewisham High Street,
London SE13. ✆ 01 690 8925.
Vixen Ale (1038)
Bruce's Bitter (1045)
Dogbolter (1060)
Blanket pressure.

FOX & HOUNDS, Stottesdon,
Shropshire. ✆ 074 632 222.
Dasher's Draught (1040)
Christmas Special (1070)
Also available in a few other
pubs.

FOX & HOUNDS, Barley,
Royston, Herts. ✆ 076 384
459.
Nathaniel's Special (1046)
Hogshead (1041)
Home-brew pub with rare
'gallows' sign across the road.

FOX & NEWT, Burley Road,
Leeds 3. ✆ 0532 432612.
Burley Bitter (1036)
Old Willow (1046)
Festival (1060)
Whitbread – malt extract.

FROG & FIRKIN, 41 Tavistock
Crescent, London W11. ✆ 01
727 9250.

Tavistock Ale (1038)
Bullfrog (1045)
Dogbolter (1060)
Blanket pressure. Viewing
panel to the brewery – in the
floor.

FROG & FRIGATE, 33 Canute
Road, Southampton, Hants.
✆ 0703 332231.
Frog's Original (1038)
Croaker (1050)
Captain Frigate (1060)
Now serves two pubs in
Southampton plus another
Frog & Frigate in Portsmouth.

FROG & PARROT, Division
Street, Sheffield. ✆ 0742
21280.
Old Croak Ale (1035)
Reckless Bitter (1046)
Roger's Conqueror (1066)
Roger's Specials (1080) +
Whitbread – malt extract. In
1985 brewed the strongest
draught beer in the world,
Roger & Out (1125).

GLOBE, Main Street,
Fishguard, Dyfed, Wales.
✆ 0348 872500.
Black Fox Bitter (1038)
Malt extract. Blanket pressure.

The Brewery Tap & Brewery

GOLDEN LION, Market Place,
Leyburn, N. Yorks. ✆ 0969
22161.
Oliver John's Bitter (1037)
Former Harrogate home-brew
pub moved further north.

GOOSE & FIRKIN, 47
Borough Road, Southwark,
London SE1. ✆ 01 403 3590.
Goose Bitter (1038)
Borough Bitter (1045)
Dogbolter (1060)
London's first pub to revive
brewing on the premises, in
1979. Malt extract. Blanket
pressure.

GREYHOUND, 151
Greyhound Lane, Streatham,
London SW16. ✆ 01 677
9962.
XXX Pedigree (1035)
Greyhound Special (1037)
Streatham Strong (1048)
Streatham Dynamite (1056)
Clifton Inns. Blanket pressure.

HALL CROSS, 33 Hallgate,
Doncaster, S. Yorks. ✆ 0302
28213.
Stocks Best Bitter (1038)
Stocks Select (1045)
Old Horizontal (1055)

Stock's beers now also
supplied to a second pub, The
Turnpike, Bawtry.

JOHN LANDREGAN, Reigate
Brewery, 46 Glovers Road,
Reigate, Surrey. ✆ 42317.
Reigate Bitter (1042).
Ten Fifty Five (1055)
Brewery in an off-licence –
malt extract.

JOLLY FENMAN, 64 Blackfen
Road, Sidcup, Kent.
✆ 01 850 6664.
Blackfen Bitter (1037)
Fenman Fortune (1047)
Clifton Inns. Blanket pressure.

LASS O'GOWRIE, Charles
Street, Manchester.
✆ 061 273 6932.
Bitter (1035)
Strong (1042)
Whitbread – malt extract.

LION, 182 Pawsons Road,
Croydon, Surrey.
✆ 01 684 2978.
Burke's Best Bitter (1041)
Also available at the Hole in
the Wall and the Wellington,
Waterloo.

MAPLE LEAF, Winthorpe
Road, Newark, Notts.
✆ 0636 703485.
Maple Leaf Bitter (1037)
Ind Coope home-brew.

MARISCO TAVERN, Lundy
Island, Bristol Channel,
✆ Woolacombe (0271)
870870.
John O's Bitter (1037)
John O's Special (1055)
Malt extract island brewery.

MARKET PORTER, 9 Stoney
St., Borough Market, London
SEI. ✆ 01 407 2495.
Market Bitter (1038)
Market Special (1048)
Malt extract brewery
supplying the pub and two
other 'Market Taverns' with
the same beers under different
names – Pearly King,
Bromley-by-Bow (Bow Bitter/
Seven Bells) and Paper Moon,
Blackfriars Road (Blackfriars
Bitter/ Strong).

Mr CHERRY'S, Marina Court,
St. Leonards, Sussex. ✆ 0424
422705.
Hastings (1042)
Conqueror (1066)
Sea-front brewhouse.

NEW FERMOR ARMS, Station
Road, Rufford, Lancs. ✆ 0704
821713.
Fettlers Bitter (1037)
Home-brew pub since 1976
owned by Tetley-Walker for
four years but now back with
original owners. Malt extract.

NEW INN, Otley Road,
Harrogate, W. Yorks. ✆ 0423
503501.
Gate Ale (1040)
Tetley home-brew pub.
Blanket pressure.

NEW INN, Cropton, Pickering, N. Yorks. ☎ 075 15 330.
Two Pints (1036)
Special (1060)

OLD ANCHOR, High Street, Upton-on-Severn, Worcs. ☎ 068 46 2146.
Anchor Bitter (1034)
Severn X (1040)
Old Anchor (1060) – winter only.

OLDE BULL & BUSH, 9 Hartshill Road, Stoke-on-Trent. ☎ 0782 49782.
Potters Bitter (1039)
Saggars Special (1052)
Rough (1070)
New Victorian-style home-brew pub.

OLD SWAN, (Ma Pardoe's), Halesowen Road, Netherton, Dudley, W. Midlands. ☎ 0384 53075.
Bitter (1034)
One of the great institutions of Black Country drinking, currently being enlarged.

OLD SWAN, High Street, Cheltenham, Glos. ☎ 0242 584929.
Old Swan Bitter (1038)
Whitbread – malt extract.

ORANGE Brewery, 37 Pimlico Road, London SW1. ☎ 01 730 5378.
Pimlico Light (1036) – summer only.
SW1 (1040)
SW2 (1050)
Pimlico Porter (1046) – winter only.
Clifton Inns oldest in-house brewery, since early 1983. Blanket pressure.

PHEASANT & FIRKIN, 166 Goswell Road, London EC1. ☎ 01 253 7429.
Barbarian Bitter (1038)
Pheasant Bitter (1045)
Dogbolter (1060)
Blanket pressure.

PHOENIX & FIRKIN, Windsor Walk, London SE5. ☎ 01 701 8282.
Rail Ale (1038)
Phoenix Bitter (1045)
Dogbolter (1060)
Former Denmark Hill station. Blanket pressure.

PIG & WHISTLE, Privett, Alton, Hants. ☎ 073 088 323.
Privett Bitter (1039)
BDS (1049)
Also now brewing for the free trade.

PIG & WHISTLE, McNeil Street, Glasgow. Gorbals. Home-brew pub serving pressurised beer.

PLOUGH, Bodicote, Banbury, Oxon. ☎ 0295 62327.
Bodicote Bitter (1035)
Old English Porter (1045)
No. 9 (1045)
Brews from its own well for the pub and free trade.

QUEEN VICTORIA, 118 Wellington Street, London SE18. ☎ 01 854 3838.
Country Bitter (1036)
Sidekick (1047)
Sledgehammer (1058)

RAISDALE HOTEL, Raisdale Road, Penarth, S. Glamorgan. ☎ 707317.
Eight-Bore Special (1041)
Beer only served to hotel residents.

ROSE & CROWN, Lawrence Street, York. ☎ 0904 28560.
Viking Bitter (1043)
Tetley home-brew pub. Blanket pressure.

ROSE STREET Brewery, Rose Street, Edinburgh. ☎ 031 225 1660.
Auld Reekie 80/- (1041)
Auld Reekie 90/- (1046)
Scotland's first home-brew pub, run by Alloa Brewery. Malt extract.

ROYAL CLARENCE, The Esplanade, Burnham-on-Sea, Somerset. ☎ 0278 783138.
Clarence Bitter (1036)

ROYAL INN, Horsebridge, Tavistock, Devon. ☎ 082 287 214.
Tamar Ale (1039)
Horsebridge Best (1045)
Heller (1060)
15th century country pub on Cornish border.

SAIR, Lane Top, Linthwaite, Huddersfield, W. Yorks. ☎ 0484 842370.
Linfit Mild (1032)
Linfit Bitter (1035)
Linfit Special (1041)
English Guineas Stout (1040)
Old Eli (1050)
Leadboiler (1063)
Enoch's Hammer (1080)
Extensive range of beers due to tiny 1½ barrel brew length.

SOUTH EASTERN, 51 Station Road, Strood, Kent. ☎ 0634 719958.
Pirate Porter (1035)
Clipper (1040)
Gravedigger (1050)
Buccaneer (1060)
Lifebuoy (1075)

Only remaining 'Hilton' brewery; the one at the Pier Hotel, Gravesend, closed in 1985.

STAG & HOUNDS, Burrough on the Hill, Melton Mowbray, Leics. ☎ 066 477 375.
Parish Special or **PSB** (1036)
Poachers Ale (1066)
Probably Britain's smallest commercial brewery. Tiny half-barrel plant.

STATION, Otley Road, Guiseley, Leeds, W. Yorks.
Guiseley Gyle (1045)
Tetley's first home-brew pub set up in 1982. Now have four. Malt extract.

TAVERN, Newnham Bridge, Worcs. ☎ 058 479 331.
Bartlett's Mild (1036)
Bartlett's Bitter (1042)
Set up by former Black Country family brewer Bob Bartlett.

JOHN THOMPSON Inn, Ingleby, Derbyshire. ☎ 033 16 3426/2469.
JTS XXX (1043)
Award-winning pub brewery named after the landlord. JTS XXX is sold in the free trade as **Lloyd's Best Bitter**. Also **Lloyd's Skullcrusher** (1065) at Christmas.

THREE CROWNS, Ashurstwood, E. Grinstead, Sussex. ☎ 0342 21597.
Session Bitter (1038)
The (Watney) Phoenix Brewery's only brewery!

THREE TUNS, Bishop's Castle, Shropshire. ☎ 0588 638797.
Mild (1035)
XXX (1042)
Castle Steamer (1045)
Historic home-brew pub.

VICTORIA, Earl Soham, Suffolk. ☎ 072 882 758.
Gannet Mild (1034)
Victoria Bitter (1037)
Also supplies a few other pubs. Malt extract.

WARRIOR, Coldharbour Lane, London SW9.
Brixton Bitter (1036)
Brixton Best (1040)
Warrior Strong Ale (1050)
Owned by Conway Taverns and supplies other Conway pubs in London with local beers like Balmoral Bitter (1040), Castle Bitter (1040) and Anchor Strong Ale (1050).

YORKSHIRE GREY, 2 Theobalds Road, London WC1. ☎ 01 405 2519.
City Bitter (1035)
Headline Bitter (1037)
Holborn Best (1047)
Regiment Bitter (1055) – winter only.
Clifton Inns. Malt extract. Blanket pressure.

BY the end of the century, Britain's remaining breweries will produce between them no more than a dozen bottled beers. Most will be brewed by whichever multinational corporation takes over Whitbread. New uses will have to be found for the shelves which decorate the space between the optics and the floor. Britain will have lost a large chunk of its brewing heritage.

There are said to be nearly thirty distinct styles of beer brewed in the United Kingdom. Yet even a detailed perusal of the brewery section of this year's Guide will yield less than half that number. Of those, several will represent little more than the final stand of a small pocket of consumer resistance or else the entrepreneurial hunch of a micro-brewer, chancing his customers' arms on an unusual pint.

The truth is that the bulk of British beer styles have survived the ravages of takeover and rationalization by hiding in bottles. You won't find strong brown ale or, rarer still, oatmeal stout served by handpump.

The last fifteen years have seen the old brown bottle come under threat of extinction from two quarters. In pubs the drift has been towards draught beers. In the burgeoning supermarket trade, the demand has been for cans of low-cost, highly watered 'special bitters' and lagers.

The aluminium ring-pull can has the advantage that when thrown into the gutter, it can be stamped on without risk to the consumer's footwear. It can also double as a percussion instrument for cricketing calypsos. But don't think that it's kind to beer because it ain't.

American beer 'gourmet' Howard Hillman writes theses on the subject. He believes not only that cans impair the taste of beer but that flavour defects can be detected in bottled brews if clear glass is employed or even, wait for it, bottled beers are stored under incorrect lighting. To my palate canned beer always has a background flavour of burnt coffee and rusty nails.

A CAMRA survey last year revealed that the total number of UK bottled beers in production had all but halved since 1974. Just over 300 remain but the tendency is to concentrate on the production of all-weather very light ales and dilute browns. It is difficult to stamp a brewer's 'thumbprint' flavour on a container beer which is 97 parts water, so the trend to uniformity is inevitable.

The most distinctive beer styles are suffering badly. Only twenty breweries produce any form of stout – and a third of these brew at a strength that would have wrought scorn from traditional stout drinkers. Less than half the independent brewers retain a truly *strong* golden ale or dark barley wine. The number offering both can be counted on the fingers of one hand. *Whitbread's Gold Label* is the uniquitous replacement.

Strong brown ales, both sweet and dry, are holding their own north of a line from the Mersey to the Humber, whilst premium pale ales – modern day equivalents of the old India Pale Ales – survive in the East Midlands and South Eastern England.

Most bottled beers are *not* 'naturally conditioned'. That is to say that they do not contain a yeast sediment and so cannot continue to mature in the bottle. There is no doubt that quality can and does suffer as a result. *Worthington White Shield* (1052) is a rare example of a sediment beer and as a premium pale ale leads the field in flavour. One need only drink it side by side with the bottled version of a fine beer like *Ruddles County* (1050) to recognise the advantages of allowing a degree of secondary fermentation in the bottle. The subtleties of palate are immediately clear and make White Shield an infinitely superior drink. *Young's Ramrod* (1046), *Shepherd Neame Abbey* (1045), *Ridley's Old Bob* (1050) and *Home's Robin Hood IPA* (1045) have similar shortfalls but nonetheless are good examples of the style.

Courage's Bulldog Pale Ale (1068) is a beer in the Churchillian mould. It has a crisp, clean, full flavour and retains its hop aroma. To my mind it is matched only by the more mellow *Greene King St. Edmund Ale* (1060) or perhaps *Adnams Broadside* (1068).

Brown ales come in all shapes and shades. *Whitbread's Forest Brown* (1032) and *Manns Brown* (1034) are starting to mop up the lower end of the market. Neither is memorable. This is the territory of the old Nut Browns, still produced by many breweries. The mid-gravity brown ales tend to be sweeter but are an endangered species. Bass Runcorn produce *M & B's Sam Brown* (1035). In Nottingham, *Home's Home Brewed* (1036) and *Hardy's & Hanson's Special Brown* (1036) still live. Other strongholds include the offshore islands such as Jersey, Guernsey and the Isle of Man where each brewer's brown ales maintain a decent gravity.

Strong brown ales are a speciality of the North East. The best known and least impressive is *S & N's Newcastle Brown* (1045), a burnt sugar brew. At the time of writing the fate of the Vaux Group's bottled bevvies post-rationalisation is not clear but should *Vaux Double Maxim* (1044) survive the pogrom it deserves a try. *Sam Smith's Strong Brown* (1045) is a beauty, as is *North Clubs Fed Strong Brown* (1047). The South's leading contenders are *Adnams Fisherman Brown* (1042) and the distinctive *King & Barnes Old XXXX* (1046). Both are bottled versions of draught winter brews.

Stout should be black by virtue of the full roast malt used in its mash. It should be bitter but may vary in sweetness. There were once a dozen different styles of stout but nowadays the term refers almost exclusively to two brands – Guinness and Whitbread's Mackeson. *Guinness* (1042) is the dry one, *Mackeson* (1042) the sweet. Bottled Guinness is still found in naturally conditioned form in England, Wales and Ireland, provided one sticks to the traditionally shaped pint and half-pint bottles. There is no doubting it is a first class drink in this form, although I strongly suspect that the old barroom edict about Guinness being better in Ireland is nonsense. More likely the standard of bitter beers in Ireland is so low that it *seems* so much better over there. Mackeson is tolerable, and English.

The best place to drink British stout is Italy, where a number of companies like Belhaven and Courage export fine brews unavailable to the home market. British drinkers can, however avail themselves of *Sam Smith's Nourishing Sweet Stout* (1042) and wonderful *Strong Stout* (1050), *Hardy's & Hanson's Blackamoor* (1044), *Tim Taylor's Black Bess* (1043) and *Morrell's Malt Stout* (1042) whilst they still exist.

Courage Imperial Russian Stout (1102) is naturally conditioned and in a class of its own. The best place to drink it is in a specialist beer bar in continental Europe alongside the best in Belgian, German and Czech beers. Having sidled one's way through a Weissbier, a couple of Lambics, via increasing strengths of Pilseners and Dortmunders to a Doppelbock, take a slurp of this mighty brew and you will taste the reason why Britain's perverse systems of brewing beer have survived the centuries.

Strong ales in general and barley wines in particular can be found in decreasing number across the British Isles. *St. Austell* produce two – *Smugglers Ale* (1070) is a delicious dark creamy brew that is presumably administered to coastguards on nights of no moon. *Prince's Ale* (1100), was first brewed in the Duchy of Cornwall to celebrate their Duke's 21st birthday and comes with the prettiest of purple and gold labels. If thrown on the embers of a dying fire it is said to be inflammable.

In the West Midlands, Wolverhampton & Dudley advertise their *Banks's Imperial Old Ale* (1096) on posters and placards – it is 'Old and Unimproved', saints be praised. *Davenports* promote their golden *Top Brew de Luxe* (1074), perhaps at the expense of the dark and impressive *Top Brew Original* (1071). *Sam Smiths* head their excellent bottled range with *Golden Strong* (1100). Local advice is to extinguish cigarettes and fasten seat belts before journeying too far with that one. *Morrells* of Oxford brew a scholarly dark brew called *College Ale* (1073). In the North West *John Willie Lees Moonraker* (1074) and *Robinsons Old Tom* (1080) can also be found in cask in the winter months whilst *Holts Sixex* (1064) and *Higsons Stingo* (1078) survive in bottle only.

Along the south coast, *Harveys* are remarkable in that they produce two beers at a gravity of 1090 – *Elizabethan* and *Christmas Ale*. But a few miles to the west are the kings of the strong bottled ales. *Gales Prize Old Ale* (1095) in its uniquely eccentric cork-stoppered bottle and *Eldridge Pope's Thomas Hardy Ale* (1125) with its equally unusual plea to the consumer to wait ten years before opening the bottle, represent the happy marriage of brewer's art and marketing man's dream. Both are sediment beers.

One final indulgence before ending this whistle stop tour of the nation's alternative ales. If any beer can be said to stand in a category all its own then it is *Greene King's Strong Suffolk* (1056). Imagine taking a gigantic, hand hewn wooden cask, placing it on end, filling it with fermentable material at an og of 1106, covering the top with sand and leaving it for over a year. Contemplate such a sight in the stainless steel, screwtop, military order of Greene King's Westgate brewery. Imagine taking the resulting antiseptic potion – I can assure you the neat version tastes foul – and mixing it with ten parts of dark winter ale.

The result is a masterpiece called Strong Suffolk, a connoisseur's delight and a damning testimony against those who feel bottled beers should be allowed quietly to die.

But then as Wilsons, North Country, Darleys, Lorimer & Clark, Yates & Jackson and Simpkiss will tell you, producing a first rate product in this day and age confers no right to survival.

Tim Webb

CAN YOU THINK OF A TOPIC OF CONVERSATION – I'M AFRAID WE'VE COMPLETELY RUN OUT

Almondsbury 14E8

10.30–2.30; 6–11

Bowl Inn
Church Road, Lower
Almondsbury ℰ 612757
Courage BA, Best Bitter,
Directors; John Smiths Bitter
Old village local next to
church ▲🅑🅿️🅖♈👤🅱️

Aust 14D8

10.30–2.30; 6–10.30 (11 F, S and summer)

Boars Head
Off A408 near M4 Jct 21
ℰ Pilning 2278
Courage Best Bitter,
Directors Ⓗ
Historic pub with emphasis on
food, no meals Sun
▲Q🅑🅿️🅖♈🅰️

Backwell 14D9

11.0–2.30; 6–11

Rising Sun
West Town Road (A370)
ℰ Flax Bourton 2215
Draught Bass; Hancocks HB Ⓗ
Warm friendly atmosphere,
skittle alley 🅖♈👤

Bath 15E9

10.30–2.30; 5.30–10.30 (11 F, S,)

Barley Mow
32 Bathwick Street ℰ 330416
Draught Bass Ⓗ
Cosy pub with darts room and
skittle alley 🅖♈👤

Bladud Arms
Gloucester Road, Lower
Swainswick (A46) ℰ 20152
Butcombe Bitter; Marston
Pedigree; Smiles Best Bitter;
Whitbread WCPA; Youngers
Scotch Ⓗ
Named after a local Swineherd
and Prince who cured himself
and his pigs of leprosy 🅿️🅖👤

Coeur De Lion
17 Northumberland Place
ℰ 65371
John Devenish Bitter, Wessex
Best Bitter Ⓗ
Tiny, intimate pub in town-
centre alley. Good convers-
ation, popular with tourists
Q🅿️🅱️

Fairfield Arms
Fairfield Park Road (off
Camden Road) ℰ 310594
Courage Bitter, Best Bitter Ⓗ
Welcoming local in north-
eastern outskirts of city 🅿️👤

Garricks Head
8 St Johns Place, Sawclose
Courage Best Bitter, John
Smiths Bitter, Wadworth 6X Ⓗ
Town centre pub near Theatre
Royal. Popular with thespians
🅖

Hatchetts
6–7 Queen Street ℰ 25045
Butcombe Bitter; Fuller
London Pride; Smiles

Exhibition; Uley Old Spot Ⓗ
Regular guest beers
Lively bar with upstairs room.
Popular with younger set 🅖♈

King William
Thomas Street (A4)
Brain Dark; Marston Burton
Bitter, Pedigree; Smiles Best,
Exhibition; Usher Founders
Ale Ⓗ Regular guest beers
Lively street corner freehouse
👤

Larkhall Inn
The Square, Larkhall (off A4)
Courage Bitter, Best Bitter,
Directors Ⓗ
Distinctive pub of character
with unique beer engines ▲🅿️👤

New Westhall
Upper Bristol Road (A4)
ℰ 25432
Butcombe Bitter; Marston
Pedigree, Owd Rodger;
Westons Original Cider Ⓗ
Popular local, pool, darts, and
occasional live music 🅿️🅖

Olde Farmhouse
Lansdown Road ℰ 316162
Butcombe Bitter; Marston
Pedigree; Miners Arms Own
Ale; Theakston Best Bitter;
Uley Old Spot; Wadsworth
6X Ⓗ Regular guest beers
Celebrated boozer of great
character, regular live jazz 👤

Pulteney Arms
37 Daniel Street ℰ 63923
Usher PA, Best Bitter Ⓗ & Ⓖ
Side-street local with gas
lighting 🅿️🅖♈

Railway Brewery
Wells Road (A367) ℰ 25202
Draught Bass; Flowers
Original Ⓗ
Cheerful local, with
comfortable lounge 👤≷

Rose & Crown
6 Brougham Place,
St Saviours Road,
Larkhall (off A4)
Butcombe Bitter; Marston
Pedigree; Usher Founders Ale;
Thatchers Cider Ⓗ
Friendly out of town local,
worth finding 👤

Rose & Laurel
118 Rush Hill ℰ 837500
Courage Bitter, Best Bitter,
Directors Ⓗ
Local with fine views of west
side of city 🅿️🅖👤

Star
23 The Vineyards (A4)
ℰ 25072
Draught Bass Ⓖ; Butcombe
Bitter; Golden Hill Exmoor
Ale; Hall & Woodhouse
Tanglefoot; Miners Arms Own
Ale Ⓗ Regular guest beers
Enjoy the atmosphere in this
old wood-panelled inn Q👤

Blagdon 5F1

11–2.30; 7–11

New Inn
Church Street
Draught Bass; Wadworth
Devizes Bitter, 6X Ⓗ, Old
Timer (winter) Ⓖ
Cosy stone pub in idyllic
setting overlooking lake
▲Q🅿️🅖

Bridgeyate 14E9

11–2.30; 6.30–10.30 (11 F, S)

White Hart
East of Kingswood (A420)
Courage BA, Best Bitter Ⓗ
Unspoilt friendly local on
common ▲Q🅿️👤

Bristol 14D9

10.30–2.30; 5.30–10.30 (11 F, S)

Avon Packet
185–187 Coronation Road,
Bedminster (A370) ℰ 663985
Courage BA; Best Bitter,
Directors Ⓗ
Urban riverside local
🅖♈ (till 7 pm) 👤🅱️

Bay Horse
Lewins Mead
Opens 11 am
Davenports Mild, Bitter Ⓔ
Large and plush, close to
shopping centre and bus
station. Restaurant bar 🅖

Cattle Market Tavern
Cattle Market Road, St Philips
Marsh ℰ 776983
Closed Sun and Bank Holidays
Draught Bass; Butcombe
Bitter; Davenports Bitter Ⓗ
Occasional guest beers
Basic pub, popular with
postmen 👤🅱️≷ (Temple Meads)

Farm
Hopetoun Road,
St Werburghs
Opens 11.30 & 6
Usher Best Bitter, Founders Ⓗ
Rural pub by St Werburghs
City Farm Q🅿️🅖

Grosvenor Arms
3 Coronation Road,
Bedminster (A370) ℰ 663325
Opens 7 evenings
Draught Bass Ⓗ
Working-class local

Highbury Vaults
164 St Michaels Hill,
Kingsdown
Evenings opens 6
Brain SA; Smiles Best,
Exhibition Ⓗ Regular guest
beers
Down to earth, old-fashioned
pub, popular with students
🅿️🅖

Horse & Groom
17 St George's Road
Opens 11.30 am; closed Sun
lunch
Courage BA, Best Bitter Ⓗ
Small lively local behind

College Green and Council House ♿ ✎

Kings Head
80 Victoria Street
Courage BA, Best Bitter Ⓗ
Small Victorian pub with
delightful snug Q♿🎱♨≋

Kings Head
Whitehall Road (B4465)
Opens 11 & 6
**Courage BA, Best Bitter,
Directors** Ⓗ
Attractive local with
competitive prices ♨Q✎♿🎱

Knowle Hotel
Leighton Road, Knowle
Opens 11 & 6.30
**Halls Harvest Bitter; Ind
Coope Burton Ale; Tetley
Bitter** Ⓗ
Large and friendly local,
popular with quiz teams ✎♿🎱

Nova Scotia
Nova Scotia Place, Hotwells
☎ 22751
Opens 11 & 6
**Courage BA, Best Bitter,
Directors** Ⓗ
Quayside pub, nautical theme,
folk club, busy in summer ✎🖾

Old Globe
117 East Street, Beminster
(A38)
Evenings opens 6
Courage BA, Best Bitter Ⓗ
Basic old fashioned local 🎱

Old Market Tavern
29–30 Old Market Street
☎ 28232
**Wadworth Devizes Bitter, 6X,
Farmers Glory** Ⓗ
Large open plan gas-lit pub
Q✎♿🎱♨

Phoenix
15 Wellington Road
Opens 11.30, Sat eve opens
6.30
Draught Bass Ⓖ & Ⓗ; **Halls
Harvest Bitter** Ⓗ; **Wadworth
IPA, 6X, Farmers Glory, Old
Timer** (winter) Ⓖ
Busy corner local, full of
character(s). Singalong Sats ✎

Queens Head
286 Fishponds Road, Eastville
Evenings opens 6
**Halls Harvest Bitter; Ind
Coope Burton Ale; Tetley
Bitter** Ⓗ
Huge main road local, mixed
architecture and clientele ♿🎱

Royal George
2 Filton Road, Horfield (A38)
Opens 11 & 6
**Courage Best Bitter,
Directors** Ⓗ
Locals pub by Horfield
Common ✎♿🎱♨♲

Ship Inn
Lower Park Row
Evenings opens 6
Boddingtons Bitter; Butcombe

Bitter; Hook Norton Best
Bitter; Marston Pedigree;
Smiles Best; Wadworth 6X Ⓗ
Occasional guest beers
Near University, popular with
lunching office workers ♿

Three Horse Shoes
359 Church Road, St George
(A420) ☎ 556818
**Draught Bass; Whitbread
WCPA** Ⓗ
Large popular roadside pub
♿♨🎱

Camerton   5G1
12–2.30; 6.30–11

Camerton Inn
Meadgate (B3115)
**Smiles Best Bitter; Wadworth
6X** Ⓗ
Welcoming roadside house
with busy public bar ✎🎱

Chipping
Sodbury   15E8
10.30–2.30; 5.30–10.30 (11 F, S)

Portcullis
Horse Street (A432)
☎ 312004
**Courage Best Bitter, Directors;
Taunton Cider** Ⓗ
Friendly locals pub, no food
Sunday ♨Q🖾♿♨

Churchill   5F1
10.30–2.30; 6–11

Crown Inn
The Batch, Skinners Lane
Cotleigh Bitter, Tawny;
Felinfoel Double Dragon;
Fuller London Pride; Marston
Pedigree; Oakhill Farmers
Ale Ⓗ **Regular guest beers**
Enlarged rural pub ♨Q🖾✎♿

Clapton-in-
Gordano   14D9
10.30–2.30; 6–11

Black Horse
Clapton Lane
Courage BA, Best Bitter Ⓗ
Unspoilt country pub with
original stone floor ♨🖾✎🎱

Clevedon   14E9
10.30–2.30; 6.30–11

Reading House
11 Alexandra Road ☎ 873545
**Courage BA, Best Bitter,
Directors** Ⓗ
Well run local, popular with
all ages ♿🎱

Compton Martin   5F1
11–2.30; 7–11

Ring O' Bells
A368
**Butcombe Bitter; Marston
Pedigree** Ⓗ
Cosy locals bar. Large 'Beams
& Brass' lounge. Winner of
family pub award
♨Q🖾✎♿🎱♨

Dundry   14D9
10.30–2.30; 6.30–11

Carpenters Arms
Wells Road ☎ Bristol 640415
**Butcombe Bitter; Courage BA,
Best Bitter; Smiles Best
Bitter** Ⓗ **Occasional guest
beers**
Friendly stone-built pub with
panoramic views of Bristol
and Chew Valley Lake ✎🖾♿✎

Engine
Common   15F8
12–2.30; 6–10.30 (11 F, S)

Cross Keys
North Road
**Courage BA, Best Bitter,
Directors** Ⓗ
Picturesque 17th century ivy-
clad pub ♨♿ (not Sun) 🎱♨

Frampton
Cottrell   14E8
11–2.30; 7–11

Rising Sun
Ryecroft Road (off A432 &
B4058)
**Draught Bass; Marston
Pedigree; Smiles Best Bitter;
Wadworth 6X** Ⓗ
Popular free house, no food
Sunday ♨♿✎

Hewish   14C9
10.30–2.30; 6–11

Full Quart
A370 ☎ Yatton 833077
**Draught Bass; Eldridge Pope
Royal Oak; Hall & Woodhouse
Badger Best Bitter** Ⓗ
Pleasant pub, large garden
and restaurant ✎♿✎♨

Hinton   15E8
10.30–2.30; 6.30–10.30 (11 F, S)

Bull
Off A46 OS735768
☎ Abson 2332
Wadworth IPA, 6X Ⓗ, **Old
Timer** (winter) Ⓖ
Country local with splendid
garden for children ♨✎♿🎱♨

Hinton
Charterhouse   5H1
11–2.30; 6–10.30 (11 F, S)

Rose & Crown
B3110
**Draught Bass; Marston
Capital, Pedigree; Wadworth
6X, Old Timer** Ⓖ
Busy local with oak panelled
bar ♨✎♿

Keynsham   14E9
11.30–2.30; 6–11

Crown Inn
63 Bristol Road ☎ 2150
**Courage BA, Best Bitter; John
Smith's Bitter** Ⓗ
Popular regulars pub. Walls

covered with local photographs and memorabilia
🏠♿🅿🕐🛏🍴🎯≷

Littleton-on-Severn 14E7

12.30–2.30; 7–11 (closed Tue)

White Hart
OS596898
☎ Thornbury 412275
Flowers Original; Smiles Best Bitter, Exhibition, Old Vic Ⓗ
16th century pub. Don't forget to duck, petanque played here, Sunday snacks
🏠Q🅿🕐🛏🍴🎯

Marshfield 15F9

12–2.30; 7–10.30 (11 F, S)

Lord Nelson Inn
Market Place (off A420)
☎ Bath 891282
Eldridge Pope Dorset Original IPA Ⓗ, Royal Oak (winter) Ⓖ; Palmer IPA; Wadworth 6X Ⓗ
Old coaching inn/restaurant with nautical theme 🏠🅿🕐🍴

Midford 5H1

11–2.30; 6.30–10.30 (11 F, S)

Hope & Anchor
B3110
☎ Combe Down 832296
Draught Bass; Butcombe Bitter; Marston Burton Bitter, Pedigree, Owd Rodger Ⓗ
Oak-beamed lounge in 300-year-old pub 🏠♿🕐🍴

Midsomer Norton 5G1

10.30–2.30; 6–11

White Hart
The Island ☎ 412957
Draught Bass; Welsh Brewers Hancocks HB Ⓗ Taunton Cider Ⓖ
Deservedly popular traditional town pub, friendly atmosphere, local memorabilia
🏠🅿🍴

Monkton Combe 15F9

12–2.30; 6–10.30 (11 F, S)

Wheelwrights Arms
☎ Limpley Stoke 2287
Butcombe Bitter; Flowers IPA Ⓖ; Wadworth 6X; Whitbread WCPA Ⓗ
Pleasant village local in picturesque valley 🏠♿🍴🎯🍴

Oldbury-on-Severn 14E7

11.30–2.30; 30–10.30 (11 F, S & summer)

Anchor Inn
Church Road
☎ Thornbury 413331
Draught Bass; Boddington Bitter; Butcombe Bitter; Marston Pedigree; Theakston

Best Bitter Ⓗ, Old Peculier Ⓖ
Occasional guest beers
Old local with well worn steps near site of Roman fort. Fine food 🏠Q🅿🕐🍴

Old Down 14E8

10.30–2.30; 6–10.30 (11 F, S & summer)

Fox
The Inner Down (off A38)
OS617873
Draught Bass; Davenports Traditional Bitter; Flowers IPA Ⓗ
Popular old stone village pub with excellent garden 🏠Q🅿

Paulton 5G1

11–2.30; 6.30–11

Red Lion
High Street
Halls Harvest Bitter; Ind Coope Burton Ale; Taunton Cider Ⓗ
Lively and spacious open-plan bar 🛏🕐🍴🎯

Radstock 5G1

10.30–2.30; 6–11

Waldegrave Arms
Market Place (A367) ☎ 34359
Courage Best Bitter Ⓗ
Large, comfortable ex-mining town hotel 🛏🕐🍴🎯

Rickford 5F1

11–2.30; 6–11

Plume of Feathers
(off A368) ☎ Blagdon 6249
Courage BA, Best Bitter Ⓗ; Taunton Dry Cider Ⓖ
One bar pub in picturesque hamlet in lee of the Mendips
🏠Q🅿🍴

Ridgehill 14D9

10.30–2.30; 6.30–11

Crown Inn
Regil Lane (off B3130)
Draught Bass; Wadworth IPA, 6X, Old Timer (winter) Ⓗ
Cosy stone country pub. Small popular restaurant
🏠Q🅿🕐🍴

Shepperdine 14E7

10.30–2.30; 6–10.30 (11 F, S & summer)

Windbound
OS613961
☎ Thornbury 414343
Archers Village Bitter Ⓖ; Davenports Traditional Bitter; Hall & Woodhouse Badger Bitter Ⓗ, Tanglefoot Ⓖ; Wadworth 6X; Whitbread WCPA Ⓗ
Remote but popular pub by Severn Estuary 🅿🕐🍴🎯

Stanton Drew 14D9

10.30–2.30; 6.30–11

Druids Arms
Courage BA, Best Bitter, Directors Ⓗ

Cosy stone cottage pub close to famous Stone Cove 🏠Q🅿🍴

Thornbury 14E7

10.30–2.30; 6–10.30 (11 F, S & summer)

White Lion
High Street ☎ 412126
Courage Best Bitter, Directors (winter); John Smiths Bitter Ⓗ
Georgian town pub in busy main street, unmistakable inn sign ♿🅿🛏🕐🍴🎯

Weston-super-Mare 14C9

10.30–2.30; 6–11

Britannia Inn
118 High Street
Courage Best Bitter, Directors; John Smiths Bitter Ⓗ
Old fashioned pub atmosphere, vast array of stock car trophies 🅿 (part covered) 🕐

The Heron
358-368 Locking Road
☎ 22218
Opens 11 am
Courage Best Bitter Ⓗ
Spacious brick pub, comfortable interior
🏠Q🛏 (summer) 🅿🕐🍴🎯≷

Market House
High Street ☎ 20834
Winter evenings opens 7
Draught Bass Ⓗ
Comfortable wood-panelled pub, theatrical flavour
🏠♿🅿🕐🍴🎯♿

Regency
22-24 Lower Church Road
Draught Bass; Butcombe Bitter; Wadworth 6X, Old Timer Ⓗ
Comfortable local pub 🅿🕐

Willsbridge 14E9

10.30–2.30; 5.30–10.30 (11 F, S)

Queens Head
Willsbridge Hill (A431)
Courage BA, Best Bitter Ⓗ
Unspoilt pub by Willsbridge Mill Wildlife Trust. Q♿🍴

Worle 14C9

11–2.30, 6–11

Nut Tree
Ebdon Road
Wadworth 6X; Younger Scotch Bitter, IPA Ⓗ
Recently converted Cotswold-stone farmhouse ♿🕐🍴🎯

Yatton 14D9

10.30–2.30; 6–11

Butchers Arms
High Street (off B3133)
Courage BA, Best Bitter; Bulmers Cider Ⓖ
Small cosy village local. Ten minutes from M5 (Jct 21)
🏠🕐🍴≷

Ampthill 17E6

11–2.30; 6–11
Old Sun
87 Dunstable Street ✆ 403101
Flowers Original; Wethered Bitter; Samuel Whitbread Ⓗ
Regular guest beers
Two small popular bars; games room ⚟ ⚥ ☺ (Mon–Fri) 🍴

Barton-le-Clay 17E7

10–2.30; 6–11
Speed the Plough
Pulloxhill Turn (A6)
✆ Silsoe 60205
Tolly Cobbold Bitter, Original Ⓗ, **Old Strong** Ⓖ
Well-kept and comfortable
⚟ ⚥ ☺ 🍴 ♿

Bedford 17E6

10.30–2.30; 5.30–11
Fleur de Lis
12 Mill Street (off High Street)
Wells Eagle Bitter Ⓗ
Well-run town pub with excellent mix of clientele
☺ (Mon–Sat)

Rose
45 High Street ✆ 53749
Greene King IPA, Abbot; Samuel Whitbread Ⓗ
Occasional guest beers
Beefeater restaurant ☺ 🍴

Try also: Flower Pot (Greene King)

Biddenham 17E6

11.30–2.30; 6–11
Three Tuns
Main Road (off A428)
✆ Bedford 54847
Greene King Simpsons Ale, IPA, Abbot Ⓗ
Delightful village inn with excellent range of food
⚥ ⚟ ☺ 🍴 🍴

Biggleswade 17F6

10.30–2.30; 6–11
Coach & Horses
Shortmead Street (road to A1 N) ✆ 312043
Greene King IPA, Abbot Ⓗ
Busy town pub with games-oriented public and small comfortable lounge ⚟ ⚥ 🍴

Try also: Rising Sun (Wells)

Bromham 17E6

10.30–2.30; 5.30–11
Prince of Wales
Northampton Road (A428 near A422 Junction)
✆ Oakley 2447
Wells Eagle Bitter, Bombardier Ⓗ
Large modern pub in centre of village near renovated water mill/country museum ⚥ 🍴

Broom 17F6

11.30–2.30; 7–11

Cock

High Street (just N of B658)
OS172430
Greene King IPA Ⓖ
As pubs used to be—multi roomed village local with a skittles room and beer served direct from cellar ⚟ ⚥ ⚥

Campton 17F6

11–2.30; 7–11
White Hart
Mill Lane (off A507)
✆ Hitchin 812657
Wells Eagle Bitter Ⓗ
Fine village pub, lots of games in the bar⚟ ⚥ ☺ (not Sun) 🍴 🍴 ♿

Clophill 17F6

11.30–2.30; 6–11
Green Man
The Green (off A6)
✆ Silsoe 60352
Greene King IPA, Abbot Ⓗ
Attractive old oak-beamed pub by the village green, with splendid public bar ⚟ ⚥ ☺ 🍴

Stone Jug
Back Street (2nd right north of A6/507 roundabout)
✆ Silsoe 60526
Opens 11
Banks & Taylor Shefford Bitter; Courage Directors; Fuller London Pride Ⓗ **Regular guest beers**
Popular back street local with friendly atmosphere and sensible prices ⚟ ⚥ ⚥ ☺

Deadmans Cross 17F6

10.30–2.30; 6–11
White Horse
A600 OS112419
✆ Haynes 634
Banks & Taylor Shefford Bitter, SPA, SOS Ⓗ
Friendly roadside pub with excellent food (supper licence)
⚟ ⚥ ☺ 🍴 (not Sun)

Dunstable 17E7

10.30–2.30; 5.30–11
Plume of Feathers
6 West Street (A505) ✆ 61035
Ind Coope Burton Ale Ⓗ
Fine town pub near A5
☺ (not weekend) 🍴

Eggington 16E7

10.30–2.30; 6–11
Horseshoes
High Street
✆ Leighton Buzzard 210282
Benskins Bitter Ⓗ
Fine little pub with friendly service, vintage M.Gs and upstairs snug ⚟ Q ⚥ ☺ 🍴 🍴

Elstow 17E6

10.30–2.30; 5.30–11
Red Lion
High Street ✆ Bedford 59687

Flowers Original, Wethered Bitter; Whitbread Castle Eden Ⓗ **Occasional guest beers**
Roast Inn with plush lounge. Near John Bunyan's birthplace and ancient Moot Hall ⚥ ☺ 🍴

Great Barford 17F6

11.30–2.30; 5.30–11
Golden Cross
Bedford Road (A428)
✆ Bedford 870928
Regular guest beers
Mini-beer exhibition; constantly changing range of beers. Lively locals' public and summer barbecues ⚟ ⚥ 🍴 Ⓖ 🍴 🍴

Kempston West End 17E6

10.30–2.30; 5.30–11
Three Horseshoes
West End Road (B560)
OS997482 ✆ Bedford 854377
Greene King KK, IPA Ⓖ
Small rural locals' pub ⚟ Q ⚥

Keysoe 17F5

11–2.30; 6.30–11
Chequers
Kimbolton Road (B660)
OS076636 ✆ Riseley 678
Adnams Bitter Ⓗ **Regular guest beers**
Large, popular, comfortable pub with open-plan bar and fireplace. Restaurant
⚟ ⚥ ☺ 🍴

Leighton Buzzard 16E7

10.30–2.30; 6–11
Wheatsheaf
57 North Street (A418)
✆ 374611
Usher Founders Ale; Wilsons Original Bitter Ⓗ
The best juke box in town!
⚟ ⚥ 🍴

Luton 17F7

10.30–2.30; 5.30–11
Gardeners Call
151 High Town Road
✆ 29037
Greene King KK, IPA, Abbot Ⓗ
Pleasant pub with comfortable lounge and straightforward public bars
⚥ ☺ (not Sat/Sun) 🍴 ⇄

Harrow
85 Hitchin Road ✆ 24284
Wells Eagle Bitter, Bombardier Ⓗ
Traditional street-corner local. Darts and pool in public and small lounge
⚟ ⚥ ☺ (not Sun) 🍴 ♿ ⇄

Mother Redcap
80 Latimer Road (off A6)
✆ 30913

Greene King Simpsons Ale, IPA, Abbot H
Successfully renovated one-bar pub ⌖⌖ (not Sat/Sun) ⌖

Try also: Bricklayers Arms, (Banks & Taylor)

Milton Ernest 17E5

10.30–2.30; 5.30–11

Queens Head
1 Rushden Road (A6)
⌖ Oakley 2250
Wells Eagle Bitter, Bombardier H
Friendly pre-Tudor pub. Comfortable lounge; "hole in the floor" darts in public ⌖⌖⌖

Moggerhanger 17F6

11–2.30; 6–11

Guinea
Bedford Road (A603)
⌖ Biggleswade 40388
Wells Eagle Bitter, Bombardier G
Spacious and welcoming main road pub; brasses in large lounge and pool in public ⌖⌖⌖⌖ (not Mon) ⌖

Odell 16E5

10.30–2.30; 5.30–11

Mad Dog
Little Odell OS955575
⌖ Bedford 720221
Greene King IPA, Abbot H
Thatched pub to west of village with home-cooked food. Children's roundabout in garden ⌖⌖⌖⌖

Pavenham 17E5

11.30–2.30; 5.30–11

Cock
High Street OS989554
⌖ Oakley 2834
Greene King IPA, Abbot H
Lively village pub with a warm welcome. One through bar and skittles ⌖⌖

Pegsdon 17F7

11–2.30; 6–11

Live & Let Live
Pegsdon Way (B655)
⌖ Luton 881739
Greene King XX, IPA, Abbot E
Low-beamed pub in scenic surroundings. Good food ⌖⌖⌖⌖ (not Sun)

Pulloxhill 17E7

10.30–2.30; 6–11

Cross Keys
High Street ⌖ Flitwick 712442
Wells Eagle Bitter, Bombardier H
500-year-old inn with restaurant. Excellent value ⌖Q⌖⌖⌖⌖⌖⌖

Ridgmont 17E7

10–2.30; 6–11

Rose & Crown
89 High Street (A418 near M1 Jct 13) ⌖ 245
Wells Eagle Bitter; Bombardier H
Excellent pub catering for all tastes ⌖⌖⌖⌖⌖⌖⌖⌖

Riseley 17E5

11–2.30; 5.30–11

Fox & Hounds
High Street OS038624 ⌖ 240
Wells Eagle Bitter, Bombardier H
Imposing 16th century oak-beamed village pub with wide selection of home-made food, restaurant and family room
Q⌖⌖⌖⌖

Salford 16E6

10.30–2.30; 6–11

Red Lion
Wavendon Road (near A421) OS934392
⌖ Milton Keynes 583117
Wells Eagle Bitter, Bombardier H
350-year-old inn; comfortable lounge and restaurant. Four poster bedrooms and generous garden ⌖⌖⌖⌖⌖⌖

Sandy 17F6

11–2.30; 5.30–11

Bell
Station Road (off B1042 to Cambridge) ⌖ 80267
Greene King IPA, Abbot H
Friendly one-bar local. Handy for RSPB HQ; opposite station. No meals Sun ⌖⌖⌖⌖⌖⌖

Sharnbrook 17E5

10.30–2.30; 6–11

Fordham Arms
Templars Way OS002595
⌖ Bedford 781357
Wethered Bitter H Regular guest beers
Large and attractive village pub with good food, comfortable lounge; darts and skittles in the public ⌖⌖⌖⌖⌖

Shefford 17F6

10.30–2.30; 6–11

White Hart
2 North Bridge Street (at Jct of A507 & A600)
⌖ Hitchin 811144
Greene King XX, IPA, Abbot H
Friendly pub with spacious through bar and restaurant ⌖Q⌖⌖⌖⌖⌖

Try also: Bridge (Wells)

Shillington 17F7

10.30–2.30; 6–11

Crown
High Road ⌖ Hitchin 711667
Flowers Original, Wethered Bitter, Winter Royal; Whitbread Castle Eden,

Samuel Whitbread H Regular guest beer
Welcoming pub; fine fireplace in public ⌖⌖⌖⌖ (not Sun) ⌖⌖

Musgrave Arms
Aspley End Road OS122328
⌖ Hitchin 711286
Greene King IPA, Abbot G
Superb country local, little touched by progress—in the same family for 90 years
⌖Q⌖⌖⌖

Silsoe 17F7

11–2.30; 6–11

Star & Garter
16 High Street (off A6)
⌖ 60250
Wethered Bitter H
Welcoming village local
⌖⌖⌖⌖

Slip End 17F8

10.30–2.30; 5.30–11

Rising Sun
1 Front Street ⌖ Luton 21766
Courage Best Bitter, Directors H
Village local with busy public bar and pleasant lounge
⌖⌖ (not Sun) ⌖ (not Sat, Sun) ⌖

Southill 17F6

11–2.30; 6–11

White Horse
High Road (West of B658)
OS148418 ⌖ Hitchin 813364
Wethered Bitter; Whitbread Castle Eden H
Large comfortable country pub on Whitbread Estate and near cricket ground. Shove ha'penny, restaurant, and miniature railway
⌖⌖⌖⌖⌖⌖ (not Sun) ⌖

Stagsden 16E6

11–2.30; 6–11

Royal George
High Street (A422)
⌖ Oakley 2801
Wells Eagle Bitter, Bombardier H
Friendly village pub with vast garden, children's amusements and animals, near well-known Bird Gardens
⌖⌖⌖⌖

Streatley 17F7

11–2.30; 6–11

Chequers
Sharpenhoe Road (off A6)
⌖ Luton 882072
Greene King Simpsons Ale, IPA, Abbot H
Spacious comfortable, 1-bar village local ⌖⌖ (not Sun)

Tebworth 17E7

11–2.30; 6–11

Queens Head
The Lane ⌖ Toddington 4101
Wells Eagle Bitter H, Bombardier G

Splendid village local, full of character(s) 🏠 ⚑ ⅃ (not Sun) 🍷

Toddington 17E7

10.30–2.30; 5.30–11

Angel Inn
1 Luton Road (A5120, near M1 Jct 12) ☎ 2380
Flowers Original, Wethered Bitter Ⓗ
Comfortable and friendly, with frequent live music 🏠 ⅃ ➐

Bedford Arms
64 High Street ☎ 2401
Wells Eagle Bitter Ⓗ
Attractive exterior, two pleasant lounge bars. No meals weekends 🏠 ⚑ ⅃ ➐

Sow & Pigs
Church Square (A5120) ☎ 3089
Greene King XX (winter), IPA, Abbot Ⓗ
Unique institution catering for local artists (!) 🏠 Q ⚑ ⅃ (not Sun)

Totternhoe 17E7

10.30–2.30; 5.30–11

Old Farm
Church Road ☎ Dunstable 61294
Benskins Bitter; Ind Coope Burton Ale Ⓗ

Former Tudor farmhouse with original fireplaces 🏠 ⚑ ⅃ 🍷🍴

Upper Dean 17E5

12–2.30; 7–11 (closed lunch Mon–Fri)

Prince of Wales
High Street (2 miles S of A45) OS048678 ☎ Riseley 551
Greene King IPA, Abbot; Marston Pedigree Ⓗ **Regular guest beers**
Bustling village pub with pleasing combination of local and passing trade. Pool and skittles 🏠 ⚑ ⅃ ➐ (not Tue) 🍷

Upper Sundon 17E7

11–2.30; 6–11

Crown
Harlington Road
Brakspear Pale Ale; Wethered Bitter Ⓗ
Darts and dominoes in the bar, spacious lounge with bar billiards. Live music weekends 🏠 ⚑ ⅃ (not Sat/Sun) 🍷👦

Westoning 17E7

10.30–2.30; 6–11

Bell
Greenfield Road ☎ Flitwick 712511
Greene King XX, IPA, Abbot Ⓗ

15th century inn. Traditional timbered lounge with inglenook fireplaces 🏠 ⚑ ⅃ ➐ (Mon–Thu) ⅄

Chequers
Park Road (A5120) ☎ Flitwick 713125
Flowers Original, Wethered Bitter Ⓗ
Comfortable thatched pub with restaurant 🏠⅛ ⚑ ⅃ ➐ (not Mon) 🍷

Woburn 16E7

10.30–2.30; 6–11

Black Horse
1 Bedford Street (A418) ☎ 210
Adnams Bitter; Ind Coope Burton Ale; Marston Burton Bitter; Ⓗ
One-bar free house with restaurant. Superb value food and beer Q ⚑ ⅃ ➐ ⅄

Wootton 17E6

10.30–2.30; 5.30–11

Chequers
Hall End (off A421) OS001458 ☎ Bedford 768394
Wells Eagle Bitter, Bombardier Ⓗ
Comfortable 16th century village pub 🏠 ⚑ ⅃ ➐🍷

Try also: **Black Horse** (Wells)

"HONESTLY, I DON'T KNOW WHAT THEY SEE IN THAT NEW PLACE ACROSS THE ROAD!"

KenPyne

Aldworth 6E2

11–2.30; 6–11 (closed Mon)

Bell
Off B4009 ✆ Compton 272
**Arkell BBB, Kingsdown Ale;
Hall & Woodhouse Badger
Best Bitter; Morland Mild** Ⓗ
Occupied by same family for at
least 200 years and unaltered
for most of that time. See the
old one-handed clock in the
tap room. Near Ridgeway
Path ▲ Q ⓔ ⓖ ▮

Try also: Four Points (Free)

Aston 7F1

11–3; 6–11

Flower Pot
Ferry Lane (off A432)
OS784842 ✆ Henley 574721
**Brakspear Mild, Bitter, Special
(summer), Old (winter)** Ⓗ
Out of the way ex-hotel with
stuffed fish now in residence.
Handy for the river. Darts,
shove ha'penny ▲ Q ⓔ ▮ Ⓐ

Binfield 7G2

11–3; 5.30–11

Jack o' Newbury
Terrace Road North, ¾ mile N
of village OS845709
✆ Bracknell 54881
**Flowers Original; Wethered
Bitter, SPA; Bulmers Cider** Ⓗ
Comfortable country pub with
skittle alley
▲ Q ⓔ ⓖ (not Sun) ↝

Try also: Stag & Hounds
(Courage)

Bracknell 7G2

11–3; 5.30–11

Market Inn
Station Road ✆ 51734
**Friary Meux Bitter; Ind Coope
Burton Ale** Ⓗ
Friendly, town centre pub
next to bus station. Live music
Thu and Fri nights. No food
Sun ⓔ ⓔ ⓖ ↝ ▮ ⇄

Burchetts Green 7F2

10–2.30; 6–11

Red Lion
Applehouse Hill, Hurley
(A423)
✆ Littlewick Green 4433
**Brakspear Bitter, Special,
Old** Ⓗ
Very good country local
▲ Q ⓔ ⓖ ↝

Caversham 7F2

10.30–2.30; 5.30–11

Prince of Wales
76 Prospect Street (Nr
A4074) ✆ Reading 472267
Brakspear Bitter, Special Ⓗ
Honest local, occasional live
music ⓔ ▮

Try also: White Horse, Emmer
Green (Courage)

Charvil 7F2

10–2.30; 6–11

Lands End
Lands End Lane OS781748
✆ Twyford 340700
**Brakspear Bitter, Special,
Old** Ⓗ
Deservedly popular, smart
out-of-the-way pub. Bar
billiards, darts. Children's
playground ⓔ ⓔ ⓖ ▮

Chievely 6D2

10.30–2.30; 5.30–11

Wheatsheaf
High Street (near A34)
OS476738 ✆ 378
Morland Bitter, Best Bitter Ⓗ
Small but lively open-plan
village local. Darts, bar
billiards ▲ ⓖ ↝ ▮

Colnbrook 7H2

10.30–2.30; 5.30–11

Red Lion
High Street ✆ Slough 682695
Courage Best Bitter Ⓗ
Small, cosy pub, slat panelling
and Tudor beams; on old
London to Bath coaching road
▲ ⓔ ⓖ (Mon–Fri) ⓖ

Crazies Hill 7F2

11–3; 6–11

Horns
Off A4/A423 OS799809
✆ 3226
**Brakspear Bitter, Special
(summer), Old (winter)** Ⓗ
Picturesque country pub;
darts, interesting menu
▲ Q ⓔ ⓖ ↝ (not Sun/Mon) Ⓐ

East Ilsley 6D2

11–2.30; 5.30–11

Crown & Horns
Off A34 ✆ 205
**Arkell BBB; Draught Bass;
Charrington IPA; Morland
Bitter; Theakston XB;
Wadworth 6X** Ⓗ **Regular
guest beers**
A treasure, dedicated to good
food, whisky and racing. Sells
draught milk. Skittle alley
▲ ⓔ ⓔ ⓖ ↝ (not Sun) ▮

Eton 7G2

10.30–2.30; 5.30–11

Crown & Cushion
High Street ✆ Windsor 61531
**Courage Best Bitter,
Directors** Ⓗ
Busy pub, public decorated
with Heraldic badges. No food
weekends ▲ ⓔ ⓔ ⓖ ▮
⇄ (Windsor Riverside)

Eton Wick 7G2

11–2.30; 5.30–11

Pickwick
32 Eton Wick Road (B3026)
✆ Windsor 861713

**Brakspear Bitter; Flowers
Original; Wethered SPA** Ⓗ**,
Winter Royal** Ⓖ
Enterprising free house
ⓔ ⓖ (not Sun) ⓖ

Fifield 7G2

10.30–2.30; 5.30–11

Rising Sun
Forest Green Road (B3022)
**Morland Mild, Bitter, Best
Bitter** Ⓗ
Good value local
▲ ⓔ ⓖ (Mon–Fri) ▮

White Hart
Fifield Road
**Morland Mild, Bitter, Best
Bitter** Ⓗ
Deservedly popular locals'
pub, games bar
ⓔ ⓖ (Mon–Fri) ↝ (Fri–Sat) ▮

Finchampstead 7F3

11–3; 6–11

Queen's Oak
Church Lane OS793639
✆ Eversley 733686
**Brakspear Bitter, Special,
Old** Ⓗ
Lovely village pub in
picturesque setting next to
church. Large lounge, small
cosy snug. Live music Tue
▲ ⓔ ⓖ ↝

Try also: Greyhound
(Wethered)

Frilsham 6E2

12 (11.30 Sat)–2.30; 6–10.30 (11 F, S)

Pot Kiln
Yattendon/Bucklebury Road
OS553731
✆ Hermitage 201366
**Arkell BBB; Morland Bitter,
Best Bitter; Theakston XB** Ⓗ
Remote village pub, in same
family for 150 years
▲ Q (folk Sun) ⓔ
ⓖ (not Sun) ↝ ▮

Hamstead Marshall 6D3

11–2.30; 6.30–11

White Hart
✆ Kintbury 58201
**Hall & Woodhouse Badger
Best Bitter, Tanglefoot;
Wadworth 6X** Ⓗ
Relaxing, upmarket free
house. Italian restaurant
▲ Q ⓔ ⓔ ⓖ ↝

Hare Hatch 7F2

11–3; 5.30–11

Queen Victoria
Blakes Lane (just off A4)
OS809783
✆ Wargrave 2477
**Brakspear Mild, Bitter,
Special, Old** Ⓗ
Busy 17th century country
pub, food always available
▲ ⓔ (if eating) ⓔ ⓖ ↝

Hermitage 6D2

10.30–2.30; 5.30–11
Fox
B4009 (Newbury/Goring
Road) ℰ 201545
**Courage Best Bitter, Directors;
Morland Bitter;
Wadworth 6X** Ⓗ Occasional
guest beers
Spacious and friendly. Popular
with young people and locals.
Comfortable lounge, saloon
and restaurant ♨ ℐ ᵺ ♥ ♿

Hungerford 6C3

11–2.30; 6–11
Sun
Charnham Street (A4)
ℰ 82162
**Morland Mild, Bitter, Best
Bitter** Ⓗ
Unpretentious locals pub.
Visitors welcome. Pool, table
skittles, shove ha'penny and
solitaire ℐ ᵺ ♥

Try also: Bear Hotel (Free),
Railway Tavern (Ushers)

Hurley 7G2

10.30–2.30; 6–11
Black Boy
Henley Road (A423)
ℰ Littlewick 4212
Brakspear Bitter, Old Ⓗ
16th century, beamed pub,
near the Thames. Emphasis
on food ♨ Q ℐ ᵺ ♥

Dew Drop
Batts Green OS824815
ℰ Littlewick Green 4327
**Brakspear Bitter, Old; Coates
Cider** Ⓗ
Turn at Grassland Research to
find this remote country pub,
about 2 miles up Honey Hill
♨ Q ℐ ᵺ (Mon–Sat)
♥ (Tues–Sat)

Hurst 7F2

11–3; 6–11
Elephant & Castle
Lodge Road, Whistley Green
(A321/B3030) OS792743
ℰ Twyford 340886
Closes 2.30 & 10.30
**Morland Mild, Bitter, Best
Bitter** Ⓗ
Village pub, smart lounge,
busy public bar. Darts, bar
billiards ♨ ℐ ᵺ (not Sun) ♟

Green Man
Hinton Road (off A321)
OS801741
**Brakspear Bitter, Special
Bitter, Old** Ⓖ
Attractive 17th century
country pub with lots of
character. Boules, Aunt Sally.
No food Sun ♨ ℐ ᵺ ♥

Try also: Cricketers (Courage)

Inkpen 6C3

11–2.30; 6–11
Swan

Lower Green OS359643
ℰ 326
**Brakspear Bitter; Hall &
Woodhouse Badger Best
Bitter; Wethered Bitter, SPA** Ⓗ
Regular guest beers
Hard to find but worth the
effort. 3 real fires; good food
and pleasant welcome
♨ ℐ ᵺ ♥ (Tue–Sat)

Kintbury 6D3

10.30–2.30; 5.30–11
Blue Ball
OS380668 ℰ 58515
Courage Best Ⓗ
Friendly local ♨ ℐ ᵺ ♥ ♟

Crossways
Inkpen Road OS385653
ℰ 58398
Opens 11 & 6 (closes 10.30 ex
F, S) Closed Tue lunch
**Marston Burton Bitter; Ruddle
Rutland Bitter;
Wadworth 6X** Ⓗ **Regular
guest beers**
Smart, remote open-plan pub.
No food Sun ♨ Ⓓ ℐ ᵺ ♥

Knowl Hill 7F2

11–3; 5.30–11
Seven Stars
Bath Road (A4)
ℰ Littlewick Green 2967
**Brakspear Mild, Bitter,
Special, Old** Ⓗ
16th century coaching inn;
lot of interest in pub games
♨ Q Ⓓ ℐ ᵺ ♥ ♟

Maidenhead 7G2

10.30–2.30; 5.30–11
Jack of Both Sides
81 Queen Street ℰ 20870
**Flowers Original, Wethered
Bitter; Samuel Whitbread** Ⓗ
Busy town centre pub with
good reputation for food ᵺ ≷

North Star
North Town Road
Wethered Bitter, SPA Ⓗ
Pub sign depicts the first GWR
locomotive to reach the town
in 1845 ♟ ≷ (Furze Platt)

Pond House
Bath Road (A4 W of town)
ℰ 27178
**Wethered Bitter, SPA, Winter
Royal** Ⓗ
Modern suburban house. The
pond is now the garden
ℐ ᵺ ♥ ♟

Vine
Market Street (off A4)
**Brakspear Mild, Bitter,
Special, Old** Ⓗ
Lively town centre pub
ℐ ᵺ ♥ ♟ ≷ ≷

Marsh Benham 6D3

10.30–2.30; 6–10.30 (11 F, S)
Red House
Off A4 ℰ Newbury 41637
Adnams Bitter; Brakspear

**Bitter, Special; Ringwood Best
Bitter** Ⓗ **Cider** Ⓖ **Occasional
guest beers**
Thriving thatched pub in old
estate hamlet. Miniature
railway in garden, children's
summer house, superb food
ℐ ᵺ ♥

Newbury 6D3

10.30–2.30; 5.30 (6.30 S)–11
Bacon Arms Hotel
Oxford Street ℰ 31822
**Courage Best Bitter,
Directors** Ⓗ
Friendly former coaching inn.
Popular lounge, restaurant
and wine bar. Very good bar
snacks, Mon–Sat ♨ ℐ ᵺ ♥ ♥

Try also: Bricklayers Arms
(Courage)

Old Windsor 7G2

10.30–2.30; 5.30–11
Oxford Blue
Crimp Hill ℰ Windsor 861954
**Friary Meux Bitter; Ind Coope
Burton Ale** Ⓗ
Welcoming pub on hillside
with balcony for drinkers.
Children's playground Ⓓ ᵺ ♥

Pangbourne 7E2

10–2.30; 6–11
Star
Reading Road ℰ 2566
**Courage Best Bitter,
Directors** Ⓗ
Village pub near Thames.
Lounge once a ginger beer
factory ♨ ℐ ᵺ ♥ ♟ ≷

Reading 7F2

10.30–2.30; 5.30–11
Blagrave Arms
35 Blagrave Street ℰ 590920
Closes 10.30 Mon–Thu
**Courage Best Bitter,
Directors** Ⓗ
Gas lighting, marble topped
tables and wood floors give a
fine impression of a Victorian
ale house. Near town centre
Q Ⓓ ≷ (Reading General)

Eldon Arms
Eldon Terrace (near A4)
ℰ 53857
**Wadworth IPA, 6X, Farmers
Glory, Old Timer** (winter) Ⓗ
All a good boozer should be.
Parking difficult ᵺ (not Sun) ♟

Greyhound
4 Mount Pleasant (A33)
ℰ 863023
**Courage Best Bitter,
Directors** Ⓗ
Popular pub south of town
ℐ ᵺ

Retreat
8 St. Johns Street (off Queens
Road)
Evening opens 6
**Wethered Bitter, SPA, Winter
Royal; Samuel Whitbread** Ⓗ
Superb back-street pub with
bar billiards, darts ᵺ ♥ ♟

Remenham 7F2

10.30–2.30; 6–11

Two Brewers
Wargrave Road (A321)
✆ Henley 574375
Brakspear Bitter, Old Ⓗ
Pleasant panelled pub. Good
children's room. Darts
🅰️🆔🅿️Ⓖ🍴

Sandhurst 7F3

11–3; 6–11

Wellington Arms
Yorktown Road (A321)
✆ Yately 872408
Brakspear Bitter, Special Ⓗ,
Old Ⓖ
Friendly atmosphere. Piano
player at weekends 🅿️🅰️Ⓖ🍴

Shefford 6D2
Woodlands

10.30–2.30; 5.30–11

Pheasant
Baydon Road (B4000/A338)
✆ Great Shefford 284
Wadworth IPA, 6X Ⓗ Bulmer
Cider Ⓖ
Charming tile-hung country
inn with "ring the bull", hard
by M4 Jct 14. Once known as
"The Paraffin House!"
🅰️Q🆔🅿️Ⓖ🍴🍴

Shurlock Row 7F2

11–3; 6–11

Royal Oak
Hungerford Lane OS833745
✆ Twyford 345133
**Morland Mild, Bitter, Best
Bitter** Ⓗ
Comfortable village pub; Aunt
Sally 🅰️Q🅿️Ⓖ🍴 (not Tue) 🍴

Slough 7G2

10.30–2.30; 5.30–11

Alpha Arms
Alpha Street ✆ 22727
**Courage Best Bitter,
Directors** Ⓗ
Basic town centre pub. Small
and cheerful; darts 🅿️Ⓖ🍴≷

Stanford 6E2
Dingley

12–2; 6–10.30 (11 F, S)

Old Boot Inn
Bucklebury, Common Road
✆ Bradfield 744292
**Adnams Bitter; Arkell BBB;
Fuller London Pride; Ruddle
County** Ⓗ
Tastefully decorated, up-
market free house. Inglenook
fireplace. Restaurant 🅰️🅿️🍴

Sunningdale 7G3

11–3; 6–11

Nag's Head
OS953677 ✆ Ascot 22725
Ind Coope Bitter, Burton Ale Ⓗ
Pleasant village pub 🅰️🅿️Ⓖ🍴

Thatcham 6D3

10.30–2.30; 6–10.30 (11 F, S)

Swan
Longbridge OS526664
**Courage Best Bitter,
Directors** Ⓗ
Old fashioned pub, unaffected
by new development nearby
🍴≷

Theale 7E2

10–2.30; 6–11

Lamb
Church Street (near M4
Jct 12) ✆ 302216
**Courage Best Bitter,
Directors** Ⓖ
Friendly village pub
🅰️Q🆔🅿️Ⓖ🍴🍴≷

Tilehurst 7E2

11–3; 5.30–11

Royal Oak
69 Westwood Glen
OS661739 ✆ 417300
**Halls Harvest Bitter; Ind
Coope Burton Ale** Ⓗ
Worth the climb up the steep
driveway to escape
surrounding suburban spread
🅿️Ⓖ (not Sun) 🍴

Twyford 7F2

11–3; 5.30–11

Duke of Wellington
High Street (A3032)
✆ 340456
**Brakspear Mild, Bitter,
Special** Ⓗ, **Old** Ⓖ
Friendly reasonably-priced
village pub. Comfortable
lounge, darts 🅿️Ⓖ🍴≷

Upper 6E2
Bucklebury

10.30–2.30; 6–10.30 (11 F, S)

Three Crowns
Broad Lane OS543686
✆ Thatcham 62153
**Courage Best Bitter,
Directors** Ⓖ
Pleasant village pub with pet's
corner and children's
playground 🅰️🆔🅿️🍴🍴

Waltham St. 7F2
Lawrence

11–3; 6–11

Bell
Near B3024 OS830769
✆ Twyford 341788
**Adnams Bitter; Brakspear
Bitter; Hall & Woodhouse
Badger Best Bitter; Theakston
XB; Wadworth 6X; Wethered
Winter Royal** Ⓗ **Regular guest
beers**
Excellent 14th century wood-
panelled pub in village square;
darts, no dogs
🅰️Q🆔🅿️Ⓖ (not Sun) 🍴🍴

Plough
West End OS824757
✆ Twyford 340015

Morland Bitter, Best Bitter Ⓖ
Attractive low-ceilinged 16th
century country pub, no food
Sun/Mon 🅰️Q🅿️Ⓖ (not Sat) 🍴🍴

Warfield 7G2

11–3; 6–11

Cricketers
Cricketers Lane OS891713
✆ Winkfield Row 882910
**Brakspear Bitter; Flowers
Original; Wethered SPA,
Winter Royal; Samuel
Whitbread** Ⓗ **Occasional guest
beers**
Busy, country free house,
good food, barbecue summer
weekends 🅰️🅿️🍴🍴

Three Legged Cross
Battle Bridge (A3095)
✆ Bracknell 421673
**Courage Best Bitter,
Directors** Ⓖ
14th century foresters
cottage. Pleasant pub, noted
for good food 🅿️Ⓖ (not Sun)

Wargrave 7F2

11–3; 6–11

Bull
High Street (A321) ✆ 3120
**Brakspear Bitter, Special,
Old** Ⓗ
Large, 17th century village
pub, big fire and good food
🅰️🆔 (if eating) 🅿️🅰️Ⓖ🍴♿≷

White Hart
High Street (A321) ✆ 2590
**Flowers Original; Wethered
Bitter, SPA, Winter Royal** Ⓗ
Comfortable village pub; darts,
busy food trade
🅰️🆔 (if eating) Ⓖ🍴♿≷

Try also: Greyhound
(Courage)

West Ilsley 6D2

10.30–2.30; 5.30–11

Harrow
Off A34 ✆ East Ilsley 260
**Morland Mild, Bitter, Best
Bitter** Ⓗ
Overlooks cricket pitch; ideal
for watching last overs on a
summer evening. Children's
play area separate from
garden. Good food 🅰️Ⓖ🍴🍴

Windsor 7G2

10.30–2.30; 5.30–11

Carpenters Arms
Market Street ✆ 863695
**Charrington IPA; Draught
Bass** Ⓗ
Comfortable pub on cobbled
street. Games include bar
billiards
🆔🅿️Ⓖ (not Sun) ≷ (Central)

Prince Christian
Kings Road ✆ 60980
**Brakspear Bitter; Fuller
London Pride; Young Bitter** Ⓗ
Convivial company; efficient,
bright and cheerful
Ⓖ (not Sun) ≷

Star
Peascod Street
Draught Bass; Charrington IPA Ⓗ
Always lively—both tourists and local visitors. Indoor games a speciality Ⓖ✿

Winterbourne 6D2
11.30–2.30; 6 (7 winter)–11
New Inn
Off B4494 OS455722
✆ Chieveley 248200
Flowers Original; Wethered Bitter, SPA, Winter Royal; Whitbread Pompey Royal (summer) Ⓗ Regular guest beers
Warm, friendly free house in riverside hamlet. Bar billiards
Ⓐ✿Ⓖ❧

Wokingham 7F3
11–3; 5.30–11
Crooked Billet
Honey Hill, 2 miles S of town OS826668 ✆ 780438
Brakspear Mild, Bitter, Special, Old Ⓗ
Country pub ⒶQ✿Ⓖ❧

Queens Head
23 The Terrace (A329)
✆ 781221
Morland Mild, Bitter, Best Bitter Ⓗ
Unspoilt town pub without gimmicks. Deservedly popular
✿Ⓖ❧ (not Sun) ✿

Woolhampton 6E3
11–2.30; 5.30–11
Angel Inn
Bath Road (A4)
✆ Reading 713307
Flowers Original; Fremlins Bitter; Wethered Bitter, SPA; Samuel Whitbread, Winter Royal Ⓗ
Smart old coaching inn with skittle alley; has managed to avoid horrible olde worlde brewery treatment
Ⓐ✿▣Ⓖ❧ (not Mon) ⅁
✿ (Midgham)

Rising Sun
Bath Road (A4)
✆ Reading 712717
Opens 11.30
Adnams Bitter; Arkells BBB; Hall & Woodhouse Badger

Best Bitter; Ringwood Fortyniner, Old Thumper; Theakstons XB Ⓗ Regular guest beers
Two-bar free house, smart saloon and cosier public
Ⓐ✿Ⓖ❧❡✿ (Midgham)

Wraysbury 7H2
10.30–2.30; 5.30–11
Perseverance
High Street ✆ 2375
Courage Best Bitter, Directors Ⓗ
Low-beamed old pub
✿Ⓖ
❧ (Thurs–Sat) ❡✿

Yattendon 6E2
12–2.30; 6.30–11
Nut & Bolt
Burnt Hill OS568743
Fuller London Pride, ESB; Morland Bitter, Best Bitter; Ruddles Rutland Bitter, County Ⓗ
Welcoming rural pub near M4. Exotic range of baked spuds! Ⓐ✿Ⓖ❧

Try also: **Royal Oak** (Free)

Akeley 16C6

12–2.30;; 6–11

Bull & Butcher
The Square (A413)
☎ Lillingstone Dayrell 257
**Hook Norton Best Bitter;
Marston Pedigree; Bulmer
Cider** Ⓗ **Regular guest beers**
Deservedly popular village
pub; comfortable, with warm
welcome. Restaurant area
🍴 ✿ (not Sun)
🍴 (not Sun/Mon) ✿

Amersham 16E9

11–2.30; 6–11

Queens Head
Whielden Gate (A404)
OS942957
**Benskins Bitter; Ind Coope
Burton Ale** Ⓗ
Very pleasant country pub set
back off main road. No food
Sun 🍴✿✿ ✿✿✿

Aston Abbotts 16D8

11–2.30; 5.30 (6 Sat)–11

Royal Oak
Wingrave Road
☎ Aylesbury 681262
**Aylesbury ABC Bitter;
Draught Bass** Ⓗ
16th century half-thatched
inn. Evening meals must be
booked 🍴✿✿✿
✿ (not Sun) 🍴 (Wed–Sat)

Astwood 16E6

11.30–2.30; 6–11

Old Swan Inn
Main Road (near A422)
☎ North Crawley 272
**Adnams Bitter; Courage Best
Bitter, Directors; Tetley Bitter;
Usher Founders Ale; Wilsons
Original Bitter** Ⓗ
17th century thatched inn
with open plan and separate
restaurant. NB Main Road now
bypasses village 🍴✿✿✿✿✿

Aylesbury 16D8

10.30–2.30; 5.30 (6 Sat)–11

Bell Hotel
Market Square ☎ 89835
Wethered Bitter, SPA Ⓗ
Occasional guest beers
THF hotel, with real ale in
oak-beamed market bar. Food
in bar (lunchtime) or
restaurant 🍴Q✿✿✿✿✿

Old Millwright's Arms
Walton Road ☎ 23405
Opens 11 & 6
**Aylesbury ABC Bitter;
Chiltern Beechwood Bitter;
Morrell Light Mild** Ⓗ
Friendly 30s-style house,
away from town centre
✿✿ (not Sat/Sun) ✿

White Swan
Walton Street ☎ 23933
**Aylesbury ABC Bitter;
Draught Bass; Chiltern**

**Beechwood Bitter; Morrell
Light Mild** Ⓗ
Lively 16th century town pub
near County Offices. Happy
hour: 5.30–6.30; booking
advisable for evening meals
✿✿🍴✿

Try also: Harrow &
Barleycorn (ABC)

Beachampton 16D6

11–2.30; 6–11

Bell
Main Street B4033
☎ Milton Keynes 563861
**Aylesbury ABC Bitter; Greene
King Abbot** Ⓗ **Regular guest
beers**
Popular popular free
house, adventure playground
in garden. Motel extension
✿✿✿✿

Beaconsfield 7G1

10.30–2.30; 5.30–11

Old Hare
Aylesbury End (near A40)
☎ 3380
**Benskins Bitter; Ind Coope
Burton Ale** Ⓗ
Oddly-shaped bar, with
unpredictably varying ceiling.
No meals Sundays 🍴Q✿✿🍴

Bennett End 7F1

12–2.30; 7–11

Three Horseshoes
OS783973 ☎ Radnage 3273
**Young Bitter, Special, Winter
Warmer** Ⓗ
18th century inn tucked away
in attractive Chiltern Valley.
No food Mon 🍴Q✿✿✿✿✿🍴✿

Bledlow 16C9

11–2.30; 6–11

Lions of Bledlow
Off B4009
☎ Princes Risboro' 3345
**Courage Directors; Marston
Pedigree; Wadworth 6X;
Young Bitter** Ⓗ **Regular guest
beers**
Large rambling 16th century
inn on edge of Chilterns—very
popular 🍴Q✿✿✿✿✿🍴 (not Sun)

Bolter End 7F1

11–2.30; 6–11

Peacock
B482 OS797923
☎ High Wycombe 881417
**Aylesbury ABC Bitter;
Draught Bass** Ⓗ
Popular country pub with
good value food 🍴Q✿✿✿🍴

Buckingham 16C7

10.30–2.30; 6–11

Grand Junction
13 High Street ☎ 813260
**Aylesbury ABC Bitter;
Draught Bass; Everard Tiger** Ⓗ
Typical market town pub,

---

open all day Tuesdays.
Landlord is Town Crier ✿✿✿ ✿

White Hart
Market Square ☎ 815151
**Courage Directors; Hook
Norton Best Bitter** Ⓗ
Substantial hotel with country
town atmosphere. Popular
with locals and visitors to
Stow 🍴✿✿✿🍴

Burnham 7G2

10.30–2.30; 5.30–11

Pheasant
Lent Rise Road ☎ 5843
**Courage Best Bitter,
Directors** Ⓗ
Comfortable popular split-bar
pub in rural setting; darts
🍴✿✿ (not Sun) ✿

Try also: Crispin (Bass)

Cadmore End 7F1

10.30–2.30; 6–11

Old Ship
B482 OS785927
**Brakspear Bitter, Special
Bitter, Old** Ⓖ
Tiny, unspoilt, traditional
country pub 🍴Q✿

Try also: Blue Flag (Free)

Calverton 16D6

11.30–2.30; 6–11

Shoulder of Mutton
Lower Weald (Nr B4033)
☎ Milton Keynes 562183
**Usher Founders Ale; Wilsons
Original Bitter; Bulmers Cider
(summer)** Ⓗ
Very popular pub with open
plan lounge/dining area; well
situated in picturesque village
🍴✿✿🍴

Chalfont 7G1
St. Giles

10–2.30; 6–11

Feathers
Dean Way (High Street) off
A413
**Wethered Bitter, SPA; Samuel
Whitbread**
Comfortable old inn close to
Milton's cottage 🍴

Chesham 16E9

11–2.30; 5.30–11

Queens Head
Church Street (B485)
OS956013 ☎ 783769
**Brakspear Bitter, Special
Bitter** Ⓗ**, Old** Ⓖ**, (winter)**
Traditional public,
comfortable lounge; a
deservedly popular hostelry in
interesting old part of town
🍴✿✿ (not Sun) ✿ ✿

Denham 7H1

10–2.30; 5.30–11

Falcon
Village Road (off A40)

✆ 832125
Wethered Bitter, SPA, Winter Royal Ⓗ
Unspoilt local with inglenook fireplace, opposite village green Q Ⓖ (not Sun)

Dorney 7G2

10.30–2.30; 5.30–11
Pineapple
Lake End Road (B3026)
Friary Meux Bitter; Ind Coope Burton Ale Ⓗ
Deservedly popular country pub in attractive setting. Darts, crib and dominoes in public bar ♿ ☕ Ⓖ (not Sun) ⚓

Drayton Parslow 16D7

11–2.30; 6–11
Three Horseshoes
Main Road ✆ Mursley 296
Aylesbury ABC Bitter; Draught Bass Ⓗ
Friendly village local with horse brasses and attentive pub cat at mealtimes. No food Sunday ♿ ☕ Ⓖ ⚓ ♿

East Burnham 7G2

10.30–2.30; 6–11
Crown
Crown Lane
✆ Farnham Common 4125
Courage Best Bitter, Directors Ⓗ
Old pub/restaurant fronted by 300 year-old wisteria. Shire horses in field at rear. Prices above average
☕ Ⓖ ♿ (not Sun/Mon)

Farnham Royal 7G2

10.30–2.30; 5.30 (6 Sat)–11
Emperor of India
Blackpond Lane (off A355)
Wethered Bitter, SPA, (summer), Winter Royal Ⓗ
Fine pub, reputedly haunted. Called King of Prussia until 1914
♿ Q ☕ Ⓖ (not weekends) ⚓

Fawley 7F1

11–2.30; 6–11
Walnut Tree
Off B480 & A4155 OS757872
✆ Turville Heath 360
Brakspear Bitter, Special Bitter Ⓗ, **Old** (winter) Ⓖ
Very popular pub, noted for exotic food in restaurant (Booking: Tel. 617)
♿ Ⅲ (not weekends) ☕ Ⓖ ♿ ⚓ ♿

Forty Green 7G1

10.30–2.30; 5.30–11
Royal Standard of England
Near B474 OS923919
✆ Beaconsfield 3382
Eldridge Pope Royal Oak; Marston Pedigree, Owd Rodger Ⓗ

Characterful, popular free house with nine centuries of history, approached by narrow lanes ♿ Q ☕ Ⓖ ♿

Frieth 7F1

11–2.30; 6–11
Prince Albert
Moor Common OS799907
✆ High Wycombe 881683
Brakspear Mild, Bitter, Special Bitter, Old Ⓗ
Delightful, homely pub in attractive countryside, just off road from Frieth to Lane End
♿ ☕ Ⓖ (not Sat/Sun)

Great Hampden 16D9

12–2.30; 7–11
Hampden Arms
OS844015
✆ Hampden Row 255
Morland Best Bitter; Ruddle County; Watney Combes Bitter; Webster Yorkshire Bitter Ⓗ
Situated in splendid wooded country. Varied menu, notable for real ham!
♿ Q ☕ Ⓖ ♿ ⚓

Great Missenden 16D9

11–2.30; 6–11
Barley Mow
Chesham Road, Hyde End (B485) OS911012 ✆ 6253
Fuller London Pride; Marston Pedigree; Morrell Bitter Ⓗ
Pleasant, rural roadside inn. Occasional live music ♿ ☕ Ⓖ ♿

Black Horse
Mobwell (off A413) OS891021
Aylesbury ABC Bitter; Chiltern Beechwood Bitter; Morrell Light Mild Ⓗ
Welcoming pub with sing-song evenings. Hot air balloons used to be launched in field next to pub. No food Sun/Mon ♿ ☕ Ⓖ ♿ ⚓ ▲ ♿

Hambleden 7F1

11–2.30; 6–11
Stag & Huntsman
3 miles NE of Henley, off A4155 OS783866
✆ Henley 571227
Brakspear Bitter, Special Bitter; Eldridge Pope Royal Oak; Flowers Original; Wadworth 6X; Bulmer Cider Ⓗ **Occasional guest beers**
Unspoilt pub with restaurant, in picturesque brick-and-flint Trust village
♿ Ⅲ (lunchtime) ☕ Ⓖ ♿ ⚓

Hartwell 16D8

11–2.30; 6–11
Bugle Horn
A418 ✆ Aylesbury 748209

Benskins Bitter, Ind Coope Burton Ale Ⓗ
Smart, attractive, 17th century country inn
♿ Q Ⅲ ☕ Ⓖ ♿

Hawridge 16E8

11–2.30; 6–11
Full Moon
Hawridge Common OS935069
Wethered Bitter, SPA, Winter Royal Ⓗ
Quiet country local, next to windmill. Often busy ♿ Q ☕ ⚓

Try also: **White Lion**, St. Leonards

High Wycombe 16D9

10.30–2.30; 5.30–11
Bell
Frogmoor (A4128) ✆ 21317
Fuller Chiswick Bitter, London Pride, ESB Ⓗ
Town centre pub near viaduct and shop construction sites. Cosy, smart bar—mind the step ♿ Ⓖ ♿

Happy Wanderer
Arnison Avenue ✆ 25093
Evening opens 6
Wethered Bitter, SPA, Winter Royal Ⓗ
Large estate pub opposite shops, with goat in beer garden ☕ Ⓖ (not Sun) ⚓

Iron Duke
Duke Street (along Totteridge Road) ✆ 29644
Morning opens 11; Sat eves 6
Courage Best Bitter, Directors Ⓗ
Large corner pub on road above rail station. Bar billiards, darts and pool; regular socials and raffles
Ⓖ ♿ ⚓ ⇌

Wendover Arms
Desborough Avenue ✆ 26476
Brakspear Mild, Bitter, Special Bitter, Old Ⓗ
Bright suburban corner house—only draught mild in the town. Superb selection of hors d'oeuvres—part of good quality low priced meals
Q ☕ Ⓖ ♿ ⚓

Try also: **Queen** (Fuller)

Iver 7H2

10.30–2.30; 5.30–11
Gurkha
Langley Park Road (B470)
✆ 4257
Courage Best Bitter, Directors Ⓗ
Smart pub with two gardens, one exclusively for children
♿ Q ☕ Ⓖ ♿ (Tues–Sat)

Ley Hill 16E9

10.30–2.30; 6–11
Swan
OS989019

Benskins Bitter; Ind Coope Bitter, Burton Ale ⊞
Tiny old inn overlooking the common ⚓Q✦🅖✆❉

Little Hampden 16D9

12–2.30; 6 (7 winter)–11
Rising Sun
OS857040
✆ Hampden Row 393
Adnams Bitter; Brakspear Special Bitter; Greene King Abbot; Samuel Smith OBB ⊞
Delightful pub in idyllic surroundings. Good bar food at all times ⚓Q✦🅖❉

Little Horwood 16D7

10.30–2.30; 6–11
Shoulder of Mutton
Church Street (off A421)
✆ Winslow 2514
Aylesbury ABC Bitter; Everard Tiger; Morrell Light Mild ⊞
Lively 14th century village pub with popular restaurant area and large garden
⚓✦🅖❉ (not Mon/Tue)

Little Missenden 16E9

11–2.30; 6–11
Crown
Off A413 OS928988
Adnams Bitter; Marston Pedigree; Morrell Varsity ⊞
Very popular village local; excellent garden
⚓Q✦🅖 (not Sun)

Littleworth Common 7G1

10.30–2.30; 5.30–10.30
Beech Tree
Dorney Wood Road
OS934860 ✆ Burnham 61328
Wethered Bitter, SPA ⊞
Pleasant, friendly pub in Burnham Beeches
⚓Q✦🅖 (not Sun)

Try also: Blackwood Arms (Free)

Longwick 16D9

12–2.30; 6–11
Red Lion
Thame Road (Jcn A4129/ B4444)
✆ Princes Risboro' 4980
Aylesbury ABC Bitter; Hook Norton Best Bitter ⊞
Surprisingly spacious roadside pub, recently renovated
🅱🅖❉ (not Sun)

Loudwater 7G1

10.30–2.30; 5.30–11
Bricklayers Arms
Derehams Lane (near A40)
✆ High Wycombe 30965
Wethered Bitter, Samuel Whitbread ⊞

Warm welcome in small cosy pub up narrow lane just off A40 roundabout. Charity roasts in garden ⚓✦

Marlow 7G1

10.30–2.30; 5.30–11
Red Lion
West Street (A4155) ✆ 2957
Winter opening 11 & 6
Aylesbury ABC Bitter; Draught Bass; Ind Coope Burton Ale ⊞
Spotless and friendly town pub with many games. Large garden welcoming all the family. No food Sun ✦🅖❉≷

Royal Oak
Chalkpit Lane, Bovingdon Green (half mile off A4155)
✆ 3875
Mornings opens 11
Wethered Bitter, Samuel Whitbread, Winter Royal ⊞
Friendly one-bar pub next to village duckpond. Petanque played in garden ⚓✦🅖

All Marlow's 20 pubs sell real ale

Marsworth 16E8

11–2.30; 6–11
Red Lion
Vicarage Road (off B489)
OS918146
Aylesbury ABC Bitter; Everard Tiger; Morrell Light Mild ⊞, Westons Vintage Scrumpy 🅖
Regular guest beers
Attractive village inn near Grand Union Canal
⚓🅱✦❉ (summer) ❢

Milton Keynes 16D6

10.30–2.30; 6–11
Cricketers
Oldbrook Boulevard ✆ 678844
Mornings opens 11
Greene King KK, Simpsons Ale, IPA, Abbot ⊞
Excellent estate pub with (obviously) cricketing theme. Check the autographed bats, and find Bradman's! ✦🅖❉☙≷

Cross Keys
Newport Road, Great Woolstone ✆ 679404
Morning opens 11
Wells Eagle Bitter, Bombardier ⊞
Thatched pub with prize-winning garden. Look out for fantail doves and goat ✦🅖❉❢

New Inn
Bradwell Road, New Bradwell
✆ 312094
Wells Eagle Bitter, Bombardier ⊞
Friendly canalside pub. Homely lounge. Good value food in restaurant ✦🅖❉❢

Suffolk Punch
Saxon Street, Heelands
✆ 311166

Evenings opens 5.30
Tolly Cobbold Mild, Bitter, Original, Old Strong ⊞
Interesting new city pub with Suffolk theme. Split-level carvery restaurant 🅱✦🅖❉❢

Newton Blossomville 16E6

12–2.30; 7–11
Old Mill Burnt Down
Olney, (near A428 Turvey)
✆ Turvey 433
Marston Mercian Mild, Burton Bitter, Border Bitter, Pedigree, Owd Rodger; Younger IPA ⊞
Superbly rebuilt, open plan village pub. Skittles room
🅱✦🅖❉

Northall 16E8

10.30–2.30; 5.30–11
Swan
Leighton Road OS959198
✆ Eaton Bray 22044
Flowers Original; Wethered Bitter ⊞
Comfortable and friendly roadside pub. Occasional live music ⚓🅱✦🅖❉♪

Prestwood 16D9

10.30–2.30; 5.30–11
Kings Head
Wycombe Road (A4128),
½ mile S of village
Brakspear Mild, Bitter, Special Bitter, Old; Courage Best Bitter; Marston Pedigree ⊞
Regular guest beers
Genuine locals' local
⚓Q🅱✦🅖❢

Princes Risborough 16D9

10.30–2.30; 5.30 (Sat 6)–11
Whiteleaf Cross
Market Square (near A4010)
✆ 6834
Morland Mild, Bitter, Best Bitter ⊞
Bright town centre tavern, catering for most tastes—only Morland house in county
✦🅖❉ (not Sun) ≷

Saunderton 16D9

10.30–2.30; 5.30–11
Golden Cross
Wycombe Road (A4010)
✆ Naphill 2293
Aylesbury ABC Bitter; Ind Coope Burton Ale; Morrell Light Mild ⊞
Friendly roadside pub; substantial bar menu
✦🅖❉ (not Mon) ❢≷

Rose & Crown
Wycombe Road (A4010)
✆ Princes Risboro' 5299
Opens 11; Sat eves 6
Morland Bitter; Morrell Varsity; Wethered Bitter ⊞
Occasional guest beers

Comfortable country hotel beside Aylesbury-Wycombe road. Large garden
🍺 Q ✿ 🏠 🕒 ✹ (not Sun/Mon)

Skirmett 7F1

11–2.30; 5.30–11

Old Crown
OS775908
✆ Turville Heath 435
Brakspear Mild, Bitter, Special Bitter, Old G
Unspoilt country pub with friendly atmosphere. Excellent food 🍺 Q 🎪 ✿ 🕒 ✹ ♪ ▮

Stewkley 16D7

10.30–2.30; 5.30–11 (6 Sat)–11

Swan
High Street North (B4032)
✆ 285
Courage Best Bitter, Directors H
Attractive Georgian exterior; inglenook fireplace. No food Sun 🍺 🕒 ♪

Stoke 16D8
Mandeville

11.30–2.30; 6–11

Woolpack
Risborough Road (A4010)
✆ 3447
Aylesbury ABC Bitter; Draught Bass H
Friendly and comfortable half-thatched inn, very popular, large well-appointed garden
Q 🍺 ✿ 🕒 ▮ ⅗ ≷

Stoke Poges 7G2

11–2.30; 5.30–11

Rose & Crown
Hollybush Hill (off B416)
✆ Fulmer 2148
Courage Best Bitter; Directors H
Comfortable village local with two separate bars; homemade fayre on menu
🍺 ✿ 🕒 ♪ (not Sun) ▮ ⅗

Try also: Plough (Ind Coope)

Stony 16D6
Stratford

12–2.30; 5.30–11

Bull (Vault's Bar)
66 High Street
✆ Milton Keynes 567104
Aylesbury ABC Bitter; Draught Bass; Fuller London Pride; Hook Norton Best Bitter H **Regular guest beers**
Splendid Victorian bar adjoining historic coaching house. Many curios, frequent live bands ✿ 🏠 🕒 ♪ ▮

Taplow 7G2

10.30–2.30; 5.30–11 (6 Sat)–11

Horse & Groom
735 Bath Road (Jcn of A4/B3026) ✆ Burnham 5952
Draught Bass; Charrington IPA H

Enterprising 300 year-old roadhouse ✿ 🕒 (not Sun)

Twyford 16C7

11–2.30; 6–11

Red Lion
Church End
✆ Steeple Claydon 339
Aylesbury ABC Bitter; Ind Coope Burton Ale H
Unique 17th century pub in tranquil country setting. Renowned for its home cooking (booking advisable); no food Sun/Mon
🍺 Q 🕒 ♪

Weedon 16D8

10.30–2.30; 6 (7 Sat)–11

Five Elms
Stockaway (off A413)
✆ Aylesbury 641439
Aylesbury ABC Bitter; Draught Bass; Everard Tiger H
Small, low-beamed country pub, full of character—a warm welcome on all levels
🍺 Q ✿ 🕒 (not Sun) ♪ (not Mon)

Weston 16D8
Turville

11.30–2.30; 6–11

Five Bells
Main Street (B4544)
✆ Stoke Mandeville 3131
Aylesbury ABC Bitter; Everard Tiger; Webster Yorkshire Bitter; Young Special; Younger IPA, No. 3 H
Occasional guest beers
Comfortable village inn with two bars, restaurant and purpose-built hotel ✿ 🏠 🕒 ♪ ▮

Whaddon 16D7

10.30–2.30; 6–11

Lowndes Arms
High Street
✆ Milton Keynes 501706
Aylesbury ABC Bitter; Everard Tiger H
Old village pub with wealth of original beams and inglenook fireplace. Stables now converted to luxurious motel rooms 🍺 ✿ 🏠 🕒 ♪ (not Sun)

Whiteleaf 16D8

11.30–2.30; 6–11

Red Lion
Upper Icknield Way (off A4010)
✆ Princes Risboro' 4476
Brakspear Bitter, Special Bitter; Morland Bitter H
Attractive country pub in secluded Chiltern village. Good for food (not Sun) and quiet conversation
🍺 Q ✿ 🕒 ♪

Wing 16D7

10.30–2.30; 6–11

Cock
High Street (off A418)
✆ Aylesbury 688214
Wethered Bitter; Whitbread Castle Eden H
Exuberant public bar with separate dart and pool areas—sedate comfortable lounge; restaurant (not Sun)
🍺 ✿ 🏠 🕒 ♪ ▮

Winslow 16D7

10.30–2.30; 6.30–11

Nag's Head
Sheep Street (A413) ✆ 2037
Aylesbury ABC Bitter; Everard Tiger H
Attractive split-level pub with raised games area; large garden-barbecues at weekends; live music 🍺 ✿ 🕒 ♪

Wolverton 16D6

10.30–2.30; 6–11

North Western
Stratford Road
Wells Eagle Bitter H
Modernised busy Victorian pub opposite railway works ▮ ≷

Wooburn Moor 7G1

10.30–2.30; 5.30–11

Falcon
Watery Lane (near A40)
✆ Bourne End 22752
Wethered Bitter, SPA, Samuel Whitbread H
Three-part room round central bar with traffic lights. Beware raised floor and low beam. No food Sun ✿ 🕒 ♪

How to Use the Guide

Facilities

🍺	real fire
Q	quiet pub–no electronic music, TV or obtrusive games
🎪	indoor room for children
✿	garden or other outdoor drinking area
🏠	accommodation
🕒	lunchtime meals
♪	evening meals
▮	public bar
⅗	facilities for the disabled

🅐	camping facilities close to the pub or part of the pub grounds
≷	near British Rail station
⊖	near Underground Station.

The facilities, beers and pub hours listed in the Good Beer Guide are liable to change but were correct when the Guide went to press. Many pubs do not serve meals at weekends.

Abington Piggots 17G6

12–2; 6–11

Darby & Joan
OS306455
✆ Steeple Morden 852273
Adnams Bitter; Greene King XX, IPA, Abbot; Hall & Woodhouse Badger Best Bitter; Marston Pedigree [H]
Regular guest beers
Large country pub, well worth finding ⌂Q✿◗▮

Alwalton 17F3

11–2.30; 6–11

Wheatsheaf
Oundle Road (off A605/A1)
✆ Peterborough 231056
Ind Coope Burton Ale [H]
Unspoilt village pub near East of England Showground
⌂✿◔▮

Ashley 18C6

11–2.30; 6–11

Crown
24 Newmarket Road
✆ Newmarket 730737
Greene King XX, IPA, Abbot [H]
Colourful village local. Large busy public bar; cosy lounge for meals
⌂✿◔◗ (not Wed) ▮♿

Barnack 17F2

11–2.30; 6–11

Millstone
Millstone Lane
✆ Stamford 740296
Adnams Bitter; Everard Tiger, Old Original [H] **Regular guest beers**
Hidden down small lane. Colourful landlord ⌂✿◔◗▮

Bartlow 18C7

11.45–2.30; 6.30–11

Three Hills
Off A604
✆ Cambridge 891259
Greene King IPA, Abbot [H]
Cosy timbered country pub; growing reputation for food
⌂Q✿◔◗

Bluntisham 17G4

11.30–2.30; 7–11

White Swan
High Street (off A1123)
✆ Ramsey 842055
Tolly Cobbold Bitter, Original, Old Strong [H]
Pleasant two-bar pub in heart of fruit-growing area ⌂✿▮

Bottisham 18C6

11–2.30; 7–11

Bell
High Street
✆ Cambridge 811483
Adnams Bitter; Greene King IPA [H]
Unpretentious low-ceilinged pub; marvellous value home cooking ⌂✿◔◗▮♿

Brampton 17F4

10.30–2.30; 6–11

Black Bull
Church Road
✆ Huntingdon 54193
Usher Founders Ale; Wilsons Original Bitter [H]
Lively 2-bar village local
✿◔◗▮

Buckden 17F5

10.30–2.30; 6.30–11

Falcon
Mill Road (off A1)
✆ Huntingdon 811612
Wells Eagle Bitter [H], **Bombardier** [G]
Friendly comfortable village pub; games room
⌂▣◔◗ (Wed–Sat)

Burwell 18C6

11–2.30; 7–11

Fox
Causeway
✆ Newmarket 741267
Norwich S & P Best Bitter; Webster Yorkshire Bitter [H]
Class and style amongst surrounding mediocrity
⌂✿◔▮

Bythorn 17E4

11.30–2.30; 6.30–11

White Hart
A604 ✆ 226
Liddingtons Litchborough Bitter; Marston Pedigree [H]
Village local on county boundary ⌂▣◔◗

Cambridge 18B6

10–2.30; 6–11

Cambridge Blue
85 Gwydir Street ✆ 356408
Opens 12
Earl Soham Victoria; Elgood Bitter; Tolly Cobbold Bitter, 4X [H] **Regular guest beers**
Well renovated Victorian local with tiny snug, petanque played ⌂Q✿◔◗⇄

Champion of the Thames
King Street
Mornings opens 10.30
Greene King XX, IPA [H] **Abbot** [G]
Ace little local, splendid etched windows
⌂◔ (not Sun) ▮♿

County Arms
43 Castle Street (A604)
✆ 353285
Opens 11; opens 7 Sat eve
Brakspear Bitter; Flowers Original; Whitbread Castle Eden [H]
Warm welcoming pub opposite Shire Hall
⌂✿◔◗ (not Tue)

Cow & Calf
Pound Hill ✆ 311919
Opens 11.30
Tolly Cobbold Bitter, Original, 4X
Smashing street corner local in improving part of the city
⌂✿◔ (not Sun)

Fleur-de-Lys
73 Humberstone Road
✆ 356095
Opens 11.30 and 7
Tolly Cobbold Mild, Bitter, Original, Old Strong [H]
Convivial pub with a real "locals" feel, try the mild
✿◔▮♿

Kingston Arms
33 Kingston Street ✆ 61868
Opens 11.30
Greene King IPA, Abbot Rayment BBA [H]
Lively back-street local in good drinking area
⌂Q✿◔ (not Sun) ▮⇄

Maypole
Park Street ✆ 352999
Opens 10.30
Tolly Cobbold Mild, Bitter Original, Old Strong [H]
Comfortable two-bar pub run with Latin flair and charm by champion-cocktail-mixer landlord ✿◔▮

Merton Arms
25 Northampton Street
✆ 359236
Opens 11.30 and 6.30
Greene King IPA, Abbot [H]
Lively front bar, quiet cosy lounge. A nice place to stay
✿▣◔◗▮

Royal Standard
292 Mill Road ✆ 247877
Opens 11
Tolly Cobbold Mild, Bitter Original, Old Strong [H]
Once upon a time most locals were like this ⌂✿▮♿

Try also: Alma (Free) **Zebra** (Greene King)

Castor 17F3

11–2.30; 6–11

Royal Oak
24, Peterborough Road (A47)
✆ 217
Ind Coope Bitter, Burton Ale [H]
Regular guest beers
Listed, thatched building of considerable character and charm. Friendly atmosphere makes this a popular business and family rendezvous
⌂Q✿◔ (not Sun) ▮

Chatteris 18B4

11.30–2.30; 6–11

Cock
41 London Road (B1050)
✆ 2026
Websters Yorkshire Bitter [H]
Former mansion with ornate ceilings and large key ring

collection; Petanque
courts ✿♿➤♿

Chippenham   18B6

11–2.30; 6–11

Tharp Arms
High Street
✆ Newmarket 720234
**Greene King XX, IPA,
Abbot** Ⓗ
Family pub with a lot to offer
♨✿♟

Conington   18A6

11–2.30; 6–11

White Swan
(Off A604) ✆ Elsworth 251
Greene King KK Ⓖ**, IPA** Ⓗ**,
Abbot** Ⓖ
Victorian pub in splendid
pastoral setting; traditional
pub games ♨✚✿➤♟

Cottenham   18B6

11–2.30; 7–11

Chequers
297 High Street ✆ 50307
**Tolly Cobbold Bitter,
Original** Ⓗ
Classily renovated pub near
War Memorial
♨✿➤ (not Tue, Sun)♿

Earith   17G4

10.30–2.30; 6–11

Crown
High Street ✆ Ramsey 841442
**Manns Bitter; Usher Founders
Ale; Webster Yorkshire Bitter;
Wilsons Original Bitter** Ⓗ
Pleasant riverside pub with its
own moorings ✿➤♟

Eaton Socon   17F5

10.30–2.30; 5.30–11

Crown
Great North Road
✆ Huntingdon 212232
Adnams Bitter Ⓗ **Regular
guest beers**
Busy freehouse at southern
end of town bypass ✚✿➤

Elton   17F3

10.30–2.30; 6–11

Black Horse
Overton Road (A605) ✆ 240
**Samuel Smith OBB, Museum
Ale** Ⓗ
Old maps and prints adorn
walls, pub is about 400 years
old. A previous landlord was
Kirk the Hangman. Pool and
darts ♨♟

Try also: Crown

Ellington   17F4

11.30–2.30; 6–11

Mermaid
Boddingtons Bitter Ⓗ
Occasional guest beers
Busy village freehouse full of
characters ✿

Ely   18C5

10.30–2.30; 6–11

Prince Albert
62 Silver Street ✆ 3494
Opens 11 and 6.30
**Greene King XX, IPA,
Abbot** Ⓗ
Cosy little local ✿➤≷

Royal Standard
Forehill ✆ 2613
Opens 11 and 7
**Greene King XX, IPA,
Abbot** Ⓔ
City centre pub, popular for
lunches ♨✿➤ (not Sun)♟

Eynesbury   17F5

11.30–2.30; 6–11

Coneygeare
Hardwicke Road
**Adnams Bitter; Ruddle
County; Samuel Smith OBB** Ⓗ
Regular guest beers
Large modern free house, by
St Neots Riverside Park ✿➤

Fenstanton   17G5

10.30–2.30; 6–11

George
High Street
**Flowers Original, Wethered
Bitter; Whitbread Castle
Eden** Ⓗ
Modernised village local;
games and childrens areas
✚✿➤♟

Foxton   18B7

11.30–2.30; 6–11

White Horse
High Street (off A10)
✆ Cambridge 871948
**Brakspear Pale Ale; Flowers
Original; Fremlins Bitter;
Wethered Bitter; Whitbread
Castle Eden** Ⓗ **Occasional
guest beers**
Enterprising, welcoming
pub—something for everyone
♨✚✿➤♟≷

Fulbourn   18B6

10.30–2.30; 6–11

Six Bells
High Street
**Tolly Cobbold Mild, Bitter, Old
Strong** Ⓗ
Bustling local at centre of
village ♨✿➤♟

Glatton   17F3

11.30–3; 7–11

Addison Arms
Sawtry Road (off B660)
✆ Ramsey 830410
**Manns Bitter; Usher Founders
Ale; Wilsons Original Bitter** Ⓗ
Quiet, popular village pub
♨Q✿➤♿

Godmanchester   17G4

10.30–2.30; 6–11

Exhibition
London Road
✆ Huntingdon 59134
**Manns Bitter; Usher Founders
Ale; Wilsons Original Bitter** Ⓗ
Victorian shopfronts in
lounge, railway paraphernalia
in public. Garden has
petanque pitch and animals
✿➤♟♿

Grantchester   18B6

11–2.30; 6–11

Rupert Brooke
The Broadway
✆ Cambridge 840295
**Flowers IPA, Original,
Wethered Bitter; Whitbread
Castle Eden** Ⓗ
Smart, popular pub named
after former village resident
♨✿➤

Great Eversden   18A7

11 (12 winter)–2.30; 6 (7 winter)–11

Hoops
High Street
✆ Comberton 2185
Wells Eagle Bitter Ⓗ
Bombardier Ⓖ
Wells flagship in the county.
Home cooking (not Tue)
served beneath timber beams
♨✿Ⓔ➤♟♿

Great Gransden   17G5

12–2.30; 6–11

Crown & Cushion
✆ 214
Wells Eagle Bitter Ⓗ**,
Bombardier** Ⓖ
Cosy, welcoming village pub
♨Q✿➤

Great Wilbraham   18C6

11–2.30; 6.30–11

Carpenters Arms
10 High Street
✆ Cambridge 880202
**Greene King XX, IPA,
Abbot** Ⓗ
17th century pub; selection of
Islay malt whiskies
♨✿Ⓔ➤♟

Guyhirn   17H2

10.30–2.30; 5.30–11

Chequers
Main Road (A47) ✆ 352
Elgood Bitter Ⓗ
Built 1913 smart lounge
leading to garden. Small
public with pool. Only pub in
area with Ringing the Bull
♨✿➤♟♿

Hartford   17G4

10.30–2.30; 6–11

Barley Mow
A141 ✆ Huntingdon 50557
**Wells Eagle Bitter,
Bombardier** Ⓗ
Comfortable lounge bar ✿➤Å

Hinxton 18B7

11.30–2.30; 6.30–11

Red Lion
High Street
☎ Saffron Walden 30601
**Flowers Original; Fremlins
Bitter; Wethered Bitter;
Whitbread Castle Eden** Ⓗ
Lovely old pub in picture-book
village ♨ ✿ ⌕ ➤

Holme 17F3

10.30–2.30; 6–11

Admiral Wells
41 Station Road (B660, off
A1) ☎ Ramsey 830798
**Ind Coope Burton Ale, Tetley
Bitter** Ⓗ **Regular guest beers**
Lowest pub in England;
petanque played ♨ ♙ ✿ ⌕ ➤ ❢ ⅙

Holywell 17G4

10.30–2.30; 6–11

Olde Ferryboat Inn
☎ Huntingdon 63227
**Draught Bass; Gibbs Mew
Wiltshire Bitter; Greene King,
IPA, Abbot** Ⓗ
Thatched riverside pub,
reputedly haunted
♨ ♙ ✿ Ⓟ ⌕ ➤

Horningsea 18B6

11.30–2.30; 7–11

Plough & Fleece
High Street (off A45)
☎ Cambridge 860795
Greene King IPA, Abbot Ⓗ
Superb public bar with stuffed
fox; excellent food (Tue–Sat)
♨ Q ✿ ⌕ ➤ ❢

Huntingdon 17G4

11–2.30; 6–11

Victoria
Ouse Walk ☎ 53899
James Paine XXX, EG Ⓗ
More like a country pub; hard
to find in this Watney-
dominated town ✿ ⌕ ➤

Ickleton 18B7

11–2.30; 7–11

New Inn
10 Brookhampton Street
☎ Saffron Walden 30497
**Greene King KK, IPA,
Abbot** Ⓖ
As name suggests, an old inn!
Antique jukebox in lounge ✿ ❢

Kirtling 18C6

11–2.30; 7–11

Queens Head
☎ Newmarket 730253
**Tolly Cobbold Mild, Bitter,
Original, Old Strong; Bulmer
West Country Cider** Ⓗ
Unspoilt Elizabethan inn run
with energy and charm in
delightful surroundings
♨ ♙ ✿ Ⓖ ⌕ ➤ (not Thu/Sun) ❢ ⅙

Litlington 17G6

10.30–2.30; 6–11

Crown
Silver Street
Greene King IPA Ⓗ, **Abbot** Ⓖ
Bustling village local, on
unusual village one-way
system. Has appeared in every
edition of the GBG ♨ ✿ ⌕ ➤ ❢

March 18B3

10–2.30; 6–11

Acre
9 Acre Road ☎ 57116
Wed lunch 10–4
Greene King IPA Ⓔ
Town centre pub with unique
riverside country flavour.
Famous locally for its
homecooked lunches ✿ ⌕ ➤ ⅙

Great Northern
Norwood Road ☎ 54736
Elgood Bitter Ⓗ
Cosy little pub described
locally as a mini railway
museum ✿ ⌕ ➤ ⅙ ᚙ ⚓ ➤

Ship
Nene Parade ☎ 56999
**Greene King XX, IPA,
Abbot** Ⓗ
Occasional guest beers
Thatched riverside pub.
Carved ceiling beams were
reputedly intended for Ely
Cathedral ♙ ♨ Ⓟ ⌕ ➤ ❢

Newton 18B7

11.30–2.30; 6–11

Queens Head
Off B1368
☎ Cambridge 870436
**Adnams Bitter, Old; Bulmer
Medium Cider** Ⓖ
Idyllic local; variety of pub
games ♨ Q ✿ ⌕ ➤ ❢

Over 18B5

12–2.30; 7–11

Exhibition
2 King Street
☎ Swavesey 30790
**Tolly Cobbold Mild, Bitter,
Original** Ⓗ **Old Strong** Ⓖ
Beautifully restored and
extended village local ✿ ⌕ ➤

Peterborough 17F3

10.30–2.30; 6–11

Bluebell
Welland Road, Dogsthorpe
Elgood Bitter Ⓗ
Oldest city pub. Monkey's
skull behind panelling in
porch. Small totally unspoilt
snug ✿ ⌕ ❢

Crown
749 Lincoln Road (off A15)
New England ☎ 41366
Music licence to midnight
**Charrington IPA; Draught
Bass** Ⓗ **Occasional guest beers**
Large lively corner pub, live
music and discos in lounge
most eves. Some entrance fees
♨ ♙ ✿ ⌕ ➤ ❢

Dragonfly
Herlington Centre, Orton,
Malborne
**Tolly Cobbold Bitter, Original,
Old Strong** Ⓗ
Sandpiper Bar has interesting
roof ✿ Ⓖ ❢ ⅙

Fountain Inn
2 Burghley Road (old A47)
☎ 54533
Opens 11 am
**Manns Bitter; Usher Founders
Ale; Wilsons Original Bitter** Ⓗ
Evening locals pub, built on
site of former "fountain" in
early 1950s—bar music,
lounge comfortable ✿ Ⓖ ➤ ❢ ❢ ⌕

Greenkeeper
Thorpe Wood (off A47)
☎ 267601
Greene King IPA, Abbot Ⓗ,
Christmas Ale Ⓖ
19th hole of public golf
course. Panoramic view of
Nene Valley. Friendly house
with low key golfing theme
Q ✿ ⌕ ➤

The Harrier
Gunthorpe Road, Gunthorpe
(near A47) ☎ 75362
Opens 11 am & 6.30 pm
Greene King IPA, Abbot Ⓗ;
Taunton Cider
Winner of CAMRA pub
preservation group new pub
award 1985. Modern family-
type pub ✿ Ⓖ ⅙

Peter Pan
Eastern Avenue, Dogsthorpe
Home Mild, Bitter Ⓔ
Large estate pub. Basic public,
2 lounges, one quiet. Main
lounge has live music. Many
international jazz stars have
performed here ✿ ❢

Still
Cumbergate ☎ 68531
Closed Sun and Bank holidays
**Bateman XXXB; Elgood Bitter;
Greene King Abbot, Marston
Pedigree; Owd Rodger; Ruddle
County** Ⓖ & Ⓗ **Regular guest
beers**
An oasis marooned in the
Queensgate Shopping Centre.
Beer delivered by lift Q ✿ Ⓖ ❢ ➤

*Try also: Gladstone, Limetree,
White Hart*

Purls Bridge 17H3

12–2.30; 7–11 (closed Mon)

Ship
Manea 578
Greene King IPA Ⓗ
Isolated Fenland pub by
Bedford River. Popular with
ornithologists ♨ Q ✿ Ⓖ ➤

Rampton 18B6

11–2.30; 7–11

Black Horse
High Street
**Greene King KK, IPA,
Abbot** Ⓗ

Welcoming village local with one of the county's last remaining outside gents 🏠 🌳 ♀

Ramsey 17G4

10.30–2.30; 6–11

Jolly Sailor
Great Whyte
Usher Founders Ale; Wilsons Original Bitter H
Look out for photos of the Great Whyte River in this Fenland town pub Q 🌳 ♀

Reach 18C6

12–2.30; 7–11

Kings
Fair Green (off B1102)
☎ Newmarket 741745
Benskins Bitter; Greene King IPA; Tetley Bitter H Regular guest beers
Well-restored pub on historic village green, famous for its fair 🏠 🌳 🕒 (not Mon)
➔ (not Sun/Mon)

Rings End 17H2

10.30–2.30; 5.30–11

Black Hart
A141
Elgood Bitter G
Unspoilt Fenland pub. Beer fetched from the cellar. Popular with fishermen. The juke box dates from 1958 and gives 3 plays for a shilling
🏠 ♀ 🕭

St Ives 17G4

10–2.30; 6.30–11

Royal Oak
High Street ☎ 69644
Ind Coope Bitter, Burton Ale H
Multi-roomed pub with lots of beams and settles 🏠 🕒

St Neots 17F5

10.30–2.30; 7–11

Wheatsheaf
Church Street
Greene King XX, IPA, Abbot H, **Christmas Ale** G
Busy terraced town local 🏠 ♀

Sawston 18B7

10–2.30; 6–11

University Arms
84 London Road
☎ Cambridge 832165
Adnams Bitter; Marston Pedigree; Webster Yorkshire Bitter H Regular guest beers
Ever-changing cornucopia of exotic real ales
🏢 🌳 🕒 ➔ (not Tue)

Somersham 17G4

10.30–2.30; 6–11

Rose & Crown
High Street ☎ Ramsey 840328
Wethered Bitter; Whitbread Castle Eden H

Town pub; handpumps in lounge ♀

Southoe 17F5

10.30–2.30; 6–11

Three Horseshoes
High Street
Wells Eagle Bitter H, **Bombardier** G
Cosy village local 🏠 🌳 🕒

Teversham 18B6

10.30–2.30; 6–11

Rose & Crown
High Street ☎ 2245
Flowers Original H
Village local with sporting feel to it. Watch out for George
🏠 🌳 ➔ 🕭

Thorney Toll 17G2

10.30–2.30; 6 (7 winter)–11

Black Horse
A47 ☎ Knarr Cross 218
Elgood Bitter H
Public bar with lounge area. Pool room 🏠 🌳 ➔ ♀ 🕭

Ufford 17F2

10.30–2.30; 6–11

Olde White Hart
☎ Stamford 740250
Home Bitter H
Attractive old coaching inn. Friendly atmosphere makes this a popular rendezvous for locals and travellers. No food Sun or Mon 🏠 Q 🌳 🕒 ♀

Waterbeach 18B6

11–2.30; 6.30 (6 F, S)–11

Star
40 Station Road
☎ Cambridge 861287
Greene King IPA, Abbot H
Very friendly local. No food Suns 🏠 🏢 🌳 🕒 ➔ ≷

Whittlesey 17G3

10.30–2.30; 6–11

Boat Inn
2 Ramsey Road
☎ Peterborough 202488

Elgood Bitter H
Friendly town pub, one of the original inns of England mentioned in Domesday Book. Beware! Pub uses false handpulls for keg beers
🏠 🌳 🎦 🕒 ➔ ♀ 🕭 ≷

Try also: Bricklayers Arms

Willingham 18B5

10.30–2.30; 6–11

Three Tuns
Church Street
Greene King XX, IPA, Abbot G
Straightforward village local; ale fetched from back 🌳 ♀ 🕭

Wisbech 17H2

10.30–2.30; 6–11

Kings Head
13 Old Market
☎ 65402
Elgood Bitter H
Old pub by River Nene, popular with the young. Nautical lounge; pool
🌳 🕒 ➔ ♀ 🕭

Red Lion
North Brink ☎ 582022
Opens 11 am
Elgood Bitter H
Popular pub near the Brewery. Collection of plates, foreign currency notes, matchboxes and brassware. Dining room 🏠 🕒 ➔ 🕭

Try also: Blackfriars (Norwich/Ruddles) Turnpike, Walsoken (Greene King)

Witcham 18B5

11–2.30; 6–11

White Horse
7 Silver Street
☎ Ely 778298
Bateman XB, Elgood Bitter; Greene King IPA, Abbot G Regular guest beers
Splendid village free house with beer straight from the cask 🏠 🌳 🕒 ➔ (must book) ♀

How to Use the Guide

Facilities

🏠 real fire
Q quiet pub–no electronic music, TV or obtrusive games
🏢 indoor room for children
🌳 garden or other outdoor drinking area
🎦 accommodation
🕒 lunchtime meals
➔ evening meals
♀ public bar
🕭 facilities for the disabled

A camping facilities close to the pub or part of the pub grounds
≷ near British Rail station
⊖ near Underground Station.

The facilities, beers and pub hours listed in the Good Beer Guide are liable to change but were correct when the Guide went to press. Many pubs do not serve meals at weekends.

Alpraham 22C5

11–3 (closed Mon–Fri) 6–11
Travellers Rest
Chester Road (A51)
✆ Bunbury 260523
**Tetley Mild, Bitter, McEwan
70/-** ℍ
Popular pub with a variety of
small rooms 🏚Q🏠🍴🅰

Audlem 22D6

11–3; 5.30–11
Bridge
12 Shropshire Street (A525)
✆ Crewe 811267
**Marston Burton Bitter,
Pedigree, Merrie Monk** ℍ**,
Owd Rodger (winter)** 🅖
Friendly canalside pub,
mooring facilities nearby
🏚Q🎱🏠🍴🍺🔨

Barbridge 22D5

11–3; 5.30–11
Barbridge Inn
Chester Road (A51)
✆ Nantwich 73266
Boddingtons Mild, Bitter ℍ
Attractive, busy canalside pub
with restaurant Q🏠🍴🍺🅰

Barthomley 22E5

11–3; 5.30–11
White Lion
Audley Road (off A52)
Burtonwood Bitter ℍ
Unspoilt, 17th century
thatched pub in picturesque
village 🏚Q🏠🍴

Bollington 23F4

11–3; 5.30–10.30 (11 F, S)
Meridian
48 Palmerston Street ✆ 73883
Boddingtons Mild, Bitter ℍ
Old town-centre local, popular
with all age groups 🏚🍴

Vale
Adlington Road ✆ 75147
**Marston Burton Bitter; Taylor
Landlord; Thwaites Mild,
Bitter** ℍ
Comfortable old stone-built
pub, once 3 terraced houses,
by long distance footpath
🏚🅖 (not Mon)

Bosley 23F4

11–3; 5.30–10.30 (11 F, S)
Queens Hotel
A523 ✆ North Rode 267
Boddingtons Bitter ℍ
Popular country pub. Small
dining room open 7–9.15 pm
🏚🏠🅖🍴

Buglawton 23E4

11.30–3; 5.30–11
Robin Hood
Buxton Road (A54)
OS887647
✆ Congleton 273616
**Marston Burton Bitter,
Pedigree** ℍ

Comfortable, friendly old pub
near canal. No food Mon
🏚Q🏠🅖🍴

Burleydam 22D6

11.30–3; 7–11
Combermere Arms
A525 (near Jct with A529)
**Draught Bass; M&B
Springfield Bitter; Younger's
Scotch Bitter** ℍ
16th century pub with
restaurant 🏚Q🏠🍴🍴

Butley 23F4

11–3; 5.30–10.30 (11 F, S)
Ash Tree
London Road (A523)
✆ Prestbury 829207
Boddingtons Bitter ℍ
Comfortable rural pub,
excellent selection of food
🏚🅖🍴🍴

Chester 22B4

11–3; 5.30–10.30 (11 F, S)
Albion
Park Street
**Greenall Whitley Mild, Local
Bitter, Original Bitter** ℍ
Liberally decorated with bric-
a-brac and relics. Imaginative
lunchtime menu (no chips).
Live jazz Sunday nights
🏚🅖🍴 (weekends) 🍴

Bridgewater Arms
Crewe Street, off City Road
**Greenall Whitley Mild,
Bitter** ℍ
Friendly, comfortable two
room back street local 🍴🍴🅰≷

Carlton Tavern
Hartington Street, Handbridge
**Peter Walker Mild, Bitter, Best
Bitter** ℍ
Art-deco suburban pub with
distinctive lounge and bar 🏚🍴

Olde Custom House
Watergate Street
**Marston Border Mild,
Exhibition, Burton Bitter,
Pedigree** ℍ
Historic half-timbered
building opposite original
Custom House 🅖🍴

Ship Victory
George Street ✆ 376453
**Ind Coope Burton Ale;
Jennings Bitter; Tetley Bitter** ℍ
Prominent white building
near bus station 🅖 (not Sun)

Childer Thornton 22B4

11.30–3; 5.30–10.30 (11 F, S)
White Lion
New Road (off A41)
Thwaites Best Mild, Bitter ℍ
Unspoilt friendly village local
Q🎱🏠

Comberbach 22D4

11–3; 5.30–11

Drum & Monkey

Off A559
Tetley Mild, Bitter ℍ
Formerly "The Avenue".
Monkey tends to lose his
bearings in cold weather!
Q🅖🍴

Congleton 23E5

11.3; 5.30–11
Lion & Swan Hotel
Swan Bank (West Street)
✆ 273115
**Burtonwood Bitter; Marston
Burton Bitter, Pedigree** ℍ
16th century half timbered
coaching inn; superb carved
oak fireplace in cocktail
lounge 🏚🎱 (lunchtime) 🅖🍴🍴

Wharf Inn
121 Canal Road (by
Macclesfield Canal Aqueduct)
**Greenall Whitley Local
Bitter** ℍ
Comfortable, friendly old-
fashioned local. Glass bottle
collection 🏚Q🏠🍴

Crewe 22D5

11–3; 5.30–11
Belle Vue
Earle Street ✆ 584578
**Ind Coope Burton Ale; Peter
Walker Mild, Bitter** ℍ
Warm friendly, traditional
local. Unusual town centre
garden with summer
barbeques 🏚🎱🏠🍴

Horseshoe
North Street ✆ 584265
Evenings opens 6 (6.30 Sat)
**Robinson Best Mild, Best
Bitter** ℍ
Multi-roomed comfortable and
cosy pub 🏚🎱🅖🍴

Kings Arms
Earle Street
Evening opens 7
Chesters Best Mild, Bitter ℍ
Medium-sized popular pub
with good atmosphere; pool
🎱🏠🍴🅰≷

Royal Scot
Plane Tree Drive ✆ 584328
Evening opens 6
**Ind Coope Burton Ale; Tetley
Mild, Bitter** ℍ
Large, basic estate pub 🏚🍴

Croft 22D3

12–3; 7–10.30 (11 F, S)
Plough
Heath Lane
**Greenall Whitley Mild,
Bitter** 🅔
Small popular local, friendly
homely atmosphere. Waitress
service in vault only 🏚Q🍴🍴

Culcheth 22D3

11.30–3; 5.30–10.30 (11 F, S)
Pack Horse
Church Lane (off A574)

Greenall Whitley Mild,
Bitter E, Original H
Small multi-roomed pub;
busy, with friendly
atmosphere Q🍺⏴🕭

Disley   23F3

11–3; 5.30–10.30 (11 F, S)

Crescent
Buxton Road (A6) ✆ 2638
Robinson Best Mild, Best
Bitter H
Thriving village local, friendly
atmosphere, pool table
🏠🍴 (if eating) 🍺⏴🕭🚲⏴≷

Mousetrap
Buxton Old Road (off A6)
Webster Yorkshire Bitter,
Wilsons Original Mild,
Bitter H
Small comfortable local
tucked away in old part of
village 🍴🍺⏴🕭≷

Try also: White Horse; Dandy
Cock

Eaton   23E4

11–3; 5.30–11

Plough
A536 ✆ Congleton 280207
Winkles Saxon Cross Bitter H
Pleasant low-beamed rural
pub 🏠

Ellesmere Port   22B4

11.30–3; 5.30–10.30 (11 F, S)

Grosvenor Hotel
2 Upper Mersey Street (by
M53)
Tetley Mild, Bitter H
Dockland pub, recently
improved to pull in visitors
from nearby National Boat
Museum 🏠🕭🍴≷

Elworth   22D5

11–3; 5.30 (7 Sat)–11

Midland
5 New Street
Robinson Best Mild E,
Bitter H, Best Bitter E
Friendly locals pub. Warm
atmosphere with patriotic
clientele 🏠🕭🍴≷

Farndon   22B5

11–3; 5.30–10.30 (11 F, S)

Greyhound Hotel
High Street (A534) ✆ 270244
Greenall Whitley Mild, Bitter,
Original H
Local caught fresh Dee salmon
meals a speciality. No food Sun
🏠Q🍺🕭⏴🍴

Frodsham   22C4

11–3; 5.30–11

Belle Monte
Bellemonte Road, Overton (off
B5152) OS521769
Samuel Smith OBB H
Guaranteed boisterous
welcome in friendly, many-
roomed comfortable local.

Children's playground, good
views 🏠Q🏠🍺⏴ (summer) 🕭

Netherton Hall
Chester Road (A56) ✆ 32342
Ind Coope Burton Ale; Tetley
Mild, Bitter H
Converted farmhouse
replacing demolished
"Whalebone Inn". Pub
history illustrated throughout
Q🍺🏠⏴🍴⏴&

Gawsworth   23E4

11–3; 5.30–10.30 (11 F, S)

Harrington Arms
Congleton Road (off A536)
OS887695
Robinson Best Mild, Best
Bitter H
Old pub, part of a farm. Close
to half-timbered Gawsworth
Hall Q🍺🕭

Goostrey   22E4

11–3; 5.30–10.30 (11 F, S)

Crown
Main Road
Marston Mercian Mild,
Burton Bitter E, Pedigree H
Comfortable pub near Jodrell
Bank radio telescope. No food
Mon 🍺⏴🍴

Great Budworth   22D4

11–3; 5.30–11

George & Dragon
High Street (off A559)
✆ Comberbach 891317
Tetley Mild, Bitter H
Attractive pub opposite
church. Hinge and Bracket's
local restaurant 🏠🍺⏴🍴🕭

Heatley   22D3

12–3; 5.30–10.30 (11 F, S)

Railway
Mill Lane (B5159—between
A56 & A6144) ✆ Lymm 2742
Boddingtons Mild, Bitter H
Several rooms, handy for
family visitors to Lymm area
🏠🍺⏴🕭

Henbury   22E4

11–3; 5.30–10.30 (11 F, S)

Cock Inn
Chelford Road
✆ Macclesfield 23186
Robinson Best Mild, Best
Bitter, Old Tom (winter) H
Large comfortable pub on
main road just outside
Macclesfield. Friendly tap
room Q🍴🍺⏴🍴🕭

Knutsford   22E4

11–3; 5.30–10.30 (11 F, S)

Builders Arms
Mobberley Road (off A537)
Marston Mercian Mild,
Burton Bitter, Pedigree H
Small and busy local 🕭≷

White Lion
King Street ✆2018
Tetley Mild, Bitter H
Convivial town centre pub
🏠⏴≷

Langley   23F4

12–3; 7–10.30 (11 F, S)

Leather's Smithy
Clarke Lane OS952715
✆ Sutton 2313
Ind Coope Bitter, Burton Ale;
Tetley Mild, Bitter H
Friendly old country pub with
scenic views across reservoir
towards Macclesfield Forest
🏠⏴🕭🍴🏕

Try also: St Dunstan
(Marston)

Little Leigh   22D4

11–3; 5.30–11

Holly Bush
Runcorn Road (A49, just S of
A533 junction)
Greenall Whitley Local Mild,
Bitter H
Simple farm pub, thatched
and timber-framed, notably
unspoilt and rare. Autumn
steam event, Morris Men and
Soul Cakers. Short walk from
canals 🏠Q🍺🕭🏕 (1 mile)

Lymm   22D3

11–3; 5.30–10.30 (11 F, S)

Bulls Head
The Cross (A6144) ✆ 2831
Hydes Mild, Bitter H
Spruce bar and comfortable
lounge. Next to picturesque
canal bridge ⏴🕭

Spread Eagle
Eagle Brow (A6144) ✆ 3139
Opens 11.30
Lees GB Mild, Bitter H,
Moonraker (winter) E
Near lower dam in village
centre. Small busy snug, large
welcoming lounge
🏠⏴🍴 (not Sun)

Macclesfield   23F4

11–3; 5.30–10.30 (11 F, S)

Baths Hotel
Green Street (behind station)
Closed weekday lunchtime
Boddingtons Mild, Bitter H
Well hidden friendly local 🕭≷

Bridgewater Arms
Buxton Road ✆ 22660
Wilsons Original Mild,
Bitter H
Friendly locals pub next to
Macclesfield Canal ⏴🕭≷

Britannia
260 Hurdsfield Road (A5002)
✆ 23954
Evening opens 6
Greenall Whitley Local Mild,
Bitter H
Stone-built terraced local close
to Macclesfield Canal Q

British Flag
42 Coare Street (off A523)
✆ 25500
Robinson Best Mild, Best Bitter Ⓗ
Cosy friendly local

Evening Star
James Street ✆ 24093
Marston Mercian Mild, Burton Bitter, Pedigree Ⓔ
Busy and comfortable local in back street ▲Ⓖ🕯🚻≢

Star Inn
London Road (A523) ✆ 26738
Marston Mercian Mild, Burton Bitter, Pedigree Ⓗ
Popular, yet quiet local close to football ground ▲Q♨

Wharf
Brook Street
Tetley Mild, Bitter Ⓗ
End-terrace local close to Canal Marina ▲Ⓖ🍽≢

Marbury 22C6
12–3; (closed Mon) 7–11
Swan Inn
Near Whitchurch OS561457
✆ 3715
Greenall Whitley Bitter; Wem Best Bitter Ⓗ
Comfortable, picturesque and friendly old pub. Hard to find, but well worth it
▲♨Ⓖ (not Mon) 🍽🕯♿⚘

Middlewich 22D4
11–3; 5.30–11
Boars Head
Kinderton Street (A54)
✆ 3191
Robinson Best Mild, Best Bitter Ⓔ
Spacious pub near canal. Many rooms, good value food. Pool table. No food weekends
🚻♨▲Ⓖ🍽🕯

Newton Brewery
Webbs Lane (off A54 via Pepper Street) ✆ 3502
Marston Mercian Mild, Burton Bitter, Merrie Monk Ⓗ
Small, red-brick local by Trent and Mersey Canal. Thriving bar, cosy lounge ♨🕯

Mobberley 22E4
11–3; 5.30–10.30 (11 F, S)
Bulls Head
Town Lane (just off B5085 3 miles E of Knutsford) ✆ 3134
Jennings Bitter; Tetley Mild, Bitter Ⓗ
Welcoming village pub to suit all tastes, featuring central open fireplace. Bowling green at the back
▲🚻 (lunchtime) ♨Ⓖ🕯♿

Mow Cop 22E5
11–3; 5.30–11
Cheshire View
Top Station Road

Marston Bitter, Pedigree Ⓗ,
Owd Rodger (winter) Ⓖ
Stone pub, lounge has good view of Cheshire Plain and collection of hill climb photographs 🕯

Nantwich 22D5
11–3; 5.30–11
Oddfellows
97 Welsh Row
Tetley Mild, Bitter Ⓗ
Small, busy pub with good garden ♨Ⓖ🍽 (summer) ♿

Red Cow
Beam Street
Robinson Best Mild, Best Bitter, Old Tom Ⓗ
Recently extended pub opposite the bus station. Try home made steak and kidney pie ▲🚻♨Ⓖ🍽🕯♿

Neston 22B4
11.30–3; 5.30–10.30 (11 F, S)
Brown Horse
The Cross
Tetley Bitter Ⓗ
Friendly pub with varied clientele ▲Ⓖ≢

Coach & Horses
Bridge Street
Whitbread Castle Eden Ⓗ
Extended friendly local
▲♨Ⓖ≢

Newbold 23E5
11–3; 5.30–11
Horse Shoe
Fence Lane OS863602
✆ Congleton 272205
Robinson Best Mild, Best Bitter Ⓔ, **Old Tom** Ⓖ
Remote comfortable country pub ▲♨Ⓖ🍽

Northwich 22D4
11–3; 5.30–11
Cock
Off Chesterway (A559)
✆ 48717
Greenall Whitley Bitter Ⓗ
Open-plan pub near ring road ≢

Freemasons Arms
Chester Road
Webster Yorkshire Bitter; Wilsons Mild, Bitter Ⓗ
Small friendly pub on Castle Hill

Lion & Railway
Station Road ✆ 6080
Greenall Whitley Mild, Bitter Ⓗ
Spacious multi-roomed town pub with railway theme
♨Ⓖ (not Sun) 🍽≢

Over Peover 22E4
11–3; 5.30–10.30 (11 F, S)
Whipping Stocks
Stocks Lane (just off A50)
✆ Lower Peover 2332

Samuel Smith OBB Ⓗ
Large pub with many rooms and good food ▲🚻♨Ⓖ🍽♿

Pickmere 22D4
11–3; 5.30–10.30 (11 F, S)
Red Lion
B5391 off A556
Tetley Bitter Ⓗ
Cosy village pub near lake. No food Mon Q♨Ⓖ🍽🕯

Plumley 22D4
11–3; 5.30–10.30 (11 F, S)
Golden Pheasant
Plumley Moor Road (between A556 & B5081)
✆ Lower Peover 2261
Lees GB Mild, Bitter Ⓗ
Comfortable relaxing country pub. Live music some evenings. Restaurant, pool, bowling green, children's play area ▲🚻♨🚻Ⓖ🍽≢

Smoker
Manchester Road (A556)
✆ Lower Peover 2338
Robinson Best Mild, Best Bitter Ⓔ
Many-roomed roadside inn. Dates from reign of Elizabeth I. Named after a horse
▲Q🚻 (lunch) ♨Ⓖ🍽≢ (¾ mile)

Poynton 23F3
5.30–10.30 (11 F, S) Mon, Thu, Fri, Sat evenings only
Centre
Park Lane (off A523)
Entertainment entrance fee payable when folk provided
Boddingtons Bitter; Thwaites Bitter; Marston Pedigree; Ruddle County Ⓗ **Varied Cider** Ⓖ
Local entertainment centre. Mecca for folk and Morris dance enthusiasts. Membership required but free on application. Table tennis and snooker ♿≢

Try also: Boars Head; Bulls Head

Rainow 23F4
11–3; 5.30–10.30 (11 F, S)
Highwayman
A5002 N of Rainow
✆ Bollington 72345
Thwaites Bitter Ⓗ
400 year-old country pub with magnificent views
▲🚻♨Ⓖ🍽

Runcorn 22C3
11–3; 5.30–10.30 (11 F, S)
Masonic
Devonshire Place, Old Town
✆ 72964
Boddingtons Mild, Bitter Ⓗ
Town centre pub close to bus station Ⓖ🍽≢

Royal Oak
Heath Road South, Weston Village (off A557) ✆ 65839

Marston Mercian Mild,
Burton Bitter, Pedigree Ⓗ
Bustling local, interesting
views nearby of river and
chemical complex by night ⓒ🍴

Sandbach   22E5

11–3; 5.30–11

Iron Grey
Middlewich Road
**Robinson Best Mild, Best
Bitter Ⓗ, Old Tom Ⓖ**
Small and homely friendly
locals pub. Multi-roomed with
darts and bar skittles—strong
on traditional pub games
🏚Q🍴

The Lower Chequer
Hawk Street
Open till 4 Thu lunchtimes
**Tetley Bitter; Boddingtons
Bitter Ⓗ**
Small town pub, just off the
Cobbles. Collection of brasses,
oak beams 🏚🍴Ⓒ🍴

Try also: Wheatsheaf
(Youngers)

Sarn   22C6

11.30–3; 5.30–11

Queens Head
Queens Head (off B5069)
OS440447
**Marston Border Mild, Burton
Bitter Ⓗ**
Small two-roomed pub on
river bank. Worth finding
🏚Q🌿Ⓒ🍴🍴

Scholar Green   22E5

11–3; 5.30–11

Travellers Rest
Congleton Road (A34)
✆ Kidsgrove 2359
**Ind Coope Burton Ale; Tetley
Bitter Ⓗ**
Large open-plan pub 🏚🌿Ⓒ🍴

Stockton Heath 22D3

11–3; 5.30–10.30 (11 F, S)

Red Lion
London Road (A49)
**Greenall Whitley Mild,
Bitter Ⓔ, Original Ⓗ**
Popular many-roomed pub
with floodlit bowling green
Q🌿Ⓒ🍴

Tabley   22D4

11–3; 5.30 (may vary)–10.30 (11 F, S)

Windmill
Chester Road (A556 off M6 Jct
19) ✆ Knutsford 2670
**Robinson Best Mild, Bitter,
Best Bitter Ⓗ, Old Tom Ⓖ**
Large multi-roomed pub.
Beware of the fox! 🏚🌿Ⓒ🍴🍴

Tarporley   22C5

11–3; 7–11

Rising Sun
High Street (A49/A51)
**Robinson Best Mild, Best
Bitter Ⓗ**

Unspoilt attractive interior.
This old established pub is
deservedly busy
🏚QⒸ🍴 (not Sun)

Tattenhall   22C5

11–3; 5.30–10.30 (11 F, S)

Sportsmans Arms
Burwardsley Road (off A41)
Thwaites Mild, Bitter Ⓗ
Village local with bowling
green 🏚🌿🍴🍴

Warrington   22D3

11–3; 5.30–10.30; (11 F, S)

Borough Arms
Mersey Street (A57)
Wilsons Mild, Bitter Ⓗ
Small ex-Greenalls pub,
pleasantly refurbished
Ⓒ🍴🚆 (central)

Manx Arms
31 School Brow (off A57)
✆ 38460
**Tetley Mild; Walker Best
Bitter Ⓗ**
Small, friendly, local's pub
with pool table in lounge 🍴🚆

Ring O'Bells
Church Street (A57) ✆ 34332
**Greenall Whitley Mild, Bitter,
Original Ⓗ**
Tastefully renovated historic
pub, near impressive parish
church 🏚🌿Ⓒ

Try also: Bewsey Farm, Old
Hall (Higsons)

Wheelock   22D5

Closed lunch except Sun; 8–11

Commercial
Crewe Road (A534)
**Boddingtons Bitter; Marston
Pedigree Ⓗ; Bulmer Cider Ⓖ**
Old free house, one time home-
brew pub, close to canal 🏚Q🍴

Widnes   22C3

11–3; 5.30–10.30 (11 F, S)

Griffin

Peel House Lane/Derby Road
(between A568 & A5080)
**Greenall Whitley Mild, Bitter,
Original Ⓔ**
Popular local, cosy lounge,
strong Rugby League
following, near historic
Farnworth Church
🌿Ⓒ🍴🚆 (north)

Horse & Jockey
18 Birchfield Road (A568)
✆ 34332
Evening opens 6
**Greenall Whitley Mild,
Bitter Ⓔ**
Small, friendly two roomed
local of character Q🌿🍴🚆

Wilmslow   23E4

11–3; 5.30–10.30 (11 F, S)

Farmers Arms
Chapel Lane
Boddingtons Mild, Bitter Ⓗ
Friendly, popular local
🏚Q🏚(upstairs)🌿Ⓒ(not Sun)🍴

Unicorn Inn
Dean Row
Sat evening opens 7
Boddingtons Mild, Bitter Ⓗ
Comfortable pub in semi-rural
outskirts of town
🌿Ⓒ (not Sun)

Wincle   23F5

11–3; 5.30–10.30 (11 F, S)

Wild Boar Inn
A54 ✆ 219
**Robinsons Best Mild, Best
Bitter Ⓗ**
Popular pub on edge of moors
🏚🏚🌿Ⓒ🍴

Winsford   22D4

11–3; 5.30–11

Gate Inn
Delamere Street ✆ 2303
Bass Cask Bitter Ⓔ
Honest and welcoming local;
basic bar, cosy lounge. Pity
the handpumps are redundant
🏚🌿🍴

"IT'S THE PUB GHOST— HE ONLY MANIFESTS DURING OPENING HOURS"

Cleveland

Billingham 30D3
11–3; 5.30–10.30
Billingham Arms Hotel
The Causeway
✆ Stockton 553661
McEwan 80/-; Newcastle Cask Exhibition; Younger No. 3 Ⓗ
1950's hotel in new town centre, real ale in Pride bar
🏠Ⓖ♿🍽♨≷

Brotton 30E3
11–3; 5.30–10.30 (11 F, S)
Green Tree
High Street
✆ Guisborough 76377
Evenings opens 7
Cameron Strongarm Ⓗ
Quiet and friendly local with several rooms 🏠🖭🅿Ⓖ♿🍽&

Cowpen Bewley 30D3
11.30–3; 7–10.30
Three Horseshoes
Off A689 ✆ Stockton 561541
Cameron Strongarm Ⓗ
Traditional village local with interesting history 🏠🅿Ⓖ♿🍽♨≷

Egglescliffe 30C4
12–3; 5.30–10.30
Pot & Glass
Church Road
✆ Stockton 780145
Bass Ⓔ
Charming village local, with whitewashed exterior. Long and fascinating history
🖭🅿Ⓖ♿🍽

Eston 30D3
11–3.30; 6–10.30
Eston Hotel
Fabian Road (off A175)
✆ Middlesbrough 453256
Samuel Smith OBB Ⓗ
Large popular pub opposite Langbaurgh town hall
🅿🖭Ⓖ♿

Queens Head
Guisborough Street
✆ Eston Grange 452498
Evening opens 7
Cameron Strongarm Ⓗ
Small, friendly pub in old industrial village 🍽

Guisborough 30E3
11–3; 5.30–10.30 (11 F, S)
Abbey Inn
37, Redcar Road ✆ 32802
Samuel Smith OBB Ⓗ
Typical locals' terraced pub near to town centre and ancient priory 🏠🅿Ⓖ♿🍽

Globe
Northgate (A173) ✆ 32778
Opens 11 & 6.30
Cameron Strongarm Ⓗ & Ⓔ
Friendly, busy street corner local with bustling public bar and large lounge 🅿🍽♨

Ship
145 Westgate (A171)
Opens 11.30
Bass Ⓗ
Busy, friendly town centre pub; former coaching inn. Maritime relics 🏠🅿🍽♿♨

Hartlepool 30D2
11–3; 5.30–10.30
Causeway
Stranton ✆ 273954
Cameron Strongarm Ⓗ
Busy, popular local between Stranton Church and Cameron's Brewery!
🏠🖭Ⓖ♿(must book)♿≷

Mill House
Ryan Terrace ✆ 260329
Cameron Strongarm Ⓗ
Two-roomed local with quiet lounge and busy bar. Very busy when Hartlepool F.C. are at home! 🍽≷

New Inn
Durham Street ✆ 267797
Evening opens 7 Sun to Thu
Cameron Strongarm Ⓗ
Busy friendly local on the road to the headland 🍽

High Leven 30C4
11–3; 7 (6 summer)–10.30
Fox Covert
Low Lane (A1044)
✆ Stockton 760033
Vaux Samson; Wards Sheffield Best Bitter Ⓗ
Popular open-plan pub in cluster of old farmhouse buildings. Caravan site nearby
🏠🅿Ⓖ♿

Lazenby 30D3
11–3.30; 7–10.30
Nags Head
High Street (off A174)
✆ Eston Grange 453479
Bass Ⓗ
Unspoilt village local with friendly welcome 🏠🍽

Marske-by-the-Sea 30E3
11.30–3; 5.15 (6 Sat)–10.30 (11 F, S)
Clarendon
90 High Street (A1085)
Tetley Bitter; Theakston Best Bitter, XB, Old Peculier Ⓗ
Lively and popular old pub. Known as the "Middle House"
≷

Middlesbrough 30D3
11–3; 5.30–10.30
Apple Tree
38, The Derby, Marton
✆ 310564
Bass Ⓗ
Friendly comfortable estate pub built 1984. An example of what can be done! 🖭🅿Ⓖ♿&

Linthorpe Hotel
The Crescent, Linthorpe Village ✆ 819287
Samuel Smith OBB Ⓗ
Converted from large house. Real ale only in public bar
🅿🖭Ⓖ♿

Redcar 30D3
11–3; 5.30–10.30
Newbigging Hotel
Queen Street/Turner Street
✆ 482059
Opens 12 & 6.30
Theakston Best Bitter, XB, Old Peculier Ⓗ
Old-world bar interior with something for everybody! Fine restaurant. Caravan park
🅿🖭Ⓖ♿(not Sun) 🍽

Try also: Kingfisher, Dormanstown

Yorkshire Coble
West Dyke Road ✆ 482071
Samuel Smith OBB Ⓗ
Smart modern estate pub near Racecourse 🏠🅿🍽≷

Saltburn 30E3
11–3; 5.30–10.30 (11 F, S)
Victoria
Dundas Street
Bass; Theakston Best Bitter, XB, Old Peculier Ⓗ
Lively, comfortable pub, excellently converted from an old warehouse Ⓖ🍽♿≷

Skelton Green 31E3
12–3; 7–10.30 (11 F, S)
Miners Arms
Boosbeck Road
✆ Guisborough 50372
Vaux Samson Ⓗ
Fine village pub with comfortable bar and spacious games room. No food Sun
🖭Ⓖ🍽♿

South Bank 30D3
11–3; 5.30–10.30
Prince Harry
Station Road
✆ Middlesbrough 460908
John Smith's Bitter Ⓗ
Free house in former steelmaking area Ⓖ🍽♿&≷

Stockton-on-Tees 30C3
11–3; 5.30–10.30
Cricketers Arms
Portrack Lane ✆ 675468
Theakston Old Peculier; Whitbread Castle Eden Ale Ⓗ
Busy refurbished local offering two beers rare in the area! Ⓖ🍽

Green Dragon
Finkle Street ✆ 672798
Samuel Smith OBB Ⓗ
Impressive former coaching inn, part of Stockton's oldest complex of buildings 🅿Ⓖ♿

Parkwood Hotel
64–66, Darlington Road, Hartburn ✆ 580800
Lorimer & Clark 80/-
Smart conversion of large house in leafy village suburb. Former home of shipowning Ropner family ⊞ ✿ ▣ ◔ ◗

Stockton Arms
Darlington Road, Hartburn ✆ 580104
Bass [H]
Busy, deservedly popular suburban pub with several rooms ♔ ⊞ ✿ ▣ ◔ ◗

Wild Ox
136 Norton Road ✆ 611655
Cameron Strongarm [H]
Lively 3-roomed local with friendly atmosphere ◔ (Fri) ▮

Try also: Red Lion, Ramsgate (S & N)

Thornaby 30C4

11.30–3; 5.30–10.30

Cleveland Hotel
Bridge Street ✆ 676917
Sat eves opens 7
Younger No. 3 [H]
Warm and friendly local with distinctive facade. Opposite railway station ◔ ▮ ⇌

Collingwood
Trafalgar Street
✆ Stockton 673010
Cameron Strongarm [H]
Small well-modernised pub near railway station. Off the beaten track but well worth finding ✿ ◔ ▮ ⇌

Yarm 30C4

11–3; 5.30–10.30

Ketton Ox
High Street (A67)
✆ Stockton 788311
Lorimer & Clark 80/-; Vaux Samson [H]
Marvellous historic coaching inn in village conservation area ⊞ ✿ ◔ ◗ (Tue–Sat)

Try also: Black Bull (Bass)

" OF COURSE HE'S MY MOST REGULAR CUSTOMER – HE CAN'T GET OUT OF THE DOOR!"
Ken Pyne

Altarnun 3G5

11–2.30; 5.10–10.30 (11 F, S & summer)

Rising Sun
Off A30/A395 1 mile from
village OS825215
Butcombe Bitter; Cotleigh
Kingfisher; Flowers IPA;
Marston Pedigree; Samuel
Whitbread; Stallion Bitter Ⓗ
Regular guest beers
Popular, 16th century
country pub on fringe of
Bodmin Moor 🏠🅱️🎵🔔⛰️

Blackwater 2C7

11–2.30; 5.30–10.30 (11 F, S & summer)

Red Lion
A30 ✆ Truro 560289
John Devenish Bitter, Cornish
Best Bitter Ⓗ
Friendly roadside inn, beamed
ceilings 🏠🅱️🔔⛰️

Blisland 3F6

11–2.30; 6–10.30 (11 F, S & summer)

Royal Oak
Off A30 ✆ Bodmin 850739
Flowers IPA; Tetley Bitter;
Inch's Cider Ⓗ
In picturesque moorland
setting by village green
🏠Q🅱️🔔 (not Sun) 🍴⛰️

Bodmin 3F6

10.30–2.30; 6–10.30 (11 F, S & summer)

Masons Arms
Higher Bore Street ✆ 2607
Usher Best Bitter, Founders
Ale Ⓗ
Small but comfortable old
town pub
🏠🅱️🔔 (summer) 🍴⛰️

Boscastle 3F4

11–2.30; 6–10.30 (11 F, S & summer)

Napoleon
B3266 ✆ 204
Draught Bass; St. Austell
Hicks Special Ⓗ & Ⓖ
16th century inn set above
the village 🏠Q🔔🍴

Camborne 2C8

10.30–2.30; 6–10.30 (11 F, S & summer)

Red Jackets
Trevenson Street ✆ 712682
John Devenish Bitter, Cornish
Best Bitter Ⓗ
Comfortable town local, host
to local rugby, football and
fishing clubs 🔔🍴🍴⇌

Camelford 3F5

11–2.30; 6–10.30 (11 F, S & summer)

Masons Arms
Market Place ✆ 213309
St. Austell Tinners Bitter Ⓗ,
Hicks Special Ⓖ
Centre of life in this busy little
town 🔔🍴

Cargreen 3H6

11–2.30; 6–10.30 (11 F, S & summer)

Spaniards
Off A388 OS435627
Fuller London Pride; St.
Austell Mild, Tinners Bitter;
Theakston XB; Wadworth
6X Ⓗ; Hills Cider Ⓖ Regular
guest beers
Excellent riverside inn set in
beautiful Tamar Valley
🏠Q🅱️🔔🍴🍴⛰️

Charlestown 3E7

11–2.30; 6–10.30 (11 F, S & summer)

Rashleigh
St. Austell Best Bitter, Tinners
Bitter Ⓗ
2-bar village pub in
piituresque seaside village
🏠🔔🍴⛰️

Chilsworthy 3H6

11.30–2.30; 6.30–10.30 (11 F, S & summer)

White Hart Inn
Latchley Road (off A390)
Bishops PA (Chilsworthy
Special); Butcombe Bitter;
Flowers Original; Marston
Pedigree; Theakston Old
Peculier; Wadworth 6X Ⓗ
Regular guest beers
Friendly, popular old country
pub. Superb views over Tamar
Valley 🏠Q🅱️🔔⛰️

Comford 2C8

11–2.30; 6–10.30 (11 F, S)

Fox & Hounds
Draught Bass, St. Austell Best
Bitter
Fine country pub; granite
fireplaces and splendid
atmosphere 🏠Q🔔

Cremyll 3H7

10.30–2.30; 5.30–10.30 (11 F, S & summer)

Edgcumbe Arms
B3247 OS454535
Courage Best Bitter, Directors
(summer) Ⓗ
18th century inn by
Stonehouse Ferry Quay. Near
Country Park and coastal
paths 🏠🅱️🍴

Cripplesease 2B8

10.30 (12 winter)–2.30; 5.30 (7 winter)–10.30
(11 F, S & summer)

Engine Inn
OS500368
John Devenish Bitter, Cornish
Best Bitter Ⓗ
Entertaining, 17th century
inn in the heart of moorland;
tasty menu 🏠🅱️🔔🍴⛰️

Falmouth 2D8

10.30–2.30; 6–10.30 (11 F, S)

Seven Stars
The Moor ✆ 312111
Draught Bass; Courage
Directors; Flowers Original;
Samuel Whitbread Ⓗ Regular
guest beers
Free house in same family for
five generations Q🔔🍴

Fraddon 2E6

11–3; 6–10.30 (11 F, S & summer)

Blue Anchor
A30 ✆ St. Austell 860352
St. Austell Tinners Bitter;
Hicks Special Ⓗ
Convient stop. Live groups
most Sats
🅱️ (summer) 🔔🍴🍴

Golant 3F7

11–2.30; 6–10.30 (11 F, S & summer)

Fishermans Arms
Courage Best Bitter;
Directors Ⓗ
Charming village pub in
superb setting
🏠Q🅱️🔔🍴⛰️⇌

Goldsithney 2B8

10.30–2.30; 6–10.30 (11 F, S)

Crown
B3280 ✆ Penzance 710494
St. Austell BB, Mild, Hicks
Special Ⓗ
Pleasant pub with friendly
village atmosphere. Good food
🏠🅱️🔔🍴

Gunwalloe 2C9

11–2.30; 6–10.30 (11 F, S)

Halzephron
Off A3083 ✆ Mullion 240406
John Devenish Bitter, Cornish
Best Bitter Ⓗ
Old smugglers' inn takes its
name from nearby cliff
🏠🅱️🔔🍴

Hayle 2B8

11 (12 winter)–2.30; 6–10.30 (11 F, S)

Bird in Hand
Trellisick Road (off B3302)
Paradise Bitter, Artists Ale Ⓗ
Regular guest beers
Home-brew pub in grounds of
bird paradise garden. Meals
summer only 🅱️🔔🍴⇌

Helston 2C8

10.30–2.30; 6–10.30 (11 F, S)

Blue Anchor
50 Coinagehall Street
Blue Anchor Mild (summer),
Medium, Best, Special Ⓗ
Superb, world-famous 15th
century thatched pub. Skittles;
regular jazz 🏠Q🔔🍴

Holywell Bay 2D6

10.30–2.30; 6–10.30 (11 F, S & summer)

Treguth Inn
(off A3075)
Courage Best Bitter Ⓗ
Thatched inn near sandy
beach and leisure park
🏠🅱️🔔🍴

Kingsand 3H7

10.30–2.30; 6–10.30 (11 F, S & summer)

Devonport Inn
The Cleave, Sea Front
Courage Best Bitter Ⓗ

Traditional 1-bar pub with panoramic views 🏛♨♟

Lanlivery 3F6

11–2.30; 6–10.30 (11 F, S)

Crown Inn
Off A390 ☎ Bodmin 872707
Draught Bass; Hancock HB Ⓗ
Comfortable 12th century
inn. Excellent food
🏛Q♨Ⓖ♟♨💺♿Å

Lanner 2C8

11–2.30; 6–10.30 (11 F, S & summer)

Coppice
A393 ☎ Redruth 216668
Burton Ale; Tetley Bitter Ⓗ
Pleasant pub, spacious
grounds. Excellent food
🏛Q💺♨Ⓖ♟♨💺Å

Lanreath 3F7

10.30–2.30; 6–10.30 (11 F, S & summer)

Punch Bowl
Off B3359, 6 miles NW of
Looe ☎ Lanreath 20218
Draught Bass Ⓗ Occasional
guest beers
Famous old coaching inn in
delightful village. Meals April–
Oct only 🏛💺♨Ⓖ♟♿

Launceston 3G5

11–2.30; 6–10.30 (11 F, S & summer) (open all
day Tue)

Westgate Inn
21, Westgate Street ☎ 2493
Courage Best Bitter Ⓗ;
Taunton Traditional Cider
Old coaching inn near Castle.
Ⓖ♟(not Sun/winter) ♟💺

Lerryn 3F7

12–2.30; 6–10.30 (11 F, S)

Ship Inn
Draught Bass; Flowers
Original Ⓗ
Old village pub in delightful
Fowey Valley 💺♨Ⓖ♟♟💺Å

Liskeard 3G6

10.30–2.30; 6–10.30 (11 F, S & summer)

Fountain Hotel
The Parade ☎ 42154
Courage Best Bitter,
Directors Ⓗ
Comfortable old oak-beamed
town centre hotel. Restaurant
💺♨♨Ⓖ♟(not winter Sun)

Lostwithiel 3F6

10.30–2.30; 5.30–10.30 (11 F, S)

Royal Oak
Duke Street ☎ Bodmin 872552
Gibbs Mew Bishops Tipple;
Eldridge Pope Royal Oak;
Flowers Original; Fuller
London Pride; Hall &
Woodhouse Tanglefoot; Usher
Best Bitter Ⓗ Regular guest
beers
Busy friendly 13th century
inn. Good restaurant
Q💺♨♨Ⓖ♟♟Å≷

Mabe Burnthouse 2D8

10.30–2.30; 6–10.30 (11 F, S)

New Inn
Church Road
John Devenish Bitter, Cornish
Best Bitter
300-year old pub at heart of
granite country
🏛Q💺♨♨Ⓖ♟♟

Manaccan 2D9

11–2.30; 6–10.30 (11 F, S)

New Inn
John Devenish Bitter, Cornish
Best Bitter Ⓖ
Traditional thatched village
pub. Good food, peaceful
atmosphere 🏛Q💺♨Ⓖ♟

Metherell 3H6

11.30–2.30; 7–10.30 (11 F, S & summer)

Carpenters Arms
Off A390 OS409695
Draught Bass; Bishops Best
Bitter, Flowers Original; Fuller
London Pride;
Wadworth 6X Ⓖ Regular
guest beers
14th century inn off the
beaten track. Exceptional food
🏛Q♨♨Ⓖ♟♟

Mevagissey 3E7

11–2.30; 6–10.30 (11 F, S)

Fountain Inn
Cliff Street
St. Austell BB, Tinners
Bitter Ⓗ
Cosy pub near harbour.
Excellent home-made pasties
(winter Sat lunch) 🏛Q💺♨♟

Morwenstow 3F3

11–2.30; 6–10.30 (11 F, S & summer)

Bush Inn
Off A39 OS151208 ☎ 242
Devenish Wessex Best Bitter;
Ⓗ St. Austell BB Ⓖ
Fine 12th century inn, near
rugged Atlantic cliffs
🏛♨♨Ⓖ♟(Book) ♟

Mullion 2C9

11–2.30; 6–10.30 (11 F, S)

Old Inn
John Devenish Bitter, Cornish
Best Bitter Ⓗ
Partly-thatched 16th century
village pub 🏛Q💺♨♨Ⓖ

Nancenoy 2D8

10.30–2.30; 6–10.30 (11 F, S)

Trengilly Wartha
Draught Bass; Courage
Directors; John Devenish
Bitter; Flowers Original;
Golden Hill Exmoor Ale;
Bulmers Cider Ⓖ Regular
guest beers
Beautifully sited in extensive
grounds. Regular live music
🏛💺♨♨Ⓖ♟♟Å

Newlyn 2B8

10.30–2.30; 6–10.30 (11 F, S)

Fishermans Arms
Fore Street ☎ Penzance 3399
St. Austell Hicks Special Ⓗ
Magnificent views across
Mounts Bay to Lizard Ⓖ♟

Padstow 2E5

10.30–2.30; 6–10.30 (11 F, S & summer)

London Inn
6–8 Lanadwell Street
St. Austell Best Bitter, Tinners
Bitter, Hicks Special Ⓗ
Unspoilt interior fronting on
to one of many narrow streets
Q💺Ⓖ♟♟

Pendogget 3E5

10.30–2.30; 5.30–10.30 (11 F, S & summer)

Cornish Arms
B3314 ☎ Port Isaac 263
Draught Bass; Flowers
Original; St. Austell Hicks
Special; Weston Cider Ⓖ
Occasional guest beers
Good local and holiday trade.
Restaurant
🏛💺(Lunch) ♨Ⓖ♟

Penzance 2B8

10.30–2.30; 6–10.30 (11 F, S)

Turks Head
Chapel Street ☎ 63093
John Devenish Bitter, Cornish
Best Bitter Ⓗ
Oldest inn in town. Good food
💺♨Ⓖ♟

Phillack 2B8

11–2.30; 6–10.30 (11 F, S & summer)

Bucket of Blood
Churchtown (off A30)
St. Austell BB, Tinners Bitter,
Hicks Special Ⓗ
Unspoilt, historic village inn.
Meals summer only
🏛💺♨Ⓖ♟♟Å

Philleigh 2D8

11–2.30; 6 (7 winter)–10.30 (11 F, S & summer)

Roseland Inn
Off A3078 on King Harry
Ferry Road ☎ Portscatho 254
John Devenish Bitter, Cornish
Best Bitter Ⓗ; Taunton Cider Ⓖ
Superb low-beamed village
pub 🏛Q♨Ⓖ♟(summer)

Pillaton 3G6

11–2.30; 6–10.30 (11 F, S & summer)

Weary Friar
Near A388 ☎ Liskeard 50238
Draught Bass; Courage
Directors; St. Austell Tinners
Bitter Ⓗ
Comfortable old pub. Popular
for food ♨♨Ⓖ♟

Polkerris 3F7

11–2.30; 6–10.30 (11 F, S)

Rashleigh Inn
St. Austell Best Bitter, Tinners
Bitter, Hicks Special Ⓗ

Delightful setting; good beach, good food 🏠 Q ✿ ❧ ❶ ♥

Polperro 3F7

10.30–2.30; 5.30–10.30 (11 F, S & summer)

Three Pilchards
The Quay ☏ 72233
Courage Best Bitter, Directors
Old pub in picturesque fishing village 🏠 ⚓ ❶ ♠

Port Isaac 3E5

10.30–2.30; 6–10.30 (11 F, S & summer)

Golden Lion
12 Fore Street ☏ 336
St. Austell Tinners Bitter, Hicks Special Ⓗ
Beside slipway of old smuggling harbour

Portscatho 2D8

11.30–2; 6.30–10.30 (11 F, S & summer)

Plume of Feathers
The Square (off A3078) ☏ 321
St. Austell BB; Tinners Bitter; Bulmers Traditional Cider Ⓗ
Old smugglers pub. Extensive menu 🏠 ⚓ ✿ ❧ ❶ ♥ ♠

Praze-an-Beeble 2C8

11 (10.45 summer)–2.30; 6.30 (6 summer)–10.30 (11 F, S & summer)

St. Aubyn Arms
B3303 ☏ 831425
John Devenish Bitter, Cornish Best Bitter Ⓗ
Large, friendly village pub; try the traditional home-made pasties 🏠 ⚓ ✿ ❧ ❶ ♥ ♦

Redruth 2C8

11–2.30; 6–10.30 (11 F, S & summer)

Mount Ambrose Inn
Mount Ambrose ☏ 215809
St. Austell BB, XXXX, Hicks Special Ⓗ
Lively oasis 🏠 ✿ ❧ ❶ ♥

Restronguet Creek 2D8

11–2.30; 6–10.30 (11 F, S)

Pandora
Draught Bass; St. Austell BB, Tinners Bitter, Hicks Special Ⓗ
Superb 13th century thatched pub in beautiful water-side setting 🏠 Q ✿ ❧ ❶ ♥ ♦

Roche 2E6

11–2.30; 5.30–10.30 (11 F, S)

Rock Inn
John Devenish Bitter, Cornish Best Bitter Ⓗ
Lively local with good restaurant ❧ ❶ ♥ ♦

St. Austell 3E7

10.30–2.30; 5.30–10.30 (11 F, S & summer)

Queens Head
Fore Street ☏ 75452

Courage Best Bitter, Directors; St. Austell Tinners Bitter Ⓗ
Occasional guest beers
Comfortable hotel. Live music; ale and wine cellar bar 🎵 ❧

St. Breward 3F5

11–2.30; 6–10.30 (11 F, S & summer)

Old Inn
Churchtown
Stallion Bitter Ⓖ & Ⓗ **Usher Best Bitter, Founders Ale** Ⓗ
Slate floors and homely atmosphere on edge of Bodmin Moor 🏠 ⚓ ✿ ❧ ❶ ♥ ♦

St. Columb Major 2D6

11–3; 6.30 (7 winter)–10.30 (11 F, S & summer)

Ring o' Bells
Bank Street
Flowers IPA Ⓗ, **Original**
15th century slate-clad front belies extensive interior 🏠 Q ⚓ ❧ 🎵 ❶ ♥

St. Just 2A8

11–2.30; 6–10.30 (11 F, S)

Star Inn
1 Fore Street (B3306)
St. Austell Tinners Bitter, Hicks Special Ⓖ
St. Just's oldest inn 🏠 Q ⚓ ❧ 🎵 ❶ ♥

St. Kew 3E5

10.30–2.30; 6–10.30 (11 F, S & summer)

St. Kew Inn
St. Austell Tinners Bitter, Hicks Special; Bulmers Cider Ⓖ
Picturesque 15th century village inn 🏠 Q ✿ ❧ ❶ ♥ ♦

St. Neot 3F6

11–2.30; 6–10.30 (11 F, S & summer)

London Inn
Off A38 ☏ Liskeard 20263
Usher Best Bitter, Founders Ale Ⓗ
16th century pub in attractive moorland village 🏠 Q ⚓ ✿ 🎵 (s/c flat) ❧ ❶ ♥

Saltash 3H6

10.30–2.30; 6–10.30 (11 F, S & summer)

Boatman
3 Old Ferry Road (near A38)
Courage Best Bitter, Directors Ⓗ
By old ferry slipway, under Tamar bridges ✿ ❧ ❶ ♥ ⚡

Stratton 3G9

10.30–2.30; 6–10.30 (11 F, S & summer)

Kings Arms
Howls Road (A3072)
Courage Best Bitter, Directors Ⓗ
Popular old coaching inn ✿ ❧ ♥ ♦ ♠

Torpoint 3H7

10.30–2.30; 6–10.30 (11 F, S & summer)

Kings Arms
37 Fore Street (A374)
Courage Best Bitter, Directors Ⓗ
Traditional pub, friendly relaxed atmosphere 🏠 ✿ ❧ ❶

Treen 2A9

10.30–2.30; 5.30–10.30 (11 F, S)

Logan Rock Inn
Off B3315 ☏ St. Buryan 495
St. Austell BB, Tinners Bitter, Hicks Special Ⓗ
On outstanding coastline 🏠 Q 🎵 ✿ ❧ ❶ ♥ ♦ ♠

Trevarrack 2B8

Tyringham Arms
Draught Bass; Courage Best Bitter Ⓗ
Comfortable free house, good meals. Caravan site nearby 🏠 🎵 ✿ ❧ ♥ ♠

Truro 2D7

11–2.30; 5.30–10.30 (11 F, S)

City Inn
Pydar Street ☏ 72623
Courage Best Bitter, Directors Ⓗ
Superb town pub, excellent whisky selection 🏠 🎵 ✿ ❶ ♥ ⚡

St. Clement Inn
St. Austell Street ☏ 72218
Draught Bass; Courage Best Bitter, Directors; St. Austell Tinners Bitter; Usher Best Bitter, Founders Ale
Regular guest beers
Known as the Round House. Good restaurant ❧ ❶ ⚡

Tywardreath 3F7

10.30–2.30; 6–10.30 (11 F, S & summer)

New Inn
Off A3082 ☏ Par 3901
Draught Bass; St. Austell BB, Tinners Bitter (summer) Ⓖ; **Bulmers Cider** Ⓔ
Very popular village local in quiet area near coast Q ✿ 🎵 ❧ (not Sun) ❶ ♥ ⚡

Upton Cross 3G6

11–2.30; 5.30–10.30 (11 F, S & summer)

Caradon Inn
B3254 ☏ Liskeard 62391
Flowers Original; St. Austell Hicks Special; Stallion Bitter Ⓗ; **Haymaker Cider** Ⓖ
Occasional guest beers
18th century country inn 🏠 🎵 ❧ ❶ ♥

Veryan 2E8

11–2.30; 6–10.30 (11 F, S & summer)

New Inn
Off A3078 ☏ Truro 501362
St. Austell BB, Tinners Bitter Ⓖ
Friendly 18th century local. Near beaches and famous Roundhouses 🏠 Q ✿ 🎵 ❧ ❶ ♥ ♦

Allonby 28C2

11–3; 5.30–10.30 (11 F, S)
Grapes Hotel
✆ 344
Jennings Mild, Bitter H
Comfortable seaside pub, old
State Brewery posters
Q⊞ (lunchtime) ✿▣Ⓖ➐♥& Å

Alston 29G2

11–3; 6–10.30 (11 F, S)
Angel Inn
Main Street ✆ 81363
Drybrough's Eighty;
Newcastle Exhibition H
Popular 17th century pub in
England's highest market
town ♨⊞✿▣Ⓖ➐Å

Try also: Swans Head

Ambleside 28D4

11–3; 6–11
**Stringers Bar
Waterhead Hotel**
A591 S of town
Jennings Bitter; Marston
Pedigree H Regular guest
beers
Comfortable, hospitable bar in
hotel overlooking Lake
Windermere ✿▣Ⓖ➐

Try also: Golden Rule

Appleby-in- 29F3 Westmorland

11–3; 6–10.30 (11 F, S & summer)
Gate
Bongate ✆ 51498
Younger Scotch Bitter,
No. 3 H
Small and friendly roadside
restaurant and bar
♨Q✿Ⓖ➐♥≈

Midland Hotel
Clifford Street
Marston Burton Bitter H
Large town pub with railway
prints. By station on Settle–
Carlisle line ♨⊞✿▣➐♥≈

Try also: Golden Ball, High
Wiend; Royal Oak, Bongate

Armathwaite 29E2

11–3; 5.30–10.30 (11 F, S)
Fox & Pheasant
✆ 400
Tetley Bitter, Younger Scotch
Bitter H
Very busy (book meals);
popular with fishermen
♨✿▣Ⓖ➐♥

Askham 29E3

11–3; 5.30 (7 winter)–11
Queens Head
✆ Hackthorpe 225
Vaux Samson; Ward Sheffield
Best Bitter H Regular guest
beers
Hospitable 17th century
coaching inn. Beams, brass,
real fires. Excellent food.

Working model railway
behind pub ♨⊞✿▣Ⓖ➐

Aspatria 28C2

11–3; 5.30–10.30 (11 F, S)
Fox & Hounds
King Street (A596) ✆ 20860
Jennings Mild, Bitter H
Friendly village pub. Delicious
home made "sarnies" ♨Q♥≈

Barbon 29F6

11–3; 6–11
Barbon Inn
✆ 233
Theakston Best Bitter, Old
Peculier H
Whitewashed old coaching
inn; cosy small bar, lounge
with armchairs and settles.
Imaginative menu; 4-poster
beds available ♨⊞✿▣Ⓖ➐

Barngates 28D4

11–3; 5.30–10.30 (11 F, S)
Drunken Duck
Off B5286 OS351012
✆ Hawkshead 347
Jennings Mild, Bitter; Marston
Pedigree; Tetley Bitter;
Theakston XB, Old Peculier H
Regular guest beers
Well-patronised free house in
splendid countryside. Name
comes from an amusing
legend ♨Q⊞✿▣Ⓖ➐♥

Barrow-in- 28C6 Furness

11–3; 5.30–
Crown Hotel
North Scale, Walney Island
Evening opens 6
Hartleys Mild, Bitter, XB E;
Robinson Old Tom G
Popular pub, much used by
the island's fisherfolk. Starting
point of annual raft race
(August) ♨♥

Victoria Tavern
Oxford Street
Hartleys XB; Whitbread Castle
Eden E
Well patronised, typical
Victorian local. Snooker table
♥≈

Wheatsheaf Hotel
Anson Street ✆ 37175
John Smith's Bitter H
Busy with Navy personnel
and locals of all ages who
enjoy the nautical theme of
this historic listed building
✿▣Ⓖ♥

Bassenthwaite 28C3

10.30–3; 5.30–10.30 (11 F, S)
Sun Inn
✆ 059 681 439
Jennings Bitter H
Busy village pub. Good food,
pleasant layout
♨Q⊞✿Ⓖ➐♥& Å

Beckermet 28B4

11–3; 5.30–10.30 (11 F, S)
Royal Oak
Off A595 ✆ 551
Hartleys XB; Younger Scotch
Bitter H
Popular, pleasant village local,
very friendly landlord.
Definitely not a nuclear free
zone! ♨⊞✿▣Ⓖ➐♥

Beetham 29E6

11–3; 6–11
Wheatsheaf
Off A6 ✆ Milnthorpe 2123
Thwaites Bitter H
Characterful 19th-century inn
with oak-beamed bars ▣Ⓖ➐♥

Blencow 28E3

11–3; 6–10.30 (11 F, S)
Clickham Inn
B5288 OS466311
Marston Burton Bitter, Merrie
Monk, Pedigree H
Attractive roadside inn on
fringe of Lake District National
Park. Friendly service,
occasional live music
♨⊞✿Ⓖ➐& Å

Braithwaite 28C3

11–3; 5.30–10.30 (11 F, S)
Coledale Inn
Near A66 ✆ 272
Younger Scotch Bitter H
Friendly hostelry, fine view of
Skiddaw from garden. Several
walks start from the village
♨✿▣Ⓖ➐♥Å

Try also: Royal Oak
(Jennings)

Brigham 28C3

11–3; 5.30–10.30 (11 F, S)
Wheatsheaf
Low Road (off A66)
Jennings Mild, Bitter H
Occasional guest beers
Comfortable and friendly
village pub ♨Q✿Ⓖ➐♥

Brough 29G4

11–3; 6–10.30 (11 F, S & summer)
Golden Fleece
Main Street ✆ 314
Whitbread Trophy H
Cheerful, well appointed
village pub. Popular bar and
lounge/dining room
♨✿▣Ⓖ➐♥& Å

Broughton-in- 28C5 Furness

10.30–3; 6–11
Old Kings Head
Church Street/Station Road
(A595) ✆ 293
Hartleys Bitter, XB; Chesters
Best Bitter; Whitbread Trophy,
Castle Eden (summer) H
Regular guest beers
Friendly village inn. Cosy
lounge, pool table and good
value restaurant ✿▣Ⓖ➐

Burton-in-Kendal 29E6

11–3; 6–11

Kings Arms
Main Street (A6070)
✆ 781409
Mitchells Mild, Bitter ⒣
Large, popular village pub.
Some walls retained, creating
small drinking areas ⊞⌂⌟⌖⏺

Calderbridge 28B4

11–3; 5.30–10.30 (11 F, S & summer)

Golden Fleece
A595 ✆ Beckermet 250
Matthew Brown Lion Mild,
Lion Bitter ⒣
Friendly pub opposite church.
Rugby League spoken in the
bar Q⌟⊞⌖⏺⏹

Carlisle 28D1

11–3; 5.30–10.30 (11 F, S)

Boardroom
Castle Street
Younger Scotch Bitter, No. 3 ⒣
Popular old pub nestling
alongside 11th century
Cathedral and city centre
⌖ (not Sun)

Coach & Horses
Kingstown Road (A7/A74) nr
M6 Junction 44
Matthew Brown Lion Mild,
Lion Bitter, John Peel ⒣
Popular 2-room pub on
northern city outskirts
⌂⏺⌖⏺⏹

Friars Tavern
Devonshire Street ✆ 23757
Evening opens 6.30
Whitbread Castle Eden;
Bulmer Cider ⒣
Lively city centre pub (real ale
in downstairs bar).
Comfortable atmosphere ⌖⏹⏺⏹

Howard Arms
Lowther Street ✆ 32926
Matthew Brown Lion Mild;
Theakston Best Bitter, XB, Old
Peculier ⒣
Superb city centre pub with
theatrical memorabilia. Music
in toilets! ⌂⏺⌖⏹⏺

Pippins
Lowther Street (opposite bus
station)
Greenall Whitley Original
Bitter ⒣
City centre "fun pub" on edge
of Lanes shopping centre
⏺⌖⏹

Theakston
43 London Road (A6)
✆ 43820
Matthew Brown Lion Mild;
Theakston Best Bitter, XB, Old
Peculier ⒣
Busy pub just off city centre.
State Management
memorabilia
⌂⏺⌖⏺ (summer) ⏹

Woolpack Inn
Milbourne Street (near
Brewery off A595)
✆ 32459
Jennings Mild, Bitter,
Marathon ⒣
Popular, lively local. Friendly
service, excellent value meals.
Beware of "Kangaroo" at
"walkies" time! ⌂⌖⏺

Cartmel Fell 28E5

10.30–3; 6–11

Masons Arms
Strawberry Bank (off A5074)
OS413895
McEwan 70/- ⒣; Westons
Cider ⒢ Regular guest beers
Set in beautiful valley. World-
wide range of bottle-
conditioned beers. Excellent
meals ⌂Q⊞⏺⌖⏺⏹⛺

Castle Carrock 29E1

11–3 (12–2 winter); 6–10.30 (11 F, S)

Duke of Cumberland
Off B6413 OS542555
✆ Hayton 341
Marston Mercian Mild,
Burton Bitter, Pedigree ⒣
Friendly pub in attractive
village on edge of Pennines.
Basic bar, comfortable lounge
⌂Q⊞ (lunchtime) ⏺⌖⏺⏹

Cleator Moor 28B4

11–3; 5.30–10.30 (11 F, S)

New Crown
Bowthorn Road (B5295)
Hartleys Bitter, XB ⒣
Popular town local with
friendly atmosphere ⌂⏹

Cockermouth 28C3

11–3; 5.30–10.30 (11 F, S)

Swan
Kirgate ✆ 822425
Jennings Mild, Bitter,
Marathon ⒣
Eric prides himself on his
grand selection of whiskies.
Smart town pub, difficult to
find ⌂Q⊞⌖⏺⏹

Tithe Barn
Station Road ✆ 822179
11–5 Mondays (market)
Jennings Mild, Bitter,
Marathon ⒣
Neat snug, comfortable
lounge. Norman is noted for
his good value fare ⊞⌂⌖⏺⏹

Try also: Brown Cow
(Theakston)

Coniston 28D5

11–3; 5.30 (7 winter)–10.30 (11 F, S)

Crown Hotel
Off A593 ✆ 41243
Hartleys XB ⒣
Small village centre hotel,
popular with locals and
visitors ⌂Q⊞⏺⌖⏺⏹⛺

Try also: Yewdale Hotel

Dalton-in-Furness 28C6

11–3; 7–11

Britannia Inn
Skelgate (A5911) ✆ 62733
John Smith's Bitter ⒣
Pleasant local on town
outskirts. Good food, darts
Q⏺⌖⏺ (not Mon) ⏹⛺⏹⏹

Try also: Red Lion; Prince of
Wales

Dent 29F5

11–3; 6–11

Sun
Main Street ✆ 208
Younger Scotch, No. 3 ⒣
Popular with locals and
visitors. Old pub with
remarkable sign
⌂⊞⏺⌂⌖⏺⏹⛺

Drigg 28B5

11–3; 5.30–10.30 (11 F, S)

Victoria Hotel
Off B5344 ✆ Holmrook 231
Jennings Mild, Bitter ⒣
Excellent village pub next to
station ⌂⊞⏺⌂⌖⏺⏹⛺⏹⏹

Eaglesfield 28C3

11–3; 6–10.30 (11 F, S)

Blackcock
1 mile off A5086
Jennings Mild, Bitter ⒣
Quiet village local, worth a
visit if you can find it! ⌂Q⏺⏹

Egremont 28B4

11–3; 5.30–10.30 (11 F, S & summer)

Blue Bell
6 Market Place (A595)
Hartleys Mild, XB ⒣
Busy town pub with Rugby
League connections, opposite
War Memorial ⌂Q⏹

Elterwater 28D4

11–3; 6.30–10.30 (11 F, S)

Britannia Inn
Off B5343 OS285061
✆ Langdale 210
Bass Cask Bitter; Hartleys XB;
Tetley Mild, Bitter; Bulmers
Cider ⒣
Very popular inn in beautiful
village setting
⌂Q⊞⏺⏺⌖⏺⏹⛺

Eskdale Green 28C5

11–3; 5.30–10.30 (11 F, S)

Bower House Inn
OS131003 ✆ 244
Hartleys XB; Younger Scotch
Bitter; Olde English Cider ⒣
17th century pub of great
character in scenic valley.
Good bar and dining room
food ⌂Q⏺⌂⌖⏺⏹⛺

Flookburgh 28D6

11–3; 5.30–10.30

Hope & Anchor (Pals)

10 Market Street (B5278)
℘ 733
Hartleys Mild, XB Ⓗ
Large busy village local. Very
welcoming atmosphere. 4 dart
boards, pool table ▦🄳🅟🅖

Try also: **Engine Inn**, Cark;
Royal Oak; **Cavendish Arms**,
Cartmel

Gaitsgill 28D2

11–3 (weekends only); 6–10.30 (11 F, S)
Royal Oak
OS388468
℘ Raughton Head 422
Matthew Brown Lion Bitter Ⓗ
If you are looking for a typical
Cumberland country pub this
is it. No bar, just a serving
hatch ▦Q🅟❦

Goose Green 28D2

11–3; 5.30–10.30 (11 F, S)
String of Horses
B5299/B5305
℘ Raughton Head 358
**Marston Mercian Mild,
Burton Bitter, Pedigree** Ⓗ
Small country inn, horse
racing connections. Busy at
weekends. Darts and pool
▦🄳🅟🅖❦

Grasmere 28D4

11–3; 5.30–10.30 (11 F, S)
Tweedies Bar
Off A591 (rear of Dale Lodge
Hotel) ℘ 300
**Matthew Brown John Peel;
Theakston XB, Old Peculier** Ⓗ
Lively pub popular with the
young, pool table in family
room. Dining area 🄳🅟🅖❦

Great Asby 29F3

11–3; 6–10.30 (11 F, S & summer)
Three Greyhounds
Wilsons Original Bitter Ⓗ
Village local, very popular
with nearby caravan site
▦🄳🅟🅖❦Å

Great Langdale 28D4

11–3; 5.30–10.30 (11 F, S)
Old Dungeon Ghyll
B5343 OS285061
℘ Langdale 272
**McEwan 80/-; Theakston Best
Bitter, XB, Old Peculier;
Younger No. 3** Ⓗ Occasional
guest beers
Very popular, basic, climbers
and walkers bar at the head of
beautiful valley. Excellent
home-cooked meals
▦Q🅟🅖❦Å

Try also: **New Dungeon Ghyll,
Stickle Barn**

Great Urswick 28D6

11–3; 6–11 (10.30 S)
General Burgoyne Inn
Off A590 OS746269
℘ Bardsea 394

Hartleys Mild, XB Ⓗ
Popular village inn ▦🅟❦

Hale 29E6

11–3; 6–11
Kings Arms
A6 OS505786
Milnthorpe 3203
Mitchells Bitter Ⓗ
Cosy rural pub, popular with
car trade. Bowling green.
Single bar, several rooms
▦🄳🅟🅖❦

Hawkshead 28D5

11–3; 5.30–10.30 (11 F, S)
Queens Head
Off B5286 ℘ 271
Hartleys Mild, XB Ⓗ; **Robinson
Old Tom** Ⓖ
Comfortable pub with good
food. The village has four real
ale pubs—try them all!
▦Q🄳🅟🅖❦Å

Hayton 29E1

11–3; 7–10.30 (11 F, S)
Stone Inn
Off A69 ℘ 498
Tennent Heriot 80/- Ⓗ
Village pub with friendly
atmosphere. Bar in keeping
with pub's name ▦Q❦

Helton 29E3

12–3 (closed Tue & winter); 7–11
Helton Inn
Theakston Best Bitter Ⓗ
Small, homely village local. A
friendly welcome for all. Good
bar meals ▦Q🄳🅟🅖❦

Heversham 29E6

11–3; 6–11
Blue Bell
Princes Way (A6)
℘ Milnthorpe 3159
Hartley XB Ⓔ
Hotel with comfortable lounge
and pleasant stone-floored
public bar. Well-kept garden
Q🄳🅟🅖❦

Hoff 29F3

11–3; 6–10.30 (11 F, S & summer)
New Inn
B6260
Marston Pedigree
Small roadside tavern
▦Q🅟🅖❦Å

Kendal 29E5

11–3; 6–11
Cock & Dolphin
Milnthorpe Road (A6)
℘ 28268
**Vaux Sunderland Draught,
Samson** Ⓗ
Large hotel in neo-Edwardian
style. Old metal advertising
signs on way to gents!
Stabling 🅟 (playground) 🄳
🅖 (Mon–Fri) ❦

Golden Lion
Market Place ℘ 24116
**Lorimer & Clark 70/-; Vaux
Sunderland Draught Bitter;
Wards Sheffield Best Bitter** Ⓗ
Long-established homely
hostelry with award-winning
cellar 🄳 (dining room) 🅖≈

Keswick 28D3

11–3; 5.30–10.30 (11 F, S)
Dog & Gun
Lake Road
Eves opens 6
**Theakston Best Bitter, XB, Old
Peculier** Ⓗ
Popular pub within walking
distance of Derwent Water.
Excellent food ▦🅖❦

Twa Dogs
Penrith Road (A591) ℘ 72599
**Jennings Mild, Bitter,
Marathon** Ⓗ
Bogart Preservation Society
HQ. Don't believe all you hear,
landlord was once "Biggest
Liar" in the world
▦Q🄳🅟🅖❦Å

Try also: **Pack Horse**
(Jennings)

Kirkby
Lonsdale 29F6

Snooty Fox
Main Street (B6254)
℘ 71308
Hartley XB; Younger Scotch Ⓗ
Busy dining room in front bar;
more "pubby" atmosphere in
back bar 🅟🅖❦

Kirkby Stephen 29G4

11–3; 6–10.30 (11 F, S & summer)
White Lion
Main Street
**Marston Mercian Mild,
Burton Bitter**
Busy, small town pub close to
Market Place

Try also: **Croglin Castle**

Leece 28D6

12.3 (Sat only); 7–11
Queen's Arms
Off A5087 OS244695
**Matthew Brown Lion Mild,
Lion Bitter** Ⓗ
Thriving village local, very
friendly atmosphere. Pool,
darts, quiz teams (Trivial
Pursuits very popular) 🅟

Levens 29E5

11–3; 6–11
Hare & Hounds
Causeway End (off A590)
℘ Sedgwick 60408
Vaux Samson Ⓗ **Ward
Sheffield Best Bitter** Ⓔ
Local in self-assured, village; 3
low-beamed rooms around a
central bar Q🄳🅟🅖❦

Lindal-in-Furness 28D6

12–3; 7–11

Railway Inn
London Road (off A590)
Matthew Brown Lion Mild,
Lion Bitter, John Peel Ⓗ
Friendly village local, very
welcoming atmosphere. Fine
watering hole for travellers ♨

Lorton 28C3

11–3; 5.30–10.30 (11 F, S)

Wheatsheaf Inn
Low Lorton (B5289) ✆ 268
Jennings Bitter Ⓗ
Cosy pub in scenic valley.
Caravan site ♨ Q ▤ ⑃ ♿ 🍴 ♟

Try also: Horseshoe (Jennings)

Melmerby 29F2

11–3; 6–10.30 (11 F, S)

Shepherds Inn
Marston Mercian Mild,
Burton Bitter, Pedigree Ⓗ
Multi-roomed restaurant &
bar at foot of Hartside Pass
♨ ▤ ⑃ 🍴 ♟ ≹

Monkhill 28D1

11–3; 5.30–10.30 (11 F, S)

Drovers Rest
Carlisle/Burgh-by-Sands road
(off B5307)
Jennings Mild, Bitter Ⓗ
Friendly, popular village local
with half netting connections
♨ ▤ (lunchtime) ♿ ♟

Moota 28C2

11–3; 5.30–10.30 (11 F, S)

Laal Moota
A595
Tetley Mild, Bitter Ⓗ
Occasional guest beers
Recently modernised pub,
toilets now inside. Landlord
reputed to be shortest in
Cumbria. Ask for a pint of
jaspers. Don't mention
dominoes ♨ Q ▤ ⑃ ♿ 🍴 ♟ & ⅄

Morland 29F3

11–3; 6–10.30 (11 F, S)

Kings Arms
Water Street
Marston Burton Bitter,
Pedigree Ⓗ
Village pub on outskirts of
Lake District ♨ ⑃ 🍴 ♟ ⅄

Near Sawrey 28D5

11–3; 5.30–11

Tower Bank Arms
B5288 ✆ Hawkshead 334
Jennings Bitter; Matthew
Brown Lion Mild, John Peel Ⓗ
Popular NT pub near Beatrix
Potters house. Shove
ha'penny ♨ Q ▤ ⑃ ♿ 🍴 ⑃

Try also: Sawrey Hotel, Far
Sawrey

Nether Wasdale 28C4

11–3; 5.30–10.30 (11 F, S & summer)

Screes Hotel
OS124041 ✆ 262
Hartleys XB; Theakston Best
Bitter, Old Peculier Ⓗ
Occasional guest beers
A mile from Wastwater, ideal
starting point for walks
around Wasdale. Homely pub
with excellent food
♨ ▤ ⑃ ▣ ⑃ 🍴 ♟ ⅄

Oulton 28D1

11–3; 5.30–10.30 (11 F, S)

Bird in Hand
Wigton/Kirkbride Road (off
B5302) OS245515
Jennings Mild, Bitter Ⓗ
Homely, welcoming rural inn
just north of the village
♨ ⑃ ♟ &

Oxen Park 28D5

11–3; 6–11

Manor House
Nr A590 OS316873
Hartleys Mild, XB Ⓗ
Converted manor house.
Unusual high oak-beam and
plaster ceiling. Regular folk
nights ♨ Q ⑃ ⅄

Penrith 29E3

11–3; 5.30–10.30 (11 F, S)

Agricultural Hotel
Cromwell Road (Castlegate)
✆ 62622
Evening opens 7
Marston Burton Bitter,
Pedigree, Owd Rodger Ⓗ
Tastefully refurbished
Victorian bar. Direct access
from the bar to the auction
mart next door ♨ ⑃ ♿ 🍴 ≹

Board & Elbow
Cornmarket
Open till 5 Tues lunchtime
Matthew Brown Lion Bitter;
Theakston Old Peculier Ⓗ
Town centre pub popular with
youngsters, especially at
weekends ♨ ⑃ 🍴 ≹

Waverley
Crown Square
Evening opens 7
Wilsons Original Bitter Ⓗ
Well-appointed town centre
hotel. Popular restaurant.
Own leisure centre upstairs
⑃ 🍴 ≹

Rockcliffe 28D1

11–3; 5.30–10.30 (11 F, S)

Crown & Thistle
Off A74, 4½ miles NW of
Carlisle ✆ 378
McEwan 70/-; Younger IPA Ⓗ
Friendly, comfortable local,
everything a village pub
should be. Excellent bar meals
♨ ⑃ ♿ 🍴

Rowrah 28B3

11–3; 5.30–10.30 (11 F, S & summer)

Stork Hotel
A5086
Jennings Mild, Bitter Ⓗ
Friendly local, open fires,
numerous hunting and hound
trailing trophies. Many
"sports" teams ♨ ⑃ ♟

St. Bees 28B4

11–3; 5.30–10.30 (11 F, S)

Manor House
Main Street (B5345)
✆ Egremount 822425
Matthew Brown Lion Mild
(summer), Lion Bitter, John
Peel (summer) Ⓗ
Popular friendly village pub,
plush lounge. Good meals and
accommodation
♨ ▤ ⑃ ♿ 🍴 ♟ ≹

Sandwith 28B4

11–3; 6.30–10.30 (11 F, S & summer)

Dog & Partridge
Nr B5345 SW of Whitehaven
Matthew Brown Lion Mild,
Lion Bitter; Theakston Best
Bitter, Old Peculier Ⓗ
Popular village local. Just off
Coast to Coast walk, worth a
detour ♨ Q ⑃ ♿ 🍴 ♟ ⅄

Seathwaite 28C5

11–3; 6–11

Newfield Inn
6 miles N of Broughton
OS227960 ✆ Broughton 208
McEwan 70/- Ⓗ
16th century inn of great
character in beautiful Duddon
Valley. Slate floor and oak
beams. Renowned for its steak
dinners ♨ Q ▤ ⑃
▣ (self-catering) ⑃ 🍴 ♟ ⅄

Sedbergh 29F5

11–3; 6–11

Red Lion
Finkle Street ✆ 20433
Marston Mercian Mild;
Burton Bitter; Pedigree Ⓗ
Attractive friendly 1-room
local. No food Mon Q ⑃ ♿ 🍴

Silecroft 28C6

11–3; 6–10.30 (11 F, S & summer)

Miners Arms
Off A595 ✆ Millom 2325
Younger No. 3 Ⓗ
Lively village pub, popular for
meals. Pool table
♨ ▤ ⑃ ▣ ♿ 🍴 ♟ & ⅄ (1 mile) ≹

Sizergh 29E5

11–3; 6–11

Strickland Arms
Old A6 (now by-passed by
new A590) OS500872
Younger Scotch, No. 3 Ⓗ
Originally the dower house for
the nearby Sizergh Castle
♨ ▤ ⑃ ♿ 🍴

Spark Bridge   28D5

11–3; 6–11
Royal Oak
Off A5084 ℰ Greenodd 286
**Hartleys XB; Thwaites Best
Mild, Bitter** Ⓗ
Large country pub, good food
🏚Q🅷🅿️🅶🌂🍴🚭👥♿🏕️

Talkin   29E1

12–2.30 (July–Aug & bank hols only) 7–10.30
(11 F, S)
Hare & Hounds
ℰ Brampton 3456
**Hartleys XB; Theakston Best
Bitter, XB, Old Peculier;
Bulmer Cider** Ⓗ
Charming award-winning
village inn near Talkin Tarn.
Intimate atmosphere,
comfortable, traditional decor,
superb bar 🏚Q🅷🅿️🅶🌂🍴🚭♿🏕️

Tarraby   28E1

11–3; 5.30–10.30 (11 F, S)
Near Boot
B6264 (Back Brampton Road)
ℰ Carlisle 29547
**Matthew Brown Lion Mild;
Theakston Best Bitter, XB, Old
Peculier** Ⓗ
Roadside inn with original
19th century fireplaces.
Bowling green
🏚🅷 (lunchtime) 🅿️🅶
🌂 (summer) 🍴🏕️

Uldale   28C2

11–3; 5.30 (7 winter)–10.30 (11 F, S)
Snooty Fox
ℰ Low Ireby 479
Wilsons Original Bitter Ⓗ
Friendly village local near
Bassenthwaite Lake
🏚🅷🅿️🅶🌂🏕️

Ulverston   28D6

10.30–3; 6–11 (open all day Thu)
Bay Horse
Canal Foot ℰ 53972
Mornings opens 11
Mitchells Mild, Bitter Ⓗ
Picturesque local on tidal
estuary, popular with locals
and visitors. Fresh water and
sea fishing facilities
🏚🅷🅿️🅶🌂🍴🏕️ (1 mile)

Beehive Inn
Three Bridges (A590 ½ mile W
of Ulverston)
Closed lunch Mon–Fri;
eves opens 7
Hartleys XB Ⓗ
Extremely friendly local—
small, homely pub well worth
a visit 🏚Q🅷🍴

Devonshire Arms
Victoria Road (off A590)
ℰ 52537
**Thwaites Best Mild, Best
Bitter** Ⓗ
Popular local near town
centre. Very friendly welcome
assured. A haven 🅿️🅶🌂🍴

Kings Head Hotel
Queen Street
Theakston Best Bitter Ⓗ
Regular guest beers
Busy town centre pub. Crown
green at rear. Woods available
🏚🅿️🍽️🍴

**Try also: Waterwheel; Hope &
Anchor**

Whitehaven   28B3

11–3; 5.30–10.30 (11 F, S & summer)
Central
104 Duke Street ℰ 2796

**Matthew Brown Lion Mild;
Theakston Best Bitter, XB, Old
Peculier** Ⓗ
Lounge bar is "Central"
Station Whitehaven with
famous rodents in residence!
Quiet locals bar around the
back 🅶🍴🍽️

Sun Inn
Hensingham Square (A595)
Jennings Mild; Bitter Ⓗ
Cosy and relaxed, dominoes a
popular pastime. Parking
difficult Q🍴

Try also: Welsh Arms
(Hartleys)

Wigton   28D1

11–3; 5.30–10.30 (11 F, S)
Throstles Nest
Kings Street (A596)
ℰ 43139
**Marston Burton Bitter,
Pedigree** Ⓗ
Modern town centre pub next
to bus station 🏚🅿️🅶🌂🍴♿🚋

Workington   28B3

11–3; 5.30–10.30 (11 F, S)
Ancient Mariner
Church Street ℰ 3616
Vaux Sampson Ⓗ
Enlightening for those who
seek adventure! 🍽️🍴🚋

Henry Curwen
Bridge Street ℰ 67355
**Matthew Brown Lion Mild,
Bitter, John Peel Bitter;
Theakston Old Peculier** Ⓗ
Busy efficient pub. Very good
food at a fair price
🍽️ (lunchtime) 🅿️🅶🌂🍴♿🚋

Acresford 23H8

10.30–2.30; 6–11

Cricketts Inn
A444 ☎ Burton 760359
Draught Bass Ⓗ
Popular roadside pub by
county boundary. Good food
🍴♿⚲🅿🍷🍴♿

Alfreton 23J5

11.30–3; 6–11

Robin Hood
26 Nottingham Road
☎ 833588
**Hardys & Hansons Best Mild,
Best Bitter** Ⓔ
Unpretentious friendly local.
Skittle alley in garden
🅿⚲🍷♿⚋

Swan & Salmon
Derby Road ☎ 832870
John Smith's Bitter Ⓗ
Modern pub with front and
back lounges. Very popular at
lunchtimes ⚲🅿♿🍷 (book) ⚋

Try also: Devonshire Arms
(Shipstone)

Apperknowle 23J4

11–3; 6–11

Yellow Lion
High Street (A61)
☎ Dronfield 413181
Tetley Bitter Ⓗ Occasional
guest beers
Friendly village local. Organ
in lounge; restaurant
Q🅿⚲♿🍷♿

Ashbourne 23G6

10.30–3; 6–11

Bowling Green
Buxton Road ☎ 42511
Draught Bass Ⓗ
On hilltop just out of town.
Ideal starting/finishing place
for Tissington Trail ♿🍷

Ashover 23H5

11–3; 6.30–11

Black Swan
Church Street
☎ Chesterfield 590305
Draught Bass Ⓗ
Fine old coaching house in
picturesque village
🍴Q🅿⚲♿🍷♿

Crispin Inn
Church Street (off A632)
Evening opens 7
Home Bitter Ⓗ
Picturesque old village inn,
once frequented by
Cromwell's men 🍴Q🅿⚲🍷

Aston on 23J7
Trent

10–2.30; 6–11

Malt Shovel
The Green ☎ Derby 792256
Ind Coope Bitter, Burton Ale Ⓗ

Friendly and popular village
local specialising in meals
♿🍷🍴

Try also: White Hart
(Marston)

Bakewell 23G4

10.30–3 (4 Mon); 6–11

Peacock Hotel
Market Place (off A6/A619)
☎ 2994
Ward Sheffield Best Bitter Ⓔ
Stone-fronted pub in Market
Square. Very comfortable and
friendly 🍴🅱♿🍷♿

Bamford 23G3

11–3; 5.30–11

Derwent Hotel
Main Road (A6013)
☎ Hope Valley 51395
**Stones Best Bitter; Ward
Sheffield Best Bitter** Ⓗ
Friendly pub with home
cooking. Collection of sewing
machines 🅱⚲♿🍷🅰⚋

Birchover 23H5

12–3; 6–11

Red Lion
Main Street (off B5056)
☎ Winster 229
**Marston Pedigree; Tetley
Bitter** Ⓗ
Traditional village pub with
indoor well 🍴Q⚲🍷🅰

Birch Vale 23F3

12–3; 5.30–11

Sycamore
Sycamore Road (off A6015)
☎ New Mills 42715
**Boddingtons Bitter; Marston
Pedigree; Winkle BVA** Ⓗ
Freehouse/restaurant catering
for children, with large picnic
area 🅱⚲♿🍷♿

Boylestone 23G6

11–2.30; 7–11

Rose & Crown
Off A515 OS177356
☎ Great Cubley 518
Marston Pedigree Ⓗ; **Bulmer
Cider** Ⓖ Regular guest beers
Small white-washed pub in
pleasant setting. Low beamed
ceiling and small bar 🅱⚲🍷

Brassington 23H5

10.30–3; 6–11

Olde Gate
Off B5035
☎ Carsington 448
Marston Pedigree Ⓗ
Built 1616; scrubbed tables
and black-leaded fireplace. Off
High Peak Trail 🍴🅱⚲♿🍷🍴

Bretby 23H7

11–2.30; 6–11

Chesterfield Arms
Ashby Road (main A50)
☎ Burton 211606

Ind Coope Bitter, Burton Ale Ⓗ
Comfortable modernised pub.
Former gatehouse to Bretby
Estate. Childrens play area
outdoors ⚲♿🍷🍴

Buxton 23F4

11–3; 5.30–11

Bakers Arms
West Road
Evening opens 6
Draught Bass Ⓔ
Cottage pub with lots of
atmosphere 🍷🍴

Cheshire Cheese
High Street ☎ 5371
**Hardys & Hansons Best Mild,
Best Bitter** Ⓗ
Renovated pub close to
market place. Interesting
façade ♿

Castleton 23G3

12–3; 5.30 (7 winter)–11

Bulls Head Hotel
Cross Street (A625)
☎ Hope Valley 20256
Robinson Best Bitter Ⓔ, **Old
Tom** Ⓖ
Friendly pub with restaurant,
large lounge and pool room.
Hikers welcome 🍴🅱⚲♿🍷♿🅰

Try also: George (Stones)

Chapel-en-le- 23G4
Frith

11–3; 5.30–11

Old Pack Horse
Town End (A6) ☎ 812135
**Robinson Best Mild, Best
Bitter** Ⓗ, **Old Tom** Ⓖ
Comfortable market town
pub, with mild in both dark
and light form 🅱♿🍷🍴

Roebuck
Market Place (off A6)
Tetley Mild, Bitter Ⓗ
Market pub of great character
near village stocks ♿🍷

Chesterfield 23J4

11–3; 5.30–11

Derby Tup
Sheffield Road, Whittington
Moor (off A61)
**Bateman XXXB; Marston Owd
Rodger; Ruddle County;
Taylor Landlord; Theakston
XB, Old Peculier** Ⓗ
12 hand-pulled beers, friendly
unspoilt free house 🍴Q♿♿

Devonshire
Mansfield Road, Hasland (off
A617) ☎ 32218
Opens 12 (11.15 Sat)
Tetley Bitter Ⓗ
Unassuming local; pool and
darts 🅱⚲♿ (Mon–Fri) 🍷♿

Grouse
136 Chatsworth Road,
Brampton (A619) ☎ 79632
**Bass 4X Mild, Draught Bass;
Stones Best Bitter** Ⓗ

Popular local, just off town centre, on route to Peak District ✏🚭🍴

Market Hotel
New Square ☎ 73641
Evening closes 10.30 (11 F, S)
Tetley Mild, Bitter ⑭
Open-plan town centre pub overlooking market; opens 9.30 am for coffee ♿ (not Sun)

Walton Hotel
59 St Augustines Road
☎ 32480
Home Bitter Ⓔ
Large mock-Tudor estate pub opened Coronation Day 1937 ✏♿🍻 (Tue–Sat) ♿

Try also: Hare & Greyhound (Youngers)

Chinley 23F4

11–3; 5.30–11
Old Hall Inn
Whitehough ☎ 50529
Marston Pedigree; Thwaites Best Mild, Bitter ⑭
Comfortable restaurant-style pub in historic building ✏♿🍻

Try also: Oddfellows (Marston)

Clay Cross 23J5

12–3; 7–11
New Inn
Market Street
Tetley Mild, Bitter ⑭
Deceptively large market town pub. Coaches welcome ✏🍴

Try also: Shoulder of Mutton (Tetley)

Crich 23H5

10.30–3; 6–11
Cliff Inn
Cromford Road (B5035)
☎ Ambergate 2444
Hardys & Hansons Best Mild, Best Bitter ⑭
Popular local, near National Tramway Museum ✏♿🍻🍴

Cromford 23H5

11.30–3; 6–11
Bell Inn
The Hill ☎ Wirksworth 2102
Hardys & Hansons Best Mild, Best Bitter ⑭
Friendly three-roomed local 🍴

Darley Dale 23H5

11–3; 7–11
Grouse Inn
Dale Road North (A6) ☎ 2297
Hardys & Hansons Best Mild, Best Bitter ⑭
Friendly local on tourist route 🏠✏♿♿

Derby 23H6

10.30–3; 6–11
Dolphin Inn
Queen Street ☎ 49115

Draught Bass Ⓔ
Picturesque timber-framed pub, built 1530. Near Derby Cathedral ♿🍴

Furnace
Duke Street
Hardys & Hansons Best Mild, Best Bitter ⑭ & Ⓔ
Popular Victorian foundrymans slaker, near St Mary's Bridge ✏

Grampian
Grampian Way ☎ 764385
Marston Mercian Mild, Burton Bitter, Pedigree ⑭,
Owd Rodger Ⓖ
Modern pub in newly developed area of Sinfin, on southern outskirts of city ♿

Maypole
Brook Street ☎ 44560
Home Mild, Bitter Ⓔ
Pleasantly fronted, one-roomed tavern with bustling social club atmosphere 🚭♿🍻

Olde Spa Inne
204 Abbey Street ☎ 43474
Ind Coope Bitter, Burton Ale ⑭
Cosy, well-modernised popular locals' pub. CAMRA 1985 pub preservation award winner ✏♿

Wardwick Tavern
The Wardwick ☎ 32677
Ansells Mild; Aylesbury ABC Bitter; Ind Coope Bitter, Burton Ale ⑭
Early 18th-century listed building with timbered ceilings 🚭♿ (Mon–Sat)

White Horse
The Morledge ☎ 42352
Ansells Mild; Ind Coope Bitter, Burton Ale ⑭
Distinctive building near bus station. Large bar and split-level lounge ♿ (Mon–Sat) 🍴

Try also: Half Moon (Bass); Exeter Arms (Marston)

Dove Holes 23G4

12–3; 6–11
Railway
Hardys & Hansons Best Mild, Best Bitter ⑭
Pleasant pub with many rooms in upland village 🏠♿🍴♿

Draycott 23J7

11–2.30; 6–11
Travellers Rest
Derby Road (A6005) ☎ 2332
Marston Mercian Mild, Pedigree ⑭
Lively local with traditional layout. Sing-song Saturday night 🍴♿

Dronfield 23H4

11–3; 6–11
Blue Stoops
High Street (near A61)

Ward Sheffield Best Bitter Ⓔ
Comfortable village inn. 2 wood-panelled lounges and room with dartboard Q✏♿♿

Try also: Old Sidings (Free)

Dronfield Woodhouse 23H4

11–3; 6–11
Gorsey Brigg
Pentland Road, Gosforth Valley
Shipstone Bitter ⑭
Comfortably furnished large modern estate pub, with friendly atmosphere ✏🍴♿

Duffield 23H6

11–3; 6–11
Bridge
Makeney Road (off A6)
☎ Derby 841073
Home Bitter Ⓔ
Large and comfortable lounge, lively bar and pleasant terrace overlooking river ✏🍴♿

Earl Sterndale 23G4

11–3; 5.30–11
Quiet Woman
B5053 ☎ Longnor 211
Marston Mercian Mild, Burton Bitter ⑭
Superb example of a village green pub on the "White Peak Way" walk route 🍴♿

Eckington 23J4

11–3; 6–11
Prince of Wales
11 Church Street ☎ 432966
Marston Burton Bitter, Pedigree Ⓔ, **Owd Rodger** (winter) Ⓖ
Lively village local, popular with the young. Livestock in garden ✏♿🍴

Try also: White Hart (Home)

Edale 23G3

12–3 (closed winter); 6–11
Rambler Inn
☎ Hope Valley 70268
Marston Burton Bitter, Pedigree ⑭
Large comfortable inn near start of Pennine Way. Owned by Ramblers Association 🏠Q🚭 (in restaurant) ✏🚌♿🍴♿

Try also: Old Nags Head (Free)

Foolow 23G4

12–3 (2.30 winter); 7 (7.30 winter)–11
Bulls Head Inn
Off A623
☎ Hope Valley 30873
Whitbread Castle Eden; Bulmer Cider ⑭
Village pub and restaurant. Oak beams and brasses. Only underwater car park in the county! Q✏♿🍻🍴♿⛺

Glossop 23F3

11–3; 5.30–11

Crown Inn
Victoria Street (A624)
Samuel Smith OBB ℍ
Comfortable thriving local
near town centre ☞♥

Grapes
High Street West ☎ 4147
Evening opens 6
Boddingtons Mild, Bitter ℍ
Unspoilt friendly pub. A gem
of a northern local ▥Q♥

Prince of Wales
Mill Town (off A57)
Opens 11.30 & 5
**Marston Mercian Mild,
Burton Bitter, Pedigree** ℍ
Cosy three-room pub with
original furnishings ☞♥♿≠

Star
Howard Street
Boddingtons Bitter ℍ
Busy stone-built corner local,
outside station ☞♥≠

Hartshorne 23H7

11–2.30; 6–11

Rodney Inn
Main Street (A514)
☎ Burton 216482
Draught Bass Ⓔ
Friendly village pub with own
cricket pitch ▥♥♥

Hathersage 23H4

11–3; 6–11

Plough Inn
Leadmill Bridge (A622)
OS805305
Stones Best Bitter Ⓔ
Converted farm and cottages
on banks of River Derwent.
Small taproom and split-level
lounge ▥♥♥♿▲≠

Try also: Scotchmans Pack
(Stones)

Hayfield 23F4

11–3; 5.30–11

George
Church Street (off A624)
☎ New Mills 43691
Burtonwood Bitter ℍ
Low beamed 16th century
pub modernised in 1750!
Stained glass windows
▥▣☞▲

Lantern Pike
Little Hayfield Village (A624)
☎ New Mills 44102
**Wilsons Mild, Original
Bitter** ℍ
Comfortable 18th century inn
overlooked by Pennine Hills
▥▣☞♥♿

Heage 23H6

11–3; 6–11

Black Boy
Old Road (B6013)
☎ Ambergate 2779

Whitbread Castle Eden
Friendly and popular local,
specialising in meals ♥☞♥♥♿

White Hart
2 Church Street
☎ Ambergate 2302
Opens 11.30
Draught Bass Ⓖ (Ⓔ summer)
Large many-roomed pub at
crossroads overlooking
village. Bar billiards ♥♥♿

Heanor 23J6

11–3; 7–11

New Inn
Derby Road (A608)
☎ Langley Mill 719609
Home Mild; Bitter Ⓔ
Busy compact local with
friendly atmosphere ♥☞♥

Try also: Erewash Hotel
(A610)

Hope 23G3

11–3; 6–11

Old Hall Hotel
Market Place (A625)
☎ Hope Valley 20160
Stones Best Bitter ℍ
Occasional guest beers
Opposite church; oak-panelled
lounge with grand piano.
Restaurant ▥♥▣☞♥♥♿▲≠

Horsley 23J6

11–2.30; 6–11

Coach & Horses
47 Church Street
☎ Derby 880581
**Marston Capital Ale, Merrie
Monk, Pedigree** ℍ, **Owd
Rodger** Ⓖ
Popular open-plan village
pub. Model railway in garden
♥☞

Horsley Woodhouse 23J6

11–3; 7–11

Jolly Colliers
27 Main Street
☎ Derby 880425
**Ward Best Mild, Sheffield Best
Bitter** Ⓔ
Friendly village local.
Weekend singalongs always
end with the house anthem
♥♥♿

Ilkeston 23J6

11–3; 7–11

Durham Ox
Durham Street (off A6007)
☎ 324570
**Lorimer & Clark 70/-; Ward
Best Mild, Sheffield Best
Bitter** ℍ
Busy backstreet local, friendly
and comfortable ▥♥☞♥♿

Rutland Cottage
Heanor Road (A6007)
☎ 304875

Shipstone Mild, Bitter ℍ & Ⓔ
Delightful roadside inn, full of
old world charm and
character ▥▣♥♥

Try also: Bridge Inn (Hardys &
Hansons); Flowerpot
(Shipstones)

Knockerdown 23H5

11–3; 6–11

Knockerdown Inn
B5035 near Hogmaston
☎ Carsington 209
**Marston Pedigree, Merrie
Monk** Ⓖ
Isolated, modernised
roadhouse. Popular and
comfortable Q♥☞➔

Little Hucklow 23G4

12 (closed winter)–3; 5.30–11

Old Bulls Head
Off B6049 OS169786
☎ Tideswell 871097
May close early if trade slack
**Winkle Ivanhoe, Saxon
Cross** ℍ
Connoisseur's pub. Geological
collection and display of
African carvings ▥Q♥▲

Long Eaton 26A8

11–3; 6–11

Prince of Wales
High Street
☎ 732492
Home Mild, Bitter Ⓔ
Modernised, one-roomed local
☞

Lullington 23H8

10.30–2.30; 6–11

Colville Arms
Coton Road
Draught Bass ℍ
Friendly 18th century village
local with own bowling green
▥Q♥♥

Makeney 23H6

12–3; 7–11

Hollybush
Hollybush Lane (near A6)
☎ Derby 841729
**Marston Pedigree, Owd
Rodger; Ruddle County;
Theakston Old Peculier** Ⓖ & ℍ
Late 17th-century listed
beamed pub of exceptional
character. Limited parking
▥♥☞♥

Matlock 23H5

10.30–3; 6–11

White Lion Inn
195 Starkholmes Road
☎ 2511
Home Mild, Bitter ℍ
Old coaching inn over-
looking Derwent Valley
▣♥☞➔♥♿

Matlock Bath   23H5

11–3; 6–11
Princess Victoria
176 South Parade
℡ 57462
Draught Bass; Marston Pedigree; Ruddle County; Ward Sheffield Best Bitter Ⓗ
Regular guest beers
One of Matlock Bath's oldest buildings, now restored to its former glory ▲Q❻❼&≋

Melbourne   23H7

10.30–3; 6–11
Blue Bell Inn
Church Street
℡ 2606
Ind Coope Burton Ale Ⓗ
Small but lively local, real ale in bar only. No car park ❺❼❢

Try also: Alma Inn (Marston)

Middle Handley   23J4

11–3; 6–11
Devonshire Arms
Westfield Lane (near B6052)
Stones Best Bitter Ⓗ
Lively village local with three comfortable rooms round central bar Q♨

Milton   23H7

10.30–3; 6–11
Swan Inn
Main Street
℡ Burton-on-Trent 703188
Marston Mercian Mild, Pedigree Ⓗ
Popular village pub with pleasant garden ♨❢

New Mills   23F3

11–3; 5.30–11
Crescent
Market Street
℡ 43889
Evening opens 6
Tetley Mild, Bitter Ⓗ
Attractive, stone-built pub in crescent shaped terrace
❺❼❢≋

Fox
Brookbottom Hamlet (Strines)
Robinsons Best Mild, Best Bitter Ⓗ
Old whitewashed pub in small hamlet; comfortable and friendly; difficult to find
♨❺≋ (Strines)

Ockbrook   23J6

10.30–3; 6–11
Royal Oak
Off A52 ℡ Derby 662378
Draught Bass; M&B Springfield Bitter Ⓗ
Characterful village meeting place with four small rooms
▲Q♨❺ (Mon–Sat) ❢&

Old Brampton   23H4

11–3; 7–11
George & Dragon
Old Brampton
℡ Chesterfield 566728
Marston Burton Bitter, Pedigree Ⓗ
Pleasant and friendly village local in delightful surroundings
▲Q⊞ (lunchtimes) ❺❼❢

Try also: Fox & Goose (Stones)

Openwoodgate   23H6

11–3; 6–11
Bulls Head
A60 Ilkeston Road, E. of Belper
Hardys & Hansons Best Bitter Ⓔ
Exceptionally well-run village local with warm and friendly atmosphere ❺❢

Over Haddon   23G5

11.30–3; 6–11
Lathkil Hotel
Near A6/B5055
℡ Bakewell 2501
Darley Dark Mild, Thorne Best Bitter; Ward Sheffield Best Bitter Ⓗ
Welcoming hostelry with panoramic views over Lathkil Dale and beyond
▲Q⊞ (lunchtime) ♨❢❺❼❢

Peak Forest   23G4

11–3; 5.30–11
Devonshire Arms
℡ Buxton 3875
Ward Sheffield Best Bitter Ⓗ
Pleasant welcoming roadside inn ▲❢♨❢❺❼❢&❢▲

Pilsley   23J5

11–3; 7–11
Gladstone Arms
Morton Road (off B6039)
℡ Ripley 872285
Home Mild, Bitter Ⓗ
Lively local in village centre. Organ at weekends
❢♨❢

Riddings   23J5

11–3; 6–11
Moulders Arms
Church Street
℡ Leabrooks 602445
Draught Bass Ⓗ
Attractive, white-washed pub with snug interior, beamed ceiling and thatched roof
♨❢

Seven Stars
Church Street
℡ Leabrooks 602715
Ward Best Mild, Sheffield Best Bitter Ⓗ
Historic house of considerable character dating from 15th

century and set in the oldest part of the village ♨❢

Ripley   23J5

11–3; 6–11
Hollybush
Brook Lane, Marehay (off A61) ℡ 42558
Shipstone Bitter; Bulmer Cider Ⓗ
Spacious pub with good view of cricket ground ♨❼❢&

Jolly Colliers
Jessop Street, Waingroves
℡ 46341
Home Mild, Bitter Ⓔ
Comfortable local off the beaten track, with skittles team in summer ▲♨❢

Sawley   23J7

11–3; 6–11
Bell Hotel
Tamworth Road
℡ Long Eaton 732566
Shipstone Mild, Bitter Ⓗ
A real locals' local ♨❢❢≋

Try also: Nag's Head (Marston)

Scarcliffe   23J4

11–3; 7–11
Horse & Groom
B6417
℡ Chesterfield 823152
Home Bitter Ⓗ
Beamed coaching inn ▲♨❺❢

Shardlow   23J7

10.30–3; 6–11
Dog & Duck
London Road (A6)
℡ Derby 792224
Marston Mercian Mild, Merrie Monk, Pedigree Ⓗ**, Owd Rodger** Ⓖ (winter)
Much extended, cruck-built original, with good choice of rooms ❢♨❺❢&▲

Navigation
London Road
℡ Derby 792918
Lunchtime closes 2.30
Davenports Bitter Ⓗ **Regular guest beers**
Large roadside pub at the turn to the wharf. The only gas-lit lounge in Derby ❢♨❺▲

Shirebrook   23J4

11–3; 7–11
Station Hotel
Station Road (B6407)
℡ Mansfield 742210
Shipstone Mild, Bitter Ⓔ
Modernised 1896 hotel
❺❼ (must book) ❢

Shirland   23J5

11–3; 6–11
Duke of Wellington
Main Road (A61)

Derbyshire

88

Home Mild, Bitter E
Busy roadside pub, good
atmosphere 🏮🍺

Somercotes 23J5

11–3; 7–11

Horse & Jockey
Leabrooks Road (B6016)
✆ Leabrooks 602179
Home Mild, Bitter E
Deservedly popular, unspoilt
local 🏮Q🍺

Spinkhill 23J4

11–3; 6–11

Angel
College Road (off A616; near
M1 Jct. 30)
✆ Eckington 432315
Tetley Bitter H
Friendly, lively, country inn
and village local. Large games
room with snooker table
🍺📺🕕🍷

Spondon 23J6

10.30–3; 6–11

Malt Shovel
Potter street
✆ Derby 674203
Draught Bass E
Characterful, unspoilt village
local fronted by glorious
flower-beds in summer 🏮🍷🍺

Stone Edge 23H4

11–3; 5.30 (6.30 summer)–11

Red Lion
B5057
✆ Chesterfield 566142
**Darley Dark Mild, Thorne
Best Bitter; Ward Sheffield
Best Bitter** H
Smart pub/restaurant; four
real fires provide warm
welcome 🏮📺🍷🕕🍷🍴Å

Stoney 23G4
Middleton

12–3; 6–11

Royal Oak
The Dale (A623)
✆ Hope Valley 31392
**Marston Pedigree; Tetley
Bitter** H Regular guest beers

♦ A REAL FIRE PUB ♦

The 🏮 symbol denotes a pub
with a real solid fuel fire

Traditional village pub with
friendly atmosphere. Hikers
welcome. Open all hours for
well-dressing week in July
🏮🍷🕕🍷Å

Sutton-cum- 23J4
Duckmanton

11–3 (closed winter S); 6–11

Arkwright Arms
Bolsover Road (A632)
**Marston Burton Bitter,
Pedigree; Whitbread Castle
Eden** H Occasional guest beers
Convivial roadside pub with
beer garden and donkeys. Bar
billiards 🏮🍷🕕

Tideswell 23G4

11–3; 6–11

Anchor Inn
Four Lane Ends
(A623/B6049) ✆ 871371
**Robinson Best Mild, Best
Bitter** E, **Old Tom** G
Spacious oak-panelled lounge;
small taproom with dartboard
and aquarium. Friendly
atmosphere 🏮Q🍷🕕🍷🍴👟

Horse & Jockey
Queen Street (B6049)
✆871597
Tetley Mild, Bitter H
Friendly village pub with local
atmosphere. Home cooking.
Piano player Saturday and
Sunday evening Q🍷🕕🍷

Try also: **George** (Hardys &
Hansons)

Wardlow 23G4
Mires

11–3; 6–11

Three Stags Heads
A623/B6465
✆ Tideswell 871251
Younger's Scotch Bitter H
Family-run farmhouse pub
that time has passed by.
Petrified cat watches from
glass case in corner
🏮Q🍷Å

Whaley Bridge 23F4

11–3; 5.30–11

Jodrell Arms
Buxton Road (A6)
**Wilson's Original Mild,
Bitter** H
Imposing village centre
building with comfortable,
well laid-out interior
🏮🍷📺🕕🍷⇌

Shepherds Arms
Old Road (off A6)
**Marston Mercian Mild,
Burton Bitter, Pedigree** H
Excellent local with good
vault and garden
🍷🕕🍷🍴⇌

Try also: **Board Inn**
(Robinsons)

Willington 23H7

10.30–3; 6 (7 winter)–11

Green Dragon
The Green
Ind Coope Bitter, Burton Ale H
Small-roomed pub near canal
and railway. Very popular in
summertime for its large lawn
🏮🍷🕕🍷 (Mon–Fri)

Windley 23H6

10.30–3; 6–11

Puss in Boots
Nether Lane (B5023)
✆ Cowers Lane 316
Draught Bass H
An isolated, characterful
country pub with low-beamed
ceiling 🏮🍷🍺

Wirksworth 23H5

11–3 (4 Tue); 6–11

Hope & Anchor
Market Place
✆4620
Home Bitter E
Old, stone-built pub with
small lounge dominated by
carved 17th-century
chimneypiece 🏮🍷🕕🍷🍴

Woolley Moor 23H5

11.30–3 (2.30 winter); 6 (7 winter)–11

White Horse
White Horse Lane (off B6014)
✆ Chesterfield 590319
**Draught Bass; M&B
Springfield Bitter** H
Friendly country inn, good
value meals; adventure
playground
Q🍷🕕🍷 (not Sun) 🍴👟

Youlgreave 23G5

10.30–3; 6.30–11

Bulls Head Hotel
Church Street (off A6)
✆ 307
**Marston Burton Bitter,
Pedigree** H
16th century coaching house,
in Peak District National Park
🍷📺🕕🍷🍴👟Å

Try also: **George** (Home)

Help keep real ale alive by
joining CAMRA. Your voice
helps encourage brewers big
and small to brew cask beer
and offer all beer drinkers a
better choice. Send £9 for a
year's membership or use the
form on page 319.

Appledore   3H2

11–2.30; 6–11

The Beaver
Irsha Street (off A39)
Flowers Original G
Waterfront pub with nautical
flavour ⚓ 🏠 🍴

Ashburton   4A6

11–2.30; 5–11

London Hotel
11 West Street ☎ 52478
Thompsons Aysheburton
Mild, Bitter, IPA H; Hills
Cider G
Old comfortable coaching
house; large but intimate bar
🏠 ⌂ 🍴

Try also: Exeter Inn

Axminster   4E5

10.30–2.30; 5.30–11

George Hotel
George Street (off A357)
☎ 32209
Draught Bass H
Well-appointed hotel bars in
town centre 🏠 ⌂ 🍴 ➤

Try also: Millwey (Palmers)

Axmouth   4E5

10.30–2.30; 5.30–11

Ship Inn
Church Street (B3172)
☎ Seaton 21838
John Devenish Bitter, Wessex
Best Bitter; Taunton Cider G
Seaside village pub with
excellent food 🏠 Q ⚓ ⌂ 🍴 ▲

Aylesbeare   4C5

11–2.30; 5.30–11

Halfway Inn
A3052/B3180 Crossroads
☎ Woodbury 32273
Devenish Wessex Best Bitter H
Popular crossroads pub,
varied food selection, unique
range of malt whiskies
⚓ ⌂ 🍴 ▲

Barnstaple   3J2

11–2.30; 5.30–11

Barnstaple Inn
Trinity Street
Courage Best Bitter H
Lively local near river ⌂ 🍴

Corner House
Boutport Street
Draught Bass H
Wood-panelled town centre
pub with old bottle collection.
Skittles Q 🏠 🍴

Beer   4D5

10.30–2.30; 6–11

Barrel o' Beer
Fore Street ☎ Seaton 20099
Draught Bass H; Taunton
Cider G
Busy one-bar pub catering for
all ages. Jumbo sausages

recommended, mind the
brook when you emerge!
⌂ 🍴 ▲

Try also: Anchor

Bideford   3H2

Portobello
Silver Street (A39) ☎ 2991
Courage Best Bitter; Taunton
Cider H
Corner house local, popular
with the young 🏠 ⚓ ⌂ 🍴 ▲

Blackawton   4B8

10.30–2.30; 5.30–10.30 (11 F, S & summer)

Normandy Arms
Off B3207 ☎ 316
Blackawton Best Bitter, 44,
Inde Coope Burton Ale H
Comfortable 15th century
village pub. Restaurant
🏠 ⚓ ⌂ 🍴 ▲

Branscombe   4D5

10.30–2.30; 6–10.30 (11 F, S & summer)

Three Horseshoes
Outside village A3052 ☎ 251
Draught Bass; Hall &
Woodhouse Badger Best
Bitter; Ind Coope Burton Ale;
Wadworth 6X, Old Timer;
Hills Cider H
Large and comfortable, with
good family facilities
🏠 Q 🏠 ⚓ ⌂ 🍴 ▲

Brixham   4C7

11–3; 5.30–11

Burton Hotel
23 Burton Street ☎ 2805
Courage Best Bitter,
Directors G
Small but very attractive
lounge bar, busy public
🏠 ⚓ ⌂ 🍴

Broadclyst   4C5

11–2.30; 5.30–11

Red Lion
(B3181) ☎ Exeter 61271
Draught Bass; Eldridge Pope
Royal Oak; Hancocks HB H
Attractive and picturesque
16th century inn

Broadhembury   4D4

10.30–2.30; 6–11

Drewe Arms
Off A373 ☎ 267
Draught Bass; Cotleigh Tawny
Bitter; Bulmer Cider G
Picturesque ancient thatched
pub 🏠 Q 🏠 ⚓ ⌂ 🍴 ▲

Burlescombe   4C3

10.30–3; 6 (6.30 winter)–10.30 (11 F, S & summer)

Ayshford Arms
☎ Greenham 672429
Cotleigh Tawny Bitter H
Occasional guest beers
Spacious and lively pub. Good
food 🏠 🏠 ⚓ ⌂ 🍴

Chagford   4A5

11–2.30; 6–11

Bullers Arms
Mill Street ☎ 2348
Greene King Abbot Ale;
Marston Pedigree; Usher Best
Bitter H Occasional guest
beers
Traditional unspoilt local
🏠 Q ⚓ 🏠 ⌂

Challacombe   4A2

11–2.30; 6–10.30 (11 F, S & summer)

Black Venus
(B3358) ☎ Parracombe 251
Flowers IPA G
Low-beamed country inn, in
the heart of Exmoor walking
country 🏠 Q ⚓ 🏠 ⌂ 🍴 ▲

Cheriton   4B4
Fitzpaine

11–2.30; 6.30–10.30

Half Moon
Flowers IPA H
Homely village pub with
comfortable lounge 🍴

Chittlehampton   3J2

10.30–2.30; 6–11

Bell
(Off B3227)
Hall & Woodhouse Badger
Best Bitter H
Stone-built; opposite ancient
ruined churchtower ⚓

Colaton   4D5
Raleigh

10.30–2.30; 6–10.30 (11 F, S)

Otter Inn
(A376) ☎ 68434
Usher Best Bitter, Founders
Ale H
Large-gardened roadside pub.
Spruce comfortable bars. Ideal
for summer family visits—
play area in garden 🏠 ⚓ ⌂ 🍴

Colyton   4E5

11–2.30; 6–11

Kingfisher
Dolphin Street ☎ 52476
Axe Vale Axe Bitter, Eldridge
Pope Royal Oak; Flowers IPA;
Hall & Woodhouse Badger
Best Bitter; Bulmers Cider H
Characteristic village pub.
Good tasty food. Unusual use
of wagon wheel for glass
storage 🏠 🏠 ⚓ ⌂ 🍴

Try also: Bear

Coombe in   4B6
Teignhead

11–2.30; 6.30–11

Wild Goose
☎ Newton Abbot 872241
Golden Hill Exmoor Ale; Mill
Brewery Janners Ale;
Wadworth 6X H Regular
guest beers
17th century old farm house
still retains its character, trad
jazz Monday nights 🏠 ⚓ ⌂ 🍴

Cornwood 3J6

10–2.30; 6–10.30 (11 Th, F, S summer)

Cornwood Inn
Near A38
Bates Bitter; Bishops Best
Bitter; Blackawton Squires;
Marston Pedigree; Palmer
IPA; Wadworth 6X Regular
guest beers
Well worth a visit. Weekend
organ music ✿ ☾ ⚌♪

Croyde 3H1

10.30–2.30; 6–11

Thatched Barn Inn
Off A361 ☎ 890349
Courage Best Bitter,
Directors Ⓗ
Beautiful 15th century inn,
seafood a speciality
⊞▦☾➔♣& Å

Cullompton 4C4

11–2.30; 5–11

Manor House
Fore Street ☎ 32281
Flowers Original Ⓗ
16th century town centre
hotel ⊞✿▦☾➔♣&

Try also: Pony & Trap

Culmstock 4D4

11–2.30; 5 (7 winter)–11

Illminster Stage
Near B3391
☎ Craddock 40872
Cotleigh Tawny Bitter Ⓗ
Welcoming and sociable
village pub ▦✿☾➔♣&

Dartmouth 4B8

10.30–2.30; 5.30–11

Floating Bridge
Sand Quay ☎ 2354
Usher Best Bitter, Founders
Ale; Bulmers Cider Ⓗ
Old fashioned pub by the river,
near Higher Ferry ⊞✿☾➔♣&

Dawlish 4C6

11–2.30; 5–11

Prince Albert
28 The Strand ☎ 862132
Draught Bass Ⓔ Flowers
IPA Ⓗ
Cosy and convivial; also
known as the "Hole in the
Wall" Q☾⇄

Dittisham 4A8

10.30–2.30; 6–11

Red Lion
☎ 235
Courage Best Bitter; Usher
Best Bitter, Founders Ale Ⓗ;
Hills Cider Ⓖ
Popular pub near the River
Dart ▦⊞✿☾➔ Å

Doddiscombsleigh 4B5

11–2.30; 6–11

Nobody Inn

☎ Christow 52394
Draught Bass; Bates Bitter Ⓖ
Hall and Woodhouse Badger
Best Bitter Ⓗ Occasional guest
beers
Renowned 16th century inn.
Excellent range of wines; over
120 whiskies ▦Q✿⚌☾➔♣

Drewsteignton 4A5

10.30–2.30; 6–10.30

Drewe Arms
Flowers IPA; Bulmers Cider Ⓖ
Original unspoilt village pub
with longest-serving landlady
in the country ▦Q⚌

Ermington 3J7

11–2.30; 6–10.30 (11 F, S & summer)

First & Last
B3210 ☎ Modbury 830671
Usher Best Bitter, Founders
Ale (summer) Ⓗ
Cosy country pub
▦⊞✿☾➔♣& Å

Exeter 4B5

11.2.30; 5.30–10.30 (11 F, S & summer)

Double Locks
Canal Banks, Marsh Barton
OS933900 ☎ 56947
Eldridge Pope Royal Oak,
Golden Hill Exmoor Ale;
Marston Pedigree; Wadworth
6X, Old Timer; Hills Cider Ⓖ
Regular guest beers
Lively canalside pub with
huge garden. Excellent value
bar meals ▦⊞✿☾➔♣& Å

Duke of York
Sidwell Street ☎ 56515
Draught Bass; Bates Bitter;
Flowers IPA, Original; Hall &
Woodhouse Tanglefoot;
Wadworth 6X Ⓗ
Popular refurbished pub near
cinema ☾➔♣⇄

Great Western Hotel
St Davids Approach
Draught Bass Ⓗ
Busy hotel, 2 comfortable
bars, railway paraphernalia
⊞▦☾➔⇄

Mill on the Exe
Bonhay Road ☎ 214464
Evenings opens 5 pm
(summer) 7 pm (winter)
Ind Coope Burton Ale; Halls
Harvest Bitter Ⓗ
Large roadside pub-cum-
restaurant, overlooking the
River Exe ▦Q✿☾➔⇄

Poltimore Arms
Pinhoe (B3181) ☎ 67517
John Devenish Bitter, Wessex
Best Bitter Ⓗ
Lively local on outskirts of city
⊞✿✔▦

Well House
Cathedral Yard ☎ 58464
Evenings opens 5 pm
Bishops Best Bitter; Flowers
IPA Ⓗ
On site of old city well. Good
value food Q▦☾⇄

Exmouth 4C6

10.30–2.30; 5.30–10.30 (11 F, S summer)

Beach
Victoria Road
Draught Bass; Eldridge Pope
Royal Oak Ⓗ
Two-bar locals' pub near
harbour ☾➔♣

Royal Oak
31 Exeter Road
John Devenish Bitter, Wessex
Best Bitter; Taunton Cider Ⓗ
Friendly and traditional local
near town centre
☾ (not Sun) ➔♣⇄

Feniton 4D4

11–2.30; 6–11

Nog Inn
Ottery Road
☎ Honiton 850210
Axe Vale Axe Bitter,
Battleaxe; Draught Bass;
Cotleigh Tawny; Hancocks
HB; Taunton Dry Cider Ⓗ & Ⓖ
Occasional guest beers
Friendly village local with
squash court, ballroom and
cat ▦⊞▦✔♣⇄

Georgeham 3H1

10.30–2.30; 6–11

Rock Inn
Off B3231
Usher Best Bitter; West
Country Cider Ⓗ
Food, beer and welcome
immaculate in this ancient
free house ▦Q⊞✿☾➔

Great Torrington

11–2.30; 6–11

Black Horse Inn
The Square
Usher Founders Ale Ⓗ
Bar of an ancient coaching
inn in town centre ▦☾➔

Hartland 3G2

10.30–2.30; 6.30–11 (late licence F, S)

Anchor
Fore Street ☎ 414
Usher Best Bitter, Founders
Ale Ⓗ
Modernised friendly local
⊞▦☾➔♣

Hatherleigh 3J4

10.30–2.30; 6–11

George Hotel
Square
☎ Okehampton 810454
Opens lunch Mon 10–4;
Tue 10–5
Bass; Courage Best, Devenish
Cornish Best Bitter Ⓗ, St
Austell HSD; Inch's Cider Ⓖ
14th century historic hotel
with four-poster beds. 3 bars
including very traditional
Market bar ▦Q⊞✿▦☾➔♣&

Try also: Tally Ho (free)

Haytor Vale 4B6

11–2.30; 6–11
Rock Inn
✆ 208
Draught Bass, Eldridge Pope
Dorchester Bitter, IPA, Royal
Oak Ⓗ
Superb old Dartmoor village
inn, large lounge, tiny public
bar ⌂ ⌘ ⌾ Ⓖ ⏃ ⏁

Heathfield 4B6

11–2.30; 5.30–11
Sportsmans
Draught Bass; St Austell
HSD Ⓗ
Old ale and cider house
reopened after 60 years. Set in
nine acres ⌂ Q Ⓖ ⏁

Hemerdon 3J7

11–2.30; 6–10.30 (11 F, S & summer)
Miners Arms
Near A38
✆ Plymouth 343252
Bass Ⓗ & Ⓖ Countryman
Cider Ⓖ
Former tin miners pub with
dartboard ⌂ Q ⌾ ⏃

Holbeton 4C7

11–2.30; 6–10.30 (11 F, S & summer)
Mildmay Colours
Off A379 ✆ 248
Bass Draught Bitter;
Blackawton Bitter; Ind Coope
Burton Ale; Usher Best Bitter
Occasional guest beers
Good value carvery; pets and
swing in garden ⌂ ⌾ ⏁ ⏃

Honiton 4D5

11–2.30; 6–11
White Lion
High Street
John Devenish Bitter; Wessex
Best Bitter Ⓗ
Friendly local with active pub
games teams
⌂ ⌾ Ⓖ (not Sun) ⏃

Try also: Angel & Volunteer

Horndon 3H6

11.30–2.30; 6.30–10.30 (11 F, S & summer)
Elephants Nest
Near A386
✆ Mary Tavy 273
Palmer IPA Ⓗ St Austell
Tinners Bitter, HSD, Usher
Best Bitter, Founders Ale
Occasional guest beers
Traditional Dartmoor pub.
Caters for healthy moorland
appetites ⌂ Q ⌾ Ⓖ ⏁ (not Thu)

Horns Cross 2G2

Coach & Horses
A39
Devenish Wessex Best Bitter Ⓗ
Small friendly pub handy for
Parracombe ⌂ Q Ⓗ Ⓖ ⏁

Try also: Hoops Inn

Horrabridge 3H6

11–2.30; 6–10.30 (11 F, S)
Leaping Salmon
Whitchurch Road off A386
✆ Yelverton 852939
Courage Best Bitter,
Directors Ⓗ
Popular with fishing
fraternity. Garden unsuitable
for young children ⌂ Q ⌾ Ⓖ ⏁

Try also: Rock Inn

Horsebridge 3H5

12–2.30; 7–10.30 (11 F, S)
Royal Inn
Near A384
Eldridge Pope Royal Oak;
Flowers IPA; Horsebridge
Tamar Ale, Best Bitter,
Heller Ⓗ; Countryman Cider
Occasional guest beers
Home-brew country pub by
ancient bridge ⌂ ⌾ Ⓖ ⏁ ⏃ ⏀

Ide 4B5

11–2.30; 5.30–11
Huntsman
High Street (off A30)
John Devenish Bitter, Wessex
Best Bitter Ⓗ; Taunton Cider Ⓖ
Ancient thatched village pub,
longest sign in Devon
⌂ Q ⌾ Ⓖ ⏁

Ilfracombe 3H1

11–2.30; 5–11
**Wellington Arms
Hotel**
High Street (A361) ✆ 62206
Courage Best Bitter Ⓗ
Beamed town pub with Iron
Duke theme ⌘ ⌾ Ⓖ ⏁ ⏃

Kennford 4B5

11–2.30; 6.30–11
Anchor
A38 ✆ Exeter 832344
Courage Best Bitter,
Directors Ⓗ
Large "Brewers Tudor" style
roadhouse. Good range of bar
meals ⌾ Ⓖ ⏁ ⏃ ⏀

Kilmington 4E5

10.30–2.30; 5.30–11
New Inn
The Hill (off A35)
✆ Axminster 33376
Palmer BB, IPA Ⓖ
Attractive thatched village
pub ⌂ ⌘ ⌾ Ⓖ ⏁ ⏃

Kingsbridge 4A8

10.30–2.30; 5.30–10.30 (11 F, S & summer)
Hermitage Bar
8 Mill Street ✆ 3234
Draught Bass, Flowers IPA;
Bulmers Cider Ⓗ
Smart town pub with unique
carved woodwork
⌘ Ⓖ ⏁ (summer)

Kingsteignton 4B6

11–2.30; 6–11

Old Rydon

Rydon Lane
✆ Newton Abbot 4626
Draught Bass; Mill Brewery
Devon Special; Wadworth
6X Ⓗ Occasional guest beers
Very old pub, small bar with
cosy corners and upstairs
drinking area. Good food
⌂ Q ⌾ Ⓖ ⏁

Kingswear 4B8

11–2.30; 6–11
Steam Packet Inn
✆ 208
Courage Best Bitter,
Directors Ⓗ Occasional guest
beers
Small friendly local with good
views over the river Dart.
Food available summer only
⌂ Ⓖ ⏁

Knowle 4C6

11–2.30; 7–11 (closed Sun/Mon)
**Tidwell House
Country Hotel**
(B3178) OS059834
✆ Budleigh Salterton 2444
Cotleigh Tawny Bitter,
Devenish Wessex Best
Bitter Ⓗ; Hills Cider Ⓖ
Family-run country hotel, bar
in old cellar, specialising in
home cooked meals Q ⌾ ⌘ ⏁

Lapford 4A4

11.30–2.30; 6–11
Yeo Vale
A377 ✆ 452
Hall & Woodhouse Badger
Best Bitter; Usher Best Bitter Ⓗ
Pleasant main road pub with
restaurant ⌘ ⌾ Ⓖ ⏁ ⏀ ⏃ ⏂

Luton 4B6

10.30–2.30; 6–11
Elizabethan Inn
Off A380 ✆ Teignmouth 5425
John Devenish Bitter, Wessex
Best Bitter; Flowers IPA Ⓗ
Occasional guest beers
400 years old; small public
bar, low ceilings, larger wood
panelled lounge ⌂ ⌘ ⌾ Ⓖ ⏁ ⏃ ⏀

Lympstone 4C6

11–2.30; 6.30–11
Redwing
Church Road (off A376)
✆ Exmouth 271656
Devenish Wessex; Flowers
IPA, Original Ⓗ
Friendly village local with
aviary at rear in pretty
riverside village
Q ⌘ ⌾ Ⓖ ⏁ ⏃ ⏀ ⏂ ⏂

Marlborough 4A8

11–2.30; 5.30–10.30 (11 F, S & summer)
Royal Oak
Off A381
✆ Kingsbridge 561481
Courage Best Bitter, Directors
(summer) Ⓗ

Traditional, old-fashioned pub, regular folk-nights Weds ⊞✿🏠🕭🔥🍴🍺🍷

Mary Tavy 3H5

11–2.30; 6–10.30 (11 F, S & summer)
Royal Standard
(A386)
Palmer IPA; St Austell HSD ⊞
Pleasant one-bar village pub
🏠🕭🍴

Mary Tavy Inn
St Austell HSD; Usher Best Bitter ⊞
Inglenook fireplace in lounge bar; dining room 🏠🍴🕭🍴🍺

Merrivale 3J5

11–2.30; 6–10.30 (11 F, S)
Dartmoor Inn
B3357 ☎ Princetown 340
Courage Best Bitter, Directors; Wadworth 6X ⊞; Countryman Cider ⊡
Typical Dartmoor pub
🏠Q🍴🕭🍴🍺

Milton Combe 3M6

11–2.30; 6–10.30 (11 F, S)
Who'd of Thought It
(Near A386)
☎ Yelverton 853313
Eldridge Pope Royal Oak; Golden Hill Exmoor Ale; Palmer IPA; Wadworth 6X; Bulmers Cider ⊞
16th century village pub, folk singing Sunday nights
🏠Q🍴🕭🍴

Newton Abbot 4B6

11–2.30; 5–11
Devon Arms
67 East Street ☎ 68725
Bates Bitter; Wadworth 6X ⊞
Occasional guest beers
Old but modernised, busy and lively 🍴🕭🍴🚆

Two Mile Oak
Totnes Road, Abbotskerswell (A381) ☎ Ipplepen 812411
Evenings opens 6 pm
Draught Bass ⊞; Eldridge Pope Royal Oak ⊡; Flowers IPA ⊞
15th century coaching house. Very little changed over the centuries 🏠⊞🍴🕭🍴🍺

Newton St Cyres 4B5

11.30–2.30; 6–11
Beer Engine
Sweetham (off A377) ☎ 282
Beer Engine Rail Ale, Piston Bitter, Sleeper Strong Ale ⊞
Popular pub-brewery next to railway station, 20p off 1st pint on production of valid train ticket 🏠Q⊞🍴🕭🍴🚆

Ottery St Mary 4D5

10.30–2.30; 5.30–11
Volunteer

Broad Street, Town Square
☎ 2445
John Devenish Bitter, Wessex Best Bitter ⊡
16th century posting house. Small homely lounge, larger public bar. Excellent food. Visit it Nov. 5th at your peril!
🍴🕭🍴🍺

Parkham 3H3

12–2.30; 6.30–11 (winter hours vary)
Bell
(Off A39) ☎ Horns Cross 201
Draught Bass; Flowers IPA, Original ⊞
Delightful thatched inn 🍴🕭🍴

Paignton 4B7

11–3; 5–30–11
Parkers Arms
343 Totnes Road (A385)
☎ 551011
Plympton Best, Plympton Pride ⊞
Smart, large local pub
⊞ (summer) 🍴🕭🍴🍺🍴

Parracombe 4A2

10.30–2.30; 6–11
Hunters Inn
Heddons Mouth (off A39) ☎ 230
Draught Bass; Flowers IPA Original, Golden Hill Exmoor Bitter; Samuel Whitbread Strong Ale ⊞; Local Cider ⊡
Surprisingly large but nonetheless charming pub. Surroundings reflected in high prices ⊞🍴🕭🍴🍴

Pennymoor 4B4

12–2.30; 6.30–11
Cruwys Arms
☎ Cheriton Fitzpaine 347
Draught Bass; Bishops Best Bitter ⊞
Unspoilt country pub with splendid open fire 🏠⊞🍴🕭🍴🍴

Plymouth 3H7

10–2.30; 6–10.30 (11 Th, F, S & summer)
Archer Inn
Archer Terrace (off North Road West)
Opens 11 am
Draught Bass ⊡
Friendly city centre local
🍴🕭🚆

The Bank
Lockyer Street
Plympton Best Bitter, Plympton Pride ⊞
Spacious city centre pub

Complex
Keyham Road Devonport (opp Albert Gate RN base)
☎ 560293
Courage Best Bitter, Directors; Cotleigh Tawny Bitter; Goldenhill Exmoor Ale; Marston Pedigree; St Austell HSD ⊞ Regular guest beers
Lively pub 🕭🍴🍴

Ferry House
888 Wolseley Road, Saltash Passage St Budeaux
☎ 361659
Opens 11 & 6
Courage Best Bitter ⊞
Fine views of Brunels railway bridge and river ⊞🍴

Kings Head
Bretonside
Courage Best Bitter, Directors ⊞
Next to main bus and coach station 🕭🍴

Minerva
Looe Street
Courage Best Bitter ⊡
Oldest pub in Plymouth between town centre and Barbican 🍴

Pennycomequick
Alma Road
Plympton Best Bitter, Plympton Pride ⊞
Popular pub between central park and city centre 🍴🕭🍴🍴🚆

Pym Arms
16, Pym Street, Devonport (behind Aggie Westons)
Opens 11 am
Eldridge Pope Royal Oak, St Austell HSD; Ushers Best Bitter; Wadworth 6X ⊡
Regular guest beers
Basic one-bar pub. Where young clientele create brash & breezy atmosphere
🍴🚆 (Devonport Albert Road)

Royal Adelaide Arms
9 Adelaide Street, Stonehouse
☎ 665348
Opens 12 noon and 7 pm
Golden Hill Exmoor Ale; Wadworth 6X ⊞
Civilised oasis twixt Union Street and RN hospital, handy for cross channel port ⊞

Royal Oak
Hooe
Opens 11 & 7
Courage Best Bitter, Directors ⊞
Comfortable pub by river. No car park 🕭🍴

Seven Stars
Seven Stars Lane, Tamerton Foliot
Opens 11
Courage Best Bitter, Directors ⊞
Rambling low-ceiling pub
🏠Q⊞🍴🕭🍴🍴

Shipwrights Arms
Sutton Road, Coxside
Courage Best Bitter, Directors ⊞
Comfortable pub near city centre 🏠🍴

Stopford Arms
172 Devonport Road, Stoke
Opens 10.30
Courage Best Bitter, Directors ⊞

Sets the best of CAMRA standards in quality and price which others find hard to match. Popular, small bars 🍴🎵🎧 (Devonport Albert Road)

Three Crowns
The Barbican
Courage Best Bitter Ⓗ, **Directors**
Busy, good value pub on the Barbican 🍴🕔🍺🎵

Thistle Park Tavern
Sutton Road, Coxside
Opens 12 noon (Mon, Tue, Wed); 11.30 (Th and Sat)
Eldridge Pope Royal Oak; Marston Owd Rodger; St Austell HSD; Usher Best Bitter; Wadworth 6X Ⓗ **Regular guest beers**
Basic pub near commercial port 🍴🍺

Swan Inn
Cornwall Beach, Cornwall Street, Devonport
Opens 11 am
Bates Bitter; Courage Best Bitter, Directors; St Austell HSD; Wadworth 6X Ⓗ **Regular guest beers**
Plymouth's oldest real ale pub, folk music and jazz 🍴

Try also: Royal Albert Bridge Inn; Kings (Courage)

Plymtree   4C4

Blacksmith's Arms
Plymtree, Nr Cullompton
OS053028ℰ 322
Opens 11 & 7 (May vary according to season)
Golden Hill Exmoor Ale Ⓗ; **Wadworth 6X, Old Timer** Ⓖ
Cosy country pub. Heavy horse in beer garden occasionally. Best value pub in East Devon 🍴Q
🍺🎧🕔🎵 (booking advisable) ♿

Poundsgate   4A6
11–2.30; 6–11

Tavistock Inn
(A384)ℰ 251
Courage Best Bitter Ⓗ; **Taunton Cider** Ⓖ
Very old traditional granite moorland pub 🍴🍺🎧🕔🎵

Princetown   3J6
11–2.30; 6–10.30 (11 F, S)

Prince of Wales
Tavistock Road B3357 ℰ 219
Flowers Original; Wadworth 6X Ⓗ; **Inches Cider**
Unspoilt pub on Dartmoor 🍴Q🎧🍺🕔

Try also: Plume of Feathers

Putts Corner   4D5
12–2.30; 7–11

Hare & Hounds
A375 ℰ Honiton 41760
Axe Vale Battleaxe; Courage

Directors; Flowers Original; Gibbs Mew Premium Bitter; Hardington Best Bitter; Marston Pedigree
Regular guest beers
Comfortable, low-beamed rural decor. Children's play area and pets corner. Beers rather expensive 🍴Q🎧🍺🕔♿⛺

Rockbeare   4C5

Bidgood Arms
A30 ℰ Whimple 822262
Flowers IPA; Samuel Whitbread Strong Ale; Bulmer Cider Ⓗ
Lively roadside local. Salad bar and other good food in lounge
🍴 (summer) 🎧🍺🕔🎵⛺

Try also: Jack in the Green (Bass)

Salcombe   4A8
10.30–2.30; 5.30–11

Victoria Inn
Fore Street ℰ 2604
Draught Bass; Hills Cider Ⓖ
Old yachting pub; basic bar, comfortable lounge
🎧🍺🎧🕔🎵

Shaldon   4C6
11–2.30; 5–11

Ferry Boat
ℰ 872340
Courage Best Bitter, Directors Ⓗ
One-bar pub with beer garden right on estuary beach 🎧🕔🎵

Sheepwash   3H3
11–2.30; 6–11

Half Moon Inn
Draught Bass; Courage Best Bitter Ⓗ
Friendly village hotel with genial host 🍴Q🎧🎧🕔♿

Sidford   4D5
10.30–2.30; 5.30–11

Blue Ball
A3052 ℰ Sidmouth 4062
John Devenish Bitter, Wessex Best Bitter Ⓗ; **Taunton Cider** Ⓖ
Flagstone-floored public bar, inglenook fireplace, cosy lounge. Order ploughmans lunch only if ravenous! Summer weekend barbecues
🍴Q🎧🎧🍺🕔🎵

Sidmouth   4D5
10.30–2.30; 5.30–11

Balfour Arms
Woolbrook ℰ 3742
John Devenish Bitter, Wessex Best Bitter Ⓗ
Well-appointed, large yet snug, lounge. Busy public. Pub games much in evidence 🎧🕔🎵

Silverton   4C4
11–2.30; 6–11

Three Tuns
ℰ Exeter 860352
Barrons Exe Valley; Draught Bass, Eldridge Pope Dorchester Bitter; Wadworth 6X Ⓗ **Occasional guest beers**
Well kept free house, bottle collection 🍴🎧🕔🎵

Slapton   4B8
11.30–2.30; 6–11

Tower Inn
ℰ Kingsbridge 580216
Blackawton Bitter; Gibbs Mew Bishops Tipple; Golden Hill Exmoor Ale; Palmer IPA; Wadworth 6X; Hills Cider Ⓗ
Regular guest beers
Very attractive 14th century free house. Two childrens rooms, large selection of bottle conditioned beers
🍴🎧🎧🍺🕔🎵🍴⛺

South Brent   4A7
11–2.30; 6–11

Royal Oak
Station Road ℰ 2133
Draught Bass; Hall & Woodhouse Badger Best Bitter; Halls Harvest Bitter; Hills Cider Ⓗ
Large old-fashioned village local, skittle alley by appointment 🍴🍺🕔🎵

South Molton   4A3
11–2.30; 5.30–10.30 (11 F, S & summer)

Goose & Gander Hotel
Usher Best Bitter
Comfortable hotel bar 🛏🍺🕔🎵

South Zeal   3J4

Oxenham Arms
Off A30, near Sticklepath
Everards Bitter Ⓖ
12th century rambling ex-monastery in old mining village on edge of Dartmoor 🍴Q🛏🕔

Starcross   4C6
11–2.30; 5.30–11

Alexandra Inn
The Strand (A379) ℰ 890312
Bates Bitter; Mill Brewery Janners Ale Ⓗ; **Hills Cider; Inches Cider** Ⓗ
Cosy friendly one bar pub with pool and darts; good cooking. Midnight lodge (annex) open till 12 pm 🍴🎧🍺🕔🎵♿⛺🎧

Sticklepath   3J4
10.30–2.30; 6–11

Devonshire Inn
A30 ℰ 626
Courage Best Bitter; Usher Best Bitter Ⓗ; **Grays Cider** Ⓖ
Friendly family run local on edge of Dartmoor 🛏🎧🍺🕔🎵

Teignmouth   4C6
11–2.30; 5–11

Teign Brewery Inn

Teign Street *☎* 2684
**Courage Best Bitter,
Directors** Ⓗ
Small and cosy lounge, busy
public bar near docks 🅿Ⓖ♿♨🚲

Try also: Kings Arms

Tiverton 4C4

11–2.30; 5–11
Four in Hand
Fore Street *☎* 252765
Draught Bass Ⓗ
Busy bar near cinema and bus
station Ⓖ

Racehorse
Wellbrook Street *☎* 252606
**Usher PA, Best Bitter; Bulmers
Cider** Ⓗ
Popular recently modernised
local 🏚🅿Ⓖ♨

Try also: White Ball Bridge
Street

Topsham 4C5

11–2.30; 5–10.30 (11 F, S)
Globe
Fore Street *☎* 3879
Draught Bass; Hancocks HB Ⓗ
Occasional guest beers
Cheerful 16th century local.
Home of Topsham R.F.C
🏚🅿Ⓖ♨🚲

Try also: Bridge Inn and Kings
Head

Torbryan 4B7

11–2.30; 5.30–11
Church House Inn
☎ Ipplepen 812372
**Bates Bitter; Cotleigh Old
Buzzard, Gibbs Mew Bishops
Tipple; Mill Brewery Devon
Special; Palmer Tally Ho;
Theakston Old Peculier
Regular guest beers**

Superb example of an old,
large village inn 🏚🅿🌳🅿Ⓖ♨♨

Torquay 4B7

11–3; 5.30–11
Crown & Sceptre
2 Petitor Road St Marychurch
☎ 38290
**Courage Best Bitter,
Directors** Ⓗ
200-year old popular local.
Folk oriented, Cockney
humour abounds
🏚🅿🌳Ⓖ♨♨♿

Clarence Hotel
Newton Road, Torre *☎* 24417
**Halls Harvest Bitter; Ind
Coope Burton Ale** Ⓗ
Large pub on main route into
Torquay 🅿Ⓖ♨♨🚲 (Torre)

**Saxon Bar,
Courtlands Hotel**
Rawlyn Road, Chelston
Evenings opens 6
Draught Bass Ⓗ
Comfortable hotel bar
🌳🅿🅿Ⓖ♨

Totnes 4B7

10.30–2.30; 5.30–11
Bay Horse
8 Cistern Street *☎* 862088
Courage Best Bitter Ⓗ
Small, very old pub at the top
of the town with a tame ghost!
🏚🅿🅿Ⓖ♨♨

Trusham 4B6

11.30–2.30; 6 (winter 7)–11
Cridford Inn
☎ Chudleigh 853694
**Bates Blaster; Cotleigh Old
Buzzard; Golden Hill Exmoor
Ale** Ⓖ **Regular guest beers**
Originally an old barn,

became a pub in 1983, good
bottled beers 🏚🅿🌳Ⓖ♨

Upottery 4D4

11–2.30; 6.30–11 (summer) 12.2; 7–11 (winter)
Sidmouth Arms
☎ 252
Flowers IPA, Original Ⓗ
Recently discovered inglenook
fireplace 🏚Q🅿Ⓖ♨♨♿

Ugborough 4A7

10–2.30; 5–10.30 (11 F, S)
Anchor Inn
1 Lutterburn Street (near
B3210) *☎* Plymouth 892283
Opens 11 & 6
**Draught Bass; Wadworth
6X** Ⓖ
Good village pub 🏚Q Ⓖ♨♨

Ship Inn
Near B3210
☎ Plymouth 892565
Opens 11 & 6
Draught Bass; Hancocks HB Ⓗ
New old pub 🏚🅿Ⓖ♨♨

Westcott 4C4

11–2.30; 5–11
Merry Harriers
B3181
**Usher Best Bitter; Founders
Ale** Ⓗ
Friendly local 🏚🅿Ⓖ♨♨

Westleigh 3H2

11–2.30; 6.30–11 (summer) 11.30–2; 6–10.30
(winter)
Westleigh Inn
Off A39 *☎* Instow 860867
**Usher Best Bitter, Founders
Ale (summer)** Ⓗ
16th century pub, as pretty as
the village it stands in
🌳🅿Ⓖ♨♿⚓

"WE'VE DECIDED TO IMPROVE THE PUB"

United Breweries Ltd

Askerswell 5F5

10–2.30; 6–11

Spyway Inn
Off A35 OS528934
✆ Powerstock 250
**Poole Dolphin Bitter, Usher
PA, Best Bitter, Founders Ale;
Bulmers Cider** 🅗
Very popular pub with lovely
views and good children's
room ♨ Q 🚻 🏵 🕭 ❤ 🍴 ♿

Birdsmoorgate 5E5

10–2.30; 6–11

Rose & Crown
B3165 OS391009
✆ Hawkchurch 527
**Wadworth 6X; Taunton
Cider** 🅗 & 🅖 Regular guest
beers
Isolated pub in beautiful
surroundings ♨ 🚻 🏵 🕭 ❤ 🍴 ♿ ▲

Blandford Forum 5J4

10.30–2.30; 6–10.30 (11 F, S & summer)

Wheatsheaf
6, Albert Street (off A354)
**Hall & Woodhouse Hectors
Bitter, Badger Best Bitter** 🅗
Friendly old beamed
backstreet pub ♨ 🏵 🕭 ♿

Try also: Stour Inn (Hall &
Woodhouse)

Bournemouth 6B7

10.30–2.30; 5.30–10.30 (11 F, S & summer

Brunswick Hotel
199 Malmesbury Park Road
(off B3063) ✆ 20197
**Flowers Original, Whitbread
Strong Country Bitter;** 🅗
Friendly backstreet local. Folk
music alternate Suns ♨ 🕭 🍴

Cricketers Arms
Windham Road,
Springbourne (near A338)
✆ 21589
Lunchtime opens 11.30 am
**Flowers Original; Whitbread
Strong Country Bitter** 🅗
Occasional guest beers
Victorian pub of character
🏵 🍴 ≹

**Criterion (Victoria
Bar)**
Old Christchurch Road
✆ 20070
Draught Bass 🅗
Victorian town centre lounge.
Parking difficult

Old Thumper
113, Poole Road, Westbourne
✆ 768586
**Ringwood Best Bitter,
Fortyniner, Old Thumper, 4X
(winter); Wadworth 6X** 🅗
Occasional guest beers
Cosy cosmopolitan one bar
pub with Liverpudlian
landlord 🕭 ❤ (by
appt.) ≹ (Branksome)

Bridport 5F5

10–2.30; 6–11

Bull Hotel
West Street (A35) ✆ 22878
**Bass Draught; Eldridge Pope
Royal Oak; Hall &
Woodhouse Badger Best
Bitter** 🅗
Comfortable coaching inn in
centre of town ♨ Q 🚻 🏵 🕭 ❤

Crown Inn
West Bay Road (B3157)
✆ 22037
Palmer BB, IPA 🅗
Popular pub on outskirts of
town 🚻 🏵 🕭 ❤ ▲

Burton Bradstock 5F5

10.30 (11 winter)–2.30; 6–11

Anchor
High Street ✆ 897228
**Courage Best Bitter,
Directors** 🅗 **Coates Cider** 🅖
Popular village local, built
1560, emphasis on darts
🚻 🕭 ❤ 🍴 ❤

Cattistock 5G5

11–2.30; 7.11

Fox & Hounds
OS593997
✆ Maiden Newton 20444
**John Devenish Bitter, Wessex
Best Bitter; Taunton Cider** 🅗
Friendly local opposite church
♨ 🚻 🏵 🕭 ❤ ▲

Cerne Abbas 5G5

10.30–2.30; 6–11

Red Lion
Long Street ✆ 441
Wadworth IPA, 6X 🅗 Regular
guest beers
Spacious village pub with
superb leaded windows
♨ 🏵 🕭 ❤ ▲

Charminster 5G5

11–2.30; 7–11

New Inn
(A352) ✆ Dorchester 64694
Draught Bass 🅗 **Taunton
Cider** 🅖
Smart and popular locals pub
with large garden 🏵 🕭 ❤

Charmouth 5E5

11–2.30; 6–11

Coach & Horses
The Street (A35) ✆ 60321
Palmer BB, IPA 🅗; **Coates
Cider** 🅖
Large Victorian pub on main
road ♨ Q 🚻 🏵 🕭 ❤ 🍴 ♿

Chickerell 5G6

11–2.30; 6.30–11

Fishermans Arms
Lower Putton Lane (off
B3157) OS651805
✆ Weymouth 785136
Devenish Wessex Best Bitter 🅖

Friendly local off beaten track.
Restaurant ♨ Q 🚻 🏵 🕭 ❤ ♿

Child Okeford 5H4

11–2.30; 6.30–11

Union Arms
Station Road (off A357)
✆ 860540
**Hall & Woodhouse Hectors
Bitter** 🅗 Occasional guest
beers
One-bar country local ♨ Q 🏵 🍴

Christchurch 6B7

10.30–2.30; 6–10.30 (11 F, S & summer)

Castle Tavern
7 Church Street ✆ 485199
**Draught Bass; Ringwood Best
Bitter, Fortyniner, Old
Thumper** 🅗 Regular guest
beers
Popular lounge bar near
church. Parking difficult
🕭 ❤ ≹

Corfe Mullen 6A7

11–2.30; 6.30–10.30 (11 F, S & summer)

Coventry Arms
(A31) ✆ Sturminster Marshall
857284
**John Devenish Bitter, Wessex
Best Bitter** 🅖
Interesting old low beamed
two-bar pub; good food
♨ Q 🏵 🕭 ❤ 🍴 ▲

Dorchester 5G5

10–2.30; 6–11

Kings Arms
High East Street (A35)
✆ 65353
**John Devenish Bitter, Wessex
Best Bitter** 🅗
Big old coaching inn featured
in 'Mayor of Casterbridge'
♨ Q 🚻 🕭 ❤ 🍴 ♿ ≹

White Hart
London Road (A35) ✆ 63545
11–2.30; 6 (7 winter)–11
**Hall & Woodhouse Badger
Best Bitter, Tanglefoot
(summer)** 🅗
Friendly hotel on way out of
town
♨ 🏵 🕭 ❤ (summer) 🍴 ♿ ≹

East Knighton 5H5

11–2.30; 6–11

Rising Sun
(off A352)
✆ Warmwell 852980
**John Devenish Bitter, Wessex
Best Bitter** 🅗 **Taunton Cider** 🅗
Warm and friendly place
down a track
♨ Q 🚻 🏵 🕭 ❤ 🍴 ♿ ▲

East Lulworth 5H6

11–2.30; 6–10.30 (11 F, S & summer)

Weld Arms
(B3070) ✆ West Lulworth 211
**John Devenish Bitter, Wessex
Best Bitter** 🅗
Picturesque pub in tourist
area ♨ Q 🚻 🏵 🕭 ❤ 🍴 ♿ ▲

Evershot 5G4

11–2.30; 7–11

Acorn
(off A37) ✆ 228
Palmer IPA; Wadworth 6X;
Burrow Hill Cider Ⓗ Regular
guest beers
Attractive popular small hotel
with four-poster beds
🏠🅿🏨🌲❄🛏

Gillingham 5H3

10.30–2.30; 6.30–11

Phoenix
High Street ✆ 2120
Hall & Woodhouse Badger
Best Bitter Ⓗ
Smart pub in town centre
🌲🍴➤≷

Highcliffe 6B7

10.30–2.30; 6–10.30 (11 F, S & summer)

Globe
266 Lymington Road (A337)
✆ 71360
Flowers Original; Whitbread
Strong Country Bitter Ⓗ
Old coaching inn on main
road 🏨🌲🍴🐕

Horton 6A6

11–2.30; 6–10.30 (11 F, S & summer)

Horton Inn
B3078 OS017086
✆ Witchampton 840252
Ind Coope Burton Ale; Poole
Dolphin Bitter; Wadworth
6X Ⓗ Regular guest beers
A fine country inn, relaxing
atmosphere 🏠Q🏨🅿🌲🍴

Kings Stag 5H4

11–2.30; 6.30–11

Green Man
(B3143) OS724105
✆ Hazelbury Bryan 338
Draught Bass Ⓖ; Goldenhill
Exmoor Ale; Wadworth 6X Ⓗ
Comfortable country pub;
good food and skittle alley
🏠Q🍴🌲🍴

Langton Matravers 5J6

10.30–2.30; 6.30–11

Kings Arms
(B3069) ✆ Swanage 422979
Flowers Original; Whitbread
Strong Country Bitter; Ⓗ
Bulmers Cider Ⓖ
Excellent village local built in
Purbeck style with many
small interconnecting rooms
🏠Q🏨🌲🍴🍺🛏

Try also: Ship (Whitbread)

Laymore 5F4

10.30–2.30; 6–11

Squirrel Inn
Near Thorncombe B3162
OS387048 ✆ Winsham 298
Axe Vale Battle Axe; Hall &
Woodhouse Badger Best

Bitter; Usher Founders Ale;
Vickerys Farmhouse Cider Ⓖ
Regular guest beers
Pleasant country pub
🏠Q🏨🌲🍴🌲🛏

Litton Cheney 5G5

10.30–2.30; 6–11

White Horse
OS549900 ✆ Long Bredy 539
Palmer BB, IPA; Coates
Cider Ⓖ
Friendly village local with bar
billiards. Youth hostel next
door 🏠🏨🌲🍴🐕🛏

Lyme Regis 5E5

10–2.30; 6 (7 winter)–11

Royal Standard
Marine Parade ✆2637
Palmers BB, IPA Ⓗ
Interesting old harbourside
pub 🏠🌲🍴🐕🛏

Lytchett Minster 6A7

10.30–2.30; 6–10.30 (11 F, S & summer)

St Peters Finger
(off A35) ✆ 622275
Draught Bass; Hall &
Woodhouse Hectors Bitter,
Badger Best Bitter Ⓗ
Cheerful historic inn with
contrasting bars 🏠🌲🍴➤🍺🛏

Milton Abbas 5H5

11–2.30; 6.30–11

Hambro Arms
Off A354 ✆ 880233
John Devenish Bitter, Wessex
Best Bitter Ⓗ
Thatched pub in unspoilt
model village; good food
🏠🌲🅿🍴🍺

Morden 5J5

11–2.30; 7–11

Cock & Bottle
B3075 (½ mile north of A35)
✆ 238
Hall & Woodhouse Hector's
Bitter, Badger Best Bitter Ⓗ
Pleasant rural pub 🏠Q🌲

Mosterton 5F4

11–2.30; 6–11

Admiral Hood
(A3066)
✆ Broadwindsor 68394
Usher Best Bitter; Founders
Ale Ⓗ
Large open-plan thatched pub
🏠🏨🌲🍴➤🛏

North Wootton 5G4

10.30 (11 winter)–2.30; 6 (7 winter)–11

Three Elms
(A3030) ✆ Sherborne 812881
Wadworth 6X Ⓗ Regular
guest beers
Cheerful roadside pub; good
food 🏨🌲🅿🍴➤

Poole 6A7

10.30–2.30; 6–11

Bulls Head
Parr Street, Parkstone (off
A35) ✆ Parkstone 748087
Whitbread Strong Country
Bitter Ⓖ
Charming small pub with
luxury toilets Q🍴≷ Parkstone

Dorset Knob
164, Alder Road, Parkstone
✆ Bournemouth 745918
Hall & Woodhouse Hector's
Bitter, Badger Best Bitter,
Tanglefoot Ⓗ
Friendly pub serving residen-
tial area 🏠🏨🌲 (weekdays)
🍴≷ (Branksome)

Inn in the Park
26 Pinewood Road,
Branksome Park
✆ Bournemouth 761318
Wadworth IPA, 6X, Farmers
Glory; Ringwood Best Bitter Ⓗ
Plush, comfortable pub near
the sea
🏠🏨 (dining room) 🌲🅿🌲🍴

Lord Nelson
The Quay ✆ 673774
Hall & Woodhouse Hectors
Bitter, Badger Best Bitter,
Tanglefoot Ⓗ
Popular quayside pub with
regular live music. Large
collection of nautical items
🏠🏨🌲🍴

Sweet Home Inn
25 Ringwood Road, Parkstone
(A348) ✆ 676297
Hall & Woodhouse Badger
Best Bitter, Taunton Cider Ⓗ
Friendly local; rare bar
billiards, Saturday piano
singsong 🌲🍴➤🍺

Try also: King Charles
(Whitbread)

Portland 5G6

10.30–2.30; 6–11

Clifton Hotel
The Grove (off Easton Street)
✆ 820473
Evenings opens 7 pm
John Devenish Bitter, Wessex
Best Bitter Ⓗ
Pleasant local with skittle
alley. Home of Ivan the arm
wrestler
🏠🏨 (skittle alley) 🌲🍴🐕

George Inn
Reforne, Easton ✆ 820011
John Devenish Bitter, Wessex
Best Bitter Ⓗ
Old, low-ceilinged, stone pub
opposite church and cricket
ground. Value-for-money
menu 🌲🍴➤🍺🐕

Rampisham 5G4

11–2.30; 6.30–11

Tigers Head
Off A356 ✆ Evershot 244
Butcombe Bitter; Draught

Bass; Wadworth 6X ⊞ Perry
Cider ⒼG
Super small pub in heart of
Dorset; unusual food
🏠Q⊞♿⌖🅿

Shaftesbury 5H6

11–2.30; 6–10.30 (11 F, S & summer)

Royal Chase Hotel
Salisbury Road (A30/A350)
✆ 3355
Hall & Woodhouse Badger
Best Bitter ⊞ Usher Best Bitter;
Wadworth 6X Regular guest
beers
Friendly hotel offering real ale
weekends. Bar has old fire
range 🏠⊞♿🅿⌖🍴Å (400 yds)

Ship Inn
Bleke Street (near B3081/
B3091) ✆ 3219
Hall & Woodhouse Hector's
Bitter, Badger Best Bitter;
Taunton Cider ⊞
Super stone local dating from
1605 🏠⌖🍴🍺

Two Brewers
St James Street ✆ 2210
Courage Directors; Usher PA,
Best Bitter; Wadworth 6X ⊞
Regular guest beers
Fine local at the bottom of
Gold Hill ♿⌖🍴🍺

Sherborne 5G4

10–2.30; 6–11

Britannia
Westbury ✆ 813300
Coopers Cask Ale; Ind Coope
Burton Ale; Marston
Pedigree ⊞
Once a school for wayward
girls 🅿⌖🍴🍺🍴≋

Digby Tap
Cooks Lane ✆ 813148
Hardington Best Bitter; Smiles
Best Bitter; Wadworth 6X; ⊞
Taunton Cider ⊞; Farmhouse
Cider Ⓖ Regular guest beers
Side street tavern close to
Abbey ⊞♿ (not Sun) ≋

Shillingstone 5H4

10.30–2.30; 6.30–11

Seymer Arms
A357 ✆ Child Okeford 860488
Hall & Woodhouse Hector's
Bitter, Badger Best Bitter ⊞
Main road local in attractive
Stour Valley ♿🅿🍴

Stoke Abbott 5F5

11–2.30; 7–11

New Inn
Off B3162 OS454008
✆ Broadwindsor 68333
Palmer BB, IPA ⊞
Pleasant one-bar inn
🏠Q⊞♿🅿🍴

Stourton Caundle 5G4

11–2.30; 6.30–11

Trooper

Off B3030 ✆ Stalbridge 62405
Hall & Woodhouse Badger
Best Bitter ⊞
Village local; small but cosy
🏠Q♿

Swanage 6A8

10.30–2.30; 6–11

Red Lion
High Street ✆ 422533
Flowers Original; Whitbread
Strong Country Bitter, Bulmer
Cider Ⓖ
Popular with Swanage Steam
Railway enthusiasts,
rebuilding the Purbeck Line
🏠⊞♿🍴

Royal Oak
High Street, Herston (A351)
✆ 423303
Open till 3 summer lunch
John Devenish Bitter, Wessex
Best Bitter; Bulmer Cider ⊞
Friendly local pub convenient
for Herston halt on Swanage
Steam Railway 🏠⊞♿🍴Å

Try also: Globe (Whitbread)

Symondsbury 5F5

10.30–2.30; 6–11

Ilchester Arms
Off A35 OS445935 ✆ 22600
John Devenish Bitter, Wessex
Best Bitter; Taunton Cider ⊞
Old beamed village pub
🏠Q⊞♿🅿🍴Å

Thornford 5G4

11–2.30; 7–11

Kings Arms
Off A352/A37
✆ Yetminster 872294
Hall & Woodhouse Hector's
Bitter, Badger Best Bitter ⊞
Comfortable village pub with
glass fronted beer engines
Q♿🍴≋

Trickett's Cross 6B7

12–2.30; 7–10.30 (11 F, S & summer)

Forest Edge Motel
Ringwood Road (A31)
✆ Ferndown 874221
Draught Bass; Wadworth
6X ⊞ Occasional guest beers
Popular motel on edge of New
Forest ⊞🅿♿🍴Å

Wareham 6A8

11–2.30; 7–11

Railway Tavern
Northport (off A351) ✆ 2006
John Devenish Bitter, Wessex
Best Bitter ⊞
Two good bars; railway theme
in lounge ♿🍴≋

Try also: Antelope (Whitbread)

West Bay 5F5

10.30–2.30; 6–11

Bridport Arms Hotel
Off B3157 ✆ Bridport 22994

Palmer BB, IPA ⊞
Hotel near the beach
🏠Q⊞🅿🍴Å

West Bexington 5F5

10.30–2.30; 6–11

Manor House Hotel
Off B3157
✆ Burton Bradstock 897785
Eldridge Pope Royal Oak;
Palmer BB (Manor Bitter);
Wadworth 6X ⊞
Cellar bar in attractive hotel.
Large garden overlooking
Chesil Beach and sea
🏠Q♿🅿🍴Å

West Stafford 5H5

11.30–2.30; 6.30 (7 winter)–11

Wise Man Inn
OS726896
✆ Dorchester 63694
John Devenish Bitter, Wessex
Best Bitter; Taunton Cider ⊞
Smart country village pub,
winter home of Frome Valley
Morris Men
🏠Q⊞ (family dining area)
♿🍴🍺

Weymouth 5G6

10.30–2.30; 6–11

Golden Eagle
Lower Bond Street ✆ 783280
Hall & Woodhouse Badger
Best Bitter ⊞
Lively one-room, side-street,
locals boozer ♿≋

Kings Arms
Trinity Road ✆ 770055
John Devenish Bitter, Wessex
Best Bitter ⊞
Harbourside pub full of
nautical bric-a-brac 🏠🅿♿≋

Waterloo
Grange Road ✆ 784488
John Devenish Bitter, Wessex
Best Bitter ⊞
Lively one-room pub with
separate restaurant ♿🍴≋

**Weatherbury Hotel
(Winstons Bar)**
7 Carlton Road North (off
Dorchester road A354)
✆ 786040
Poole Dolphin Bitter;
Wadworth 6X ⊞ Regular
guest beers
Popular local. Live music
weekends ♿🅿🍴≋

Wimborne Minster 6A7

10–2.30; 6–10.30 (11 F, S & summer)

Cricketers Arms
Park Lane ✆ 882846
John Devenish Bitter, Wessex
Best Bitter ⊞
Lively friendly town centre
pub next to river and cricket
ground ♿ (not Sun)

Vine Inn
Vine Hill, Pamphill,
OS995004 ✆ 882259
Opens 11
Whitbread Strong Country Bitter [H]
Very small village pub with large beer garden

Try also: Albion (Hall & Woodhouse) **Bell** (Whitbread)

Wimborne St Giles 6A6

11–2.30, 6–10.30 (11 F, S & summer)

Bull
(off B3081) ✆ Cranborne 284
Hall & Woodhouse Badger Best Bitter [H]
Rural pub with extensive menu and games room

Winkton 6B7

11–2.30; 6–10.30 (11 F, S & summer)

Lamb Inn
Burley Road (off B3347)
OS166962
✆ Bransgore 72427
Arkell BBB; Gale HSB; Hall & Woodhouse Badger Best Bitter; Marston Pedigree; Wadworth 6X [H] **Regular guest beers**
Friendly rural local, sympathetically extended due to its popularity

Winterborne Kingston 5H5

10.30–2.30; 6.30–11

Greyhound
North Street (off A31)
✆ Bere Regis 471332
Hall & Woodhouse Badger Best Bitter [H]
Lively village pub

Winterborne Whitechurch 5H5

11–2.30; 6–11

Milton Arms
Dorchester Hill (A354)
✆ Milton Abbas 880306
John Devenish Bitter, Wessex Best Bitter [H]
Small village pub on main road

Worth Matravers 6A8

10.30–2.30; 6–10.30 (11 F, S & summer)

Square & Compass
(off B3069) ✆ 229
Whitbread Strong Country Bitter, Pompey Royal; Bulmers Cider [G]
Ancient stone pub in fine setting. A real bastion of the Purbecks with extensive coastal views
Q (ring landlord)

THE FREEMASON'S ARMS
"ANY OF THE REGULARS WANT A DRINK BEFORE I SERVE THIS BLOKE?"
KenPyne

Aycliffe Village   30B3

12–2; 7–10.30

North Briton
High Street
Vaux Samson Ⓗ
Large, popular village pub
with pool table, darts in bar
🍺🍴🕒🍷🏅♿

Barnard Castle   29J3

11–3; 5.30–10.30 (11 S)

Three Horseshoes
Galgate (A67)
✆ Teesdale 38774
Draught Bass Ⓔ
Solid old pub with a large
comfortable lounge and a
games room. Near the Castle
🍷🕒

Try also: **Cricketers**
(Cameron); **Old Well, White
Swan** (free)

Billy Row   30B2

Closed lunch; 6–10.30

Dun Cow (Cows Tail)
Old White Lea (off A689)
OS149372
**Tetley Scotch, Flastaff;
Theakston Best Bitter** Ⓗ
A time capsule, off the beaten
track. Landlord has held the
licence for 56 years 🍺Q🍷

Bishop Auckland   30B3

11–3; 6–10.30

Sportsman
Market Place
**Theakston Bitter; Whitbread
Castle Eden** Ⓗ
Popular with younger set,
often crowded. Cellar has its
own ghost 🍺🍴≷

Try also: **Newton Cap**
(Cameron)

Bishop Middleham   30C2

11–3; 6 (6.30 winter)–10.30

Red Lion
3 Bank Top (off A177)
✆ Ferryhill 51298
Whitbread Castle Eden Ⓗ
Traditional country pub
overlooking the village
🍺Q🍷🕒🍷♿

Bishopton   30C3

11.30–3; 6–11

Talbot
The Green ✆ Sedgefield 30371
**Cameron Lion Bitter,
Strongarm** Ⓗ & Ⓔ
Pleasant old local in leafy
village. Long, modernised
lounge, small snug off 🍺🍷♿

Blackhouse   30B1

11–3; 6–10.30

Charlaw Inn

Wheatley Green, Edmondsley
(B6532)✆ Stanley 232085
**McEwan 80/-; Younger's
No. 3** Ⓗ
Lively country pub with
restaurant 🍴🍷🕒🍷🏅♿

Canney Hill   30B3

11–3; 6–10.30

Sportsman
A689
**Cameron Lion Bitter,
Strongarm** Ⓗ
Tidy and popular roadside inn
with warm atmosphere
🍺🍷🕒 Mon–Fri) 🍷

Chester-le-Street   30B1

11–3; 6–10.30

Wheatsheaf
Pelaw Grange (A6127)
✆ 883104
Stones Bitter Ⓗ
Lively bar and smart lounge
on outskirts of town. Good
value food 🍷🕒🍷🏅♿

Coatham Mundeville   30B3

11.30–3; 6–11

Stables
Hallgarth Hotel (off A167;
near A1(M))
✆ Aycliffe 319595
**Newcastle Exhibition; Tetley
Bitter** Ⓗ
Stone outbuildings neatly
converted to country hotel.
Pleasant lounge with section
for non-smokers 🍷🍴🕒🍷🏅♿

Try also: **Foresters Arms** (John
Smiths)

Consett   30A1

11–3; 6–10.30

Bellamys
Newmarket Street
**Theakston XB, Old Peculier;
Bulmer Cider** Ⓗ
Tastefully modernised for the
over 25's! Not over the top
and not too expensive 🍴🕒🍷

Cornsay   30B2

11.30–2.30; 6.30–10.30

Blackhorse Inn
B6311 ✆ 734211
**Theakston Best Bitter, XB, Old
Peculier** Ⓗ
Set in rural Durham, cheerful
atmosphere and good value
food 🍴🕒🍷

Cornsay Colliery   30B2

11–3; 6–10.30

Firtree
Hedley Hill Lane (B6301)
OS167425
Lorimer Best Scotch Ⓗ
Isolated and basic country

local. Known as "The
Monkey". Cheap pint
🍺Q🍴🍷🍷♿

Cowshill   29G2

11–3; 6–10.30 (11 S)

Cowshill Hotel
A689 ✆ Weardale 537236
Tetley Bitter Ⓗ
Fine 19th century alehouse in
picturesque Weardale. Good
food 🍺Q🍴🍷🍷🍷Å

Crook   30B2

11–3; 7–10.30

Millhouse
24 North Terrace
✆ Bishop Auckland 766873
Tetley Bitter Ⓗ
Cosy 3-room pub including
separate disco room for young
at heart 🍴 (lunchtime) 🍷🍷

Try also: **Travellers Rest**
(Camerons)

Crossgate Moor   30B2

11–3; 5.30–10.30 (11 summer)

Pot & Glass
Newcastle Road (A167 Great
North Road)
✆ Durham 64556
**Darley Thorne Best Bitter;
Vaux Samson** Ⓗ
Popular and friendly road
house. Locals' bar and
characters, comfortable
lounge. Real food 🍴🍷🕒🍷🍷

Croxdale   30C2

11.3; 6–10.30

Coach & Horses
Low Butcher Race
✆ Durham 814484
Vaux Samson Ⓗ **Occasional
guest beers**
Old coaching inn with
interesting history
🍺🍴 (if eating) 🕒🍷Å

Darlington   30B4

11–3; 5.30–11

Black Swan
Parkgate (A67) ✆ 466104
Open till 4 Mon Lunch
Newcastle Exhibition Ⓗ
Urban pub with some style. 3
rooms and "drinking
corridor" 🍷🍷≷

Britannia
Archer Street (A68/inner ring
road Jct) ✆ 463787
Opens 11.30; closes 10.30 pm
Mon–Wed
Cameron Strongarm Ⓗ
Warm relaxed atmosphere
and no pretentions in 125-
year old town centre pub Q

Falchion
Blackwellgate ✆ 462541
Evening opens 6
Cameron Strongarm Ⓗ
Cosy local in central shopping
street. Named after a
legendary "worm"-killing
sword 🍷

Glittering Star
Stonebridge ✆ 483455
Opens 12 Tue–Thur; open till
4 Mon lunch
Samuel Smith OBB 🅷
One U-shaped room with lots
of secluded corners.
Traditional lunchtimes, disco-
style evenings 🌣≹

Pennyweight
Bakehouse Hill (Market Place)
✆ 464244
Evening opens 6.30
**Lorimer & Clark 80/-; Wards
Sheffield Best Bitter** 🅷 **Regular
guest beers**
Attractive modern pub in an
18th-century building 🌣≹

Try also: Central Borough
(Cameron)

Durham City 30B2

11–3; 6–10.30 (11 F, S summer)

Colpitts Hotel
Hawthorne Terrace ✆ 69913
Samuel Smith OBB 🅷
Busy bar attracts students to
mix with locals 🅰🔟≹

Dun Cow
37 Old Elvet ✆ 69219
Evening opens 5.30
Whitbread Castle Eden 🅷
Quaint "old-world" city pub
opposite the prison Q🔟🅖

Fighting Cocks
4 South Street ✆ 364822
Evening opens 5.30
**Draught Bass; Stones Best
Bitter** 🅷
Busy city centre pub, popular
with young people. Pool table
and darts 🎲 (lunchtime) 🌣≹

Half Moon
New Elvet ✆ 64528
**Draught Bass; Stones Best
Bitter** 🅷
Popular city pub with unique
circular bar 🔟

Nevilles Cross Hotel
Darlington Road (A167)
✆ 43872
Stones Best Bitter 🅷
Unique coal fire in centre of
small cosy bar; lounge and
games room 🅰🅔🌣🅟🔟

Queens Head Hotel
2/4 Sherburn Road Gilesgate
✆ 65649
**Marston Pedigree; Tetley
Bitter** 🅷 **Regular guest beers**
Busy small hotel, contrasting
bar and lounge 🖋🅔🌣🅟

Shakespeare
Saddler Street ✆ 69709
Evening opens 5.30
**McEwan 80/-; Newcastle
Exhibition; Younger's No. 3** 🅷
Very popular, friendly and
well-run city centre pub,
frequented by regulars,
tourists and students Q🔟≹

Victoria
88 Halgarth Street ✆ 65269

**McEwan 80/-; Newcastle
Exhibition**
Cosy, unspoilt Victorian pub,
lively, friendly atmosphere.
Popular with locals and
students—don't worry,
service is fast! 🅰Q🅔🔟🅖

Try also: Swan & 3 Cygnets;
Market Tavern; Duke of
Wellington; Old Elm Tree;
Garden House

Ebchester 30A1

11–3; 6–10.30

Chelmsford
Front Street (A694) ✆ 560213
Vaux Samson 🅷
Friendly village local, bustling
bar and comfortable lounge,
close to country walks
🅰🅔🖋🌣🅟🔟

Evenwood 30B3

11–3; 6–10.30

Bay Horse
✆ 832697
Whitbread Castle Eden 🅷
Comfortable family-run pub.
Lively clientele and home
cooking 🌣🅟🔟

Ferryhill 30B2

11–3; 6–10.30

Black Bull
2–3 Main Street ✆ 51676
**McEwan 80/-; Newcastle
Exhibition; Younger's No. 3;
Bulmer Cider** 🅷
Large village pub—site of
annual pub olympics 🔟🅖

Framwellgate 30B2
Moor

11–3; 6.30–10.30 (11 F, S & summer)

Marquis of Granby
Front Street (off A167)
✆ Durham 69382
Samuel Smith OBB 🅷
Busy 2-room pub with strong
community ties 🅰🖋🌣

Try also: Queens Head
(Cameron)

Great Stainton 30C3

11–3; 5.30–11

Kings Arms
✆ Sedgefield 30361
Whitbread Castle Eden 🅷
White-painted old pub in tiny
village. Unspoilt wood-beamed
bars; emphasis on food in the
lounge. Renowned for its
varied menu! 🅰Q🌣🅟🔟

Haswell 30C2

11–3; 6.10.30

Oddfellows Arms
86 Front Street
✆ Hetton-le-Hole 261014
Big Lamp Bitter 🅷
Basic 2-room local, successful
brewery flagship. Pool room
🅰🔟

Heighington 30B3

11–3; 5.30–11

Dog Inn
Cross Lanes (A68 1 mile S of
village) ✆ Darlington 312152
Vaux Samson 🅷 **Occasional
guest beers**
Basic bar popular with
families for good food.
Children welcome in pleasant
lounge 🅰🖋🌣🅟🔟🅐

High 30C2
Shincliffe

11–3; 6–10.30 (11 F, S & summer)

Avenue
Off A177
**Lorimer Best Scotch; Vaux
Samson** 🅷
Old road house marooned by
new bypass, now serving a
large private estate 🅰Q🅔🅟

Holmside 30B2

11–3; 6–10.30

Wardles Bridge
**McEwan 70/-, 80/-;
Newcastle Exhibition;
Younger's No. 3** 🅷
A friendly local in rural
setting. Wed folk and country
nights. Quiz and regular sing-
along nights 🅰Q🖋🌣🅟🔟

Holwick 29H3

11–3; 6–10.30

Strathmore Arms
Middleton-in-Teesdale (off
B6277) OS909268
✆ Middleton 40362
Theakston Best Bitter 🅷
Off the beaten track, popular
with summer hikers
🅰Q🅔🖋🅔🌣🅟🅐

Howden-le- 30B2
Wear

11–3; 6–10.30 (11 S)

Australian
Church Street
**Cameron Lion Bitter,
Strongarm** 🅷
Small friendly local. Pool and
jukebox 🅰🔟

Try also: Plantation
(Theakstons)

Hunwick 30B2

11–3; 7–10.30

Wheatsheaf
Village Green (B6286)
✆ Bishop Auckland 603642
**Cameron Lion Bitter,
Strongarm** 🅷
Popular, friendly village local
with cosy bar and pool room
🅰🔟

Langley Park 30B2

12–2; 7–10.30 (11 F, S & summer)

Centurion
Wall Nook Lane ✆ 731323

Vaux Samson ⊞
Smart country pub with
French restaurant. Expensive
beer Q ✿ ⅁ ⚬

Low Pittington 30C2

11.30–3; 6–10.30 (11 F, S & summer)

Blacksmiths Arms
Front Street (off A690)
✆ Durham 7202871
Vaux Samson ⊞
Friendly village local. Lively
bar, pool table ⚓ ✿ ⅁ ⚬ ⚋ ⚌

Medomsley 30A1

11–3; 6–10.30

Miners Arms
Manor Road
✆ Ebchester 560428
**Vaux Sunderland Draught
Bitter** ⊞
Cosy pub in former mining
village ⚏ ✿ ⅁ ⚬ ⚋

Middlestone
Moor 30B2

11–3; 6–10.30

Masons Arms Hotel
Durham Road
✆ Spennymoor 816169
**Cameron Lion Bitter,
Strongarm** ⊞
Neat lounge, bar games
room—snooker, pool and
darts. Caters for most tastes
⚓ ⚏ ✿ ⚋

Neasham 30C4

11–3; 6.30–11

Fox & Hounds
24 Teesway
✆ Darlington 720350
**Vaux Samson; Ward Sheffield
Best Bitter** ⊞ Occasional guest
beers
Village pub near scenic part of
river. Busy bar with darts and
dominoes. Popular for evening
meals. Childrens' play
equipment ⚏ ✿ ⅁ ⚋ ⚌

Pity Me 30B2

11–3; 6–10.30 (11 F, S & summer)

Lambton Hounds
62 Front Street (off A167)
✆ Durham 64742
Lorimer Best Scotch ⊞
Friendly traditional 3-room
local, collection of shooting
sticks, live music Sunday eve
⚓ ✿

Romaldkirk 29H3

11–3; 6–10.30 (11 S)

Rose & Crown
Romaldkirk (B6277)
✆ Teesdale 50213
Theakston Best Bitter ⊞
Hospitable hotel and eating
place in heart of Teesdale
⚓ Q ✿ ⚏ ⚆ ⅁ ⚋ ⚌ ⚊

Seaton 30C1

11–3; 6–10.30

Dun Cow
✆ Seaham 813075
Whitbread Castle Eden ⊞
Lively and friendly local in
quiet cul de sac. Beware the
villagers—park carefully!
⚓ Q ⚋ ⚊

Seaton Lane Inn
✆ Seaham 812038
Opens 12
**Theakston Best Bitter, Old
Peculier** ⊞
Free house, unusual beers for
area ⚓ Q ✿ ⚋

Sedgefield 30C3

11–3; 6–10.30

Nags Head
8, West End (near A177)
✆ 20234
Draught Bass ⊞
Pleasantly refurbished inn
near village green. Good food
⚏ ✿ ⅁ ⚋ ⚊

Shildon 30B3

11–3; 6–10.30

King William
Eldon Road
Cameron Strongarm ⊞
Large bustling local ⚋ ⚌

Timothy Hackworth
107 Main Street
**Cameron Lion Bitter,
Strongarm** ⊞
Compact and welcoming with
accent on games ✿ ⅁ ⚌

Shincliffe 30C2

11–3; 6–10.30 (11 F, S & summer)

Seven Stars
A177 ✆ Durham 48454
**Lorimer Best Scotch; Vaux
Sunderland Draught Bitter** ⊞
Cosy friendly pub with bistro
cuisine, a pleasant walking
distance from Durham City
⚓ Q ✿ ⚏ ⅁ ⚋ ⚋

South Church 30B3

11–3; 6–10.30

Red Alligator
**Vaux Sunderland Draught
Bitter** ⊞
Interesting decor in smart
lounge pub beneath England's
largest parish church Q ✿ ⅁ ⚬

Stanhope 29H2

11–3; 6–10.30

Phoenix
Front Street (A689) ✆ 528214
**Cameron Lion Bitter,
Strongarm (summer)** ⊞
No frills Dales market town
pub ⚓ Q ⚏ ⚆ ⅁ ⚊

Summerhouse 30B3

11.30–3; 6.30–11

Raby Hunt
B6279 ✆ Piercebridge 604
**Cameron Strongarm;
Theakston Best Bitter** ⊞
Occasional guest beers

Neatly-extended old stone free
house in a whitewashed
hamlet ⚓ ⚏ ✿ ⅁ (not Sun) ⚋ ⚊

Tantobie 30B1

11–3; 6–10.30

Bird Inn
White-le-Head (B6311)
Opens 12 & 7
**Belhaven 80/-; Marston
Pedigree, Merrie Monk, Owd
Rodger** ⊞ Regular guest beers
Popular local, lively bar,
comfortable lounge ⚋ ⚋

Commercial
Front Street (B6311)
✆ Stanley 23875
Whitbread Castle Eden ⊞
Lively basic village pub ⚋

Waskerley 29J2

11–3; 7–10.30

Moorcock Inn
Off A68
Marston Pedigree ⊞
Remote friendly hostelry.
Impromptu folk venue.
Children welcome
⚓ ⚏ ✿ (3000 acres) ⅁ ⚬

West Cornforth 30C2

11–3; 6–10.30

Square & Compass
The Green (off B6291)
**Bass Extra Light; Stones Best
Bitter** ⊞
Excellent village local on
attractive green Q ✿ ⅁ ⚋ ⚋ ⚊

Witton Gilbert 30B2

11–3; 6–10.30 (11 F, S & summer)

Glendenning Arms
Front Street (A691) ✆ 710321
Vaux Samson ⊞
Village pub with sporting
connections and horse racing
theme ⚓ Q ✿ ⚋

Travellers Rest
Front Street (A691)
**McEwan 70/-; Newcastle
Exhibition; Theakston Best
Bitter** ⊞, **XB** ⊞, **Old Peculier** ⊞;
Younger's No. 3 ⊞
Smart traditional pub with
live music, darts and petanque
pitch ⚓ Q ⚏ ✿ ⅁ ⚬

WARMEST WELCOME

♦ A REAL FIRE PUB ♦

The ⚓ symbol denotes a pub
with a real solid fuel fire

Aldham 18E8

10.30–2.30; 6–11

Queens Head
Ford Street (A604)
✆ Colchester 241291
**Adnams Bitter; Greene King
IPA, Abbot** ⊞
Popular inn with vast
collection of water jugs. Large
garden with donkey. Fishing
by arrangement. Restaurant
🏚🍴🕭🍺

Althorne 11F2

11–2.30; 6–11

Huntsman & Hounds
Green Lane (off B1038)
OS906004 ✆ Maldon 740387
Greene King IPA, Abbot ⊞
Thatched pub with attractive
gardens 🏚🍴🕭🍺🅿️🛏️

Arkesden 18B8

11.30–2.30; 6–11

Axe & Compasses
(2 miles N of B1038)
OS483344 ✆ Clavering 272
**Greene King Abbot; Rayment
BBA** ⊞
Traditional 17th century
village local
🏚Q🍴🕭🍺 (Tue–Sat) 🍴

Aveley 10C3

10.30–2.30; 6–10.30 (11 F, S)

Sir Henry Gurnett
Romford Road (near B1335)
✆ Purfleet 864042
**Tolly Cobbold Mild (summer),
Bitter, Original, Old Strong** ⊞
700 year-old converted
farmhouse with stream in
garden. No food Sun 🏚🍴🕭🍺

Bannister Green 18D9

10.30–2.30; 6–11

Three Horseshoes
Near A120 OS696206
✆ Great Dunmow 820467
Ridley Bitter, HE ⊞ & Ⓔ
Picturesque pub on the green
with ring the bull game,
barbeques in summer
🏚🍴🕭🍺🍴

Basildon 10D2

10–2.30; 6–10.30 (11 F, S)

Towngate Theatre
Towngate (off Roundacre
roundabout)
**Crouch Vale Best Bitter;
Greene King IPA, Abbot** ⊞
Part of town-centre theatre
complex 🍴🕭🍺

Battlesbridge 10E2

10–2.30; 6–11

Barge
Hawk Hill
**Ind Coope Bitter, Burton
Ale** ⊞; **Bulmer Cider** Ⓖ
Small popular pub on bank of
River Crouch 🏚🎿🍴🕭🍺

Baythorn End 18D7

10.30–2.30; 6–11

Swan
A604/A1092
✆ Hedingham 60649
Greene King IPA, Abbot ⊞
Pleasantly restored old
roadside inn 🍴🕭🍺

Billericay 10D2

10–2.30; 6–10.30 (11 F, S)

Railway
High Street (B1007)
Greene King IPA, Abbot ⊞
Popular one-bar local 🕭🍺

Birchanger 18B8

10.30–2.30; 6–11

Three Willows
Off A120/M11 Jct 8
✆ Bishops Stortford 815913
**Greene King Abbot; Rayment
BBA** ⊞
Excellent village local. Home
of the Three Willows Amateur
Theatrical Society. No food
Sun 🍴🕭🍺🍴

Birdbrook 18D7

11–2.30; 6–11

Plough
1 mile off A604
✆ Ridgewell 336
**Adnams Bitter; Greene King
IPA; Mauldon Special** Ⓖ
Traditional village local
🏚Q🍴🕭🍺🍴🛏️

Blackmore End 18D8

10.30–3; 6–11

Red Cow
(4 miles E of B1053)
OS738310
✆ Great Dunmow 85337
Ridley Bitter, HE ⊞
Excellent split level village pub
with games area 🏚🍴🕭🍺🛏️

Black Notley 18D9

11–3; 6–11

Green Dragon
Upper London Road (A131)
✆ Chelmsford 361030
**Greene King XX, IPA,
Abbot** ⊞
Sympathetic restoration, old
barn now restaurant. Good
food 🏚🍴🕭🍺🍴

Boreham 18D9

10.30–2.30; 6–11

Queens Head
Church Road
Greene King IPA, Abbot ⊞
Excellent, friendly traditional
17th century village pub. In
same family for 50 years.
Q🍴🕭🍺🍴

Braintree 18D8

10–3; 6–11

Fountain
103 High Street ✆ 45544

**Adnams Bitter; Courage Best
Bitter, Directors; Greene King
Abbot; Mauldon Bitter** ⊞; **Zum
Cider** Ⓖ Regular guest beers
Old, renovated pub; noisy and
often crowded 🏚🍴🎿🍺🕭🍺

Brentwood 10C2

10–10.30 (11 F, S)

Victoria Arms
50 Ongar Road (A128)
Greene King IPA, Abbot ⊞
Friendly and popular one-bar
pub; parking difficult
🍴🕭 (Mon–Fri)

Broads Green 18C9

10.30–2.30; 6–11

Walnut Tree
Off A130 OS694125
Ridley Bitter ⊞
Victorian pub facing green;
unusual snug bar 🏚🍴🕭🍺

Bulmer Tye 18D7

10.30–2.30; 6–11

Fox
A131 ✆ Sudbury 77505
Greene King IPA, Abbot ⊞
Comfortable welcoming
roadside inn. Pool room
🏚🍴🕭🍺🛏️🍴

Bures 18E8

11–2.30; 6–11

Swan Inn
1 Station Hill ✆ 227815
**Greene King XX, IPA,
Abbot** ⊞
Friendly village local (1490).
Restaurant area, lounge and
public; darts 🏚🍴🕭🍺🍴🍺

Burnham-on-Crouch 11F2

10–2.30; 6–11

New Welcome Sailor
74 Station Road
Greene King IPA, Abbot ⊞
Basic, friendly local Q🕭🛏️🍺

Victoria
1 Belvedere Road (off B1010)
✆ Maldon 783583
Greene King IPA, Abbot ⊞
Spacious Victorian pub
🏚Q🎿🍴🕭🍺🛏️

Canvey Island 10E3

10–2.30; 6–11

Oyster Fleet
21 Knightswick Road
(B1014)
**Greene King Abbot; Shepherd
Neame Bitter; Tolly Cobbold
Bitter; Wethered Bitter** ⊞
Well stocked free house with
nautical theme 🍴🕭🍺

Castle Hedingham 18D8

10.30–2.30; 6–11

Bell
St James Street

Greene King IPA, Abbot Ⓖ
Splendid old timbered Grays
pub near Norman Castle and
Colne Valley Railway
🏚️🍴🕒🍺🍷

Chappel   18E8

10.30–2.30; 5.30–11

Swan Inn
The Street (off A604)
✆ Earls Colne 2353
**Greene King XX (winter), IPA
Abbot; Mauldon Bitter** Ⓗ
Lovely old inn and restaurant
on River Colne, in the shadow
of Chappel Viaduct
🏚️🍺🕒🍷🍴🍽️≷

Chelmsford   10D1

10–2.30; 6–11

Endeavour
351 Springfield Road ✆ 57717
Opens 10.30
Greene King IPA, Abbot Ⓗ,
Christmas Ale Ⓖ
Friendly, three-roomed locals'
pub 🏚️Q🕒🍷🍷

Partners
30 Lower Anchor Street
✆ 265181
Opens 11
**Adnams Bitter; Greene King
IPA, Abbot; Mauldon Bitter;
Marston Pedigree; Ridley
Bitter** Ⓗ
Friendly, renamed street
corner local
🍴🍺🕒🍷(7–9 pm)≷

Red Lion
147 New London Road
Ridley Bitter, HE Ⓗ
Popular workingmen's local;
comfortable lounge, busy
public with pool table 🕒🍺≷

Ship
18 Broomfield Road (A130)
Ridley Mild, Bitter, HE Ⓗ
Popular, family-run pub, just
outside town centre.
Comfortable lounge; busy
cheerful public bar 🕒🍺≷

Sir Evelyn Wood
Widford Road, Widford (off
A12)
Greene King IPA, Abbot Ⓗ
Lovely simple back-street pub
Q🍺

Coggeshall   18E8

10.30–2.30; 6–11

Earls Colne Road
Opens 11
**Ridley Bitter; Truman Bitter;
Webster Yorkshire Bitter** Ⓗ
A locals' pub 🏚️

Fleece Inn
West Street ✆ 61412
Greene King IPA, Abbot Ⓗ
Lively 16th century inn near
NT Tudor house 🏚️🍺🕒🍷

Colchester   11F8

10.30–2.30; 5.30–11

Artilleryman
54–56 Artillery Street
**Greene King XX, IPA,
Abbot** Ⓗ
Friendly local; lounge and
public both popular
Q🍺🕒🍺🍺≷

Bricklayers Arms
Bergholt Road
**Tolly Cobbold Original, Old
Strong** Ⓗ
Busy town pub; contrasting
bars 🍺🕒🍺≷

Crown Inn
Lexden Road
Opens 11.30; & 6
**Truman Bitter; Webster
Yorkshire Bitter** Ⓗ
Popular, comfortable pub.
Good value food
🍺🕒 (not Sun) 🍺🍽️

Norfolk
North Station Road ✆ 45257
Greene King IPA, Abbot Ⓗ
Popular town pub Q🍺🕒🍺🍺≷

Oliver Twist
Golden Noble Hill ✆ 562453
Opens 12 & 6
**Greene King IPA, Abbot;
Webster Yorkshire Bitter** Ⓗ
Victorian decor with gas
lighting. Live music Wed to
Sun 🏚️Q🍺≷

Prettygate
The Commons ✆ 573060
**Ridley Bitter; Truman Bitter;
Webster Yorkshire Bitter** Ⓗ
Modern estate pub.
Comfortable saloon; pool and
darts 🍺🍺🍺

Coopersale   10C2

10–2.30; 6–11

Garnon Bushes
Coopersale Common (off
B181) ✆ Epping 73096
**Charrington IPA; Draught
Bass** Ⓗ
Popular local, formerly two
terraced cottages
Q🍺🕒 (not Sun) 🍺

Copford   18E8

Alma
Copford Green (off A120)
Greene King IPA, Abbot Ⓗ
Rural pub, traditional values
🏚️🍺🕒🍺

Coxtie Green   10C2

10–2.30; 6–10.30 (11 F, S)

White Horse
Coxtie Green Road (1 mile off
A128)
**Benskins Bitter, Ind Coope
Burton Ale** Ⓗ Occasional
guest beers
Cosy, friendly country local
Q🍺🍺🍽️

Dedham   19F8

12–2.30; 7–11

Lamb Inn
Lamb Corner, Birchwood
Road ✆ Colchester 322216
**Tolly Cobbold Bitter, Old
Strong** Ⓖ
Excellent rural boozer. Small
basic bar with darts; pleasant,
comfortable lounge. Must
book meals on Sun Q🍺🕒🍺🍷

Dengie   11F2

White Horse
Tillingham Road
✆ Tillingham 288
**Crouch Vale Best Bitter;
Greene King IPA, Abbot; Tolly
Cobbold Bitter, Original** Ⓗ
17th century coaching inn
🍴🍺🕒🍺

Dobbs Wier   17H8

10.30–2.30; 5.30–11

Fish & Eels
Three Quarter Mile Road
✆ Hoddesdon 41385
Benskins Bitter Ⓗ; **Ind Coope
Burton Ale** Ⓖ
Popular pub on River bank in
Lea Valley Park 🍺🕒🍷🍷

Duton Hill   18C8

10.15–2.30; 6–11

Rising Sun
W of B184 ✆ Great Easton 204
Ridley Bitter, HE Ⓗ
Comfortable, well-appointed
old pub with oak studwork
🏚️🍺🕒🍷

Earl's Colne   18E8

10.30–2.30; 6–11

Coachman Inn
Upper Holt Street (A604)
✆ 2330
Greene King IPA Ⓗ
14th century coaching inn,
full of beams and atmosphere.
Emphasis on meals
🏚️🍴🍺🕒🍺🍽️

Drum
High Street (A604)
**Adnams Bitter; Greene King
IPA, Abbot** Ⓗ
Much ornamented, many
beamed, popular, rustic pub
🏚️🍺🍴

Eastwood   11E2

10–2.30; 6–11

Bellhouse
321 Rayleigh Road (A1015)
**Courage Best Bitter,
Directors** Ⓗ
Old rectory, set in spacious
grounds 🍺🕒🍷

Oakwood
Rayleigh Road (A1015)
Charrington IPA Ⓗ
Popular 50's pub with pool
room 🕒🍺

Elmdon   18B7

12–2.30, 6–11

Kings Head
Heyden Lane
✆ Royston 838358
Ind Coope Bitter Ⓗ
Comfortable pub with dining room and games room. Take-away fish and chips Fri eves
🏠🍴🅿🕓🍺 (not Thu) 🍷🏕

Elsenham 18C8
10.30–2.30; 6–11

Crown
High Street (B1051)
✆ Bishop Stortford 812827
Benskins Bitter Ⓗ
Busy village pub with oak studwork 🏠Q🍺🕓 (not Sun)
🍺 (not Sun/Mon) 🍷≷

Epping 10C2
10–2.30; 6–11

Forest Gate
Bell Common (off B1393)
✆ 72312
Adnams Bitter; Rayment BBA; Bulmer Cider Ⓗ Regular guest beers
Good, honest pub on edge of Epping Forest 🏠Q🍺🕓🍺

Merry Fiddlers
Fiddlers Hamlet, Hobbs Cross Road (1 mile off B1393)
OS473010 ✆ 72142
Ind Coope Bitter, Burton Ale Ⓗ
Pleasant 17th century pub
Q🍺🕓🍺

Feering 18E9
10.30–2.30; 6–10.30 (11 summer)

Bell Inn
The Street (off A12)
Greene King IPA, Abbot Ⓗ
Occasional guest beers
Unspoilt, 14th century rural inn with adjoining shop 🍺🍷

Felsted 18C9
11–2.30; 6–11

Swan
At village crossroads
Ridley Bitter Ⓗ
Comfortable pub and restaurant in attractive village; home of famous public school 🏠🅿🕓🍺🍷

Finchingfield 18D8
10.30–3; 6–11

Red Lion
Church Lane (B1053)
✆ Great Dunmow 810400
Ridley Bitter, HE Ⓗ
Friendly pub in attractive village. Games room with snooker. Pets corner in garden
🏠🍺🅿🕓🍺

Fobbing 10D3
10–2.30; 6–10.30 (11 F, S)

White Lion
Lion Hill (off B1420)
Ind Coope Bitter, Burton Ale Ⓗ
Regular guest beers
300 year-old pub, connections

with Peasants Revolt.
Petanque played 🏠🕓🍺

Fuller Street 10E1
10–2.30; 6–11

Square & Compasses
Off A131 OS747161
✆ Chelmsford 361477
Ridley Bitter Ⓖ
Traditional welcoming country pub with good food and twice monthly folk nights.
Toss penny stool 🏠🍺🕓🍺🍷

Fyfield 10C1
10.30–2.30; 6–11

Queens Head
Queen Street (off B184) ✆ 231
Ind Coope Bitter, Burton Ale Ⓗ
Welcoming, well-run old village pub 🏠Q🍺🕓 (not Sun)
🍺 (not Mon/Tue)

Great Bardfield 18D8
10.30–3; 6–11

Vine
Vine Street (B1057)
✆ Great Dunmow 810355
Ridley Mild, Bitter, HE Ⓗ
Well-kept, welcoming pub in pretty village
🍺🕓 (not Sun) 🍺🍷

Great Burstead 10D2
10–2.30; 6–10.30 (11 F, S)

Kings Head
Southend Road (A129)
Charrington IPA Ⓗ
Recently refurbished family pub 🍺🕓🍷

Great Chesterford 18B7
10.30–2; 6–11

Plough
High Street (near M11 Jct 9)
Greene King IPA, Abbot Ⓖ
Excellent 18th century village local; beer carried up from cellar 🏠🍺🕓 (not Sun) ≷

Great Dunmow 18C8
10.30–2.30; 6–11

Cricketers Arms
22 Beaumont Hill (B184)
✆ 3359
Ridley Bitter Ⓗ
Busy pub with old fashioned ovens built into saloon bar wall. Near sports centre
🍺🕓 (not Sun) 🍺 (not Wed) 🍷&

Great Saling 18D8
11–3; 6–11

White Hart
(2 miles N of A120)
✆ Great Dunmow 850341
Ridley Bitter, HE Ⓗ
Superb Tudor pub with timber gallery 🏠🍺🕓🍺🍷

Hadstock 18C7
11–2.30; 6–11

Kings Head
B1052 ✆ Cambridge 893473
Tolly Cobbold Bitter, Original Ⓗ
17th century village pub
🏠🍺🕓🍺

Harwich 19G8
10.30–2.30; 6–11

Alma
Kings Head Street (off Quay)
Tolly Cobbold Mild, Original Ⓗ
Pleasant unpretentious watering-hole Q🎯🍺🍷🍺≷

Hatfield Heath
10.30–2.30; 5.30–11

White Horse
The Heath (A1060)
Greene King Abbot; Rayment BBA Ⓗ
Fine old timbered pub on village green 🏠Q🍺🕓🍺🍷&

Hazeleigh 10E1
10–2.30; 6–11

Royal Oak
Fambridge Road OS848047
Greene King IPA, Abbot Ⓗ
Popular country pub 1 mile south of Maldon 🏠🍺🕓🍷🏕

Hempstead 18C7
11–2.30; 6–11

Rose & Crown
High Street ✆ Radwinter 221
Greene King IPA; Mauldon Special Ⓗ Regular guest beers
Excellent village inn, enormously popular landlord
🏠🍺🕓 (not Sun)
🍺 (not Sun/Mon)

Henny Street 18E7
10.30–2.30; 6–11

Swan Inn
A131 2 miles OS879386
✆ Twinstead 238
Greene King IPA, Abbot Ⓗ
Remote cosy pub; large beer garden on the Stour 🍺🕓🍺

High Beach 10B2
10.30–2.30; 6–10.30 (11 F, S)

Duke of Wellington
Wellington Hill (near A104/A121) OS407985
Ind Coope Bitter, Burton Ale Ⓗ
Friendly, 1-bar pub on fringe of Epping Forest 🏠Q🍺🕓🏕

Leigh-on-Sea 11E3
10–2.30; 6–11

Crooked Billet
51 High Street, Old Town
Ind Coope Bitter, Burton Ale Ⓗ
Waterfront pub with original smokeroom 🏠🍺🍷≷

Grand Hotel
131 The Broadway
Courage Best Bitter, Directors Ⓗ
Large, multi-room pub 🎯🍺🍷

Little Baddow   18D9

11.30–2.30; 6–11

Generals Arms
The Ridge (off A414)
**Charrington IPA; Draught
Bass** Ⓗ
Friendly roadside pub in rural
surroundings ⌂ Q ✿ Ⓖ ♡

Little Braxted   18D9

10.30–2.30; 6–11

Green Man
Off A12 OS849130
✆ Maldon 891659
Ridley Bitter Ⓗ
Pretty country pub with cosy
traditional lounge in
delightful rural surroundings.
Good value food ⌂ Q ✿ Ⓖ ♡♥

Little Tey   18E8

11–2.30; 7–11

Kings Arms
Coggeshall Road (A120)
✆ Coggeshall 61581
Greene King IPA, Abbot Ⓗ
Pleasant roadside pub ⌂ Ⓖ ♡♥

Little Walden   18C7

11–2.30; 6–11

Crown
B1053
✆ Saffron Walden 27175
**Adnams Bitter; Courage Best
Bitter, Directors; Ruddle
Rutland Bitter** Ⓖ Occasional
guest beers
Immaculate village pub. No
food Sun ⌂ ✿ Ⓖ ♥

Littley Green   18D9

10–2.30; 6–11

Compasses
OS698172
Ridley Bitter Ⓖ
Simple, country pub.
Landlord's home for 70 years.
Ridley brewery tap ⌂ Q ✿

Maldon   11E1

10–2.30; 6–11

Blue Boar
Silver Street (near A414)
✆ Maldon 52681
**Adnams Bitter; Draught
Bass** Ⓖ
Historic THF hotel Q ❖ Ⓖ ♥♡

Queens Head
The Hythe
Greene King IPA, Abbot Ⓗ
Strong nautical atmosphere;
three bars overlooking sailing
barge moorings ⌂ ✿ Ⓖ ♥♡

Manningtree   19F8

11–2.30; 6–11

Station Buffet
The Station
**Adnams Bitter, Old; Greene
King IPA, Abbot** Ⓗ
A must for railway buffs.
Magnificent bar and food
❖ ✿ Ⓖ ♥ ♧ ≋

Margaretting   10D2

Red Lion
Main Road (B1002 off A12)
Ridley Mild, Bitter, HE Ⓖ
Fine old pub with live jazz Tue
and Fri ⌂ Q ✿ ♥ Å

Mashbury   18C9

11–2.30; 6–11

Fox
Fox Road OS650127
✆ Good Easter 573
Ridley Bitter, HE Ⓗ & Ⓖ
Delightful, isolated old
country pub ⌂ Q ✿ Ⓖ ♥♡

Mill End Green   18C8

10.30–2.30; 6–11

Green Man
East of B184
✆ Great Easton 286
**Adnams Bitter; Greene King
Abbot; Mauldon Bitter** Ⓗ
Ridley Bitter Ⓖ
Very old pub with oak
studwork and log fire
⌂ ✿ Ⓖ ♧ (must book Sun)

Mill Green   18C9

10–2.30; 6–10.30 (11 F, S)

Viper
Highwood Road (off A12)
**Truman Bitter, Best Bitter;
Webster Yorkshire Bitter** Ⓗ
Unspoilt country pub in
woodland setting, good for
rambles ⌂ Q ✿ ♥

Mundon   11E2

11–2.30; 6–11

Roundbush
Fambridge Road OS858019
Greene King IPA, Abbot Ⓖ
Friendly, uncrowded locals'
pub; interesting history,
pleasant rural setting
⌂ Q ❖ ✿ ♥ ♿

Nazeing   10B2

11–2.30; 6–11

Coach & Horses
Waltham Road (near B194)
Ind Coope Bitter Ⓗ
Public bar has old Christie's
glasswork, saloon was once a
tearoom ✿ ♥

Orsett   10D3

10.30–2.30; 6–10.30 (11 F, S)

Foxhound
18 High Road (B188)
**Courage Best Bitter,
Directors** Ⓗ
A pub for all tastes; live music
Sun eves ⌂ ❖ ✿ Ⓖ ♥♡

Kings Arms
Stifford Clays Road (B188)
**Benskins Bitter; Ind Coope
Bitter, Burton Ale** Ⓗ Regular
guest beers
Friendly local. Country/folk
music Thu eves ✿ Ⓖ ♥♡

Quendon   18B8

11–2.30; 6–11

Quendon Arms
Cambridge Road (B1383)
**Adnams Bitter; Younger's
IPA** Ⓗ
Comfortable free house
Q ✿ Ⓖ ♩

Rayleigh   10E2

10–2.30; 6–11

Old White Horse
39–41 High Street (A129)
Charrington IPA Ⓗ
Friendly, comfortable pub Ⓖ ≋

Rettendon   10E2

10–2.30; 6–11

Wheatsheaf
Rettendon Common, A130
Ridley Bitter Ⓗ, **HE** Ⓖ
Superb, weatherboarded inn,
a former bakery; large garden
⌂ ✿ Ⓖ ♥

Rochford   11E2

10–2.30; 6–11

Golden Lion
35 North Street
**Adnams Bitter; Greene King
Abbot** Ⓗ Regular guest beers
Small busy freehouse Ⓖ

Saffron Walden 18C7

10.30–2.30; 6–11

Railway Arms
Station Road ✆ 22208
Benskins Bitter Ⓗ **Ind Coope
Burton Ale** Ⓖ
Plain, but very comfortable
and friendly pub
✿ Ⓖ (not Sat/Sun) ♥

Sun
Gold Street (off High Street)
Ridley Bitter, HE Ⓗ
A welcoming old town pub
with character ⌂ ✿ Ⓖ

Shoeburyness 11F3

10–2.30; 6–11

Parsons Barn
Frobisher Way (North
Shoebury village)
Adnams Bitter Ⓖ; **Greene King
IPA, Abbot; Webster
Yorkshire Bitter** Ⓗ
Spacious freehouse in 200
year-old converted barn,
supposedly haunted ❖ ✿ Ⓖ ♩

South Benfleet 10E3

10–2.30; 6–11

Half Crown
27 High Street (B1014)
**Charrington IPA; Draught
Bass** Ⓗ
Popular local near station ♥ ≋

Southend-
on-Sea   11E3

10–2.30; 6–11

Esplanade

Western Esplanade
Truman Bitter, Sampson H
Large seafront pub, pool and
darts; live jazz Thu 🎵♿☕

South Weald 10C2

10–2.30; 6–10.30 (11 F, S)

Tower Arms
Weald Road OS572938
**Adnams Bitter; Fenman
Fortune; Greene King IPA,
Abbot; Webster Yorkshire
Bitter; Young Special** H
Occasional guest beers
Imposing pub opposite
church, large garden;
petanque and ring the bull
🏡Q🎵♿☕ (not Sun)🍽

Stanford-le-Hope 10D3

10.30–2.30; 5.30–10.30 (11 F, S)

Rising Sun
Church Hill (near A1014)
**Courage Best Bitter,
Directors** H
Cosy local in shadow of 900
year-old church ♿🍽≢

Stanford Rivers 10C2

10–2.30; 6–10.30 (11 F, S)

White Bear
London Road (by A113)
Ind Coope Burton Ale H
Excellent country pub; large
garden. ♿🍽🏕

Stansted Mountfitchet 18B8

10–2.30; 6–11

Dog & Duck
Lower Street (B1351)
**Greene King Abbot; Rayment
BBA** H
Excellent village local; bar
billiards ♿☕ (not Sun)♿ ⊖

Stock 10D2

10–2.30; 6–11

Hoop
21 High Street (B1007)
Adnams Mild, Bitter H**, Extra;
Archers Headbanger; Hook
Norton Old Hookey; Marston
Pedigree** H **Regular guest
beers**
Small, comfortable village pub
Q♿🍽♿

Stondon Massey 10C2

10–2.30; 6–10.30 (11 F, S)

Bricklayers Arms
Ongar Road
Greene King IPA, Abbot H
Popular, Grays pub 🏡🍽🍽

Thaxted 18C8

10.30–2.30; 6–11

Star
Mill End ☎ 830368
Ind Coope Bitter H

Exposed beams and vast brick
fireplaces, in village with
spectacular church, Guildhall
and windmill 🏡♿🍽🍽

Tillingham 11F2

10–2.30; 6–11

Fox & Hounds
12 The Square ☎ 416
Greene King IPA; Abbot H
Friendly pub on village green
🏡Q🏡♿🍽🍽♿

Tolleshunt d'Arcy 11F1

11–2.30; 6–11

Queen's Head
North Street (B1023)
Greene King IPA; Abbot H
Authentic parlour and
comfortable saloon 🏡♿♿

Toppesfield 18D8

10.30–2.30; 6.30–11

Green Man
OS739374
Greene King IPA, Abbot H
Excellent friendly village pub
off the beaten track
♿♿🍽 (not Sun)🍽

Waltham Abbey 10B2

10–2.30; 6–10.30 (11 F, S)

Coach & Horses
1 Green Yard
**McMullen AK Mild, Country
Bitter** H
Basic, no frills local 🏡♿🍽

Woodbine
Honey Lane (A121, E of M25
Jct 25) ☎ Lea Valley 713050
Ind Coope Bitter, Burton Ale H
Popular pub with attractive
conservatory
🎵♿☕🍽 (not Sun)

Westcliff-on-Sea 11E3

10–2.30; 6–11

Melrose
168 Hamlet Court Road (off
A13)
Truman Bitter, Best Bitter H
Welcoming Victorian-style
local ♿☕≢

Palace Theatre Centre
London Road (A13)
**Crouch Vale Palace Premier
Ale; Greene King IPA,
Abbot** H **Regular guest beers**
Part of theatre complex ☕♿

West Thurrock 10C3

10.30–2.30; 5.30–10.30 (11 F, S)

Ship
470 London Road (A126)
**Charrington IPA; Draught
Bass; Fuller ESB** H
Friendly pub in industrial
area. Bar billards ♿☕🍽

West Tilbury 10D3

10–2.30; 5.30–10.30 (11 F, S)

King's Head
The Green (off Blue Anchor
Lane) OS661780
**Charrington IPA; Draught
Bass** H
Convivial village pub Q♿🍽

White Notley 18D9

10.30–2.30; 6–11

Cross Keys
1 The Street
Ridley Mild, Bitter H
Fine village local 🏡♿☕🍽🍽≢

White Roding 18C9

10–2.30; 6–10.30 (11 F, S)

Black Horse
A1060 ☎ 322
Ridley Bitter, HE H
Fine country pub, excellent,
good value food 🏡♿☕🍽🍽🏕

Witham 11E1

10–2.30; 6–11

Victoria
Powers Hall End (off A1389)
Opens 10.30
Ridley Bitter, HE H
Spacious old country house
on edge of town Q♿☕🍽🍽

George
36 Newland Street ☎ 511098
Ridley Mild E**, Bitter, HE** H
Good value town centre pub.
Games/music room and quiet
16th century timber-framed
saloon 🎵☕🍽♿≢

Wivenhoe 19F9

11–2.30; 6–11

Black Buoy
Black Buoy Hill (near B1028)
**Tolly Cobbold Bitter, Original,
Old Strong** H
Quaint nautical pub
🏡Q♿☕🍽♿

Wix 19F8

11–2.30; 6–11

White Hart
Harwich Road (off A120)
Greene King IPA, Abbot H
Tolly Cobbold Original H
Fine 17th century weather-
boarded inn ♿☕🍽🍽♿🏕

Wormingford 19E8

10.30–2.30; 6–11

Queens Head
**Adnams Bitter, Extra, Greene
King IPA** H
Rural Essex, warm and
beamed. Caters for the
younger taste 🏡♿🎵☕🍽♿

Writtle 10D1

11–2.30; 6–11 (may close 10.30 Mon–Thu)

Wheatsheaf
The Green (A122, off A414)
Greene King IPA, Abbot G
Small, unspoilt village local 🍽

Ampney Crucis 15H7
11–2.30; 6–11

Butchers Arms
Off A417 ✆ Poulton 486
Flowers IPA, Original;
Whitbread WCPA ⊞ Regular
guest beers
Good old fashioned two-bar
village local ✿☯✆⚓♥

Ashleworth 15F5
11–2.30; 6–11

Arkle
Off A417 ✆ Hartpury 395
Donnington BB, SBA ⊞
Regular guest beers
One-bar free house named
after famous racehorse Q✿

Awre 15E6
12–2.30; 7–11

Red Hart
Off A48 ✆ Blakeney 220
Bass; Hawthorn Dean Strong
Ale; Uley Bitter ⊞
Smart pub with restaurant,
small garden. Worth a detour!
✿☯♥

Bibury 15H6
10.30–2.30; 6–11

Catherine Wheel
A433 (Arlington) ✆ 250
Courage Best Bitter ⊞
Cosy Cotswold pub with
pleasant garden ⌂✿⊞☯♥⚓

Bishops Cleeve 15G5
10.30–2.30; 6–11

Royal Oak
Church Road (off A435)
✆ 2664
Halls Harvest Bitter; Ind
Coope Burton Ale; Ruddle
County ⊞
Popular thatched pub near
church ⌂✿☯⚓

Broadwell 15H5
10–2.30; 6–11

Fox
½ Mile East of A429
OS202276 ✆ Cotswold 30212
Donnington BB, SBA;
Westons Cider ⊞
Small pub in lovely village.
Aunt Sally in garden, good
food, booking advised (not
Tue)
⌂⊞ (lunch only) ✿⊞☯♥Å

Brockweir 14D7
11–2.30; 7 (6 summer)–11

Brockweir Inn
Off A466 ✆ Tintern 548
Flowers Original; Hook
Norton Best Bitter, Old
Hookey; ⊞ Bulmer Cider ⊞
Comfortable Wye Valley inn,
pleasant atmosphere, good
food. Tintern Abbey nearby
⌂✿⊞☯♥⚓

Chedworth 15G6
12–2.30 7–11

Seven Tuns
Off A429 ✆ Fossebridge 242
Courage Best Bitter,
Directors ⊞
Stone-built pub in delightful
village ⌂✿☯⚓

Cheltenham 15G5
11–2.30; 6–11

Bayshill
St Georges Place ✆ 524388
Wadworth IPA, 6X, Farmers
Glory, Old Timer (winter) ⊞
Plain exterior hides a
welcoming interior—an ever
popular town local ☯⚓≱

Duck & Pheasant
North Place ✆ 41978
Boddingtons Bitter; Courage
Best Bitter, Directors; Hook
Norton Best Bitter; John
Smiths Bitter ⊞
Busy comfortable town centre
pub ✿☯

Haymaker
Windyridge Road, Wymans
Brook ✆ 44728
Courage BA, BB, Directors ⊞
Modern estate pub adorned
with agricultural implements
✿☯

Jolly Brewmaster
Painswick Road
Flowers IPA, Original,
Whitbread WCPA ⊞
Well ordered, lively and
popular pub ⌂✿☯⚓

Malvern Inn
Leckhampton Road (B4070)
✆ 526763
Flowers Original; Whitbread
WCPA ⊞
Out-of-town local at foot of
Leckhampton Hill
✿☯ (not Sun)

Cirencester 15G7
10.30–2.30; 6–11

Brewers Arms
Cricklade Street ✆ 3763
Evenings opens 6.30
Arkell BB, BBB, Kingsdown
Bitter ⊞
Busy but plain town pub
⊞✿☯⚓

Drillmans Arms
A417 ✆ 3892
Archers Village, Best,
Special ⊞ Regular guest beers
Cosy old roadside local
offering a warm welcome,
no food Sundays
⌂Q⊞✿☯♥⚓

Woodbine Inn
Chesterton Lane (off A419)
✆ 3646
Courage BA, BB, Directors ⊞
Quiet pub just off the ring
road. No meals Sundays
Q✿☯♥⚓

Clearwell 14D6
11–2.30; 7–11

Wyndham Arms
✆ Dean 33666
Marston Pedigree; Theakston
Best Bitter ⊞
Built in 1340. Good food
(snacks and restaurant meals)
⌂Q✿⊞☯♥

Cleeve Hill 15G5
10.30–2.30; 7–11

High Roost
A46 ✆ Bishops Cleeve 2010
Hook Norton Best Bitter, Old
Hookey; Wadworth 6X ⊞
Good views over Severn Valley
from this hilltop free house ✿

Coates 15G7
11–2.30; 7–11

Tunnel House
Off A433 up side lane between
Tarlton and Coates
OS965005 ✆ Kemble 280
Archers Best; Flowers
Original; Bulmers Cider ⊞
Regular guest beers
At entrance to Sapperton
Canal Tunnel. Built 1780 for
canal diggers' accommo-
dation. Worth finding
⌂⊞✿☯♥⚓Å

Cockleford 15G6
10.30–2.30; 6–11

Green Dragon
Off A435 near Cowley
✆ Coberley 271
Butcombe Best Bitter; Hook
Norton Best Bitter; Wadworth
6X ⊞ Occasional guest beers
Much improved lively inn.
Jazz on Mondays ⌂⚓♥⚓

Dymock 15E5
11–2.30; 7–11

Crown
B4215 ✆ 660
Hook Norton Best Bitter ⊞
Regular guest beers
Quiet village pub Q☯⚓

Elkstone 15G6
11–2.30; 6–11

Highwayman
A417 (Beechpike)
✆ Miserden 221
Arkell BB, BBB, Kingsdown
Ale ⊞
Isolated, but popular roadside
inn with restaurant ⌂⊞☯♥

Fairford 15H7
12–2.30; 6.30–10.30 (11 F, S)

Marlborough Arms
Cirencester Road (A417)
✆ Cirencester 712566
Flowers Original; Hook
Norton Best Bitter; Marston
Pedigree; Theakston Best
Bitter ⊞ Regular guest beers
Fine two-bar pub, near village
centre ☯⚓

Foss Cross 15H6
11–2.30; 6–11
Hare & Hounds
Foss Way (A429)
✆ Fossebridge 288
**Hook Norton Best Bitter;
Robinson Best Bitter;
Theakston Old Peculier;
Wadworth 6X** ⊞
Remote country pub with
dining room ▲Q⌂➧

France Lynch 15G7
12–2.30; 7–11
Kings Head
✆ Brimscombe 882225
**Bass; Butcombe Bitter;
Theakston Best Bitter** ⊞
First-rate village pub Q⌂⌂

Glasshouse 15E6
11–2.30; 6–11
Glass House
May Hill (off A40)
✆ Gloucester 830529
**Morrell Varsity; Theakston
BB; Whitbread WCPA;
Weston Cider** Ⓖ
Totally unspoilt pub at the
foot of local landmark ▲Q⌂

Gloucester 15F6
11–2.30; 6–11
Cross Keys
Cross Keys Lane off Southgate
Street ✆ 23358
**Flowers IPA, Original;
Whitbread WCPA** ⊞
Good atmosphere, live
"middle of the road" music 5
nights. Historic pub in historic
lane ⇌

Linden Tree
73 Bristol Road ✆ 27869
**Butcombe Bitter; Hook Norton
Best Bitter; Marston Pedigree;
Wadworth 6X** ⊞ Regular
guest beers
Friendly pub, with L shaped
bar, good value for money
meals. A pub for all tastes
Q⌂⌂

Northend Vaults
Northgate Street ✆ 23560
**Flowers Original, Pompey
Royal, Whitbread WCPA** ⊞
Pleasant ale house, busy at
lunchtimes. Cosy snug
panelled with Whitbread
wooden bottle cases ⌂⇌

Pint Pot
Station Road ✆ 416840
**Courage Directors; Hook
Norton Best Bitter; Marston
Pedigree; Wadworth 6X**Ⓖ
Busy, cosy pub, opposite
leisure centre ⇌

Great Barrington 15H6
11–2.30 (2 winter); 6–11
Fox

Off A40 OS205131
✆ Windrush 385
Donnington XXX, BB, SBA ⊞
Coates Cider (summer) Ⓖ
Stone built pub in splendid
position by River Windrush.
Skittle alley ▲Q⌂⌂➧

Great Rissington 15H6
11–2.30; 6.30–11
Lamb
OS200173 ✆ Cotswold 20388
**Boddington Bitter; Glenny
Wychwood Best, Wadworth
6X** ⊞ Regular guest beers
Comfortable modernised
country pub with restaurant
⌂⌂➧

Guiting Power 15H5
12–2.30; 5.30–11
Olde Inne
OS092250 ✆ 392
**Hook Norton Mild, Best Bitter;
Marston Pedigree** ⊞
Occasional guest beers
Friendly free house. No food
Mondays ▲Q⌂⌂➧

Joyford 14D6
11–2.30; 7–11
Dog & Muffler
Off B4432 OS579132
✆ Dean 32444
**Samuel Smith OBB; Bulmer
Cider** ⊞
Warm and cosy pub well
worth finding. Old cider press
in garden ⌂⌂➧

Kineton 15H5
10.30–2.30; 6.30 (6 summer)–11
Halfway House
2 miles south of Ford (B4077)
OS097267
✆ Guiting Power 344
Donnington BB, SBA ⊞
Bulmer Cider Ⓖ
Delightful country pub, near
Cotswold Farm Park
▲⊞ (lunch) ⌂⌂➧

Longborough 15H5
11–2.30; 6–11
Coach & Horses
Near A424 OS180297
✆ Cotswold 30325
Donnington XXX, BB, SBA ⊞
Friendly pub in quiet Cotswold
village ▲⌂⌂

Lower Swell 15H5
11–2.30; 6–11
Golden Ball
B4068 OS175255
✆ Cotswold 30247
Donnington XXX, BB, SBA ⊞
Weston Cider Ⓖ
Pleasant pub in attractive
Cotswold stone village
▲⊞⌂⌂➧ (not Sun)

Minchinhampton 15F7
11.30–2.30; 6 (7 winter)–11
Old Lodge Inn
Minchinhampton Common
OS853008 ✆ Nailsworth 2047
**Archers Village; Arkells BBB;
Fuller ESB; Hook Norton Best
Bitter; Smiles Best Bitter;
Theakston Best Bitter** ⊞
Regular guest beers
Isolated large 16th-century
beamed hunting lodge. Golfers
oasis, in middle of common.
Lovely views ▲Q⊞⌂⌂➧▲

Moreton-in-Marsh 15H5
10–2.30; 6–11
Black Bear Inn
High Street ✆ 50705
Opens 10.30
Donnington XXX, BB, SBA ⊞
Busy town pub ⌂⊞⌂➧▲⇌

Wellington
London Road (A44) ✆ 50396
Evenings open 6.30
Hook Norton Best Bitter ⊞;
Bulmer Cider Ⓖ
Unpretentious local on edge of
town ⌂⌂▲⇌

Nailsworth 15F7
11–2.30; 7–11
Weighbridge Inn
B4014 between Nailsworth
and Avening OS863994
✆ 2520
**Wadsworth IPA, 6X, Farmers
Glory (summer), Old Timer
(winter)** ⊞ Regular guest beers
Popular, beautifully situated
17th-century country inn.
Collection of ironware;
splendid food ▲Q⊞⌂⌂➧

Naunton 15H5
10.30–2.30; 6–11
Black Horse
North of B4068 OS120235
✆ Guiting Power 378
Donnington BB, SBA ⊞;
Weston Cider Ⓖ
Typical Cotswold stone pub
▲⌂⌂➧▲ (side door)

Nether Westcote 15J6
11–2.30; 6–11
New Inn
Off A424 ✆ Shipton-u-
Wychwood 830827
Morrell Bitter; Bulmer Cider ⊞
The only Morrells pub (just)
in Gloucestershire. Warm
welcome, bar billiards
Q⌂⌂➧

Newland 14D6
11–2.30; 6–11
Ostrich
B4231 ✆ Dean 33260

Butcombe Bitter; Flowers
Original; Uley Bitter Ⓗ;
Bulmers Cider Ⓖ
Friendly village pub opposite
church known as the
Cathedral of the Forest
⌂QⒽ⌂Ⓖ🚶

North Nibley   15F7

11 (12 winter)–2.30; 6 (7 winter)–11

New Inn

Waterley Bottom OS758963
✆ Dursley 3659
Cotleigh WB; Greene King
Abbot; Smiles Best Bitter Ⓗ,
Exhibition; Theakston Old
Peculier; Inch's Cider Ⓖ
Occasional guest beers
Friendly, popular but remote,
set in magnificent country-
side. Large garden, children's
play area ⌂⌂⌂Ⓖ🚶🍴

Oakridge   15G7
Lynch

11–2.30; 6 (7 winter)–11

Butchers Arms

✆ Frampton Mansell 371
Butcombe Best Bitter; Marston
Burton Bitter, Pedigree; Uley
Bitter, Old Spot Ⓗ Regular
guest beers
Renovated village pub. Meals
weekdays only ⌂Q⌂Ⓖ🚶🍴⌂

Oddington   15J5

11–2.30; 6–11

Horse & Groom

Upper Oddington (off A436)
✆ Cotswold 30584
Wadworth Devizes Bitter, 6X;
Bulmer Cider Ⓗ
Large, pleasant village pub
with restaurant and Aunt
Sally ⌂⌂⌂Ⓖ🚶🍴

Paxford   15H4

11–2.30; 7–11

Churchill

B4479 OS185379 ✆ 203
Hook Norton Best Bitter, Old
Hookey; Bulmers Cider Ⓗ
Pleasant country local
⌂⌂Ⓖ🚶⌂

Prestbury   15G5

10.30–2.30; 6–11

Plough

Mill Street (off A46)
Flowers IPA, Original;
Whitbread WCPA Ⓖ Regular
guest beers
Unspoilt old village pub near
church ⌂Q⌂Ⓖ🍴

Purton   15E7

10.30–2.30; 7–11

Berkeley Hunt

Off A38 ✆ Dursley 811217
Theakston Best Bitter;
Wadworth 6X; Bulmer Cider
Quaint canalside pub ⌂🍴

Quedgeley   15F6

11–2.30; 6–11

Basket Maker

B4008 ✆ Gloucester 720124
Banks's Mild, Bitter Ⓔ
Extensive contrasting bars in
a new estate pub ⌂Ⓖ🚶🍴⌂

Sapperton   15G7

11–2.30; 7–11

Daneway

Off A419
✆ Frampton Mansell 297
Archers Best Bitter;
Wadworth IPA Ⓗ, 6X, Old
Timer (winter) Ⓖ; Bulmers
Medium Cider (summer)
Occasional guest beers
Superb old canal workers' inn
set in beautiful surroundings
⌂QⒽ⌂Ⓖ🚶🍴

Sheepscombe   15F6

10.30–2.30; 6.30–11

Butchers Arms

Off A46 near Painswick
✆ Gloucester 812113
Flowers Original; Whitbread
PA; ⒽBulmer Medium Cider Ⓔ
Nicely decorated village local
⌂Q⌂Ⓖ

Siddington   15G7

10.30–2.30; 7–11

Greyhound

Ashton Road (off A419)
✆ Cirencester 3573
Wadworth IPA, 6X, Old
Timer Ⓗ
Friendly pub with good food
⌂Q⌂Ⓖ🚶🍴

Stow-on-the-   15H5
Wold

10.30–2.30; 6–11

Queens Head

The Square ✆ Cotswold 30563
Donnington XXX; BB; SBA Ⓗ
Fine old Cotswold town centre
pub Q⌂Ⓖ🚶🍴

Stroud   15G7

11–2.30; 6–11

Clothiers Arms

Bath Road (A46) ✆ 3801
Archers Village; Smiles Best
Bitter; Uley Bitter; Wadworth
6X, Farmers Glory Ⓗ Regular
guest beers
Go-ahead free house ⌂Ⓖ🚶≋

Duke of York

Nelson Street ✆ 78715
Arkell BBB, Kingsdown;
Butcombe Bitter; Marston
Pedigree; Smiles Best Bitter;
Wadworth 6X Ⓗ Regular
guest beers
Comfortable 18th-century
one-bar pub Ⓖ≋

Tetbury   15F7

11–2.30; 6–11

Crown Inn

Gumstool Hill ✆ 52469

Flowers Original; Whitbread
WCPA Ⓗ Occasional guest
beers
16th-century friendly, busy,
market town coaching inn
⌂Q⌂⌂Ⓖ🚶

Tewkesbury   15F5

10–2.30; 6–11

Berkeley Arms

Church Street (A38)
✆ 293034
Opens 10.30
Wadworth Devizes Bitter, 6X,
Farmers Glory, Old Timer Ⓗ;
Bulmers Cider Ⓖ
Interesting 17th-century pub
QⒽⓄ🚶🍴

Britannia

High Street (A38) ✆ 294208
Davenports Bitter Ⓗ
One-bar town pub Ⓖ🍴⌂

Winchcombe   15G5

10.30–2.30; 6–11

Corner Cupboard

Gloucester Street (A46)
✆ Cheltenham 602303
Flowers IPA, Original;
Whitbread WCPA; Bulmers
Cider Ⓗ Regular guest beers
Cosy pub in town centre, self-
catering accommodation
Q⌂🚶🍴

Woodchester   15F7

11–2.30; 6–11

The Ram

South Woodchester (off A46)
Archers Village, Best;
Boddingtons Bitter; Holdens
Black Country; Hook Norton
Old Hookey; Uley UB40, Old
Spot Ⓗ Regular guest beers
Village pub with friendly
atmosphere and splendid
views ⌂Q⌂Ⓖ🚶⌂

Woolaston   14D7
Common

12–2.30; 6.30–11

Rising Sun

Off A48 (through village)
Closed Wed lunchtimes
Hook Norton Best Bitter;
Theakston Best Bitter Ⓗ
Occasional guest beers
Comfortable country pub with
good views and good food
⌂Q⌂Ⓖ🍴⌂

Wotton-   15F7
under-Edge

11–2.30; 6–11

Falcon

20 Church Street
✆ Dursley 842138
Courage Bitter, Best Bitter,
Directors Ⓗ
Comfortable, friendly town
pub, old bar dates from 1659
⌂Ⓖ🚶🍴

Aldershot 7G4

11–2.30; 6–11

Albion
Waterloo Road (off High Street)
Gales XXXD, BBB, XXXXX, HSB Ⓗ
Compact and welcoming; hive of social activity
Ⓖ (not Sat/Sun) 🍴⇄

Alton 7F4

10–2.30; 6–10.30 (11 F, S & summer)

Bakers Arms
High Street 𝄞 82232
Flower's Original; Whitbread Strong Country Bitter Ⓗ
Old town pub
Ⓖ🍺🍴⇄ (lounge) ⇄

Kings Head
Market Street 𝄞 82313
Courage Best Bitter, Directors Ⓗ
Country pub atmosphere in town centre
QⓅⒼ (not Sun) 🍴⇄

Andover 6C4

11 (10.30 Sat)–2.30; 6–11

Railway Tavern
Weyhill Road 𝄞 62474
Flowers Original; Samuel Whitbread; Whitbread Strong Country Bitter Ⓗ
Large roadside local, welcoming atmosphere
🏠Ⓟ🅿Ⓖ🍴🍺

Basingstoke 7E4

10.30–2.30; 5.30–10.30 (11 F, S & summer)

Bounty
81 Bounty Road 𝄞 20071
Courage Best Bitter, Directors Ⓗ
Cosy local next to County Cricket Ground. No meals Sun
🏠QⓅⒼ🍴🍺

George (Hole in the Wall)
London Street 𝄞 465168
Evenings opens 6
Courage Best Bitter, Directors Ⓗ
Value for money town pub near market ⓅⒼ (not Sun) 🍴

Magnums
The Parade, Basing View, Eastrop
Eldridge Pope Dorchester Bitter, Royal Oak; Fuller London Pride; Gales HSB; Ringwood Fortyniner, Old Thumper Ⓖ
Unusual pub in main office area of town Ⓖ (not Sun) ⇄

Queens Arms
Bunnian Place
Courage Best Bitter, Directors Ⓗ
Cosy local ⓅⒼ (not Sun) 🍴⇄

Baughurst 6E3

11–2.30; 5.30 (6 Sat)–10.30 (11 F, S & summer)

Badgers Wood
Wolverton Road
Flowers Original; Whitbread Strong Country Bitter Ⓗ
Friendly village local. Large public. Darts, pool
🏠🅿Ⓖ (not Sun) 🍴

Beaulieu 6D7

10–2.30; 6–10.30 (11 F, S)

Royal Oak Inn
Hilltop 𝄞 612228
Flowers Original; Whitbread Strong Country Bitter Ⓗ
Popular forest pub on outskirts of village 🅿Ⓖ

Beauworth 6E5

10.30–2.30; 6–10.30 (11 F, S & summer)

Milbury's
OS570246 𝄞 Bramdean 248
Flowers Original; Gales BBB, HSB; Wethered Bitter; Whitbread Strong Country Bitter Ⓗ Occasional guest beers
Remote old inn: huge treadmill, 300 ft well in bar. Open 9.30 am Sun for (non-alcoholic) breakfasts
🏠Q🅿🍽️🅿🏠Ⓖ🍴

Binsted 7F4

10.30–2.30; 6–10.30 (11 F, S & summer)

Cedars
The Street (off A31)
𝄞 Bentley 22112
Restaurant licence till 3.30 & midnight
Courage Directors Ⓗ
Old pub in farming area. Good restaurant; games room
🏠🏨🅿Ⓖ🍴 (not Tues) 🍴🍺

Bishopstoke 6D6

11.30–2.30; 6–10.30 (11 F, S & summer)

Longmead Arms
Longmead Avenue (off B3037)
Marston Mercian Mild, Burton Bitter, Pedigree Ⓗ
Good locals' pub
🏠🅿Ⓖ (not Sun) 🍴🍺

Bishops Waltham 6E6

10.30–2.30; 6.30–11

Barleycorn Inn
Lower Basingwell Street
Marston Mercian Mild, Burton Bitter, Pedigree Ⓗ
Unspoilt 3-bar village local
🏠🅿Ⓖ (not Sun) 🍴

Bunch of Grapes
St Peter's Street 𝄞 2935
10–2 (2.30 Sat); 6–10.30 (11 F, S)
Courage Best Bitter, Directors Ⓖ
Superb, unspoilt alehouse with a very warm welcome
Q🍴

Blacknest 7F4

11.30–2.30; 6–10.30 (11 F, S & summer)

Jolly Farmer
Off A325 𝄞 Bentley 22244
Adnams Bitter; Courage Best Bitter; Eldridge Pope Royal Oak; Hall & Woodhouse Badger Best Bitter; Bulmer Cider Ⓗ Regular guest beers
Large pub with skittle alley and restaurant 🅿Ⓖ🍴🍺

Botley 6D6

10–2.30; 6–10.30 (11 F, S & summer)

Brewery Bar
10 Winchester Street (A3051)
Marston Mercian Mild, Burton Bitter, Pedigree Ⓗ, Owd Rodger Ⓖ
Popular village local with contrasting bars
🏠Ⓖ (not Sun) 🍴⇄

Broughton 6C5

11–2.30; 6–10.30 (11 F, S & summer)

Greyhound
High Street (off B3084)
𝄞 Romsey 301464
Marston Mercian Mild, Burton Bitter, Pedigree, Owd Rodger (winter) Ⓗ
Welcoming village pub. Lively public bar, Cunard Liner theme in lounge
🏠Ⓖ🍴 (not Mon) 🍴

Buriton 7F5

10–2.30; 6–10.30 (11 F, S & summer)

Five Bells
48 High Street
𝄞 Petersfield 63584
Friary Meux Bitter, Burton Ale Ⓗ
17th century pub. Popular public, cosy lounge.
Restaurant Tues–Sat 🏠Ⓖ🍴

Chalton 7F6

11–2.30; 6–10.30 (11 F, S & summer)

Red Lion
(off A3) 𝄞 Horndean 592246
Gales XXXD, BBB, XXXXX, HSB Ⓗ
Remote, thatched 13th century inn with inglenooks
🏠Q🅿Ⓖ🍴

Chawton 7F4

10.30 (11 winter)–2.30; 6–10.30 (11 F, S & summer)

Greyfriar
Winchester Road
Flowers Original; Whitbread Strong Country Bitter, Pompey Royal Ⓗ
Beamed village pub. Jane Austen's local?
🏠🅿Ⓖ🍴 (Tue–Sat) 🍴🍺

Cheriton 6E5

10–2.30; 6–10.30 (11 F, S & summer)

Flower Pots
Off A272 𝄞 Bramdean 318
Flower's Original; Whitbread Strong Country Bitter Ⓖ
Cosy, unspoilt local in pretty village 🏠Q🅿🅿🍴⛺

Chilbolton 6D4

11–2.30; 6–10.30 (11 F, S & summer)

Abbots Mitre
☎ 384
Flowers Original; Samuel
Whitbread; Whitbread Strong
Country Bitter ⊞
Friendly, lively village pub;
excellent food,
accommodation and outdoor
children's facilities ▲ ♨ 🖩 ᐧ 🍴 🍺

Crawley 6D5

10.30–2.30; 6–10.30 (11 F, S & summer)

Rack & Manger
Stockbridge Road (A272)
☎ Winchester 72281
Marston Mercian Mild,
Burton Bitter, Pedigree,
Merrie Monk, Owd Rodger ⊞
Cosmopolitan pub—quiet
lounge, public bar with many
games ▲ ♨ ᐧ 🍴🍺

Crondall 7F4

10.30–2.30; 6–10.30 (11 F, S & summer)

Hampshire Arms
Pankridge Street (off A287)
☎ Aldershot 850418
Courage Best Bitter,
Directors ⊞
Comfortable village pub
Q 🖩 ♨ ᐧ 🍺

Crookham Village 7F3

12–2.30; 6–11

Chequers
Crondall Road
Courage Best Bitter; Hall &
Woodhouse Badger Best
Bitter Ⓖ
Timeless rural pub near
Basingstoke Canal Q 🍴

Damerham 6B6

10.30–2.30; 6–10.30 (11 F, S & summer)

Compasses Inn
B3078 OS105162
☎ Rockbourne 231
Courage Best Bitter, Directors
⊞
Fine old inn in pleasant rural
setting ▲ 🖩 ♨ 🖩 ᐧ 🍴🍺 🅰

Droxford 7E6

10–2.30; 6–11

White Horse
High Street (A32) ☎ 877490
Courage Directors, Best,
HSB; Gibbs Mew Bishops
Tipple; Ringwood Best Bitter;
Wadworth 6X, Old Timer
(winter) ⊞ Occasional guest
beers
Cosy 17th century inn
opposite Court House.
Cheerful atmosphere, home-
made food ▲ 🖩 ♨ 🖩 ᐧ 🍴🍺 🅰

Dundridge 6E6

11–2.30; 6.30–11

Hampshire Bowman

Dundridge Lane (1 mile off
B3035) OS579185
☎ Bishops Waltham 2940
Gale BBB, XXXXX, HSB Ⓖ
Friendly country inn off the
beaten track
▲ ♨ ᐧ 🍴 (not Sun) 🅰

East Meon 7F5

10–2.30; 6–10.30 (11 F, S & summer)

George
Church Street ☎ 481
Ind Coope Bitter, Burton Ale;
Gales BBB, HSB; Wadworth
6X ⊞
Free house in pleasant village.
Magnificent fireplaces in
restaurant ▲ ᐧ 🍴🍺

East Stratton 6E4

10.30–2.30; 6–10.30 (11 F, S & summer)

Plough
☎ Micheldever 464
Gales BBB, HSB; Marston
Burton Bitter; Whitbread
Strong Country Bitter ⊞
Converted 18th century
farmhouse. Skittle alley
▲ 🖩 ♨ 🖩 ᐧ 🍺

East Worldham 7F4

11–2.30; 5.30–11

Three Horseshoes
B3004 ☎ Alton 83211
Gales BBB, XXXXX, HSB ⊞
Well-run, friendly pub at top
of steep hill! ♨ ᐧ 🍺

Eling 6D6

11–2.30; 6.30–10.30 (11 F, S)

Village Bells
Eling Hill (off A326)
Gales HSB; Usher Best Bitter ⊞
Popular village local near
working tidal mill ♨ ᐧ 🍴🍺 🅰

Ellisfield 7E4

11–2.30; 6–10.30 (11 F, S & summer)

Fox Inn
OS632455 ☎ Herriard 210
Bishop's Best Bitter; Hall &
Woodhouse Badger Best
Bitter; Gales HSB; Marston
Pedigree; Wadworth 6X ⊞
Excellent country local. Pool &
darts in small public ▲ ♨ ᐧ 🍴🍺

Emsworth 7F6

10–2.30; 6–10.30 (11 F, S & summer)

Lord Raglan
Queen Street (off A27)
☎ 372587
Gales BBB, HSB, XXXXX ⊞
Small comfortable flint pub on
Sussex border ▲ ♨ 🍴🍺 🅯

Smugglers
The Square ☎ 373314
Gales HSB; Usher Bitter;
Webster Yorkshire Bitter ⊞
Large pub in town centre.
Restaurant has "do-it-
yourself" barbeque
🖩 ♨ ᐧ 🍴🍺 🅯

Fareham 6E6

10–2.30; 6–10.30 (11 F, S & summer)

Cob & Pen
Wallington Shore Road
(off A27) ☎ 221624
Flowers Original; Wethered
Bitter; Samuel Whitbread;
Whitbread Strong Country
Bitter ⊞
Successfully improved village
pub with wood decor ▲ ♨ ᐧ 🍴

Golden Lion
28 High Street (A32)
Gales XXXD, BBB, XXXXX,
HSB ⊞
Smart, lively pub in historic
street. Bar billiards & darts ᐧ

Farnborough 7G3

10.30–2.30; 5.30–11

Imperial
12 Farnborough Street
☎ 542573
Courage Best Bitter,
Directors ⊞
Old 3-bar village inn. Pool
room. No food Sun
ᐧ 🍴🍺 🅯 (North)

Prince of Wales
184 Rectory Road ☎ 545578
Opens 11.30 & 6
Eldridge Pope Royal Oak;
Flowers Original; Fuller
London Pride; King & Barnes
Sussex Bitter; Wadworth 6X;
Wethered Bitter ⊞ Regular
guest beers
Popular, friendly, comfortable
and expensive
ᐧ (not Sun) 🅯 (North)

Farringdon 7F5

10–2.30; 6–10.30 (11 F, S & summer)

Rose & Crown
Upper Farringdon (off A32)
☎ Tisted 231
Draught Bass; Flowers
Original; Fuller ESB; Marston
Pedigree, Owd Rodger ⊞
Pleasant village pub with
restaurant. Strong, pricey
ales, but lighter house beer
available ▲ Q ♨ ᐧ 🍴🍺

Finchdean 7F6

10–2.30; 6–10.30 (11 F, S & summer)

George Inn
☎ Rowlands Castle 2257
Ind Coope Bitter, Burton Ale ⊞
Attractive country pub,
thatched public bar and cosy
lounge. Relaxing atmosphere
▲ ♨ ᐧ (not Mon) 🍴🍺 🅰

Fritham 6C6

10–2.30; 6–10.30 (11 F, S & summer)

Royal Oak
Off B3078 OS242141
Flowers Original; Whitbread
Strong Country Bitter Ⓖ
Rustic thatched alehouse, no
brewery "improvement"
▲ Q 🖩 ♨ 🅰

Froyle 7F4

11–2.30; 6–10.30 (11 F, S & summer)

Hen & Chicken
A31 ✆ Bentley 22115
Brakspear Special Bitter;
Courage Best Bitter; Draught
Bass; Hall & Woodhouse
Badger Best Bitter Ⓗ Regular
guest beers
A welcome and worthwhile
stop ☖ 🅿 �P Ⓖ ♫ ♣

Prince of Wales
Lower Froyle (off A31)
Opens 11.30 winter lunch
Ballards Best Bitter; Brakspear
Special Bitter; Courage Best
Bitter; Gales HSB; King &
Barnes Sussex Bitter Ⓗ
Occasional guest beers
Edwardian country pub in
scenic village ☖ 🅿 Ⓖ ♣

Funtley 6E6

11–2.30; 6–10.30 (11 F, S & summer)

Miners Arms
112 Funtley Road
✆ Fareham 232065
Gales BBB, XXXXX, HSB Ⓗ
Friendly, well-kept village pub
Q 🅿 Ⓖ ♣ (not Sun) ♣

Gosport 7E7

10–2.30; 6–10.30 (11 F, S & summer)

Queens Hotel
143 Queens Road ✆ 582645
Opens 11.30 weekdays
Gales HSB; Marston Pedigree;
Palmer IPA Ⓗ Occasional
guest beers
Lively, street corner local,
occasional live music ☖ Ⓖ ♣

Village Home
Village Road, Alverstoke
Mornings opens 11
Flowers Original; Whitbread
Pompey Royal Ⓗ
Lives up to its name! Live
music Tue & Sun eve 🅿 Ⓖ

Windsor Castle
33 St Thomas's Road,
Hardway
Gales XXXD, BBB, XXXXX,
HSB Ⓖ; Taunton Cider Ⓗ
Basic, friendly street corner
local with original well-
stocked off sales hatch.
Occasional piano music 🅿 ♣

Hamble 6D6

10 (10.30 winter)–2.30; 6–10.30 (11 F, S &
summer)

Olde Whyte Harte
High Street (B3397)
✆ Southampton 452108
Gales XXXD, BBBM XXXXX,
HSB Ⓗ
Popular 16th-century pub in
famous yachting village
☖ 🅿 🚶 Ⓖ ♣

Hambledon 7E6

11–2.30; 6–11

Vine
West Street (off B2150) ✆ 419

Courage Directors; Flowers
Original; Gales BBB, HSB;
Marston Pedigree; Wadworth
6X Ⓗ Regular guest beers
Friendly village local with
shove ha'penny ☖ Q 🅿 Ⓖ ♣ ♣ Å

Hammer Vale 7G5

11–2.30; 6–10.30 (11 F, S & summer)

Prince of Wales
Off A3 OS868326
✆ Haslemere 52600
Gales XXXD, BBB, XXXXX,
HSB Ⓖ
Unique rural red brick and
stained glass building. Bags of
atmosphere
☖ Q 🅿 Ⓖ ♣ (not Sun) ♣ ♿

Havant 7F6

10–2.30; 6–10.30 (11 F, S & summer)

Old House at Home
South Street ✆ 483464
Gales BBB, XXXXX, HSB Ⓗ
14th century timber building
behind graveyard
☖ 🅿 Ⓖ (not Sun) ♣ ✦

Robin Hood
6 Homewell ✆ 482779
Gales XXXL, BBB, XXXXX,
HSB Ⓖ
Unpretentious, welcoming
one-bar pub in town centre
☖ Q 🅿 Ⓖ ✦

Hayling Island 7F7

10–2.30; 6–10.30 (11 F, S & summer)

Ferryboat Inn
Ferry Road
Friary Meux Bitter, Ind Coope
Burton Ale Ⓗ
Fine sandy beach outside back
door. Wet suits not allowed in
bar 🚶 🅿 Ⓖ ♣ ♣

Maypole
9 Havant Road ✆ 463670
Gales XXXL. BBB, XXXXX,
HSB Ⓗ
Country atmosphere on
popular holiday island
🅿 ♣ (not Sun) ♣ ♣ Å

Hedge End 6D6

10–2.30; 6–10.30 (11 F, S & summer)

Barleycorn
Lower Northam Road (off
A334)
Marston Mercian Mild,
Burton Bitter, Pedigree Ⓗ
Busy village pub 🅿 Ⓖ (not Sun)

Horndean 7F6

11–2.30; 6–10.30 (11 F, S & summer)

Brewers Arms
Five Heads Road (off A3)
Gales BBB, HSB Ⓗ
Smart village local 🅿 Ⓖ ♣ Å

Horsebridge 6C5

11–2.30; 6–10.30 (11 S, F & summer)

John o'Gaunt
Horsebridge, ½ mile off A3057
✆ Romsey 388394
Eldridge Pope Dorchester

Bitter, Dorset Original IPA,
Royal Oak; Palmer BB Ⓗ
Welcoming country pub.
Shove ha'penny and real
cornish pasties ☖ 🅿 🚶 Ⓖ ♣

Horton Heath 6D6

10.30–2.30; 6–10.30 (11 F, S & summer)

Rising Sun
Botley Road (B3051)
Flowers Original; Whitbread
Strong Country Bitter Ⓗ
Friendly roadside pub
🅿 Ⓖ (not Sun)

Hurstbourne Priors 6D4

10–2.30; 6–10.30 (11 summer)

Hurstbourne
(B3400) ✆ Whitchurch 2000
Flowers Original; Wadworth
6X; Whitbread Strong
Country Bitter; Bulmers
Cider Ⓗ
Formerly the Portsmouth
Arms. Now a pub-restaurant
with a games area
☖ Q 🚶 🅿 Ⓖ ♣

Hythe 6D6

10–2.30; 6–10.30 (11 F, S)

Lord Nelson
High Street ✆ 842169
Flowers Original; Whitbread
Strong Country Bitter; Samuel
Whitbread Ⓗ; Bulmers Cider Ⓖ
Waterfront pub with quaint
bars 🅿 Ⓖ ♣ ♿

Kings Somborne 6C5

10–2.30; 7–10.30 (11 F, S & summer)

Crown
A3057 ✆ 360
Whitbread Strong Country
Bitter Ⓖ
Unspoilt, 15th century,
thatched picture-postcard inn
☖ 🅿 Ⓖ ♣ ♿

Kings Worthy 6D5

10–2.30; 6–10.30 (11 F, S & summer)

Cart & Horses
A3090/A33
✆ Winchester 882360
Marston Burton Bitter,
Pedigree, Owd Rodger Ⓗ
Bulmers Cider Ⓖ
Large thatched roadhouse
with restaurant, childrens'
garden and skittle alley
☖ 🅿 Ⓖ ♣ ♣

Leckford 6D4

10–2.30; 6–10.30 (11 F, S)

Leckford Hutt
Near Stockbridge (A30)
✆ Andover 810787
Marston Mercian Mild,
Burton Bitter, Pedigree,
Merrie Monk (summer), Owd
Rodger Ⓗ
Bustling, isolated, main road
inn ☖ 🚶 🅿 Ⓖ ♣ ♿ Å

Liss 7F5

10–2.30; 6–10.30 (11 F, S & summer)

Temple Inn
82 Forest Road, Liss Forest
✆ 892134
Gales BBB, XXXXX, HSB ⓗ
Friendly local with live music
Sat eves. Pool, shove
ha'penny
🏠🍴♨🕭🎵 (not Sun) 🎵

Little London 7E3

10.30–2.30; 5.30–10.30 (11 F, S & summer)

Plough
Silchester Road OS621597
**Wethered Bitter, Winter
Royal** ⓗ
Small cosy country pub. Bar
billiards 🏠♨🕭 (Mon–Fri)

Long Sutton 7F4

10.30–2.30; 6–10.30 (11 F, S & summer)

Four Horseshoes
The Street (½ mile E. of village)
**Gales XXXD, BBB, XXXXX,
HSB** ⓗ
Rural pub, warm atmosphere
and unusual exterior 🏠🍴♨🕭

Lymington 6C7

10–2.30; 6–10.30 (11 F, S & summer)

King's Arms
St. Thomas Street (off A337)
✆ 72594
**Flowers Original; Whitbread
Strong Country Bitter** ⓖ
Popular 15th century
coaching inn. Friendly
atmosphere, good value food
🏠Q♨🕭🎵🎵🍴♿≈

Lyndhurst 6C6

11–2.30; 6–10.30 (11 F, S & summer)

Mailmans Arms
71 High Street ✆ 2257
**Marston Burton Bitter,
Pedigree** ⓗ
Friendly, comfortable local.
Frequent live entertainment
🏠🍴♨🕭

Marchwood 6D6

11–2.30; 6–10.30 (11 F, S)

Pilgrim Inn
Main Road (off A326)
✆ Southampton 867752
**Draught Bass; Courage Best
Bitter, Directors** ⓗ
Beautiful thatched pub with
immaculate garden 🏠Q♨🕭🎵

Mattingley 7F3

10.30–2.30; 5.30–10.30 (11 F, S & summer)

Leather Bottle
B3349 (near Hook)
✆ Heckfield 371
Courage Best Bitter ⓖ,
Directors ⓗ
Beamed pub, good food
♨🕭🎵

Micheldever 6D4

10.30–2.30; 6–10.30 (11 F, S & summer)

Half Moon & Spread Eagle

Winchester Road
**Flowers Original; Whitbread
Strong Country Bitter** ⓗ
Hub of village life. Own cricket
pitch & piano sing songs 🏠Q♨

Minstead 6C6

10–2.30; 6–10.30 (11 F, S & summer)

Trusty Servant
Between A31 and Lyndhurst–
Cadnam Road
✆ Southampton 812137
**Flowers Original; Wethered
Bitter** ⓗ
Unspoilt, friendly New Forest
village local 🏠🕭🎵🎵

Mortimer West End 7E3

10.30–2.30; 5.30–10.30 (11 F, S & summer)

Turners Arms
West End Road (near
Mortimer) ✆ Reading 332961
**Brakspear Bitter, Special,
Old** ⓗ
Comfortable, roadside inn;
emphasis on food.
N.B. Landlord has tongue in
cheek! ♨🕭🎵 (not Sun)

Nether Wallop 6D4

10–2.30; 6–11

Five Bells
✆ Andover 781572
**Marston Mercian Mild,
Burton Bitter, Pedigree** ⓗ
Classic rural local with skittle
alley 🏠Q♨🏠🕭🎵♿

North Warnborough 7F4

10.30–2.30; 6–11

Anchor
The Street ✆ Odiham 2740
**Courage Best Bitter,
Directors** ⓗ
Quiet, friendly local; large
choice of games 🏠Q♨🕭🎵🎵

Oakhanger 7F5

10–2.30; 6–11

Red Lion
Off B3004 ✆ Bordon 2232
**Courage Best Bitter,
Directors** ⓗ
Classic village local 🏠♨🕭🎵

Odiham 7F4

10.30–2.30; 5.30–11

Waterwitch
Colt Hill ✆ 2778
**Gales HSB; Usher Best Bitter;
Webster Yorkshire Bitter;
Bulmer Cider** ⓗ
In pleasant setting near canal
(boat hire trips) 🏠Q♨🕭🎵

Overton 6D4

10–2.30; 6–10.30 (11 F, S)

Old House at Home
Station Road (off B3400)
✆ Basingstoke 770335

**Courage Best Bitter,
Directors** ⓗ
Thriving local. Crib, darts,
good family garden 🕭♨🕭🎵

Owslebury 6D5

11–2.30; 6–10.30 (11 F, S & summer)

Shearers Arms
Owslebury Bottom (off A333)
OS514242 ✆ 296
**Gales BBB, HSB; Hall &
Woodhouse Badger Best
Bitter; Wadworth 6X, Farmers
Glory** ⓗ
Quiet rural setting 🏠♨🕭🎵🅰

Passfield 7F5

11–2.30; 5.30–10.30 (11 F, S & summer)

Passfield Oak
Passfield Common, Liphook
✆ 205
**Ballards Best Bitter; Bunce's
Best Bitter; Joshua Privett
Bitter, BDS; Marston
Pedigree** ⓗ
Convivial pub on village
green. Large garden
🏠Q♨🕭🎵♿

Pennington 6C7

11–2.30; 6–10.30 (11 F, S & summer)

Musketeer
26 North Street (near A337)
✆ Lymington 76527
**Brakspear Bitter; Felinfoel
Double Dragon; Gales HSB;
Gibbs Mew Salisbury Best;
Ringwood Best Bitter** ⓗ **&** ⓖ
Regular guest beers
Friendly comfortable pub.
No food Sun 🏠Q♨🕭🎵

Petersfield 7F5

10–2.30; 6–10.30 (11 F, S & summer)

Market Inn
The Square ✆ 63723
**Flowers Original; Whitbread
Strong Country Bitter** ⓗ
Small listed building Q🕭🎵🎵≈

Portsmouth 7E7

10–2.30; 6–10.30 (11 F, S & summer)

Artillery Arms
1 Hester Road, Milton
**Friary Meux Bitter; Ind Coope
Burton Ale** ⓗ
Friendly popular back street
local. Piano player Fri eves 🎵

Brewers Arms
170 Milton Road, Milton
Gales BBB, XXXXX, HSBⓖ **&**ⓗ
Interesting town local near
Fratton Park 🏠♨

Brewery Tap
17 London Road, North End
✆ 699943
**Draught Bass; Fuller London
Pride, ESB; Taunton Medium
Cider, Dry Cider** ⓗ **Regular
guest beers**
Shopping centre pub near old
Southsea Brewery
🕭🎵 (Mon–Fri) ♿

Fifth Hants Volunteer Arms
Albert Road, Southsea
Gale BBB, XXXXX, HSB Ⓗ
Popular street-corner local
🏚🍺

George
84 Queens Street, Portsea
Flowers Original; Fuller London Pride, ESB Ⓗ
Historic pub with well in the bar. Near Mary Rose and HMS Victory Q Ⓖ ≥ (Harbour)

George Inn
Portsdown Hill Road, Cosham
Whitbread Strong Country Bitter, Pompey Royal, Samuel Whitbread Ⓗ
Old coaching inn; panoramic views; shove ha'penny
Q 🍴 Ⓖ (not Sun) Å

Mermaid
222 New Road, Copnor
Whitbread Strong Country Bitter, Samuel Whitbread Ⓗ
Occasional guest beers
Fine local with Victorian wrought iron canopy and unusual façade 🏫 ♨ 🍺

Pembroke
Pembroke Road, Old Portsmouth ☎ 823961
Flowers Original; Whitbread Strong Country Bitter Ⓗ
Comfortable pub with Naval flavour, near the Cathedral. No meals Sun
Ⓖ 🍴 ≥ (Harbour)

Red White & Blue
150 Fawcett Road, Southsea
Gales BBB, XXXXX, HSB Ⓗ
Small, busy local ≥ (Fratton)

R M A Tavern
58 Cromwell Road, Eastney ☎ 820896
Gales XXXD, BBB, XXXXX, HSB Ⓗ
Lively local with rare toad in the hole game. Good value food 🏫 ♨ Ⓖ 🍴 🍺

Scotts
51 King Street, Southsea ☎ 826018
Courage Best Bitter, Directors; Fuller London Pride; Gales HSB; Marston Pedigree; Wadworth 6X Ⓗ Regular guest beers
Smart town pub. Good selection of beer
Ⓖ 🍴 ≥ (Portsmouth & Southsea)

Priors Dean
7F5

11–2.30; 6–10.30 (11 F, S & summer)

White Horse (Pub with no name)
Off A32 OS714290
Ballards Best Bitter; Draught Bass; Gales HSB; Marston Pedigree; Ringwood Fortyniner; Wadworth 6X Ⓗ
Occasional guest beers

Remote free house. Unsigned, in the middle of a field
🏚 Q ♨ 🍺 Å

Privett
7E5

10–2.30; 6–11

Pig & Whistle
A32 ☎ 323
Flowers Original; Gibbs Mew Bishops Tipple; Marston Pedigree; Joshua Privett Bitter, BDS; Ringwood Fortyniner Ⓗ
Large home brew pub. Comfortable sitting area around open fire 🏚 ♨ 🏫 Ⓖ 🍴

Ringwood
6B6

11.30–2.30; 6–10.30 (11 F, S & summer)

Hunter's Lodge
154 Southampton Road (Old Road)
Hall & Woodhouse Badger Best Bitter Ⓗ
Comfortable popular local; stripped pine decor 🏫 ♨ Ⓖ

Romsey
6C6

10–2.30; 6–10.30 (11 F, S)

Tudor Rose
3 The Cornmarket ☎ 512126
Courage Best Bitter, Directors Ⓗ
Convivial, welcoming 15th century town pub 🏚 Q ♨ Ⓖ

Selborne
7F5

10–2.30; 6–10.30 (11 F, S & summer)

Selborne Arms
High Street (B3006) ☎ 247
Courage Best Bitter, Directors Ⓖ
Splendid, unspoilt pub near N.T. Selborne. Zig-zag
🏚 ♨ Ⓖ 🍴 🍺

Queens Hotel
High Street (B3006)
Courage Best Bitter, Directors; Taunton Cider Ⓗ
Village-style public bar; hotel lounge bar ♨ 🏫 Ⓖ 🍴 🍺

Silchester
7E3

10.30–2.30; 5.30–10.30 (11 F, S & summer)

Calleva Arms
Silchester Common
OS627621 ☎ Reading 700305
Gales BBB, XXXXX, HSB Ⓗ
Near common and remains of Roman town
🏚 ♨ Ⓖ 🍴 (not Sun) 🍺

Sopley
6B7

10.30–2.30; 6–10.30 (11 F, S & summer)

Woolpack
B3347 ☎ Bransgore 72252
Whitbread Strong Country Bitter, Pompey Royal Ⓗ
Attractive thatched pub. Patio overlooks stream; ducks, geese, playground 🏚 🏫 Ⓖ 🍴 ♿

Southampton
6D6

10–2.30; 6–10.30 (11 F, S & summer)

Bay Tree
10 New Road ☎ 333187
Gales BBB, XXXXX, HSB Ⓗ
Lively city-centre pub with games room; near College & Mountbatten Theatre
Ⓖ 🍺 ♿ ≥

Crown & Sceptre
168 Burgess Road, Bassett (A35)
Flowers Original; Whitbread Strong Country Bitter; Pompey Royal; Samuel Whitbread Ⓗ
Finewood panelled bars, friendly atmosphere, good food Q ♨ Ⓖ 🍴 🍺

Mason's Arms
45 St. Mary's Street, St. Mary's ☎ 32398
Opens 11 & 6.30
Gales XXXD, BBB, XXXXX, HSB Ⓗ
Excellent, small pub near market; darts 🏚 Q Ⓖ 🍴

New Inn
14 Bevois Valley Road ☎ 228437
Mornings opens 11; eves 6.45
Gales BBB, XXXXX, HSB Ⓗ
Popular, friendly local. Good atmosphere. Darts Ⓖ ♿

Park Inn
37 Carlisle Road, Shirley ☎ 787835
Opens 10.30 & 6.30
Wadworth IPA, 6X, Farmer's Glory, Old Timer (winter) Ⓗ
Popular, friendly, sidestreet local; darts 🏚 🍺

Richmond Inn
Portswood Road, Portswood
Marston Mercian Mild, Burton Bitter, Pedigree Ⓗ
Good town local with superb old LSD cash till ♨ 🍺

Salisbury Arms
126 Shirley High Street, Shirley ☎ 774624
Opens 7 Sat eves
Marston Mercian Mild, Burton Bitter, Pedigree Ⓗ
Unpretentious working-class local; darts Ⓖ 🍴 🍺

Wellington Arms
56 Park Road, Freemantle
Mornings opens 11
Courage Directors; Gales HSB; Gibbs Mew Salisbury Best; Ringwood Best Bitter, Old Thumper; Wadworth IPA, 6X Ⓗ
Small, popular free house full of Wellington memorabilia
♨ Ⓖ

Southwick
7E6

10–2.30; 6–10.30 (11 F, S & summer)

Golden Lion
High Street ☎ Cosham 379134
Courage Best Bitter, Directors Ⓗ

Comfortable local with old brewhouse restored as a "dry" museum—visits by appointment—Tel. Cosham 380978 🏠🍴🕕🅿🍺🍴

Steep   7F5

10–2.30; 6–10.30 (11 F, S & summer)

Harrow
Flowers Original; Whitbread Strong Country Bitter; Samuel Whitbread Ⓖ
Fine old country pub. Inglenook fireplace in public. Polyphon in lounge 🏠Q🅿🍴

Stratfield Saye   7F3

10.30–2.30; 5.30–10.30 (11 F, S & summer)

Four Horseshoes
West End Green OS668616
Morland Mild, Bitter Ⓗ Best Bitter Ⓖ
Unspoilt village local 🏠Q🅿🍴

New Inn
Fair Oak Lane, Burt Norton
Off A33 OS684616
Arkell BBB; Burt VPA; Hook Norton Best Bitter, Old Hookey; Ringwood Old Thumper; Theakston XB Ⓗ
Regular guest beers
Remote pub with traditional games 🏠🚲🅿🍴

Swanmore   6E6

10–2.30; 6–11

New Inn
Chapel Road (off A333)
🕿 Bishops Waltham 3588
Marston Mercian Mild, Burton Bitter, Pedigree, Owd Rodger Ⓗ
Very popular village inn with lots of bric-a-brac; excellent menu 🏠Q🚲🅿🕕🍴🍴♿

Tadley   6E3

11–2.30; 5.30–10.30 (11 F, S & summer)

Treacle Mine Hotel
Silchester Road (off A340)
🕿 4857
Arkell BBB; Courage Best Bitter; Hall & Woodhouse Badger Best Bitter; Theakston XB Ⓗ
Named after popular Tadley legend. Home cooked food Q🅿🚲🕕

Titchfield   6E7

11–2.30; 6–10.30 (11 F, S & summer)

Wheatsheaf
East Street 🕿 42965
Gales HSB; Usher Best Bitter; Webster Yorkshire Bitter Ⓗ
Small, very cosy pub; excellent food Q🚲🍴🕕🍴 (Tue–Sat) ♿ 🅰

Twyford   6D5

11–2.30; 6–10.30 (11 F, S & summer)

Phoenix
High Street (A333) 🕿 713322
Marston Mercian Mild,

Burton Bitter, Pedigree, Owd Rodger Ⓗ
Welcoming inn, excellent food. Skittle alley & bar billiards 🏠🚲🕕🍴

Upton Grey   7F4

11–2.30; 6–10.30 (11 F, S & summer)

Hoddington Arms
Upton Grey
🕿 Long Sutton 371
Courage Best Bitter, Directors Ⓗ
Pleasant local in pretty village, near pond 🏠🚲🅿🕕🍴🍴

Vernham Street   6C3

12–2.30 (closed Mon); 6–10.30 (11 F, S)

Boot
Littledown OS351581
🕿 Linkenholt 213
Hall & Woodhouse Badger Best Bitter; Marston Burton Bitter, Pedigree Ⓖ
Thatched pub with new eating area 🏠Q🅿🕕🍴🍴

West Dean   6C5

10–2.30; 6–10.30 (11 F, S)

Red Lion
(Off A27/B3084)
🕿 Lockerley 40469
Flowers Original; Whitbread Strong Country Bitter; Samuel Whitbread Ⓗ
Friendly village local straddling two counties. River frontage 🏠🚲🅿🚲🕕🍴🍴♿🅰≷

West Wellow   6C6

11–2.30; 6.30–10.30 (11 F, S)

Red Rover
Salisbury Road (A36)
🕿 22266
Flowers Original; Whitbread Strong Country Bitter Ⓗ
Friendly village local 🚲🕕🍴

Weyhill   6C4

11.30–2.30; 6 (7 Sat)–11

Weyhill Fair
A303 🕿 3631
Flowers Original; Morrell Dark Mild Ⓖ Bitter, Varsity; Wethered Bitter; Westons Cider Ⓗ Regular guest beers
Good beer drinkers' pub. Mural of historic Weyhill Fair 🏠Q🚲🕕🍴

Whitchurch   6D4

11–2.30; 6–10.30 (11 F, S & summer)

Harvest Home
Winchester Road 🕿 892217
Marston Mercian Mild, Burton Bitter, Pedigree, Owd Rodger Ⓗ
Popular local near silk mill. Specialises in excellent sea food and frogs' legs 🏠🚲🕕🍴

Wickham   6E6

10–2.30; 6–11

Roebuck

Kingsmead (A32) 🕿 832150
Gales BBB, XXXXX, HSB Ⓗ&Ⓖ
Popular and friendly roadhouse with accent on food 🚲🕕🍴🍴🅰

Winchester   6D5

10.30–2.30; 6–10.30 (11 F, S & summer)

Bell
83 St. Cross Road (A333)
Marston Mercian Mild, Burton Bitter, Pedigree Ⓗ
Splendid ancient inn in historic St. Cross. Huge bottle collection 🏠🚲🕕🍴♿

County Arms
85 Romsey Road (A3090)
🕿 51950
Marston Mercian Mild, Burton Bitter, Pedigree Ⓗ
Friendly inn close to prison and hospital 🏠🚲🅰🕕🍴🍴

Fulflood Arms
28 Cheriton Road (off A272)
Mornings opens 11
Marston Burton Bitter, Pedigree Ⓗ
Traditional street corner local. Sign still proclaims "Winchester Brewery" 🚲🕕 (Sat) 🍴≷

Green Man
53 Southgate Street (A333)
🕿 65429
Marston Mercian Mild, Burton Bitter, Pedigree, Merrie Monk Ⓗ
Solid corner city-centre local. Table skittles and skittle alley 🅰🕕🍴≷

King Alfred
8 Saxon Road, Hyde
Marston Mercian Mild, Burton Bitter, Pedigree Ⓗ
Busy traditional local in residential area 🚲🕕🍴🅰≷

Olde Market
The Square (next ot precinct)
Flowers Original; Whitbread Strong Country Bitter Ⓗ
Thriving, one-bar tourist pub near cathedral. Jazz mon 🕕

Rising Sun
14 Bridge Street 🕿 62564
Courage Best Bitter, Directors Ⓗ
Timber-framed Tudor town inn; cellar once a prison 🏠🚲🅰🕕🍴

Wolverton   6E3

10.30–2.30; 5.30–10.30 (11 F, S & summer)

George & Dragon
Towns End (off A339)
OS566587
🕿 Kingsclere 298292
Brakspear Special; Hall & Woodhouse Tanglefoot; Wadworth IPA, 6X Ⓗ
Occasional guest beers
Old rambling pub
🏠🚲🕕 (not Sun) 🍴♿

Astwood Bank 15G3

12–2.30; 6–10.30

Oddfellows Arms
Foregate Street (off A441)
access via Retreat Street
☎ 2806
M & B Mild ⒠, Brew XI ⒣
Welcoming old back street
local. New inn sign depicts
two local odd fellows! You
may spot them drinking in the
pub. No food Sun
🏠 Q ✿ ᠖ ➐ (till 8.30) ❢

Bartestree 14D4

10.30–2.30; 6–11

New Inn
A438
Marston Burton Bitter,
Pedigree ⒣
Imposing Victorian mock
Gothic roadhouse 🏠 ✿

Bewdley 15F2

11–2.30; 7–10.30 (11 F, S)

Black Boy
50 Wyre Hill (off A456)
Banks's Mild, Bitter ⒠
Excellent small pub, mecca for
mild drinkers ᠖ ❢

Hop Pole Inn
Cleobury Road (A456)
Marston Mercian Mild,
Burton Bitter ⒣
Friendly pub on hill above
town Q ✿ ❢

Pack Horse Inn
High Street ☎ 403762
Ansells Bitter; Ind Coope
Burton Ale; Tetley Bitter ⒣
Small, cosy pub in narrow side
street 🏠 ᠖ ❢

Thurston Hotel
Severn Side South ☎ 403267
Ansells Mild, Bitter; Ind Coope
Burton Ale ⒣
Plush riverside lounge.
Regular live jazz
🔳 ᠖ ➐ (not Sun) ❢

Bournheath 15G2

11–2.30; 6–10.30 (11 F, S)

New Inn
10 Doctors Hill (off
Stourbridge Road)
☎ Bromsgrove 73094
Draught Bass; M & B Mild,
Springfield Bitter, Brew XI ⒣
Cosy locals' bar with new
lounge 🏠 ✿ ➐ ❢

Bransford 15F4

11–2.30; 6–11

Fox Inn
Hereford Road (A4103)
☎ Leigh Sinton 32247
Davenports Bitter ⒣
Comfortable, friendly roadside
inn 🏠 ✿ ᠖ ➐ ❢

Bretforton 15H4

10.30–2.30; 6–11

Fleece
The Square (off B4035)
Hook Norton Best Bitter;
Marston Pedigree; M & B
Brew XI ⒣ Regular guest beers
Famous village inn owned by
the National Trust. No outside
sign board to disturb its
originality 🏠 ✿ ᠖ ❢

Broadwas 15F3

11–2.30; 6–11

Royal Oak
A44
Marston Mercian Mild,
Burton Bitter, Pedigree ⒣
Welcoming wayside tavern
with fine views ✿ 🔳 ᠖

Broadway 15H5

10–2.30; 6–11

Crown & Trumpet
Snowshill Road ☎ 853202
Flowers IPA Original,
Whitbread WCPA; Bulmers
Cider ⒣
Fine cotswold stone pub in a
tourist mecca. Wide variety of
traditional games 🏠 ✿ 🔳 ᠖ ➐ ⅄

Bromsgrove 15G2

10.30–2.30; 6–10.30 (11 F, S)

Red Lion
High Street
Banks's Mild, Bitter ⒠
Busy bar in pedestrianised
shopping area ✿ ᠖ (not Sun)

Canon Pyon 14D4

10.30–2.30; 6–11

Nags Head
A4110 ☎ 252
Wye Valley Hereford Bitter,
Supreme ⒣; Dunkertons
Cider ⒢
Bustling village pub with
home cooking and brewing
🏠 🔳 ✿ ᠖ ➐ ❢

Carey 14D5

10.30–2.30; 6.30–11 winter opens later

Cottage of Content
OS565310 ☎ 242
Flowers Original; Hook
Norton Old Hookey; Wye
Valley Hereford Bitter,
Supreme ⒣ Occasional guest
beers
Idyllic country pub
🏠 Q 🔳 ✿ 🔳 ᠖ ➐ ❢

Catshill 15G2

10.30–2.30; 7–10.30 (11 F, S)

Plough & Harrow
Stourbridge Road
☎ Bromsgrove 77355
Ansells Mild, Bitter; Gaymers
Cider ⒣
Cosy and comfortable roadside
inn. Sing-songs in the lounge.
Plush split-level bar ✿ ᠖ ➐ ❢

Chaddesley Corbett 15F2

11–2.30; 7–10.30 (11 F, S)

Swan
High Street (off A448) ☎ 302
Evening opens 6.30
Batham Mild, Bitter, Delph
Strong Ale ⒢; Bulmers Cider ⒢
Quiet village pub, three rooms
to suit all tastes. Dining room
🏠 ✿ ᠖ ➐

Talbot
High Street (off A448) ☎ 388
Banks's Mild, Bitter ⒠
Large, lively 15th century inn,
original oak beams and
panelling. Restaurant
🏠 ✿ ᠖ ➐ ❢

Claines 15F3

11–2.30; 6–11

Mug House
The Churchyard (off A449)
Banks's Mild, Bitter ⒠
Excellent and ancient pub ✿ ❢

Clifton upon Teme 15E3

11–2.30; 7–11

Lion
B4204
☎ Shelsley Beauchamp 238
Adnams Bitter; Draught Bass;
Hook Norton Best Bitter;
M & B Springfield Bitter ⒣
Old village inn. Pleasant
garden, interesting fireplace
✿ ᠖ ➐ ❢

Colwall 15E4

11–2.30; 7–11

Chase Inn
Upper Colwall
☎ Upper Colwall 40276
Donnington Best Bitter, SBA;
Wye Valley Hereford
Supreme; Tate's Traditional
Bitter ⒣
Unspoilt, traditional local on
Malvern Hill Q ✿ ᠖ ➐ ❢

Dodford 15G2

11–2.30; 6.30–10.30 (11 F, S)

Dodford Inn
Whinfield Road (off A448)
OS939729
☎ Bromsgrove 32470
Davenports Mild, Bitter ⒣
Attractive one-roomed pub.
Large garden with barbeque
at weekends 🏠 ᠖ ➐ ⅄

Drayton 15G2

12–2.30; 7–10.30 (11 F, S)

Robin Hood
(off B4188) OS908758
☎ Belbroughton 730255
Ansells Bitter; Ind Coope
Burton Ale ⒣
Popular country pub with
cosy atmosphere. Extensive
menu—some vegetarian
meals 🏠 ᠖ ➐ ❢

Droitwich 15F3

11–2.30; 6–11

Gardeners Arms
Vine Lane

Hansons Mild, Bitter E
Small pub, local's bar and
comfortable lounge
🏃&(not Sun) 🍺

Dulas 14C5

11–2.30; 6.30–11

Trout (Found Out)
Off B4347 OS361302
☎ Golden Valley 240356
**Tates Traditional Bitter;
Woods Special; Wye Valley
Hereford Supreme** H**; Bulmers
Cider** H
Isolated, marvellous and
totally unspoilt 🏚Q🏃&🍺🍴🏕

Eldersfield 15F5

Greyhound
Lime Street (off B4211)
OS814305
☎ Staunton Court 381
Flowers Original G
Excellent, unspoilt pub on
county boundary. Skittle alley
🏃🍺

Elmley Castle 15G4

11–2.30; 6–11

Queen Elizabeth
Marston Burton Bitter H
16th century inn with cosy,
traditional bars 🏃&🍺🍴

Evesham 15G4

11–2.30; 6–11

Trumpet
Merstow Green
**Draught Bass; M & B Mild,
Brew XI** H**; Weston Cider** G
Town house, close to Market
Square and town centre 🏃&≷

Forhill 15G2

10.30–2.30; 6–10.30 (11 F, S)

Peacock
Icknield Street (off A441)
OS054755 ☎ Wythall 823232
**Draught Bass; M & B Mild,
Springfield Bitter** H
Friendly country pub with
large gardens. Bar billiards.
Picnic area opposite pub
🏚🏃&(not Sun) 🍺🏕

Fownhope 14D5

10.30–2.30; 6–11

Forge & Ferry
Ferry Lane (off B4224 ☎ 391
**Davenports Bitter; Marston
Pedigree; Usher Best Bitter,
Founders Ale** H**; Wye Valley
Hereford Supreme; Westons
Cider** G **Occasional guest
beers**
Lively village local 🏚🏨🏃&🍺🍴

Green Man
B4224 ☎ 243
**Hook Norton Best Bitter; Sam
Smith OBB; Wadworth 6X** H**;
Westons Cider** G
Comfortable, timber-framed
village inn 🏚Q🏃🏨🍺🍴🏕

Franche 15F2

11–2.30; 7–10.30 (11 F, S)

**Three Crowns &
Sugarloaf**
Wolverley Road
Banks's Mild, Bitter E
Large modern, suburban pub
popular with the young &🍺🍴

Grimley 15F3

11–2.30; 6–11

Camp House Inn
Camp Lane (off A443)
OS835592
Flowers Original H**;
Whitbread WCPA; Bulmer
Cider** G
Unspoilt riverside inn with
spacious garden 🏚🏃&🍺🍴

Hanley Castle 15F4

11–2.30; 6–11

Three Kings
B4211
☎ Upton on Severn 2686
**Butcombe Bitter; Wadworth
6X** H
Excellent pub on village green,
small but classic 🏚Q🏃🍺

Hardwicke 14B4

10.30–2.30; 6–11

Royal Oak
B4348 OS273438
☎ Clifford 248
**Flowers Original; Fuller ESB;
Westons Cider** H
Isolated, roadside inn
🏚Q🏃&🍺🍴

Hay on Wye 14B4

11–3; 6–11

Blue Boar
Castle Street ☎ 820884
Flowers IPA Original H
Regular guest beers
Comfortable town pub 🏚Q&🍺

Hereford 14D4

10.30–2.30; 6–11

Bay Horse
Kings Acre Road (A438)
**Flowers IPA, Original;
Whitbread WCPA** H
Popular and convivial pub on
outskirts of town 🏃&🍺

Saracens Head
☎ 275480
**Draught Bass; Marston
Pedigree; Herefordshire Ales
Tennants Old Original; Wye
Valley Hereford Bitter,
Supreme; Westons Cider** H
Regular guest beers
Popular freehouse overlooking
the Wye 🏃&🍺

Vaga Tavern
Vaga Street ☎ 273601
Banks's Mild, Bitter E
Two-bar local. Difficult to find
but worth it 🍺

Try also: Oxford Arms & New
Harp (Whitbread)

Himbleton 15G3

12–2.30; 6–11

Galton Arms
☎ 672
Banks's Mild, Bitter H
Splendid village local in
beautiful setting 🏃&🍺🍴

Holy Cross 15G2

11–2.30; 6–10.30 (11 F, S)

Bell & Cross
Off A491
☎ Belbroughton 730319
M & B Mild, Brew XI H
Timeless pub with a warm
welcome 🏚Q🏃🍺

Ismere 15F2

11–2.30; 7–10.30 (11 F, S)

Waggon & Horses
A451
Hansons Mild, Bitter E **&** H
Popular roadside house. Live
jazz Mon nights 🏚🏃🍺🍴

Kidderminster 15F2

11–2.30; 7–10.30 (11 F, S)

Hare & Hounds
Stourbridge Road,
Broadwaters (A449)
☎ 751819
Bathams Mild, Bitter H
Spartan bar, split-level lounge
&🍺🍴

King & Castle
Comberton Hill ☎ 744667
**Bathams Mild, Bitter; Courage
Best Bitter; Pardoes Bitter** H
Regular guest beers
Large one-room pub on
Severn Valley Railway Station
🏚Q🏃&🍺≷

Station Inn
Fairfield (off A448)
Davenports Bitter H
Handy for Severn Valley
Steam Railway. Pictures of old
Kidderminster 🏨🏃&🍺🍴≷

Ye Old Seven Stars
Coventry Street
**Courage Best Bitter,
Directors** H
Large town centre pub;
regulars keen on charity work
&🍺≷

Yew Tree
Chester Road North ☎ 751786
Banks's Mild, Bitter E
Small, busy pub &🍺🍴≷

Try also: Horsefair (John
Smiths)

Kingsland 14D3

11.30–2.30; 6.30–11

Angel Inn
B4360 (off A4110) ☎ 355
**Marston Pedigree; Wye Valley
Hereford Bitter** H **Occasional
guest beers**
Excellent friendly 16th
century inn 🏚Q🏃🏨🍺🍴🏕

Kington 14C3

10.30–2.30; 6–11

Olde Tavern (Railway Tavern)
Victoria Road (off A44)
Opens lunch 12 Sat/Sun only;
eves 7.30
Ansells Bitter ℍ
Totally unspoilt boozer ⌂ ℘

Swan Hotel
Church Street (off A44)
✆ 230510
Ansells Bitter; Tetley Bitter ℍ
Comfortable family hotel
🛏️ ℘ ℍ ⏣ ♪ ▮

Knightwick 15E3

10.30–2.30; 6–11

Talbot Hotel
A44 ✆ 21235
Banks's Bitter; Draught Bass;
Donnington BB ℍ
Impressive 14th century hotel
🛏️ ℘ ℍ ⏣ ♪ ▮

Leigh Sinton 15F4

11–2.30; 6–11

Somers Arms
Hereford Road (A4103)
✆ 32343
Banks's Mild, Bitter; Wye
Valley Hereford Bitter; Tates
Traditional Bitter ℍ; Norbury
Cider Ⓖ Regular guest beers
Busy village local. Jazz and
folk nights. Quoits, skittles,
shove halfpenny ℘ ⏣ ♪ ▮

Try also: Royal Oak (Marston)

Leintwardine 14C2

10.30–2.30; 6–11

Sun Inn
Rosemary Lane (off A4113)
Ansells Mild, Bitter Ⓖ
A real gem, left over from the
last century 🛏️ Q ▮

Malvern 15F4

11–2.30; 6–11

Retired Soldier
83 Newtown Road ✆ 2313
Marston Burton Bitter ℍ
Small, friendly local ℘ ▮

Mathon 15E4

10.30–2.30; 6–11

Cliffe Arms
OS737458
✆ Ridgeway Cross 782
Hook Norton Best Bitter ℍ;
Bulmers Cider ℍ Regular
guest beers
Village focal point, well
hidden away ℘ ⏣ ♪ ▮ ⏚

Menith Wood 15E2

11–2.30; 7–10.30 (11 F, S)

Cross Keys
Between A443 & B4202
OS709690
Marston Mercian Mild,
Burton Bitter, Pedigree ℍ

Roadside pub in quiet
countryside ℘ ⏣ ♪

Much Marcle 14E5

10.30–2.30; 6–11

Slip Inn
OS652333
✆ 246
Draught Bass; Whitbread
WCPA ℍ Occasional guest
beers
Picturesque country pub,
named after a nearby landslip
🛏️ ℘ ⏣ ♪ ▮

Try also: Westons Cider Mill

Munderfield 14E4

10.30–2.30; closed some winter weekdays; 6–11

Hollybush
Munderfield Row (B4214)
✆ 349
Ansells Bitter; Ind Coope
Burton Ale; Bulmers Cider ℍ
Isolated country pub
commanding good views
🛏️ ℍ ℘ ⏣ ♪ ▮ ⏚

Norton 15G4

10.30–2.30; 7–11

Norton Grange
A435/A439, near Evesham
✆ Evesham 870215
Marston Burton Bitter,
Pedigree ℍ
Family-run hotel,
conveniently situated
🛏️ ℘ ℍ ⏣ ♪ ⏚

Pandy 14C5

11–3; 6–11

Old Pandy
A465 OS335226
✆ Crucorney 208
Brain Dark, SA; Smiles Best
Bitter, Exhibition, Old Vic ℍ;
Westons Cider Ⓖ Regular
guest beers
Excellent pub with amusing
landlord, well worth the visit!
🛏️ Q ⌂ ℘ ℍ ⏣ ♪ ▮ ⏚

Pensax 15E2

11–2.30; 6–10.30 (11 F, S)

Bell
B4202, 1 mile from Clowes
Top
Hook Norton Best Bitter;
Robinson's Best Bitter; Timothy
Taylor Landlord; Wadworth
6X ℍ Regular guest beers
Popular country pub highly
regarded for its food
🛏️ Q ℘ ⏣ ♪

Peterstow 14D5

10.30–2.30; 6–11

Yew Tree
A49 ✆ Ross 62815
Flowers IPA; Whitbread
WCPA ℍ Regular guest beers
Welcoming roadside pub
🛏️ ℘ ⏣ ♪ ▮

Try also: Red Lion, Cradley

Poolbrook 15F4

11–2.30; 6–11

Three Horseshoes
✆ Malvern 3983
Flowers IPA, Original ℍ
Popular local on Poolbrook
Common 🛏️ Q ℘ ⏣ ♪

Powick Hams 15F4

11–2.30; 6–11

Vernon Arms
A449
Davenports Mild (summer),
Bitter ℍ
Large modernised roadside
house with darts and crib
⌂ ⏣ ♪ ▮

Redditch 15G3

12–2.30; 6–10.30 (11 F, S)

Gate Hangs Well
Evesham Road, Headless Cross
Ansells Mild, Bitter ℍ
Convivial 1-roomed pub on
outskirts of town, with patio
🛏️ Q ℘ ⏣ (Mon–Fri)

Richards Castle 14D3

10.30–2.30; 6–11

Castle
Castle Road (B4361) ✆ 678
Wem Pale Ale, Best Bitter,
Special Bitter ℍ
Lively country pub 🛏️ ℘ ▮ ⏚

St Owens Cross 14D5

10.30–2.30; 6–11

New Inn
A4137/B4521
✆ Harewood End 274
Draught Bass; Marston
Pedigree; Herefordshire Ales
Tennants Hereford Bitter ℍ;
Westons Cider Ⓖ
Pleasant country pub

Sellack 14D5

10.30–2.30; 6–11

Lough Pool
Upper Grove Common
OS558268
✆ Harewood End 236
Draught Bass; M & B
Springfield; Wye Valley
Hereford Supreme ℍ
Very pleasant and picturesque
country pub. Good food
🛏️ Q ⏣ ♪

Shenstone 15F2

10–2.30; 7–10.30 (11 F, S)

Plough
Off A448/A450
✆ Chaddesley 340
Batham Bitter, Delph Strong
Ale ℍ; Weston Cider Ⓖ
Friendly country pub off the
beaten track 🛏️ Q ℘ ▮ ⏚

Stoke Works 15G3

11–2.30; 6–10.30 (11 F, S)

Boat & Railway
Shaw Lane (1½ miles M5 Jct 5)
Hansons Mild, Bitter E
Popular canalside pub.
Meeting place for many
societies and clubs. Skittles
🔥🎯🍴

Bowling Green
Shaw Lane
Opens 7 winter eves
Banks's Mild, Bitter E
Friendly locals' pub with
bowling green
🔥🎯👣 (not Sun) 🍴🔵

Stourport 15F2

11–2.30; 6–10.30 (11 F, S)

Bell
Lion Hill
Hansons Mild, Bitter E
Roadhouse on one-way
system. Easy access to
pleasant canalside walk
🎯👣🍴

Suckley 15F4

10.30–2.30; 6–11

Cross Keys
OS715532
**Marston Mercian Mild,
Burton Bitter** H
Basic rural local. Pub games 🍴

Try also: Nelson (Free)

Symonds Yat 14D6

10.30–2.30; 6–11

Wye Knot
B4164 ✆ 890501
Davenports Bitter H Regular
guest beers
Fine pub commanding views
over the River Wye
🔥🎲🎯👣🍴🅿

Tenbury Wells 14E3

11–2.30; 6–11

Pembroke House
Cross Street (B4214)
Wem Mild, Best Bitter H
Substantial half-timbered pub.
Lively atmosphere 👣🍴

Titley 14C3

10.30–2.30; 6–11 may open late in winter

Help keep real ale alive by
joining CAMRA. Your voice
helps encourage brewers big
and small to brew cask beer
and offer all beer drinkers a
better choice. Send £9 for a
year's membership or use the
form on page 319.

Stagg
B4355 OS330598
✆ Kington 230221
M & B Brew XI H
Friendly country inn 🔥Q🎯🍴

Ullingswick 14E4

10.30–2.30; 6–11

Three Crowns
Bleak Acre OS605497
✆ Burley Gate 279
**Ansells Bitter; Ind Coope
Burton Ale; Tetley Bitter;
Bulmer Cider** H
Unspoilt country pub with the
emphasis on food 🔥🎯👣🍴

Upper Sapey 15E3

11–2.30; 6–11

Gate Hangs Well
High Lane (B4203) ✆ 638
**Draught Bass; Hook Norton
Best Bitter** H
Cosy country inn 🎯👣🍴

Upper Welland 15F4

10.30–2.30; 6–11

Hawthorn Inn
Upper Welland Road
✆ Malvern 63519
Hook Norton Bitter H
Pleasant homely pub with
restaurant and barbecue
🎯👣🍴

West Malvern 15F4

11–2.30; 6–11

Lamb Inn
West Malvern Road
✆ Malvern 2994
**Flowers Original; Fremlins
Bitter; Samuel Whitbread** H
Large, busy local with skittle
alley 🎯👣🍴

Whittington 15F4

11–2.30; 6–11

Swan
Whittington Road (off A44;
100 yards M5 Jct 7)
✆ Worcester 351361
Banks's Mild, Bitter E
Basic bar, plush lounge
🎯👣🍴

Wolverley 15F2

11–2.30; 7–10.30 (11 F, S)

Queens Head
Off B4189 OS829794
Banks's Mild, Bitter E
Friendly village local in
picturesque setting 🎯👣🍴

Woolhope 14E5

10.30–2.30; 6–11

Butchers Arms
OS618358 ✆ Fownhope 281
**Hook Norton Best Bitter, Old
Hookey; Marston Pedigree** H;
Westons Cider G
Busy, 14th century inn
🔥🎯🔵👣🍴

Try also: Crown (Free)

Worcester 15F3

11–2.30; 6–11

Cardinals Hat
Friar Street ✆ 21890
Davenports Bitter H
Historic half-timbered pub in
old street near Cathedral 🍴

Farriers Arms
Fish Street ✆ 27569
Courage Directors H
Old inn near cathedral, with
superb cold table
🎯👣🍴🎿 (Foregate St.)

Herefordshire House
Bransford Road (A4103)
M & B Mild, Brew XI H
Warm, cheerful local; darts,
pool and doms leagues 🎯🍴

Kings Head Inn
Sidbury ✆ 26204
Banks's Mild, Bitter E
Pleasant, popular inn. Pub
games; regular live music in
annexe 🎲👣🍴

Lamb & Flag
30 The Tything (A38)
**Marston Burton Bitter,
Pedigree** H
Lively and welcoming
🎯🍴🎿 (Foregate St.)

Long Stop
Broad Street
**Ansells Mild, Bitter; Tetley
Bitter** H
Lively city centre hostelry
🍴🎿 (Foregate St.)

Paul Pry Inn
The Butts
Banks's Mild, Bitter E
One basic bar, one more
comfortable. Pub name means
Peeping Tom
👣🎿 (Foregate St.)

Try also: **Bridge**, Lowesmoor
(M & B); **Imperial Hotel**
(Courage)

Yarpole 14D3

10.30–2.30; 6–11

Bell Inn
Off B4361 ✆ 359
**Woods Special; Bulmer
Cider** H
Pleasant 17th century village
pub 🔥Q🎯👣🍴

♦ A REAL FIRE PUB ♦

The 🔥 symbol denotes a pub
with a real solid fuel fire

Abbots Langley 17F9

11–3; 5.30–11

Kings Head
Bridge Road, Hunton Bridge
(just off A41)
**Benskins Bitter; Ind Coope
Burton Ale** H
Large garden backing on
Grand Union Canal,
pleasantly refurbished pub
🏨🅿🕭🍽 (7–9, not Sun)

Swan
College Road, Leavesden
Evenings opens 6
**Greene King KK, IPA,
Abbot** H
Traditional friendly local, with
lively public bar
🅿🕭 (not Sat/Sun) 🍽

Aldbury 16E8

11–2.30; 6–11

Valiant Trooper
Trooper Lane (off A41)
OS966124
☎ Aldbury Common 203
**Adnams Bitter; Fuller London
Pride, ESB; Greene King
Abbot; Marston Pedigree;
Bulmer Cider** H
Busy picturesque inn in
attractive village 🏨Q🅿🕭🍽

Ardeley 17G7

12–2.30; 6.30–11

Jolly Waggoner
OS310272 ☎ Walkern 350
Greene King IPA, Abbot G
16th-century cottage pub in
rural setting. Good food
🏨🅿🕭🍽

Ayot Green 17F8

10.30–2.30; 5.30–10.30 (11 F, S)

Waggoners
Brickwall Close (near A1M)
OS222139
☎ Welwyn Garden 324241
**Fremlins Bitter; Wethereds
Bitter** H Occasional guest
beers
Cosy old pub on the old Great
North Road 🏨Q🅿🕭🍽

Baldock 17G7

10.30–2.30; 5.30–11

George IV
London Road (A6141)
☎ 892367
**Greene King Simpsons Ale,
IPA, Abbot** H
Unpretentious and roomy.
Pleasant garden beneath
Weston Hills
🏨Q🅿🕭 (not Sun) 🍽

Barley 17H6

11–2.30; 6.30 (7 winter)–11

Fox & Hounds
High Street (B1368)
☎ Barkway 459
**Barley Brewery Nathaniel's
Special, Hogshead; Flowers**

Original; Wethered Bitter H
Regular guest beers
Own brewery and one of only
two gantry signs in Herts
🏨🕭🍽

Berkhamsted 17E8

10.30–2.30; 5.30 (6 Sat)–11

George
High Street (A41) ☎ 2950
**Aylesbury ABC Bitter;
Draught Bass; Everard Tiger;
Morrell Light Ale** H
Attractive Georgian style
lounge bar; dartboard in
public bar. Popular town
centre pub Q🍴🅿🛏🕭🍽≷

Bishops Stortford 18B8

10.30–2.30; 5.30–11

Fox
Rye Street (B1004) ☎ 51623
**Courage Best Bitter, Directors;
Rayment BBA** H Occasional
guest beers
Traditional basic pub with
riverside garden 🏨Q🅿🕭🍽

Bourne End 17E8

10.30–2.30; 5.30–1

Anchor
London Road (A41)
OS022063
☎ Berkhamsted 6220
**Benskins Bitter; Friary Meux
Bitter; Ind Coope Burton Ale** H
Reputedly used by
highwayman Robert Snooks.
Clientele has changed since
then 🏨🅿🕭🍽

Braughing 17H7

10.30–2.30; 5.30–11

Axe & Compasses
28 The Street (off B1368)
☎ Ware 821610
**Wethered Bitter; Samuel
Whitbread** H Regular guest
beers
Village pub by cricket field.
Excellent food
🏨🅿🕭 (not Sun) 🍽🍽

Buntingford 17G7

11–2.30; 5.30–11

Crown
High Street (A10)
☎ Royston 71422
Mon lunch closes 4 (market
day)
Greene King IPA, Abbot H
Regular guest beers
Excellent small free house, no
keg bitter 🏨🅿🕭🍽

Burnham Green 17G8

10.30–2.30; 6–10.30 (11 F, S)

White Horse
1 White Horse Lane
OS262166 ☎ Bulls Green 416
**Benskins Bitter; Ind Coope
Burton Ale** H

Traditional village local on
large green with OS
triangulation pillar. No meals
Sun 🏨Q🅿🕭🍽&

Bushey 17F9

11–3; 5.30–11

Swan
Park Road (off A411)
**Benskins Bitter; Ind Coope
Burton Ale** H
Small public bar only pub.
Always sold real ale 🏨🍽

Chapmore End 17G8

12–2.30; 6–11

Woodman
Off B158 OS328163
☎ Ware 3143
Greene King IPA, Abbot G
Snug cottage pub. Ideal
summer garden with
barbecue 🏨Q🅿🕭🍽🍽

Charlton 17F7

10.30–2.30; 5.30–11

Windmill
Charlton Lane ☎ 2096
**Wells Eagle Bitter,
Bombardier** H
Idyllic riverside pub 🅿🕭🍽

Chipperfield 17E9

11–2.30; 6–11

Royal Oak
The Street OS042081
**Benskins Bitter; Friary Meux
Bitter** H; Ind Coope Burton
Ale G
Friendly, comfortable pub in
attractive village
🏨🕭 (not Sun)

Chorleywood 17E9

11–2.30; 6–11

Rose & Crown
The Common OS026963
Ind Coope Bitter H
Small quiet pub on edge of
common 🅿🕭🍽⊖

Coleman Green 17F8

11–2.30 (3 Sat/Sun); 6–11

John Bunyan
Coleman Green Lane
(off A6129) OS189128
☎ Wheathampstead 2037
**McMullen AK Mild, Country
Bitter** H
One-bar pub with games area.
Good fast food. Large garden
play area. Landlady likes a jug
or two! 🏨Q🅿🕭🍽&

Colney Heath 17F8

11–3; 5.30–11

Crooked Billet
88 High Street OS202060
☎Bowmansgreen 22128
**Adnams Bitter; Greene King
Abbot; Wethered Bitter** H
Regular guest beers

Popular free house converted from two cottages. Weekend barbecues in summer. Covered patio ✿ ᐸ ♈🍴 ⟁

Queens Head
1 High Street OS206058
✆ Bowsmangreen 23656
Wethered Bitter; Samuel Whitbread Ⓗ **Occasional guest beers**
Comfortable, friendly pub with gregarious landlord. Summer barbecues. Unique menu display
🍴✿ ᐸ (not Sat/Sun) 🍴⚥ ⟁

Croxley Green 17E9
11–3; 5.30–11

Fox & Hounds
New Road
Greene King KK, IPA, Abbot Ⓗ
Large saloon with upstairs drinking area overlooking public bar. Pool and darts in public
✿ ᐸ🍴⊖

Datchworth 17G8
11–2.30; 5.30 (6.30 in winter)–11

Plough
5 Datchworth Green
✆ Stevenage 813000
Greene King KK, IPA, Abbot Ⓗ
Thriving cottage local near village green
🍴Q✿ ᐸ (not Sun)

Essendon 17G8
11–2.30; 6–11

Rose & Crown
22 High Road (B158)
OS275084 ✆ Hatfield 61229
Ind Coope Bitter, Burton Ale Ⓗ
Friendly village local with warm welcome. Table skittles. Childrens play area in garden
🍴Q✿🍴⚥

Flaunden 17E9
10–2.30; 6–10.30 (11 F, S)

Bricklayers Arms
Hogspit Bottom OS017013
✆ Hemel Hempstead 833322
Arkell BBB; Everards Tiger; Ind Coope Bitter; Tetley Bitter Ⓗ
Small low-beamed country pub in attractive setting
🍴Q✿ ᐸ

Furneux Pelham 17H7
11–2.30; 6–11

Star
The Causeway (off B1368)
OS431278
✆ Brent Pelham 227
Greene King KK, Abbot; Rayments BBA Ⓗ
Welcoming old pub in picturesque brewery village. No food Sun 🍴Q✿ ᐸ ♈

Green Tye 17H8
11–2.30; 5.30 (6 winter)–11

Prince of Wales
Much Hadham
✆ Much Hadham 2517
McMullen AK Mild, Country Bitter Ⓗ
Busy country pub in farming village 🍴Q✿ ᐸ ♈🍴

Harpenden 17F8
11–3; 5.30–11

Silver Cup
St. Albans Road (A1081)
✆ 3094
Wells Eagle Bitter, Bombardier Ⓗ
Old roadside pub overlooking the common. Named after horse race that was run locally 🍴✿ ᐸ🍴≷

Hatfield 17G8
10.30–2.30; 5.30–10.30

Wrestlers
89 Great North Road (off A414) ✆ 62116
Ind Coope Bitter, Burton Ale Ⓗ
Popular pub full of timber, brass and master cellarman awards 🍴Q✿ ᐸ (not Sun) ≷

Haultwick 17G7
12–2.30; 6 (7 winter)–11

Rest & Welcome
OS339230 ✆ Dane End 323
McMullen AK Mild, Country Bitter Ⓗ
Attractive one-bar local in tiny hamlet. Games room 🍴✿

Hemel Hempstead 17E6
11–2.30; 5.30–11

Old Bell Hotel
High Street (Old Town)
✆ 52867
Benskins Bitter; Ind Coope Burton Ale Ⓗ
Heritage Inn with antique wallpaper in main bar Q ᐸ

Hertford 17G8
10.30–2.30; 5.30–11

Bell & Crown
29 Cowbridge (B158)
✆ 52121
Opens 7 Sat eves
McMullen AK Mild, Country Bitter Ⓗ
Small local near McMullen Brewery. One of the few street corner pubs left in the town
🍴≷ (North)

Great Eastern
29 Railway Place (off A119)
✆ 53570
Opens 7 Sat eves
McMullen AK Mild, Country Bitter Ⓗ
Lively local with many railway paintings and lots of pub games ✿ ᐸ🍴♈≷ (East)

Sportsman
117 Fore Street
✆ 55162
Opens 11.30 & 6
Adnams Bitter; Courage Best Bitter; Greene King Abbot Ale; Rayments BBA: Sam Smith OBB: Young Special Ⓗ
Usually busy especially weekends. This comfortable pub offers excellent food but sadly nothing for indoor sportsmen ᐸ♈≷ (East)

Hertford Heath 17G8
10.30–2.30; 6–11

East India College Arms
40 London Road (B1197)
OS350111 ✆ Hertford 52618
Benskins Bitter; Ind Coope Burton Ale Ⓗ
Likeable village pub with something for everybody. A real pint for mum and dad and a real milkshake for the kids
⚥✿🍴 ᐸ♈🍴⚥

High Wych 17H8
10.30–2.30; 5.30–11

Rising Sun
High Wych Road
✆ Harlow 726300
Courage Best Bitter, Directors Ⓖ
Basic, friendly local known as Sid's 🍴Q♈

Try also: **Half Moon** (Ind Coope)

Hitchin 17F7
11–2.30; 7–11

Cricketers
Bedford Road ✆ 2116
Benkins Bitter Ⓗ
Comfortable two-bar pub near Hitchin Town FC 🍴✿♈

Hoddesdon 17G8
11–2.30; 5.30–11

Golden Lion
23 High Street (A1170)
✆ 463146
Ind Coope Bitter, Burton Ale Ⓗ
16th century coaching inn where a table in saloon serves as bar 🍴Q✿ ᐸ♈

Rose & Crown
90 Amwell Street (A1170)
✆ 462553
Opens 7 Sat eves
Flowers Original; Fremlins Bitter; Wethered Bitter Ⓗ
Friendly, popular pub. Pub sign beam still says Fordhams
🍴✿ ᐸ (not Sun)
♈ (not Mon/Tues)

Ickleford 17F7
10.30–2; 6–11

Plume of Feathers
Upper Green ✆ Hitchin 2729

Fremlins Bitter; Wethered
Bitter H; Whitbread Castle
Eden
Smart local on village green
where landlord has a right to
graze cows & pigs ☺ ●

Try also: Cricketers (Free)

Kings Langley 17F9

11–2.30; 6–11

Saracens Head
High Street (A41)
Benskins Bitter; Ind Coope
Burton Ale H
Comfortable & improved old
inn Q≢

Langley 17F7

11–2.30; 6–11

Farmers Boy
Off B656 OS216225
✆ Stevenage 820436
Greene King IPA, Abbot H
Charming country pub in
quiet cul-de-sac.
Recommended food ✍☺●

Little 17F7
Wymondley

10.30–2.30; 5.30–11

Buck's Head
Stevenage Road (A602)
✆ Stevenage 53320
Flowers IPA, Original;
Wethered Bitter H Occasional
guest beers
Comfortable, 400-year old
pub ♨✍☺

Long Marston 16D8

11–2.30; 6–11

Queens Head
38 Tring Road OS899157
Aylesbury ABC Bitter;
Draught Bass; Everard Tiger;
Morrell Light Ale H
Pleasant, busy village pub
♨Q✡✍☺ (not Sun)

Much 17H8
Hadham

11–2.30; 6–11

Bull
High Street (B1004) ✆ 2668
Benskins Bitter; Ind Coope
Burton H
Busy old pub serving good
food. Guild of master
cellarmen for Burton
Q✡✍☺●

Oxhey 17F9

11–3; 5.30–11

Haydon Arms
76 Upper Paddock Road
Benskins Bitter; Ind Coope
Burton Ale H
Thriving village-style pub
with small public bar
✍☺●●⊖

Villiers Arms
109 Villiers Road (off A4008)
Evenings opens 6 (7 Sat)

Benskins Bitter; Ind Coope
Burton Ale H
Pleasant corner house with
darts area ✍☺≢⊖

Piccotts End 17E8

11–2.30; 5.30–11

Boar's Head
✆ Hemel Hempstead 40084
Benskins Bitter; Ind Coope
Burton Ale H; Bulmers Olde
English Cider H
Cheery village local
♨✍☺ (not Sun)

Pirton 17F7

10.30–2.30; 5.30–11

Motte & Bailey
1 Great Green
✆ Hitchin 612641
Adnams Bitter; Banks &
Taylor Shefford Bitter; Everard
Old Original; Greene King
IPA, Abbot H Occasional
guest beers
Named after nearby
Earthworks ♨✍☺● (not Sun)

Preston 17F7

11–2.30; 6–11

Red Lion
The Green ✆ Hitchin 59585
Adnams Bitter; Greene King
IPA: Hall & Woodhouse
Badger Best Bitter; Marston
Pedigree; Ruddle Rutland
Bitter H Regular guest beers
Pub owned by villagers.
Unique in the country. Idyllic
setting, overlooking village
green. No meals Sun
♨Q✡ (until 8 pm) ✍☺●

Puckeridge 17H7

10.30–2.30; 5.30–11

Buffalo's Head
High Street (off A10/A120)
✆ Ware 821949
Benskins pub free to serve
additional guest beers
Lively local at end of village.
Good value food ♨✍☺●●

Pye Corner 17H8

10.30–2.30; 5.30–11

Plume of Feathers
Near A414 ✆ Harlow 24154
Courage Best Bitter,
Directors H
Large old pub serving low-
priced good food ♨✍☺●●

Redbourn 17F8

11–3; 5.30 (6 Sat)–11

Cricketers
East Common OS104120
✆ 2410
Benskins Bitter H
Friendly pub on common, well
worth a visit. African Grey
parrot in lounge ☺●●♿

Reed 17G6

10.30–2.30; 5.30–11

Cabinet

High Street (near A10)
OS364361 ✆ Barkway 366
Adnams Bitter, Extra
(summer) Old; Courage
Directors G Regular guest
beers
Weatherboarded cottage,
large garden
♨✍☺● (not Mon/Tue) ●

Rickmansworth
17E9

11–3; 5.30–11

Feathers
34 Church Street
Benskins Bitter; Ind Coope
Burton Ale H
Old-fashioned exterior,
younger atmosphere. No food
Sun ✍☺● (until 7) ≢ ⊖

Halfway House
Uxbridge Road (A412)
Closes 10.30 Mon–Thu
Courage Best Bitter,
Directors G
Large and friendly; garden
leads to river
Q✍☺ (not Sun) ≢ ⊖

Royston 17G6

11–2.30; 6–11

Jockey
Baldock Street (off A505)
✆ 4377
Wethered Bitter; Samuel
Whitbread H Regular guest
beers
Lively town house ✍▣☺●●

St. Albans 17F8

11–3; 5.30–11

Acorn
82 Victoria Street ✆ 55869
Benskins Bitter; Ind Coope
Burton Ale H
Friendly local between station
and city centre. Bar billiards
☺ (not Sun) ≢

Farriers Arms
Lower Dagnall Street
✆ 51025
Opens 6 Sat eves
McMullen AK Mild, Country
Bitter H
Quality street corner local
Q☺●

White Lion
91 Sopwell Lane ✆ 50540
Opens 7 Sat eves
Ind Coope Bitter, Burton Ale H
Friendly cottage pub in quiet
corner of town. Boules pitch
in garden Q✍☺●≢

Sarratt 17E9

11–3; 5.30–11

Boot
The Green OS043995
Benskins Bitter; Ind Coope
Burton Ale; Taylor-Walker
Bitter H
Popular and friendly inn with
inglenook, in attractive village
♨✍☺

Try also: Cock (Benskins)

Sawbridgeworth

10.30–2.30; 5.30–11

Three Horseshoes
West Road (off A1184)
☎ Bishops Stortford 722485
McMullen AK Mild, Country
Bitter Ⓗ
🏠Q🅿️🅖➐&

White Lion
London Road (A1184)
☎ Bishops Stortford 726341
Greene King Abbot; Rayment
BBA Ⓗ
Q🅖&⩙

Shenley
17F9

11–3; 5.30–11

Pinks Hotel
Rectory Lane (near M25)
OS202015
☎ Potters Bar 43106
Brakspear Bitter; Flowers
Original; Young Bitter,
Special Ⓗ
Easy-going bar in beautiful
rural surroundings.
Recommended restaurant
🏠🅿️🅖Ⓖ➐

Stevenage
17G7

10.30–2.30; 7–11

Two Diamonds
High Street, Old Town
McMullen AK Mild, Country
Bitter Ⓗ
Untouched by modern times 🅿️

Stocking Pelham
17H7

10.30–2.30; 6–11

Cock
Off B1038 OS453292
Ind Coope Bitter, Burton Ale Ⓗ
Charming thatched and
weather-boarded pub in rural
hamlet 🏠🅿️&

Tring
16E8

11–2.30; 7–11

Kings Arms
King Street ☎ 3318
Fuller ESB; Morrell Varsity;
Hook Norton Best Bitter;
Wadworth 6X; Wells Eagle
Bitter Ⓗ Occasional guest
beers
Thriving back street local
🏠🅿️🅖➐

Tyttenhanger
17F8

11.30–3; 6–11

Plough
OS183059
☎ Bowmansgreen 57777
Adnams Bitter; Brakspear
Bitter; Greene King IPA,
Abbot; McMullen Country
Bitter; Wethered Bitter Ⓗ
Lively country pub with good
food. Look at the beer mats!
🏠🅖Ⓖ🅰️

Ware
17G8

10.30–2.30; 5.30–11

Old Bulls Head
26 Baldock Street ☎ 2307
Opens 11.30; 6.30 Sat eves
Benskins Bitter; Friary Meux
Bitter; Ind Coope Burton Ale Ⓗ
16th century inn with
timbered interior & inglenook
fireplace. Reasonably-priced
food. Children's play area in
garden Landlord is a ham!
🏠Q🅖Ⓖ (not Sun)
➐ (not Sat/Sun) ⩙

Spread Eagle
37 Amwell End ☎ 2784
McMullen AK Mild, Country
Bitter Ⓗ
Unspoilt town local, a few
staggers from the station
🅖Ⓖ (not Sun) 🍴⩙

Station Hotel
Station Road ☎ 3604
Opens 7 Sat eves
McMullen AK Mild, Country
Bitter Ⓗ
Brilliant little pub opposite the
station—worth missing a few
trains in 🅖Ⓖ➐&⩙

Wareside
17H8

10.30–2.30; 5.30–11

White Horse
B1004 ☎ Ware 2582
Greene King Abbot; Rayment
BBA Ⓗ
Popular village pub
🏠🅖Ⓖ (not Sun)
➐ (Fri, Sat only) 🍴

Water End
17G9

10.30–2.30; 5.30–11

Woodman
Warrengate Road, North
Mymms (near A1M)
OS228043
Potters Bar 50502
Adnams Bitter; Courage
Directors; Marston Pedigree;
Younger's IPA Ⓗ
Quiet convivial pub near
North Mymms Park Q🅿️Ⓖ➐

Watford
17F9

11–3; 5.30–11

Tantivy
91 Queens Road
Benskins Bitter Ⓗ
Longest-standing entry in
GBG for Watford. Pool and
darts in public
🏠🅖Ⓖ➐ (not Sun) 🍴⩙ ⊖

Welham Green
17G9

10.30–2.30; 5.30–11

Hope & Anchor
Station Road (near A1000)
OS232053
☎ Hatfield 62935
Courage Best Bitter,
Directors Ⓗ
Popular village local with
lively public bar & quiet
lounge. Wallcases of
Victoriana and beer taps
🅖Ⓖ&⩙

Welwyn
17G8

11–2.30; 5.30–10.30 (11 F, S)

Baron of Beef
11 Mill Lane OS232163
☎ 4739
Opens evenings 6
McMullens AK Mild, Country
Bitter Ⓗ
Village local with characters
both sides of the bar. The
name is all that is left of its
former use. Welsh spoken
here
🏠Ⓖ (weekdays) ➐ (to order) 🍴

White Hart
2 Prospect Place ☎ 5353
Opens 7 Sat eves
Flowers Original; Wethered
Bitter Ⓗ
Splendid old coaching inn,
once used as the local Court
House. Lunches recommended
(booking advised)
🏠Ⓖ (weekdays) 🍴

Wheathampstead
17F8

11–2.30 (3 Sat); 5.30–11

Wicked Lady
Nomansland Common (B651)
OS176127 ☎ 2128
Fuller London Pride; Gales
HSB; Greene King Abbot;
Hook Norton Bitter; Robinson
Best Bitter; Wadworth 6X Ⓖ
Three drinking areas around
central bar. Children's play
area in garden. Recommended
meals. Sorry no motorcycles
🏠Q🅿️Ⓖ➐ (not Sun) &

Whitwell
17F7

11.30–2.30; 6.30–11

Maidens Head
67 High Street ☎ 392
McMullen AK Mild, Country
Bitter Ⓗ
Attractive village local.
Collection of key rings on
ceiling 🏠🅿️Ⓖ➐ (until 8) 🍴

Wild Hill
17G8

11.30–2.30; 5.30–11

Woodman
7 Wild Hill Lane (between
B158 & A1000) OS263068
Greene King IPA, Abbot Ⓗ
Classic locals' free house on
edge of Hatfield House estate
🅿️Ⓖ (not Sun)

Wormley West End
17G8

10.30–2.30; 5.30–11

Woodman
20 Wormley West End
OS339059
☎ Hoddesdon 463719
McMullen AK Mild, Country
Bitter Ⓗ
Old pub on edge of Wormley
Woods. Lounge bar & car park
recently extended 🏠🅿️Ⓖ➐🍴

Aldbrough 31H8

11–3; 6–11

George & Dragon
Main Street (B1242) ☎ 230
Younger Scotch, IPA, No. 3 Ⓗ
500 year old inn. Concentrates on food ♨🅿Ⓖ🍴🍺

Althorpe 26D3

11–3; 6–11

Dolphin
A18 ☎ Scunthorpe 783469
John Smith's Bitter Ⓗ
Accent on food. Childrens play area ♨Ⓖ🍺

Arnold 31H9

11.30–3; 7–11

Bay Horse
Near Skirlaugh (½ ml off A165)
Bateman XB, XXXB Ⓗ
Cosy rural pub with animal hospital ♨♨🍺

Barmby Moor 31F8

11.30–3; 7–11

Boot & Slipper
St Helens Square
☎ Pocklington 3328
Younger Scotch Bitter, IPA Ⓗ
Large open-plan interior with pool room ♨🅿Ⓖ🍺

Barnetby le Wold 26E3

11–3; 7–11

Station Hotel
Station Yard ☎ 688288
Ward Sheffield Best Bitter Ⓗ
Free house. Lounge decorated in railway style ♨Ⓖ🍴🍺≷

Barrow upon Humber 27E3

11–3; 6–11

Royal Oak
High Street ☎ 30318
Fri, Sat evenings opens 6.30
Bass Mild XXXX, Bass; Stones Best Bitter Ⓗ
Recently modernised village pub Ⓖ (not Sun) 🍺

Barton upon Humber 26E3

10.30–3; 6–11

Coach & Horses
High Street ☎ 32161
Tetley Mild, Bitter Ⓗ
Busy public bar, lounge. Jumbo sandwiches ♨🍺≷

Wheatsheaf
Holydyke (A1077) ☎ 33175
Evening opens 7
Ward Mild, Sheffield Best Bitter Ⓗ
Old pub, snug. Lunches popular ♨Ⓖ (Mon–Fri) 🍺≷

Beverley 31G8

11–3; 7–10.30; (11 F, S)

Moulders Arms
32 Wilbert Grove ☎ 867033
Open to 5 Sat lunch
Bass Mild XXXX, Stones Best Bitter Ⓗ
Friendly local with lending library 🎲 (lunchtime) 🍺≷

Queens Head
Wednesday Market
Opens 10–4 Wed lunch
Darley Dark Mild; Thorne Best Bitter; Ward Sheffield Best Bitter Ⓗ
Well laid out pub, comfortable alcove seating ♨Ⓖ♿≷

Rose & Crown
North Bar Without ☎ 862532
Darley Dark Mild, Thorne Best Bitter; Ward Sheffield Best Bitter Ⓗ
Spacious mock-Tudor lounge. Games room bar ♨♨Ⓖ🍴🍺

Royal Standard (Dolly's)
North Bar Within (A164)
Darley Dark Mild, Thorne Best Bitter Ⓗ
Small cosy lounge, traditional bar Q🍺

White Horse (Nellies)
Hengate ☎ 861973
Opens 10.30–5 Sat
& 10.30–4 Wed
Samuel Smith OBB, Museum Ⓗ
Basic gaslit pub. Jazz, folk and blues nights
♨Q🎲 (lunchtimes) ♨🍴🍺

Woolpack Inn
37, Westwood Road
☎ 867095
Bateman XB Ⓗ
Small unspoilt local ♨Ⓖ

Bridlington 31H7

10.30–3; 6–11

Hilderthorpe Hotel
Hilderthorpe Road ☎ 672205
Bass Mild XXXX, Bass Ⓗ
Basic local near harbour
♨🅿🍺≷

Old Ship Inn
90, St Johns Street ☎ 670466
Evenings opens 7
Darley Thorne Best Bitter Ⓗ
Thriving local retains traditional atmosphere ♨QⒼ🍴≷

Olde Star Inn
17, Westgate ☎ 676039
Younger Scotch Bitter Ⓗ
Rambling pub in the old town. Restaurant ♨Q🎲♨Ⓖ🍴🍺

Brigg 26E4

10.30–3 (4 Tue & Thu); 6–11

White Hart
57 Bridge Street (A15/A18)
Mansfield 4XXXX Bitter Ⓗ
Excellent riverside pub ♨Ⓖ🍺

White Horse
Wrawby Street (A15/A18)
Closes 2.30 lunch Fri-Wed

Ward Mild, Sheffield Best Bitter Ⓗ
Welcoming old inn, lunches very popular ♨Ⓖ (not Sun) 🍺≷

Burstwick 31H9

11–3; 6–11

Hare & Hounds
Main Street, (off B1362)
☎ Keyingham 2318
Bass Mild XXXX, Bass; Stones Best Bitter Ⓗ
Old village local. Bar lounge and restaurant ♨♨Ⓖ🍴🍺

Cleethorpes 27G4

11–3; 6–10.30 (11 F, S)

Crows Nest Hotel
Balmoral Road ☎ 698867
Samuel Smith OBB Ⓗ
Large and comfortable with a friendly atmosphere ♨🅿Ⓖ🍴🍺

No. 2 Refreshment Room
Cleethorpes Station ☎ 697951
Ruddle Rutland Bitter; Ward Sheffield Best Bitter; Younger No. 3 Ⓗ
Small and friendly, known as "Under the Clock" Q♨🍺≷

Nottingham
7, Seaview Street (off A1098)
Evenings opens 7
Tetley Mild, Bitter Ⓗ
Busy pub satisfying local and visiting custom 🍺≷

Victoria
Grant Street
Bass Mild XXXX, Bass; Stones Best Bitter Ⓗ
Popular pub near sea front ♨🍺≷

Willys
17, High Cliff Road ☎ 602145
Evenings opens 7
Bateman XB; Ruddle County Ⓗ**; Symonds Cider** Ⓖ
Regular guest beers
Superb view. Excellent, varied cuisine ♨Ⓖ♿♨≷

Flamborough 31H6

10.30–3; 7–11

Rose & Crown Hotel
High Street
Cameron Lion Bitter, Strongarm Ⓗ
Comfortable one-roomer, popular with locals ♨♨Ⓖ

Goole 26C3

10.30–3; 6–11

North Eastern
Boothferry Road
(A161/A614) ☎ 3705
Open till 5 Wed lunchtime
Darley Thorne Best Bitter Ⓗ
Cosy lounge, large bar with darts and pool Ⓖ🍴🍺≷

Royal
Aire Street ☎ 3608
Younger Scotch, No. 3 Ⓗ
Well-modernised dockside pub popular with young ♨🅿Ⓖ🍴

Vikings
Airmyn Road (A614) ☎ 2875
Bass Light, XXXXX, Bass;
Stones Best Bitter Ⓗ
Large comfortable roadhouse
🅿️🆑🎵

Grimsby 27F3

11–3; 6–10.30 (11 F, S)

County Hotel
Brighowgate ☎ 54422
Younger Scotch Bitter;
No. 3 Ⓗ
Popular town centre bar, well
worth a visit 🏨🅖🎵&≷

Friar Tuck
Friargate ☎ 58412
Evenings opens 6
Bass Mild XXXX, Bass; Stones
Best Bitter Ⓗ
Smart lounge bar in
Riverhead Centre 🅖🎵≷

Hewitts Tavern
Pasture Street ☎ 56976
Bass Mild XXXX; Stones Best
Bitter Ⓗ
Fine memorial to Hewitts
Brewery. Large, popular bar
🅿️&🎵

White Bear
137, Freeman Street ☎ 54893
Evenings opens 7
Darley Dark Mild, Thorne
Best Bitter Ⓗ
Popular with characters of all
ages. Weekend sing-a-longs
🅿️🎵≷ (docks)

Gunness 26D3

11.30–3; 5–11

Jolly Sailor
Station Road (A18)
Bass Special Bitter, Bass Ⓗ
Large basic pub, has a room
with three pool tables 🏨🎵≷

Hedon 31H9

11–3; 6–11

Shakespeare Inn
Baxtergate (off A1033)
Darley Dark Mild, Thorne
Best Bitter; Ward Sheffield
Best Bitter Ⓗ
1-room old inn. Bar billiards,
shove ha'penny, darts 🏨🎵🅖

Hessle 31G9

11–3; 6–10.30 (11 F, S)

George (Top House)
Prestongate (off Square)
Bass Mild XXXX; Stones
Bitter Ⓗ
Hospitable pub, focal point for
local community 🏨🅿️🅖🎵

Hibaldstow 26D4

11–2.30; 6–11

Wheatsheaf
Station Road (A15)
☎ Brigg 54056
Ward Mild, Sheffield Best
Bitter Ⓔ
Well decorated popular pub
with restaurant 🏨🅖🎵🎵

Holmpton 31J9

11.30–3; 6.30–11

George & Dragon
Off A1033
Bass Mild XXXX, Bass; Tetley
Bitter Ⓗ
Spacious and busy 🅐

Hook 26C3

10.30–3; 6–11

Blacksmiths Arms
High Street ☎ Goole 3482
Webster Green Label Best,
Yorkshire Bitter Ⓗ
Large comfortable lounge,
skittles 🅿️🅖🎵 (not Mon) &

Howden 31E9

12–3; 7–10.30 (11 F, S)

Board
1 Market Place (off B1228)
Selby Best Bitter Ⓗ
Listed pub serving mainly
local trade 🎵

Hull 31H9

11–3; 6–10.30 (11 F, S)

Bonny Boat
Trinity House Lane, Old Town
Batemans XB Ⓗ
Small friendly and busy 🅖

City Hotel
Lowgate, Old Town (A1033)
Bass Mild XXXX, Bass Ⓗ
Bustling one-roomer 🅖

Duke of Edinburgh
De La Pole Place, Great Union
Street ☎ 225382
Evenings opens 5.30
Bateman XB Ⓗ
Excellent lively local 🎵

East Riding
St Pauls Street/Cannon Street
Tetley Mild, Bitter Ⓗ
Basic and friendly 🅖🎵

Halfway House
595, Spring Bank West
☎ 53227
Bass Mild XXXX, Bass; Stones
Best Bitter Ⓗ
Superb beer in three
contrasting bars 🏨🅿️🎵

King Edward VII
Anlaby Road ☎ 25811
Evenings opens 7, closed Sun
lunch
Darley Dark Mild, Thorne
Best Bitter Ⓗ, XXXXXX
(winter) Ⓖ; Ward Sheffield
Best Bitter Ⓗ Regular guest
beers
Upstairs only recommended.
Expensive guest beers 🅖≷

Minerva Hotel
Nelson Street (near pier)
☎ 26909
Minerva Pilots Pride; Tetley
Mild, Bitter Ⓗ
Crowded, trendy home-brew
pub. Expensive 🏨🅚🅖🎵🎵

New Inn
Hedon Road, Marfleet
(A1033)
Evenings opens 5.30
Tetley Mild, Bitter Ⓗ
Good dockland drinking
establishment 🅿️🎵

Oberon
Queen Street (near pier)
Evenings opens 5.30
Bass Mild XXXX, Bass; Stones
Best Bitter Ⓗ
Perennial Hull favourite—a
real gem Q🎵

Old Blue Bell
Market Place, Old Town
Samuel Smith OBB, Museum
Ale Ⓗ
Excellent pub 🅖🎵

Olde White Hart
Silver Street, Old Town
☎ 26363
Younger IPA, No. 3 Ⓗ
Intriguing and ancient, strong
Civil War links 🅿️🅖 (not Sun)

Queens
Queens Road ☎ 43451
Bateman XB Ⓗ
Spacious many-roomed pub in
student area 🅿️🅖 (Tues-Sun) 🎵

Wellington
Peel Street/Wellington Lane
Tetley Mild, Bitter Ⓗ Regular
guest beers
Small and friendly with
low-priced guest beers 🅿️🅖🎵

Whalebone
165, Wincolmlee ☎ 27980
Evenings opens 5.30 Mon-Fri;
6.30 Sat
Tetley Mild, Bitter Ⓗ
Friendly, unpretentious pub.
Well worth seeking out 🅖🎵

Humberston 27G4

11–3; 6–10.30 (11 F, S)

Countryman
Fieldhouse Road (off North
Sea Lane) ☎ 812402
Whitbread Castle Eden Ⓗ
Busy well appointed pub near
camping area 🅿️🅖🎵🎵🅐

Kilham 31G7

10.30–3; 6–11

Kilham Arms
Middle Street
Webster Yorkshire Bitter Ⓗ
Modernised village local with
games-oriented bar 🅿️🅖🎵🎵

Langtoft 31G7

11–3; 6.30–10.30 (11 F, S & summer)

Ship Inn
Front Street (B1249)
☎ Driffield 87243
Cameron Lion Bitter Ⓗ
Small friendly village local
🏨🅚🅿️🅖🎵

Leven 31H8

11–3; 6–11

Hare & Hounds
1, North Street (A165)
Tetley Mild, Bitter Ⓗ
Smart country pub 🏠🅿🕑🍴🍷

Little Driffield 31G7

12–2.30; 7–10.30 (11 F, S summer)

Downe Arms
York Road (A163)
✆ Driffield 42243
Cameron Lion Bitter,
Strongarm Ⓗ
Friendly rural local 🏠🕑🍴🍷

Low Catton 31E7

11–3; 7–10.30 (11 F, S)

Gold Cup
(off A166)
✆ Stamford Bridge 71354
John Smith's Bitter; Tetley
Bitter Ⓗ
Cosy rural local with good
food 🏠🅿🕑🍴🍷

Messingham 26D4

11.30–3; 5–11

Green Tree
33, High Street (A159)
Bass Mild XXXX, Special
Bitter Ⓔ, Bass Ⓗ
Friendly busy local, children's
play area 🏠🅿🕑🍷

Newport 31F9

11–3; 7–11

Kings Arms
Main Street (A63) ✆ 40289
Tetley Mild, Bitter Ⓗ
Pleasant main road pub 🕑🍷

New Waltham 27F4

11–3; 6–10.30 (11 F, S)

Cross Keys
Station Road
Bass Mild XXXX, Bass; Stones
Best Bitter Ⓗ
Modern comfortable pub
🅿🕑🕑

North Newbald 31F8

11–3; 6.30–10.30 (11 F, S)

Gnu
The Green (off A1034)
Bateman XB; Mansfield
4XXXX Bitter Ⓗ
Traditional and hospitable
🏠🅿🅿🕑🍴🍷🍴

Owston Ferry, 26C4
Isle of Axholme

10.30–3; 7–11

Crooked Billet
Silver Street OS813000
✆ Gainsborough 72364
Darley Dark Mild, Thorne
Best Bitter Ⓗ
Trent-side village pub. Pool,
darts and boxing. Live music
Mon-Sat 🏠🅿🕑 (not Sun) 🍴

Paull 31H9

11–3; 7.30–11

Humber Tavern
Main Street ✆ 899437
Whitbread Trophy, Castle
Eden Ⓗ
4-roomer almost in the River
Humber! 🏠Q🅿 (until 9 pm) 🍴

Rawcliffe 26C3

11–3; 7–11

Creykes Arms
High Street (A614)
✆ Goole 83707
John Smith's Bitter,
Whitbread Durham Ale,
Trophy Ⓗ
Large comfortable pub by
green. Restaurant 🍴🕑🍷

Rudston 31H7

10.30–3; 6–11

Bosville Arms
B1253
Bass Mild XXXX, Stones Best
Bitter Ⓗ
Warm and welcoming with
much brasswork 🏠Q🅿🍴🍷🍴

Ryhill 31H9

11.30–3; 7–11

Crooked Billet
Pit Lane (½ mile off A1033)
✆ Keyingham 2303
Tetley Mild, Bitter Ⓗ
Attractive old smugglers
haunt 🏠🕑🍴 (not Tue) 🍷

Scawby 26D4

11–3; 6–11

Sutton Arms
West Street (B1207)
Bass Mild XXXX; Old Mill
Traditional Bitter; Stones Best
Bitter Ⓗ
Modernised old free house 🍴🍷

Scawby Brook 26D4

11–3; 6–11

King William IV
A15 ✆ Brigg 53147
Darley Dark Mild; Ward
Sheffield Best Bitter Ⓗ
Cosy pub with equestrian
flavour Q🍴🕑🍷

Scunthorpe 26D3

11.30–3; 5–11

Queen Bess
Derwent Road (off B1501)
Samuel Smith OBB Ⓗ
Modern estate pub with
concert room. C&W Thu 🍷

Tavern in the Town
143, High Street
Evenings opens 6
Darley Dark Mild, Thorne
Best Bitter; Ward Sheffield
Best Bitter Ⓗ
Popular with youngsters in
evening—may be noisy! 🕑🍸

Skerne 31G7

10.30–2.30, 6–10.30 (11 F, S)

Eagle
Wandsford Road
Cameron Lion Bitter Ⓗ
Unusual beer engine

Sledmere 31G7

11–2.30; 7–10.30 (11 F, S & summer)

Triton Inn
✆ Driffield 86644
Younger Scotch Bitter Ⓗ
Splendid pub next to Sledmere
House 🏠🅿🍴🅿🕑🍴🍷

South Dalton 31G8

12–2.30; 7–10.30 (11 F, S)

Pipe & Glass
West End (1½ miles off B1248)
Clark Traditional Bitter;
Webster Yorkshire Bitter Ⓗ
Smart, food-oriented and busy
🏠🕑🍴🍷

Stamford Bridge 31E7

10.30–3; 6–11

Bay Horse
A166 ✆ 71320
Cameron Lion Bitter Ⓗ
Open plan pub, large games
area. 🏠🅿🍴🍷 Å

Sutton on Derwent 30E8

12–2.30; 7–10.30 (11 F, S & summer)

St Vincent Arms
B1228 ✆ Elvington 349
Tetley Bitter; Theakston
Bitter; Old Peculier; Younger
Scotch Bitter, IPA Ⓗ
Popular and attractive
country inn 🏠🅿🍴🕑🍴🍷🍴 Å

Ulceby 27E3

10.30–3; 6–11

Yarborough Arms
Station Road (A160)
Bass Mild XXXX; Ruddle
County; Stones Best Bitter;
Tetley Bitter; Younger No. 3 Ⓗ
Comfortable lounge. Games
room 🏠Q🅿🍴🍷🎀

Walkington 31G8

11–3; 6–10.30 (11 F, S)

Barrel
East End (B1230)
Webster Dark Mild, Yorkshire
Bitter; Wilsons Original
Bitter Ⓗ
Small, friendly 🏠🅿🍴

Westwoodside, 26C4
Isle of Axholme

10.30–3; 6–11

Park Drain Hotel
Park Drain (off B1396)
OS726988
Stones Best Bitter Ⓗ
Unusual remote freehouse.
Good food 🏠🅿🍴🕑🍴🍷 Å

General opening hours: 10.30–3; 6–11

Arreton 6D8

Hare & Hounds
Downend (A3056)
Burt VPA Ⓗ
Delightful, ancient thatched
country pub ♨ ⊞ ♨ ☾ ➐

Try also: White Lion
(Whitbread)

Bembridge 7E8

Crab & Lobster
Forelands
✆ 2244
Whitbread Strong Country
Bitter, Pompey Royal Ⓗ
Very pleasant, comfortable
pub, good seafood ♨ ⊞ ☾ ➐ ♔ Å

Carisbrooke 6D8

Shute Inn
Clatterford Shute
Draught Bass, Hancocks HB;
Burt VPA Ⓗ
Pleasant Georgian hotel in
delightful setting ⊞ ♨ ⊞ ☾ ➐

Chale 6D8

Wight Mouse
Off A3055 ✆ Niton 730431
Burt VPA; Flowers Original;
Whitbread Strong Country
Bitter Ⓗ
Old stone family pub of great
character ⊞ ♨ ⊞ ☾ ➐

East Cowes 6D7

Victoria Tavern
62 Clarence Road
Burt VPA Ⓗ
Comfortable town pub ♔

Freshwater 6C8

Royal Standard
School Green Road
✆ 753227
Burt Mild, VPA Ⓗ
Homely pub in hotel;
good value food ⊞ ☾ ➐ ♔ Å

Godshill 6E8

Griffin
Newport Road
Whitbread Strong Country
Bitter, Pompey Royal Ⓗ
Excellent country local. Fine
views from garden Q⊞ ♨ ☾ ➐ ♔

Gurnard 6D7

Woodvale
Woodvale Road ✆ 292037
Flowers Original; Whitbread
Strong Country Bitter Ⓗ
Seaside pub. Fine views ⊞ ♨

Lake 6E8

Manor House
Sandown Road (A3055)

Draught Bass Ⓗ
Large village pub ♨

Newchurch 6E8

Pointers
High Street
Whitbread Strong Country
Bitter Ⓖ
Unspoilt 18th century pub
Q♔

Newport 6D8

Barley Mow
57 Shide Road
✆ 523318
Flowers Original; Wethered
Bitter; Whitbread Strong
Country Bitter, Samuel
Whitbread Ⓗ Occasional guest
beers
Busy roadhouse with good
food ♨ ⊞ ♨ ➐

Castle Inn
High Street
Whitbread Strong Country
Bitter, Samuel Whitbread Ⓗ
Excellent 17th century pub;
beams and flag floors ♨ ☾ ➐

Osborne 6D7

Prince of Wales
Whippingham Road
Flowers Original; Whitbread
Strong Country Bitter; Bulmer
Cider Ⓗ
Pleasant, comfortable pub by
Osborne House ⊞ ♨ ⊞ ☾ ➐ ♔ Å

Pondwell 7E7

Wishing Well
✆ Seaview 3222
Burt Mild, VPA Ⓗ
Popular, large free house with
self-catering chalets ⊞ ♨ ⊞ Å

Ryde 7E7

Castle
164 High Street
Evening opens 7
Gale XXXL, BBB, XXXXX,
HSB Ⓗ
Popular town pub ♨

Simeon Arms
Simeon Street (off sea front)
Burt VPA Ⓗ
Pleasant town pub ⊞ ♨ ☾

Yelfs Hotel
Union Street
✆ 64062
Draught Bass; BurtVPA Ⓗ
Large town centre hotel
♨ ⊞ ☾ ➐ ⇄

Try also: Esplanade Bars

Sandown 7E8

Commercial
15 St. Johns Road (off High
Street)

Gale XXXL, BBB, XXXXX,
HSB Ⓗ
Superb, comfortable pub
⊞ ♨ ♔

Try also: Castle

Seaview 7E7

Seaview Hotel
High Street
✆ 2278
Burt VPA Ⓗ
Popular seafront hotel, superb
public bar ⊞ ♨ ⊞ ☾ ➐ ♔ ♿

Shalfleet 6D7

New Inn
A3054
✆ Calbourne 314
Flowers Original; Wethered
Bitter; Whitbread Strong
Country Bitter Ⓖ
Lovely old village pub. Superb
food; seafood a speciality
♨ ☾ ➐ ♔

Shanklin 6E8

Crab
Old Village
Flowers Original; Whitbread
Strong Country Bitter Ⓗ
Very photogenic, ancient
thatched pub ⊞ ♨ ☾ ➐ ♔ ≋

Shorwell 6D8

Crown
Walkers Lane (B3399)
Flowers Original; Whitbread
Strong Country Bitter Ⓖ
Deservedly popular old pub,
fine garden ♨ Q ☾ ➐ ♔

Ventnor 6E8

Mill Bay
Esplanade
Burt Mild, VPA Ⓗ
Pleasant seafront pub ♔

Volunteer
Albert Street
Burt Mild, VPA Ⓗ
Excellent basic town bar ♔

Try also: Blenheim
(Whitbread)

Wroxall 6E8

Star
Clarence Road (B3327)
Burt Mild, VPA, 4X Ⓗ
Popular village pub, good food
♨ ☾ ➐ ♔

Yarmouth 6C7

Kings Head
Quay Street (opposite car
ferry)
Flowers Original; Whitbread
Pompey Royal Ⓗ
Splendid cosy pub ♨ ⊞ ♨ ☾ ➐

Ash 11H4

10–2.30; 6–11

Volunteer
43 Guilton (A257) ℰ 812506
**Adnams Bitter; Young
Special** Ⓗ; **Pippin Cider** Ⓖ
Regular guest beers
Popular historic pub; various
games and bat and trap
🏚🐾🎱🕒🍴🍽

Ashford 11F5

10–2.30; 6–11

Beaver
Beaver Road (B2070)
Evenings opens about 6.30
**Shepherd Neame Mild,
Bitter** Ⓗ
Pleasant two-bar pub on edge
of town 🏚🍴

Blacksmiths Arms
The Street, Willesborough
ℰ 23975
Fremlins Bitter Ⓗ
Attractive, popular old pub
🕒🍴

Kent Arms
Station Road
**Flowers Original; Fremlins
Bitter** Ⓗ Regular guest beers
No frills pub. Known to
commuters as "Platform 5"
🍴🍽

Prince Albert
109 New Street
**Draught Bass; Boddingtons
Bitter; Kentish Ales Royal
Porter** (winter); **Ruddle
County** Ⓗ Regular guest beers
Thriving one-bar pub

Smiths Arms
Rugby Gardens
Opens 11 am
**King & Barnes Festive;
Webster Yorkshire Bitter** Ⓗ
Popular with pool players. Bat
and trap pitch 🐾🍽

Bapchild 11F4

10–2.30; 6–11

Fox & Goose
2 Fox Hill (A2)
Courage Best Bitter Ⓗ
Large, attractive and busy pub
on main road 🎱🐾🕒

Bean 10C3

10–2.30; 6–11

Black Horse
High Street (B255, off A2)
ℰ Longfield 2486
**Truman Bitter, Best Bitter;
Webster Yorkshire Bitter** Ⓗ
Smart village pub. Weekend
barbeques, small zoo
🎱🕒🍴👶

Benenden 10E6

11.30–2.30; 6–11

King William IV
The Street (B2086)
ℰ Cranbrook 240636
Shepherd Neame Bitter Ⓗ

Excellent village local
🏚🐾🕒 (not Sun) 🍴(not Mon) 🍽

Benover 10D5

11–2.30; 6–11

Woolpack Inn
(B2162) OS704483
**Shepherd Neame Bitter, Stock
Ale** Ⓗ
Splendid 17th century
country pub with restaurant
🏚Ⓠ🍴🐾🕒

Bethersden 11F6

10–2.30; 6–11

Whiston Hotel
A28 ℰ Bethersden 252/693
Shepherd Neame Bitter Ⓗ
Attractive hotel converted
from an old rectory 🐾🎱🍴🍽

Biddenden 11E6

11–2.30; 6–11 (10.30 Mon–Thu winter)

Three Chimneys
Off A262 (west of village)
OS828387 ℰ 291472
**Adnams Bitter; Fremlins
Bitter; Goachers Maidstone
Light; Godsons Black Horse;
Harvey BB, XXXX; Biddenden
Cider** Ⓖ
Attractive 16th century pub,
excellent food, ideal for
families 🏚Ⓠ🎱🐾🕒🍴🍽

Bishopsbourne 11G5

10–2.30; 6–10.30 (11 F, S & summer)

Mermaid
The Street (off A2)
**Shepherd Neame Bitter, Stock
Ale** (winter); **Invicta** Ⓗ
Very attractive 🏚Ⓠ🐾🕒🍴

Borough Green 10D4

11–2.30; 6 (7 Sat)–11

Railway
Wrotham Road (A227)
ℰ 882016
**Davenports Bitter; Goacher
Maidstone Ale; Greene King
XX, IPA, Abbot; Rayment
BBA** Ⓗ Regular guest beers
Interesting local with teams
for everything. Rare mild
outlet 🏚🎱🐾🕒🍴🍽♿

Bough Beech 10C5

10–2.30; 6–11

Wheatsheaf
B2027 OS488468
ℰ Four Elms 254
**Flowers Original; Fremlins
Bitter** Ⓗ
Unspoilt 16th century pub in
rural setting
🏚🐾🕒🍴 (not Wed) 🍽

Brasted 10C5

10.30–2.30; 6–11

Bull Inn
High Street (A25)
ℰ Westerham 62551
**Shepherd Neame Mild,
Bitter** Ⓗ, **Stock Ale** Ⓖ (winter)
Invicta Ⓗ

Welcoming local; darts, shove
ha'penny, bat and trap;
vegetarian menu available
Ⓠ🐾🕒🍴

Bredgar 11E4

10–2.30; 6–11

Sun
The Street (B2163)
ℰ Wormshill 221
**Courage Best Bitter,
Directors** Ⓗ
Spacious country inn with
good selection of food 🏚🐾🕒🍴

Broadstairs 11J4

11–2.30; 5.30–11

Bradstow Mill
125 High Street
**Flowers Original; Fremlins
Bitter** Ⓗ
Interesting bar, reconstructed
as interior of windmill.
Popular with young set 🐾🕒🚃

Brown Jug
Ramsgate Road, Dumpton
Park, (A255)
**Flowers Original; Fremlins
Bitter** Ⓗ
Collection of china jugs and
animated musical clocks.
Colourful beer garden
🏚Ⓠ🐾🍴🚃 (Dumpton Park)

Neptunes Hall
1 Harbour Street
Shepherd Neame Bitter Ⓗ
Large, busy Victorian town
pub 🏚🐾🍴🚃

Royal Albion Hotel
Albion Street ℰ Thanet 68071
**Flowers Original, Fremlins
Bitter, Fullers ESB, Shepherd
Neame** Ⓗ Occasional
guest beers
Friendly hotel bar near town
centre 🏚🐾🎱🕒🍴🚃

Broomfield 11G4

10–2.30; 6–10.30 (11 F, S & summer)

Huntsman & Horn
Margate Road
Fremlins Bitter Ⓗ
End of village local by the
duckpond 🏚🎱🐾

Burham 10D4

11–2.30; 7–11

Toastmasters Inn
Church Street
ℰ Medway 61299
**Adnams Bitter; Boddingtons
Bitter; Fuller ESB; Marston
Pedigree; Robinson Best Bitter;
Young Special** Ⓗ Regular
guest beers
Bar has pews from demolished
parish church 🕒🍴

Canterbury 11G4

10–2.30; 6–10.30 (11 S, F & summer)

Eight Bells
34 London Road ℰ 454794
Opens 11

Flowers Original; Fremlins
Bitter H
Friendly local ✿ ⚲ ➴ ≉

Gentil Knyght
Shipman Avenue, London
Road Estate ✆ 65891
**Shepherd Neame Mild,
Bitter** H
Friendly estate pub
⚎ ✿ ⚲ ➴ (not Sun) ⚑ &

Royal Dragoon
100 Military Road (A28)
**Shepherd Neame Mild,
Bitter** H
Pleasant local: outdoor
drinking in old graveyard
✿ ⚲ & ≉

Capel le Ferne 11H6
10–2.30; 6–11
Royal Oak
Dover Road (A20) OS264387
**Charrington IPA; Fremlins
Bitter** H
Roadside pub with nearby
panoramic views of the
English Channel ⚎ ✿ ⚲ ⚐

Chartham 11G5
10–2.30; 6.30–10.30 (11 F, S & summer)
Artichoke
Rattington Street ✆ 316
**Shepherd Neame Bitter,
Invicta** H
Formerly an ancient "Hall
House" ⚎ ✿ ⚲ ⚑ & ≉

Chatham 10D4
10–2.30; 6–11
Von Alten
63 High Street (near A2)
**Flowers Original; Fremlins
Bitter; Wethered Bitter** H
Small town pub ⚲ ≉

Court at Street 11G6
10–2.30; 6–11
Welcome Stranger
B2067
**Hook Norton Old Hookey;
Shepherd Neame Bitter;
Wadworth 6X** H Occasional
guest beers
Small and friendly two-bar
pub near Wildlife Park Q

Cowden Pound 10C5
10–2.30; 6–10.30 (11 F, S)
Queens Arms
Cowden Cross (B2026)
OS464425
Fremlins Bitter H
Totally unspoilt Victorian
country pub. No keg or lager
sold! ⚎ ✿

Cranbrook 10E6
11–2.30; 6–11
Duke of York
High Street (B2189)
✆ 713460
**Shepherd Neame Bitter, Stock
Ale** (winter) **Invicta** G
Small friendly one-bar pub
known locally as "Deano's" ⚎

Cuxton 10D4
10–2.30; 6–11
White Hart
Rochester Road (A228)
✆ Medway 717372
**Shepherd Neame Bitter,
Invicta** H
Recently modernised roadside
inn ⚎ ✿ ⚲ ➴ (not Mon) ≉

Dargate 11G4
11–3; 6–11
Dove Inn
Plum Pudding Lane (off
A299) ✆ Canterbury 751360
**Shepherd Neame Mild,
Bitter** H
Popular village local with
garden ⚎ ✿ ⚲ ➴ (not Sun)

Dartford 10C3
10–2.30; 6–11
Malt Shovel
3 Darenth Road (off A226)
✆ Dartford 24381
**Young Bitter, Special, Winter
Warmer** H
Pub with a cosy 17th century
public bar ⚎ Q ✿ ⚲ ➴ ⚑ ≉

Masons Arms
50 Spital Street ✆ 26032
Truman Best Bitter H
Friendly town pub. Bat and
trap, darts, pool. Genuine
Italian food by arrangement
✿ ⚏ ⚲ ≉

Smiffys Bar
Orchard Street ✆ 71237
Opens 12.00 & 7.30 closed
Sun lunch
**Everard Tiger; Pitfield Hoxton
Heavy, Dark Star** G Regular
guest beers
Wine bar in converted stables
in back street ✿ ⚲ ➴ ≉

10–2.30; 6–11
Victory
East Hill (A226)
**Shepherd Neame Mild, Bitter,
Invicta** H
Cosy corner local; darts ✿ ⚲

Deal 11H5
10–2.30; 6–11
Three Compasses
Beach Street ✆ 374661
Fremlins Bitter H
Friendly unpretentious sea-
front pub ⚑ ≉ (Deal)

Doddington 11F4
10.30–3; 6–11
Chequers
The Street ✆ 269
Shepherd Neame Bitter H
Popular village inn ⚎ ✿ ⚑

Dover 11H5
10–2.30; 6–11
Arlington
Snargate Street
**Adnams Extra; Shepherd
Neame Bitter** H Occasional
guest beers

Small distinctive free house
near Western Docks
⚲ ≉ (Dover Priory)

Crown & Sceptre
25 Elms Vale Road (off A20)
Charrington IPA H
Strong local trade
⚑ ≉ (Dover Priory)

Royal Oak
Lower Road, River ✆ 822073
**Shepherd Neame Mild,
Bitter** H
Modern interior in historic
flint shell ⚲ ≉ (Kearsney)

White Horse Inn
St James Street (off A258)
✆ 202911
Fremlins Bitter H Occasional
guest beers
Parts date back to 14th
century ✿ ⚲ ➴

White Lion
Tower Street
**Shepherd Neame Mild,
Bitter** H
Pleasant local in residential
area ≉ (Dover Priory)

Dungeness 11G7
10–2.30; 6–11
Pilot
OS090185 ✆ Lydd 20314
Courage Directors H
Unusual pub on shingle
beach. Renowned for fresh
fish and chips. Ringing the
bull. Within sight of nuclear
power station. RH&DR trains
pass by (non stop) Q ⚲ ➴ ⚑

East Farleigh 10D5
10–2.30; 6–11
Walnut Tree
Forge Lane OS743531
✆ Maidstone 26368
**Shepherd Neame Bitter, Stock
Ale** H
Increasingly popular cosy
country local ⚎ Q ✿ ⚲ ➴

East Malling 10D4
10–2.30; 6–11
Rising Sun
Mill Street
✆ West Malling 843284
**Shepherd Neame Bitter, Stock
Ale** (winter) H
Friendly local with home
cooked food, games room
⚎ ✿ ⚲ ➴

East Peckham 10D5
11–2.30; 6–11
Bush, Blackbird &
Thrush
Peckham Bush OS664498
✆ 871349
Fremlins Bitter G
Unspoilt country pub set
amongst orchards ⚎ ✿

Edenbridge 10C5
10–2.30; 6–10.30 (11 F, S)
White Horse

High Street (B2026)
℘ 862208
**Friary Meux Bitter; Ind Coope
Burton Ale** ℍ
Coaching inn dating from
1574, restaurant with late
licence ⊞ (lounge bar) ⑤♥▮≷

Fairseat 10D4

12–2.30; 6–11

Vigo Inn
(A227) ℘ 822547
**Eldridge Pope Royal Oak;
Goacher Vigo Best Bitter;
Maidstone Ale; Young Bitter,
Special** ℍ Occasional guest
beers
Endearingly basic pub with
rare daddlums table ▦Q℘▮

Farningham 10C4

10–2.30; 6–11

Chequers
High Street ℘ 862223
**Adnams Bitter; Everard Tiger;
Fuller ESB; Godsons Black
Horse; Greene King IPA;
Young Special** ℍ Regular
guest beers
Warm, friendly, busy local in
picturesque riverside village
℘⑤ (Mon–Sat) ♥ (Wed–Sat)

Faversham 11F4

10.30–3; 6–11

Albion
Front Brents ℘ 533897
Fremlins Bitter ℍ
Comfortable inn on edge of
creek Q▦▮℘ℍ⑤♥

Mechanics Arms
44 West Street ℘ 532693
**Shepherd Neame Mild,
Bitter** ℍ
Splendid, unspoilt local Q▮

Phoenix
99 Abbey Street ℘ 532693
**Flowers Original; Fremlins
Bitter** ℍ
Pleasant pub in historic street.
Excellent home cooked food
▦℘⑤♥

Folkestone 11H6

10–2.30; 6–11

Clifton Hotel
The Leas ℘ 41231
Draught Bass ℍ
Large hotel, handy for Leas
Cliff Hall concertgoers. Superb
Channel views Q▦⑤♥

Lifeboat
42, North Street ℘ 43958
**Draught Bass; Courage
Directors; Fremlins Bitter;
Shepherd Neame Bitter** ℍ
Regular guest beers
Small pub close to fishmarket.
Generally busy, especially
during Easter Hockey Festival
℘

Raglan
104 Dover Road ℘ 54836
Evenings Opens 7

**Fremlins Bitter; Taylor
Landlord; Cider** (summer) ℍ
Regular guest beers
Comfortable free house

Richmond Tavern
1, Margaret Street ℘ 54857
Opens 10–30; Sat eves opens 7
**Shepherd Neame Mild,
Bitter** ℍ
Small and busy. Thriving crib
and dart teams ℘⑤ (not Sun)

Victoria
106, Risborough Lane,
Cheriton ℘ 77347
Opens 11 & 6.30
Fremlins Bitter ℍ
Friendly, busy public with
pool and darts. Comfortable,
smart lounge and restaurant
Q℘⑤♥ (not Tue) ▮&

Gillingham 10E4

10–2.30; 6–11

Cannon
15 Garden Street, Brompton
℘ Medway 41006
Webster Yorkshire Bitter ℍ
Friendly local—home of local
amateur sports teams ℘⑤♥▮

Prince Albert
80 High Street
℘ Medway 51020
**Courage Best Bitter,
Directors** ℍ
Comfortable and cosy corner
house in town centre ℘⑤▮≷

Goodnestone 11H5

10–2.30; 6–11

Fitzwalter Arms
The Street OS255546
℘ Nonington 840303
Shepherd Neame Bitter ℍ
Unspoilt Jacobean pub owned
by the Lord of Manor
▦Q⑤♥▮

Gravesend 10D3

10–2.30; 6–11

Bat & Ball
113 Wrotham Road (A227)
**Ruddle County; Watney
Combes Bitter, Stag Bitter;
Webster Yorkshire Bitter** ℍ
Balcony at rear overlooks the
cricket ground ℘⑤▮&≷

Jolly Drayman
Wellington Street (off A226)
Charrington IPA ℍ
Attractive, old pub, once part
of Wellington Brewery.
Known as the Coke Oven
Q℘▮≷

New Inn
Milton Road (A226) ℘ 66651
Fremlins Bitter ℍ
Comfortable 18th century
town centre pub ▮≷

Hadlow 10D5

10–2.30; 6–11

Fiddling Monkey
Maidstone Road (A26)
℘ 850267

**Flowers Original; Fremlins
Bitter; Ind Coope Burton Ale;
Young Special** ℍ
Plush, roomy pub divided into
several drinking areas ℘⑤♥

Halfway 11F3

10–2.30; 6–11

Oddfellows Arms
Minster Road (B2008)
Ind Coope Bitter ℍ
Popular, friendly local ▦▮

Harty 11F4
(Sheppey)

10–2.30; 6–11

Ferry House Inn
Harty Ferry Road OS015659
℘ Leysdown 510214
**Friary Meux Bitter; Ind Coope
Burton Ale** ℍ Occasional
guest beers
Remote free house on south
east tip of Sheppey. Busy in
summer ▦Q▦℘ℍ⑤♥▮&▲

Hawkhurst 10E6

10–2.30; 6–11

Oak & Ivy
Rye Road (A265), Pipsden
℘ 3293
**Flowers Original; Fremlins
Bitter** ⑥ Occasional guest
beers
Traditional English country
pub. Dining room with supper
licence ▦▮℘⑤♥&

Herne 11G4

10–2.30; 6–10.30 (11 F, S & summer)

Upper Red Lion
Herne Street (A291)
℘ Herne Bay 361083
Fremlins Bitter ℍ
Popular village local
▦▦℘⑤♥ (not Sun)

Herne Bay 11G4

10–2.30; 6–10.30 (11 F, S & summer)

Divers Arms
Central Parade ℘ 375265
**Shepherd Neame Bitter, Stock
Ale** ℍ
Lively sea front local ⑤

Heron
Station Road
Shepherd Neame Bitter ℍ
Friendly locals' pub ▦℘⑤≷

Prince of Wales
Mortimer Street ℘ 374205
Shepherd Neame Bitter ℍ
Comfortable house with fine
interior Q▮

Hernhill 11G4

11–3; 6–11

Three Horseshoes
Staple Street (off A299)
OS061602
**Shepherd Neame Mild, Bitter,
Stock Ale** (winter) ⑥
Typically Kentish; many
games, stone bottles displayed
▦Q℘▮&

Higham   10D3

11–2.30; 6–11
Railway Tavern
Chequers Street, Lower
Higham ✆ Shorne 2858
Shepherd Neame Bitter Ⓗ
Cosy bar; railway prints and
models. No meals Sun ⌂⏴➤≷

Hollingbourne   11E5

10.30–2.30; 6–11
Parkgate Inn
Ashford Road (A20)
OS839537 ✆ 582
**Boddingtons Bitter; Fremlins
Bitter; Goachers Maidstone
Light** Ⓗ **Regular guest beers**
Welcoming roadside inn with
restaurant, spit roasts in
winter. Handy for Leeds Castle
Q⊞⏴➤ (not Sun) ⅊

Windmill Inn
Eyehorne Street (B2163)
✆ 280
Fremlins Bitter Ⓗ
Friendly old pub in centre of
village, comfortable lounge.
Disco Sun eve
⌂⏴➤ (not Mon/Sun) ⬧≷

Hythe   11G6

10.30–2.30; 6.30–11
Britannia
Horn Street, Seabrook
(B2064)
Ind Coope Bitter Ⓗ**, Burton
Ale** Ⓖ
Excellent unspoilt one-bar
village pub ⌂Q⏴⏴

Kemsing   10C4

10.30–2.30; 6–11
Bell
High Street
✆ Sevenoaks 61550
**Courage Best Bitter,
Directors** Ⓗ
Friendly pub in village centre,
trad jazz Mondays; restaurant
Thu–Sun ⌂⏴⏴➤⬧⬧▲

Lamberhurst   10D6

10–2.30; 6–11
Chequers
Hastings Road (A21)
✆ 890260
**Flowers Original; Fremlins
Bitter** Ⓗ
Old coaching inn dating back
to 15th century ⌂⏴⊞⏴➤⬧

Longfield   10D4

10.30–2.30; 6–11
Railway
2 Station Road (off B260)
**Truman Bitter, Best Bitter,
Sampson; Webster Yorkshire
Bitter** Ⓗ
Popular, good value village
local ⌂⏴⏴⬧≷

Luddenham   11F4

10.30–3; 6–11
Mounted Rifleman

OS981627
Fremlins Bitter Ⓖ
Beer carried up from the
cellar. Totally unspoilt ⌂Q⏴

Maidstone   10E5

10–2.30; 6–11
Chiltern Hundreds
Sittingbourne Road (A249)
✆ 52335
**Courage Best Bitter,
Directors** Ⓗ
Lively, refurbished pub
serving housing estate ⏴⏴➤

Dog & Gun
213, Boxley Road ✆ 58748
Opens 11 Mon–Sat, 6.30 Sat
evening
**Shepherd Neame Bitter, Stock
Ale** Ⓗ
Cosmopolitan and friendly.
Ex-pop star landlord's gold
discs adorn the walls. Pool
table ⏴⬧≷ (east)

Dragoon
40, Sandling Road (A229)
Opens 11 & 6.30
**Shepherd Neame Bitter, Stock
Ale** Ⓗ
Busy and friendly local with
varied pub games ⏴≷ (east)

**Drakes Crab & Oyster
House**
9, Fairmeadow (off A229)
✆ 52531
Morning opening 11
**Flowers Original; Fremlins
Bitter; Wethered Bitter** Ⓗ
Popular ale and wine house
close to river and town centre
⏴⏴➤≷ (east & west)

First & Last
40, Bower Place (off A26)
Fremlins Bitter Ⓗ
Small, friendly street corner
local with two bars
Q⬧≷ (west)

Flowerpot
96, Sandling Road (A229)
✆ 52926
**Truman Bitter, Best Bitter;
Webster Yorkshire Bitter** Ⓗ
Comfortable, friendly house.
Excellent food (Wed–Sat).
Darts and bar billiards
⊞⏴➤≷ (east)

Wheeler's Arms
1, Perry Street (off A229)
Opens 11; & 6.30 Mon & Tue
Shepherd Neame Bitter Ⓗ**,
Stock Ale** Ⓖ
Friendly corner local, very
popular. Bar billiards and
darts ⏴⏴⬧≷ (east)

Marden   10D5

11–2.30; 6–11
Mile Bush Inn
Maidstone Road (B2079)
✆ Maidstone 831303
**Shepherd Neame Bitter, Stock
Ale (winter)** Ⓗ
Popular pub in rural setting.
Good value meals (not Sun)
⌂⏴➤

Margate   11H4

11–2.30; 5.30–11
Duke of Edinburgh
Milton Avenue
**Shepherd Neame Mild,
Bitter** Ⓗ
Popular one-bar local on
corner of Victorian terrace ⌂

Orb Inn
243 Ramsgate Road (A254)
Shepherd Neame Bitter Ⓗ
Friendly traditional 2-bar pub
⌂⏴⏴⏴

Spread Eagle
25 Victoria Road
✆ Thanet 293396
**Boddingtons Bitter; Hook
Norton Old Hookey; Ruddle
County; Wadworth 6X,
Farmers Glory; Young
Special** Ⓗ **Regular guest beers**
Splendid free house. Recom-
mended restaurant ⏴⏴➤

Victoria
104 Ramsgate Road (A254)
Charrington IPA Ⓗ
Comfortable 3-bar corner pub⬧

Marshside   11G4

10–2.30; 6–10.30 (11 F, S & summer)
Gate Inn
Boyden Gate (off A28)
OS220655 ✆ Chislet 496
**Shepherd Neame Mild, Bitter,
Stock Ale, Invicta** Ⓖ
Lively country pub, superb
value; unusual snacks
⌂Q⏴⏴➤ (not Sun) ⬧⏴

Milton Regis   11E4

10–2.30; 6–11
Foresters Arms
77, Charlotte Street
Fremlins Bitter Ⓗ
Friendly backstreet local
⏴⬧≷ (Sittingbourne)

Minster
(Thanet)   11H4

11–2.30; 5.30–11
Saddler
7–9 Monkton Road
✆ Thanet 821331
**Shepherd Neame Mild,
Bitter** Ⓗ
Popular 2-bar local in
attractive village ⊞⏴⏴➤⬧≷

Offham   10D4

10.30–2.30; 6–11
Kings Arms
Teston Road
✆ West Malling 843082
**Courage Best Bitter,
Directors** Ⓗ
Old Kentish inn opposite
village green with a warm
welcome. Live music 1st Thu
of month ⌂Q⊞⏴➤⏴⏴

Ospringe   11F4

10.30–3; 6–11
Anchor

33 Ospringe Street (A2)
**Shepherd Neame Mild,
Bitter** ⊞
Popular village local
🏠 Q 🖉 ⊞

Petteridge 10D5

12 (11 Sat)–2.30; 6–11

Hopbine Inn
Petteridge Road OS667413
✆ Brenchley 2561
Closed Weds. Lunch winter
**King & Barnes Sussex Mild,
Sussex Bitter, Old Ale,
Festive** ⊞
Small country pub in
attractive setting 🏠 🖉 ⓖ ➾

Plaxtol 10D5

10–2.30; 6–11

Papermakers Arms
The Street (off A227)
✆ 810407
**Flowers Original; Fremlins
Bitter** ⊞ Occasional guest
beers
Comfortable village local with
darts and pool table 🖉 ⓖ

Rainham 10E4

10–2.30; 6–11

Dewdrop
100 Hawthorne Avenue,
Twydall
Opens 10–30 & 6.30
Shepherd Neame Bitter ⊞
This spacious postwar pub is
heart of local life 🎲 🖉 ⓖ 🍴

White Horse
High Street ✆ Medway 31210
Courage Best Bitter ⊞
Lively locals' pub in village
centre. Monthly folk club
🖉 🍴 👤 ⓖ ➾

Ramsgate 11H4

11–2.30; 5.30–11

Foy Boat
8 Sion Hill ✆ Thanet 591198
**Flowers Original, Fremlins
Bitter** ⊞ Occasional guest
beers
Plush one-bar pub on cliff top
overlooking Royal Harbour
🎲 ➾

Rochester 10D4

10–2.30; 6–11

Bell
20/21 Cossack Street
✆ Medway 45461
Shepherd Neame Bitter ⊞
Fine wood carving and
glasswork. Warm and friendly
ⓖ ➾ 👤 🍴 ➾

Coopers Arms
10, St Margarets Street
**Courage Best Bitter,
Directors** ⊞
Interesting and ancient
building, 13th century crypt
as cellar 🏠 🖉 ⓖ (not Sun) ➾ ➾

Ruckinge 11F6

10–2.30; 6–11

Blue Anchor
B2067 ✆ Ham Street 2387
**Flowers Original; Fremlins
Bitter** ⊞
Popular village pub with open
log fire in saloon bar 🏠 ⓖ

St Margarets- 11H5
at-Cliffe

10–2.30; 6–11

Carriers Arms
High Street ✆ Dover 852434
Fremlins Bitter ⊞
Small village local, skittle
alley, darts and bar skittles 🖉

Sandgate 11G6

10–2.30; 6–11

Ship
Sandgate High Street (A259)
Ind Coope Burton Ale ⓖ
Occasionally cut off during
stormy weather. Seafaring
charts and prints in lounge,
clog dancing team ⓖ ➾ 🍴

Sandling 10E4

10–2.30; 6–11

Yew Tree
Boarley Lane (off A229)
Shepherd Neame Bitter ⊞
Popular rural pub Q 🖉 ⓖ ➾

Sandwich 11H4

10–2.30; 6–11

Greyhound
10 New Street ✆ 612675
Courage Best Bitter ⊞
Well maintained and centrally
situated ⓖ ➾

Red Cow
Moat Sole ✆ 613243
**Fremlins Bitter; Flowers
Original** ⓖ
Popular pub near Market
Place. Lunches popular with
business people. No meals Sun
Q 🎲 🖉 ⓖ ➾ ➾

Sellindge 11G6

10–2.30; 6–11

Swan
The Street (A20)
**Flowers Original; Fremlins
Bitter** ⊞; **Fuller ESB;
Biddenden Cider** ⓖ
Friendly split-level village pub
with unusual ceiling
🏠 ⓖ ➾

Shatterling 11H4

10–2.30; 6–11

Green Man
Pedding Hill (A257)
OS268584
**Fremlins Bitter; Ruddle Bitter;
Young Bitter, Special** ⊞
Comfortable, friendly pub with
restaurant 🖉 🎲 ⓖ ➾

Sheerness 11F3

10.30–2.30; 6–12

Royal Fountain Hotel
West Street, Blue Town (off
A249) ✆ 662024
**Shepherd Neame Invicta;
Younger Scotch Bitter** ⊞
Occasional guest beers
Historic Naval Hotel (c1755)
near docks. Lord Nelson and
Emma Hamilton's love nest
🏠 🎲 🖉 🎲 ⓖ ➾ ➾

Shepherdswell 11H5

10–2.30; 6–11

Bell
Church Hill OS262478
Fremlins Bitter ⊞
Picturesque pub by the village
green 🖉 ⓖ ➾ ➾

Shoreham 10C4

10–2.30; 6–11

Royal Oak
High Street (off A225)
**Flowers Original, Fremlins
Bitter** ⊞, **Merrydown Cider** ⓖ
Regular guest beers
The heart of village life
🏠 Q ⓖ 🎲 ➾

Shorne 10D3

10–2.30; 6–11

Rose & Crown
32 The Street (off A226)
**Truman Bitter, Best Bitter,
Sampson** ⊞
Most attractive and
welcoming, in pleasant
surroundings
🖉 ⓖ (not Sun) ➾ 🎲

Shottenden 11F5

10–2.30; 6–10.30 (11 F, S)

Plough
Shottenden Road (off A252)
**Adnams Bitter; Devenish
Wessex Best Bitter; Fremlins
Bitter** ⊞ Occasional guest
beers
Popular country freehouse
🏠 🖉 ⓖ

Sittingbourne 11F4

10–2.30; 6–11

Park Tavern
86 Park Road (off A2)
**Shepherd Neame Mild, Bitter,
Stock Ale (winter)** ⊞
Busy local near town centre
Q 🖉 ⓖ 🎲 ➾

Smart's Hill 10C5

10–2.30; 6–11

Spotted Dog
(Off B2188) OS522419
**Flowers Original; Fremlins
Bitter; Wethered Bitter** ⊞
Regular guest beers
Picturesque weatherboarded
pub; spectacular views from
garden; restaurant 🏠 🖉 ⓖ ➾

Snargate 11F6

10–2.30; 6–11

Red Lion
B2080
Shepherd Neame Mild,
Bitter G
Proper unspoilt pub ♨Q♟

Speldhurst 10C5

10–2.30; 6–11

George & Dragon
Off A26/A264 OS554414
Flowers Original; Fremlins
Bitter; Harvey Pale Ale, BB,
XXXX; King & Barnes Sussex
Bitter H
Classic Medieval inn, cosy
saloon; stone-flagged public
bar. Restaurant ♨Q☝♟♦

Stansted 10D4

10.30–2.30; 6 (7 winter)–11

Black Horse
Tumblefield Road (off A20)
Flowers Original; Fremlins
Bitter H
Popular village local with bat
and trap lawn. No meals Sun
♨⊞♪☝♟

Stone in Oxney 11F6

10–2.30; 6–11

Ferry Inn
Appledore Road
Courage Best Bitter,
Directors H
Pleasant former Toll House.
Home cooked meals a
speciality ♪☝♦ (not Thu)

Strood 10D4

10–2.30; 6–11

Crispin & Crispianus
London Road (A2)
Courage Best Bitter,
Directors H
13th century inn—the oldest
in Strood. No food Sun ☝♦≢

Sutton-at-Hone 10C4

10–2.30; 6–11

Greyhound
58 Main Road (A225)
Courage Best Bitter,
Directors H
Comfortable pub. Organist
Saturday night ♪☝

Tonbridge 10C5

10–2.30; 6–11

Forester's Arms
Quarry Hill (A26) ✆ 360129
Shepherd Neame Bitter, Stock
Ale (winter), Invicta
(summer) H
Friendly pub with a basic but
welcoming public and
comfortable lounge
♨Q⊞♪☝& (Public Bar) ≢

Ivy House
High Street (A26) ✆ 352382
Flowers Original; Fremlins
Bitter; Wethered Bitter H
Regular guest beers

Friendly, welcoming 15th
century inn. ♪☝

Tunbridge Wells 10C6

10–2.30; 6–11

Beau Nash Tavern
Mount Ephraim (A264)
Harvey Pale Ale; King &
Barnes Sussex Bitter; Truman
Sampson; Usher Best Bitter;
Webster Yorkshire Bitter H
Occasional guest beers
Small, busy mews pub
♨♪☝♦≢

Compasses
Little Mount Sion
Flowers Original; Fremlins
Bitter H Regular guest beers
Tucked away, comfortable,
no-frills town pub ♨Q☝♟≢

Railway Inn
106 Goods Station Road
Courage Best Bitter,
Directors H
Old fashioned, basic back-
street boozer ♪

Upper Upnor 10D4

10–2.30; 6–11

Tudor Rose
29 High Street
Young Bitter, Special H
Regular guest beers
Inglenook family rooms,
shove ha'penny, historic
castle next door. No food Sun
♨Q⊞♪☝♦

Walmer 11H5

10.2.30; 6–11

Green Beret
Canada Road ✆ Deal 362411
Draught Bass; Courage
Directors; Johnsons College H
Close to barracks, strong
Royal Marines connections.
Folk club ☝♦≢

Lord Clyde
The Strand (A258)
Shepherd Neame Mild,
Bitter H
One-bar pub; cosy atmosphere
♨♪☝♦≢ (Deal)

West Cliffe 11H5

10–2.30; 6–11

Swingate Inn
Deal Road A258 OS335440
Draught Bass H Occasional
guest beers
Cosy roadhouse ♨Q⊞♪

West Malling 10D4

10.30–2.30; 6–11

Joiners Arms
High Street (A228) ✆ 840723
Shepherd Neame Bitter, Stock
Ale H
Town pub with friendly atmos-
phere, quiet lounge ☝♟≢

Whitstable 11G4

10–2.30; 6–10.30 (11 F, S & summer)

Coach & Horses
Oxford Street (A290)
Shepherd Neame Mild,
Bitter H, Stock Ale (winter) G
Smart, busy High Street local
Q☝≢

Prince Albert
Sea Street
Fremlins Bitter H
Basic, friendly locals pub

Rose in Bloom
Joy Lane (off A290)
Flowers Original; Fremlins
Bitter H
Comfortable house, sea views
from garden ♪☝ (not Sun)

Wall Tavern
Middle Wall
Fremlins Bitter H
Friendly house behind High
Street
♪☝♦ (occasional B-B-Q)

Wickhambreaux 11G4

10–2.30; 6–11

Rose
The Green
Flowers Original; Fremlins
Bitter H
Charming 13th century pub

Wingham 11H4

10–2.30; 6–11

Anchor
High Street
Fremlins Bitter H
Rambling old house ☝♦

Wittersham 11E6

10–2.30; 6–11

Ewe & Lamb
Stocks Road (B2082) ✆ 203
Courage Best Bitter, Directors
(summer) H
Friendly village pub.
Decorated with cricketing
ephemera. Push-penny ☝♦

Wouldham 10D4

10.30–2.30; 6–11

Medway
2 High Street
Fremlins Bitter; Goacher's
Maidstone Ale H Occasional
guest beers
Friendly and welcoming;
occasional sing songs. Close to
river, no food Sun ⊞♪☝♦

Wrotham 10D4

10.30–2.30; 6–11

Three Post Boys
The Square
Courage Best Bitter,
Directors H
Old coaching inn; warm
friendly welcome ♨♪☝♦

Accrington 29G9

11.30–3; 6–11

Boars Head
51 Burnley Road (A679)
Opens 11 & 7
Thwaites Mild, Bitter Ⓗ
Town centre local, bar
billiards and pool table ᴳ⪰

Great Eastern
Arnold Street (off A679)
Thwaites Mild, Bitter Ⓗ
Friendly local in improved
part of town 🏠⪰

Adlington 22D2

10.30–3; 6–11

White Bear
5a Market Street (A6)
✆ 482357
**Matthew Brown Lion Mild;
Theakston Best Bitter, XB, Old
Peculier** Ⓗ
Large white painted local pub,
good lunches 🏠Q ᴳ🍴⪰

Altham 29G9

10.30–3; 6–11

Greyhound
Whalley Road (A680)
Samuel Smith OBB Ⓗ
Plush main road pub, warm
and inviting 🏠ᴾ🍴

Aughton 22B2

11–3; 5.30–10.30 (11 F, S)

Dog & Gun
233 Long Lane (off A59 &
B5197)
✆ Aughton Green 423303
**Burtonwood Dark Mild,
Bitter, Almonds Bitter** Ⓗ
Rural pub on edge of town.
Beware keg light mild on
handpump
🏠Q ᴾ🍴⪰ (Aughton Park)

Royal Oak
134 Liverpool Road (A59)
✆ Aughton Green 422121
**Ind Coope Burton Ale; Peter
Walker Mild, Best Bitter** Ⓗ
Comfortable suburban local
with distinctive U-shaped
public bar 🏠Q ᴾᴳ🍴

Bartle 29E9

11–3; 6.30–11

Sitting Goose
Sidegreaves Lane OS486329
✆ Catforth 690344
Thwaites Mild, Bitter Ⓗ
Old pub in pleasant wooded
Fylde country
🎫 (lunchtimes) ᴾᴳ🍷

Baxenden 29G9

10.30–3; 7–11

Alma
Manchester Road (A680)
**Matthew Brown Lion Mild,
Lion Bitter** Ⓗ
Cosy old pub on two levels,
partly 16th century 🍴

Bay Horse 29E7

10.45–3 (closed mon); 5.45–11

Bay Horse
Off A6 (just off M6 Jct. 33)
✆ 791204
Mitchells Mild, Bitter Ⓗ
Country pub with its own
rugby team. Summer
barbeque evenings.
No food Mon 🏠🎫ᴾᴳ🍷🍴

Bickerstaffe 22B2

11–3; 5.30–10.30 (11 F, S)

Stanley Gate
Liverpool Road (A570)
**Greenall Whitley Mild,
Bitter** Ⓔ
Inviting hostelry standing
guard at lonely crossroads 🍴

Bilsborrow 29E8

11 (12 winter)–3; 6–11

White Bull
Garstang Road ✆ Brock 40324
**Matthew Brown Lion Mild,
Bitter** Ⓗ
Canalside village pub, friendly
locals 🏠🎫ᴾ

Blackburn 29F9

10.30–3; 6–11

Bank
Hope Street (off Montague
Street)
**Matthew Brown Lion Mild,
Lion Bitter** Ⓗ
Comfortable local near the
park ᴳ🍴

Corporation Park
Revidge Road (off A677)
Evening opens 7
Thwaites Best Mild, Bitter Ⓗ
Highest pub in town, close to
golf course and park ᴳ

Havelock
Stancliffe Street (B6447)
Thwaites Mild, Bitter Ⓗ
Thriving, tastefully
modernised local with
sporting vault, handy for
Blackburn Rovers FC
ᴾᴳ🍴🍷⪰

Knowles Arms
Brownhill Drive (A6119)
**Matthew Brown Lion Mild,
Lion Bitter, John Peel;
Theakston Old Peculier** Ⓗ
Tastefully modernised main
road pub, often busy.
Favoured by young crowd
ᴾᴳ🍴

Black Lane Ends 29H8

11–3; 5.30–11

Hare & Hounds
Skipton Old Road OS928433
**Taylor Dark Mild, Best
Bitter** Ⓗ
Friendly hillside pub, superb
views of the Pennines 🏠ᴾᴳ

Blacko 29G8

11–3; 5.30–11

Cross Gaits
Beverley Road (off A682)
OS866415
**Burtonwood Dark Mild,
Bitter** Ⓗ
Old, comfortable inn with
good views 🏠ᴾᴳ

Blackpool 28D9

10.30–3; 6–11

Bispham
Red Bank Road (off A584)
✆ 51752
Samuel Smith OBB Ⓗ
Popular with locals and
holidaymakers ᴳ

Empress
Exchange Street, North Shore
✆ 20413
Thwaites Best Mild, Bitter Ⓗ
Large Victorian pub, basic but
friendly. 2 minutes from
Promenade. Snooker table
🎫ᴳ🍴⪰ (North)

Mount Pleasant
103 High Street, North Shore
**Matthew Brown Lion Mild,
Lion Bitter; Theakston Old
Peculier** Ⓗ
Friendly street corner local 🍴⪰

New Mariners
8 Norbreck Road, Norbreck
(off A584) ✆ 51154
Opens 11
Boddingtons Bitter Ⓗ
Large, tastefully modernised
pub, just off Promenade ᴾᴳ🍷

Ramsden Arms
Talbot Road ✆ 23215
**Ind Coope Burton Ale;
Jennings Bitter; Tetley Mild,
Bitter** Ⓗ
Excellent enterprising town
centre ale house. Popular with
motor cyclists 🏠ᴳ🍴⪰ (North)

Saddle
286 Whitegate Drive, Marton
✆ 63065
Opens 11.30
**Bass Mild, Special Bitter,
Draught Bass** Ⓗ
Old inn of character.
Collection of old pictures and
photos 🏠Qᴾ

Welcome
Vicarage Lane (1 mile W. M55
Jct. 4) ✆ 65372
**Burtonwood Bitter, Almonds
Bitter** Ⓗ
Modernised large pub; plush
bar and public with pool and
darts
🏠🎫ᴾ (children's rides) ᴳ🍴

Wheatsheaf
194 Talbot Road ✆ 25062
**Matthew Brown Lion Mild,
Theakston Best Bitter, XB, Old
Peculier** Ⓗ
Basic town centre pub
🎫🍴⪰ (North)

Bolton-le-Sands   29E7

10.45–3; 5.45–11

Blue Anchor
Main Road (off A6)
Mitchells Mild, Bitter H
Unpretentious village local
🏚🍴👶

Briercliffe   29H9

12–3; 7–11

Roggerham Gate
OS884337 ☎ Burnley 22039
Youngers IPA, No. 3 H
Remote, well-appointed pub in
attractive setting by reservoir
🏚👶🍴🎵

Brierfield   29H8

11–3; 5.30–11

Waggon & Horses
Colne Road (A56, off M65)
☎ 63962
Thwaites Best Mild, Bitter H
Past CAMRA award winner
for best refurbished pub
🏚Q👶🍴🎵➤

Brindle   22D1

10.30–3; 6–11

Cavendish Arms
Sandy Lane (B5256)
☎ Hoghton 2912
**Burtonwood Dark Mild,
Bitter** H
A very small cosy old village
pub. Interesting stained glass
windows 🏚Q👶👶

Broughton   29E9

10.30–3; 6–11

Golden Ball
521 Garstang Road (A6/
B5269 off M55 Jct. 1)
☎ 852746
**Matthew Brown Lion Mild,
Lion Bitter, John Peel;
Theakston Best Bitter** H
Comfortable renovated pub in
village centre. Pool and darts
rooms 🏚👶🍴

Bryning   28D9

11–3; 6–11

Birley Arms
Bryning Lane
☎ Freckleton 632201
**Greenall Whitley Mild, Local
Bitter, Original Bitter** H
Spacious updated village pub
🍴👶👶🎵

Burnley   29G9

11–3; 5.30–11

Grey Mare
110 Gannow Lane (off A671)
Opens 11.30 & 6
Bass Special Bitter E
Typical cosy East Lancs local
near Leeds–Liverpool canal 🍴

Old Duke
56 Briercliffe Road (off A56)
Bass Special Bitter E

Boisterous open-plan main
road local. Deservedly popular
🍴👶

Woodman
129 Todmorden Road (A671)
Evening opens 6
**Bass Special Bitter; Stones Best
Bitter** H
Deservedly popular large
corner pub. Unusual layout,
with snug concealed by
ornate wood-panelled bar
👶 (Thur/Fri) 🍴

Catforth   29E9

10.30–3; 6–11

Running Pump
Catforth Road (off B5269)
☎ 690265
**Robinson Best Mild, Best
Bitter, Old Tom** G
Deservedly popular country
inn 🏚👶🍴

Caton   29E7

10.45–3; 5.45–11

Station
2 Hornby Road (A683)
☎ 770323
Mitchells Mild, Bitter, ESB E
Large locals' pub with small
dining room and bowling
green 🏚🅿 (dining room) 👶👶🎵

Chipping   29F8

11–3; 6–11

Sun
Windy Street ☎ 206
Opens 11.30. Sat eve opens
6.30
Boddingtons Mild, Bitter H
Unspoilt old haunted pub.
Stream runs through cellar
🏚👶🎵🍴👜

Talbot
Talbot Street ☎ 260
Boddingtons Mild, Bitter H
Popular pub in centre of
picturesque village, wide
range of pub games
🏚Q🅿 (lunchtime) 👶👶👜

Chorley   22C1

10.30–3; 6–11

Crown
46 Chapel Street
**Matthew Brown Lion Mild;
Theakston Best Bitter, XB** H
Recently modernised town
centre pub 👶➤

Market
Cleveland Street ☎ 77991
Opens 11 & 7
**Ind Coope Burton Ale; Peter
Walker Mild** H**, Best Bitter**
A small, often crowded town
centre pub of character
🏚👶 (Mon–Fri) 🍴➤

Queens Tavern
6 Preston Road (A6) ☎ 75902
**Hartley XB; Whitbread Castle
Eden** H
Recently renovated and
enlarged 👶

Wheatsheaf
3 St. Thomas's Road (A581)
Opens 11 & 7
**Matthew Brown Lion Mild,
Lion Bitter** H
18th century town centre
pub, often crowded 🏚➤

Church   29G9

11–3; 6–11

Bridge
Henry Street (B6231)
**Bass XXXX Mild, Special
Bitter** H
Local near sports centre.
Splendid original gents! Irish
folk music Sun lunch 🏚👶➤

Churchtown   29E8

11–3; 6–11

Horns
The Green (A586) ☎ 3351
Whitbread Castle Eden H
Many horns—no dilemma.
Good food Q🅿👶🎵

Clayton-le-Moors   29G9

11–3; 7–11

Old England Forever
13 Church Street (off A680)
**Matthew Brown Lion Mild,
Lion Bitter** H
Small locals' pub with rare
tiled bar, worth finding 🍴

Cleveleys   28D8

11–3; 6–11

Royal
North Promenade ☎ 852143
**Boddingtons Bitter;
Moorhouses Premier Bitter,
Pendle Witches; Tetley
Bitter** H
Large sea front pub, popular
with locals 🅿🅿🅿👶🍴

Clitheroe   29G8

11–3; 5.30–11

Buck
Lowergate
Thwaites Best Mild, Bitter H
Very busy young people's pub,
catering for most tastes 👶👶

Try also: Waggon & Horses
(Thwaites)

Cloughfold   22E1

11.30–3; 7–11

Ashworth Arms
325 Bacup Road (A681)
**Bass XXXX Mild, Special
Bitter** E
Tastefully modernised local
with small rooms. Pool 👶

Cockerham

10.45–3; 7–11

Manor
Main Street (A588/B5272)
☎ Forton 791252
Mitchells Bitter E
Multi-roomed inn, stone-built
in 1871 🏚🅿👶👶🎵

Colne 29H8

11–3; 5.30–11

Crown
Albert Road (opposite station)
✆ 863580
Evening opens 7.15
**Bass XXXX Mild, Special
Bitter, Draught Bass; Stones
Best Bitter** Ⓗ
Award-winning hotel with
comfortable lounge, large
games room, snooker room
and restaurant ♨🏠🕒🍽️♿≷

Golden Ball
Burnley Road (A56)
✆ 861862
Tetley Mild, Bitter Ⓗ
Fine exterior and prize-
winning cellar ♨♿🍽️

Try also: Red Lion (Taylors)

Conder Green 28E7

10.45–3; 6.30–11

Stork
A588 OS460560
✆ Galgate 751234
**Hartley XB; Boddingtons
Bitter** Ⓗ
Single L-shaped bar with oak
panelling. Near cycleway
along old railway ♨♿🏠🍽️

Coppull Moor 22C2

12–3; 5.30–11

Plough & Harrow
Preston Road (A49)
Thwaites Best Mild, Bitter Ⓔ
Small, friendly wayside local
♿🍽️

Cowpe 23E1

11.30–3; 7–11

Buck
9 Asten Buildings, Cowpe
Road (off A681 at Waterfoot)
**Boddingtons Bitter; Taylor
Mild, Best Bitter; Thwaites
Best Mild, Bitter** Ⓗ
Terraced village local, ex-Bass,
transformed since becoming a
free-house ♨♿🍽️ (not Mon) 🍽️

Darwen 22D1

11–3; 6–11

Crown
Redearth Road ✆ 73192
**Boddingtons Mild, Bitter;
Taylor Bitter; Thwaites Mild,
Bitter** Ⓗ Regular guest beers
Enterprising free house near
town centre ♿≷

Greenfield
Lower Barn Street (off
Cranberry Lane) ✆ 73945
Thwaites Mild, Bitter Ⓗ
Classic Victorian back street
local. Basically a man's pub,
yet with ladies' darts and
dominoes 🍽️

Edenfield 22E1

11.30–3; 7–11

Coach & Horses

167 Market Street (A680)
**Wilsons Original Mild,
Bitter** Ⓗ
Pleasant village local near
church 🚌 (lunchtimes) 🍽️

Elswick 28E8

11–3; 6–11

Ship
High Street (B2569)
Boddingtons Bitter Ⓗ
Recently modernised; lively &
friendly ♨🍽️

Euxton 22C1

11.30 (12 Sat)–3; 6–11

Euxton Mills
Wigan Road (A49/A581)
✆ Chorley 64002
**Burtonwood Dark Mild,
Bitter** Ⓗ
Very comfortable and cosy
pub with excellent meals
♨🚌 (lunchtimes) 🕒🍽️🍽️

Fence 29G8

11–3; 7–11

Harpers
Harpers Lane, off Wheatley
Lane Road ✆ Nelson 66249
**Tetley Bitter; Thwaites Best
Mild, Bitter** Ⓗ
Comfortable friendly pub.
Extensively modernised with
restaurant. Handy for Pendle
Hill and rural walks ♿🕒🍽️

Fleetwood 28D8

10.30–3; 6–11

Fleetwood Arms
188 Dock Street ✆ 2787
Evening opens 6.30
Higsons Mild, Bitter Ⓗ
Dockside tavern of great
character 🍽️

Victoria
46 Dock Street
Summer opens 11–4 Mon,
Tue, Fri, Sat
Higsons Mild, Bitter Ⓗ
Pub of great character,
Fleetwood's oldest 🕒🍽️

Galgate 29E7

11–3; 6–11

New
59 Main Road (A6) ✆ 751613
Mitchells Mild, Bitter Ⓗ
Open-plan lounge with
traditional Yorkshire range
♨🏠🕒 (not Mon)

Garstang 29E8

11–3; 6–11

Farmers Arms
16 Church Street (off B6430)
✆ 2195
**Jennings Bitter; Tetley Mild,
Bitter** Ⓗ
Oak-beamed lounge leads to
basic games room. Plain but
"spick" childrens room
♨🚌♿🕒🍽️

Glasson Dock 28E7

10.45–3; 5.45–11

Victoria
Victoria Terrace (B5290)
✆ Galgate 751423
Mitchells Bitter Ⓗ
Three-roomed comfortable
local with mixed clientele and
unique carpet! ♨🚌♿🕒🍽️

Great Singleton 28D8

11–3; 6–11

Miller Arms
Great Singleton Village
(B5260)
✆ Poulton le Fylde 882668
Whitbread Castle Eden Ⓗ
Rural retreat with Beefeater
restaurant ♨Q🚌♿🕒🍽️♿

Halton 29E7

10.45–3; 5.45–11

White Lion
Church Brow ✆ 811210
Mitchells Mild, Bitter Ⓗ
17th-century village local
with snug bar
♨Q🚌♿🕒 (not Mon)
🍽️ (not Mon)

Helmshore 22E1

11.30–3; 5.30–11

Robin Hood
280 Holcombe Road (B6235)
**Wilsons Original Mild,
Bitter** Ⓗ
Excellent small pub near
Textile Museum. Painted tiles
inlaid into woodwork of tap
room ♿🕒🍽️

Hest Bank 28E7

10.45–3; 5.45–11

Hest Bank
Hest Bank Lane (off A5105)
✆ 822226
Boddingtons Mild, Bitter Ⓗ
Old coaching inn turned busy
local. Canalside garden
♨🚌♿🍽️

Heysham 28E7

10.45–3; 5.45–11

Royal
Main Street, Lower Heysham
✆ 51475
Mitchells Mild, Bitter Ⓗ
Dating from 1502, in old
village centre. Gets crowded
with tourists. Organ nights
Thu ♨♿🍽️

Higher Walton 29F9

10.30–3; 6–11

Mill Tavern
Cann Bridge Street (Blackburn
Old Road A675)
✆ Preston 38462
Burtonwood Bitter Ⓗ
Popular pub tastefully
restored ♨♿🍽️

Hoghton 22D1

11–3; 5.30–11
Royal Oak
Riley Green (A6061)
Thwaites Best Mild, Bitter H
Old pub near Hoghton Tower
🏠🐾🕭♿🍷

Holme Chapel 29H9

11–3; 5.30–11
Queens
412 Burnley Road (A646)
**Burtonwood Dark Mild,
Bitter** H
Unaltered cosy village local,
unusual passageway entry
🏠Q🕭🍷

Huncoat 29G9

10.30–3; 6–11
White Lion
1 Highergate (off A679 nr
M65)
**Matthew Brown Lion Mild,
Bitter** E; **Theakston Old
Peculier** H
Friendly local opposite village
stocks 🐾🕭≷

Hutton 29E9

10.30–3; 6–11
Anchor
Liverpool Road (off A59)
✆ Longton 614058
**Matthew Brown Lion Mild,
Lion Bitter, John Peel;
Theakston Old Peculier** H
Very large roadside pub with
good food. Handy for police
HQ!🏠🔢 (lunchtimes) 🐾🕭🍷🍴

Kirkham 28E9

11–3; 6–11
Queens Arms
Poulton Street
**Matthew Brown Lion Mild;
Theakston Bitter, XB, Old
Peculier** H
Friendly small town pub
🏠🐾🕭♿🍴

Railway
Station Road
Tetley Mild, Bitter H
Large pub near station 🍷≷

Lancaster 29E7

10.45–3; 5.45–11
Golden Lion
Moor Lane ✆ 65676
Evening opens 7
**Matthew Brown Lion Mild;
Theakston Best Bitter, XB** H
Splendid variety of pub
games—two games rooms.
Diverse clientele. Jazz
Mondays. Parking difficult 🍷

Moorlands
Quarry Road, Moorlands
Opens 12 & 7, closed Mon
lunch & 10.30 Mon eve
Mitchells Mild, Bitter H
Large turn-of-the-century
local. Variety of rooms;
stained glass. Piano Sat & Sun
🍷

Royal Oak
152/4 Mainway, Skerton
✆ 65641
Evening opens 6.30
**Chesters Bitter; Hartley XB;
Whitbread Trophy, Castle
Eden** H
Two dapper lounges, spartan
vault. Working-class
suburban local 🔢🍷

Wagon & Horses
27 St. George's Quay
Hartley Mild, Bitter, XB H;
Robinson Old Tom G
Cosmopolitan riverside pub
near Maritime Museum 🏠≷

Laneshaw Bridge 29H8

11–3; 5.30–11
Alma
Hill Lane (off A6068)
✆ Colne 863447
Tetley Mild, Bitter H
Smart friendly country pub in
pleasant surroundings 🐾♿🍷🍴

Langho 29F9

11–3; 6–11
Lord Nelson
York Village
**Matthew Brown Lion Mild,
Lion Bitter; Theakston Old
Peculier** H
Perched on hillside
overlooking River Calder 🏠♿

Leyland 22C1

11–3; 6–11
Crofters Arms
373 Leyland Lane (B5253)
✆ 22420
Opens 11 & 6.30 Sats
**Matthew Brown Lion Mild,
Lion Bitter; Theakston Old
Peculier** H
Popular pub on edge of town
🐾♿🍷

Dunkirk Hall
Dunkirk Lane ✆ 422102
John Smith's Bitter H
Tastefully converted 17th
century manor house.
Conveniently situated on new
by-pass 🔢 (lunchtimes) 🐾♿🍴

Limbrick 22C1

10.30 (11.30 Sat)–3; 7–11
Black Horse
Long Lane OS602165
✆ Chorley 64030
**Matthew Brown Lion Mild,
Lion Bitter** E, **John Peel** H
Popular stone pub in a
pleasant hamlet 1½ miles SE of
Chorley. Prize-winning,
locally-made black puddings!
🏠🐾♿🍷🍴

Longridge 29F8

11–3; 6–11
Old Oak
111 Preston Road ✆ 3648

**Matthew Brown Lion Mild;
Theakston Best Bitter, XB** H
Small welcoming pub ♿

Towneley Arms
41 Berry Lane (off B5269)
✆ 2219
Tetley Mild, Bitter E
Warm, inviting wood-
panelled pub by old railway
terminus 🍷

Longton 22C1

10.30–3 (closed Mon–Fri lunch); 7–11
Dolphin
Marsh Lane OS459254
✆ 612032
Thwaites Best Mild, Bitter H
Recently extended farmhouse
pub on edge of Longton
Marsh. Haunt of wildfowlers
and clay pigeon shooters
🏠Q🔢🐾🍷

Lostock Hall 29E9

10.30–3; 6–11
Pleasant Retreat
Watkin Lane (A582)
✆ Preston 35616
Boddingtons Bitter H
Large, comfortable pub on
main road ♿🍷≷

Victoria
Watkin Lane (A582)
✆ Preston 35338
John Smith's Bitter H
Popular mainroad pub with
large vault. Friendly welcome
assured
🔢 (lunchtimes) 🐾♿🍷≷

Lytham 28D9

11–3; 6–11
Hole in One
Forest Drive ✆ 739968
Thwaites Bitter H
Tasteful pub in new
residential area. Pool table,
darts 🐾♿🍷

Queens
Central Beach ✆ 737316
**Matthew Brown Lion Bitter,
John Peel; Theakston Old
Peculier** H
Popular, spacious sea front
pub 🐾🔢🍷≷

Mereclough 29H9

11–3; 5.30–11
Kettledrum
302 Red Lees Road
OS873306 ✆ Burnley 24591
**Matthew Brown Lion Mild,
Lion Bitter; Theakston XB, Old
Peculier; Wilsons Original
Bitter** H **Occasional guest
beers**
Attractive roadside pub with
restaurant on outskirts of
Burnley 🏠🐾♿🍷

Morecambe 28E7

10.45–3; 5.45–11
Bradford Arms
38–40 Queen Street
✆ 417952

Mitchells Bitter 🅔
Late 19th century pub on site of fishermen's cottages. Separate snug and games room. Parking difficult
🏠 ♿ ➤ ≷

George
302 Lancaster Road, Torrisholme 𝄢 418477
Thwaites Best Mild, Bitter 🅔
Large 1930's local with panelled lounge ♫ ♿ 🍴

Newchurch in Rossendale 22E1

11.30–3; 5.30–11

Blue Bell
1 Old Street
Wilsons Original Mild, Bitter 🅗
Comfortable, pleasant village local. Occasional live entertainment at weekends
🏠 ♫ ♿

Oakenclough 29E8

11–3; 6–11

Moorcock
OS460560 𝄢 Garstang 2130
Tetley Mild, Bitter; Thwaites Bitter 🅗
Motorists' pub on slopes of the fells 🏠 ♿ ♫ ♿ ➤

Ormskirk 22B2

11–3 (4 Thu); 5.30–10.30 (11 F, S)

Buck i' th' Vine
Burscough Street 𝄢 72647
Peter Walker Mild, Bitter, Best Bitter 🅗
Historic pub on pedestrian street. Entertainment in attractive courtyard in summer 🏠 ♿ ♫ ♿ (Tue–Sat) 🍴 ≷

Greyhound
Aughton Street (B5197) 𝄢 67701
Peter Walker Mild, Bitter 🅗
Traditional lively town centre local retaining several small rooms of character 🏠 ♫ 🍴 ≷

Horse Shoe
Southport Road (A570) 𝄢 72956
Tetley Mild; Peter Walker Best Bitter 🅗
Friendly alehouse in terrace opposite parish church and Civic Hall 🏠 🍴 ≷

Queen
81 Aughton Street (B5197) 𝄢 72114
Vaux Sunderland Draught, Samson 🅗
Handsome town pub, pleasant hall bar and several rooms
🏠 🍴 🍴 ≷

Snig's Foot
Church Street (off A570 near parish church)
Burtonwood Dark Mild, Almonds Bitter 🅔
Unassuming façade hides pub

of character. Remains of Knowles Brewery visible from gents! Fortnightly jazz duets
🍴 ≷

Osbaldeston 29F9

11–3; 6–11

Bay Horse
Longsight Road (A59)
Thwaites Mild, Bitter 🅗
Welcoming rural inn. Good service with waiter at weekends. Snooker table
Q ♫ ♿ 🍴

Oswaldtwistle 29G9

11–3; 6–11

Coach & Horses
Haslingden Old Road, Rams Clough (A677) OS754254
𝄢 Rossendale 213825
Tetley Mild, Bitter 🅗
Well-appointed country inn. Fine views 🏠 ♫ ♿ ➤ (not Sun)

Overton 28E7

10.45–3; 5.45–11

Ship
9 Main Street 𝄢 231
Thwaites Best Mild, Bitter 🅗
Old-fashioned village local renowned for sandwiches and Uncle Joe's mintballs. Bowling green 🏠 ♫ ♿

Padiham 29G9

11–3; 5.30 (6.30 Sat)–11

Kings Arms
2 Mill Street (off Burnley Road A671)
Boddingtons Bitter; Taylor Best Bitter; Thwaites Mild, Bitter 🅗
Busy, open-plan town centre pub. Can get crowded and noisy; regular disco nights ♿

Parbold 24C1

11–3; 5.30–10.30 (11 F, S)

Stocks Tavern
Alder Lane (A5209) 𝄢 2902
Tetley Mild, Bitter 🅗
Excellent village local
🏠 Q ♿ ➤ 🍴 ≷

Penwortham 29E9

11–3; 6–11

Sumpter Horse
235 Leyland Road (A582)
𝄢 744456
Matthew Brown Lion Mild, Lion Bitter, John Peel 🅗
Large, popular suburban pub
🎲 (lunchtimes) ♫ ♿ 🍴

Pilling 28E8

10.30–3; 6–11

Golden Ball
School Lane (off A588) 𝄢 212
Thwaites Best Mild, Bitter 🅗
Village pub with bowling greens and pool table
🎲 ♫ ♿ ➤ 🍴 🅰

Pleasington 29F9

10.30–3; 6–11

Butlers Arms
Off A674 𝄢 Blackburn 21561
Matthew Brown Lion Mild, Lion Bitter, John Peel; Theakston Old Peculier 🍺
Plush village inn with bowling green and garden. Westerly view to Hoghton Tower
🏠 ♫ ♿ ➤ 🍴 ≷

Try also: Railway (Wilsons)

Poulton-le-Fylde 28D8

11–3; 6–11

Queens
Higher Green 𝄢 88347
Opens 10.30
Bass Mild, Special Bitter, Draught Bass 🅗
Large Victorian pub opposite park ♿ 🍴 ≷

Thatched House
Ball Street (off A586)
Boddingtons Bitter 🅗
Busy town centre pub
🏠 Q ♿ 🍴 ≷

Preesall 28D8

10.30–3; 6–11

Saracens Head
Park Lane (off A588)
𝄢 Blackpool 810346
Thwaites Best Mild, Bitter 🅗
Village local, friendly atmosphere 🏠 ♫ ♿ ➤ 🍴 🅰

Preston 29E9

10.30–3; 6–11

Black Horse
166 Friargate 𝄢 52093
Evening opens 6.30 (7 Sat)
Robinson Best Bitter 🅗, **Old Tom** 🅖
Unspoilt Victorian town centre pub with ornate mahogany and tiled bar
🎲 (lunchtimes) ♿ 🍴 ≷

Fox & Grapes
Fox Street 𝄢 52448
Matthew Brown Lion Mild, Lion Bitter, John Peel 🅗
Small, popular town centre pub ♿ ≷

George
39 Church Street 𝄢 51529
Opens 11.30 & 7 (6.30 Sat)
Thwaites Mild, Best Mild, Bitter 🅔
Friendly town centre pub ♿ 🍴

Greyhound
London Road (A6)
Opens 11 (11.30 Sat) & 7
Boddingtons Bitter 🅗
Basic local with tiled exterior
🍴

Joplins
2 Stanley Street (A6)
Opens 12 & 7
Chesters Bitter; Hartleys XB; Whitbread Trophy 🅗

Town centre pub featuring a video juke box. Live entertainment

Lamb
Church Street ✆ 54478
Greenall Whitley Local Mild, Local Bitter, Original Bitter ℍ
Live music most nights. Large upstairs room
🄴 (lunchtimes) ᵍ

Lamb & Packet
91a Friargate ✆51857
Thwaites Mild, Bitter ℍ
Tiny pub popular with students ᵍ☮

Maudland
1 Pedder Street ✆ 726941
Matthew Brown Lion Mild, Lion Bitter ℍ
Small local next to third highest spire in England ☮

Mitre
90 Moor Lane ✆ 51918
Opens 11.30
Vaux Sunderland Draught, Samson ℍ
Modern, friendly pub ᵍ☮

New Welcome
Cambridge Street ✆ 53933
Opens 12 & 6.30 (7 Sat)
Thwaites Best Mild, Bitter ℍ
Small local amid new housing development ♨ᵍ

Olde Blue Bell
116 Church Street ✆ 51280
Opens 11; Sat eve opens 7
Samuel Smith OBB ℍ
Oldest pub in Preston, usually crowded ♨☮ᵍ🢛

Royal Garrison
Watling Street Road/Deepdale Road (B6242/B6241)
✆ 794470
Opens 11; Sat eve opens 6.30
**Matthew Brown Lion Mild, Lion Bitter, John Peel;
Theakston Best Bitter** ℍ
Large comfortable pub near Fulwood Barracks ᵍ☮

Ship
3 Fylde Road (A583) ✆ 51799
Opens 11; Sat eve opens 6.30
**Matthew Brown Lion Mild, Lion Bitter, John Peel;
Theakston Old Peculier** ℍ
Tastefully renovated pub next to Polytechnic ᵍ☮≷

Scarisbrick 22B1
11–3; 5.30–10.30 (11 F, S)

Heatons Bridge
2 Heatons Bridge Road (B5242)
**Peter Walker Best Bitter;
Tetley Mild** ℍ
Basic but welcoming canalside gem Q☞☮

Skelmersdale 22C2
11–3; 5.30–10.30 (11 F, S)

Victoria
Sandy Lane

Peter Walker Mild, Bitter, Best Bitter ℍ
Friendly local, good for dominoes ☮

Slaidburn 29G8
11–3; 5.30–11

Hark to Bounty
**Moorhouse's Premier Bitter, Pendle Witches Brew;
Thwaites Best Mild, Bitter** ℍ
Village free house of great character; Court sessions held here in the past. Village dances and flea market in upstairs room ☞🄴ᵍ🢛

Slyne 29E7
12–3; 5.45–11

Slyne Lodge
Main Road (A6)
✆ Hest Bank 823389
**Hartley XB; Tetley Bitter;
Theakston Best Bitter** ℍ
Quiet, relaxing atmosphere, hardly changed from when it was a private club ♨🄴☞🄴ᵍ🢛

Snatchems 28E7
11.30; 7–11

Golden Ball
On riverside bank between Lancaster and Overton
OS448615
Mitchells Mild, Bitter ℍ;
Bulmer Cider 🄶
Three homely rooms. Cut off by highest tides. Where the press gang used to come and snatch 'em for the Navy
♨🄴ᵍ🢛

Thornton 28D8
11–3; 6–11

Burn Naze
Gamble Road
Tetleys Mild, Bitter ℍ
Local near ICI Hillhouse. Live music, good cheap lunchtime food. Large, basic, yet comfortable ♨ᵍ🢛☮

Ulnes Walton 22C1
10.30–3; 5.30–11

Rose & Crown
Southport Road (A581)
OS513188
Burtonwood Mild, Bitter ℍ
Popular old country pub
♨🄴 (lunchtimes) ☞ᵍ🢛☮

Upholland 24D2
11–3 (often closed); 5.30–10.30 (11 F, S)

Old Dog
Alma Hill
Greenall Whitley Mild, Bitter 🄴
Picturesque village local, worth discovering ☮

Wharles 28E9
12–3 (closed winter Mon–Fri); 7–11

Eagle & Child
Church Road

**Boddingtons Bitter;
Moorhouses Pendle Witch** ℍ
Occasional guest beers
Remote country free house with thatched roof and beamed ceilings ♨☮

Wheelton 22D1
10.30–3; 5.30–11

Dressers
Briers Brow (off A674)
**Boddingtons Bitter; Matthew Brown Lion Mild; Hartley XB;
Theakston Best Bitter, Old Peculier** ℍ
Popular low-beamed pub in a row of cottages, new Chinese restaurant upstairs
♨🄴 (lunchtimes) ☞ᵍ🢛☮

White Coppice 22D1
11.30–3; 7–11

Railway
1 Coppice Lane OS611198
Matthew Brown Lion Mild, Lion Bitter ℍ
Isolated but comfortable and popular country pub ♨ᵍ

Whittle-le-Woods 22C1
10.30–3; 6–11

Royal Oak
216 Chorley Old Road
Opens 12; Sat eve opens 7
Matthew Brown Lion Mild, Lion Bitter ℍ
Small friendly pub in terrace at north end of village ♨☮

Sea View
2 Preston Road (A6)
Matthew Brown Lion Mild, Lion Bitter; Theakston Old Peculier ℍ
Smart main road pub on Chorley boundary. You really can see the sea on a clear day!
♨🄴 (lunchtimes) ☞ᵍ🢛

Worsthorne 29H9
11–3; 5.30 (7 Sat)–11

Crooked Billet
Smith Street (off Village Square)
Tetley Mild, Bitter ℍ
Pleasant village local with fine, unspoilt wood-panelled lounge ♨Q☞ᵍ☮

WARMEST WELCOME

♦ A REAL FIRE PUB ♦

The ♨ symbol denotes a pub with a real solid fuel fire

Anstey 16B2

11–2.30; 6.30–11

Old Hare & Hounds
34 Bradgate Road (B5327)
✆ Leicester 362496
**Marston Mercian Mild,
Burton Bitter, Pedigree** Ⓗ
Small friendly local opposite
the village church, choice of
many pub games. A pub on
this site since since 1720
🍴Q🐾♿

Ashby-de-la-Zouch 16A1

10.30–2.30; 6.30–11

White Hart
Market Street (A453 & A50)
✆ 414531
Marston Pedigree Ⓗ
Town centre pub with bar-
billiards 🍴♿ (not Sun)

Ashby Folville 16C2

10.30–2.30; 6–11

Carington Arms
Folville Street (B674)
✆ Melton Mowbray 840228
**Adnams Bitter; Everard Tiger,
Old Original; Bulmer Cider** Ⓗ
Occasional guest beers
Attractive country pub with
long alley skittles and
petanque track 🍴Q🐾♿🍷🍴♿

Bardon 16B2

11–2.30; 6–11

Birch Tree
A50 ✆ Coalville 32134
**Everard Mild, Tiger, Old
Original** Ⓗ
Friendly roadside pub with
good garden 🐾♿ (not Sun)🍴♿

Barlestone 16B2

11–2; 5.30–11

Red Lion
Newbold Road (off A447)
**Marston Mercian Mild,
Pedigree** Ⓗ
Old village pub with public
bar, large family room, cosy
comfortable lounge 🍴🐾♿🍴🍷

Barrow upon Soar 16B1

11–2.30; 6–11

Navigation
Mill Lane (off B5328)
✆ Quorn 412844
**Marston Pedigree; Shipstone
Mild, Bitter; John Smith's
Bitter** Ⓗ
Traditional Canalside hostelry
with skittle alley 🍴🐾🍷♿ 🏕

Belton 16B1

12–2.30; 6–11

George
✆ Coalville 222426
**Shipstone Mild, Bitter; Wem
Best Bitter** Ⓗ
Country inn with reasonably-
priced accommodation and
home cooking 🍴🐾🖼♿🍴♿

Blackfordby 16A1

10.30–2.30; 5.30–11

Blue Bell
Main Street (off A50)
✆ Burton 216737
Marston Pedigree Ⓗ
Lively village pub with its own
garden centre 🍴🐾♿🍷🍴

Broughton Astley 16B3

11–2.30; 7–11

George & Dragon
Green Lane
✆ Sutton Elms 282256
**Marston Mercian Mild,
Burton Bitter, Pedigree** Ⓗ
Friendly village local; table
and long alley skittles 🖼🐾🍴

Burbage 16A3

11.30–2.30; 6–11

Sycamores
Windsor Street
✆ Hinckley 39268
**Marston Mercian Mild,
Burton Bitter, Pedigree** Ⓗ
Welcoming village local
🍴Q🐾🍴

Castle Donington 16B1

10.30–2.30; 5.30–11

Cross Keys
Bond Gate (B6540)
✆ Derby 812214
**Draught Bass; Burton Bridge
Bitter; Vaux Samson; Wards
Sheffield Best Bitter** Ⓗ **Regular
guest beers**
Modernised village local,
retaining much traditional
flavour 🍴♿ (not Sun)

Coalville 16B2

10.30–2.30; 5.30–11

Snibston New Inn
Belvoir Road (Jct A50/B585)
✆ 33976
**Marston Mercian Mild, Border
Bitter, Burton Bitter,
Pedigree** Ⓗ **Occasional guest
beers**
Down-to-earth town local.
Bustling bar and comfortable
lounge with prints of old
Coalville 🍴🐾♿🍴🍷

Try also: **Cocked Hat** (John
Smith's); **Jolly Colliers**
(Marston)

Cottesmore 16E2

11–2.30; 6–11

Sun Inn
25 Main Street
✆ Oakham 812321
**Adnams Bitter; Everard Tiger,
Old Original** Ⓗ
17th century thatched village
local. Large function room
with Village Theatre Club
🍴🖼🐾♿🍷

Cropston 16B2

10.30–2.30; 5.30–11

Bradgate Arms
Station Road
✆ Leicester 362120
**Ind Coope Burton Ale; M&B
Mild; Ruddle Bitter, County;
Samuel Smith OBB** Ⓗ
400 year old building. Run by
same family for 100 years.
Long alley skittles
🍴Q🖼🐾♿🍴🏕

Desford 16B2

11–2.30; 5.30 (6 Sat)–11

Olde Lancaster Inn
Station Road ✆ 2589
**Adnams Bitter; Everard Bitter,
Tiger, Old Original; Bulmer
Cider** Ⓗ
Pleasant 4-room, oak-beamed
country inn 🍴Q🐾♿🍷

Earl Shilton 16B3

10.30–2.30; 5.30–11

Red Lion
High Street (A47) ✆ 43356
Draught Bass; M&B Mild Ⓗ
Busy 3-room local, all served
from central bar 🐾🍴

Enderby 16B3

10.30–2.30; 5.30–11

Plough Inn
Mill Hill (B582)
✆ Leicester 863307
**Hardys & Hansons Best Mild;
Ind Coope Burton Ale;
Marston Pedigree; Samuel
Smith OBB; Younger IPA** Ⓗ
Friendly pub with good
restaurant. Long alley skittles
🍴🖼🐾♿🍷

Gaddesby 16C2

10.30–2.30; 6–11

Cheney Arms
Rearsby Lane
✆ Melton Mowbray 840260
**Adnams Bitter; Everard Old
Original** Ⓗ
Former Dower House. Decor
reflects landlord's interest in
horse racing 🍴Q🐾🖼🍴♿

Groby 16B2

11.30 (11 F, S)–2; 6–11

**Earl of Stamford
Arms**
Leicester Road (off A50)
✆ Leicester 875616
**Cameron Bitter; Everard Mild,
Bitter, Tiger, Old Original** Ⓗ
At the heart of the village.
Bar, lounge and games room;
pool 🐾♿ (Mon–Fri)🍴

Harby 16C1

10.30–2.30; 6–11

Nags Head

Main Street ☎ 60209
Home Bitter Ⓔ
Traditional Vale of Belvoir pub
in rustic setting
🅰 Q 🅱 ✿ Ⓖ ➔ (Mon–Fri) 🛇

Hathern 16B1

12–2.30; 7–11

Dewdrop Inn
Loughborough Road (A6)
☎ Loughborough 842438
**Hardys & Hansons Best Mild,
Best Bitter** Ⓗ
Traditional village local; keen
darts following 🅰 Q 🛇

Hinckley 16A3

11–2.30; 6.30–11

Black Horse
Upper Bond Street
☎ 637613
**Marston Mercian Mild,
Burton Bitter, Pedigree** Ⓗ
Multi-room town pub with
fine timbered exterior
🅰 Q 🅱 Ⓖ 🛇

Castle Tavern
Castle Street ☎ 634258
**Draught Bass; M&B Mild,
Springfield** Ⓗ
Popular 2-roomed pub near
site of Hinckley Castle ✿ 🛇

Weavers Arms
Derby Road ☎ 632927
Evenings opens 5.30
**Marston Mercian Mild,
Burton Bitter, Pedigree** Ⓔ;
Merrie Monk, Owd Rodger Ⓗ
3-room town pub 🅰 ✿ 🛇

Hose 26C9

11–2.30; 7–11

Black Horse
Bolton Lane ☎ Harby 60336
Home Mild, Bitter Ⓗ
Unspoilt 3-room village local
with skittle alley 🅰 Q ✿ 🛇

Try also: Rose & Crown (Free)

Huncote 16B3

10.30–2.30; 5.30–11

Red Lion
Main Street
☎ Leicester 862233
**Everard Mild, Bitter, Tiger,
Old Original** Ⓗ
Basic front bar, plush lounge
and smoke room. Long alley
skittles 🅰 Q ✿ Ⓖ (Mon–Fri) 🛇 🅰

Hungarton 16C2

10.30–2.30; 5.30–11

Black Boy
Main Street ☎ 601
M&B Mild, Brew XI Ⓗ
Excellent village pub doubling
as village sweet shop 🅰 ✿ Ⓖ ➔ 🛇

Illston-on-
the-Hill 16C3

11–2; 7–11

Fox & Goose

Main Street (off B6047)
☎ Billesdon 340
Everard Tiger, Old Original Ⓗ
Small unspoilt pub. A treasure
trove of unusual knick-knacks
🅰 Q 🛇 🅰

Kegworth 16B1

10.30–2.30; 5.30–11

New Inn
58 Derby Road (A6)
☎ 2231
Draught Bass; M&B Mild Ⓗ
Friendly, compact local on
main road 🅰 ✿ Ⓖ (not Sun) 🛇

Kilby Bridge 16C3

11.30–2.30; 5.30–11

Navigation
A50 ☎ Leicester 882280
Ind Coope Bitter, Burton Ale Ⓗ
Old and unspoilt pub with low
beams. Situated next to Grand
Union Canal 🅰 Q 🅱 ✿ Ⓖ ➔ 🛇

Leicester 16C2

10.30–2.30; 5.30–11

Blackbird
Blackbird Road (A5125)
☎ 22678
Mon–Wed Evenings 6–10.30
**Everard Mild, Bitter, Tiger,
Old Original** Ⓗ
Large 1930's suburban pub
with quiet lounge
Q 🅱 ✿ Ⓖ (not Sun) 🛇 ♿

Black Horse
Narrow Lane, Aylestone
☎ 832811
11–2 (2.30 F, S) 6–11
**Everard Mild, Bitter, Tiger,
Old Original, Bulmer Cider** Ⓗ
Occasional guest beers
Popular pub close to Grand
Union Canal and Great
Central Way footpath
🅰 Q ✿ Ⓖ 🛇

Bricklayers Arms
Welford Road (A50)
☎ 540687
**Shipstone Mild, Bitter; Bulmer
Cider** Ⓗ
Victorian pub near Prison,
popular with students Q ✿ Ⓖ 🛇

Empire Hotel
Fosse Road North (A5125)
☎ 21602
Ansells Mild, Bitter Ⓗ
19th century mansion, small
basic bar and large
comfortable lounge. Live
entertainment most nights
🅱 🅰 Ⓖ ➔ 🛇

Globe
Silver Street ☎ 28918
**Cameron Bitter; Everard Mild,
Bitter, Tiger, Old Original;
Bulmer Cider** Ⓗ Occasional
guest beers
One of city's oldest pubs. Close
to 3 museums ✿ Ⓖ 🛇

Rainbow & Dove
Charles Street

**Holden Black Country Mild;
Hoskins Bitter, Penns Ale, Old
Nigel** Ⓗ **Regular guest beers**
Large city centre pub. Popular
and lively Q Ⓖ ♿

Salmon
Butt Close Lane ☎ 532301
Banks Mild, Bitter Ⓔ
Unspoiled local, comfortable
smoke room. Close to bus
station Q Ⓖ 🛇

Ship Inn
Soar Lane (off A50) ☎ 27765
Shipstone Mild, Bitter Ⓗ
Small, friendly locals' pub;
strong darts following ✿ Ⓖ 🛇

Tom Hoskins
131 Beaumanor Road (off
A5131) ☎ 681160
Opens 11.30 Mon–Fri; Sat
evenings opens 6
**Hoskins Bitter, Penns Ale, Old
Nigel** Ⓗ **Regular guest beers**
Friendly, lively pub. The
Brewery Tap a must. New
lounge offers a respite from
lively bar Q ✿ Ⓖ (Mon–Fri) 🛇

Tudor
100 Tudor Road ☎ 20087
Opens 11 & 6
**Cameron Bitter; Everard Mild,
Bitter, Tiger, Old Original;
Henry Wadworth IPA** Ⓗ
Victorian local with lounge
bar and games room 🅱 🛇 ♿

Littlethorpe 16B3

10.30–2.30; 6–11

Plough
Station Road
☎ Leicester 862383
**Everard Mild, Bitter, Tiger,
Old Original; Bulmer Cider** Ⓗ
Occasional guest beers
Cosy thatched local. Long
alley skittles ✿ Ⓖ ➔ 🛇 ♿

Loughborough 16B1

10.30–2.30; 5.30–11

Albion
Canal Bank (off Bridge St)
☎ 213952
Opens 11 & 6
**Shipstone Mild, Bitter; Wem
Best Bitter** Ⓗ **Regular guest
beers**
Convivial inn, reached by
towpath. Good locals' bar &
cosy lounge ✿ Ⓖ 🛇

Boat
Meadow Lane
☎ 214578
**Marston Mercian Mild, Merrie
Monk, Pedigree** Ⓗ
Friendly 3-room pub with
canalside drinking area
✿ Ⓖ 🛇 ♿

Gate
Meadow Lane
☎ 263779
Opens 11 & 6
**Marston Mercian Mild,
Pedigree** Ⓗ

Small popular pub near the canal ♿ 🅿 ⌂ (not Sun) ⏐ ≷

Peacock
Factory Street (off A6 Leicester Road) ☎214215
Opens 11 & 7
M&B Mild, Springfield Bitter ⊞
Popular, cosy traditional 3-room local near steam railway ♿ 🅿 ⏐

Three Nuns
Churchgate ☎ 232061
Evenings opens 7
Adnams Bitter; Everard Mild, Bitter, Tiger, Old Original ⊞
Large, comfortable town pub, popular with young people 🅿 ⌂ ≷

Windmill
Sparrow Hill (near parish church) ☎ 216314
Opens 11 & 7
Ansells Mild; Ind Coope Bitter, Burton Ale ⊞
Oldest pub in town—friendly welcome for strangers ♿ 🖪 🅿 ⌂ ⏐ ⏐

Try also: Blackbird (Bass); Jack o' Lantern (Ind Coope/ Ansells); Old Pack Horse (Hardys & Hanson)

Lount 16A1
11–2.30; 6–11

Ferrers Arms
A453 ☎ Ashby/Zouch 412982
Marston Pedigree ⊞
Busy pub on main Ashby/ Nottingham Road ♿ 🅿

Lyddington 16D3
12–2.30; 6–11

Old White Hart
Main Street (near A6003)
☎ Uppingham 823810
Greene King XX, IPA, Abbot ⊞
18th century village pub with comfortable, wood-panelled lounge. Excellent Stilton cobs ♿ Q 🖪 🅿 ⌂ ⏐ ⏐

Try also: Marquis of Exeter Hotel

Medbourne 16D3
12–2.30; 6–11

Neville Arms
Waterfall Way ☎ 288
Adnams Bitter; Hook Norton Best Bitter; Marston Pedigree; Ruddle County ⊞
400 year-old stone pub by the village stream. Grade II listed building ♿ 🅿 ⌂ ⏐

Melton Mowbray 16D1
11–2.30; 6–11

Cherry Tree
Edendale Road (off A607 Leicester Road) ☎ 60856

Draught Bass ⊞; M&B Mild ⊞ & ⒺⒺ
Popular, comfortable modern estate pub ⌂ (not Sun) ⏐

Try also: Black Swan (Home); Fox (Whitbread)

Mountsorrel 16B2
11–2.30; 7 (6 Summer)–11

Dog & Gun
Leicester Road (A6)
☎ Leicester 303316
Draught Bass; M&B Mild ⊞
Homely 2-roomer on main road ♿ 🅿 (not Sun) ⏐

Try also: Prince of Wales (Free)

Muston 26C8
10.30–2.30; 6–11

Gap
Muston Gap (A52)
Marston Pedigree ⊞
Very friendly 300 year-old pub, full of character ♿ Q 🅿 ⛺

Osgathorpe 23J7
12–2.30; 6.30–11

Royal Oak
Main Street (off B5324)
☎ Coalville 222443
Draught Bass; M&B Mild; Marston Pedigree ⊞
Characterful country pub, off the beaten track ♿ 🅿 ⏐ ♿

Peggs Green 16A1
11–2.30; 5.30–11

New Inn
B587 ☎ Coalville 222293
Draught Bass; M&B Mild ⊞
Excellent country pub with large garden catering for families ♿ 🅿 ⏐ ♿

Quorn 26B9
11.30–2.30; 5.30–11

Blacksmith's Arms
Meeting Street (off A6)
☎ 412751
Marston Pedigree ⊞, Owd Rodger Ⓖ
Bustling village local with friendly atmosphere ♿ 🖪 🅿 ⏐

Try also: Royal Oak (Bass)

Ravenstone 16A2
10.30–2.30; 5.30–11

Kings Arms
Church Lane (off A447)
☎ Coalville 34759
Marston Mercian Mild; Pedigree ⊞
Bustling village local with welcoming atmosphere 🅿 ⏐ ♿

Ryhall 17E2
10.30–2.30; 6–11

Green Dragon
The Square (off A6121)
☎ Stamford 53081

Samuel Smith OBB ⊞
Popular old village local; collection of heads in bar. No food Sunday ♿ 🅿 ⌂ ⏐

Shepshed 16B1
11–2.30; 7–11

Richmond Arms
Forest Street (off B5330)
☎ 503309
Draught Bass; M&B Mild ⊞
Hospitable, traditional hostelry. Renowned among mild drinkers 🅿 ⏐

Try also: Jolly Farmers (Bass); Railway (Marston)

Sileby 16C2
10.30–2.30; 5.30–11

Free Trade Inn
Cossington Road (B5328)
☎ 2411
Adnams Bitter; Cameron Best Bitter; Everard Mild, Tiger, Old Original ⊞ Regular guest beers
Very old thatched pub with low oak beams ⌂ (not Sun)

Skeffington 16C2
10.30–2.30; 6–11

Fox & Hounds
Uppingham Road (A47)
☎ Billesdon 250
Davenports Mild, Bitter ⊞
Busy pub with deserved reputation for food. No meals Sunday ♿ 🅿 ⌂ ⏐ ⏐

South Croxton 16C2
11–2.30; 6–11

Golden Fleece
Main Street
☎ Melton Mowbray 840275
Ruddle Bitter, County; Bulmer Cider ⊞ Occasional guest beers
Built in 1740, once a blacksmiths and Methodist School ♿ Q 🅿 ⌂ ⏐ ⏐

South Wigston 16C3
11–2.30; 6–11

Grand Hotel
Canal Street
☎ Leicester 782561
Shipstone Mild, Bitter ⊞
Down to earth, friendly Victorian local
🅿 ⌂ (Mon–Fri) ⏐

Swannington 16A2
11–2.30; 7–11

Fountain
Main Street (A447)
☎ Coalville 32257
Marston Pedigree ⊞
Roadside pub with comfortable lounge and busy bar 🅿 ⏐ ♿

Swithland 16B2

11–2.30; 6–11

Griffin Inn
Main Street
✆ Woodhouse Eaves 890535
**Adnams Bitter; Everard
Mild, Bitter, Tiger, Old
Original; Henry Wadworth
IPA** Ⓗ
Pleasant inn in Charnwood
Forest, wood-panelled lounge.
Long alley skittles
🕮 ✍ Ⓖ (not Sun) Ⓐ

Thrussington 16C2

10–2.30; 6–11

Blue Lion
Rearsby Road
✆ Rearsby 256
**Ind Coope Bitter, Burton
Ale** Ⓗ
Friendly village pub, popular
with diners
✍ Ⓖ ☞ (not Tue) ◗ Ⓐ

Thurcaston 16B2

11–2; 6–11

King William IV
Mill Road (near B5328)
✆ Leicester 302287
Ind Coope Bitter Ⓗ
Modern exterior conceals cosy
lounge and bustling bar.
Friendly pub 🕮 ✍ Ⓖ (not Sun) ◗

Thurmaston 16C2

10.30–2.30; 5.30–11

Unicorn & Star
796 Melton Road (off B667)
✆ Leicester 692849
Shipstone Mild, Bitter Ⓗ
Popular corner pub, basic bar
and small comfortable lounge
🕮 ✍ ◗

Tinwell 17E2

11–2.30; 7–11

Crown
A6121
✆ Stamford 62492
Samuel Smith OBB Ⓗ
Popular village pub
🕮 ✍ Ⓖ ☞ ◗ Ⓖ

The 🔥 symbol denotes a pub
with a real solid fuel fire

Tugby 16D2

11–2.30; 6–11

Fox & Hounds
Hallaton Road (off A47)
✆ 282
**Greene King XX Mild, Abbot;
Marston Burton Bitter, Owd
Rodger (Winter); Blands Cider
(Summer)** Ⓗ Regular guest
beers
Lounge with central fireplace
and thatched bar! Bar billiards
table, restaurant
🕮 ✍ Ⓖ ☞ ◗ Ⓐ

Tur Langton 16C3

12–2.30; 6–11

Bulls Head
Main Street (B6047)
✆ East Langton 373
**Adnams Bitter; Marston
Pedigree; Ruddle Bitter,
County** Ⓗ
First licensed in 1744, friendly
village pub with restaurant
🕮 🕮 ✍ Ⓖ ☞ ◗ Ⓖ Ⓐ

Walcote 16B4

11–2.30; 5.30–11

Black Horse
Lutterworth Road (A427 near
M1 Jct 20)
✆ Lutterworth 2684
**Flowers Original; Hook
Norton Best Bitter, Old
Hookey; Hoskins & Oldfield
Bitter** Ⓗ Regular guest
beers
Friendly village inn
specialising in Thai food
🕮 Q 🕮 ✍ Ⓖ ☞ Ⓐ

Walton-by-Kimcote 16C3

10.30–2.30; 5.30–11

Dog & Gun
Main Street
✆ Lutterworth 2808
Banks Mild, Bitter Ⓔ
Large village local. Lounge
used to be a butchers' ✍ ◗

Whetstone 16B3

10.30–2.30; 6–11

Wheatsheaf
85 High Street
✆ Leicester 864891
**Ansells Mild; Ind Coope
Bitter** Ⓗ
Locals' bar in need of
enlarging, cosy lounge
✍ Ⓖ (Mon–Fri) ◗

Whissendine 16D2

10.30–2.30; 6–11

White Lion
Main Street ✆ 233
**Adnams Bitter; Everard Bitter,
Tiger, Old Original** Ⓗ
Friendly village pub. Games
area includes devil-among-
the-tailors. No food Sun or
Mon ✍ 🕮 Ⓖ ☞

Whitwell 16E2

10.30–2.30; 6–11

Noel Arms
A606 ✆ Empingham 334
**Marston Pedigree; Ruddle
Bitter, County** Ⓗ
17th century free house with
cosy snug. Close to Rutland
Water 🕮 ✍ 🕮 Ⓖ ☞ ◗

Whitwick 16B2

11–2.30; 7–11

Duke of Newcastle
North Street (B587)
✆ Coalville 32547
Shipstone Mild Ⓗ; **Bitter** Ⓗ & Ⓔ
Popular locals pub with good
darts following 🕮 🕮 ✍ ◗

Foresters Arms
Leicester Road (B587)
✆ Coalville 36180
Opens 11.15 & 6.30
Marston Pedigree Ⓗ
Down-to-earth local with pool
and darts ◗ Ⓖ

Try also: Forest Rock (Ind
Coope/Ansells); Kings Arms
(Marston)

Wing 16D2

11–2.30; 6–11

Kings Arms
Top Street
✆ Manton 315
**Greene King IPA; Ruddle
Bitter, County** Ⓗ
Popular stone village pub with
restaurant. Near to ancient
turf maze
🕮 Q 🕮 ✍ 🕮 Ⓖ ☞ (not Sun) ◗

Wymondham 16D1

11–2.30; 6–11

Hunters Arms
Edmondthorpe Road
✆ 633
**Draught Bass; Greene King
IPA, Abbot** Ⓗ
Cosy comfortable village local
🕮 Q ✍ Ⓖ ☞ ◗

Alford 27G6

10–2.30; 6–10.30 (11 F, S)

Half Moon
West Street (A1104) ☎ 3334
Bateman Mild, XB, XXXB ℍ
Busy and homely, this pub
deserves an Oscar for its best
supporting role as home to the
local film society ✿ ℭ ♠

Aswarby 27E8

12–2.30; 6–11

Tally Ho
A15 ☎ Culverthorpe 205
**Adnams Bitter; Bateman
XXXB** ℍ Occasional guest
beers
Comfortable friendly
roadhouse/motel.
Accommodation in converted
outhouses ✿ ✿ ✿ ℭ ♠

Barholm 17F2

11–2; 7–11

Five Horseshoes
**Adnams Bitter; Bateman
XXXB** ℍ Regular guest beers
Lovely stone pub in quiet
village. Inside adorned with
Shire Horse tack ✿ ✿ ✿ ✿ Å

Bassingham 26D7

10.30–2.30; 6–11

Five Bells
Main Street ☎ 269
Ind Coope Bitter, Burton Ale ℍ
Busy village local with good
food ✿ ✿ ℭ ♠

Belchford 27F6

11–2.30 (closed Mon); 7–11

Blue Bell
Off A153 ☎ Tetford 602
Ind Coope Burton Ale ℍ
Regular guest beers
Comfortable village pub on
the Viking Way ✿ Q ✿ ✿ ℭ ♠

Blyton 26D4

11–2.30; 6–11

Black Horse
98 High Street (A159)
Bass Mild, Draught Bass ℍ
Comfortable village pub,
smart but not swish ✿ ✿ ✿ ℭ ♠

Boston 27G8

10.30–3; 6.30–11

Burton House Hotel
Wainfleet Road (main A52
coast road) ☎ 62307
Draught Bass; Bateman XB ℍ
Two-star hotel, good food,
boules in car park ✿ ✿ ℭ ♠

Carpenters Arms
Witham Street ☎ 62840
Bateman Mild, XB, XXXB ℍ
Back-street local; exotic
lunchtime menu. A lively
meeting place ✿ ✿ ✿ ℭ

Railway
London Road

**Usher Founders Ale; Wilsons
Original Bitter** ℍ
Smart town local near old
railway cottages. No trains
courtesy Dr. Beeching ✿

Ropers Arms
Horncastle Road
Bateman Mild, XB ℍ
Friendly street corner local.
Popular with anglers; pool ♟

Town Pump
Craythorne Lane (off Market
Place) ☎ 68594
**Greene King IPA, Abbot;
Ruddle County; Younger's
Scotch** ℍ
Loud colours, popular with
the young. Food bar with
interesting menu ✿ ℭ ♠

Bourne 17F1

10.30–2; 7–11

Golden Lion
49 West Street (A151)
Samuel Smith OBB ℍ
Popular town local
✿ ✿ ✿ ✿ ℭ ♠ ♟ ♿

Burgh le Marsh 27H6

10.30–3 (2.30 winter); 6–11

White Hart Hotel
High Street (A158)
☎ Skegness 810321
**Bateman Mild, XB, XXXB,
Ruddle Bitter, County** ℍ
Occasional guest beers
Comfortable friendly and
popular pub ✿ ✿ ✿ ℭ ♠ ♟

Caenby Corner 26D5

10–2.30; 6.30–11

Moncks Arms
A15 (roundabout with A631)
☎ Normanby-by-Spital 363
**Bass Special Bitter; Tetley
Mild, Bitter** ℍ
Roomy roadhouse ✿ ℭ ♠

Caythorpe 26D7

10.30–3; 6–11

Red Lion
High Street (off A607)
☎ Loveden 72632
**Draught Bass; Everards Old
Original; Marston Pedigree,
Ruddle County** ℍ Regular
guest beers
Attractive 17th century
country pub ✿ ✿ ✿ ℭ ♠ ♟

Chapel St. Leonards 27H6

10.30–3 (2.30 winter); 6–11

Ship
Sea Road ☎ Skegness 72362
Bateman Mild, XB, XXXB ℍ
Friendly atmosphere, popular
with locals and holiday-
makers. No food winter
✿ ✿ ℭ ♠

Coleby 26D7

10.30–2.30; 6–11

Bell Inn

Far Lane ☎ Lincoln 810240
**Samuel Smith OBB, Museum
Ale; Bulmer Cider** ℍ
Modernised village pub with
excellent meals ✿ ✿ ✿ ℭ ♠

Coningsby 27F7

10–2.30; 6.30–11

Leagate Inn
Boston Road (B1192)
**Adnams Bitter; Ruddle
County; Taylor Landlord;
Whitbread Castle Eden** ℍ
Regular guest beers
Historic coaching inn with
large restaurant, cosy bars
and garden catering for
families and Koi Carp
admirers ✿ ✿ ℭ ♠

White Swan
Old Boston Road (off A153)
Bateman Mild, XB ℍ
Frequented by the young from
around and within the local
RAF camp. Good jukebox and
pub games create a lively,
cheerful atmosphere ✿ ℭ

Corby Glen 26E9

10.30–2.30; 6.30–11

Woodhouse Arms
A151
Bateman XB, XXXB ℍ Regular
guest beers
Roadside inn with attractive
interior ✿ ℭ ♠ ♟

Croft 27H7

10.30–3 (2.30 winter); 6–11

Old Chequers
Lymn Bank
Bateman XB, XXXB ℍ
Former 15th century posting
house—isolated but worth
finding ✿ ✿ ♟

Donington 27F8

11–3; 6–11

Queen Inn
49 Station Street (A52)
**Usher Founders Ale; Wilsons
Original Bitter** ℍ
Popular village local, basic but
comfortable ✿ ✿ ℭ

Dyke 27E9

10.30–2.30; 6.30–11

Wishing Well
Off A15 ☎ Bourne 2970
Adnams Bitter Ⓖ; **Greene King
IPA, Abbot; Tetley Bitter** ℍ
Attractive pub in pleasant
surroundings ✿ ✿ ♠ ♟

East Kirkby 27G6

10–2.30 (3 summer); 6–11

Red Lion
Main Road (A153) ☎ 406
Bateman XB, XXXB ℍ
The circular table engraved by
WW2 aircrews is a reminder
of the pub's connections with
nearby disused airfields
✿ ✿ ✿ Å (caravan club)

Edenham 27E9

11–2.30; 6–11
Five Bells
Main Street (A151) ☎ 235
Samuel Smith OBB ⊞
Friendly village pub with
restaurant ✿ ⑤ ♥ ♀

Fishtoft 27G8

10.30–3; 6.30–11
Ball House
Wainfleet Road (A52)
Bateman Mild, XB ⊞
Comfortable pub on the main
coast road. Children's play
area in garden ✿ ⑤ ♥

Folkingham 27E8

Closed weekday lunch; 6–11
New Inn
West Street (off A15) ☎ 371
**Hardys & Hansons Best Mild,
Best Bitter** ⊞
Pleasant friendly inn with
good value restaurant. Food
weekends only ✿ ⑤ ♥

Fosdyke 27G8

10.30–3; 7–11
Ship
Main Road (A17) ☎ 628
Bateman Mild, XB ⊞
Friendly pub with nautical
links by swing bridge over
River Welland
✿ ⑤ ♥ (summer)

Frampton 27G8

10.30–3; 6.30–11
Moores Arms
Church End OS328392
Adnams Bitter; Bateman XB ⊞
Occasional guest beers
Cosy and busy, idyllic on a
summer evening, restaurant
✿ ⑤ ♥

Freiston 27G8

10.30–3; 6.30–11
Castle Inn
Haltoft End (Main A52 coast
road) ☎ 760393
Bateman Mild, XB ⊞
Attractive exterior, smart
interior and superb adventure
playground—aerial runway
and fishing boat amuse
children and adults alike!
✿ ▣ ⑤ ♥

Fulbeck 26D7

11–2.30; 7–11
Hare & Hounds
The Green (A607)
☎ Lovedon 72441
Bateman XB, XXXB ⊞
Old stone coaching inn ✿ ▣ ♥ ♀

Gainsborough 26C5

10.30–2.30; 6–11
Drovers Call
Lea Road ☎ 2044
Bass Mild, Special Bitter ⒠,

**Draught Bass; Stones Best
Bitter** ⊞
Large and cheerful estate pub
⑤ ♥ ≉

Elm Cottage
Church Street ☎ 5474
Bass Mild, Special Bitter ⊞
Popular, quiet town pub for
drinkers Q ✿ ⑤

Grantham 26D8

11–3; 6–11
Angel & Royal
High Street ☎ 5816
**Draught Bass; Greene King
Abbot** ⊞
Historic coaching inn; note
fireplace, masonry and
tapestries ✿ ✿ ▣ ⑤ ♥ ♀

Chequers
Butcher's Row, Market Place
**Everards Old Original;
Marston Burton Bitter,
Pedigree, Merrie Monk;
Bulmer Cider** ⊞
Popular town pub with very
friendly atmosphere ♀

Granby
Market Place ☎ 63309
Open 11–4 Sat lunchtime
Home Mild; Bitter ⒠
Popular market pub ♀

Odd House
4 Fletcher Street (off Wharf
Road) ☎ 65293
**Marston Mercian Mild, Border
Bitter, Pedigree; John Smith's
Bitter** ⊞ Regular guest beers
Warm, friendly, typically
British pub. Excellent
lunchtime meals ✿ ✿ ⑤ ♥ ≉

Shirley Croft
Harrowby Road (off A52)
☎ 3260
Bateman XB, XXXB ⊞
Victorian local set in own
grounds ✿ ▣ ⑤ ♥

Heckington 27E8

10.30–2.30; 6.30–11
Nags Head
High Street (off A17)
☎ Sleaford 60218
Wilsons Original Bitter ⊞
Popular old village inn
✿ ✿ ▣ ⑤ ♥ ≉

Heighington 26E6

10.30–2.30; 6–11
Butcher & Beast
High Street ☎ Lincoln 790386
Bateman XB ⊞
Very friendly village inn,
glittering brasses. Immaculate
toilets—should be in the good
loo guide too! ✿ ▣ ⑤ ♥ ♿

Holbeach 27G9

10.30–3 (4 Thurs); 6–11
Bell
High Street (A151) ☎ 23223
Elgood Bitter ⊞
Popular friendly town centre
local ✿ ✿ ▣ ⑤ ♥

Horncastle 27F6

10–2.30; 6.30–11
Red Lion
Bull Ring ☎ 3338
Shipstone Bitter ⊞
Pleasant and friendly town
pub, home of town's art and
drama groups ✿ ✿ ▣ ⑤

Rodney Hotel
North Street ☎ 3389
Whitbread Castle Eden ⊞
Sandwiched between the
lively bar and the comfortable
lounge, the snug bar reflects
bygone days ✿ ✿ ▣ ⑤ ♥ ♀

Ingham 26D5

11–3; 6 (7 winter)–11
Windmill
B1398 ☎ Lincoln 730249
**Bass Mild, Draught Bass;
Stones Best Bitter** ⊞
Isolated, basic roadside pub
✿ Q ✿ ♥ ⚑

Limber 27E3

10.30–2.30; 7–11
New Inn
High Street (A18)
☎ Roxton 60257
**Bateman XXXB; Ward
Sheffield Best Bitter** ⊞
Occasional guest beers
Substantial building, very
popular with all ages
✿ Q ✿ ✿ ♥ ▣ ⚑ ♿

Lincoln 26D6

11–3; 5.30–11
Blue Anchor
High Street ☎ 21022
**Draught Bass; Stones Best
Bitter** ⊞
Friendly town pub close to
National bus station ⑤ ♥ ≉

Cornhill Vaults
Cornhill ☎ 35113
Evening opens 6
**Samuel Smith OBB, Museum
Ale** ⊞
Cellar bar, live music
weekends ▣ (lunchtimes) ⑤ ≉

Golden Eagle
21 High Street ☎ 21058
Opens noon winter
Bateman Mild, XB, XXXB ⊞
Bateman's only tied house in
city ✿ ⑤ ♥ ≉

Jolly Brewer
Broadgate ☎ 28583
Evening opens 7; closed Sun
lunch
**Draught Bass; Bateman XB;
Everards Tiger; Hardys &
Hansons Best Bitter; Bulmer
Cider** ⊞ Regular guest beers
1930's Art Deco style free
house, in easy reach of city
centre ✿ ✿ ⑤ ≉

Monks Abbey
Monks Road ☎ 44416
John Smith's Bitter ⊞
Small friendly local ⑤ ♥ ≉

Lincolnshire 146

Queen in the West
Moor Street ✆ 26169
Evening opens 6
Ward Sheffield Best Bitter;
Youngers Scotch, No. 3 Ⓗ
Regular guest beers
Smart pub with comfortable
lounge ⚅♿

Small Beer (off licence)
91 Newland Street West
Opens 10.30–10.30
Bateman XXXB; Taylor
Landlord; Ward Sheffield Best
Bitter Ⓗ; Symonds Strong Vat
Cider; Scrumpy Jack Ⓖ
Regular guest beers

Stag's Head
68 Newport ✆ 34495
Evening opens 6
Home Mild, Bitter Ⓔ
Large, basic locals' pub Q⚅♿

Strugglers
83 Westgate ✆ 24702
Bass Mild, Draught Bass Ⓗ
Busy basic and bursting with
people. A little gem ♿

Turk's Head
Newport ✆ 23742
Whitbread Trophy, Castle
Eden Ⓗ
Popular house, opposite local
radio station ⚅♿

Victoria
Union Road ✆ 36048
Everards Mild, Old Original;
Old Mill Bitter; Taylor
Landlord; Ward Sheffield Best
Bitter; Bulmer Cider Ⓗ Regular
guest beers
Busy pub, pumpclip collection.
Excellent bar meals Q♿⚅♿

Little Bytham 26D9
11–2; 6–11
Mallard
Greene King Abbot Ⓗ
Friendly village local

Little Cawthorpe 27G5
10.30–3; 7–11
Royal Oak (Splash)
Watery Lane ✆ Louth 603204
Bass Mild, Draught Bass;
Bateman XB, XXXB; Stones
Best Bitter Ⓗ
Traditional country pub
approached via a ford
⚅Q♿⚅♿

Long Sutton 27G9
10.30–3 (4 Fri); 7–11
Bull
Market Place (A17)
✆ Holbeach 362258
Draught Bass Ⓗ
Interesting old hotel; few
changes since 1920's when
landlady (who may fine you
for bad language) took up
residence Q⚅♿♿♿

Louth 27G5
11–3; 6.30–11
Old Whyte Swanne
45 Eastgate
Evening opening 7 (6 Sat)
Bass Mild, Draught Bass;
Stones Best Bitter Ⓗ
Small 17th century low-
beamed pub. Worth a visit
⚅♿⚅♿

Wheatsheaf
Westgate ✆ 603159
Draught Bass; Stones Best
Bitter Ⓗ
17th century inn near historic
church Q♿⚅♿

Woolpack
Riverhead Road ✆ 606568
Evening opens 7
Bateman Mild, XB, XXXB Ⓗ
Traditional, friendly inn with
universal appeal ⚅♿♿♿

Market Rasen 27E5
10.30–2.30 (4 Tue); 6.30 (7 winter)–11
Red Lion
King Street ✆ 842424
Darley Thorne Best Bitter;
Vaux Samson; Ward Sheffield
Best BitterⓗH
Friendly free house, pool very
popular ⚅♿♿♿≷

Moulton Chapel 17G1
11–3 (closed Wed); 7–11
Wheatsheaf
4 Fengate (B1357)
Bateman XB, Elgood Bitter Ⓗ
Regular guest beers
300 years old, lounge on site
of former brewhouse
⚅♿♿♿♿

Nettleham 26E6
10–2.30; 6 (7 Sat)–11
Plough
The Green ✆ Lincoln 750275
Bateman Mild, XB Ⓗ
Comfortable welcoming
village pub ♿♿♿

North Hykeham 26D6
11–2.30; 6–11
Harrows
Lincoln Road
Whitbread Castle Eden Ⓗ
Popular local; piano on
Saturdays ♿♿

North Kelsey 26E4
12–2.30; 7–11
Royal Oak
High Street (near B1334)
Adnams Bitter; Tetley Mild,
Bitter; Wards Sheffield Best
Bitter Ⓗ
Typical village inn, games
room ⚅♿♿♿

North Somercotes 27H5
12–2.30; 6.45–11
Bay Horse Inn
Keeling Street ✆ 373
Bass Mild, Draught Bass;
Younger's IPA Ⓗ
Pleasant and friendly. Near
Lakeside Holiday Park
⚅Q♿⚅♿♿⚅

Old Bolingbroke 27G6
10–2.30 (3 summer); 6–11
Black Horse
Mill Lane OS349651
Ind Coope Burton Ale Ⓗ
Does King Henry still visit this
comfortable pub from his
nearby castle ruins? ⚅♿♿♿

Old Somerby 26D8
10.30–3; 6–11
Fox & Hounds
Marston Pedigree, Merrie
Monk; Ruddle County Ⓗ
Popular village pub, large
garden, superb meals ⚅♿♿♿

Raithby 27G6
10–2.30 (3 summer); 6–11
Red Lion
Main Street ✆ Spilsby 53727
Home Bitter; Ind Coope
Burton Ale; Tetley Bitter Ⓗ
On the edge of Tennyson
country, a 400 year-old pub
with good value food ⚅♿⚅♿

Rippingale 27E9
11–2; 7–11 (food licence till 3 & 12)
Bull
High Street (off A15)
Samuel Smith OBB Ⓗ
Excellent all-round local, very
good beer garden
⚅♿♿♿♿⚅

Rothwell 27F4
12–2.30; 7–11
Nickerson Arms
Near Caistor (A46)
Bateman XB, XXXB; Old Mill
Bitter; Taylor Landlord; Tetley
Bitter Ⓗ Regular guest beers
Friendly village local in the
Wolds ⚅Q♿⚅♿ (Mon–Fri) ♿

Ruskington 27E7
10.30–2.30; 6.30–11
Black Bull
Rectory Road (B1188)
Bateman XB Ⓗ
Friendly village local ♿

Saracen's Head 27G9
10.30–3; 6–11
New Saracen's Head
Washway Road (A17)
✆ Holbeach 22708
Greene King IPA, Abbot Ⓗ
Welcoming and comfortable
pub on sharp bend ⚅♿♿♿♿

Scamblesby 27F5
10.30–2.30; 6.30–11
Green Man
Old Main Road ☎ Stenigot 282
Bateman Mild, XB, XXXB Ⓗ
Comfortable old village pub
near Cadwell Park ♨ Q ♿ ⌂ ◐ ♪ 🍴

Scotter 26D4
11.30–2.30; 7–11
White Swan
9 The Green
**Bass Mild, Draught Bass;
Bateman XXXB; Tetley Mild,
Bitter** Ⓗ
Restaurant and smart lounge.
Bar meals very popular ♨ ⌂ ◐

Scotton 26D4
10.30–2.30; 6.30–11
Three Horse Shoes
Westgate (off A159)
Bass Mild, Special Bitter Ⓗ
Welcoming village pub ♨ ◐ 🍴

Skegness 27H6
10.30–3 (2.30 winter); 6–11
Vine Hotel
Vine Road (off Drummond
Road) ☎ 3018
Bateman Mild, XB Ⓗ
Attractive hotel in wooded
setting ♨ ♨ ⌂ ◐ ♪ 🍴 ≷

Welcome Inn
Burgh Road (A158)
Shipstone Bitter Ⓗ
Smart large pub, well back off
main road ♨ ♨ ◐ ≷

Skendleby 27G6
Blacksmiths Arms
Spilsby Road (off A158)
Bateman XB Ⓗ
A cosy one-roomed pub, too
good to miss. ♨ Q ♨

Sleaford 27E7
10.30–2.30; 6.30–11
Waggon & Horses
Eastgate ☎ 303388
Draught Bass Ⓗ
Busy open-plan pub. Separate
restaurant ♨ ⌂ ◐ ≷

White Hart
Southgate ☎ 302612
John Smith's Bitter Ⓗ
Busy pub with mews
converted to shops
♨ ♨ ⌂ ⌂ ◐ ≷

Spalding 27F9
10.30–3; 6–11
Bull
Churchgate ☎ 67749
Evening opens 7
Home Mild, Bitter Ⓔ
Large modern pub
overlooking River Welland.
Caravan site ⌂ 🍴 ♨

Olde White Horse
Churchgate ☎ 3529

Samuel Smith OBB Ⓗ
Thatched 16th century pub
opposite High Bridge
♨ ♿ (daytime) ⌂ ◐ ♪

Spilsby 27G6
10–2.30 (3 summer) 16–11
George Hotel
Market Place ☎ 52528
Home Mild, Bitter Ⓔ
Busy crossroads hotel with
comfortable atmosphere
♿ ♨ ⌂ ⌂ ◐ ♪

Nelson Butt
Market Place ☎ 52258
Bateman Mild, XB Ⓗ
Small locals' local full of
character and characters ♪

Stamford 17E2
11–2.30; 6–11
Dolphin
60 East Street ☎ 55494
**Wells Eagle Bitter,
Bombardier** Ⓗ
Tasteful modern pub with 4
small rooms ♨ ⌂ ♪

Green Man
29 Scotgate (old A1 going
north) ☎ 53598
Opens 10.30
**Draught Bass; Greene King
IPA; Marston Pedigree;
Ruddle County; Taylor
Landlord** Ⓗ
Small and cosy. Pub games.
No food Sun ♨ ⌂ ⌂ ◐

Hurdler
93 New Cross Street
☎ 63428
Evening opens 6.30
Adnams Bitter Ⓗ**; Everards
Mild** Ⓔ**, Bitter, Tiger** Ⓗ**, Old
Original** Ⓔ **Regular guest
beers**
Fine estate pub close to fire
station ♨ ⌂ ◐

Lord Burghley
17 Broad Street ☎ 63426
Opens 11–4 Fri lunch
**Adnams Bitter; Fuller London
Pride; Greene King IPA,
Abbot; Marston Pedigree,
Merrie Monk** Ⓗ **Regular guest
beers**
Popular town centre free
house. ♨ Q ♨ ⌂ (not Sun) ≷

Sturton-by-Stow 26D5
11–2.30; 7–11
Red Lion
Marton Road
Whitbread Caste Eden Ⓗ
Open fires in winter, beer
garden in summer ♨ ♨ ⌂ ◐ ♪

Surfleet 27F9
10.30–3; 6.30–11
Crown
Gosberton Road (A16)
Bateman XB Ⓗ

Village local. Comfortable
snug ♨ ♨ ⌂ ⌂ ◐ ♪

Swineshead Bridge 27F8
10.30–3; 6.30–11
Barge
A17 ☎ Boston 820267
Home Bitter Ⓗ
Smart hotel, good fishing
nearby ♨ ⌂ ◐ ♪ 🍴 ♨ ≷

Tetney Lock 27G4
11–3; 6.30–11
Crown & Anchor
Bass Mild, Draught Bass Ⓗ
Anglers' and wildfowlers'
pub. Live music weekends
♨ ⌂ ♪

Throckenholt 18A3
12–2 Sat & Sun; 7–11 (10.30 S)
Four Horeshoes
South Eau Bank B1166
Elgood Bitter Ⓖ
Remote, unspoilt Fenland pub
♨ Q ♨ ♨ ♿

Wainfleet 27H7
10.30–2.30; 6–11
Royal Oak
High Street
Bateman XB Ⓗ
Cosy village local, building
once belonged to Bethlehem
Hospital for the insane, now
the landlord creates the
Bedlam ♨ Q ♨ ⌂ ◐ ♪ ≷

Welton 26E5
10–2.30; 6.30–11
Black Bull
The Green ☎ 60220
Ind Coope Bitter Ⓗ
Large, busy old coaching inn
♨ ♨ ⌂ ◐ ♪

Wigtoft 27F8
10.30–3; 6.30–11
Golden Fleece
Main Road (A17)
Bateman Mild, XB Ⓗ
Comfortable and friendly
village local. Pool ♨ ⌂ ◐ ♪

Wilsford 26E8
12–2; 7–11
Plough
Main Road (A153)
Draught Bass; Bulmer Cider Ⓗ
Regular guest beers
Delightful country pub with
superb value for money meals
♨ ♨ ⌂ (not Mon) ◐ ♪ ♨

Withern 27G5
10.30–2.30; 6–11
Red Lion Hotel
Main Road (A157) ☎ 50365
Home Mild, Bitter Ⓗ
Large family pub with
restaurant ♿ ♨ ⌂ ◐ ♪

IF this is your first experience of the Good Beer Guide &/or real ale, you may be wondering a variety of things. What time is closing time? Whose round is it? What is real ale? to name but three. The answers to the first two you're going to have to find out for yourselves but we'll help you with the third.

Real ale is traditional British beer, brewed only from pure natural ingredients – malted barley, good English hops, yeast and naturally pure water, and naturally conditioned in the cask until the moment it is served. Keg beer can be brewed from the same ingredients, but often has other, cheaper ones substituted for part of the malt. It may also have some of the several hundred additives referred to elsewhere in this Good Beer Guide, which some brewers dump in their beer to improve the eye-appeal, lengthen the shelf-life, etc, etc, etc. They may make it last longer, but they certainly don't make it taste any better.

Bitter Taste

To make beer, malted barley is ground to form grist and then mixed with hot water (called 'liquor' in brewing terminology) to form a mash. The natural sugars dissolve out of the grist, and the liquid (now called 'wort') is run off into a copper, where it is boiled with hops which give the beer its characteristic bitter taste. Hops also act as a preservative and help to kill any bacteria present in the beer.

The wort is now transferred to a fermentation vessel and the brewery's own unique strain of yeast is added. This fermentation process, lasting about five days, converts the sugars into alcohol and carbon dioxide.

It is at this point that the true difference between real and keg beer begins. Keg (brewery-conditioned) beer is chilled, filtered and pasteurised, removing all traces of yeast and preventing any secondary fermentation. Keg beer keeps well and is easy to store, but lacks the mature flavour of real beer. It is kept and

AND DON'T WORRY ABOUT THE NAMES – THEY ALL COME FROM ONE BIG TANK IN THE CELLAR

dispensed under carbon dioxide pressure and is usually served chilled to disguise its lack of flavour.

At the end of fermentation, real (cask-conditioned) beer is allowed to mature in conditioning tanks for a few days before being racked into casks, often with the addition of a handful of hops to increase the aroma and flavour. Secondary fermentation continues in the cask, and it is this cask-conditioning which develops the flavour, character and maturity of real ale in the pub cellar until the cask is ready for use.

Perishable

Even the best real ale can be spoilt by a lack of care or hygiene by the pub landlord. Pipes and pumps must be regularly cleaned (and that means at least every week, not, like the apocryphal landlord who cleaned his pipes 'as regular as clockwork, every six months, whether they need it or not!'). The beer cellar must also be kept scrupulously clean; real ale is a perishable product and should be looked after as carefully as food in the kitchen.

Real ale means a bit more work for landlords, but their customers are rewarded with a distinctive, deliciously different and completely natural product – a refreshing alternative to the chemical-ridden stuff that the giants churn out under the once-proud name of beer. Leave keg beer to the people it suits – the tasteless – drink the real stuff, you know it makes sense!

Central London

(See also 'South West London' for SW1 Westminster and 'West London' for W1 West End)

EC1: 9G1
Clerkenwell

11–3; 5.30–11

City Pride
28 Farringdon Lane
☎ 01-608 0615
Closed Sat eves
Fuller Chiswick Bitter, London Pride, ESB Ⓗ
Noted for Sunday lunches
🏠Ⓖ✿⇄ ⊖ (Farringdon)

Hat & Tun
3 Hatton Wall
Closed weekends
Charrington IPA Ⓗ
Large, busy one-bar pub with wrought iron around the bar
⇄ ⊖ (Farringdon)

Horseshoe
24 Clerkenwell Close
Courage Best Bitter; Directors Ⓗ
Deceptively large pub; quiet in the evening but very busy lunchtime
Ⓖ⇄ ⊖ (Farringdon)

EC1: Finsbury 9H1

11–3; 5–11

Artillery Arms
102 Bunhill Row
☎ 01-253 4411
Sat eves opens 7
Fuller London Pride, ESB Ⓗ
Small, lively 1-bar pub near Honourable Artillery Company and Bunhill Cemetery. Jazz Friday eve
Ⓖ✿ (Not Sun) ⇄
⊖ (Old Street)

Lord Nelson
262 Old Street
Closed Sat eves and Sun
Ruddle County; Watney Combes Bitter; Stag Bitter; Webster Yorkshire Bitter Ⓗ
Large, friendly and busy pub; very crowded lunchtime
Ⓖ✿⇄ ⊖ (Old Street)

EC1: Holborn 9G2

11–3; 5.30–11

Olde Mitre
Ely Court (between Hatton Garden and Ely Place)
Closed weekends
Friary Meux Bitter; Ind Coope Burton Ale Ⓗ
Hard to find alleyway pub. Old furniture in snug
🍴⇄ (Holborn Viaduct)

EC1: Smithfield 9G2

11.30–3; 5–11

Bishops Finger
8 West Smithfield
Closed weekends

Shepherd Neame Bitter Ⓗ
2-level two-bar pub, popular with Smithfield Market workers 🍴⇄ (Holborn Viaduct)

Hand & Shears
1 Middle Street
Closed weekends
Courage Best Bitter, Directors Ⓗ
Small, friendly and historic pub 🍴 ⊖ (Barbican)

EC2: 9J1
Finsbury

11–3; 5.30–11

Fleetwood
36 Wilson Street
☎ 01-247 2242
Closes 10 pm Mon–Fri; closed Sat eve, Sun, Bank hols
Fuller Chiswick Bitter, London Pride, ESB Ⓗ
Modern split-level pub under new office development
Ⓖ🍴♿⇄ ⊖ (Moorgate)

Windmill
27 Tabernacle Street (off A501)
Closed weekends
Arkell Kingsdown Ale; Charrington IPA; Fuller London Pride; Greene King Abbot; King & Barnes Sussex Bitter; Shepherd Neame Bitter Ⓗ
Busy, friendly pub with interconnecting bars. Prices high even by City standards
Ⓖ✿ ⊖ (Old Street)

EC3: City 9J2

11.30–3; 5–11

East India Arms
67 Fenchurch Street
Closes 9.30 eves; closed weekends
Young Bitter, Special Ⓗ
Very popular, always packed pub in heart of City
⇄ (Fenchurch St.)
⊖ (Aldgate E)

Lamb Tavern
10 Leadenhall Market
Young Bitter, Special Ⓗ
Large, lively Victorian pub
🍴⇄ (Fenchurch Street)
⊖ (Aldgate E)

EC4: Blackfriars 9G2

11.30–3; 5–11

Black Friar
174 Queen Victoria Street
Closed Sat eve and Sun
Adnams Bitter; Draught Bass; Boddingtons Bitter; Tetley Bitter Ⓗ
Beautifully restored 1903 Art Nouveau pub in alabaster, marble and mosaic Ⓖ⇄ ⊖

EC4: City 9H2

11.30–3; 5–11

Shades
5 Bucklersbury (off Queen Victoria Street)

☎ 01-248 0523
Eves closes 9; closed weekends
Samuel Smith OBB, Museum Ale Ⓗ
Panelled bar in back street, dates back to 18th century
QⒼ✿ (not Sun) ⇄ ⊖ (Bank)

Monument Tavern
60 King William Street
Eves closes 9.30
Fuller Chiswick Bitter, London Pride, ESB Ⓗ
Very busy, small, one-bar alehouse 50 yards from Monument. Rare Sunday opening for City pub
Ⓖ✿ (Fenchurch Street)
⊖ (Monument)

EC4: Fleet 9G2
Street

11.30–3; 5–11

Cock Tavern
22 Fleet Street ☎ 01-353 8570
Closes 9 pm eves; closed weekends
Truman Bitter, Best Bitter, Sampson Ⓗ
Smart, heavily beamed show pub with bare floor and low lighting Ⓖ✿ ⊖ (Temple)

Old Bell
95 Fleet Street
Closed Sat eve and Sun
Belhaven 80/-; Boddingtons Bitter; Old Bell Bitter; Tetley Bitter Ⓗ
Basic one-bar pub near Ludgate Circus. Sloping wooden floors
🍴♿⇄ ⊖ (Blackfriars)

Tipperary
66 Fleet Street ☎ 01-353 0130
Closed Sat eve and Sun
Greene King IPA, Abbot; Rayment BBA Ⓗ
Long thin bar with upstairs lounge Ⓖ✿⇄ ⊖ (Blackfriars)

WC1: 9G1
Bloomsbury

11–3; 5.30–11

Lamb
94 Lambs Conduit Street (off A5201) ☎ 01-405 0713
Young Bitter, Special, Winter Warmer Ⓗ
Popular and unspoilt, with snob screens and old theatrical prints
Q♺ (no children) Ⓖ✿
⊖ (Russell Sq)

WC1: Holborn 9G2

11–3; 5.30–11

Cittie of Yorke
22 High Holborn
☎ 01-242 7670
Closed Sat eve and Sun
Samuel Smith OBB, Museum Ale Ⓗ
Famous Holborn landmark with downstairs vaults and remarkable triangular stove
🏠Ⓖ✿⇄ (Holborn Viaduct)
⊖ (Chancery Lane)

Dolphin Tavern
44 Red Lion Street
(off A5201)
**Brakspear Bitter; Flowers
Original; Greene King Abbot;
Wethered Bitter** Ⓗ Regular
guest beers
Comfortable modernised pub
Ⓖ (not Sun) ⊖

WC1: Mount Pleasant 9G1

11–3; 5.30–11

Calthorpe Arms
252 Grays Inn Road (A5200)
**Young Bitter, Special, Winter
Warmer** Ⓗ
Straightforward and friendly;
upstairs dining room
QⒼ꩜ ⊖ (Kings Cross)

Pakenham Arms
1 Pakenham Street
✆ 01-278 5582
**Arkell BBB; Brakspear Special;
Fuller London Pride, ESB;
Greene King Abbot; Samuel
Smith OBB** Ⓗ Regular guest
beers
Old established free house.
Popular with postmen from
nearby sorting office
Ⓖ꩜ (not Sun) 🍴
⊖ (Kings Cross)

WC2: Covent Garden 9F2

11–3; 5.30–11

Marquess of Anglesey
39 Bow Street ✆ 01-240 3216
**Young Bitter, Special, Winter
Warmer** Ⓗ & Ⓔ
Busy corner pub near Market
Hall with upstairs bar
Ⓖ꩜⇌ (Charing Cross) ⊖

Nags Head
10 James Street
**McMullen AK Mild, Country
Bitter** Ⓗ
Large, crowded pub near
Opera House
Ⓖ⇌ (Charing Cross) ⊖

WC2: St Giles 9F2

11–3; 5.30–11

Angel
61 St Giles High Street
Closed Sun
**Courage Best Bitter,
Directors** Ⓗ
Historic pub with reputedly
haunted cellar; dartboard
Ⓖ ⊖ (Tottenham Ct Rd)

WC2: Trafalgar Square 9F3

11–3; 5.30–11

Chandos
29 St Martins Lane
✆ 01-836 2592
**Samuel Smith OBB, Museum
Ale** Ⓗ
Large, popular, wood-panelled
pub with upstairs restaurant
Ⓖ꩜⇌ ⊖ (Charing Cross)

East London

E1: Aldgate 9E7

11–2.30; 5–11

Castle
44 Commercial Road/Alie
Street (A13)
Sat eve opens 7
**Courage Best Bitter,
Directors** Ⓗ
Friendly pub with boxing
connections
Ⓖ꩜⇌ (Fenchurch Street)
⊖ (Aldgate E)

E1: Spitalfields 9E7

11–2.30; 5–11

Pride of Spitalfields
3 Heneage Street (just off
Brick Lane)
**Fuller London Pride, ESB;
Young Bitter, Special** Ⓗ
In an area famous for its
curries this small pub
admirably lives up to its name
🖼♪Ⓖ꩜⇌ (Liverpool St)
⊖ (Aldgate E)

E1: Stepney 9E7

11–2.30; 5–11

Fish & Ring
141A Whitehorse Road
**Davenports Bitter; Fuller
London Pride, ESB; Young
Special** Ⓗ
Comfortable, corner locals'
pub; very friendly
🍴⇌ (Stepney E)
⊖ (Stepney Green)

White Horse
48 White Horse Road
(off A13)
Sat eve opens 6.15
Charrington IPA Ⓗ
Small, friendly, one-bar pub.
Wood panels, cheap prices
Q♪⇌ (Stepney E)

E1: Wapping 9E7

11–2.30; 5–11

Town of Ramsgate
62 Wapping High Street
✆ 01-488 2685
Sat eve opens 7
**Draught Bass; Charrington,
IPA** Ⓗ
Narrow, panelled riverside
pub ♪Ⓖ꩜ ⊖

E2: Bethnal Green 9E7

11–2.30; 5–11

Approach Tavern
47 Approach Road
**Chudley Local Line; King &
Barnes Sussex Bitter; Pitfield
Bitter; Young Special** Ⓗ
Regular guest beers
Lively, friendly and basic two-
bar locals' pub. Widely
divergent clientele
🍴⇌ (Cambridge Heath) ⊖

Duke of Sussex
94 Goldsmiths Row
(off A1208)
Shepherd Neame Bitter Ⓗ
Tiny two-bar, friendly street
corner local in mock Tudor
style 🍴⇌ (Cambridge Heath)

E4: Chingford 9F5

11–3; 5.30–10.30 (11 F, S)

Larkshall
Larkshall Road (off A1009)
**Courage Best Bitter;
Directors** Ⓗ
Interesting combination of old
buildings in Tudor and
Victorian styles
🖼♪⇌ (Highams Park)

E5: Clapton 9E6

11–2.30; 5 (6 Sat)–11

Anchor & Hope
15 High Hill Ferry,
Harrington Hill
Fuller London Pride, ESB Ⓗ
Busy riverside pub; packed in
summer ♪🖼🍴⇌

E6: Becton 9F7

11–3; 5.30–10.30 (11 F, S)

Tollgate Tavern
16 Mary Rose Mall, Frobisher
Road
**Greene King Abbot Ale;
Wethered Bitter** Ⓗ
Large new pub in open-plan
style. Lively darts following.
Live music weekends

E6: East Ham 9F7

11–3; 5.30–10.30 (11 F, S)

Roding
Southend Road/Leigh Road
✆ 01-472 9291
Sat eve opens 7
**Ind Coope Burton Ale; Taylor
Walker Bitter**
Renovated, large comfortable
Victorian boozer in residential
area 🖼Ⓖ꩜ ⊖

E8: Hackney 9E7

11–2.30; 5–11

Lady Diana
95 Forest Road (off A1207)
**Adnams Bitter; Fuller London
Pride; Greene King Abbot;
Samuel Smiths OBB; Young
Special** Ⓗ Occasional guest
beers
Friendly, plush one-bar pub in
up-and-coming suburb ♪
⇌ (Hackney Downs & Central)

Prince George
40 Parkholme Road
(off A1207)
**Brakspear Best Bitter; Flowers
Original; Greene King
Abbot** Ⓗ
L-shaped, popular local deep
in Hackney. Pricey for area 🍴

E9: Homerton 9E7

11–2.30; 5.30 (Sat 6)–11

Chesham Arms

15 Mehetabel Terrace (off
Isabella Road)
**Fuller London Pride; Greene
King Abbot; Wethered Bitter,
Regular guest beers**
Hidden pub backing on to
North London Link Railway.
Varied clientele ☞ ⇌

E10: Leyton 9F6

11 (12 Mon–Thu)–3; 7–10.30 (11 F, S)

Holly Bush
32 Grange Road (off A1006)
**Greene King Abbot; Rayment
BBA; Young Special ⊞**
Occasional guest beers
Renovated, friendly free house
☞⇌ (Leyton Midland Rd)

E11: 9F4
Snaresbrook

11–3; 5.30 (6 Sat)–10.30 (11 F, S)

Eagle Hotel
76 Hollybush Hill (A11)
Charrington IPA ⊞
Large, imposing pub in
prominent position ☞☆ ⊖

E14: Limehouse 9F7

11–2.30; 5–11

Grapes
76 Narrow Street
☎ 01-987 4396
**Friary Meux Bitter; Ind Coope
Burton Ale; Taylor Walker
Bitter ⊞**
Busy, historic riverside pub.
Print lined ground-floor bar,
back balcony with Thames
bar. Seafood restaurant
Q🅿☞☎☆

E15: Stratford 9F7

11–3; 5.30–11

Bacchus's Bin
7/9 Leytonstone Road (A11)
10–10 weekdays; 10–11 F, S
**Godsons Black Horse; Greene
King Abbot; Ind Coope Burton
Ale; Rayment BBA ⊞**
Occasional guest beers
Off-licence attached to wine
bar and restaurant
⇌ (Maryland) ⊖

Dew Drop Inn
22 Brydges Road (off A112)
Sat eves opens 7
Charrington IPA ⊞
Small, street corner local with
relaxing low-lit atmosphere
⇌ (Maryland)

Railway Tavern
131 Angel Lane (off A11)
Closes 10.30 weekdays
**Draught Bass; Charrington
IPA ⊞**
Large, comfortable Victorian
pub with spartan games room
☞☆ (Mon–Fri) ⇌ ⊖

Greyhound
136 West Ham Lane (A112)
**Courage Best Bitter,
Directors ⊞**
Large, modern two-bar pub
with comfortable lounge ⇌ ⊖

E16: Canning 9F7
Town

11–3; 5.30–11

Essex Arms
92 Victoria Dock Road
(A1020) ☎ 01-476 2726
**Courage Best Bitter;
Directors ⊞**
Isolated, friendly dockland
pub. Pool and darts following
🚗☞☆☎☆⇌

E17: 9F6
Walthamstow

11–3; 5.30–10.30 (11 F, S)

Flowerpot
128 Wood Street (off A503)
Draught Bass ⊞
Popular one-bar boozer with
basic comforts
⇌ (Wood Street)

Lord Brooke
47 Shernhall Street (off A503)
Charrington IPA ⊞
Basic, but very pleasant three-
bar local ☞☆
⇌ ⊖ (Walthamstow Central)

Barking 9G7

11–3; 5.30–10.30 (11 F, S)

Jolly Fisherman
108 North Street (off A124)
Webster Yorkshire Bitter ⊞
Small, friendly family pub,
once a coaching inn ☞☆⇌ ☆

Barkingside 9F6

11–3; 5.30–10.30 (11 F, S)

Doctor Johnson
175 Longwood Gardens (near
A406)
**Courage Best Bitter,
Directors ⊞**
Imposing classical-style pub
with revolving door
🚗Q🅿☞☆

Collier Row 9G6

10–2.30; 6–10.30 (11 F, S)

Bell & Gate
250 Collier Row Lane (B174)
**Courage Best Bitter,
Directors ⊞**
Popular, lively local pub.
Comfortable through lounge
☞☆ (Mon–Fri)

Cranham 9H6

10–2.30; 6–10.30 (11 F, S)

Golden Crane
117 Avon Road
Charrington IPA ⊞
Unspoilt, 3-room suburban
pub of character Q☞☆

Thatched House
348 St. Mary's Lane (B187)
**Draught Bass; Charrington
IPA ⊞**
Friendly 1930s pub on fringe
of countryside
🚗🅿☞☆ (not Sun)

Creekmouth 9G7

11–3; 5.30–10.30 (11 F, S)

Crooked Billet
113 River Road, Barking
(1¼ miles S of A13)
Charrington IPA ⊞
Excellent local in industrial
area. Bar billiards, piano
singalongs at weekends
🚗Q☞☆ (Mon–Fri) ☆

Dagenham 9G6

11–3; 5.30–10.30 (11 F, S)

Three Travellers
Wood Lane, Becontree Heath
(A124)
Ind Coope Bitter ⊞
Unspoilt local near massive
housing estate. Bar billiards
☞☆

Havering- 9H5
atte-Bower

10.30–2.30; 6–10.30 (11 F, S)

Royal Oak
North Road (B175)
**Flowers Original; Wethered
Bitter ⊞**
Friendly village pub.
Comfortable split-level, rustic
lounge ☞☆☆

Hornchurch 9H6

10.30–2.30; 6–10.30 (11 F, S)

Harrow
130 Hornchurch Road
(A124)
Ind Coope Bitter, Burton Ale ⊞
Traditional local, near
swimming pool Q☞☆☆

Ilford 9G6

11–3; 5.30–10.30 (11 F, S)

Angel
Station Road (near A123)
Charrington IPA ⊞
Smart, new pub built behind
the original Angel ☞☆⇌

Newbury Park 9G6

11–3; 5.30–10.30 (11 F, S)

Avenue
902 Eastern Avenue (A12)
☎ 01-590 3465
**Courage Best Bitter,
Directors ⊞**
Basic public and plush lounge
with carvery ☞☆☎☆ ⊖

North 9J7
Ockenden

10.30–2.30; 6–10.30 (11 F, S)

Old White Horse
Ockenden Road (B186)
Ind Coope Bitter ⊞
Traditional, friendly local.
London's most Easterly pub
☞☆

Rainham 9H7

10.30–2.30; 6–10.30 (11 F, S)

Phoenix
Broadway (B1335)

Courage Best Bitter,
Directors Ⓗ
Pleasant pub, Society for
Preservation of Beer from the
Wood meet here ⚐Ⓖ🍴≹

Romford 9H6

10.30–2.30; 6–10.30 (11 F, S)

Victoria
122 Victoria Road (off A125)
Draught Bass; Charrington
IPA Ⓗ
Pleasant 2-bar edge of town
local ⚐Ⓖ🍴≹

Upminster 9H6

10.30–2.30; 6–10.30 (11 F, S)

White Hart
Hacton Lane (1½ miles off
A124) OS547851 ✆ 20252
Draught Bass; Charrington
IPA Ⓗ
Very popular country pub.
Children's play area
⚐Ⓖ🍺 (Sat)

Woodford Bridge 9F5

11–3; 5.30–10.30 (11 F, S)

Crown & Crooked Billet
13 Cross Road (B173)
Draught Bass; Charrington
IPA Ⓗ
Smart, friendly pub,
overlooking pleasant green
QⒼⒼ🍴

North London

N1: Barnsbury 8E7

11–3; 6–11

George IV
60 Copenhagen Street (off
A5203)
Thwaites Best Mild, Bitter Ⓗ
Home from home for
expatriate Lancastrians
⚐Ⓖ (not Sun)

N1: Canonbury 8E7

11–3; 5.30–11

Four Sisters
25 Canonbury Lane (off A1)
Courage Best Bitter,
Directors Ⓗ
One-bar pub with unusual
mural
≹ ⊖ (Highbury & Islington)

Marquess Tavern
32 Canonbury Street (off
A104)
Young Bitter, Special, Winter
Warmer Ⓗ
Large, elegant pub
🍴Ⓖ🍺≹ (Essex Road)

N1: Hoxton 9J1

11–3; 5.30–11

George & Vulture
63 Pitfield Street (off A5201)
Fuller London Pride, ESB Ⓗ
Unspoilt pub on edge of City
Ⓖ (not Sun) 🍴≹ ⊖ (Old St)

Prince Arthur
49 Brunswick Place (off East
Road A1200)
Shepherd Neame Bitter Ⓗ
Friendly, back street local
with East End flavour
≹ ⊖ (Old St)

N1: Islington 8E7

11–3; 5.30–11

Clothworkers Arms
52 Arlington Avenue (off
A1200)
Greene King IPA, Abbot;
Marston Pedigree; Rayment
BBA; Weston Cider
Comfortable back street free
house
Ⓖ (not Sun) ≹ (Essex Road)

Lord Wolseley
55 White Lion Street (near
A501)
Samuel Smith OBB, Museum
Ale Ⓗ
Much enlarged, near Chapel
Market. Good value food
🍲🍴⚐Ⓖ🍺 ⊖ (Angel)

Prince Albert
16 Elia Street
Sat Eves opens 7
Charrington IPA Ⓗ
Unspoilt pub in Georgian
terrace. Bar billiards
🍴 ⊖ (Angel)

N1: Kings Cross 9F1

11–3; 5.30–11

Malt & Hops
33 Caledonian Road (A5203)
Boddingtons Bitter; Everards
Tiger; Felinfoel Double
Dragon; Marston Pedigree;
Paine XXX; Wadworth 6X Ⓗ
Regular guest beers
Noisy, dark and spartan.
Handy for Kings X/St. Pancras
Ⓖ≹ ⊖

N2: East Finchley 8D6

11–3; 5.30–11

Old White Lion
Great North Road (A1000)
Draught Bass, Charrington
IPA Ⓗ
Brewers' Tudor pub. Spacious
but convivial interior
🍲⚐Ⓖ🍴🍺🚃 ⊖

N2: Fortis Green 8D6

Clissold Arms
A504
Courage Best Bitter,
Directors Ⓗ
Traditionally-run suburban
local QⒼ (not Sun) 🍴

N4: Stroud Green 8E6

11–3; 5.30–11

Marlers

29 Crouch Hill (A1201)
House Beers; Marston Border
Mild, Pedigree; Webster
Yorkshire Bitter Ⓗ Regular
guest beers
Converted shop, part of
expanding North London free
house chain ≹ (Crouch Hill)

N6: Highgate 8D6

11–3; 5.30–11

Red Lion & Sun
25 North Road
Draught Bass, Charrington
IPA Ⓗ
Upmarket historic pub in old
London village ⚐Ⓖ ⊖

Victoria
28 North Hill
Brakspear Bitter; Flowers
Original; Greene King Abbot;
Wethered Bitter Ⓗ Occasional
guest beers
Pleasant local, popular with
orchestral musicians QⒼⒼ ⊖

N7: Barnsbury 8E7

11–3; 5.30–11

Railway Tavern
10 Roman Way
Fuller Chiswick Bitter, London
Pride, ESB Ⓗ
Excellent, tiny local Ⓖ
≹ (Caledonian Rd/Barnsbury)

N9: Lower Edmonton 9E5

11–3; 5.30–11

Beehive
Little Bury Street (off A10)
Ind Coope Bitter, Burton Ale Ⓗ
Busy, one-bar locals' pub;
darts area ⚐Ⓖ (not Sun)

N15: Turnpike Lane 8E6

11–3; 5.30–11

Green Gate
492 West Green Road (A504)
Watney Stag Bitter; Webster
Yorkshire Bitter; Ruddle
County Ⓗ
Large single bar but separate
drinking areas. Good
community spirit
Ⓖ (not Sun) ⊖

N16: Stoke Newington 9E6

11–3; 5.30–11

Prince of Wales
59 Kynaston Road (off A10)
Draught Bass, Charrington
IPA Ⓗ
First-rate community local
offering good value. Pool room
upstairs 🍴≹

Rose & Crown
199 Stoke Newington Church
Street (B104)
Truman Bitter, Best Bitter,
Sampson Ⓗ Bulmer Cider Ⓖ
Attractive period interior.
Members-only pool room Ⓖ🍺

N17: Tottenham
9E6

11–3; 5.30–11

Chequers
841 High Road (A1010)
Draught Bass, Charrington IPA H
Plush 1-bar local near Spurs FC ✿ Ꮺ ⇌ (White Hart Lane)

N18: Upper Edmonton
9E5

11–3; 5.30–11

White Horse
103 Fore Street (A1010)
Ruddle County; Watney Combes Bitter; Webster Yorkshire Bitter H
Lively local near shopping area ✿ ᏪᏪ (not Sun) 🍴
⇌ (Silver Street)

N20: Whetstone
8D5

11–3; 5.30–11

Cavalier
67 Russell Lane (off A109)
Courage Best Bitter, Directors H
Spacious, comfortable 2-bar pub with large garden ⛺✿ ᏪᏪ🍴

Griffin
1262 High Road (A1000)
Ind Coope Bitter, Burton Ale H
Smart, imposing wood-panelled pub. Historic Whetstone outside
✿ ᏪᏪ♿ ⊖ (Totteridge)

N21: Winchmore Hill
8E5

11–3; 5.30–11

Dog & Duck
74 Hoppers Road
Wethered Bitter; Samuel Whitbread H **Regular guest beers**
Fine locals pub. ⛺✿ ᏪᏪ♿⇌

Green Dragon
883 Green Lanes (A105)
Courage Best Bitter, Directors H
Well-appointed pub. Garden has children's play area and barbecue Q⛺✿ ᏪᏪ🍴⇌

N22: Wood Green
8E6

11–3; 5.30–11

Starting Gate
Buckingham Road
Ind Coope Bitter, Burton Ale; Taylor Walker Bitter H
Busy, Victorian pub near Alexandra Palace ⇌ ⊖

Barnet
8D5

11–3; 5.30–11

Alexandra
135 Wood Street (A411)
Truman Bitter, Best Bitter, Sampson H

Extrovert landlord hosts live jazz Mon nights. Prizewinning garden Q✿ ᏪᏪ (Mon–Fri)

Olde Monken Holt
193 High Street (A1000)
Courage Best Bitter, Directors H
Fine, wood-panelled pub. Sunday lunches recommended Q✿ ᏪᏪ🍴

Weaver
27 Greenhill Parade (A1000)
Sat eve opens 6.30
Fuller London Pride, ESB; Ruddle County; Webster Yorkshire Bitter H **Regular guest beers**
Tastefully converted intimate, genuine free house
Q ᏪᏪ (Mon–Fri)

Enfield
9E5

11–3; 5.30–11

Crown & Horseshoes
15 Horseshoe Lane (off Chase Side, near A110)
Flowers Original, Wethered Bitter H
In secluded setting off town centre, access by bridge over New River only. No Food Sun
⛺✿ ᏪᏪ🍴⇌ (Enfield Chase)

Old Wheatsheaf
3 Windmill Hill (A110)
Ind Coope Burton Ale; Taylor Walker Bitter H
Attractive, turn of the century pub ✿ ᏪᏪ (not Sun) 🍴
⇌ (Enfield Chase)

Southbury Hotel
253 Southbury Road (A110)
Ind Coope Burton Ale; Taylor Walker Bitter H
Fine brewers' Tudor pub opposite Enfield FC
✿ ᏪᏪ🍴⇌ (Southbury)

New Barnet
8D5

11–3; 5.30–11

Builders Arms
3 Albert Road (off A110)
Greene King IPA, Abbot H
Hard to find and hard to fault
Q✿ ᏪᏪ (not Sun) 🍴⇌

North-west London

NW1 Camden Town
8D7

11–3; 5.30–11

Victoria
2 Mornington Terrace (off A400)
Boddingtons Bitter; Fuller London Pride, ESB; Greene King Abbot; Hall & Woodhouse Badger Best Bitter; Zum Cider H **Regular guest beers**
Enterprising Whitbread "Free House" ✿ ᏪᏪ⇌ (Euston)
⊖ (Mornington Cres)

NW1: Marylebone
8D1

11–3; 5.30–11

Gloucester Arms
5 Ivor Place (off A41)
Taylor Walker Bitter; Ind Coope Burton Ale H
Lively and unspoilt. Near Planetarium and Madame Tussaud ᏪᏪ (not Sun) ⇌
⊖ (Baker St)

NW1: Regents Park
8E1

11–3; 5.30–11

Prince George of Cumberland
195 Albany Street (A4201)
Greene King Abbot; Young Bitter, Special H
Popular free house, impressive exterior. Handy for Regents Park and Zoo ᏪᏪ⇌ (Euston)
⊖ (Gt. Portland St)

NW3: Hampstead
8D6

11–3; 5.30–11

Flask Tavern
14 Flask Walk (off A502)
Young Bitter, Special, Winter Warmer H
A Hampstead institution. Plush lounge, basic bar Ꮺ🍴 ⊖

Holly Bush
Holly Mount (pedestrian access from Heath Street)
Benskins Bitter; Taylor Walker Bitter; Ind Coope Burton Ale H
Old atmospheric pub, partially gas-lit. Can be crowded
⛺Ꮺ ⊖

NW4: Hendon
8D6

11–3; 5.30–11

Greyhound
Church End (off A504)
Brakspear Bitter; Flowers Original; Greene King Abbot; Wethered Bitter; Bulmer Cider H
Hendon's oldest pub, excellent food. Good pub games. Handy for RAF Museum ⛺✿ ᏪᏪ

Midland Hotel
29 Station Road (A504)
Courage Best Bitter, Directors H
Friendly, comfortable pub with games room Ꮺ🍴⇌

NW5: Dartmouth Park
8D6

11–3; 5.30–11

Lord Palmerston
33 Dartmouth Park Hill (off A400)
Courage Best Bitter, Directors H
Lively, popular oasis
✿ ᏪᏪ (Tufnell Park)

NW5: Kentish Town 8E7

11–3; 5.30–11

Duke of Cambridge
64 Lawford Road
**Truman Bitter, Best Bitter,
Sampson** Ⓗ
Good street-corner local
✿≹⊖

NW6: Kilburn 8D7

11–3; 5.30–11

Queen's Arms
1 Kilburn High Road (A5)
**Young Bitter, Special, Winter
Warmer** Ⓗ
Large and friendly, mid-fifties
pub ♨Ⓖ❡≹(Kilburn High Rd)
⊖ (Kilburn Park)

NW7: Mill Hill 8C5

11–3; 5.30–11

Railway Tavern
129 Hale Lane (off A5109)
**Truman Bitter, Best Bitter,
Sampson** Ⓗ
Delightful cottage-style pub.
Railway memorabilia,
children's play-ground
✿Ⓖ≹(Mill Hill Bwy)

Rising Sun
Highwood Hill (A5109)
**Ind Coope Burton Ale; Taylor
Walker Bitter** Ⓗ
Reputedly the oldest pub in
Middlesex and still the wisest
in London Q✿Ⓖ❡❡

NW8: St. John's Wood 8D7

11–3; 5.30–11

Blenheim Arms
21 Loudoun Road (off A41)
**Greene King KK, IPA,
Abbot** Ⓗ
Comfortably furnished
L-shaped bar
✿Ⓖ≹(S Hampstead)
⊖ (Swiss Cottage)

Ordnance Arms
29 Ordnance Hill
**Draught Bass; Charrington
IPA** Ⓗ
Smart lounge bar with
military theme. Beers served
with Northern heads. No food
Sun ✿Ⓖ❡(not Sun) ⊖

Rossetti
23 Queens Grove (off A41)
Fuller London Pride, ESB Ⓗ
Pre-Raphaelite trattoria with
restaurant ✿Ⓖ❡⊖

NW9: Kingsbury 8C6

11–3; 5.30–11

George
234 Church Lane (B454)
**Friary Meux Bitter; Ind Coope
Burton Ale; Taylor Walker
Bitter** Ⓗ
Lively mock-Tudor oasis in
pub desert ✿Ⓖ(not Sun)

NW10: Harlesden 8C7

11–3; 5.30–11

Grand Junction Arms
Acton Lane (at canal bridge),
B4492)
**Young Bitter, Special, Winter
Warmer** Ⓗ
Four-bar canal-side pub caters
for all tastes. Garden (children
welcome) ✿Ⓖ❡≹

Harefield 8A6

11–3; 5.30–11

Plough
Hill End Road ☏ 2129
**Chiltern Beechwood; Ruddle
Bitter, County; Wadworth 6X;
Younger No. 3** Ⓗ
Friendly pub behind famous
transplant hospital ♨✿Ⓖ

Harrow 8C6

11–3; 5.30–11

Kingsfield Arms
111 Bessborough Road
(A312)
**Courage Best Bitter,
Directors** Ⓗ
Comfortable pub ✿
Ⓖ (Mon–Fri) ⊖ (Harrow/Hill)

Harrow Weald 8C6

10.30–2.30; 5.30–11

Seven Balls
749 Kenton Lane (off A410)
Benskins Bitter Ⓗ
Almost a country pub.
Award-winning garden
Q✿Ⓖ❡

Pinner 8B6

11–3; 5.30–11

Oddfellows Arms
2 Waxwell Lane
(off A404)
**Benskins Bitter; Ind Coope
Burton Ale** Ⓗ
Cosy, popular 1-bar pub
✿Ⓖ⊖

Sudbury Hill 8C6

11–3; 5.30–11

Black Horse
1018 Harrow Road (A4005)
☏ 01-904 1013
**Benskins Bitter; Ind Coope
Burton Ale; Taylor Walker
Bitter** Ⓗ
Old, friendly pub
Q❖✿Ⓖ❡≹⊖

Wealdstone 8C6

11–3; 5.30–11

Royal Oak
60 Peel Road (off A409)
☏ 01-427 3122
Sat eves opens 7
**Benskins Bitter; Ind Coope
Burton Ale; Taylor Walker
Bitter** Ⓗ
Large friendly pub, no-frills
public bar ✿Ⓖ❡≹

Wembley 8C6

11–3; 5.30–11

Norfolk Arms
96 Llanover Road (off A4088)
**Truman Bitter, Best Bitter;
Webster Yorkshire Bitter** Ⓗ
Large side-street pub. Games
room, comfortable saloon,
basic public
✿Ⓖ❡≹(N. Wembley)

South-east
London

SE1: Bermondsey 9J3

11–3; 5.30–11

Copper
208 Tower Bridge Road
(A100)
**Courage Best Bitter,
Directors** Ⓗ
Popular pub with tourists to
Tower Bridge. Regular live
theatre in cellar bar
Ⓖ❡(weekends) ≹
⊖ (London Bridge)

Leather Exchange
15 Leathermarket Street (off
A2198)
Sat & Sun eves opens 7.30
**Fuller Chiswick Bitter, London
Pride, ESB** Ⓗ
Old photos of the leather
industry. Singalong quartet
Thu–Sun Ⓖ (Mon–Fri) ≹
⊖ (London Bridge)

SE1: Southwark 9J3

11–3; 5.30–11

Bunch of Grapes
2 St. Thomas Street (A200)
☏ 01-403 2070
Closed Sat & Sun
**Brakspear Bitter; Young
Bitter** Ⓗ
Excellent range of wines.
Upstairs restaurant/bar
✿Ⓖ❡♿⊖ (London Bridge)

Founders Arms
52 Hopton Street (behind flats
on riverside, off A3200)
**Young Bitter, Special, Winter
Warmer** Ⓗ
Normally crowded; splendid
river view. Restaurant
Q✿Ⓖ❡≹⊖ (Blackfriars)

George
77 Borough High Street (A3)
**Flowers Original; Greene King Abbot;
Wethered Bitter** Ⓗ **Regular
guest beers**
Last galleried coaching inn in
London. Full of atmosphere,
always popular, a must on
summer evenings. Restaurant
Q✿Ⓖ❡≹⊖ (London Bridge)

SE1: Waterloo 9G3

11–3; 5.30–11 (Sun 12–2; 7.30–10.30)

Hole in the Wall
5 Mepham Street (off A3200)

Adnams Bitter; Brakspear
Special; Chudley Local Line;
King & Barnes Sussex Bitter;
Young Bitter, Special H
Occasional guest beers
Hidden away under railway
arches. Good food any time, so
forget the station burgers!
⛬🍴🍺⊖

SE3: Blackheath 9F8

11–3; 5.30–11

British Oak
109 Old Dover Road (off
A207)
Courage Best Bitter,
Directors H
Large, popular, unpretentious
two-bar pub 🌿🍴

SE3: Lee Green 9F8

Bitter Experience
(Off Licence)
129 Lee Road (off A205)
Mon–Fri 12–10; Sat 10–2 &
4–10; Sun 12–2 & 7–9
Fuller London Pride, ESB;
Greene King Abbot; King &
Barnes Festive G Regular
guest beers
🍺 (Lee)

SE5: 8E8
Camberwell

11–3; 5.30–11

Grove House Tavern
26 Camberwell Grove (off
A202)
Sat eves opens 7
Friary Meux Best Bitter; Ind
Coope Burton Ale; Taylor
Walker Bitter H
Very busy local. Large,
comfortable lounge, small
public bar, patio garden
Q🌿🍴🍺 (Denmark Hill)

Station Tavern
18 John Ruskin Street (off
A215)
Sat eves opens 7
Charrington IPA H
Unspoilt 3-bar haven just off
Walworth Road) 🏠🍴

SE7: Charlton 9F7

11–3; 5.30–11

Anchor & Hope
2 Riverside, Anchor & Hope
Lane (off A206)
Charrington IPA H
Basic riverside pub; views of
Thames Barrier from terrace
🌿🍺

SE9: Eltham 9G8

11–3; 5.30–11

Farmhouse
52 Jason Walk (near A208)
Ind Coope Burton; Taylor
Walker Bitter H
Comfortable estate pub caters
for community. Barbecues in
spacious garden. Very friendly
🌿🍴⛬

White Hart
2 Eltham High Street
Courage Best Bitter,
Directors H
Near Eltham Palace. Darts in
conservatory; very convivial
Q🏠🌿⛬ (not Sun) 🍺

SE10: 9F8
Greenwich

11–3; 5.30–11

Coach & Horses
13 Greenwich Market (A206)
☎ 01-858 2882
Benskins Bitter; Friary Meux
Best Bitter; Ind Coope Burton
Ale; Taylor Walker Bitter H
Traditional pub in busy
Greenwich Market (Sat/Sun).
Trad jazz Thur and Sun lunch,
other live groups Wed
🌿 (covered) ⛬🍸 (Mon–Thu)
⛬🍺

Cricketers
22 King William Walk
Sat eves opens 6.30
Charrington IPA H
Small, friendly two-bar house,
near Greenwich Market (Sat/
Sun) when pub is very busy
⛬ (Mon–Fri) 🍺

Richard I
52 Royal Hill (off A206)
☎ 01-692 2996
Young Bitter, Special, Winter
Warmer H
Very popular, good
conversational, two-bar pub.
Long established licensees
Q🌿⛬ ((Mon–Fri)
🍸 (Tue–Thu) 🍺

Royal George
2 Blissett Street (off A2211)
Shepherd Neame Bitter H
Warm, welcoming pub. Near
fire station ⛬🍺

SE12: Lee 9F8

11–3; 5.30–11

Summerfield Tavern
60 Baring Road (A2212)
Courage Best Bitter,
Directors H
Busy family local; private bar
🍴🍺 (Grove Park)

SE13: Ladywell 9F8

11–3; 5.30–11

Ladywell Tavern
80 Ladywell Road (off A21)
Charrington IPA, Draught
Bass H
Very pleasant pub with
reasonable prices, darts, shove
ha'penny; splendid old photos
of Ladywell ⛬🍴⛬🍺

SE13: 9F8
Lewisham

11–3; 5.30–11

Duke of Cambridge
32 Lewisham High Street

Ind Coope Bitter, Burton Ale;
Taylor Walker Bitter H
Corner pub, no frills but
handy for bus, rail and
shopping centre. Food basic
but excellent value. Darts
Q⛬🍺

Royal Oak
1 Lee Church Street (off A20)
Courage Best Bitter,
Directors H
300 year-old coaching inn—
hidden away 🌿

SE15: Peckham 9E8

11–4; 5.30–12 (Sun 12–3; 7–11.30)

Montpelier
43 Choumert Road (off
A2215) ☎ 01-639 1736
Ruddle County; Watney
Combes Bitter; Webster
Yorkshire Bitter H
Good lunchtime venue. Live
music Wed, Fri and Sat eves,
disco Thu
🌿⛬🍴⛬🍺 (Peckham Rye)

SE16: 9E7
Bermondsey

11–3; 5.30 (7.30 Sat)–11

Old Justice
94 Bermondsey Wall E (off
A200)
Charrington IPA H
Isolated but worth searching
out. Traditional panelled
interior. Good river views
🌿⛬ (Mon–Fri) 🍴
⊖ (Rotherhithe)

SE16: 9E7
Rotherhithe

11–3; 5.30–11

Blacksmiths Arms
257 Rotherhithe Street
(off B205) OS365805
Fuller Chiswick Bitter, London
Pride, ESB H
Large, friendly pub off the
beaten track, games room.
Seafood a specialty for Sun
lunch. Restaurant
⛬ (Mon–Fri) 🍸

Mayflower
117 Rotherhithe Street
☎ 01-237 4088
Charrington IPA, Draught
Bass H
Historic 17th century inn
overlooking River Thames.
Restaurant 🌿 (jetty) ⛬🍴🍸⊖

Ship
39 St Marychurch Street (off
A200) ☎ 01-237 4103
Young Bitter, Special, Winter
Warmer H
Friendly backstreet pub.
Modern but comfortable
🏠🌿⛬🍸⊖

SE18: Plumstead
Common 9G8

11–3; 5.30–11

Who'd A Thought It

7 Timbercroft Lane
Truman Bitter, Best Bitter, Sampson 🄷
Comfortable spacious, one-bar pub, ornately decorated ℘↻

SE18: Shooters Hill 9F8

11–3; 5.30–11

Red Lion
6 Red Lion Place (A207)
Courage Best Bitter, Directors 🄷
Comfortable L-shaped pub, once the haunt of highwaymen ℘

SE18: Woolwich 9G7

11–3; 5.30–11

Earl of Chatham
15 Thomas Street
Ruddle County; Watney Combes Bitter; Webster Yorkshire Bitter 🄷 **Occasional guest beers**
Decorative town centre pub, popular garden ℘≷ (Arsenal)

Princess of Wales (Little Bull)
18 Wilmount Street
Wethered Bitter 🄷
Genuine friendly cosy local, close to town centre
♜℘🍺≷ (Arsenal)

SE19: Upper Norwood 9E8

11–3; 5.30–11

Royal Albert
42 Westow Hill (A214)
Draught Bass; Charrington IPA 🄷
Comfortable saloon near National Recreation Centre and Park
↻🍺▲≷ (Crystal Palace)

White Swan
79 Westow Hill (A214)
Draught Bass; Charrington IPA 🄷
Victorian one-bar pub
℘↻▲≷ (Crystal Palace)

SE20: Anerley 9E9

10.30–2.30; 5.30–10.30 (11 F, S)

Anerley Arms
2 Ridsdale Road (off A214)
✆ 01-659 5552
Samuel Smith OBB, Museum Ale 🄷
Excellent backstreet local. Bar billiards ℘↻●≷

SE20: Penge 9E9

10.30–2.30; 5.30–10.30 (11 F, S)

Golden Lion
61 Maple Road (off A214)
✆ 01-778 3951
Draught Bass; Fuller London Pride, ESB; Harvey Best Bitter; Young Bitter, Special 🄷
Regular guest beers
Busy, popular freehouse. Toad in the Hole game
℘↻●≷ (Anerley)

SE22: East Dulwich 9E8

11–3; 5.30–11

Clockhouse
196A Peckham Rye (off A2214)
Young Bitter, Special, Winter Warmer 🄷
Comfortable pub, clock theme. Overlooks the Rye
Q℘↻ (not Sun)

Grove Tavern
522 Lordship Lane (A205/A2216)
Courage Best Bitter, Directors; John Smith's Bitter; Young Special 🄷
Large pub includes steak house with good family facilities ♜℘↻●

SE23: Forest Hill 9E8

11–3; 5.30–11

Railway Telegraph
112 Stanstead Road (A205)
Shepherd Neame Mild, Bitter, Stock Ale 🄷
Unassuming local on South Circular Road ℘↻🍺≷

SE24: Herne Hill 8E8

11–3; 5.30–11

Commercial
210 Railton Road (off A2214)
Draught Bass; Charrington IPA 🄷
Spacious local. Rugby mementoes in comfortable wood-panelled lounge 🍺≷

SE25: South Norwood 9E9

11–3; 5.30–11

Albert Tavern
65 Harrington Road (off A215)
Courage Best Bitter, Directors; Young Special 🄷
Modern pub where friends meet friends and strangers make friends
℘↻🍺≷ (Norwood Jcn)

Goat House
2 Penge Road (A213)
Fuller Chiswick Bitter, London Pride, ESB 🄷
Large, busy 3-bar local at Railway Bridge
Q℘↻🍺≷ (Norwood Jcn)

SE25: Woodside 9E9

11–3; 5.30–11

Beehive
47 Woodside Green (off A215)
Charrington IPA; Fuller ESB (winter)
Good value local; comfortable lounge; basic public with darts. Always busy Q℘↻🍺≷

SE26: Sydenham 9E8

11–3; 5.30–11

Dolphin
121 Sydenham Road (A212)
Courage Best Bitter, Directors; John Smith's Bitter; Young Special
Garden and childrens' playroom create family atmosphere in this Tudor-style pub ⊞℘↻≷

Dulwich Wood House
39 Sydenham Hill (off A205)
Young Bitter, Special, Winter Warmer 🄷 & 🄴
Very popular pub; large garden bar, boules team and children's play area
♜℘↻●🍺▲≷ (Sydenham Hill)

Albany Park 9G8

10.30–2.30; 6–11

Albany
13 Steynton Avenue, (A222)
Courage Best Bitter, Directors 🄷
Large inter-war roadhouse by station ℘↻ (not Sun) 🍺≷

Beckenham 9F9

10.30–2.30; 5.30–10.30 (11 F, S)

Coach & Horses
Burnhill Road (off A222)
Courage Best Bitter, Directors 🄷
Popular local off high street
℘↻≷ (Beckenham Jct)

Jolly Woodman
Chancery Lane (off A222)
✆ 01-650 3664
Draught Bass; Charrington IPA 🄷
Small traditional local, live music Sun eves
♜Q℘↻●≷ (Beckenham Jct)

Belvedere 9G7

10.30–2.30; 6–11

Victoria
2 Victoria Street (near A206)
Draught Bass; Charrington IPA 🄷
Top quality back street local—a warm welcome for all
℘↻ (Mon–Fri)

Bexley 9G8

10.30–2.30; 6–11

Black Horse
Albert Road (off A223)
Courage Best Bitter, Directors 🄷
Lively back street local. Entertainment Thu eve ℘↻≷

Bexleyheath 9G8

10–2.30; 6–11

Royal Oak (Polly Clean Stairs)
Mount Road/Alers Road (near A221)
Opens 11

Courage Best Bitter,
Directors ℍ
Delightful weatherboarded
local with rural atmosphere.
Darts Q ✿ ⏁ (Mon–Fri)

Volunteer
46 Church Road (off A207)
**Truman Bitter, Best Bitter;
Webster Yorkshire Bitter** ℍ
Quiet cosy back street pub;
darts Q ✿ ⏁ (not weekends) ⇌

Blackfen 9G8

10.30–2.30; 6–11

Jolly Fenman
64 Blackfen Road (A210)
℡ 01-850 6664
**Blackfen Bitter; Fenman
Fortune** ℍ **Occasional guest
beers**
Spacious attractive home
brew pub. Brewery visits can
be arranged for parties (up
to 8) Q ▤ ✿ ⏁ ◕ ▮ ⅓

Bromley 9F9

10.30–2.30; 5.30–10.30 (11 F, S)

Palace Tavern
1 Napier Road (off A21)
**Flowers Original; Wethered
Bitter** ℍ
Backstreet local, nautical
theme. Hard to find
✿ ⏁ ⇌ (Bromley S)

Bricklayers Arms
143 Masons Hill (A21)
Shepherd Neame Bitter ℍ
Refurbished street corner local
Q ⏁ ⇌ (Bromley S)

Freelands Tavern
31 Freelands Road
(off A222)
**Courage Best Bitter,
Directors** ℍ
Friendly suburban local
✿ ⏁ ⇌ (Bromley N)

Chislehurst 9G9

10.30–2.30; 5.30–10.30 (11 F, S)

Imperial Arms
1 Old Hill (off A222)
**Courage Best Bitter,
Directors** ℍ
Excellent hillside local ✿ ⏁ ⇌

Queens Head
High Street (A208)
**Benskins Bitter; Friary Meux
Bitter; Ind Coope Burton Ale;
Taylor Walker Bitter** ℍ
Friendly pub. Attractive
forecourt drinking area, next
to village pond ✿ ⏁ (not Sun)

Crayford 9H8

10.30–2.30; 6–11

White Swan
143 Crayford Road
(A207)
**Felinfoel Double Dragon;
Fuller London Pride, ESB;** ℍ
Westons Cider ⅊ & ℍ
Modern Swiss chalet-style pub
near Crayford Stadium ✿ ⏁ ⇌

Croydon 8E9

11–3; 5.30–11

Dog & Bull
24 Surrey Street (off A235)
**Young Bitter, Special, Winter
Warmer** ℍ
No frills ale house serving
street market
▮ ⇌ (E/W Croydon)

Eagle
Reeves Corner (off A235/
A236)
Sat eves opens 6.15
**Flowers Original; Greene King
Abbot; Wethered Bitter** ℍ
Distinctive lounge with
well-equipped games bar
⅓ ⇌ (E/W Croydon)

Golden Lion
144 Stanley Road (near
A23/A236)
**Courage Best Bitter,
Directors** ℍ
Thriving corner local; strong
darts following ✿ ▮

Lion
182 Pawsons Road (off A212)
Sat eves opens 7
**Adnams Bitter; Everard Tiger;
King & Barnes Sussex Bitter,
Festive; Godsons Black Horse;
Ward Sheffield Best Bitter** ℍ
Occasional guest beers
Free house with darts, juke
box, pin table and dog ⏁

Royal Standard
1 Sheldon Street (off A235)
℡ 01-688 9749
Sat eves opens 6.30
Fuller London Pride, ESB ℍ
Tiny, busy 2-bar pub, dwarfed
by fly-over (A232) and multi-
storey car-park. No food Sun
Q ✿ ⏁ ◕ ▮ ⇌ (E/W Croydon)

Two Brewers
221 Gloucester Road
(off A213)
Evenings opens 6
Shepherd Neame Bitter ℍ
Lively back street local near
Crystal Palace FC
✿ ⏁ ▮ ⇌ (Selhurst)

Downe 9F9

10.30–2.30; 5.30–10.30 (11 F, S)

George & Dragon
High Street
**Draught Bass; Charrington
IPA** ℍ
The natural selection—
Charles Darwin lived nearby
▨ Q ✿ ⏁ ◕

Foots Cray 9G8

10–2.30; 6–11

Seven Stars
40 Foots Cray High Street
(A211)
**Draught Bass; Charrington
IPA** ℍ **Occasional guest beers**
Historic 16th century local,
excellent value ✿ ⏁ ▮

St Mary Cray 9G9

10.30–2.30; 5.30–10.30 (11 F, S)

Beech Tree
75 Wellington Road
(off A223)
Wethered Bitter ℍ
Friendly backstreet local ✿

South Croydon 8E9

11–3; 5.30–11

Windsor Castle Hotel
415 Brighton Road (A235)
℡ 01-680 4559
Charrington IPA ℍ
Historic pub with hotel
extension. Noisy public,
comfortable lounge
▤ ⏁ ◕ ▮ ⅓ ⇌ (Purley Oaks)

South-west London

SW1: Belgravia 8D4

11–3; 5.30–11

Antelope
22 Eaton Terrace (off A3217)
℡ 01-730 7781
Sat eves opens 7
**Benskins Bitter; Ind Coope
Burton Ale** ℍ
Unspoilt haven in select
residential area, upstairs
food/wine bar. No food Sun
Q ⏁ ◕ (not Sat) ⊖ (Sloane Sq)

Star Tavern
6 Belgrave Mews West
**Fuller Chiswick Bitter, London
Pride, ESB** ℍ
Busy, unspoilt mews pub,
2 real fires
▨ Q ⏁ ⊖ (Hyde Pk Cnr)

SW1: St James's 9E3

11–3; 5.30–11

Red Lion
23 Crown Passage (off Pall
Mall)
Closed Sundays
**Ruddle County; Watney
Combes Bitter; Webster
Yorkshire Bitter** ℍ
Tiny pub in passageway,
home-cooked food
⏁ ⊖ (Green Park)

Red Lion
2 Duke of York Street
Closed Sundays
**Ind Coope Burton Ale; Taylor
Walker Bitter** ℍ
Magnificent small Victorian
Gin Palace. Engraved glass
mirrors, mahogany island bar
⏁ ⊖ (Piccadilly)

SW1: Sloane Square 8D4

11–3; 5.30–11

Fox & Hounds
29 Passmore Street

Draught Bass; Charrington
IPA Ⓗ
Small, cosy local; no spirits,
pub games Q ⊖

SW1: Trafalgar   9F3
Square

11–3; 5.30–11

Old Shades
37 Whitehall
Draught Bass; Charrington
IPA Ⓗ
Wood-panelled long bar opens
into cosy lounge, unspoilt by
tourism ⚲Ⓖ (not Sun) ≥
⊖ (Charing X)

SW1:   9F4
Westminster

11–3; 5.30–11

Barley Mow
104 Horseferry Road
✆ 01-222 2330
Watney Combes Bitter;
Webster Yorkshire Bitter Ⓗ
Large, comfortable pub. Fine
collection of Hogarth
drawings, grand piano and
restaurant Ⓖ♥ (Mon–Fri) ♿
⊖ (St. James's Park)

Buckingham Arms
62 Petty France
✆ 01-222 3386
Young Bitter, Special, Winter
Warmer Ⓗ
Well-run, long-mirrored,
L-shaped pub, near Passport
Office Ⓖ♥≥ (Victoria)
⊖ (St. James's Park)

Morpeth Arms
58 Millbank (off A202)
✆ 01-834 6442
Young Bitter, Special, Winter
Warmer Ⓗ
Comfortable pub with small
snug facing river, near Tate
Gallery QⒼ♥ ⊖ (Pimlico)

Red Lion
48 Parliament Street
✆ 01-930 5826
Benskins Bitter; Ind Coope
Burton Ale; Taylor Walker
Bitter Ⓗ
Ornate pub near Parliament
Division Bell and electronic
information panel. Cellar bar,
upstairs restaurant Ⓖ♥ ⊖

SW2: Tulse Hill   8E8

11–3; 5.30–11

Two Woodcocks
45 Tulse Hill (A204)
Battersea Nine Elms Mild,
Brixton Best, Warrior Ⓗ
Basic but friendly and
comfortable single bar
Ⓖ (Mon–Fri)

SW3: Chelsea   8C4

11–3; 5.30–11

Princess of Wales
145 Dovehouse Street
Courage Best Bitter,
Directors Ⓗ

Small pub tucked behind
Royal Marsden Hospital
Q♥Ⓖ (Mon–Fri) ⊖ (S. Ken)

Surprise
6 Christchurch Terrace
Draught Bass; Charrington
IPA Ⓗ
Genuine local with interesting
frieze; games QⓌ (Mon–Sat)

SW4: Clapham   8E8

11–3; 5.30–11

Railway Tavern
18 Clapham High Street
✆ 01-627 1696
Draught Bass; Charrington
IPA Ⓗ
Large one-bar pub, popular
with young. Folk club
Ⓖ♥ (not Sun) ≥
⊖ (Clapham N)

SW5: Earls   8B4
Court

11–3; 5.30–11

Drayton Arms
153 Old Brompton Road
(A3218) ✆ 01-373 4089
Draught Bass; Charrington
IPA Ⓗ
Decorative, cosmopolitan pub
away from bustle of Earls
Court
♥Ⓖ♥ ⊖ (Gloucester Rd)

SW6: Fulham   8D8

11–3; 5.30–11

Jolly Brewer
308 North End Road
Ruddle County; Webster
Yorkshire Bitter Ⓗ
Busy street market local;
plenty of atmosphere
Ⓖ🍴♿ ⊖ (Fulham Bwy)

SW6: Parsons   8D8
Green

11–3; 5.30–11

White Horse
1 Parsons Green (off A308)
✆ 01-736 2115
Draught Bass; Charrington
IPA; M & B Highgate Dark,
Springfield Bitter Ⓗ
Large, popular upmarket pub
facing green ♥Ⓖ♥ ⊖

SW6: West   8B4
Brompton

11–3; 5.30–11

Atlas
16 Seagrave Road (off A3218)
Truman Best Bitter; Webster
Yorkshire Bitter Ⓗ
Popular local in side street
near Earls Court exhibition
site ⚲♥Ⓖ🍴 ⊖

SW7: South   8C4
Kensington

11–3; 5.30–11

Anglesea Arms

15 Selwood Terrace
(off A308) ✆ 01-373 1207
Adnams Bitter; Boddingtons
Bitter; Brakspear Special;
Fuller London Pride; Greene
King Abbot; Young Special Ⓗ
Well known, comfortable and
popular free house ♥Ⓖ♥ ⊖

SW8: South   8E8
Lambeth

11–3; 5.30–11

Surprise
16 Southville (off
Wandsworth Road, A3036)
Young Bitter, Special, Winter
Warmer Ⓗ
Surprise not only by name.
Worth the effort to find
⚲Q♥≥ (Wandsworth Rd)

SW9: Brixton   8E8

11–3; 5.30–11

Warrior
242 Coldharbour Lane
(A2217)
Brixton Bitter, Best, Warrior Ⓗ
Large, basic locals' pub selling
own good value beer
♿≥ (Loughborough Jct)

SW9: Stockwell   8E8

11–3; 5.30–11

Landor
70 Landor Road
(off A3/A203)
Truman Bitter, Best Bitter,
Sampson; Webster Yorkshire
Bitter Ⓗ
Games oriented one-bar pub
♥≥ (Clapham)
⊖ (Clapham N)

SW10: West   8D8
Chelsea

11–3; 5.30–11

Chelsea Ram
22 Burnaby Street
(off A3212)
Young Bitter, Special, Winter
Warmer Ⓗ
Comfortable local, built 100
years ago but not licensed
until 1984 QⓌ (not Sun) ♿

**Ferret & Firkin in the
Balloon up the Creek**
114 Lots Road (off A3212)
Webster Yorkshire Bitter;
Young Special Ⓗ Regular
guest beers
Popular Bruces home-brew
pub, music nightly. House
beers under blanket of CO_2
Ⓖ (Mon–Sat)

SW11:   8D8
Battersea

11–3; 5.30–11

Anchor (Charlies)
61 Holgate Avenue (off
Plough Road, off A3205)
Webster Yorkshire Bitter Ⓗ
Never a dull moment, always
a friendly welcome
Ⓖ🍴≥ (Clapham Jct)

Duke of Cambridge
228 Battersea Bridge Road
(A3220)
Young Bitter, Special Bitter,
Winter Warmer ⊞
Large, friendly corner pub
with public bar prices Q ⅏ 🍴

Prince of Wales
339 Battersea Park Road
(A3205)
Battersea Nine Elms Mild,
Bitter, Best Bitter,
Powerhouse ⊞
Large single gas-lit bar leads
to own brewery. Live music
Wed, Thu, Sun eves and
lunch ✿ ⅏ (Mon–Fri)
⇄ (Battersea Park)

SW11: Clapham 8D8
Junction

11–3; 5.30–11

Beehive
197 St. Johns Hill (A3036)
Fuller Chiswick Bitter, London
Pride, ESB ⊞
Almost a country pub in
town. Excellent atmosphere
⅏⇄

SW12: Balham   8D8

11–3; 5.30 (7 Sat)–11

Duke of Devonshire
39 Balham High Road (A24)
Young Bitter, Special, Winter
Warmer ⊞
Superb pub, one of the best.
Magnificent glazing and
woodwork. No food Sun
Q ✿ ⅏ 🍴 (not Sat) 🍴🍴 ⊖

SW13: Barnes   8D8

11–3; 5.30–11

Coach & Horses
27 Barnes High Street
Young Bitter, Special, Winter
Warmer ⊞
Small, popular local near river
🏠 Q ✿ ⇄ (Barnes Bridge)

Red Lion
2 Castelnau (A306)
✆ 01-748 2984
Fuller Chiswick Bitter, London
Pride, ESB ⊞
Large pub, imaginative
selection of food ✿ ⅏ 🍴🍴

SW15: Putney   8D8

11–3; 5.30–11

Arab Boy
289 Upper Richmond Road
(A205) ✆ 01-788 3586
Ruddle County; Webster
Yorkshire Bitter ⊞
Busy locals' pub. Darts. No
food Sun ✿ ⅏ 🍴 (not Sat) ⇄

Fox & Hounds
167 Upper Richmond Road
(A205)
Sat eves opens 7
Flowers Original; Wethered
Bitter; Whitbread Castle Eden,
Samuel Whitbread ⊞ Regular
guest beers

Fine 1-bar pub, vaulted
ceiling. Good selection of
games
✿ ⅏ (Mon–Fri) ⇄ ⊖ (E Putney)

White Lion
14 Putney High Street (A219)
✆ 01-785 3081
Arkell Kingsdown Ale;
Brakspear Old; Darley Thorne
Best Bitter; Vaux Samson;
Ward Sheffield Best Bitter ⊞
Regular guest beers
Comfortable 5-storey relic;
can be busy late evenings. No
food Sun ⅏ (Not Sat) 🍴
⇄ ⊖ (Putney Bridge)

SW18:   8D8
Wandsworth

11–3; 5.30–11

Grapes
39 Fairfield Street (off A3/
A205)
Sat eves opens 7
Young Bitter, Special, Winter
Warmer ⊞
Superb local near brewery
✿ ⅏ ⇄ (Wandsworth Town)

Ship
41 Jews Row (off A217)
Sat eves opens 6
Young Bitter, Special, Winter
Warmer ⊞
Bustling pub with two bars
and restaurant in sailing
barge 🏠 ✿ ⅏ (not Sun) 🍴🍴 &
⇄ (Wandsworth Town)

SW19: Merton   8D9

11–3; 5.30–11

Prince of Wales
98 Morden Road (A24)
Young Bitter, Special, Winter
Warmer ⊞
Busy, friendly local
✿ ⅏ 🍴 ⊖ (S. Wimbledon)

Princess Royal
25 Abbey Road (off A24)
Opens late Sat evenings
Courage Best Bitter,
Directors ⊞
Small, smart corner pub,
family atmosphere. Good
value ✿ ⅏ (Not Sun) 🍴
⊖ (S Wimbledon)

SW19:   8D8
Wimbledon

11–3; 5.30–11

Brewery Tap
68 High Street (A219)
Flowers Original; Wethered
Bitter, Winter Royal;
Whitbread Castle Eden ⊞
Unspoilt pub in middle of
village. Darts Q ⅏ (Mon–Fri) 🍴

Hand In Hand
7 Crooked Billet (near
Wimbledon Common, on
B281) ✆ 01-946 5720
Ruddle Best Bitter; Young
Bitter, Special, Winter
Warmer ⊞

Caters for all the family.
Packed summer weekends
🏠 Q ⊞ ✿ ⅏ 🍴 (Mon–Fri) &

King of Denmark
85 The Ridgway
(off A219)
Opens 11.30 Mon–Sat, 7 Sat
eves
Courage Best Bitter,
Directors ⊞
One-bar pub with growing
reputation ✿ ⅏ (Mon–Fri)

Beddington   8E9

10.30–2.30; 5.30–10.30 (11 F, S)

Plough
Croydon Road (A232/B272)
Young Bitter, Special ⊞
Large, comfortable saloon,
lively atmosphere
Q ✿ (stable yard) ⅏ 🍴 &

Carshalton   8D9

10.30–2.30; 5.30–10.30 (11 F, S)

Greyhound
2 High Street
Young Bitter, Special, Winter
Warmer
Fine old pub in picturesque
setting. Meeting place of Eddie
Grundy Fan Club 🏠 ✿ ⊞ ⅏ 🍴 ⇄

Cheam   8D9

10.30–2.30; 5.30–10.30 (11 F, S)

Bell
Ewell Road (A232)
Draught Bass; Charrington
IPA ⊞
Busy two-bar pub with
games. Close to Nonsuch Park
✿ ⅏

Prince of Wales
28 Malden Road (A2043)
Friary Meux Bitter; Ind Coope
Burton Ale ⊞
Spotless, friendly two-bar local
Q ✿ ⇄

Chessington   8C9

10.30–2.30; 5.30–11

North Star
271 Hook Road (A243)
Draught Bass; Charrington
IPA; M & B Highgate Mild ⊞
Popular and friendly,
traditional pub games. Good
lunchtime food
⊞ ✿ ⅏ (Mon–Fri)

Kingston   8C9

10.30–2.30; 5.30–11

Bricklayers Arms
53 Hawks Road
(off A2043)
Courage Best Bitter,
Directors ⊞
Two cosy bars of separate
characters Q ✿ ⅏ 🍴

Druids Head
3 Market Place
Flowers Original; Wethered
Bitter, ⊞, Winter Royal Ⓖ
A true market pub ⅏ 🍴 ⇄

Wych Elm
93 Elm Road
Fuller Chiswick Bitter, London Pride, ESB Ⓗ
Pleasant and welcoming
Q🍴🄲ⓖ🄵🍺≉

New Malden 8C9

10.30–2.30; 5.30–11
Prince of Wales
279 Kingston Road (A2043)
Truman Best Bitter, Sampson; Webster Yorkshire Bitter Ⓗ
Often busy local with quick friendly service 🍴ⓖ

Richmond 8C8

11–3; 5.30–11
Angel & Crown
5 Church Court
☎ 01-940 1568
Fuller London Pride, ESB Ⓗ
Popular pub in one of town's delightful lanes. No food Sun
ⓖ🍴≉🍺

Orange Tree
45 Kew Road (A307)
☎ 01-940 0944
Young Bitter, Special, Winter Warmer Ⓗ
Spacious, traditional pub in Victorian building with theatre and restaurant. Good food
🏠Q🍴ⓖ🍴 (not Sun)🄳≉⊖

White Cross Hotel
Water Lane ☎ 01-940 0909
Young Bitter, Special, Winter Warmer Ⓗ
Attractive riverside pub of character. Good bar food and restaurant
🏠Q🄴🍴ⓖ🍴 (not Sun)

Surbiton 8C9

10.30–2.30; 5.30–11
Black Lion
58 Brighton Road (A243)
Young Bitter, Special Ⓗ
Large 2-bar pub at crossroads
🍴ⓖ≉

Waggon & Horses
1 Surbiton Hill Road (A240)
Young Bitter, Special, Winter Warmer Ⓗ
Popular pub noted for charity collections ⓖ🄲≉

Sutton 8D9

10.30–2.30; 5.30–10.30 (11 F, S)
Green Man
37 High Street (off A232)
Draught Bass; Charrington IPA Ⓗ
Large, split-level popular pub; darts 🍴ⓖ≉

Windsor Castle
13 Greyhound Road
(off A232)
Fuller London Pride, ESB Ⓗ
Comfortable, popular 1-bar pub Qⓖ🍴≉

West London

W1: Fitzrovia 9F2

11–3; 5.30–11
Bricklayers Arms
31 Gresse Street
Samuel Smith OBB, Museum Ale Ⓗ
Pleasant pub, upstairs bar
ⓖ ⊖ (Tottenham Ct Rd)

George & Dragon
151 Cleveland Street
Draught Bass; Charrington IPA Ⓗ
Small, corner one-bar local
Qⓖ ⊖ (Warren St)

W1: 8C2 Marylebone

11–3; 5.30–11
Beehive
7 Homer Street (off A4209)
Flowers Original; Wethered Bitter Ⓗ
Small, cosy side-street pub
Qⓖ≉ ⊖ (Edgware Rd)

Devonshire Arms
21A Devonshire Street
Friary Meux Bitter; Ind Coope Burton Ale Ⓗ
Friendly local with tiles and mirrors ⓖ ⊖ (Regents Park)

Duke of Wellington
94A Crawford Street
Draught Bass; Charrington IPA Ⓗ
Small pub, Wellington memorabilia ≉ ⊖

W1: Mayfair 8E2

11–3; 5.30–11 (closed Sun)
Guinea
30 Bruton Place
☎ 01-629 5971
Young Bitter, Special Ⓗ
Small mews pub/restaurant
ⓖ🍴 ⊖ (Green Park)

Red Lion
1 Waverton Street
☎ 01-629 1738
Ruddle County; Watney Combes Bitter; Webster Yorkshire Bitter Ⓗ
Historic pub in quiet street near Berkeley Square.
Restaurant, Mayfair prices
Q🍴ⓖ🍴 ⊖ (Green Park)

W1: Soho 9F2

11–3; 5.30–11
Dog & Duck
18 Bateman Street
Closed Sunday evening
Ind Coope Burton Ale; Taylor Walker Bitter Ⓗ
Small friendly pub, decorative tiles and mirrors
Q ⊖ (Leicester Sq)

Star & Garter
62 Poland Street
Closed Sunday
Courage Best Bitter, Directors Ⓗ

Small pub in heart of Soho
ⓖ ⊖ (Oxford Circus)

Sun & 13 Cantons
21 Great Pulteney Street
Ruddle County; Watney Combes Bitter; Webster Yorkshire Bitter Ⓗ
Small, comfortable local
Qⓖ ⊖ (Piccadilly Circus)

W2: Maida 8C1 Vale

11–3; 5.30–11
Hero of Maida
435 Edgware Road (A5)
☎ 01-723 0516
Benskins Bitter; Ind Coope Burton Ale Ⓗ
Island bar pub near Regents Canal ⓖ🍴 ⊖ (Edgware Rd)

W2: Paddington 8C2

11–3; 5.30 (7 Sat)–11
Marquis of Clanricarde
36 Southwick Street (off A4209)
Courage Best Bitter, Directors Ⓗ
Long basic one-bar pub
ⓖ≉ ⊖

Queens Railway Tavern
15 Chilworth Street
Ind Coope Burton Ale; Taylor Walker Bitter Ⓗ
Comfortable side-street pub.
Darts, noisy jukebox ⓖ≉ ⊖

W3: Acton 8C7

11–3; 5.30–11
Red Lion & Pineapple
281 High Street (A4020)
Fuller Chiswick Bitter, London Pride, ESB Ⓗ
Spacious pub, tree in garden bar. Traditional pub games
🄴ⓖ🄲 ⊖ (Acton Town)

W4: Chiswick 8C7

11–3; 5.30–11
Bell & Crown
72 Strand on the Green (off A205) ☎ 01-994 4164
Fuller Chiswick Bitter, London Pride, ESB Ⓗ
Busy Thames-side pub, conservatory bar, good home cooking (Mon–Fri)
Q🍴ⓖ🍴≉(Kew Bridge)

Crown & Anchor
374 Chiswick High Road (A315)
Young Bitter, Special, Winter Warmer Ⓗ
Large lounge, excellent first-floor carvery (not Tues & Sat)
Q🍴ⓖ🍴 ⊖ (Chiswick Park)

George IV
185 Chiswick High Road (A315) ☎ 01-994 4624
Fuller London Pride, ESB Ⓗ
Spacious lounge, unusual

cubicles, good food, pub games ♠ Q ♪ ♿ ♪ ♞
⊖ (Turnham Green)

W5: Ealing 8C7

11–3; 5.30–11

Greystoke
7 Queens Parade (off Hanger Lane, A406) ✆ 01-997 6388
Courage Best Bitter, Directors Ⓗ
Friendly two-bar local
♪ ♿ ♞♟⚌ ₴ (Ealing Bwy) ⊖

Kings Arms
55 The Grove, (behind shopping centre, off A3001)
Courage Best Bitter, Directors Ⓗ
Marvellous old-fashioned local. Same landlady since 1945. Fresh flowers daily. Best value Russian Stout around! Q ₴ ⊖ (Ealing Bwy)

Red Lion
13 St. Marys Road (A3001)
Closes 2.30 Mon–Thu lunch; Sat eves opens 7
Fuller London Pride, ESB Ⓗ
Friendly house near Ealing Studios. Film and TV connections Q ♪ ♿
₴ (Ealing Bwy) ⊖ (S Ealing)

W6: Hammersmith 8D7

11–3; 5.30–11

Black Lion
2 South Black Lion Lane (off A4 westbound)
Ruddle County; Watney Combes Bitter, Stag Bitter; Webster Yorkshire Bitter Ⓗ
Charming 17th century inn near river. Pleasant garden under 300 year-old chestnut tree Q ♪ ♿ ♞ (Mon–Sat)
⊖ (Stamford Brook)

Thatched House
115 Dalling Road
(off A315)
Young Bitter, Special, Winter Warmer Ⓗ
Comfortable, friendly local
Q ♿ ⊖ (Ravenscourt Park)

W7: Hanwell 8C7

11–3; 6–11

Fox
Green Lane (off A3002)
Courage Best Bitter, Directors Ⓗ
Canalside pub. Popular in summer Q ♪ ♿

W8: Kensington 8A4

11–3; 5.30–11

Britannia
1 Allen Street (off A315)
Young Bitter, Special, Winter Warmer Ⓗ
Busy local, large lounge, small public
Q ♪ ♿ ♞♟ ⊖ (High St Ken)

W8: Notting Hill Gate 8A3

11–3; 5.30–11

Uxbridge Arms
13 Uxbridge Street (off A40)
Brakspear Bitter; Flowers Original; Wethered Bitter; Whitbread Strong Country Bitter Ⓗ **Occasional guest beers**
Small, lively upmarket local
Q ♪ ♿ (Mon–Fri) ⊖

W9: Little Venice 8B1

11–3; 5.30–11

Warwick Castle
6 Warwick Place
Draught Bass; Charrington IPA Ⓗ
Unspoilt local in side street near Canal Basin
Q ♪ ⊖ (Warwick Ave)

W9: Maida Vale 8B1

11–3; 5.30–11

Truscott Arms
55 Shirland Road
Arkell BBB; Greene King IPA, Abbot; Shepherd Neame Bitter; Tetley Bitter; Thwaites Bitter Ⓗ **Regular guest beers**
Comfortable freehouse
♿ ⊖ (Warwick Ave)

W10: North Kensington 8D7

11–3; 5.30–11

Narrow Boat
346 Ladbroke Grove (B450)
Fuller London Pride, ESB Ⓗ
Small, friendly canalside local
Q ♪ ♿ ⊖ (Ladbroke Grove)

W11: Holland Park 8D7

11–3; 5.30–11

Duke of Clarence
203 Holland Park Avenue (A40) ✆ 01-603 5431
Draught Bass; Charrington IPA Ⓗ
Spacious pub, large, heated conservatory. Ideal for families
❦ ♪ ♿ ♞ ⊖ (Shepherds Bush)

W11: Westbourne Park 8A2

11–3; 5.30–11

Frog & Firkin
41 Tavistock Crescent
Westons County Cider; Borough Hill Cider Ⓗ **Regular guest beers**
Popular home-brew pub, live music nightly. House beers kept under blanket of CO_2
♿ ₴ ⊖

W12: Shepherds Bush 8D7

11–3; 5.30–11

Crown & Sceptre
57 Melina Road
Fuller London Pride, ESB Ⓗ
Popular back street local ♿ ♟

W13: West Ealing 8C7

11–3; 5.30–11

Drayton Court Hotel
2 The Avenue (off A4020)
Fuller London Pride, ESB Ⓗ
Large pub ♪ ♿ ♟ ₴

Forester
2 Leighton Road (off B452)
Sat eves opens 7
Courage Best Bitter, Directors Ⓗ
Imposing Edwardian edifice. Unusual wood & tiled exterior, many original features inside. Snooker room
♪ ♟ ₴ ⊖ (Northfields)

W14: West Kensington 8A4

11–3; 5.30–11

Britannia Tap
150 Warwick Road (A3220)
Young Bitter, Special, Winter Warmer Ⓗ
Friendly narrow 1-bar locals' pub. Shove ha'penny. No food Sun Q ♪ ♿ ♞ (not Sat) ₴
⊖ (Kensington Olympia)

Warwick Arms
160 Warwick Road (A3220)
Fuller Chiswick Bitter, London Pride, ESB Ⓗ
Upmarket one-bar pub with darts and eating area ♪ ♿ ♞ ₴
⊖ (Kensington Olympia)

Bedfont 8B8

10.30–2.30; 5.30 (7 Sat)–10.30 (11 F, S and summer)

Beehive
333 Staines Road (A315)
Fuller London Pride, ESB Ⓗ
Popular, friendly pub with rose garden. No food Sun
♪ ♿ ♞♟

Brentford 8C8

11–3; 5.30–11

O'Riordan's Tavern
3 High Street (A315)
Gibbs Mew Salisbury Best Bitter; Greene King Abbot Ale; Marston Pedigree; Wadworth 6X; Wiltshire Brewery Regency Bitter, Strong Ale Ⓗ **Regular guest beers**
Comfortable free house opposite Living Steam Museum ♪ ♿ ₴ (Kew Bridge)

White Horse
25 Market Place (A315)
Draught Bass; Charrington IPA Ⓗ

Greater London

Modernised cosy pub on River
Brent ♨ Q ✍ ♿ ⏎

Cranford 8B8

11–3; 5.30–11

Queens Head
123 High Street (off A312)
**Fuller Chiswick Bitter, London
Pride, ESB** Ⓗ
First pub in country to have
liquor licence ♨ ✍ ♿

Greenford 8B7

11–3; 5.30 (7 Sat)–11

Black Horse
425 Oldfield Lane N (off
A4127)
Fuller London Pride, ESB Ⓗ
Cosy, popular canalside pub
Q ✍ ♿ (not Sat) ⬛⏎ ⊖

Hampton Court 8C9

11–3; 5.30–11

Kings Arms
Lion Gate, Hampton Court
Road (A308)
**Flowers Original; Greene King
Abbot; Hall & Woodhouse
Badger Best Bitter, Tanglefoot;
Kings Arms Ale; Wadworth
6X** Ⓗ
Fine historic pub by Palace
grounds and Bushy Park.
Restaurant (not Sun eves/
Mon) ✍ ♿ ⬛❦⏎

Hampton Hill 8B8

11–3; 5.30–11

Windmill
80 Windmill Road (off A312)
**Charrington IPA; Draught
Bass** Ⓗ
Small, comfortable pub,
ornate terracotta front ✍ ♿

Hayes 8B7

11–3; 5.30–11

Woolpack
Dawley Road (A437)
**Courage Best Bitter,
Directors** Ⓗ
Comfortable lounge. Games
area, smart pool room ⬛✍♿❦

Hillingdon 8B7

11–3; 5.30–11

Star
Blenheim Parade, Uxbridge
Road (A4020)
**Draught Bass; Charrington
IPA** Ⓗ
Comfortable, friendly local
✍♿⬛

Hounslow 8B8

11–3; 5.30–11

Cross Lances
236 Hanworth Road (A314)
**Fuller London Pride, ESB;
Bulmer Cider** Ⓗ
Popular, friendly public; pool,
darts. Excellent lunches
♨✍♿⬛❦⏎⊖ (Hounslow Cen)

Earl Russell
274 Hanworth Road
(A314)
Sat eves opens 7
Fuller London Pride, ESB Ⓗ
Excellent local. Comfortable
saloon, friendly public. Darts
✍♿⬛⏎

Ickenham 8B6

11–3; 5.30–11

Soldiers Return
High Road (B466)
**Courage Best Bitter,
Directors** Ⓗ
Friendly, comfortable local,
good value food
✍♿❦⬛♿⊖ (W. Ruislip)

Isleworth 8C8

11–3; 5.30–11

Castle
18 Upper Square
(off A3004)
Young Bitter, Special Ⓗ;
Winter Warmer Ⓖ
Traditional family local
♨✍♿⏎

Coach & Horses
183 London Road (A315)
Young Bitter, Special Ⓗ;
Winter Warmer Ⓖ
Roomy old coaching inn near
Syon Park
♨Q✍♿❦⏎ (Syon Lane)

New Brentford 8C7

11–3; 5.30 (7 Sat)–11

Globe
104 Windmill Road
(B452)
Fuller London Pride, ESB Ⓗ
Very comfortable local, superb
floral displays. Weekend
pianist ♨Q✍♿⏎ (Brentford)

Norwood Green 8B7

11–3; 5.30–11

Lamb
Norwood Road (A3005)
**Courage Best Bitter,
Directors** Ⓗ
Busy canalside pub. Lively
atmosphere and a singing
landlord! Good value food
⬛✍♿❦

Ruislip 8B6

10.30–2.30; 5.30–11

Six Bells
Ducks Hill Road (A4180)
**Benskins Bitter; Ind Coope
Burton Ale; Taylor Walker
Bitter** Ⓗ
Popular pub near Lido
♨Q✍♿

Sipson 8A8

11–3; 5.30–11

King William IV
392 Sipson Road (A408)
Sat eves opens 6
**Courage Best Bitter,
Directors** Ⓗ

16th century village inn.
Restaurant and bar meals (not
Sun) ♨♿❦

Plough
Sipson Road (A408 Nr M4
Jct 4)
Sat eves opens 7
**Ruddle County; Watney
Combes Bitter, Stag Bitter;
Webster Yorkshire Bitter**
Small cosy pub behind
Post House Hotel
Q♿ (not Sun)

Southall 8B7

11–3; 6–11

Beaconsfield Arms
63 West End Road (off
A4020)
**Chudley Local Line; Timothy
Taylor Landlord** Ⓗ **Regular
guest beers**
Friendly pub ✍♿⬛⏎

Teddington 8C8

11–3; 5.30–11

Queen Dowager
49 North Lane (off A313)
**Young Bitter, Special, Winter
Warmer** Ⓗ
Comfortable pub off Broad
Street. Popular with local
Rugby and Hockey Clubs
Q✍♿⏎

Twickenham 8C8

11–3; 5.30–11

Eel Pie
9 Church Street (off A305)
**Flowers Original; Greene King
Abbot; Hall and Woodhouse
Badger Best Bitter, Tanglefoot;
Wadworth 6X, Old Timer** Ⓗ
Occasional guest beers
Popular pub near river
♿⏎

Prince Albert
30 Hampton Road (A311)
**Fuller Chiswick Bitter, London
Pride, ESB** Ⓗ
Excellent Victorian pub,
often crowded. Award-
winning floral decorations.
Shove ha'penny
Q✍♿ (not Sun)
⏎ (Strawberry Hill)

Popes Grotto
Cross Deep (A310)
**Young Bitter, Special, Winter
Warmer** Ⓗ
Large, comfortable pub
overlooking Radnor Gardens
and river, near St. Mary's
College
✍♿❦⏎ (Strawberry Hill)

Uxbridge 8A7

11–3; 5.30–11

General Elliott
St. Johns Road (A4007)
**Benskins Bitter; Ind Coope
Burton Ale** Ⓗ
Popular canalside local
Q✍⬛

Altrincham 25F4

11–3; 5.30–10.30 (11 F. S)

Railway
153 Manchester Road,
Broadheath
Boddingtons Bitter ⊞
Basic former ale-only house ▮

Old Roebuck
Victoria Street
Opens 11.30 am; Sat eve
opens 7 pm
**Wilsons Original Mild,
Bitter** ⊞
Cosy multi-roomer with
superb vault ᗑ▮≈

Ancoats 25G2

11–3; 5.30–

White House
122 Great Ancoats Street
(A665)
**Holt Mild, Bitter; Boddingtons
Bitter** ⊞
Comfortable and simply
refurbished free house. ᗑ▮≈

Ardwick 25G3

11–3; 5.30–11

King's Head
Chancellor Lane (A665)
**Greenall Whitley Local Mild,
Bitter** ⊞
Well-kept 2-roomer.
Breakfasts served (non-
alcoholic) from 9.30 am
weekdays
ᗑ▮≈ (no service evenings/
weekends)

Ashton-in-Makerfield 24D2

11.30–3.30; 5.30–11

Red Lion
Gerrard Street
**Greenall Whitley Local Mild,
Bitter** ⒠
Good basic pub. The cheapest
Greenalls for miles Q▮

Ashton-under-Lyne 25H3

11.30–3; 5–11

Gamecock
152 Old Street
**Boddingtons Bitter; Holt
Bitter; Old Mill Bullion;
Oldham Mild; Taylor Golden
Best, Landlord** ⊞ Regular
guest beers
Popular free house near town
centre. Live jazz and folk in
concert room ᗑ▮&≈

Oddfellows
Kings Road, Hurst
Robinson Mild, Best Bitter ⒠
Comfortable suburban pub ▮

Old Ball
Broadoak Road
Marston Mild, Burton Bitter ⊞
Popular, thriving local.
Regular live music ≈

Aspull 24D2

11.30–3.30; 5.30–11

Gerrard Arms
Bolton Road
Boddingtons Mild, Bitter ⊞
Modernised local, well out of
Aspull centre ▮

Astley 25F2

12–3.30; 5.30–11

Cart & Horses
221 Manchester Road (A572)
Holt Mild, Bitter ⊞
Homely pub with exquisite
tiled passageway ▮

Atherton 25E2

11.30–3.30; 5.30–11

Station Hotel
Bolton Road (A579)
**Greenall Whitley Local Mild,
Bitter** ⒠
Ex-Magee's house, celebrating
its 60th year ᗴᗑ▮≈

Billinge 24D2

12–3.30; 7–11

Hare & Hounds
144 Upholland Road (B5206)
Opens 1 pm
Walker Mild, Best Bitter ⊞
Large comfortable pub ▮

Holts Arms (Foot)
Crank Road (Near Hospital)
Burtonwood Mild, Bitter ⊞
Superb, traditional rural inn
with bowling green ᗴQᗴ▮

Blackley 25G2

11–3; 5.30–11

Golden Lion
47 Old Market Street (off
A664)
Holt Mild, Bitter ⊞
Well balanced 3-room local
ᗴ▮

Old House at Home
Bottomley Side, between Slack
Road and Delaunays Road
Evenings opens 7 pm
**Wilsons Original Mild,
Bitter** ⊞
Friendly cottage style village
local. Hidden away and best
approached on foot ⊞ᗑ▮

Bolton 25F1

Ainsworth Arms
606 Halliwell Road (A6099,
off A58) ☎ 0204 40671
**Peter Walker Mild, Best
Bitter** ⊞
Pleasant, out of town locals
pub ᗴ⊞ᗑ▮

Bob's Smithy
1448 Chorley Old Road
(B6226)
**Tetley Mild, Bitter; Peter
Walker Best Bitter** ⊞
Small moorland pub,
panoramic views of the town
ᗴᗴ▮⚎

Dog & Partridge
26 Manor Street ☎ 388596
Evenings opens 7
Thwaites Mild, Bitter ⊞
Well-run town centre pub
ᗑ▮≈

Howcroft
36 Pool Street, off Topp Way
☎ 26814
Opens 12 noon
**Peter Walker Mild, Best
Bitter** ⊞
Superb winner of CAMRA Pub
Preservation Award. Easier to
see than to reach ᗴᗴᗑ➐▮

Lodge Bank Tavern
264 Bridgeman Street
Opens 12 & 7
Lees Mild, Bitter ⊞
Friendly well-run local ᗑ▮≈

Sunnyside Hotel
Adelaide Street, off St Helens
Road (A579) ☎ 0204 616 01
Opens 12 & 7 (5.30 summer)
**Boddingtons Mild, Bitter;
Oldham Bitter** ⊞ Regular
guest beers
Large pub off beaten track ᗴ▮

White Lion
171 Deansgate ☎ 0204 27639
**Wilsons Original Mild,
Bitter** ⊞
Unusually-shaped pub close to
bus station ᗑ➐▮≈

York
112/114 Newport Street (off
A579)
Evenings opens 7
**Burtonwood Dark Mild,
Bitter; JBA Premium** ⊞
Town pub with strong
emphasis on games ᗴᗑ≈

Boothstown 25F3

11–3; 5.30–10.30 (11 F. S)

Royal Oak
20 Leigh Road (A572)
**Wilsons Original Mild,
Original Bitter** ⊞
Friendly and popular village
local ᗴ▮

Bradford 25G3

11.30–3; 7–11

Duke of Edinburgh
366 Mill Street (A635/A662)
Tetley Mild, Bitter ⊞
Large Victorian pub near
Market. Vault with TV and
Manchester log-end
dartboard. Large lounge, pool
room ⊞ᗴᗑ (summer) ▮
≈ (Ashburys)

Bradshaw 25F1

11.30–3; 7–11

Royal Oak
122 Bradshaw Brow (A676)
**Greenall Whitley Local Mild,
Bitter** ⊞
Large, comfortable pub; scenic
views from bowling green
ᗴᗴᗑ▮

Bredbury 25H3

11.30–3; 5.30–11
Rising Sun
Stockport Road
**Wilsons Original Mild,
Bitter** Ⓗ
Active pub suiting all tastes
℘Ⓖⓘⓩ

Broadbottom 25F3

11.30–3; 6.30–11
Shoulder of Mutton
138 Lower Market Street
Thwaites Mild, Bitter Ⓗ
Unpretentious pub catering
for all local tastes ⓘⓩ

Burnage 25G3

11–2; 5.30–11
Sun in September
Burnage Lane
**Samuel Smith Tadcaster
Bitter, OBB** Ⓗ
Smart former hotel. Wide
range of good food Ⓖⓘⓩ

Bury 25G1

11–3; 5.30–11
Help Me Thro'
Crostons Road (B6214)
Opens 12 noon; Sat eve opens 7
Thwaites Mild, Bitter Ⓗ
Welcoming terraced pub ⓐQⓘ

Trafalgar
12 Manchester Old Road (off
A56)
Burtonwood Mild, Bitter Ⓗ
Popular pub with two large
rooms. Just out of town centre
ⓐⒼ (weekday) ⓘⓩ

Walmersley Arms
741 Walmersley Road (A56)
Weekdays 11.30–2; Sat 12–3;
evenings opens 7
Wilson Original Mild, Bitter Ⓗ
Large emporium set back from
main road. L-shaped lounge,
pool table in vault
Q℘Ⓖ (not Sat) ⓘ

Carrington 25F3

11.30–3; 5.30–10.30 (11, F, S)
Windmill
Manchester Road (A6144)
**Samuel Smith Tadcaster
Bitter, OBB** Ⓗ
300 year old semi-rural local
℘Ⓖ (not Sun) ⓘⓩ

Cheadle 25G4

12–3; 5.30 (6.45 Sat)–11
Queen's Arms
177 Stockport Road (A560)
Robinson Best Mild, Bitter Ⓗ,
Old Tom Ⓖ
Comfortable unspoilt local
ⓐ℘ⓘ

Printers Arms
220 Stockport Road (A560)
Sat evenings opens 6.30
**Robinson Best Mild, Best
Bitter** Ⓔ

Thriving locals' pub with
active games teams ℘ⓘ

Cheetham 25G2

11–3; 5.30–11
Derby Brewery Arms
95 Cheetham Hill Road
(A665)
Holt Mild, Bitter Ⓗ
Large brewery tap, popular
with Holt's workers
ⓘⓩ (Victoria)

Chorlton-cum- 25G3
Hardy

11–3; 5.30–11
Southern Hotel
Mauldeth Road West (A6144)
Boddington Mild, Bitter Ⓔ
Large popular pub catering for
all tastes ℘Ⓖⓘ

Compstall

11.30–3; 5.30–11
Andrew Arms
George Street
Robinson Mild, Best Bitter
Friendly cosy pub close to the
Etherow Nature Reserve
ⓐQⓖⓘ

Daisy Hill 25E2

11–3; 5.30–11
**Rose Hill Tavern
(Bug)**
321 Leigh Road (B5235)
Holts Mild, Bitter Ⓗ
Large comfortable pub Ⓖⓘⓩ

Delph 25J2

1–3 closed weekdays; 7–11
Horse & Jockey
Stanedge (A62/A670)
OS990090
**Marston Owd Rodger;
Moorhouse Pendlewitch; Oak
Bitter; Theakston Mild, Best
Bitter, Old Peculier; Ward
Bitter** Ⓗ **Regular guest beers**
Lone moorland outpost with
40's atmosphere
ⓐQ🅿 (lunchtimes) Ⓐ

Denshaw 25J1

Closed Mon–Sat; 6.30–11
**Rams Head (Owd
Tupp's)**
Rippenden Road (A672)
1 mile N of village. Near M62
Jct 22 OS980130
**Theakston Mild, Bitter, XB,
Old Peculier** Ⓗ/Ⓖ **Regular
guest beers**
A magnificent moortop pub
enjoying commanding views
ⓐQ℘Ⓐ

Denton 25H3

11.30–3; 5.30–11
Bay Horse
Haughton Green Road (½ mile
off A6017)
Evenings opens 6.30

**Wilsons Original Mild,
Bitter** Ⓗ
Spacious well-appointed local.
Old photos and brassware ℘ⓘ

Dog & Partridge
Ashton Road
**Robinson Best Mild, Bitter,
Best Bitter** Ⓗ
Small terraced local ⓘ

Red Lion
Crown Point
Hydes Mild, Bitter Ⓔ
Spacious pub on busy
junction caters for all tastes
Ⓖⓩ

Didsbury 25G3

11–3; 5.30–11
Station
682 Wilmslow Road (B5093)
**Marston Mercian Mild,
Burton Bitter** Ⓗ
Small, basic and deservedly
popular Qⓘ

Dukinfield 25H3

11.30–3; 5.30–11
Lamb Inn
Crescent Road
Boddingtons Bitter Ⓗ
Locals pub with good tap
room. Emphasis on games Ⓖⓘ

Dunham 25F4
Massey

11.30–3; 5.30–10.30 (11 F, S)
Rope & Anchor
OS372388
Boddingtons Mild, Bitter Ⓔ
Large former station hotel in
rural setting Q🅿℘Ⓖⓘ

East Didsbury 25G3

11.30–3; 5.30–11
Gateway Hotel
882 Wilmslow Road (A5145/
A34)
Hydes Mild; Bitter Ⓔ
Large multi-roomed 1930's
pub on commuter route
ⓐⒼⓘⓩ

Eccles 25F3

11–3; 5.30–10.30 (11 F, S)
Duke of York
89 Church Street (A57)
℘ 061 707 5409
**Chester's Mild, Bitter; Marston
Pedigree; Taylor Golden Best,
Landlord, Ram Tam** Ⓗ
Large, busy and basic. Regular
live music. No-smoking
lounge. Deservedly popular
ⓐ🅿ⒼⒼ (not Sun) ⓘⓩ

Lamb Hotel
33 Regent Street (A57)
Sat evening opens 7
Holt Mild, Bitter Ⓗ
Splendid Edwardian
mahogany and cut glass. Full-
size snooker table Q🅿ⓘⓩ

Park Hotel
142 Monton Road, Monton
(B5229)
Holt Mild, Bitter E
Pleasant, modern 3-room
village local ♠☷ (Patricroft)

Stanley Arms
295 Liverpool Road, Patricroft
(A57) ☎ 061 788 8801
Holt Mild, Bitter H
Basic street corner local.
Occasional live music
⊞ (lunchtime) ▣Ġ♠
☷ (Patricroft)

Gatley 25G4

11.30–3; 5.30–11
Horse & Farrier
Gatley Road (A560)
Hydes Best Mild, Bitter E,
Anvil Strong Ale G
Multi-room village local. Lots
of character
Q☙Ġ (Mon-Fri) ☷

Golborne 24E3

12–3.30; 7–11
**Sir Charles Napier
(Tippings)**
High Street (A573)
Peter Walker Mild, Best
Bitter H
Large, popular town-centre
local ♠

Gorton 25G3

11–3; 5.30–11
Vale Cottage
Kirk Street (off A57)
☎ 061 223 2477
Lunchtime opens 12 noon;
winter evening opens 7
Wilsons Original Mild,
Bitter H
Comfortable open-plan pub.
Well worth finding ☙Ġ➤

Waggon & Horses
736 Hyde Road (A57)
Sat evening opens 7
Holts Mild, Bitter H
Imposing pub, cheapest beer
in the area. Live music Sats ♠

Hale 25F4

11.30–3; 5.30 (7 Sat)–10.30 (11 F, S)
Cheshire Midland
Ashley Road (opposite station)
Samuel Smith OBB H
Large former railway hotel,
comfortable lounge
☙Ġ (not Sun) ♠☷

Hazel Grove 25H4

11–3; 5.30–11
Grades
London Road (A6)
Robinson Best Mild, Best
Bitter E
Friendly, multi-room, oak-
panelled pub. Excellent bacon
and black pudding, barm
cakes Ġ (not Sun) ♠☷

Three Tunnes Hotel
London Road (A6)

Robinson Best Mild, Best
Bitter H, Old Tom G
Comfortable, busy pub Ġ♠☷

Heaton Norris 25G3

11–3; 5.30–11
Nursery
Green Lane (Near A6)
☎ 061 432 2044
Hydes Mild, Bitter E
Large, comfortable back-street
pub. Fine wood-panelled
lounge. Superb bowling green
Q☙Ġ (Mon-Fri) ➤ (Fri-Sat) ♠

High Lane 25H4

11.30–3; 5.30–11
Royal Oak
Buxton Road (A6)
☎ Disley 2380
Burtonwood Mild, Bitter H
Comfortable roadside inn ▣Ġ

Hindley 24E2

11.30–3.30; 7–11
Bridgewater Hotel
Liverpool Road (A58)
Burtonwood Mild, Bitter E
Small thriving pub with cosy
lounge Ġ➤♠

Cumberland Arms
Chapel Green Road
Tetley Mild; Walkers Best
Bitter E
Basic popular boozer ♠

Hollinwood 25H2

11.30–3; 5–11
Old Post Office
439 Manchester Road (A62)
Oldham Mild, Bitter H
Boisterous drinkers boozer.
Soon to be demolished for
M66 extension Ġ♠☷

Horwich 25G2

11–3; 5.30–11
Toll Bar
2 Chorley New Road (A673)
Thwaites Best Mild, Bitter E
Large pub at the end of town.
Convenient for walks to
Rivington Pike ▣⊞Ġ♠♠

Hulme 25G3

11–3; 5.30–11
Cornbrook Inn
256 Chester Road
Evenings opens 6
Tetley Mild, Bitter H
Traditional working mans
local. Pub games dominate ♠

Grand Junction
1 Rolls Crescent (off A6144)
Opens 11.30
Hydes Best Mild, Bitter E
Comfortable triangular local
with students and interesting
exterior Ġ➤♠

Hyde

11.30–3; 5.30–11
Cotton Tree
Markham Street, Newton

Wilsons Original Mild,
Bitter H
Genial pub in suburb
Ġ♠☷ (Flowery Field)

Crown
Market Street
Robinson Best Mild, Best
Bitter E, Old Tom G
Traditional-style local caters
for most tastes ♠☷ (Central)

Globe Inn
Lumn Road
Wilsons Original Mild,
Bitter H
Corner local near football
ground ☙♠☷ (Central)

Ince 24D2

11.30–3.30; 7–11
Engineers
Belle Green Lane, Ince Bar (off
A57)
Tetley Mild, Bitter H
Friendly local of character ♠

Walmesley
465 Warrington Road, Spring
View
Opens 12 noon
Tetley Mild, Bitter H
Imposing building with
comfortable interior ♠

**Irlam &
Cadishead** 25F3

11–3; 5.30–10.30 (11 F, S)
Boathouse
Ferry Road (off A57)
Boddingtons Mild, Bitter E
Popular riverside pub.
Traditional vault, comfortable
lounge. Large enclosed play
garden for children
☙Ġ (Mon-Fri) ♠♠

Leigh 25E2

12–3.30; 7–11
Railway Hotel
160 Twist Lane (A578/9)
Ind Coope Burton Ale;
Jennings Bitter; Peter Walker
Best Bitter; Tetley Mild H
In same family for 55 years;
handy for canal Q♠

Sportsman Hotel
1 Firs Lane (A578)
Greenall Whitley Local Mild,
Bitter E
Active participation on the
green ☙♠

Standard Mower
88 Chapel Street (A572) Near
St Joseph's Church
Bass 4X Mild, Cask Bitter E
Ex-Cornbrook house ▣♠

Littleborough 25H1

11.30–3; 5–11
Queens Hotel
Church Street (A58)
Thwaites Mild, Bitter H
Friendly Multi-room local
▣⊞♠☷

White House
Blackstone Edge Road (A58, 3 miles from town) ☎ 78456
Evenings opens 7
Thwaites Mild, Bitter ⊞
Magnificent moorland inn, panoramic views, by Pennine Way. Restaurant
🅰Ⓠ🅷🏱Ⓖ🏵🍴⅋𝄄Å

Little Hulton 25F2
11–3; 5.30–10.30 (11 F, S)

Kenyon Arms
99 Manchester Road West (A6) ☎ 061 790 4207
McEwan's 70/-; Younger No 3 ⊞
Large modern roadhouse in elegant style ⅋Ⓖ🏱🏵&

Little Lever 25F2
11–3; 5.30–11

Horseshoe
71, Lever Street (B6209)
Hydes Best Mild, Bitter Ⓔ, **Anvil Strong Ale** Ⓖ
Popular, friendly local, lively vault, comfortable lounge 🏵

Manchester City Centre 25G3
11–3; 5.30–11

City Arms
48 Kennedy Street, 2
Ind Coope Burton Ale; Jennings Bitter; Walker Best Bitter ⊞
Two-roomer popular with business community. Good food, TV in vault ⅋Ⓖ🏵&≋

Circus Tavern
86 Portland Street
Opens 11.30; Sat evenings opens 8.30
Tetley Bitter ⊞
Tiny pub of real character, minute bar. Only lagerless pub in city. Door may be shut when busy
Ⓠ≋ Picadilly/Oxford Road

Crown & Anchor
41 Hilton Street (between A6 & A665)
Sat evenings opens 7
Chester's Mild & Bitter; Trophy; Taylor Golden Best, Landlord; Ruddle County ⊞
Regular guest beers
Emerging from nautical theme pub at a gentle pace 🚲Ⓖ≋

Jolly Angler
47 Ducie Street (off A665)
Hyde Best Mild, Bitter ⊞
Tiny backwater near canal basin. Unique ambience 🅰🏵≋

Marble Arch
73 Rochdale Road, 4 (A664)
Opens 12 noon, Sat evenings opens 7, closed Sun lunch
Hydes Bitter; Holt Bitter; Marston Pedigree; Fuller London Pride; Moorhouse Pendle Witch ⊞ Regular guest beers

Victorian pub with unique barrel-vaulted tiled ceiling and frieze 🅰Ⓖ≋ (Victoria)

Peveril of the Peak
127 Great Bridgewater Street
Wilsons Original Mild, Bitter ⊞
Superb tiled Victorian pub saved from demolition. Round corner from GMEX. Table football 🅰🏵≋

Unicorn
26 Church Street, 4
Bass Mild, Light, Draught Bass, Stones Best Bitter ⊞
Comfortable oak panelled pub 🏵&≋

Wheatsheaf
30 Oak Street, off Oldham Street (A62)
Jenning's Bitter; Tetley Mild, Bitter ⊞
Comfortable wood-panelled inn tucked away near Craft Village 🚲Ⓖ🏵≋ (Victoria)

White Lion
Liverpool Road (off Air Museum)
Sat evenings opens 7
Chester's Mild, Bitter ⊞
Comfortable pub in Castlefield conservation area ⅋Ⓖ🏵≋

Marple 25H4
11.30–3; 5.30–11

Crown Inn
Hawk Green
☎ 061 449 8533
Robinson Best Mild, Best Bitter ⊞
Smart restaurant-style pub in attractive building ⅋Ⓖ🏱

Hatters Arms
Church Lane
Evenings opens 6.30
Robinson Best Mild, Best Bitter ⊞
End of terrace local. Traditional tap-room and vault 🏵

Middleton 25G2
11–3; 5–11

Gardners
114 Sandy Lane (off A669)
Lees GB Mild, Bitter ⊞
Comfortable family local. HQ of the local pigeon fanciers club ⅋Ⓖ🏵≋ (Mills Hill)

Kenyon
71 Kenyon Lane, Tonge (off A669)
Wilsons Original Mild, Bitter ⊞
Friendly family pub, paintings by the landlord
⅋🏵≋ (Mills Hill)

White Hart
86 Rochdale Road (A664)
Lees GB Mild, Bitter Ⓔ
Traditional local with busy vault ⅋🏵

Milnrow 25H1
11.30–3; 5–11

Waggon Inn
Butterworth Hall (via New Street off B6225; ½ mile M62 Jct 21)
Burtonwood Mild, Bitter ⊞
Extravert landlord assures a warm welcome in this bustling 18th century village pub 🚲≋

Mossley
11.30–3; 5.30–11

Tollemache Arms
Manchester Road (A635)
Robinson Mild, Best Bitter ⊞
Deservedly popular local, cosy and welcoming. Alongside Huddersfield Narrow Canal ⅋

Moss Nook 25G4
11.30–3; 5.30–10.30 (11 F, S)

Tatton Arms
Ringway Road (B5166, 1 mile from airport) ☎ 061 437 2505
Robinson Best Mild, Best Bitter Ⓔ
Old coaching house, carved fireplace 🅰Ⓠ⅋Ⓖ🏵

Moston 25G2
11–3; 5.30–11

Dean Brook Inn
St Marys Road, off Oldham Road (A62)
Marston Mercian Mild, Burton Bitter ⊞
Long terraced pub, central bar and rooms off. Caters largely for locals Ⓖ🏵≋ (Dean Lane)

Newhey 25H1
11.30–3; 5–11

Bird in the Hand (Top Bird)
113 Huddersfield Road (A640, 1 mile M62 Jct 21)
Samuel Smith OBB ⊞
Hospitable stone 2-room village local, busy vault Ⓠ🏵≋

New Springs 24D2
11.30–3.30; 5.30–11

Colliers Arms
Wigan Road
Burtonwood Mild, Bitter ⊞
18th century friendly local 🅰Ⓠ🏵

Newton Heath 25H2
11–3; 5.30 (7 Sat)–10.30 (11 F, S)

Railway
82 Dean Lane, off Oldham Road (A62)
Holt Mild, Bitter Ⓔ
Renovated Victorian local in twilight area. Live jazz on Wednesdays
🅰🏵⅋Ⓖ≋ (Dean Lane)

Northenden 25G3

Crown

Ford Lane (off B5167 next to police station)
Boddingtons Mild, Bitter E
Very popular traditional local ⌂♥♟

Oldham 25H2

11.30–3; 5–11

Bridge Inn
616 Lees Road, Salem (A669)
☎ 061 624 6055
Closed weekday lunch;
evenings opens 7
Tetley Walker Mild, Bitter H
Welcoming pub in Lowry-type setting. Small snug, games room, pool table. Organist at weekend ⌕♥♟

Clarksfield Hotel
38 Ronald Street via Balfour Street (off A669)
Opens 12 & 6.30
**Boddington Mild, Bitter;
Oldham Mild, Bitter** H
Edwardian pub with a strong local following. Well worth finding ♥♟≈ (Mumps)

Friendship
495 Lees Road, Salem (A669)
**Wilsons Original Mild,
Bitter** H
Plushly revamped roadside pub ♥⌕♟

Hark to Topper
Bow Street (off Yorkshire Street) ☎ 061 624 7950
Closed Sun lunch
Samuel Smith OBB H
Busy city centre hostelry hidden away on town's oldest thoroughfare ⌕♥♟≈ (Mumps)

Openshaw 25G3

11.30–3; 5.30 (6 Sat)–11

Travellers Call
525 Ashton Old Road (A635, near A6010 Jct)
**Boddingtons Bitter; Marston
Burton Bitter, Owd Rodger;
Thwaites Bitter** H
Inner city haven of warmth and comfort; excellent food, friendly welcome ⌕♥≈ (Ashburys)

Partington 25F3

11–3; 5.30 (7 Sat)–10.30 (11 F, S)

King William IV
Manchester Road (A6144)
**Marston Mercian Mild,
Burton Bitter** E**, Pedigree** H
Village pub in overspill estate ♟

Platt Bridge 24E2

12–3.30; 7–11

Victoria
592 Liverpool Road (A58)
**Peter Walker Mild, Bitter, Best
Bitter** H
Large locals' pub with tiled passage ♨♟

Prestwich 25G2

11–3; 6.30–11

Plough
Rainsough Brow, Hilton Lane (A6044)
Wilson Original Mild, Bitter H
Cosy comfortable local
Q♥⌕ (Mon-Fri) ♟

Radcliffe 25F2

11–3; 5.30 (6.30 Sat)–11

Wellington
48 Stand Lane (A665)
Bass Light E**, Mild; Stones Best
Bitter** H
Bustling 4-room town centre pub, much original tilework.
Pool table ♨♥♟≈

Reddish 25H3

11–3; 5.30–11

Union
93 Broadstone Road (B5169)
**Robinson Best Mild, Best
Bitter** E
Friendly local ♥≈ (South)

Rochdale 25H1

11.30–3; 5–11

Cemetery
470 Bury Road (B6222)
☎ 43214
**Ruddle County; Taylor Best
Bitter, Landlord; Theakston
XB, Old Peculier; Thwaites
Bitter** H**; Regular guest beers**
Vibrant pub, many foreign bottled beers ♥⌕♞

Healey
172 Shawclough Road,
Shawclough (B6377)
☎ 45453
Evenings opens 6
**Robinson Best Mild, Best
Bitter** H**, Old Tom** G
Pre-war 4-room local, tiled lounge. Football table Q♟

Merry Monk
234 College Road (B6222)
**Marston Mercian Mild,
Burton Bitter, Pedigree** H
Regular guest beers
Popular urban freehouse.
Unusual segregated darts area. Piano at weekend

Owd Betts
Edenfield Road, Cheesden (A680) OS830160 ☎ 49904
Evenings opens 7
**Greenall Whitley Local Mild,
Bitter** E
Isolated moorland pub by Ashworth Reservoir. Popular with families. Good food
♨♨♥⌕♟

Reed Hotel
Reed Hill, off Yorkshire Street
☎ 46696
Evening opening 5.30
Bass Mild, Special Bitter H
Well-preserved coaching inn, approach through archway
Q♨⌕

Windmill
440 Manchester Road,
Sudden (A58)

Burtonwood Mild, Bitter H
Attractive mock-Tudor exterior on comfortable 3-room local ♟♿

Romiley 25H3

11.30–3; 5.30–11

Duke of York
Stockport Road
John Smith's Bitter H
Attractive, comfortable pub, good tap room ⌕♞♟≈

Royton 25H2

11.30–3; 5–11

Angel
230 Shaw Road (A663)
Lees GB Mild, Bitter E
Guaranteed warm welcome awaits all ♥⌕ (Mon-Fri) ♟

Greyhound
Elly Clough, Hoden Fold (off A663)
Evenings opens 7
Lees GB Mild, Bitter E
Country pub atmosphere caters for all tastes. Good food
♥⌕ (Mon-Fri)

Sale Moor 25G3

11.30–3; 5.30 (7 Sat)–10.30 (11 F, S)

Legh Arms
Northenden Road (B5166)
Holt Mild, Bitter E
Large many-roomed Edwardian pub. Bowling green Q♥♟≈

Salford 25G2

11–3; 5.30–10.30 (11 F, S)

Church
Ford Lane, Pendleton (off A6/A576, behind church)
Opens 12 & 7
**Wilson's Original Mild,
Bitter** H
Traditional local isolated by house demolition
⌕♟≈ (Pendleton)

Horsehoe
2a Back Hope Street, off Bury New Road (A56) & Gt Clowes Street (B6187)
Evenings opens 7
Bass Mild, Special Bitter H
Back street local, tucked away in conservation area ♥♟

Oxford Hotel
11 Bexley Square, off Chapel Street (A6) next to cathedral
**Wilsons Original Mild,
Bitter** E
Popular working class corner local ♨♨♟♥♟

Spinner's Arms
4 Oldfield Road (A5066)
**Marston's Mercian Mild,
Burton Bitter** H
Spartan but friendly working class local. Occasional live music at weekends ♟≈

Union Tavern
105 Liverpool Street between A5063 & A5066

Evenings opens 7
Holt Mild, Bitter Ⓗ
Solitary but popular old
fashioned local with the
accent on pub games ♟

Wellington
Bolton Road, Irlams o'th'
Height (old A6, above new
underpass)
Holt Mild, Bitter Ⓔ
Large sixties pub ♨♟

Scouthead 25H2

11.30–3; 5–11
Three Crowns
955 Huddersfield Road (A62)
✆ 061 624 1766
**Wilsons Original Mild,
Bitter** Ⓗ
Handsome inn with
commanding views.
Attractive dining area. Good
food � (with meals) ♿�

Shaw 25H1

11.30–3; 5–11
Morning Star
107 Grains Road (off A663)
Lees GB Mild, Bitter Ⓗ
Friendly service in large pub
on edge of moors. Vault with
games and pool areas ♨♟⇄

Springhead 25J2

11.30–3; 5–11
Spinners
36 Woodbrook, off Cooper
Street (between A62 & A669)
**Lees GB Mild, Bitter,
Moonraker (winter)** Ⓔ
Homely local with busy vault.
Well worth finding Q♟

Stalybridge 25H3

11.30–3; 5.30–11
Old Hunters Tavern
Acres Lane
Robinson Mild, Best Bitter Ⓗ
Small welcoming local of truly
Northern character ♨♿⇄

Station Buffet
Stalybridge Station
**Moorhouse's Premier Bitter;
Ruddle County** Ⓗ
Privately owned, absolutely
unique atmosphere ♨♿⇄

Standish 24D1

12–3.30; 5.30–11
Crown Hotel
Platt Lane (off A5106)
Worthington ✆ 421354
**Draught Bass, 4X Mild;
Boddingtons Bitter; Thwaites
Bitter; Theakston XB** Ⓗ
Regular guest beers
Country pub with antique
furniture. Crown green
bowling; well worth finding
♨Q♨♿�

Stockport 25H3

11–3; 5.30–11
Arden Arms

Millgate
**Robinson Best Mild, Best
Bitter** Ⓗ
Classic 1930's pub. Potted
plants on the tables, light
programme on the radio
Q♿ (Mon-Fri)

Bakers Vaults
Market Place (near A6/M63)
✆ 061 480 3182
**Robinson Best Mild, Best
Bitter** Ⓔ
Classic Victorian pub, high
windows, vaulted ceiling.
Unbelievable food! (ask about
Sunday banquets!) ♿�⇄

Blossoms Hotel
2 Buxton Road, Heaviley (A6)
✆ 061 480 2246
**Robinson Best Mild, Best
Bitter, Old Tom** Ⓗ
Historic multi room pub. Folk
club Sats ♿�♟
⇄ (Stockport & Davenport)

Boars Head Hotel
Market Place (near A6/M63)
Closed Sundays
Samuel Smiths OBB Ⓗ
Bustling cosmopolitan market
pub. Regular live music
� (daytimes) ♿♿⇄

Castlewood
17 Bridge Street Brow, Market
(near A6/M63)
✆ 061 480 5529
Closed Sunday lunch. Sat eves
opens 7
**Websters Green Label Mild;
Wilson Original Mild, Bitter** Ⓗ
Traditional drink and chat
pub. Games room evenings
� (when dining) ▣♿⇄

Grapes Hotel
1c Castle Street, Edgeley
**Robinson Best Mild, Best
Bitter** Ⓗ, **Old Tom** Ⓖ
Bustling pub on shopping
precinct, handy for football
ground ♟⇄

Manchester Arms
25 Wellington Road South
(A6)
**Robinson Best Mild, Best
Bitter** Ⓗ, **Old Tom** Ⓖ
Loud, cheerful, full of unusual
characters. Good-value lunch-
time food. Live music
♿ (Mon-Fri) ⇄

New Inn
95 Wellington Road South
(A6)
**Wilsons Original Mild,
Bitter** Ⓗ
Cheerful local. Varied,
interesting clientele; busy and
noisy at weekends ♨♿♟♿

Red Bull
14 Middle Hillgate (off A6)
**Robinson Best Mild, Best
Bitter** Ⓗ
A country pub in the heart of
town. Excellent lunches
♨♿ (not Sun) ⇄

Stretford 25F3

11–3; 5.30 (6.30 Wed, Sat)–10.30 (11 F, S)
Melville Hotel
Barton Road (off A5181)
Holt Mild, Bitter Ⓔ
Large estate pub ♨♟

Swinton & Pendlebury 25F2

11–3; 5.30–10.30 (11 F, S)
Newmarket
Bolton Road, Pendlebury
(A666)
Holt Mild, Bitter Ⓔ
Late 19th century working
class boozer. Deservedly
popular ♟⇄

White Lion
242 Manchester Road (A6/
A572)
**Robinson Mild, Best Bitter,
Old Tom** Ⓔ
Old building, internally
transformed. Gave its name to
Swinton Lion RL club �♿♟

White Swan
Worsley Road (A572, off
A580)
Holt Mild, Bitter Ⓗ
5-room wood-panelled pub,
much knick-knackery and
willow pattern. Olde poole
room! ♿♟

Timperley 25F4

11.30–3; 5.30–10.30 (11 F, S)
Quarry Bank
151 Bloomsbury Lane
Hydes Mild, Bitter Ⓔ **Anvil
Strong** Ⓖ
Thriving community local
with bowling green ♨♿♟

Tottington 25F1

12–3; 6 (7 Sat)–11
Robin Hood
Market Street (B6213)
**Hartley XB; Whitbread
Trophy Cask** Ⓗ
Village centre pub appealing
to all age groups ♿

Tyldesley 25E2

11.30–3.30; 5.30–11
Collier's Arms
105 Sale Lane (A577)
Evenings opens 7
**Wilsons Original Mild,
Bitter** Ⓗ
Pleasant roadside inn; popular
with locals and travellers ♟

Mort Arms
235-7 Elliot Street (A577
facing town-hall)
Holt Mild, Bitter Ⓗ
Best value for money in
Greater Manchester ♟

Uppermill 25J2

11.30–3; 5–11
Cross Keys
Runninghill Gate-via Church
Road, 1 mile E of village

Lees GB Mild, Bitter Ⓗ
Pleasantly situated 17th
century inn. Period public bar.
Folk club Wed ♨✿⏚♿🍴⚲

Walshaw 25F1

11–3; 5.30 (7 Sat)–11

White Horse
18 Hall Street (off B6213)
Thwaites Mild, Bitter Ⓔ
The epitome of a friendly
village pub ⏚ (not Sat) 🍴

Westhoughton 25E2

11–3; 5.30–11

Brinsop Arms
590-6 Chorley Road (A6 off
M61 exit 6)
Draught Bass; Boddington's
Bitter, Stones Bitter; Thwaites
Best Mild, Bitter; Walker Best
Bitter Ⓗ Regular guest beers
Large, busy free house. Range
liable to alter ⓱✿⏚⏚🍴❀♿

Whitefield 25G2

11–3; 5.30–11

Coach & Horses
71 Bury Old Road, Besses o'
th' Barn (A665 J17 M62)
Sat evenings opens 6

Holt Mild, Bitter Ⓗ
Traditional 1930's pub with
waiter service Q✿🌿🍴⚌ (Besses)

Eagle & Child
Higher Lane (A665, off M62
Jct 17)
Holt Mild, Bitter Ⓗ
Mansion-style pub, floodlit
bowling green. Organist at
weekend
⓱ (lunchtime) 🌿⏚🍴⚌ (Besses)

Wigan 24D2

11.30–3.30; 5.30–11

Bird i' th' Hand
102 Gidlow Lane
Opens 12 & 7.30
Tetley Mild, Bitter Ⓗ
Small busy local known as
Th' En 'Ole 🍴

Bowling Green
Wigan Lane ✆ 42130
Opens 12 & 6.30
Tetley Mild, Bitter; Draught
Bass Ⓔ; Jennings Bitter Ⓗ
Large pub with strong Rugby
League connections ⏚🍴

Millstone
Wigan Lane
Opens 12 & 6.30

Thwaites Best Mild, Bitter Ⓗ
Intimate cosy local Q

Old Pear Tree
Frog Lane ✆ 43677
Burtonwood Mild, Bitter; JBA
Premium Ⓗ
Busy, popular pub near new
bus station ♨✿⏚🍴⚌

Raven
Wallgate (A49)
✆ 43865
Opens 12 noon, closed Sun
lunch
Walker Mild, Best Bitter Ⓗ
Superb Victorian town centre
pub. Smart dress weekends
♨⏚🍴⚌

Springfield
Springfield Road
✆ 42072
Walker Mild, Best Bitter Ⓗ
Large Victorian pub near
Wigan Athletic ground 🍴

Swan & Railway
Wallgate
Bass 4X Mild, Draught Bass;
John Smiths Bitter; Stones
Bitter Ⓗ
Ex-Tetley pub now restored to
its former glory ⏚⚌

" LOOK, I CAN'T HELP IT IF YOU
HAVE COME ALL THE WAY FROM
LITTLE ROCK, ARKANSAS — YOU'LL
HAVE TO COME BACK AT SEVEN O'CLOCK! "

Ken Pyne

Barnston 24A4

11.30–3; 5.30–10.30 (11 F,S)

Fox & Hounds
Barnston Road (A551)
**Wilsons Original Mild,
Bitter** Ⓗ
Unspoilt village pub with
small public bar ♨Ⓖ (Sun) 🍸

Bebington 24B4

11.30–3; 5.30–10.30 (11 F,S)

Cleveland Arms
31 Bebington Road, New
Ferry
Evening opens 5
Thwaites Best Mild, Bitter Ⓗ
Friendly town local 🍸≷

Rose & Crown
57 The Village, Lower
Bebington
Thwaites Mild, Bitter Ⓗ
Popular, friendly village local
Ⓖ (weekdays) 🍸≷

Birkenhead 24B4

11.30–3; 5–10.30 (11 F,S)

Angel
Beckwith Street (behind
Crown)
**Boddingtons Bitter; Marston
Pedigree, Merrie Monk, Owd
Rodger** Ⓗ
Large, lively freehouse with
one long bar, popular with the
young Ⓖ≷ (Hamilton Sq)

Copperfield
38 Market Street (off A552)
John Smiths Bitter Ⓗ
Vibrant, lively pub in good
drinking area
Ⓖ (Mon–Fri) ≷(Hamilton Sq)

Crown
128 Conway Street (A553)
Higsons Mild, Bitter Ⓗ
Popular town pub. Folkclub
and piano at weekends
🎵Ⓖ (Mon–Fri) 🍸≷(Central)

Lord Napier
St. Pauls Road, Rock Ferry (off
A41)
Boddingtons Mild, Bitter Ⓗ
Comfortable, friendly local.
Keen darts team
🍸≷ (Rock Ferry)

Vittoria Vaults
56 Vittoria Street (off A553)
Higsons Mild, Bitter Ⓗ
Legendary local with table
service in back lounge.
Winner of local Pub of the
Year Award. Affectionately
known as "The Piggy".
Ⓖ (not Sat) 🍸≷ (Park)

Bootle 24B3

11.30–3; 5.30–10.30 (11 F,S)

Strand
5 Strand Road, 20
Higsons Mild, Bitter Ⓗ
Large, former residential
dockland pub
Ⓖ🍸≷ (New Strand)

Formby 24A2

11.30–3; 5.30–10.30 (11 F,S)

Bay Horse
Church Road ✆ 74229
Bass Mild, Draught Bass Ⓗ
Old, smart pub with
restaurant. Warm and
inviting. Small lounge gets
very crowded ♨ⓆⒼ🍸🍴≷

Pinewoods
Wicks Crescent ✆ 72998
Higsons Mild, Bitter Ⓗ
Welcoming, well furnished
and friendly local 🌿🍸

Frankby 24A4

11.30–3; (5.30 Sat)–10.30 (11 F,S)

Farmers Arms
Hillback Road (B5140)
Whitbread Castle Eden Ⓗ
Victorian pub in countryside
near Royden Park. Large beer
garden 🌿🍸

Heswall 24A4

11.30–3; (5–10.30 (11 F, S)

Black Horse
Village Road (off A540)
**Bass XXXX Mild, Cask Bitter,
Draught Bass** Ⓗ
Three varied rooms catering
for all tastes and ages
♨Ⓖ (not Sun) 🍸

Huyton 24C3

11.30–3; 5.30–10.30 (11 F, S)

Rose & Crown
2 Derby Road
Walker Mild; Bitter Ⓗ
Large "between the wars"
roadhouse near town centre
🌿🍸≷

Liverpool: 24B3
City Centre

11.30–3; 5–10.30 (11 F, S)

Carnarvon Castle
5 Tarleton Street, 1
Closed Sun
**Draught Bass; Higsons Mild,
Bitter** Ⓗ
Small homely pub, popular
with shoppers
♨ⓆⒼ≷ (Lime St) ⊖ (Central)

Court House
3 Commutation Row, 1
Evening opens 5.30
Higsons Mild, Bitter Ⓗ
Friendly local with unusual
exterior, near Museum
🍸≷ (Lime Street)

Cracke
Rice Street, 1
**Boddington's Bitter; Marston
Pedigree, Merrie Monk** Ⓗ
Popular pub with characterful
clientele 🌿Ⓖ≷ (Lime Street)
⊖ (Central)

Grapes
25 Mathew Street, 2
Sat eves opens 7.30; closed
Sun
**Boddingtons Bitter; Higsons
Mild, Bitter** Ⓗ
Old-style pub popular with
visitors on Beatles' tours
ⓆⒼ≷ (Lime St)
⊖ (Moorfields)

Hole In Ye Wall
Hackins Hey, 2 (off Dale
Street)
Closes 9pm; Closed Sat, Sun
**Draught Bass; Ind Coope
Burton Ale; Walker Mild, Best
Bitter** Ⓖ
A gem; beer drawn down
pillars from "cellar" upstairs
Ⓖ≷ (Moorfields)

Lion
67 Moorfields, 2
Walker Mild, Bitter Ⓗ
Ornate tiles, woodwork and
dome Ⓖ🍸≷ (Moorfields)

Queens
Derby Square, 2
**Bass XXXX Mild, Special
Bitter, Draught Bass** Ⓗ
Lively city pub by Victoria
Monument, near Crown
Courts Ⓖ≷ (James St)

Roscoe Head
4 Roscoe Street, 1
**Jennings Bitter; Tetley Mild,
Bitter** Ⓗ
Splendid little four-roomer
Ⓖ🍸≷ (Lime St) ⊖ (Central)

Rose & Crown
Cheapside, 2 (off Dale Street)
**Bass XXXX Mild, Special
Bitter, Draught Bass** Ⓗ
Two-level lounge opposite
main Bridewell Ⓖ

Saddle
Dale Street (near Town Hall)
Closes 9 pm; closed Sun
**Bass XXXX Mild, Special
Bitter, Draught Bass**
Renovated pub in business
district Ⓖ≷ (Moorfields)

White House
185 Duke Street, 1
Walker Mild, Bitter Ⓗ
Chinatown pub with large
pool room, near many
restaurants
🍸≷ (Lime Street) ⊖ (Central)

White Star
2 Rainford Gardens, 2 (off
Whitechapel)
**Bass Special Bitter, Draught
Bass** Ⓗ
Between shopping and
business areas Ⓠ🍸≷

Liverpool: 24B3
East

11.30–3; 5–10.30 (11 F, S)

Clock
110 High Street,
Wavertree, 15
Higsons Mild, Bitter Ⓗ
Small split-level pub by
Wavertree Clock Tower

Gregsons Well
2 West Derby Road, 6

Higsons Mild, Bitter Ⓗ
Large multi-room pub avoided demolition but now under threat again. Curved brass bar front ♨♥

Halton Castle
86 Mill Lane, West Derby, 12
Higsons Mild, Bitter Ⓗ
Small three-room local near Croxteth Country Park Q♥

Kensington
189 Kensington, 6
Higsons Mild, Bitter Ⓗ
Recent restrained re-decoration ♨♥

Masonic
Lark Lane, 17
Walker Mild, Bitter Ⓗ
Extended pub in suburban "village", popular with students ♥

Newsham Park
108 Boaler Street, 6
Closes 10.30 F, S
Tetley Mild, Bitter Ⓗ
It really is small, friendly and local with dedicated long-standing licensee ♥

Oxford
67 Oxford Street, Edge Hill, 7
Higsons Mild, Bitter Ⓗ
Convivial little pub ♨ ᏻ ♥

Prince Alfred
77 High Street, Wavertree, 15
Draught Bass; Higsons Mild, Bitter Ⓗ
Two-room pub at end of listed terrace ♨♥

Royal Hotel
213 Smithdown Road, 15
Ind Coope Burton Ale; Tetley Mild, Bitter Ⓗ
Large, suburban pub lit by gas. Wood-panelled alcoves in lounge ᏻ♥

Royal Standard
1 Walker Street, 6
Draught Bass; Higsons Mild, Bitter Ⓗ
Lively local, demolition still pending. Piano player weekends ♥

Salisbury (Albany)
40 Albany Road, 13 (off Derby Lane)
Higson's Mild, Bitter Ⓗ
Small locals' pub with service ♥

Wheatsheaf
186 East Prescot Road (A57), Knotty Ash, 14
Higsons Mild, Bitter Ⓗ
Comfortable three-room pub with waitress service ♥

Willowbank
329 Smithdown Road, 15
Walker Mild, Bitter, Best Bitter Ⓗ
Split-level lounge with service ᏻ♥

Liverpool: North   24B3

11.30–3; 5–10.30 (11 F, S)

Abbey
153 Walton Lane, 4
Walker Mild, Bitter Ⓗ
Impressive maroon tile and half-timbered building, truly small, cosy interior. Near Everton FC ♥

Breckside "Flat Iron"
377 Walton Breck Road, 4
Tetley Mild, Bitter Ⓗ
Appropriate nick-name for unusual-shaped local; near Liverpool FC ♨♥

Breeze
66 Lancaster Street, 9 (off A59)
Higsons Mild, Bitter Ⓗ
Thriving local renowned for mild ♥

Bull
2 Dublin Street, 3
Opens 8 Sat/Sun eves
Tetley Mild; Walker Best Bitter Ⓗ
Blue-collars and suited clientele in the lively Irish atmosphere of this one-bar corner pub ᏻ

Clock
167 Walton Road, 4 (A59)
Walker Mild, Bitter Ⓗ
Bustling two-room local with clock collection. Near Everton FC ♥ ≷ (Kirkdale)

Corner House
395 Scotland Road, 5 (A59)
Walker Mild, Best Bitter Ⓗ
Imposing building close to site of former Rotunda Theatre. Large L-shaped bar, small parlour ♥

Melrose Abbey
331 Westmister Road, 4
Tetley Mild, Bitter
Lively three-room local ♨♥ ≷ (Kirkdale)

Prince Arthur
91 Rice Lane, 9 (A59)
Walker Mild, Bitter Ⓗ
CAMRA Pub Preservation Award Winner; feast of tiles mosaics, glass and wood. The locals quite like it too! ♥

Rising Sun
124 Portland Street, 5
Tetley Mild, Bitter Ⓗ
Spartan no-frills local in middle of Vauxhall Estate ♥

Sandhills
160 Regent Road, 5
Walker Mild, Bitter, Best Bitter Ⓗ
Spacious dockland ale house ♥ ≷ (Sandhills)

Stanley Bar
99 Stanley Road, 5
Walker Mild, Bitter Ⓗ
Lively three-room local. A rare survivor in locality ♥

Walton (Top House)
122 Walton Village (off A59)
Higsons Mild, Bitter Ⓗ
Popular "village" local, near Everton FC ♥

Liverpool: South   24B4

11.30–3; 5–10.30 (11 F, S)

Bleak House
131 Park Hill Road, 8
Higsons Mild, Bitter Ⓗ
Friendly old street-corner pub with views of the Mersey ♥

Cobden Vaults
Quarry Street, 25
John Smith's Bitter Ⓗ
Busy pub in conservation-conscious village ᏻ♥

King Street Vaults
74 King Street, Garston, 19
Walker Mild, Bitter Ⓗ
Popular darts oriented pub in Garston's dockland ♥ ≷ (Garston)

Mosley Arms
156 Mill Street, 8
Tetley Mild, Bitter Ⓗ
Bustling Toxteth local with "Old Walkers" signing ♥

Poet's Corner
27–29 Parkhill Road, 8
Tetley Mild, Bitter Ⓗ
Friendly little local ᏻ♥

Maghull   24B2

11.30–3; 5–10.30 (11 F, S)

Red House
Foxhouse Lane
Jennings Bitter; Tetley Mild, Bitter Ⓗ
Busy local in commuter suburb
♥ ᏻ (Mon–Fri) ≷ (Maghull)

New Brighton   74B3

11.30–3; 5–10.30 (11 F, S)

Commercial
Hope Street (off A554)
Walker Mild, Bitter, Best Bitter Ⓗ
Small, friendly local; table service in lounge ♥ ♿ ≷

Magazine Hotel
Magazine Brow
Draught Bass Ⓗ
Popular 18th century pub overlooking River Mersey, 1985 Wirral Pub of the Year ♨ Q ᏻ (not Sun) ♿

Stanley's Cask
Rake Lane (B5143)
McEwan 70/-; Younger IPA, No. 3 Ⓗ
CAMRA saved the licence of this former Whitbread pub; now thriving and well maintained ♥ ᏻ (not Sun) ♿ ≷

Telegraph
25–27 Mount Pleasant Road (off B5143)
Whitbread Castle Eden Ⓗ

Small, cosy pub with back lounge. Authentic iron range and wooden beams. Welcome assured even from Bingo, the parrot ⊞ ♫

Newton-le-Willows 24D3

11.30–3.30; 7–11

Houghton Arms
Houghton Street, Earlestown
Burtonwood Dark Mild, Bitter Ⓗ
Busy back street local—easier to see than find. Large TV screen ७≹

Vulcan Inn
Manchester Row, Vulcan Village
Burtonwood Dark Mild, Bitter
Popular urban village hostelry within a stone's throw of Manchester/North Wales railway ७

Prescot 24C3

11.30–3; 5–10.30 (11 F, S)

Clock Face
High Street (A57)
Thwaites Best Mild, Bitter Ⓗ
Converted old sandstone manor house Q♫७

Rainhill 24C3

11.30–3.30; 5.30–10.30 (11 F, S)

Commercial
Station Road (off A57)
Higsons Mild, Bitter Ⓗ
Victorian four-roomed pub opposite station ♥≹

St. Helens 24D3

11.30–3.30; 5.30–10.30 (11 F, S)

Boilermakers
Hoghton Road, Sutton
Walker Mild, Bitter Ⓗ

Comfortable local on outskirts of town. Can become rather noisy at night
♥≹ (St. Helens Junction)

Griffin
Church Lane, Eccleston
Opens noon; Sat eves opens 7
Greenall Whitley Mild, Bitter, Original Ⓗ
Fine old sandstone pub on edge of a town. Good choice of rooms and family atmosphere ♫७♪ (Thu–Sat) ♥

Hope & Anchor
City Road, Gerards Bridge
Tetley Mild, Bitter Ⓗ
Boisterous local with frequent discos ♥

Queens
Higher Parr Street
Evenings opens 7
Boddingtons Mild, Bitter Ⓔ
Popular locals pub, collection of Victorian bottles from local glass industry ♥

Sportsmans
Duke Street
Boddingtons Mild, Bitter Ⓗ
A pub with sporting connections, renamed after extensive renovations ♥

Turks Head
Cooper Street
Tetley Mild, Bitter Ⓗ
Pub with an unusual half-timbered look outside ♥

Union
Hall Street
Evenings opens 7
Boddingtons Mild, Bitter Ⓔ
Multi-roomed street corner local. Named after the old Union Plate Glass Works
♥≹ (Shaw Street)

Southport 24B1

11.30–3; 5.30–10.30 (11 F, S)

Blowick Hotel
147 Norwood Road (near A570)
Tetley Mild, Bitter Ⓔ
Friendly, inviting local on the edge of town. Lively public bar Q♫♥

Fisherman's Rest
Weld Road
McEwan 70/-; Younger IPA Ⓗ
Recently refurbished pub close to flower show site
७≹ (Birkdale)

Old Ship
43 Eastbank Street
Evenings opens 5
Ind Coope Burton Ale; Walker Mild, Bitter, Best Bitter, Winter Warmer Ⓗ
Pleasant town centre pub
♨♫७≹

Ship Inn
Cable Street
Bass XXXX Mild, Special Bitter Ⓗ
Traditional backstreet gem. Note "Walkdens" windows. Good value snacks ♨♥≹

Thatto Heath 24C3

11.30–3.30; 5.30–10.30 (11 F, S)

Vine Tavern
Elephant Lane
Evenings opens 6.10
Boddingtons Mild, Bitter Ⓔ
Lively bar with occasional singarounds ♥≹

Wallasey 24B3

11.30–3; 5–10.30 (11 F, S)

Brighton
Brighton Street (A554)
Evenings opens 5.30
Higsons Mild, Bitter Ⓗ
Good locals pub, with attractive exterior and friendly staff ♥

Farmers Arms
Wallasey Village (B5427)
Draught Bass; Higsons Mild, Bitter Ⓗ
Popular pub with public bar and snug
७♪♥≹ (Wallasey Vill.)

Mona Castle
Wheatland Lane (off A554)
Tetley Mild, Bitter Ⓗ
Lively town pub in redevelopment area ♥

Prince Alfred
Church Road (A554)
Boddingtons Mild, Bitter Ⓗ
Deservedly popular local; good lunches ७ (Mon–Fri)

Waterloo 24B3

11.30–3; 5.30–10.30

Victoria
Bath Street, 23
Ind Coope Burton Ale; Walker Mild; Best Bitter Ⓗ
Pub near Crosby Marina
♫७≹

"I DON'T KNOW ANYBODY THAT CAN AFFORD TO!"

Don't ask a man to drink and drive

Acle 19H3

11–2.30; 6–11
Reba's Riverside Inn
Old Road
☎ Gt Yarmouth 750310
**Courage Best Bitter,
Directors** Ⓗ
Comfortable refurbished pub
🏚 Q 🅿 🕒 (not Sun)
🍴 (Mon–Fri) 🔥 ᴚ ⇄

Attleborough 19F4

10.30–2.30; 5.30–11
Griffin Hotel
Church Street ☎ 452149
**Greene King Abbot; Tolly
Cobbold Bitter, Original** Ⓗ
Regular guest beers
Pleasant hotel bar, with public
house atmosphere 🅿 🖼 🕒 🍴 🔥

White Lodge
London Road ☎ 452474
**Courage Directors; Wethered
Bitter** Ⓗ
Thatched pub with
surprisingly unspoilt interior.
Near new by-pass 🏚 Q 🕒 🍴

Beechamwell 18D3

11–2.30; 6–11
Great Danes Head
The Green, 2 miles off A1122
☎ Gooderstone 443
**Adnams Bitter, Draught Bass;
Greene King IPA, Abbot;
Woodforde Wherry Best
Bitter** Ⓗ **Regular guest beers**
Country pub with meals
always available 🏚 Q 🅿 🕒 🍴 🔥

Binham 19E1

11.30–2.30; 7–11
Chequers
B1388 ☎ Binham 297
**Adnams Bitter; Woodforde
Wherry Best Bitter, Phoenix
XXX; Regular guest beers**
17th century 1-bar pub in
historic village. Good food.
Popular with locals as well as
tourists 🏚 Q 🅿 🕒 🍴

Blofield 19H3

11–2.30; 6–11
Kings Head
Norwich Road (off A47)
☎ 712545
**Flowers Original, Wethered
Bitter** Ⓗ **Regular guest beers**
Large comfortable pub with
inviting home-cooked food.
Friendly public
🏚 🅿 🕒 🍴 (not Sun) 🍽

Briston 19F2

10.30–2.30; 6–11
John H. Stracey
West End (B1354)
**Greene King Abbot; Ind Coope
Burton Ale; Reepham Granary
Bitter** Ⓗ **Occasional guest
beers**
Friendly pub with
recommended restaurant
🏚 🅿 🕒 🍴

Brundall 19H3

10.30–2.30; 5.30–11
Yare
Station Road,
☎ Norwich 713786
**Adnams Bitter; Courage Best
Bitter, Directors; Woodforde
Wherry Best Bitter** Ⓗ **Regular
guest beers**
Large pub, popular with
tourists, artefacts relating to
Broads area 🏚 🖼 🅿 🕒 🍴 🍽 ⇄

Burnham Thorpe 18E1

11–2.30; 6–11
Lord Nelson
Off A149
**Greene King XX, IPA, Abbot,
Christmas Ale** Ⓖ
Basic, unspoilt pub with
Nelson Museum. Jug service
Q 🅿 🍽

Cantley 19H3

11–2.30; 6–11
Cock Tavern
Manor Road
☎ Gt Yarmouth 700895
**Charrington IPA; Draught
Bass; Ind Coope Burton Ale;
Woodforde Phoenix XXX** Ⓗ
Regular guest beers
Friendly popular local with
petanque pitch 🏚 🅿 🕒 🍴 🍽

Castle Acre 18D3

11–2.30; 6–11
Ostrich
Stocks Green ☎ 398
**Greene King XX, IPA,
Abbot** Ⓗ
Old hostelry serving excellent
food near Castle and Priory
ruins 🏚 Q 🖼 🅰 🕒 🍴 🍽 🔥 Å

Castle Rising 18C2

10.30–2.30; 6–11
Black Horse
Off A149 ☎ 225
**Adnams Bitter; Draught Bass;
Charrington IPA** Ⓗ **Occasional
guest beers**
Popular village pub near
Castle ruins, regular live
music Sun eves 🏚 🖼 🅿 🖼 🕒 🍴

Clenchwarton 18C2

10.30–2.30; 6–11
Victory
243 Main Road (old A17)
☎ Kings Lynn 772377
Elgood Bitter Ⓗ
Quiet village local 🏚 Q 🅿 🖼 🍽

Colkirk 19E2

11–2.30; 7–11
Crown
Fakenham Road
☎ Fakenham 2172
Greene King IPA, Abbot Ⓗ
Extremely, comfortable 2-bar
pub with dining room. Good

food plus real coffee served in
pleasant atmosphere.
Guinness cartoons in lounge
🏚 Q 🖼 (dining room) 🅿 🕒 🍴 🔥

Coltishall 19G2

11–2.30; 6–11
Red Lion
Church Street (B1354)
☎ Norwich 737402
**Flowers Original, Wethered
Bitter, Winter Royal** Ⓗ
Regular guest beers
Split-level two-bar pub, with
classic top bar Q 🅿 🕒 🍴 🔥

Cromer 19G1

10.30–2.30; 6.30–11
Red Lion
Brook Street ☎ 514964
**Adnams Bitter; Charrington
IPA; Draught Bass; Greene
King Abbot** Ⓗ
Classic old bar, popular with
fishermen 🏚 🕒 🍴 🔥 ᴚ ⇄

Deopham 19F4

12–2.30; 7–11
Victoria Inn
☎ Attleborough 850783
**Adnams Bitter; Greene King
Abbot; Rayment BBA;
Woodforde Wherry Best
Bitter** Ⓗ
Country free house, very
popular at weekends.
Landlord likes a singsong
🅿 🕒 🍴 Å

Dersingham 18D2

10.30–2.30; 6–11
Feathers
Manor Road (off A149)
☎ 40207
**Adnams Bitter; Charrington
IPA** Ⓗ
Comfortable hotel near
Sandringham
House 🏚 Q 🅿 🖼 🕒 🍴

Dickleburgh 19F5

12–2.30; 7 (6 winter)–11
Crown
Norwich Road ☎ Diss 741475
**Mauldon Bitter; Woodforde
Phoenix XXX** Ⓗ **Regular guest
beers**
Deceptively large, 16th
century roadside inn
🏚 🖼 🅿 🕒 🍴 Å

Diss 19F5

11–2.30; 6–11
Two Brewers
St. Nicholas Street ☎ 2610
**Adnams Bitter; Greene King
Abbot; Mauldon Two Brewers
Best** Ⓗ
Small town pub with
interesting mural; good food
🕒 🍴

Downham Market 18C3

10.30–2.30; 6–11

Crown Hotel
Bridge Street (off A10)
Ruddle County; Tolly Cobbold
Bitter, Original ⊞ Occasional
guest beers
Old coaching inn at town
centre ▲ Q ✿ 🖺 Ᏸ ➴ ≉

Live & Let Live
22 London Road ✆ 383933
Adnams Bitter; Everards Old
Original; Greene King
Abbot ⊞ Occasional guest
beers
Popular town pub ▲ ✿ 🖺 Ᏸ ➴

East Dereham 19E3
11–2.30; 6–11

Bull
High Street ✆ 67771
Greene King XX, IPA,
Abbot ⊞
Popular pub near Market
Place ▲ ✿ Ᏸ

Phoenix Hotel (Otter Bar)
Church Street ✆ 4814
Adnams Bitter; Greene King
Abbot ⊞
Comfortable hotel bar 🏶 🖺 Ᏸ ➴

East Winch 18D3
10.30–2.30; 6.30–11

Carpenters Arms
A47
Greene King XX, IPA,
Abbot ⊞ Occasional guest
beers
Village free house. Live music
Sats ✿ Ᏸ ➴

Eccles 19F4
11–2.30; 5.30–11

Old Railway Tavern
Eccles Station (near A11)
Adnams Bitter, Old; Greene
King IPA, Abbot; Rayments
BBA ⊞ Occasional guest beers
Excellent, friendly pub. Varied
menu (not Sun) and pub
games (backgammon Mon)
▲ Q Ᏸ ➴ ≉

Erpingham 19G2
11–2.30; 6.30 (7 winter)–11

Spread Eagle
✆ Cromer 761591
Woodforde Spread Eagle Best
Bitter, Wherry Best Bitter,
Norfolk Porter, John Brown's
Erpingham Special, Phoenix
XXX ⊞
Comfortable, friendly country
pub; the Woodforde "brewery
tap". ▲ Q 🏶 🖺 Ᏸ ➴ ⚤ ▲

Fakenham 18E2
10.30–2.30; 6–11

Limes Hotel
Bridge Street ✆ 2726
Draught Bass, Charrington
IPA; Greene King Abbot;
Woodforde Wherry Best
Bitter ⊞ Occasional guest
beers

Large and friendly. Landlord
has staged own beer festival
Q 🏶 Ᏸ ➴ ♀

Foulden 18D4
11–2.30; 6–11

White Hart
White Hart Street
✆ Gooderstone 638
Greene King XX, IPA,
Abbot ⊞ Regular guest beers
Traditional lounge bar with
flagstone floor. Public bar and
restaurant ▲ Q 🏶 🖺 Ᏸ ➴ ♀

Foxley West 19G3
10.30–2.30; 6–11

Silver Jubilee
Chapel Road (near A1067)
Adnams Bitter; Tolly Cobbold
Original ⊞
Modern bungalow pub;
excellent value food, good fire
in winter. Aeroplane pictures
and models ▲

Gorleston 19J3
10.30–2.30; 6–11

Short Blue
47 High Street
Adnams Bitter ⊞
Busy free house, excellent
riverside view Ᏸ Ᏸ

Tramway
Lowestoft Road
Adnams Bitter ⊞
Fine town pub

Great Bircham 18D2
10.30–2.30; 6–11

Kings Head
Main Road (B1153)
✆ Syderstone 210
Charrington IPA; Draught
Bass ⊞ Occasional guest beers
Comfortable hotel serving
good food; Queen dines here!
▲ Q 🏶 🖺 Ᏸ ➴ ♀

Great Moulton 19F4
11–2; 6.30–11

Fox & Hounds
Frith Way ✆ Tivetshall 506
Whitbread Strong Country
Bitter 🄶
Attractive 15th century oil-lit
pub ▲ 🏶 Ᏸ ▲

Great Yarmouth 19J3
10.30–2.30; 6–11

Allens
Greyfriars Way ✆ 856758
Adnams Mild, Bitter, Extra
Old ⊞
Lively town centre pub with
very smart decor ▲ Ᏸ ➴

Dukes Head Hotel
Hall Quay ✆ 859184
Adnams Bitter, Old; Wethered
Winter Royal ⊞
Large, plush but, friendly
hotel bar and restaurant
▲ Ᏸ ➴

Ship
Greyfriars Way ✆ 855533
Flowers Original; Greene King
Abbot; Wethered Winter
Royal ⊞ Regular guest beers
Small American-style pub
🏶 🖺 Ᏸ ➴

Talbot
Howard Street ✆ 843175
Greene King Abbot; Marston
Pedigree; Samuel Smith OBB;
Woodforde John Brown
Bitter ⊞ Regular guest beers
Single bar pub Ᏸ

Happisburgh 19H2
11–2.30; 5.30–11

Victoria
Lower Street
✆ Walcott 650228
Adnams Bitter; Bateman
XXXB; Courage Directors;
Greene King IPA, Abbot;
Rayment BBA ⊞ Regular
guest beers
Friendly rural pub. Children
welcome ▲ Q 🏶 Ᏸ ➴ ♀ ⚤ ▲

Harleston 19G5
10–2.30; 6–11

Cherry Tree
London Road
Adnams Mild, Bitter, Old 🄶
Excellent, unspoilt village
local. Friendly welcome
▲ Q 🏶 Ᏸ

Hempnall Green 19G4
11–2.30; 5.30–11

Three Horseshoes
Alburgh Road
✆ Hempnall 321
Adnams Bitter, Old;
Woodforde Wherry Best
Bitter ⊞
Friendly local pub. Lounge bar
and restaurant; food
deliciously fresh, not frozen.
Children welcome ▲ 🏶 Ᏸ ➴ ⚤ ▲

Hilborough 18D4
11.30–2.30; 6–11

Swan
A1065
Adnams Mild, Bitter; Greene
King IPA, Abbot ⊞ Regular
guest beers
Attractive roadside pub in
wooded setting ▲ Q 🏶 🖺 Ᏸ ➴

Hillington 18D2
10.30–2.30; 6–11

Ffolkes Arms
Main Road (A148) ✆ 600210
Adnams Bitter; Charrington
IPA; Greene King Abbot ⊞
Large bar with secluded
alcoves ▲ 🏶 🖺 Ᏸ ➴ ♀

Hoveton 19G3
10.30–2.30; 5.30–11

Hotel Wroxham
The Bridge ✆ Wroxham 2061

Courage Best Bitter, Directors;
Woodforde Norfolk Pride,
Wherry Best Bitter, Phoenix
XXX Ⓗ
Large hotel overlooking river
Q⚲🅿🛇🛆🍴⛵

Hunworth   19F1

10.30–2.30; 6–11
Bluebell
The Green (off B1149)
✆ Holt 2300
Adnams Bitter; Woodforde
House Beer, Wherry Best
Bitter Ⓗ Occasional guest
beers
Old village green pub,
extended into former stables
🛆🏠⚲🍴

Kings Lynn   18C2

10.30–2.30; 6–11
Crossways
Valingers Road ✆ 771947
11–3
Greene King XX, IPA,
Abbot Ⓗ
Comfortable back-street local
Q⚲🛇🍴

London Porter House
78 London Road ✆ 766842
Opens 7 Wed eve
Greene King IPA, Abbot Ⓖ
Small popular street corner
local Q⚲🛇⛆

Mildenhall Hotel
Blackfriars Terrace ✆ 775146
11–3; eves opens 5.30
Ind Coope Burton Ale; Tetley
Bitter Ⓗ
Smart lounge bar. Dinner-
dances Sat nights 🏠🛇🍴⛆

Wenns Hotel
Saturday Market Place
✆ 768658
11–3; eves opens 5.30
Greene King XX, IPA,
Abbot Ⓗ
Busy town pub popular with
young people. Good food
🛇🍴⛆

Try also: Dukes Head; Tudor
Rose

Letheringsett   19F1

10.30–2.30; 6–11
Kings Head
✆ Holt 2691
Adnams Bitter; Greene King
IPA, Abbot; Ind Coope Burton
Ale Ⓗ
This friendly 2-bar pub close
to the River Glaven is popular
with locals and tourists. Good,
reasonably priced food
🏠🍽⚲🛇🍴🅿♿

Mundesley   19G1

10.30–2.30; 6–11
Royal Hotel
Paston Road
Adnams Bitter, Old;
Charrington IPA; Greene King
Abbot Ⓗ Occasional guest
beers

Comfortable, busy hotel; lots
of charm and character
🏠🚲🅿🛇🍴🛆

North Wootton   18C2

10.30–2.30; 6–11
Red Cat Hotel
Station Road
✆ Castle Rising 244
Adnams Bitter Ⓗ, Old Ⓖ;
Greene King Abbot,
Woodforde Red Cat Bitter Ⓗ
Occasional guest beers
Country hotel with sporting
links in quiet position
🏠Q🍽⚲🅿🍴🍽

Norwich   19G3

10.30–2.30; 5.30–11
Alexandra
148 Old Palace Road
✆ 625773
Opens 11 & 7
Ind Coope Burton Ale Ⓗ
Lively local with pool table
and darts

Black Horse
Earlham Road ✆ 624682
Flowers Original; Wethered
Bitter; Whitbread Strong
Country Bitter; Woodforde
Wherry Best Bitter Ⓗ Regular
guest beers
Idyllic local refurbished with
fake beams and horsebrasses
🏠🚲⚲🛇

Champion
101 Chapelfield
Lunchtime closes 2; opens
eves 7
Wethered Bitter Ⓗ
Friendly cosy city local 🛇

Ferry Boat Inn
191 King Street ✆ 622082
Greene King IPA, Abbot Ⓗ
Real ale in front bar only.
Rambling pub with riverside
garden; moorings 🏠🚲🛇🍴⛵

Freemasons
Hall Road
Courage Best Bitter,
Directors Ⓗ
Friendly locals' pub in good
drinking area

Golden Star
Duke Street
Greene King XX, IPA,
Abbot Ⓗ
Two unspoilt bars
Q🛇 (not Sun) 🍴

Horse & Dray
Ber Street ✆ 624741
Adnams Mild, Bitter, Extra,
Old Ⓗ, Bulmers Cider
Comfortable city pub. Good
food 🏠🍽⚲🛇🍴

Lawyer
12–14 Wensum Street
✆ 629878
Adnams Bitter; Courage Best
Bitter; Regular guest beers
Smart, comfortable pub on 2
floors. Close to cathedral and
Elm Hill 🍽🛇

Lord Raglan
30 Bishopbridge Road
✆ 623304
Flowers Original Ⓗ
Quiet, basic local Q⚲🛇🍴

Mill Tavern
Millers Lane
Eves opens 6 (summer), 7
(winter)
Adnams Mild, Bitter, Extra,
Old Ⓗ
Basic pub; large local trade

Plasterers Arms
Cowgate Street
Charrington IPA; Everard Old
Original; Greene King Abbot;
Ind Coope Burton Ale; Samuel
Smith OBB; Woodforde
Phoenix XXX Ⓗ
Busy, unpretentious pub;
cheap prices. Bar closes
promptly 🛇🍴

Plough
58 St. Benedicts Street
Courage Best Bitter,
Directors Ⓗ
Unspoilt pub of real character

Ribs of Beef
24 Wensum Street ✆ 619517
Bateman Mild; Flowers
Original; Rayment BBA;
Reepham Granary Bitter;
Woodforde Wherry Best
Bitter, Ribcracker Ⓗ Regular
guest beers
Edwardian style bar. River
views, moorings available
Q🍽🛇 (not Sun)

Rosary Tavern
Rosary Road ✆ 666287
Adnams Bitter; Bateman
XXXB; Marston Pedigree;
Reepham Rosary Original,
Brewhouse Ale; Woodforde
Wherry Best Bitter Ⓗ & Ⓖ
Small free house with keen
prices, near yacht stations
🚲🛇⛆

Rose Tavern
88 Rupert Street
Flowers Original, Wethered
Bitter; Whitbread Strong
Country Bitter Ⓗ Regular
guest beers
Friendly local near hospital
🛇🍴

Sir Garnet Wolseley
36 Market Place ✆ 615892
Closed Sunday eve
Courage Best Bitter,
Directors
This dominating building
which was once three pubs
belies its tiny interior 🍽🛇🍴

Vine
Dove Street ✆ 629258
Courage Best Bitter,
Directors Ⓗ
Small city centre pub in
pedestrianised area

White Cottage
Penn Grove (off A140)
✆ 410025
Eves opens 6

Greene King XX, IPA,
Abbot Ⓗ
Good friendly two-bar locals'
pub off Aylsham Road ✿Ⓖ➧♿

White Lion
73 Oak Street ☎ 620630
Eves opens 6
Adnams Bitter; Bateman
XXXB; Greene King Abbot;
Woodforde White Lion Bitter,
Phoenix XXX; Bulmers
Cider Ⓗ Regular guest beers
Deservedly popular, unspoilt
pub backing onto the river Ⓖ

York Tavern
Leicester Street ☎ 620918
Courage Best Bitter,
Directors Ⓗ
Genuine local; cribbage,
bowling green. Excellent folk
club Fridays Q✿Ⓖ🍴

Old Hunstanton 18D1

10.30–2.30–6.11

Ancient Mariner
Golf Links Road ☎ 34411
Adnams Bitter; Charrington
IPA; Draught Bass; Greene
King Abbot; Samuel Smith
OBB Ⓗ Regular guest beers
Nautical bar with extensive
drinking and eating areas
🏚Q♿✿Ⓖ🍴➧

Outwell 18B3

10.30–2.30–6.11

Red Lion
Wisbech Road (A1122)
Elgood Bitter Ⓗ
Friendly waterside pub in
village centre 🏚Q🍴

Poringland 19E3

11–2.30; 5.30–11

Royal Oak
The Street
Courage Best Bitter, Directors;
Woodforde Wherry Best
Bitter Ⓗ
Two-bar pub with real fires.
Summer barbeques and
petanque. Popular fish and
chip shop next door
🏚✿Ⓖ➧

Scole 19F5

10.30–2.30; 6–11

Scole Inn
Norwich Road
Adnams Bitter, Extra; Greene
King Abbot; Younger Scotch
Bitter Ⓗ
Excellent large historic free
house 🏚Q✿🖼Ⓖ🍴➧🅰

Sea Palling 19H2

11–2.30; 6–11

Hall Inn
☎ Hickling 323
Opens 7 winter eves
Adnams Bitter; Courage
Directors; Greene King
Abbot Ⓗ Occasional guest
beers

Cosy beamed pub; children
welcome 🏚✿🖼Ⓖ➧

Snettisham 18C1

10.30–2.30; 6–11

Rose & Crown
Old Church Lane (off A149)
☎ Dersingham 41382
Adnams Bitter, Old; Greene
King IPA, Abbot; Woodforde
Norfolk Pride Ⓗ Occasional
guest beers
14th century inn with large
restaurant serving good food
🏚🖼✿Ⓖ➧🍴

South Lopham 19F5

10.30–2.30; 5.30–11

White Horse
The Street ☎ Bressingham 252
Adnams Bitter; Woodforde
Phoenix XXX Ⓗ
Friendly 17th century local
near Bressingham Gardens
🏚✿Ⓖ➧🅰🅰

Stibbard 19E2

Ordnance Arms
A1067T ☎ Gt. Ryburgh 471
Greene King Abbot; Rayment
BBA Ⓗ
Friendly roadside estate pub;
reopened 1985 🏚Q✿Ⓖ

Stokesby 19H3

10.30–2.30; 6–11

Ferry
☎ Gt. Yarmouth 751096
Flowers Original; Whitbread
Strong Country Bitter Ⓗ
Regular guest beers
Relaxed, traditional riverside
local with moorings 🏚✿Ⓖ➧

Stow Bardolph 18C3

10.30–2.30; 6–11

Hare Arms
Off A10
☎ Downham Market 382229
Greene King Abbot Ⓗ
Comfortable pub in small
village; fine restaurant. Ivy-
clad exterior 🏚Q✿➧🍴

Swaffham 18D3

10.30–2.30; 6–11

George Hotel
Station Street ☎ 21238
Adnams Bitter; Greene King
IPA, Abbot Ⓗ Regular guest
beers
Comfortable old coaching inn
in small market town
🏚🖼✿🖼Ⓖ➧

Terrington St. 18C2
Clements

10.30–2.30; 6–11

County Arms
29 Marshland Street (off A17)
Greene King IPA, Abbot Ⓗ
Occasional guest beers
Busy 3-bar pub 🏚✿Ⓖ

Thetford 18E5

10.30–2.30; 6–11

Chase
Newtown (A11)
Greene King XX, IPA,
Abbot Ⓗ
Friendly, modern house ✿Ⓖ♿

Norfolk Terrier
Croxton Road (B1110)
Tolly Cobbold Mild, Bitter,
Original Ⓗ
Excellent modern estate pub
✿Ⓖ🍴

Thompson 18E4

10.30–2.30; 6.30–11

Chequers
Griston Road (1 mile off
A1075) ☎ Caston 360
Adnams Bitter; Courage Best
Bitter, Directors; Tolly
Cobbold Original Ⓗ
Occasional guest beers
Unspoilt large, thatched, 16th
century alehouse 🏚Q✿Ⓖ➧

Thornham 18D1

10.30–2.30; 6–11

Lifeboat
Ship Lane (off A149) ☎ 236
Adnams Bitter, Old Ⓗ & Ⓖ;
Greene King XX, IPA, Abbot;
Tolly Cobbold Bitter,
Original Ⓗ Regular guest
beers
Historic smugglers inn
overlooking marshes;
excellent food 🏚Q🖼✿Ⓖ➧

Thorpe Market 19G1

12–2.30; 7–11

Suffield Arms
Church Road (near Gunton
Station) ☎ Southrepps 461
Adnams Bitter, Old, Extra;
Greene King IPA, Abbot;
Mauldon Special Ⓗ; James
White Cider Ⓖ Occasional
guest beers
Good, friendly freehouse. Very
popular
🏚✿Ⓖ➧♿⇄ (Late train Fri)

Thorpe St. 19G3
Andrew

10.30–2.30; 5.30–11

Kings Head
Yarmouth Road (A47)
☎ Norwich 33450
Wethered Bitter Ⓗ
Appetising and competitively
priced food. Cosy bar, riverside
garden with mooring 🏚✿Ⓖ➧

Tibenham 19F4

10.30–2.30 (closed Mon–Fri); 7–11

Greyhound
The Street ☎ Tivetshall 676
Woodforde Norfolk Porter,
K9 Ⓗ Occasional guest beers
Completely unspoilt country
pub. Traditional wooden
games, beautiful quarry tiled
floor ✿Ⓖ (Sat/Sun) 🍴🅰

Tivetshall St. Mary 19G4

11–2.30; 6–11

Old Ram
Ram Lane (A140)
📞 Pulham Market 8228
Adnams Bitter; Greene King IPA, Abbot; Mauldon Bitter ⊞ **James White Cider** Ⓖ **Regular guest beers**
Large roadside hostelry with many original features
🏠 🏡 ᴄ ➜

Trowse 19G3

11–2.30; 5.30 (6.30 Sat)–11

Crown Point
A146 📞 Norwich 625689
Flowers Original; Wethered Bitter ⊞
Roadside pub with friendly public bar and comfortable lounge; good food Q 🏡 ᴄ ➜

Walpole Cross Keys 18B2

10.30–2.30; 7–11

Woolpack
A17 📞 Kings Lynn 828327
Adnams Bitter, Extra ⊞
Occasional guest beers
Pleasant roadside pub
🏠 Q 🏡 ᴄ ➜ ⃒

Weasenham All Saints 18D2

10.30–2.30; 5.30–11

Ostrich
A1065
📞 Weasenham St. Peter 221
Adnams Extra; Greene King Abbot; Tolly Cobbold Original ⊞

Typical country local; former Tolly house 🏠 Q 🏡 ᴄ ➜

Wells-next-the-Sea 19E1

10.30–2.30; 6–11

Crown Hotel
The Buttlands (near A149)
📞 Fakenham 710209
Marston Pedigree; Tolly Cobbold Bitter, Original ⊞
Occasional guest beers
Old-style hotel; truncheon-type handpumps
🏠 Q 🏡 🍴 🅿 🖼 ᴄ ➜ ⃒ ⃒ ᴧ

Edinburgh
Station Road
📞 Fakenham 710120
Draught Bass; Greene King Abbot ⊞
Smart freehouse. Previously the Fighting Cocks 🏠 🖼 ᴄ ➜

Try also: Warham Horseshoes

Welney 17H3

10.30–2.30; 6–11

Lamb & Flag
A1101 📞 242
Elgood Bitter ⊞
Cosy pub near bird sanctuary
🏠 Q 🏡 🖼 ᴄ ➜ (not Thu) ⃒ ⃒ ᴧ

West Somerton 19H2

10.30–2.30; 6–11

White Lion
Staithe Road 📞 Winterton 287
Greene King IPA, Abbot ⊞
Easy access to moorings, where country and holiday worlds meet ⊞ 🏡 ᴄ ➜

Wighton 19E1

11–2.30; 6 (summer) 7 (winter)–11

Sandpiper

Off B1105 📞 Walsingham 752
Samuel Smith OBB; Tolly Cobbold Original; Woodforde John Brown Bitter, Wherry Best Bitter ⊞ **Regular guest beers**
Pleasant atmosphere in this friendly pub. A newly built brick fireplace divides the bar into two areas. Pool and darts
🏠 Q 🏡 🖼 ᴄ ➜

Wolterton 19G2

Saracens Head
Near A140 OS172323
📞 Matlaske 287
Adnams Bitter; Greene King Abbot; Rayment BBA ⊞
Large, isolated roadside pub. Good, wholesome food
🏠 🏡 ᴄ ➜

Wood Dalling 19F2

11–2.30; 6.30–11

Wood Dalling Hall
OS074271 📞 Foulsham 832
Greene King Pedigree; Tolly Cobbold Original ⊞
Superb 16th century mansion; excellent for food
Q 🏡 ᴄ ➜ ᴧ

Wymondham 19F3

11–2.30; 7–11

Feathers
Town Green 📞 605675
Adnams Bitter; Greene King Abbot; Marston Pedigree; Reepham Feathers Bitter ⊞
Regular guest beers
Popular local; folk club Thursday nights 🏡 ᴄ ➜ ⃒ ⃒

Northamptonshire

Abthorpe 16C6

10.30 (11 winter)–2.30; 6 (7 winter)–11

New Inn
Silver Street
℡ Silverstone 857306
**Hook Norton Best Bitter, Old
Hookey** Ⓗ
Small village pub tucked up a
lane near the church
🏠 🍽 Ⓖ (not Sun)

Blakesley 16C2

11–2.30; 7–11

Bartholomew Arms
High Street ℡ 860292
Marston Pedigree Ⓗ
Attractive village local with
cricketing memorabilia, hams
and malt whiskies. Home of
soap box derby 🏠 Q 🍽 Ⓖ 🍴

Brackley 16C6

11–2.30; 5.30–11

Plumbers Arms
Manor Road (off A43)
℡ 702495
**Hook Norton Best Bitter,
Marston Burton Bitter** Ⓗ
Unpretentious back street
local 🏠 🍴

Braunston 16B5

11–2.30; 6.30–11

Old Plough
High Street (off A45)
Rugby ℡ 890000
**Ansells Mild, Bitter; Ind Coope
Burton Ale** Ⓗ
Beautiful old coaching inn
close to canal. Good menu,
skittles room 🏠 🎬 🍽 Ⓖ 🍴🍴

Burton Latimer 16D4

12–2; 7–11

Olde Victoria
Bakehouse Lane (off A6)
℡ 722786
**Adnams Bitter; Greene King
IPA, Abbot; Samuel Smith
OBB; Ruddle County** Ⓗ
Popular free house containing
much bric-a-brac, now with
adjoining restaurant. No food
Sunday 🏠 🍽 Ⓖ 🍴

Chacombe 16B6

11.30–2.30; 5.30–11

George & Dragon
Silver Street
℡ Banbury 710602
**Draught Bass, M & B Mild,
Springfield Bitter** Ⓗ Occasional
guest beers
Grade II listed building with
notable snug, stone flagged
lounge/restaurant, passage
and local's bar
🏠 Q 🎬 🍽 Ⓖ 🍴 (not Sun)🍴

Charlton 16B7

10.30–2.30; 5.30–11

Rose & Crown
Main Street
℡ Banbury 811317

**Draught Bass; Donnington
SBA; Marston Border Bitter,
Burton Bitter, Pedigree;
Bulmer Cider** Ⓗ Regular guest
beers
Quiet local in rural
conservation area with non-
smoking food bar. Food Tue–
Sat only 🏠 🎬 🍽 Ⓖ 🍴

Chipping Warden 16B6

10.30–2.30; 7–11

Rose & Crown
Banbury Road (A361) ℡ 216
**Hook Norton Mild, Best
Bitter** Ⓗ
Old coaching inn with basic
bar. Always a cheery welcome
Q 🎬 🍽 🍴

Corby 16D3

11–2.30; 6–11

Knights Lodge
Tower Hill Road (off A6003)
℡ Great Oakley 742602
**Everard Bitter, Tiger, Old
Original** Ⓗ
Large 17th century building
on modern estate, oak-
beamed interior 🎬 🍽
Ⓖ(not Sun) 🍴 (Thu–Sat) ♿

Cosgrove 16D6

11.30–2.30; 6–11

Navigation Inn
Thrupp Wharf
℡ Milton Keynes 543156
Closed Mon Oct–Easter
**Adnams Bitter; Draught Bass;
Hook Norton Best Bitter** Ⓗ
Regular guest beers
Comfortable canalside pub at
Castlethorpe Road/ Grand
Union junction. Good value
food 🏠 🍽 Ⓖ 🍴🍴♿

Cottingham 16D3

10.30–2.30; 6–11

Royal George
Blind Lane (off B670)
℡ Rockingham 771005
**Marston Pedigree, Owd
Rodger** Ⓗ
Hard to find, cosy, split-level
pub with scenic views of
village rooftops and Welland
Valley. Menu includes a
comprehensive range of
curries 🏠 🎬 🍽 🍴 (not Tue) 🍴

Daventry 16B5

10.30–2.30; 5.30–11

Coach & Horses
Warwick Street, Town Centre
℡ 76692
Opens 11 am
Ind Coope Burton Ale Ⓗ
Refurbished town pub. Live
jazz every other Tuesday.
🏠 🍽 Ⓖ (not Sun)

Dun Cow
Brook Street ℡ 771005
Opens 6 pm Sat

**Davenports Bitter; Flowers
Original** Ⓗ
Popular old coaching inn.
Unspoilt public bar
🏠 Ⓖ (not weekends) 🍴

Deanshanger 16D6

11–2.30; 6–11

Fox & Hounds
71 High Street (off A4227)
℡ Milton Keynes 563485
**Aylesbury ABC Bitter;
Draught Bass** Ⓗ
Homely pub at centre of
village life Q 🍽 Ⓖ 🍴🍴

Eastcote 16C5

12–2.30 (closed Mon); 6–10.30 (11 F, S)

Eastcote Arms
Gayton Road ℡ Pattishall 731
**Banks & Taylor Eastcote Ale;
Samuel Smith OBB; Marston
Pedigree** Ⓗ Regular guest
beers
Busy village pub with many
prints and mirrors. 🏠 Q 🍽 Ⓖ

East Haddon 16C5

10.30–2.30; 5.30–11

Red Lion
Main Street ℡ 223
**Wells Eagle Bitter,
Bombardier** Ⓗ
Thatched stone pub with
brass-festooned lounge close
to Althorp. Excellent
restaurant 🍽 🅱 Ⓖ 🍴🍴

Easton on the Hill 17E2

11–2.30; 6.30–11

Oak
Nr. Stamford (A43)
℡ Stamford 52286
**Greene King IPA, Abbot;
Marston Pedigree** Ⓗ
Smart and comfortable
restaurant with a cosy bar
area 🏠 Q 🎬 (if eating) 🍽 Ⓖ 🍴

Fotheringhay 17F3

10–2.30; 6–11

Falcon
℡ Cotterstock 254
**Elgood Bitter; Greene King
IPA, Abbot; Liddingtons
Tudor** Ⓗ Occasional guest
beers
Fine value-for-money 18th
century pub. Basic, small
public bar, busy, popular
lounge and dining room
serving excellent meals
🏠 🍽 Ⓖ 🍴🍴♿

Great Cransley 16D4

11–2.30; 7–11

Three Cranes
Loddington Road (3 miles SW
of Kettering)
Marston Capital Ale, Pedigree
Ⓗ
Excellent village local with
large garden adjoining church
🏠 Q 🍽

Great Houghton
16D5

10.30–2.30; 6–11

Old Cherry Tree
Cherry Tree Lane (hidden at
end of cul-de-sac off A428)
**Wells Eagle Bitter,
Bombardier** Ⓗ
Cosy low-beamed pub. Basic
but posh Q ✦♦♦

Grendon
16D5

10.30–2.30; 6–11

Half Moon
Main Street, (nr Grendon Hall)
✆ Wellingborough 663263
**Wells Eagle Bitter,
Bombardier** Ⓗ
Oak-beamed village local. Jazz
Tuesdays and alternate
Sundays ▦✦Ⓖ➔

Hargrave
17E4

10.30–2.30; 6–11

Nag's Head
Church Street (off A45)
✆ Wellingborough 622368
Wells Eagle Bitter Ⓗ
Quiet pub with plenty of horse
brasses, thatched roof and
inglenook ▦Q✦Ⓖ➔♦⚠

Harringworth
16E3

12–2.30; 7–11

White Swan
✆ Morcott 543
**Marston Pedigree; Ruddle
Rutland Bitter, County** Ⓗ
Fine country pub with 2
lounge bars and carvery.
Landlord was 1986 winner of
UK home-made steak and
kidney pie competition!
▦QⒺⒼ➔

Isham
16D4

11.30–2.30; 7–11

Lilacs
Church Street (off A509)
✆ Burton Latimer 3948
**Marston Burton Bitter,
Pedigree** Ⓗ
Modernised and extended old
village pub. Large games bar,
small cosy lounge ✦Ⓖ♦

Kettering
16D4

10.30–2.30; 5.30–11

Alexandra Arms
Victoria Street ✆ 512253
Opens 11 and 7
**Manns Bitter; Usher Founders
Ale; Wilsons Original Bitter** Ⓗ
Long narrow pub. Basic bar,
small comfortable lounge and
large collection of breweriana
✦Ⓖ (not Sun) ➔ (Fri, Sat) ♦

Cherry Tree
Sheep Street (opposite market)
✆ 514706
**Wells Eagle Bitter,
Bombardier** Ⓗ

Low-ceilinged busy local, with
small quiet lounge at rear
Ⓖ (not Sun) ♦≷

Cordwainer
Bath Road ✆ 518578
Opens 11 and 6
Home Bitter Ⓔ
Modern estate local, with
club-like atmosphere ✦♦&

Talbot
Meadow Road ✆ 514565
Opens 11 am
**Marston Mercian Mild, Border
Bitter, Burton Bitter, Pedigree,
Merrie Monk** Ⓗ
Victorian pub, catering for all
tastes. Lounge walls crammed
with mirrors and pictures,
including Escher prints
▦✦ⒺⒼ (not Sun) ➔♦≷

Lamport
16D4

10.30–2.30; 5.30–11

Swan
Harborough Road (A508)
✆ Maidwell 232
Whitbread Castle Eden Ale Ⓗ
Large lounge bar, separate
pool room. Good food ✦Ⓖ➔

Marston St. Lawrence
16B6

10.30–2.30; 6–11

Marston Inn
Main Street
Hook Norton Best Bitter Ⓖ
Unchanged for years, with
simple scrubbed tables ▦Q✦♦

Newnham
16C5

12–2.30; 6.30–11

Romers Arms
The Green
✆ Daventry 702221
Hook Norton Best Bitter Ⓗ
Regular guest beers
Friendly village pub, recently
refurbished ▦Q✦
Ⓖ (not Sun) ➔ (Tue, Sat)
♦& ⚠ YHA at Badby

Newton Bromswold
17E5

12–2.30; 7–11

Swan
Church Lane
✆ Rushden 314323
Greene King IPA Ⓗ, **Abbot** Ⓖ
Excellent village local with
three small bars. Well worth
finding. Northants skittles
played ✦♦

Northampton
16D5

10–2.30; 5.30–11

Barn Owl
Olden Road, off Rectory Farm
Road ✆ 416483
Opens 11 and 6.30
Greene King IPA, Abbot Ⓗ
Popular estate pub with barn
owl theme ✦&

Bat & Wickets
117 Bailiff Street ✆ 38277
**Courage Best Bitter,
Directors** Ⓗ
Basic, loud street-corner local.
Good value lunches
▦✦Ⓖ (Mon–Fri) ♦

Old Black Lion
Black Lion Hill
**Usher Founders Ale; Webster
Yorkshire Bitter; Wilsons
Original Bitter** Ⓗ
Comfortable lounge and basic
bar. Lunchtimes, packed with
local office workers. Northants
hood skittles played here
✦Ⓖ♦≷

Old House at Home
Wellingborough Road
(A4500) ✆ 33855
Opens 11 am
**Manns Bitter; Usher Founders
Ale; Wilsons Original Bitter** Ⓗ
Updated street-corner local.
Appeals to modern drinker's
needs. Function room ✦♦

Spread Eagle
147 Wellingborough Road
(A4500) ✆ 24386
**Wells Eagle Bitter,
Bombardier** Ⓗ
Good community pub with
sing-a-longs on Wed & Sun
evenings Ⓖ (Tue–Fri) ♦&

Standens Inn
Billing Brook Road, Standens
Barn ✆ 410601
Opens 11 and 6
**Hook Norton Best Bitter;
Shipstone Bitter** Ⓗ
Bustling modern estate pub,
three miles from town centre

Norton
16D5

11–2.30; 6–11

White Horse
Daventry Road (1 mile off A5)
✆ Daventry 2982
**Charles Wells Bitter,
Bombardier** Ⓗ
Pleasant village local with
skittle alley Q✦Ⓖ➔♦&

Orlingbury
16D4

10.30–2.30; 6–11

Queens Arms
Isham Road
✆ Wellingborough 678258
**Manns Bitter; Wilsons
Original Bitter** Ⓗ
Traditional 2-room village
local. No coin operated games
allowed by landlord
▦Q✦Ⓖ (not Sun) ♦

Oundle
17E3

10.30–2.30; 6–11

Rose & Crown
Market Place ✆ 73284
John Smiths Bitter Ⓗ
Small stone-built pub, with
Northants skittles
▦✦Ⓖ➔ (Summer only) ♦

Raunds 17E4

10.30–2.30; 6–11

World Upside Down
Marshalls Road (nr Square, off A605)
✆ Wellingborough 622380
Marston Mercian Mild, Burton Bitter, Pedigree Ⓗ
Regular guest beers
Basic locals pub ☺♚

Rothwell 16D4

11–2.30; 5.30–11

Red Lion
Market Square
✆ Kettering 710409
Wells Eagle Bitter, Bombardier Ⓗ
Keen sports pub. Interesting brasses around lounge
🅐☺♚

Rowell Charter Inn
Sun Hill, Kettering Road (A6)
✆ Kettering 710453
Courage Directors; Greene King IPA; Marston Pedigree; Younger Scotch Bitter Ⓗ
Friendly local caters for all tastes. Named after fair held Monday after Trinity Sunday
🅐☺♚

Rushden 16E5

10.30–2.30; 5.30–11

Feathers
High Street (off A6) ✆ 5204
Opens 11 & 6
Wells Eagle Bitter, Bombardier Ⓗ
Popular town pub, with plush lounge requiring dresss standards. Restaurant and childrens playground recently added ♘☺♚♞

King Edward VII
Queen Street ✆ 53478
Wells Eagle Bitter, Bombardier Ⓖ
Back street local popular with young. Darts, skittles in public, smaller comfortable lounge 🅐♘☺♚♞

Southwick 17E3

11–2.30; 6–11

Shuckburgh Arms
Main Street ✆ Oundle 74007
Adnams Bitter; Hook Norton Best Bitter; Ruddle County; Wadworth 6X (summer) Ⓗ
Hook Norton Old Hookey (summer) Ⓖ **Occasional guest beers**
Popular and welcoming free house. Basic public bar, open fire in lounge. Darts, dominoes and bar billiards 🅐Q♘☺♚♞

Sulgrave 16B6

11–2.30; 7–11

Star
Manor Road (off B4525)
✆ 389

Hook Norton Best Bitter, Ⓗ
Old Hookey Ⓖ **(winter)**
Unhurried and friendly, stone-flagged floor and unusual inglenook fireplace. Close to Sulgrave Manor, of George Washington fame 🅐Q

Titchmarsh 16E4

11–2.30; 6–11

Dog & Partridge
6 High Street (off A605)
✆ Thrapston 2546
Wells Eagle Bitter Ⓗ
Old stone built 'drinkers' pub with modern interior and separate games room 🅐♘♚🅗

Wadenhoe 17E4

10.30–2.30; 7–11

Kings Head
Church Street ✆ Clopton 222
Adnams Bitter; Marston Pedigree Ⓗ
Unspoilt local, popular in summer. Extensive pub gardens lead to 100 yards of River Nene bank 🅐Q♘♞

Weedon 16C5

11–2.30; 5.30–11

Globe
Watling Street (junction A5/A45) ✆ 40336
Samuel Smith OBB; Wadworth 6X Ⓗ **Regular guest beers**
Comfortable roadhouse with two lounges and restaurant
🅐♘♘🅐☺♞

Narrowboat Inn
Watling Street (A5) ✆ 40534
Wells Eagle Bitter, Bombardier Ⓗ
Popular canalside pub with garden and restaurant
♘♘♞♞🅗

Welford 16C4

11.30–2.30; 6.30–11

Shoulder of Mutton
12 High Street (A50) ✆ 375
Opens 12 & 7
Usher Founders Ale; Webster Yorkshire Bitter; Wilsons Original Bitter Ⓗ
17th century low-beamed pub now all one room, but still retaining some character. No food Thu 🅐🅗♘☺♚🅗Å

Swan Inn
49 High Street (A50) ✆ 481
Marston Burton Bitter, Pedigree Ⓗ
Friendly and homely locals pub close to Welford Basin
♘☺♞Å

Wellingborough 16D5

10.30–2.30; 6–11

Horseshoe

Sheep Street ✆ 222015
Evenings opens 7
Draught Bass; M & B Springfield Bitter Ⓗ
Town-centre pub with stained glass windows, large lounge and games room
♘☺♞

Vivian Arms
Knox Road (off B571)
✆ 223660
Wells Eagle Bitter Ⓗ
Large friendly back-street local with small lounge, large bar and games room
🅐Q♘☺♞▰

Weston 16C6

11.30–2.30; 6.30–11

Crown
By Weedon Lois OS589469
✆ Sulgrave 328
Flowers Original; Fuller ESB; Greene King Abbot; Hook Norton Best Bitter; Marston Pedigree; Ⓗ **Regular guest beers**
Very popular; Northants skittles and regular live music
🅗♘☺♞

Yardley Hastings 16D5

11–2.30; 6–11

Red Lion Inn
High Street (off A428) ✆ 210
Wells Eagle Bitter, Bombardier Ⓗ
Comfortable refurbished village pub. Northants skittles in former gents loo!
♘☺ (not Sun)

Yarwell 17F3

11–2.30; 6.30–11

Angel
Main Street
✆ Stamford 782582
Greene King IPA; Marston Pedigree Ⓗ **Regular guest beers**
Pleasant 17th century building. Near River Nene and caravan site. No food winter Mons 🅐🅗☺♞

The 🅐 symbol denotes a pub with a real solid fuel fire

Allendale 32E9

11–3; 6–10.30
Hare & Hounds
Marston Pedigree G Regular
guest beers
Small hotel with restaurant
and pool room. Friendly
atmosphere ♨Q☞🅰🖰🕭🍴

Allerdean 33F3

11–3; 6–11
Plough
B6354 West Allerdean
✆ Berwick 87206
Belhaven 80/-; Newcastle
Exhibition 🅗
Known locally as "The Folly"
but no folly to visit this
whitewashed inn. Good food
🖰🍴

Alnwick 33G5

11–3; 6–11
Fleece Inn
Bondgate Without
Drybrough's Eighty 🅗
Lively pub near ancient Town
Gate. Hat collection ♨🅰🖰🍴🍴

Oddfellows Arms
Narrowgate ✆ 602695
Vaux Samson 🅗
No oddfellows here, just
friendly locals. Food and
accommodation summer only
♨🅰🖰🍴🍴

Tanners Arms
Hotspur Place ✆ 602553
Belhaven 70/-, 80/-; Vaux
Sunderland Draught 🅗
Small, lively corner terrace
bar

Alwinton 33E6

11–3; 6–11
Rose & Thistle
✆ Rothbury 50226
Whitbread Castle Eden 🅗
Village local in National Park.
Popular with walkers Q🍴🅰

Anick 33F8

11–2.30; 6–10.30 (11 summer)
Rat Inn
✆ Hexham 602814
Tetley Bitter 🅗
Cosy pub with extensive menu
(try the "Rat Grill" if you
dare). Collections of rat objects
and chamber pots ♨Q🖰🍴🖰🕭🍴

Bamburgh 33G4

11–3; 6–11
Castle Hotel
Main Street ✆ 351
Lorimer Best Scotch; Vaux
Samson 🅗
Busy, cosy pub near castle and
beach ♨🕭🍴

Victoria Hotel
Main Street ✆ 431
Drybrough's Eighty 🅰
Compact bar in imposing
hotel. Inglenook in snug
♨🖰🕭🍴

Bedlington 33H7

11–3; 6–10.30
**Northumberland
Arms**
112 Front Street East
Drybrough's Eighty; Ruddle
Best Bitter 🅗 Regular guest
beers
Comfortable bar-lounge with
upstairs snooker room 🖰🕭

Berwick- 33F3
upon-Tweed

11–3; 6–11
Free Trade Inn
Castlegate ✆ 306498
Lorimer Best Scotch 🅗
Bonnie Berwick boozer.
Unspoilt interior; fine
woodwork, glasswork and
partitioning matched in
appeal by local banter 🍴≷

Meadowhouse
A1 Extreme N of town
✆ 304173
Lorimer & Clark 70/-, 80/- 🅗
Most northerly pub in
England. Welcoming roadside
inn, old Berwick photographs
♨🖰🍴🍴

Pilot Inn
High Greens ✆ 304214
Broughton Greenmantle Ale 🅗
Interesting pub with strong
nautical flavour

Blyth 33H7

11–3; 6–11
Ferryman
Crawford Street ✆ 353375
Matthew Brown John Peel;
Theakston Best Bitter, XB 🅗
Wood panelled lounge and bar
at waters edge. Near ferry 🍴

Top House
Matthew Brown John Peel;
Theakston Best Bitter, XB 🅗
Comfortable Street corner
lounge bar

Corbridge 33F8

11–3; 6–11
Lion of Corbridge
Bridge End ✆ 2504
Theakston Best Bitter, XB 🅗
Excellent hotel south of river
♨🖰🅰🖰🍴≷

Wheatsheaf Hotel
Watling Street ✆ 2020
Vaux Sunderland Draught 🅗
Imposing hotel, impromptu
weekend jam sessions
🍴🖰🕭🍴🍴≷

Craster 33H5

11–3; 6–11
Jolly Fisherman
✆ Embleton 218
Drybroughs Eighty 🅗
Split-level pub in fishing
village. Panoramic view to
Dunstanburgh Castle
♨🍴🕭🍴🍴

Dipton Mill 33E8

11–3; 7–10.30
Dipton Mill Inn
2 Miles S of Hexham on
Whitley Chapel Road
✆ Hexham 606577
Theakston Best Bitter 🅗
Regular guest beers
Warm, friendly pub miles
from anywhere ♨Q🖰🍴

East 33F8
Wallhouses

11–3; 6–11
Robin Hood Inn
B6318 Near Stamfordham
✆ Great Whittington 273
McEwan 80/-; Newcastle
Exhibition 🅗
Friendly cosy pub in remote
hamlet on Military Road
♨🍴🕭🍴

Etal 33E3

11–3; 6–11
Black Bull
Off B6354
Lorimer Best Scotch; Vaux
Samson 🅗
Thatched pub in picturesque
village. Attracts fox hunting
followers. Castle and working
watermill nearby 🍴🕭🍴

Falstone 32D7

11–3; 6–11
Black Cock
Falstone ✆ Bellingham 40200
Lorimer & Clark 80/-; Vaux
Samson 🅗
Very pleasant village local
near Kielder Water
♨🍴🖰🕭🍴

Haltwhistle 32D8

11–3; 6–11
Grey Bull Hotel
Main Street ✆ 20298
Theakston Best Bitter, XB, Old
Peculier 🅗
Stone-built inn with several
rooms 🖰🕭🍴🍴🅰≷

New Inn
West Road
Lorimer Best Scotch 🅔
Popular, locals' street corner
bar Q🍴≷

Hartley 33H7

11–3; 6–11
Delaval Arms
A193 South of Seaton Sluice
McEwan 80/-; Newcastle
Exhibition 🅗
Large many-roomed listed
building. Famous blue stone
near entrance 🍴

Haydon Bridge 32D8

11–3; 6–11 closed all day Monday
General Havelock
Ratcliff Road
Tetley Bitter 🅗

Pub and restaurant on main road 🅰 ⚲ ⚑ ⚞

Hedley-on-the-Hill 33F9

11–3; 6–11
Feathers
2 miles S of Prudhoe
Theakston Best Bitter, XB Ⓗ
Friendly village pub with view of Tyne Valley 🅰 Q ⚲ ⚲

Hexham 33F8

11–3; 6–11
Coach & Horses
Priest Popple ☏ 603132
Open all day Tuesday
Tetley Bitter Ⓗ
Friendly old coaching inn. Unspoilt bar and comfortable lounge/dining room 🅴 ⚲ ⚑ ⚞ ⚞

Globe
Battle Hill ☏ 603742
Newcastle Exhibition; Younger's No. 3 Ⓗ
Unspoilt locals pub of character. Unusual curving bar ⚑ ⚞

Higham Dykes 33G8

11–3; 6–11
Waggon Inn
A696 ☏ Belsay 666
Draught Bass Ⓗ
Large roadside inn. Small public bar, extended lounge Q⚑

Holy Island 33G3

11–3; 6–11
Castle Hotel
Drybrough's Eighty Ⓔ
Cosy pub near Lindisfarne Castle and Priory. A good place to be stranded at high tide. Crossing times displayed on A1 at Holy Island turnoff 🅰 Q

Horton 33H7

11–3; 6–11
Three Horse Shoes
Off A189
Drybrough's Eighty; Ruddle Best Bitter Ⓗ Regular guest beers
Surprisingly spacious yet cosy pub 🅴 ⚲ ⚲

Langley-on-Tyne 29G1

12–2; 7–11 (hours vary in winter)
Carts Bog Inn
A686 ☏ Haydon Bridge 338
Tetley Bitter Ⓗ Regular guest beers
Remote stone pub on edge of moors, its log fire is needed in winter! 🅰 ⚲ ⚑ ⚞ Å

Lowick 33G6

11–3; 8–11

Black Bull
B6353 ☏ Berwick 88228
McEwan 70/-, 80/- Ⓗ
Renowned quiet village inn. Good food and service
🅰 ⚲ ⚲ ⚑

Morpeth 33G7

11–3; 6–11
Joiners Arms
Wansbeck Street ☏ 513540
Theakston XB Ⓗ Regular guest beers
Public bar, small lounge, often crowded ⚑ ⚞

Netherton 33F5

11–3; 6–10.30 (hours may vary)
Star Inn
OS989077
Whitbread Castle Eden Ⓖ
Unspoilt gem in isolated village. Disused cock-fighting pit on hill opposite 🅰 Q⚑

Newbiggin-by-the-Sea 33H7

11–3; 6–11
Old Ship Hotel
Front Street
☏ Ashington 817212
Vaux Sunderland Draught; Lorimer & Clark 80/- Ⓗ
Occasional guest beers
Pleasant inn with bar, lounge and music room. Ships telegraph in lounge 🅴 ⚲ ⚑ ⚞

Newton-on-the-Moor 33G6

6–11 (opens evenings only)
Cook & Barker
Off A1 ☏ Shilbottle 234
McEwan 80/- Ⓗ
Warm, inviting country local, separate sitting room 🅰 ⚲ ⚑

Norham-on-Tweed 33E3

11–3; 6.30–10.30
Masons Arms
West Street (B6470)
Lorimer Best Scotch Ⓗ
Excellent traditional bar, a must. Fishing rights on the Tweed 🅰 Q 🅴 ⚲ ⚲ ⚑

Rothbury 33F6

11–3; 6–11
Railway
Station Road
McEwan 80/- Ⓗ
Former station hotel, real ale in public bar Q⚲⚑

Seahouses 33G4

11–3; 6–11
Black Swan
Union Street ☏ 720277
Lorimer Best Scotch, Vaux Samson Ⓗ
Unpretentious pub above the harbour, hidden away from

amusement arcades and candy floss 🅴 (summer) ⚑ Å

Stagshaw 33F8

11–3; 6–10.30 (11 F, S)
Errington Arms
B6318/A68 roundabout
Darley Thorne Best Bitter; Lorimer Best Scotch; Wards Sheffield Best Bitter Ⓗ
Comfortable pub near several ancient Roman sites Q⚲⚲⚑

Tweedmouth 33F3

11–3; 6–11
Harrow
Mainstreet ☏ Berwick 305451
Lorimer Best Scotch Ⓗ
Classic bar. Mellow, panelled interior 🅰 ⚲ ⚑

Twice Brewed 32E7

11–3; 6–10.30
Twice Brewed
Military Road
Marston Burton Bitter, Pedigree, Merrie Monk Ⓗ
Large pub near Roman Wall by Housesteads Fort. Suitable for walkers ⚲ ⚑ Å

Wall 33E8

11–3; 6–11
Hadrian Hotel
Wall Village, Hexham
Vaux Samson Ⓗ
Beamed Jacobean-style bar in creeper-covered hotel built with stone from Hadrians Wall 🅰 ⚲ ⚑ ⚞ ⚑ ⚲

Wooler 33F4

11–3; 6–10.30
Anchor
Cheviot Street (off A697)
Vaux Samson Ⓗ
Friendly pub, convivial atmosphere. Nearest pub to Harthope Valley and The Cheviot Q🅴⚲⚑Å

Ryecroft Hotel
A697 Ryecroft Way ☏ 459
Lorimer & Clark 70/-, 80/-; Marston Pedigree; Theakston Best Bitter Ⓗ
Well-run family hotel, reputation for good food.
🅰 Q 🅴 ⚲ ⚲ ⚑

WARMEST WELCOME

♦ A REAL FIRE PUB ♦

The 🅰 symbol denotes a pub with a real solid fuel fire

Arnold 26B7

10.30–2.30; 5.30–10.30 (11 F, S)

Horse & Jockey
Front Street
✆ Nottingham 267123
Home Mild, Bitter Ⓔ
Friendly, bustling multi-roomed town pub; just off shopping centre ♿ 🐾 🎱 🍽

Aslockton 26C8

11–2.30; 6–10.30 (11 F, S)

Old Greyhound
Main Street ✆ Whatton 50957
Home Bitter Ⓗ & Ⓔ
Cheerful, cosy country pub
Q ♿ 🐾 🕐 🍽 ▲ ≈

Try also: Cranmer (Home)

Awsworth 26A8

10.30–2.30; 6–10.30 (11 F, S)

Gate
Main Street (off A6096)
Hardys & Hansons Best Bitter Ⓔ
Isolated village pub worth finding. Near site of once famous Forty Bridges ♨ 🐾 🍽

Bagthorpe 26A7

11–3; 6–10.30 (11 F, S)

Dixies Arms
School Lane (off B600)
Home Mild, Bitter Ⓗ
Splendid unspoilt village pub in fine setting ♨ ♿ 🐾 🍽 ▲

Balderton 26C7

10.30–2.30; 6–10.30 (11 F, S)

Rose & Crown
Main Street ✆ Newark 704620
Ind Coope Bitter, Burton Ale Ⓗ
Popular well run local ♨ 🍽

Try also: Chesters (John Smith's)

Beeston 26B8

10.30–2.30; 6–10.30 (11 F, S)

Boat & Horses
Trent Road
✆ Nottingham 258589
Home Mild, Bitter Ⓔ
Traditional pub near the canal ♨ 🐾 🕐 (not Sun) 🍽 ≈

Malt Shovel Inn
Union Street
Shipstone Mild, Bitter Ⓔ
Ungutted pleasant side-street local ♿ 🐾 🍽

Queens Hotel
Queens Road
Shipstone Mild, Bitter Ⓔ
Busy Victorian pub
♨ 🐾 🕐 🍽 ≈

Blidworth 26B7

11–3; 6–10.30 (11 F, S)

Black Bull
Field Lane/Main Street
✆ Mansfield 792291
Shipstone Mild, Bitter; Bulmer Cider Ⓗ & Ⓔ

Spacious and friendly pub on edge of mining village
♨ 🐾 🕐 🍽 (not Sun or Tue) 🍽

Blidworth Bottoms 26B7

11–3; 6–10.30 (11 F, S)

Fox & Hounds
Calverton Road, ½ mile S of village ✆ Mansfield 792383
Hardys & Hansons Best Mild, Best Bitter Ⓗ & Ⓔ
Pleasant multi-roomed local, occasional outdoor entertainment on summer evenings
♨ ♿ 🐾 🕐 (not Wed) 🍽

Blyth 26B5

11–3; 6.30–11

Angel
High Street (off A1, A634)
✆ 213
Hardys & Hansons Best Bitter Ⓔ
Oldest coaching inn in North Notts with huge fires all winter ♨ ♿ 🐾 🎱 🕐 🍽

Try also: White Swan (Whitbread)

Brinsley 26A7

10.30–2.30; 6–10.30 (11 F, S)

Durham Ox
High Street, New Brinsley
✆ Langley Mill 712659
Hardys & Hansons Best Mild, Best Bitter Ⓔ
Friendly village local with comfortable lounge 🐾 🍽

Burton Joyce 26B8

10.30–2.30; 5.30–10.30 (11 F, S)

Cross Keys
Main Street ✆ 3286
Opens 11
Whitbread Castle Eden Ⓗ
Comfortable village pub Q 🍽 ≈

Wheatsheaf
Church Road (A612) ✆ 3298
Home Mild, Bitter Ⓔ
Large traditional pub with excellent restaurant, bar meals and summer barbecues
🐾 🕐 🍽 👶 ≈

Carlton 26B8

10.30–2.30; 5.30–10.30 (11 F, S)

Fox & Hounds
Station Road
✆ Nottingham 878601
Home Mild, Bitter Ⓔ
Traditional 3-roomed local next to station Q 👶 ≈

Windsor Castle
Carlton Hill (A612)
✆ Nottingham 871374
Hardys & Hansons Best Bitter Ⓔ
Popular local, live entertainment in lounge, games room upstairs
🐾 🕐 (not Sun) 🍽 ≈

Carlton-in-Lindrick 26B5

10.30 (11 Sat)–3; 6–11

Riddel Arms
Doncaster Road, Costhorpe (A60)
Home Bitter Ⓔ
Large roadside house popular for good value lunches 🐾 🕐 🍽

Caythorpe 26C7

10.30–2.30; 5.30–10.30 (11 F, S)

Black Horse
Main Street (off A612)
OS5K690456
✆ Nottingham 663520
Shipstone Bitter Ⓗ
Unspoilt 18th century inn, allegedly a hiding place of Dick Turpin, whose secret cupboard may be viewed. No food Sunday ♨ Q 🐾 🕐 🍽 🍽

Try also: Old Volunteer (Hardys & Hansons)

Cropwell Bishop 26C8

11–2.30; 6–10.30 (11 F, S)

Lime Kiln Inn
Kinoulton Road OS678345
✆ Kinoulton 540
Home Mild, Bitter Ⓔ
Fine ex-coaching inn on rural crossroads
♨ 🐾 🕐 (not Tues/Sun) 🍽

East Leake 26B9

11–2.30; 6–10.30 (11 F, S)

Bulls Head
Main Street ✆ 2393
Home Mild, Bitter Ⓔ
Pleasant, comfortable village pub, close to South Notts bus route 🐾 🍽

Try also: Three Horseshoes (Home)

Eastwood 26A7

10.30–2.30; 6–10.30 (11 F, S)

Greasley Castle
1 Castle Street, Hilltop (off A610) ✆ Langley Mill 761080
Hardys & Hansons Best Mild, Best Bitter Ⓔ
Small thriving split level one-roomer; cheapest real ale in the area 🍽

New Inn
94 Newthorpe Common, New Eastwood (off A610)
Home Mild, Bitter Ⓔ
Small relaxing 2-roomed local
🍽

Epperstone 26B7

11–2.30; 6–10.30 (11 F, S)

Cross Keys
Main Street
✆ Nottingham 663033
Hardys & Hansons Best Mild, Best Bitter Ⓔ
Friendly village inn, in

picturesque setting, complete
with local poacher
🍺Q💶🅿🏠🕐 (not Mon) 🍴🍴

Fiskerton 26C7

11.30–2.30 6 (6.30 winter)–10.30 (11 F, S)
Bromley Arms
Fiskerton Wharf
**Hardys & Hansons Best Mild,
Best Bitter** ℍ
Riverside inn. Boat moorings
and supplies nearby
🅿🕐 (Mon–Sat) 🍴

Gotham 26B8

10.30–2.30; 5.30 (6 Sat)–10.30 (11 F, S)
Sun Inn
The Square
☎ Nottingham 830484
**Adnams Bitter; Cameron Best
Bitter; Everard Mild, Bitter,
Tiger, Old Original** ℍ
Welcoming village inn
Q🅿🕐🍴&

Granby 26C8

11–2.30; 6–10.30 (11 F, S)
Marquis of Granby
Dragon Street
Home Bitter ℍ
Pleasant country inn on edge
of Vale of Belvoir 🍺Q🅿🕐🍴&

Harworth 26B5

11–3; 6–11
Galway Arms
☎ Doncaster 742219
**Hardys & Hansons Best Mild,
Best Bitter** ℍ
Large pub in mining village.
Concert room 🍺💶🅿🕐🍴🍴&

Hayton 26C5

11–3; 7–11
Boat Inn
Main Street (B1403)
☎ Retford 700158
**Bass 4X Mild; Stones Best
Bitter; Whitbread Trophy** ℍ
Regular guest beers
Country pub by Chesterfield
Canal. Carvery restaurant
🍺🅿🏠🕐🍴🅰

Hoveringham 26C7

10.30–2.30; 6–10.30 (11 F, S)
Marquis of Granby
Main Street
☎ Nottingham 663080
**Marston Pedigree; Ruddle
County** ℍ
Friendly comfortable pub. No
food Sunday. Good
accommodation in 5
bedrooms 🍺🅿🏠🕐🍴&

Hucknall 26B7

10.30–2.30; 6–10.30 (11 F, S)
Red Lion
High Street
Home Mild, Bitter 🅴
Lively town pub with many
small rooms 🍴

Huthwaite 26A7

11–3; 6–10.30 (11 F, S)
Miners Arms
Blackwell Road (B6026)
Winter evenings opens 6.30
Home Bitter ℍ
Quiet unchanged village local
Q🅿🍴🅰

Workpeoples
Chesterfield Road (off B6026)
Home Mild, Bitter 🅴
Former coaching inn, now
catering for local trade 🍴

Try also: Portland Arms
(Shipstone)

Kimberley 26A8

10.30–2.30; 5.30–10.30 (11 F, S)
Lord Clyde
Main Street (A610)
☎ Nottingham 384907
**Hardys & Hansons Best Mild,
Best Bitter** ℍ
Attractive 1-bar pub in centre
of village serving good value
food 🕐🍴 (Mon–Fri)

Nelson & Railway
Station Road, off Main Street,
opposite the brewery (off
A610) ☎ Nottingham 382177
**Hardys & Hansons Best
Bitter** ℍ
Genuine and friendly village
pub with fine wood-panelled
interior. Good value meals.
Cheap beer 5.30–7 pm
Mon–Fri 🍺🅿🏠🕐🍴 (Mon–Fri) 🍴

White Lion
The Swingate (off A610) via
Factory Lane & High Street
☎ Nottingham 383687
Opens 11 & 7
Shipstone Mild, Bitter 🅴
Excellent village local with a
vast display of horse prints
and plates 🅿🍴

Kirkby in 26B7
Ashfield

11–3; 6–10.30 (11 F, S)
Ashfields Hotel
Sutton Road (B6018)
☎ Mansfield 554074
Home Mild, Bitter ℍ
Large roadside hotel. Plush
lounge, bar dominated by pool
table 💶🅿🍴

Lambley 26B8

10.30–2.30; 6–10.30 (11 F, S)
Woodlark Inn
Church Street
☎ Burton Joyce 2535
Home Bitter 🅴
Naval curios and old beer mat
collection in bar Q🍺🅿🕐🍴&

All village pubs are "real"

Laneham 26C6

12–3 (Closed Tues lunch); 7–11
Butchers Arms
Main Street (off A57)
☎ Dunham on Trent 255

**Everard Tiger; Marston
Pedigree** ℍ **Regular guest
beers**
Unspoilt village pub.
Inglenook fireplace, warm and
friendly 🍺Q💶🅿🕐🍴🅰🅰

Lowdham 26B7

11.30–2.30; 5.30–10.30 (11 F, S)
Old Ship
Main Street (off A612)
☎ Nottingham 663049
John Smith's Bitter ℍ
Popular, friendly village inn.
Separate pool area in bar. No
food Sunday
🅿🕐🍴 (until 7.30) 🍴🚆

Mansfield 26B7

10.30–3; 7–10.30 (11 F, S)
Talbot Inn
Nottingham Road (A60, ½
mile S of town centre) ☎23357
Shipstone Bitter ℍ
Comfortable 2-room main
road pub 🍺💶🅿🕐🍴

Mansfield 26B6
Woodhouse

11–3; 6–10.30 (11 F, S)
Greyhound
High Street (off A60)
Home Mild, Bitter 🅴
Popular local with cheerful
atmosphere and a warm
welcome 🅿🍴

Maplebeck 26C7

10.30 (12 winter)–2.30; 6 (7 winter)–10.30
(11 F, S)
Beehive
Off A616 ☎ Caunton 306
**Webster Yorkshire Bitter;
Bulmer Cider** ℍ
Excellent country pub in
secluded hamlet. Smallest pub
in the county 🍺🍴

Nether 26B6
Langwith

11–3; 6–11
Jug & Glass
Queens Walk (A632)
☎ Mansfield 742283
**Hardys & Hansons Best Mild,
Best Bitter** 🅴
Attractive stone built pub by
village stream 🍺🅿🍴

Newark 26C7

10.30–2.30; 6–10.30 (11 F, S)
Kirrages
Chain Lane ☎ 703247
**Draught Bass; Ruddle Bitter,
County** ℍ
Welcoming establishment
catering for young and old
🕐🍴

Old Kings Arms
Kirk Gate (off A46) ☎ 703416
**Marston Burton Bitter, Merrie
Monk, Pedigree, Owd
Rodger** ℍ
Busy local. Folk club Sundays
🕐🍴

Nottingham 26B8

10.30–2.30; 5.30–10.30

Castle
202 Lower Parliament Street
Opens 11.30 & 6
Aylesbury ABC Bitter; Ind
Coope Bitter, Burton Ale Ⓗ
Modernised town pub with a
summerhouse half inside and
half in the garden. Do not ask
what the "F.G.A." pumpclip
means! ✿ ➷ ➐ (until 10) ⇄

Coopers Arms
Porchester Road (off A612)
✆ 502433
Evenings opens 6
Home Mild, Bitter Ⓔ
Excellent multi-roomed local
near Carlton Hill ➐

Framesmiths Arms
Main Street Bulwell
Shipstone Mild, Bitter Ⓗ & Ⓔ
Friendly street corner local
known as The Monkey ➐

Golden Fleece
Mansfield Road (A60)
Shipstone Mild, Bitter Ⓔ
Friendly street corner pub
with deepest cellars in city
➿ Q 🚻 ✿ ➷ ➐

Loggerheads
Cliff Road ✆ 580653
Home Mild, Bitter Ⓔ
Old building under cliff. Cave
at back once used for
cockfighting ✿ ➷ ➐ ⇄

Magpies
Meadow Lane ✆ 863851
Home Mild, Bitter Ⓔ
Close to Notts County and
Forest grounds. Pool table
✿ ➷ ➐ ➐ ⇄

Narrow Boat
Canal Street ✆ 501947
Shipstone Bitter Ⓗ
Popular, with pool and bar
billiards. Well used function
room 🚻 ➷ &

New Market Hotel
Lower Parliament Street
✆ 411532
Sat evenings opens 6
Home Mild, Bitter Ⓗ & Ⓔ
Railwayana in bar and
cheapest beer in town
🚻 ➷ ➐ & ⇄

Old Angel
Stoney Street ✆ 502303
Home Mild, Bitter Ⓔ
Unspoilt, centuries old pub in
historic Lace Market Q ➷ ➐ ⇄

Pheasant
Prospect Street, Radford
Opens 11 & 6
Shipstone Mild, Bitter Ⓔ
Friendly traditional local ✿ ➐ &

Quorn
Hucknall Road, Sherwood
Home Mild, Bitter Ⓔ
Suburban local in every
edition of Good Beer Guide ➐

Real Thing
186–188 Mansfield Road
(A60) ✆ 599368
Mon 5.30–8.30; Tue 11.30–
3, 5.30–8.30; Wed & Thur
1.30–3, 5.30–9.30; Fri
11.30–3, 4.30–9.30; Sat
10.30–9.30; Sun 12–2
Burton Bridge Bitter, XL;
Everard Tiger, Old Original;
Marston Pedigree; Ward
Sheffield Bitter Ⓗ & Ⓖ
Off-licence specialising in real
ale and foreign beers

Trip to Jerusalem
Castle Road
Draught Bass; Marston
Mercian Mild, Pedigree, Owd
Rodger; Samuel Smith OBB Ⓗ
"Well known throughout the
world", famed for its caves
and reputed age ➿ ✿ ➐ ⇄

Turf Tavern
Upper Parliament Street
Shipstone Mild, Bitter; Bulmer
Cider Ⓗ
Popular lounge bar in centre
near Royal Concert Hall and
Theatre ➷

Vine Inn
Handel Street, Sneinton
Sat evening opens 6
Home Mild, Bitter Ⓔ
Front parlour type pub with
corner entrance, now
extremely rare in the area Q ➐

Nuncargate 26A7

11–2.30; 6–10.30 (11 F, S)

Cricketers Arms
Nuncargate Road (off A611)
Home Mild, Bitter Ⓔ
16th century farmhouse in
mining area; retains character
and atmosphere ➿ ✿ ➐

Plumtree 26B8

11–2.30; 5.30–10.30 (11 F, S)

Griffin Inn
Main Street ✆ 5743
Hardys & Hansons Best Mild,
Best Bitter Ⓔ
Busy friendly local, good food
Q ✿ ➷ ➐

Redhill 26B8

10.30–2.30; 5.30–10.30 (11 F, S)

Ram Inn
244 Mansfield Road (A60)
✆ 267461
Sat evening opens 6
Shipstone Mild, Bitter Ⓗ & Ⓔ
Friendly local. Handpumps in
Smoke Room ➿ 🚻 ✿ ➷ & &

Waggon & Horses
246 Mansfield Road (A60)
Home Mild, Bitter Ⓗ
Friendly pub on extreme
north side of Nottingham
Q ✿ & &

Rempstone 26B9

11–2.30; 5.30–10.30 (11 F, S)

White Lion

Main Street (A6006)
Shipstone Mild, Bitter Ⓗ
Small, pleasant village pub.
Beamed ceiling, quarry-tiled
floor and much brasswork ➿ ✿

Retford 26C5

10.30–3 (4 Sat); 6–11

Albert Hotel
Albert Road ✆ 708694
Opens 11 & 7; closes 4 Thur
lunch
Webster Yorkshire Bitter;
Whitbread Castle Eden Ⓗ
Occasional guest beers
Superb cosy pub south of
town centre. Good cheap food
➷ ➐

Market Hotel
West Carr Road, Ordsall
✆ 7032
Closes 4 Thur lunch
Cameron Strongarm; Tetley
Bitter; Younger IPA, No. 3 Ⓗ
Busy pub. Excellent food
✿ ➷ ➐ ⇄

Masons Arms
Spital Hill
Home Mild, Bitter Ⓔ
Large pub favoured by an
older clientele ✿ ➐

New Sun
Spital Hill ✆ 703297
Closes 4 Thur lunch
Darley Dark Mild Ⓗ; Thorne
Best Bitter Ⓔ
Small welcoming local, close
to town centre ✿ ➷ ➐

Turks Head
Grove Street ✆ 702742
Evenings opens 7
Wards Sheffield Best Bitter Ⓔ
Town centre pub with
attractive oak panelling
➿ 🚻 ➷ ➐

Try also: Hop Pole

Ruddington 26B8

10.30–2.30; 6–10 (11 F, S)

Red Heart
Easthorpe Street
✆ Nottingham 844626
Shipstone Mild Ⓗ & Ⓔ, Bitter Ⓔ
Excellent village inn with
lively bar. All village pubs sell
real ale 🚻 ➷ (not Sun) ➐

Try also: Red Lion (Home)

Scaftworth 26C5

12–2.30 (closed Mon–Thur); 6–11

King William
Scaftworth Village (off A63)
✆ Doncaster 710292
Whitbread Castle Eden Ⓗ
Country inn with several
separate rooms. Good food
➿ Q 🚻 ✿ ➷ ➐ (Tues–Sat) ➐ & ⚘

Selston 26A7

11–3; 6–10.30 (11 F, S)

White Lion
Nottingham Road (B600)
✆ Ripley 810375

Shipstone Mild, Bitter Ⓗ
1-room roadside inn serving
good food in comfortable
surroundings
🌳Ⓖ🍴 (not Mon)

Try also: Horse & Jockey
(Shipstone)

South Clifton 26C6

10.30–2.30; 6.30–10.30 (11 F, S)
Red Lion
Front Street ☎ Spalford 660
Home Bitter Ⓔ
Rural local near the Trent
🏠Q🌳🍺

Southwell 26C7

10.30–2.30; 6–10.30 (11 F, S)
Newcastle Arms
Station Road
Shipstone Mild, Bitter Ⓔ
Friendly local close to the end
of the Southwell Trail 🌳🍺

Stapleford 26A8

10.30–2.30; 6–10.30 (11 F, S)
Old Cross
Church Street (off old A52)
Shipstone Mild, Bitter Ⓔ
Friendly, locals town pub 🏠🌳

Warren Arms
Derby Road (old A52)
☎ 392213
Ansells Mild, Bitter; Ind Coope
Burton Ale Ⓗ
Former coaching inn popular
with the young 🌳Ⓖ🍴

Staunton-in- 26C8
the-Vale

10.30–2.30; 6.30–10.30 (11 F, S)
Staunton Arms
Main Street ☎ Loveden 81062
Marston Pedigree; Tetley
Bitter Ⓗ Occasional guest
beers
Isolated hill-top local 🏠🌳Ⓖ🍺

Sutton in 26B7
Ashfield

10.30–2.30; 6–10.30 (11 F, S)
Duke of Sussex
Alfreton Road Fulwood (A38,
off M1 Junction 28)
☎ Mansfield 552560
Hardys & Hansons Best Mild,
Best Bitter Ⓔ
Popular roadside pub. Meals
served in lounge
🌳Ⓖ (Mon–Sat) 🍴 (Tues–Sat) 🍺

Market Hotel
Market Place
Evenings opens 7
Home Mild, Bitter Ⓔ
Big bustling, no frills local; full
of local characters 🍺

Try also: Shakespeare (Home)

Thurgarton 26C7

11–2.30; 6–10.30 (11 F, S)
Coach & Horses
Main Street

Home Mild, Bitter Ⓔ
Friendly village inn with
comfortable rooms
🏠🌳Ⓖ (Tues–Sat) 🍺

Upton 26C7

10.30–2.30; 6–10.30 (11 F, S)
Cross Keys
Main Street (A612)
☎ Southwell 813269
Marston Border Bitter,
Pedigree; Ruddle County Ⓗ
Inn of character in
conservation area. Regular
folk nights 🏠🌳Ⓖ🍴

Try also: French Horn (John
Smith's)

Warsop 26B8

11–3; 6–11
Hare & Hounds
Church Street (B6035)
☎ Mansfield 842440
Hardys & Hansons Best Mild,
Bitter Ⓗ
Tudor-style pub in town
centre with contrasting bar
and lounge 🏠🌳Ⓖ🍴🍺♿

Watnall 26A7

10.30–2.30; 6–10.30 (11 F, S)
Queens Head
Main Road (B600)
Home Mild, Bitter Ⓗ
Charming village pub with
pretty garden 🏠🌳Ⓖ♿

Wellow 26B6

11.30–3; 6–10.30 (11 F, S)
Olde Red Lion
Eakring Road
☎ Mansfield 861000
Whitbread Castle Eden Ⓗ
Old pub with beamed ceiling,
overlooking village green and
maypole. Good range of bar
meals Q🌳Ⓖ🍴🍺Å

West Leake 26B9

11.30–2.30; 6–10.30 (11 F, S)

Star (Pit House)
OS524261
☎ East Leake 2233
Draught Bass; M&B
Springfield Bitter Ⓗ
Splendid old coaching inn,
excellent lunchtime cold table
🏠Q🌳Ⓖ🍺

Weston 26C6

11–2.30; 6–10.30 (11 F, S)
Boot & Shoe
Old Great North Road (off A1)
☎ Newark 821257
Younger Scotch Bitter, IPA Ⓗ
Welcoming pub to suit all
tastes 🏠🌳Ⓖ🍴🍺

Worksop 26B5

11–3; 7–11
French Horn
Potter Street ☎ 472958
Stones Best Bitter Ⓔ
Fine example of a town pub.
Jostling bar, quiet snug 🍺

Greendale Oak
Norfolk Street
Stones Best Bitter Ⓔ
Cosy little pub behind main
shopping centre 🌳🍺

White Lion
Park Street (B6005)
☎ 478125
Whitbread Castle Eden Ⓗ
Excellent little pub, many low-
ceilinged rooms
🏠🎲🌳Ⓖ🍴 (Mon–Wed) 🍺

Try also: Unicorn (Stones)

Wysall 26B9

11–2.30; 6–10.30 (11 F, S)
Plough
Main Street
☎ Wymeswold 880339
McEwan 70/-; Shipstone Mild,
Bitter Ⓗ
Fine country pub in quiet
village 🏠🌳

How to Use the Guide

Facilities

🏠 real fire
Q quiet pub–no electronic
music, TV or obtrusive
games
🎲 indoor room for
children
🌳 garden or other outdoor
drinking area
🛏 accommodation
Ⓖ lunchtime meals
🍴 evening meals
🍺 public bar
♿ facilities for the disabled

Å camping facilities close
to the pub or part of the
pub grounds
≥ near British Rail station
⊖ near Underground
Station.
The facilities, beers and
pub hours listed in the
Good Beer Guide are
liable to change but
were correct when the
Guide went to press.
Many pubs do not serve
meals at weekends.

Abingdon   16B9

10–2.30; 6–11

Old Anchor
St Helen's Wharf ✆ 21726
Morland Mild, Bitter Ⓗ
Spartan ale house
complements magnificent
Thames-side setting Q❢

Ox Inn
15 Oxford Road (A4183)
✆ 20962
**Morland Mild, Bitter, Best
Bitter** Ⓗ
Popular modernised town
pub, no food Sun ♨ Ⓖ ➐

Appleton   16B9

10.30–2.30; 6–11

Plough
7 Eaton Road (off A420)
Morland Mild, Bitter Ⓗ
A perfect example of a friendly
traditional country local
🅰 Q ♨ ❢ 🅰

Bampton   15J7

11–2.30; 6–11

Jubilee Inn
Market Square (B4449)
✆ Bampton Castle 850330
**Wadworth IPA, 6X, Farmers
Glory** Ⓗ, **Old Timer** Ⓖ
Welcoming market town
inn 🅰 ♨ Ⓖ ➐

Banbury   16B6

10–2.30; 6–11

Coach & Horses
Butcher's Row ✆ 3043
Opens at 10.30 & 7
**Hook Norton Mild, Best
Bitter** Ⓗ
Pleasant town centre local
🅰 ❢ ≈

Wheatsheaf
68 George Street ✆ 66525
**M & B Mild, Springfield Bitter,
Brew XI** Ⓗ
Coaching inn, popular local
🅰 ♨ ❢ ≈

Bletchingdon   16B8

10–2.30; 6–11

Rock of Gibraltar
Enslow Bridge
**Usher Best Bitter, Founders
Ale** Ⓗ
Canalside pub; large garden
and children's play area, bar
billiards 🅰 Q ♨ Ⓖ ❢ ❢

Blewbury   6E1

10.30–2.30; 6.30–11

Red Lion
Chapel Lane, off Nottingham
Fee (off A417) ✆ 850403
**Brakspear Bitter, Special,
Old** Ⓗ
Attractive village pub, low
beams, brasses and inglenook.
Restaurant. No food Sun
🅰 Q ⊞ (lunchtimes) ♨ 🖼 Ⓖ
➐ (Wed–Sat)

Bodicote   16B6

10.30–2.30; 6–11

Plough
9 High Street ✆ Banbury
62327
**Bodicote Bitter, Porter
(Christmas), No. 9** Ⓗ
Pleasant, friendly home-brew
pub ♨ Ⓖ ➐ ❢

Britwell Salome   7E1

11–2.30; 6(7 winter)–11

Red Lion
B4009 ✆ Watlington 2304
**Brakspear Mild (summer),
Bitter, Special, Old (winter)** Ⓗ
Pleasant village pub, cosy
lounge, good food
♨ 🖼 Ⓖ ➐ (not Wed) ❢

Brize Norton   15J6

10–2.30; 6–11

Carpenters Arms
Station Road
Morland Bitter Ⓗ
Friendly no-frills local 🅰 Q ♨

Burford   15J6

11–2.30; 6–11

Highway Hotel
High Street (A361) ✆ 2136
Lunch closes 2
**Hook Norton Best Bitter;
Wadworth 6X** Ⓗ
Fine old country hotel in
picture postcard setting
🅰 Q ⊞ 🖼 🖼 ➐

Lamb
Sheep Street (off A361)
✆ 3155
Wadworth IPA, 6X Ⓗ, **Old
Timer** Ⓖ
Fine 15th century Cotswold
stone hotel. Much original
furniture, cosy atmosphere
🅰 Q ⊞ ♨ 🖼 Ⓖ (Sun) ➐ ❢

Charlbury   16A8

11–2.30; 6.30–11

Charlbury Tavern
Market Street ✆ 810103
**Glenny Witney Bitter; Hook
Norton Best Bitter; Wadworth
6X** Ⓗ **Regular guest beers**
Intimate Victorian-style town
centre pub ♨ Ⓖ ➐ ≈

Chesterton   16B7

10.30–2.30; 6–11

Red Cow
✆ Bicester 241337
**Usher Best Bitter, Founder's
Ale** Ⓗ
Pleasant, comfortable village
pub 🅰 Q ♨ Ⓖ ➐

Chilton   6D1

10.30–2.30; 7–11

Horse & Jockey
Off A34 ✆ Abingdon 834376
Morland Bitter, Best Bitter Ⓗ
Quiet hotel, popular with
ramblers from Ridgeway
Q ♨ 🖼 Ⓖ ➐

Chinnor   16D9

11–2.30; 6–11

Royal Oak
Lower Road (B4009)
✆ Kingston Blount 51307
**Adnams Bitter; Hook Norton
Best Bitter; Wadworth 6X** Ⓗ
Regular guest beers
Friendly local pub, good value
home-cooking
🅰 Q ♨ Ⓖ ➐ (Thu–Sat)

Chipping Norton   15J5

11–2.30; 7–11

Red Lion
Cattle Market ✆ 41520
**Hook Norton Mild, Best Bitter;
Bulmer Cider** Ⓗ
Small 'laugh-a-minute' local
🅰 ♨ ♿

Claydon   16B6

12–2.30 (closed winter Tue); 6–11

Sun Rising
Off A423 ✆ Farnborough 393
**Hook Norton Best Bitter;
Flowers Original (summer);
Bulmer Cider (summer)** Ⓗ
Popular, friendly local near
canal. Table skittles 🅰 ♨ Ⓖ ➐

Clifton Hampden   6E1

11–2.30; 6–11

Barley Mow
Long Wittenham Road (off
A415) ✆ 7847
**Usher PA, Best Bitter,
Founder's Ale** Ⓗ
Popular, picturesque old inn
made famous by Jerome. K.
Jerome's "3 Men in a Boat".
Restaurant
🅰 Q ⊞ ♨ 🖼 Ⓖ ➐ (not Sun) ♿ 🅰

Cumnor   16B9

10–2.30; 6–11

Bear & Ragged Staff
Appleton Road
✆ Oxford 862339
Morrell Bitter, Varsity Ⓗ
Large, comfortable 16th
century pub. First-class
restaurant 🅰 ♨ Ⓖ ➐ 🅰

Deddington   16B7

10.30–2.30; 6–11

Crown & Tuns
New Street (A423)
**Hook Norton Mild, Best
Bitter** Ⓗ, **Old Hookey
(winter)** Ⓖ
Friendly, unpretentious old
coaching inn. Knock if closed
at above times 🅰 ♨ ♿

Didcot   6E1

10.30–2.30; 6–11

Prince of Wales
Station Road (off A4130)
✆ 813027
**Morrell Light Ale, Dark Mild,
Bitter, Varsity; Bulmer Cider** Ⓗ

Large hotel lounge, basic public bar. Very close to Didcot Steam Railway Centre ♪🖾🕭🍴🍺≷

Ducklington 16A8

11–2.30; 6–11
Bell
Standlake Road (off A415)
Courage Best Bitter, Directors ⊞
Traditional village pub, parts reputed to date to 1150. Home of local folk club ⚓Q🎦🍺♪

Eynsham 16B8

10.30–2.30; 6–11
Queens Head
Queen Street
Courage Best Bitter, Directors ⊞
Friendly traditional village local, darts ⚓♪🍴

White Hart
Newland Street (off A40)
℘ Oxford 880711
Courage Best Bitter ⊞
Attractive 1-bar local on village outskirts. No food Sun 🕭🍴🍺

Faringdon 15J7

10–2.30; 6–11
Folly
54 London Street *℘* 20620
Morrell Bitter, Varsity Ⓖ
Charming little town pub ⚓Q♪🍴

Fyfield 16A9

10.30–2.30; 6–11
White Hart
Off A420 *℘* Frilford Heath 390585
Morland Bitter; Ruddle County; Theakston XB, ⊞ **Old Peculier** Ⓖ**; Wadsworth 6X** ⊞**; Weston Cider** ⊞ **Occasional guest beers**
Expensive, 15th century former almshouse. Popular for its excellent food ⚓Q🎦♪🕭🍴

Garsington 16B9

10.30–2.30; 6–11
Plough
1, Oxford Road (off B480)
℘ 395
Courage Best Bitter, Directors ⊞
Busy, friendly local. Children's play area, Aunt Sally ⚓♪🕭🍴🍺

Goring 6E2

10–2.30; 6–11
John Barleycorn
Manor Road (off B4009)
℘ 872509
Brakspear Bitter, Special, Old (winter) ⊞
Attractive 17th century, low-beamed pub; cosy saloon, good food Q♪🖾🕭🍴🍺≷

Great Tew 16A7

11–2.30 (closed Mon); 6–10.30 (11 summer)
Falkland Arms
℘ 653
Donnington Best Bitter; Hook Norton Best Bitter; Theakston XB; Wadworth 6X ⊞ **Regular guest beers**
17th century Cotswold inn, in keeping with unspoilt village ⚓♪🖾🕭

Henley-on Thames 7F2

10–2.30; 6–11
Royal Hotel
51 Station Road (off A4155)
Opens 11
Brakspear Mild, Bitter ⊞
Welcoming, spacious pub near river; pool ♪🖾🕭 (Mon-Fri)🍴≷

Three Tuns
5 Market Place (off A423)
℘ 573260
Brakspear Bitter, Special ⊞, **Old** Ⓖ
Excellent town centre pub. Open every afternoon for food and teas ♪🕭🍴🍺≷

Hook Norton 16A7

10.30–2.30; 6–11
Pear Tree
Scotland End
℘ 737482
Hook Norton Best Bitter, Old Hookey ⊞
Cheerful, welcoming local near brewery ⚓Q♪🍴🅰

Hornton 16A6

12–2; 7–11
Dun Cow
West End *℘* Edge Hill 524
Flowers Original; Hook Norton Best Bitter; Bulmer Cider ⊞ **Occasional guest beers**
Interesting blend of old and new. Reputedly haunted ⚓♪🍴

Juniper Hill 16B7

10.30–2.30; 6–11
Fox
Off A43
Hook Norton Best Bitter, Old Hookey ⊞
Family-run pub in centre of hamlet described in "Lark Rise to Candleford" ⚓Q♪

Langford 15J7

12–2.30; 6–11
Bell
Langford (east of A361)
℘ Filkins 281
Morland Bitter; Wadworth 6X ⊞ **Regular guest beers**
Quiet 17th century inn, Aunt Sally pitch ⚓Q🖾🍴

Lewknor 7F1

11–2.30; 6–11
Olde Leathern Bottel
1 High Street (off B4009/M40)
℘ Kingston Blount 51482
Brakspear Bitter, Special, Old ⊞
Homely and welcoming low-beamed pub with Cromwellian connections. Tasty food (not Mon) ⚓🍴 (over-5's only) ♪🖾🍴

Little Milton 16C9

11–2.30; 6.30–11
Lamb
High Street (A329) *℘* Great Milton 527
Halls Harvest Bitter; Ind Coope Burton Ale ⊞
Cosy, thatched 17th century pub in attractive village. Interesting menu ⚓♪🖾🍴

Long Hanborough 16A8

10.30–2.30; 6–11
Swan
Combe Road (off A4095)
Morrell Light Ale, Dark Mild, Bitter ⊞
Popular village local ♪

Long Wittenham 6E1

12–2.30; 6.30–11
Machine Man Inn
Off High Street (A415)
Ind Coope Burton Ale; Morland Bitter; Wadworth 6X ⊞ **Regular guest beers**
Pleasant village free house; try the pancakes ⚓🍴♪🖾🍴🍺

Lower Assendon 7F1

11–2.30; 6–11
Golden Ball
B480 *℘* Henley 574157
Brakspear Bitter, Special, ⊞, **Old** Ⓖ
Splendid country pub serving good value food ⚓♪🖾🍴

Nettlebed 7F1

10–2.30; 6–11
Sun
Watlington Street (B481)
℘ 641359
Brakspear Mild, Bitter, Special ⊞, **Old** Ⓖ
Popular village pub. Soup and chip butties worth trying. Garden available for "D-I-Y" barbecues ⚓Q🎦🖾🍴🍺

Noke 16B8

10.30–2.30; 6–11
Plough
Off B4027 *℘* Kidlington 3251
Courage Best Bitter, Directors ⊞
Busy country pub. Live music Sun and Tue ♪🖾🍴

North Leigh   16A8

11.30–2.30; 7–11

Woodman
New Yatt Road
✆ Freeland 881790
**Glenny Witney Bitter,
Wychwood Best; Hook Norton
Best Bitter; Wadworth 6X** Ⓗ
Occasional guest beers
Actively supported village
local 🅿🍴🕐🕓🍺⛺

Northmoor   16A9

10.30–2.30; 6–11

Dun Cow
(off A415) ✆ Standlake 295
Morland Mild, Bitter Ⓖ
Delightful and totally unspoilt
country pub. No serving
counter 🅿Q🍴🍺

Oxford   16B8

10.30–2.30; 5.30–11

Black Boy
Old High Street, Headington
**Morrell Light Ale, Bitter,
Varsity** Ⓗ **College** Ⓖ
Friendly 3-bar local. Frequent
fund-rasiing events Q🕓🍺

Cricketers Arms
43 Iffley Road ✆ 726264
Opens 11 & 6
Morland Bitter, Best Bitter Ⓗ
Popular, friendly local.
Carving on the wall is reputed
to be of Don Bradman Q🍺

Gardeners Arms
39 Plantation Road (off
Woodstock Road)
✆ 59814
Opens 11.30 (12 Sat)
Morrell Dark Mild, Bitter Ⓗ,
College Ⓖ
Friendly, traditional North
Oxford local Q🍴🕓🍺🍺

Kings Arms
40 Holywell Street
✆ 242369
**Draught Bass; Flowers
Original; Morland Bitter;
Wadworth 6X; Wethered
Bitter; Younger Scotch
Bitter** Ⓗ **Regular guest beers**
Large and deservedly popular
17th century free house at
heart of city. Delightful little
snug (Dons Bar) 🎫🕓🍺🍺

Old Tom
St. Aldates ✆ 243034
Morrell Bitter, Varsity Ⓗ
Small town pub, pleasant
secluded garden, lunches a
speciality Q🍴🕓

Oxford Beer Shops
105 Bullingdon Road
3 Osler Road
12 Western Road
11.30 am–10.30 pm (11 F, S)
Osler Road opens 10 am
**Arkell BBB; Kingsdown Ale;
Bodicote JB; Glenny Witney
Bitter; Marston Pedigree; Rich
Cider** Ⓗ **Regular guest beers**

Perch

Binsey Lane, Binsey (off Botley
Road) OS493077 ✆ 240386
**Halls Harvest Bitter; Ind
Coope Burton Ale** Ⓗ
Picturesque 17th century
thatched pub in isolated
hamlet close to Thames
Q🍴🕓🍺 (Tue–Sat)

Prince of Wales
80 Cowley Road (B480)
✆ 243069
Morrell Light Ale, Varsity Ⓗ
Street corner local with large
vault and tiny snug 🍴🍺

Royal Oak
42/44 Woodstock Road
✆ 54230
**Halls Harvest Bitter; Ind
Coope Burton Ale; Wadworth
6X** Ⓗ
Popular, former 17th century
coaching inn near Radcliffe
Infirmary Q🎫🍴🕓🍺

Temple Bar
Temple Street, off Cowley
Road
Opens 11.30 & 7
**Wadworth IPA, 6X, Farmers
Glory, Old Timer** Ⓗ
Bustling town local
🍴🕓 (not Sun) 🍺

Turf Tavern
10 St. Helens Passage/Bath
Place (off Holywell Street)
✆ 243235
**Brakspear Special; Flowers
Original; Hook Norton Best
Bitter, Old Hookey; Young
Special; Weston Cider** Ⓗ
Occasional guest beers
Famous 13th century inn,
hidden among colleges.
Beware of the price list!
Q🍴🎫🕓🍺

Westgate
12 New Road ✆ 250099
**Morrell Light Ale, Dark Mild,
Bitter, Varsity, College** Ⓗ
Modern, comfortable
city centre pub near Westgate
shopping precinct
🍴🕓🍺 (until 7.30) ♿🍴

Wheatsheaf
Wheatsheaf Yard (off High
Street) ✆ 243276
Opens 11
Morrell Bitter, Varsity Ⓗ
Comfortable, popular two-bar
pub down narrow alleyway
🕓🍺 (until 10) 🍴

White Horse
56 Broad Street ✆ 721680
**Halls Harvest Bitter; Ind
Coope Burton Ale; Wadworth
6X** Ⓗ
Popular cosy pub, squeezed
between bookshops Q🕓🍺

Postcombe   16C9

11–2.30; 6–11

Feathers
A40 ✆ Tetsworth 383
Morrell Dark Mild, Bitter Ⓗ
Friendly village local; pool,
snug saloon
🅿🎫 (summer) 🕓🍺🍺

Rotherfield Peppard   7F2

10.30–2.30; 6–11

Red Lion
Peppard Common (B481)
✆ Rotherfield Greys 329
**Brakspear Mild, Bitter,
Special** Ⓗ
Pleasant village pub over-
looking common. Extensive
menu. Children's play area
🅿🎫 (lunchtime) 🍴🍺

Sandford-on-Thames   16B9

11–2.30; 6.30–11

Fox
25 Henley Road
**Morrell Dark Mild, Light Ale,
Bitter** Ⓖ
Straightforward, unaffected
roadside local 🅿Q🍴🍺♿

Satwell   7F2

10.30–2.30; 6–11

Lamb
Off B481
**Brakspear Bitter, Special,
Old** Ⓗ
Excellent old country pub,
huge log fire, shy landlord
needs to be approached with
care! 🅿🍴🕓 (not Sun)

Shiplake   7F2

10–2.30; 6–11

Baskerville Arms
Station Road, Lower Shiplake
(off A4155) ✆ Wargrave 3332
**Fremlins Bitter; Wethered
Bitter, SPA** Ⓗ
Smart inn with rowing theme.
Restaurant
🍴🎫🕓🍺 (Tue–Sat) 🍴

Sibford Gower   16A6

11–2.30; 6.30–11

Wykham Arms
Off B4035 ✆ Swalcliffe 351
**Eldridge Pope Royal Oak;
Hook Norton Best Bitter;
Marston Burton Bitter,
Pedigree** Ⓗ **Occasional guest
beers**
Welcoming, thatched pub.
Good food 🅿Q🍴🕓🍺🍺

Sonning Common   7F2

10.30–2.30; 6–11

Bird in Hand
Reading Road (B481)
✆ Kidmore End 723230
**Courage Best Bitter,
Directors** Ⓗ
Cosy, low-beamed pub with
eating area. Enclosed garden,
ideal for children
🅿🍴🕓🍺 (Wed–Mon)

Sonning Eye 7F2

10.30–2.30; 6–11

Flowing Spring
Henley Road (A4155)
℡ Reading 693207
Fuller Chiswick Bitter, London Pride, ESB Ⓗ
Comfortable and cosy, attractive wrought-iron staircase leads to award-winning garden ♨ Q ✿ ⓒ (not Sun) Å (must book)

South Hinksey 16B8

10.30–2.30; 5.30–11

General Elliot
Manor Road ℡ Oxford 739369
Morrell Light Ale, Bitter, Varsity Ⓗ
Village pub at edge of countryside. Easy access to riverside walks
▣ ✿ ⓒ ➐ (not Mon) ❢ Å

South Leigh 16A8

11.30–2.30; 6.30–11 (closed Mon)

Mason Arms
(off A40) ℡ Witney 2485
Glenny Wychwood Best; Younger Scotch Ⓗ
Restored thatched country pub. Restaurant ♨ Q ✿ ⓒ ➐

Steeple Aston 16B7

10–2.30; 6–11

Red Lion
South Street (off A423)
℡ 40225
Hook Norton Best Bitter; Wadworth 6X Ⓗ Occasional guest beers
Friendly pub. Collection of rare whiskies ♨ Q ✿ ⓒ ➐

Steventon 16B9

10.30–2.30; 7–11

Cherry Tree
33 High Street
℡ Abingdon 831222

Brakspear Bitter; Fuller London Pride; Hook Norton Best Bitter; Morland Bitter; Wadworth 6X Ⓗ Regular guest beers
Comfortable, busy free house; fine oak-beamed lounge. No food Mon eve or Sun ♨ Q ✿ ➐

Stoke Lynn 16B7

10–2.30; 6–11

Peyton Arms
Off A43
Hook Norton Best Bitter, Old Hookey Ⓗ
Quiet, unchanged village local ♨ Q ✿ ❢

Stoke Row 7F2

10–2.30; 6–11

Cherry Tree
(Off B481)
℡ Checkendon 680430
Brakspear Mild, Bitter, Special, Old Ⓗ
Picturesque, low-beamed village pub, games room with pool; swings in garden ♨ ✿ ⓒ ➐ (not Sun) ❧

Thame 16C8

10.30–2.30; 6–11

Bird Cage
Cornmarket ℡ 2046
Closes Tue lunch 4.30
Courage Best Bitter, Directors Ⓗ
Superb 13th century building, once town Bridewell
♨ ✿ ⓒ (not Sun)

Rising Sun
26 High Street ℡ 4206
Opens 11
Archer Village Bitter; Hook Norton Best Bitter; Marston Pedigree; Wadworth 6X Ⓗ
Popular 16th century oak-beamed pub with overhanging first floor
♨ ✿ ⓒ (not Sat/Sun)

Wantage 6D1

10.30–2.30; 5.30–11

Shoulder of Mutton
Wallingford Street
Morland Mild, Bitter Ⓗ
Plain, unspoilt town local, two intimate bars; full of characters ♨ Q ❢

Warborough 7E1

11–2.30; 6–11

Six Bells
The Green South (off A329)
℡ 8265
Brakspear Bitter, Special, Old Ⓗ
Attractive 16th century thatched pub on village cricket green. Cosy beamed interior. Dining area (not Sun)
♨ Q ✿ ⓒ ➐ ❧

West Hanney 16A9

10.30–2.30; 6–11

Lamb
Main Street ℡ 540
Bar (if eating) and restaurant close 3pm & midnight
Adnams Bitter; Morland Bitter; Theakston XB Ⓗ
Occasional guest beers
Busy pub and restaurant. Live music weekends
▣ (if eating) ⓒ ➐

Witney 16A8

11–2.30; 6–11

Butchers Arms
104 Corn Street ℡ 5745
Glenny Witney Bitter, Wychwood Best; Morland Bitter Ⓗ
Smart, trendy pub popular with young. Pool, cheap food ✿ ⓒ

House of Windsor
31 West End (B4022) ℡ 4277
Opens 12
Hook Norton Best Bitter; Wadworth 6X Ⓗ Regular guest beers
Lively, popular local. Pool, bar billiards ♨ ✿ ⓒ ❢

Woodstock 16B8

10.30–2.30; 6–11

Black Prince
Manor Road (A34) ℡ 811530
Adnams Bitter; Archer Village Bitter; Flowers Original; Ringwood Fortyniner Ⓗ;
Bulmer Cider Ⓖ
Pleasant riverside pub
♨ ▣ ✿ ⓒ ➐

Woolstone 15J8

12–2.30; 6 (7 winter)–11

White Horse
℡ Uffington 566
Flowers Original; Wethered Bitter Ⓗ
Picturesque thatched pub near famous White Horse. Large open-plan bar ♨ ✿ ⓒ ➐

How to Use the Guide

Facilities

♨ real fire
Q quiet pub–no electronic music, TV or obtrusive games
▣ indoor room for children
✿ garden or other outdoor drinking area
▦ accommodation
ⓒ lunchtime meals
➐ evening meals
❢ public bar
❧ facilities for the disabled

Å camping facilities close to the pub or part of the pub grounds
≥ near British Rail station
θ near Underground Station.
The facilities, beers and pub hours listed in the Good Beer Guide are liable to change but were correct when the Guide went to press. Many pubs do not serve meals at weekends.

Albrighton 22E8
11–2.30; 6–11
Crown
High Street ✆ 2204
Banks's Mild, Bitter Ⓔ
Attractive and popular urban
pub ▲✦▣Ⓖ✿▮

Aqueduct 22D8
11–2.30; 6.30–11
Britannia
Off the Brookside Estate
✆ Telford 591488
Banks's Mild, Bitter; Hansons
Black Country Bitter Ⓔ
Comfortable pub which
retains a local character
amongst the new town
developments Q✦▮

Bicton 22C8
10.30–3; 6–11
Four Crosses Inn
A5 ✆ Shrewsbury 850258
Draught Bass Ⓗ; M & B Mild,
Springfield Bitter Ⓔ
On busy holiday route to
North Wales ▲✦▣Ⓖ▸▮&

Bishops Castle 22B9
11.30–2.30; 6.30–11
Three Tuns
Salop Street ✆ 638797
Three Tuns Mild, XXX Bitter,
Steamer, Old Scrooge;
Westons Cider Ⓗ
Medieval coaching inn at the
centre of historical town. One
of the original homebrew
pubs. Meals seasonal
▲Q✦Ⓖ▸▮

Bridgnorth 22D9
10.30–2.30; 6–11
Harp
High Street ✆ 2290
Banks's Mild, Bitter Ⓔ
Small, traditional market
town local Ⓖ▮

Railwayman's Arms
Severn Valley Railway Station
Batham Mild, Bitter; Courage
Best Bitter; Bulmer Cider Ⓗ
Regular guest beers
Smart freehouse dedicated to
the history of steam ▲✦▮

Shakespeare
West Castle Street ✆ 2403
Open until 4 Mon & Sat lunch
Banks's Mild, Bitter Ⓔ; Bulmer
Cider Ⓗ
Popular town local with two
contrasting bars and a skittle
alley Ⓖ▸▮

Try also: New Inn (Banks's)

Broseley 22D9
10.30–2.30; 6–11
Cumberland
Queen Street
✆ Telford 882301
Wem Mild, Best Bitter Ⓔ;
Special Bitter Ⓗ

Comfortable hotel near the
famous Ironbridge ✦▣Ⓖ▸▮

Church
Stretton 22C9
11–2.30; 6–11
Kings Arms
High Street ✆ 722807
Wem Mild, Best Bitter Ⓗ
Well-appointed pub; good
base for walking surrounding
Stretton Hills
Qⓖ▸ (not Tue) ≈

Cleobury
Mortimer 15E2
10.30–2.30; 6–11
Bell
Lower Street ✆ 270305
Courage Directors Ⓗ; Banks's
Mild, Bitter Ⓔ; Bulmer Cider Ⓗ
Small unspoilt inn of
character ▲▮

Clun 4C2
11–2.30; 6–11
Sun Inn
B4368
Davenports Bitter; Wood
Parish Bitter Ⓗ Occasional
guest beers
15th century listed building;
wealth of exposed beams
▲Q✦Ⓖ▸▮

Dawley 22D8
12–2.30; 7–11
Ring o' Bells
King Street
Marston Burton Bitter,
Pedigree Ⓗ
Small unspoilt pub; note the
wallplate collection ✦▮

Edgmond 22D7
11–2.30; 6–11
Lion Inn
✆ Newport 810346
M & B Highgate Mild,
Springfield Bitter Ⓔ
Pleasant village pub with
award-winning garden
✦▣Ⓖ▮

Ellesmere 22B6
10.30–2.30 (3.30 F); 6–11
Market Hotel
Scotland Street ✆ 2217
Wem Pale Ale, Mild, Best
Bitter Ⓔ
Homely town centre pub,
popular with canal users
▲▤Ⓖ▸▮

Try also: Black Lion (Marston)

Ford 22B8
11–3; 6–11
Cross Gates
A458 ✆ Shrewsbury 850332
Wem Mild, Best Bitter, Special
Bitter Ⓗ
Large roadside pub; splendid
lounge ▲▤✦Ⓖ▸▮&

Great Soudley 22D7
12–3; 6.30 (7.30 winter)–11
Wheatsheaf Inn
Off A41 ✆ Cheswardine 311
Marston Mercian Mild,
Burton Bitter, Pedigree Ⓗ,
Owd Rodger (winter) Ⓖ
Splendid village pub (1784)
one mile from Shropshire
Union Canal ▲✦▣Ⓖ▸▮&

Harley 22D9
11–3; 6–11
Plume of Feathers
A458
Flowers IPA, Original Ⓗ
Attractive pub below Wenlock
Edge ▲✦▮&

Hengoed 22C8
Closed lunch ex. Sun. 10.30–3; 7–11
Last Inn
Off A5 & B4579
✆ Oswestry 659747
Marston Pedigree Ⓗ, Owd
Rodger Ⓖ; Wood's Special;
Weston Cider Ⓗ Regular guest
beers
Large games room. Live
entertainment weekends
▲▣✦Ⓖ▮&

Hookagate 22C8
11.30–3; 7–11
New Inn
A488 ✆ Shrewsbury 860223
Draught Bass Ⓗ; M & B Mild;
Ruddle County Ⓗ
Enterprising free house at
edge of village ▲▣✦Ⓖ▮&

Try also: Royal Oak (Wem)

Horsehay 22D8
11–2.30; 6.30–11
Forester Arms
Wellington Road
Draught Bass Ⓗ; M & B
Highgate Mild, Springfield
Bitter Ⓔ
Recently modernised village
local ▲✦Ⓖ▮&

Ironbridge 22D8
11–2.30; 6–11
Malthouse
The Wharfage ✆ 3712
Davenports Mild, Bitter Ⓗ
Riverside pub with patio
garden and dining room
✦Ⓖ▸▮& Å

Jackfield 22D9
11 (12 winter)–2.30; 6–11
Boat Inn
Access by footbridge from
Coalport side of the river
✆ Telford 882178
Banks's Mild, Bitter Ⓔ;
Weston Cider Ⓖ
Superb riverside pub, pleasant
setting ▲✦Ⓖ▸▮& Å

Ketley Bank 22D8
12–2.30; 7–11

*S*hropshire

Lord Hill
Main Road (off A5)
☎ Telford 613070
Opens 6.30 F, S & summer
eves
**Draught Bass; M & B
Highgate Mild, Springfield
Bitter** H Occasional guest
beers
Popular village pub at the
heart of Telford 🏚🍴🕭🍻🍽

Rose & Crown
Holyhead Road (A5)
**Ansells Mild, Bitter; Ind Coope
Burton Ale** H Regular guest
beers
Busy roadside pub,
enterprising landlord, cosy
lounge 🍴🕭🍽

Leegomery 22D8
11–2.30; 6–11
Thomas Telford
Silkin Way ☎ Telford 57546
Wem Mild, Best Bitter E,
Special Bitter H
Well-designed new pub with
pictures of its namesake's
achievements 🍴🕭🍻🍽👶

Linley Brook 22D9
10.30–2.30; 6–11
Pheasant
Off B4373 ☎ Bridgnorth 2260
**Banks's Mild; Holden Black
Country Bitter** H Occasional
guest beers
Unspoilt rural freehouse off
the beaten track 🏚🍴🕭🍻🍽🏕

Little Stretton 14D1
11–2.30; 6–11
Ragleth Inn
B4370 (off A49)
☎ Church Stretton 22711
**Draught Bass; Courage
Directors; John Smith's
Bitter** H
17th century inn in idyllic
surroundings 🏚Q🍴🕭🍻🍽👶

Try also: Green Dragon (Free)

Longville-in-the-Dale 14D1
12–2.30 (closed Tue lunch); 7–11
Longville Arms
B4371 (between Much
Wenlock and Church
Stretton) ☎ 206
**M & B Springfield Bitter;
Wood's Special** H
Pleasant rural freehouse in
the heart of Shropshire
🏚🍴🕭🍻 (not Tue)🍽👶🏕

Loppington 22C7
10.30–3; 6–11
Blacksmith's Arms
B4397 ☎ Wem 33762
Wem Pale Ale, Best Bitter H
Thatched village pub in midst
of agricultural community
🏚Q🍴🕭🍻🍽

Try also: Dickin Arms

Ludlow 14D2
10–2.30; 6–11
Bull Hotel
Corve Street
Opens 10.30
**Marston Burton Bitter,
Pedigree** H
14th century timber-framed
building. Ludlow Fringe
Festival HQ. Local folk club.
No food Sun 🏚🍴🕭🍻🍽👶🚆

Church Inn
Buttercross
Opens 11
**Fuller London Pride; Greene
King Abbot; Hook Norton
Best Bitter; Marston Burton
Bitter, Pedigree** H Regular
guest beers
Quaintly tucked away behind
Buttercross on one of the most
ancient sites in Ludlow
🏚Q🍴🕭🍽🚆

Madeley 22D8
11–2.30; 6–11
All Nations
Coalport Road
Opens 12 & 7
All Nations Pale Ale H
Long-established home-brew
pub with strong local
following; listed building 🍴🍽

Miners Arms
Prince Street
☎ Telford 586723
Banks's Mild, Bitter E
Drinkers pub in former mining
area. Note the sculpture
outside 🍴🕭🍽

Market Drayton 22D6
10.30–3; 6–11
Coach & Horses
70 Shropshire Street (A53)
☎ 2800
Opens 11; 7 winter eves
**Marston Mercian Mild,
Burton Bitter, Pedigree** H
Friendly 18th-century local.
Small bar, cosy lounge
🏚🍴🍽

Stag's Head
Great Hales Street (A529)
Opens 12 & 7; closes 5 Wed
lunch
**Marston Mercian Mild,
Burton Bitter, Pedigree
(summer)** H
Friendly, lively atmosphere.
Etched windows and photos of
old Drayton 🏚🍴🕭 (not Sun) 🍽

Morville 22D9
11–2.30; 6–11
Acton Arms
A458 ☎ 209
Banks's Mild, Bitter E
Large, modernised country
inn; good food 🏚🍴🕭🍻🍽👶🏕

Much Wenlock 22D9
10.30–2.30; 6–11

George & Dragon
High Street ☎ 727312
Hook Norton Best Bitter H
Regular guest beers
Splendid traditional pub, real
food and breweriana 🏚🍴🕭🍻🍽

Myddle 22C7
11–3 (closed Mon lunch); 6.30–11
Red Lion
Off A528
☎ Bomere Heath 290951
**Marston Burton Bitter,
Pedigree; Wem Pale Ale, Mild,
Best Bitter, Special Bitter** H
Occasional guest beers
Interesting mix: sandstone
with timber frame 🏚🕭🍻🍽

Neen Sollars 14E2
12–2.30; 7–11
Railway Tavern
☎ Cleobury Mortimer 270254
Courage Directors H
Splendid village pub. Skittle
alley; good food 🏚🍴🕭🍻

Oakengates 22D8
11–2.30; 6.30–11
Coalport
Bridge Street
☎ Telford 612496
**Ansells Mild, Bitter; Tetley
Bitter** H
Popular and friendly pub with
good food 🏚🍴🕭🍻🍽👶🚆

Oswestry 22B7
10.30–3; 6–11
Bell Inn
Church Street ☎ 652229
Opens 11 & 7; closes 4.30
Wed lunch
**Draught Bass; M & B Mild,
Springfield Bitter, Brew XI** E
The oldest recorded pub in
Oswestry—now open-plan 🍴👶

Welch Harp
Upper Brook Street ☎ 653481
Wed & S lunch closes 4.30
**Marston Border Dark Mild,
Burton Bitter, Pedigree** H
Congenial pub just off town
centre 🍽👶

Shifnal 22D8
12–2.30; 7–11
Anvil Inn
Aston Road
Banks's Mild, Bitter E
Small unspoilt backstreet local
🏚🍽🚆

Try also; Wheatsheaf
(Banks's)

Shrewsbury 22C8
10.30–3; 6–11
Acorn
St. Julians Friars ☎ 4339
Draught Bass; M & B Mild H
Genuine ale house in historic
area of town, near river 🏚🍽🚆

Albert Hotel
Smithfield Road ☎ 3590

Banks's Mild, Bitter Ⓔ;
Marston Pedigree; Wood's
Special Ⓗ Regular guest beers
Shrewsbury's original free
house, two mins from station
🏛🥂≷

Castle Vaults
Castle Gates ℰ 58807
**Marston Mercian Mild,
Pedigree** Ⓗ Occasional guest
beers
In shadow of castle. No
smoking area. Mexican food a
speciality 🏛🎪🌿🛏🕒🍴🥂≷

Crown Inn
Longden Road, Coleham
ℰ4557
Opens 11
Ansells Mild, Bitter Ⓗ Regular
guest beers
Garden overlooks river; boats
for hire. Fishing with own
tackle permitted
🏛🎪🌿🛏🕒🍴🥂&

Old Bell
Abbey Foregate ℰ56041
Ansells Mild, Bitter Ⓗ
18th century house in family
for almost 100 years: 35 with
same landlord Q🌿🍴

Prince of Wales
Bynner Street, Belle Vue
ℰ 3301
Opens 11
**Marston Border Mild, Bitter,
Pedigree, Merrie Monk** Ⓗ,
Owd Rodger Ⓔ
Bowling green available
unless match on; woods for
hire 🏛🎪🌿🕒🍴 (not Mon) 🍴

Stottesdon   15E2
12–2.30 (closed Mon lunch); 7–11

Fox & Hounds
**Fox & Hounds DDD, Dashers
Disaster (winter)** Ⓗ Occasional
guest beers
Rural home-brew pub with a
skittle alley 🏛Q🌿🍴

Treflach   22A7
10.30–3; 6–11

Gibraltar
Off B4580 ℰ Oswestry 650111
**Draught Bass; Burtonwood
Dark Mild; Tetley Bitter** Ⓗ
Out of the way freehouse once
a farm 🏛🎪🌿🍴🏕

Wellington   22D8
11–2.30; 6–11

Smithfield
Bridge Road
Open until 3.30 Mon & Thu
lunch
Wem Mild, Best Bitter Ⓔ
Small market town pub; note
the Wrekin Brewery window
🍴&≷

Three Crowns
High Street (near bus station)
ℰ Telford 3209
Ansells Mild, Bitter Ⓗ

Welcoming town pub with
good food 🏛🌿🕒🍴≷

Welsh Frankton   22B7
11.30–3; 6–11

Narrow Boat
Ellesmere Road, Whittington
(A495) ℰ Oswestry 661051
**Ruddle County; Wadworth
6X** Ⓗ Occasional guest beers
Modern canalside pub 🏛🌿🕒🍴

Wem   22C7
10.30–3; 6–11

Dickin Arms
Noble Street ℰ 33085
Closes 5 Thu lunch
**Marston Mercian Mild,
Burton Bitter, Pedigree** Ⓗ
Useful adjunct to a town
otherwise devoted to Wem
ales 🌿🕒 (not Sun) 🍴≷

Fox
High Street
**Wem Pale Ale, Mild, Best
Bitter** Ⓗ
A short step from brewery;
Wem ales at their very best 🍴≷

Weston Rhyn   22A6
10.30–3; 6–11

Top House (Lodge)
One mile off A5
Banks's Mild, Bitter Ⓔ
Comfortable local, site of
Edward's Brewery 🏛🌿🍴

Try also: Butchers Arms
(Banks's)

Wheathill   14E2
10.30–2.30; 6–11

Three Horseshoes
B4364 near Burwarton
Wem Mild, Best Bitter Ⓔ
Remote rural pub overlooking
Brown Clee Hill 🏛🎪🕒🍴&🏕

Whitchurch   22C6
10.30–3; 7–11

The Star
Watergate Street
**Marston Mercian Mild,
Burton Bitter, Pedigree** Ⓗ
Small comfortable lounge
with aquarium 🏛🍴≷

Plume of Feathers
Bark Hill ℰ 2845
Opens at 11.30
**Greenall Whitley Local Mild,
Local Bitter; Wem Best
Bitter** Ⓗ
Dispense by set of three
Gaskell & Chambers
handpumps ≷

Whittington   22B7
10.30–3; 6–11

Penrhos Arms
Oswestry Road
ℰ Oswestry 662456
**Marston Border Bitter,
Pedigree** Ⓗ
Live entertainment and
barbecues in summer
🌿🕒🍴&

Wistanstow   14D2
12–2.30; 7–11

Plough Inn
Off A49 ℰ Craven Arms 3251
Wood Parish Bitter, Special Ⓗ
Home of Wood's beers.
Collection of royal wedding
bottles in lounge 🏛🌿🕒🍴🍴&

Woore   22D6
12–3; 6–11

Swan Hotel
Nantwich Road (A51)
ℰ Pipe Gate 220
**Wem Best Bitter, Special
Bitter** Ⓗ
Coaching inn dating from
1539. Bar meals and
restaurant. Close to
Bridgemere Garden Centre &
Wildlife Park 🏛Q🎪🌿🕒🍴🍴&

All pubs in Woore serve real
ale

How to Use the Guide

Facilities

🏛 real fire
Q quiet pub–no electronic
    music, TV or obtrusive
    games
🎪 indoor room for
    children
🌿 garden or other outdoor
    drinking area
🛏 accommodation
🕒 lunchtime meals
🍴 evening meals
🍴 public bar
& facilities for the disabled

🏕 camping facilities close
    to the pub or part of the
    pub grounds
≷ near British Rail station
⊖ near Underground
    Station.
    The facilities, beers and
    pub hours listed in the
    Good Beer Guide are
    liable to change but
    were correct when the
    Guide went to press.
    Many pubs do not serve
    meals at weekends.

Appley 4C3

11–2.30; 6.30–11

Globe
OS071215
✆ Greenham 672327
Cotleigh Kingfisher Ale,
Tawny Bitter Ⓖ; Bulmer
Cider Ⓖ
Friendly village local unspoilt
by the passage of time
🍴 Q 🏠 (summer) ⌁

Ash 5F3

11–2.30; 7–11

Bell Inn
Main Street (off A303)
✆ Martock 823387
Flowers IPA; Wadworth 6X Ⓖ
Lovely old village pub with
weekly jazz concerts 🍴 Q ⟲ �'t

Axbridge 5F1

10.30–2.30; 5.30–11

The Lamb
The Square ✆ 732253
Butcombe Bitter; Flowers
Original; Fuller London Pride
Occasional guest beers
Excellent inn and superb
historic surroundings. Bar
counter inlaid with spirit
bottles Q 🏠 ⌁ ⟲ �'t

Binegar 5G2

12–2.30; 7–11

Horse & Jockey
Near A37 ✆ Oakhill 840537
Draught Bass Ⓖ; Butcombe
Bitter Ⓗ; Thatchers Cider Ⓖ
Popular local with children's
pets corner
🍴 ⟲ �'t (not Tue or Sun) 🕮

Blackford 5F2

11–2.30; 6–11

Sexeys Arms
B3139
✆ Weston-Super-Mare
712487
Courage Bitter, Best Bitter Ⓗ
13th-century inn; excellent
dining room 🍴 Q ⌁ 🏠 ⟲ �'t 🕮

Bradford on Tone 4D3

11.30–2.30; 5.30 (6 Sat)–11

White Horse
Near A38 ✆ 239
Cotleigh Tawny Bitter;
Flowers Original; Golden Hill
Exmoor Ale; Hook Norton
Best Bitter; Occasional guest
beers Ⓗ
Tasteful pub opposite village
church 🍴 ⌁ ⟲ �'t 🕮

Brent Knoll 5E1

10.30–2.30; 6–11

Fox & Goose
Bridgwater Road (A38)
✆ 760223
Draught Bass; Flowers IPA,
Original Ⓗ

Friendly pub; good food
including vegetarian menu
🍴 ⌁ ⟲ �'t 🕮 ꜟ ⚘

Bridgwater 4E2

10.30–2.30; 5.30–11

Fountain Inn
I West Quay (off A38/A39)
✆ 424115
Opens 11 and 7
Butcombe Bitter; Cotleigh
Tawny Bitter; Golden Hill
Exmoor Ale Ⓗ
Fine town centre riverside
pub, limited street parking 🕮 ⇌

Quantock Gateway
Wembdon Road (A39)
✆ 423593
Opens 11 & 6
Draught Bass; Flowers IPA,
Original Ⓗ
Comfortable pub with large
garden play area 🚼 ⟲ �'t

Bruton 5G2

11–2.30; 5.30–11

Castle Inn
45 High Street (A359)
✆ 812211
Draught Bass; Bishop's Best
Bitter; Butcombe Bitter; Hook
Norton Old Hookey Ⓗ
Thriving one-bar local, good
food ⌁ ⟲ �'t 🕮 ⇌

Castle Cary 5G3

10.30–2.30; 5.30–11

Countryman
South Street (B3152) ✆ 50782
Oakhill Farmer's Ale Ⓖ;
Wadworth 6X; Wiltshire
Brewery Co Regency Bitter Ⓗ;
Occasional guest beers
Small freehouse; railway
theme with mock-up of steam
loco footplate in back bar
🍴 ⌁ ⟲ ➟ 🕮 ꜟ

White Hart
Fore Street ✆ 50255
Courage Bitter, Best Bitter,
Directors Ⓗ; Taunton Cider Ⓗ
Cheerful town centre pub
🚼 ⟲ ➟ 🕮

Chard 5E4

11–2.30; 6.30–11

Olde Ship Inn
Furnham Road (A358)
✆ 3135
Axe Vale Battleaxe; Golden
Hill Exmoor Ale; Wadworth
6X Ⓗ Occasional guest beers
Cosy old freehouse; pool table
and skittle alley
🍴 ⌁ ⟲ (not Sun) ꜟ

Charlton Musgrove 5H3

12–2.30; 6–11

Smithy
B3081 OS728317
✆ Wincanton 32242
Closed Mon lunch

Eldridge Pope Dorset Original
IPA; Palmer IPA; Wadworth
6X; Ⓗ
Busy roadside local with
caravan site. Dorset Original
called 'Smithy Ale' 🍴 ⟲ ➟ 🕮

Chiselborough 5F4

11–2.30; 7–11

Cat Head
Off A30 ✆ 231
Usher Best Bitter, Founder's
Ale Ⓗ
Popular old pub in charming
village. Good food 🍴 ⌁ ⟲ ➟

Coleford 5G1

12–2.30; 7–11

Rose & Crown
High Street ✆ Mells 812712
Butcombe Bitter Ⓗ Regular
guest beers
Friendly pub, worth finding
⌁ ⟲ (not Tue) 🕮

Combe Florey 4D3

11–2.30; 6–11

Farmers Arms
A358
✆ Bishops Lydeard 432267
Draught Bass Ⓗ
15th-century thatched pub
🍴 Q ⌁ ⟲ ➟

Donyatt 5E4

11–2.30; 7 (6.30 summer)–11

George Inn
A358 ✆ Ilminster 2849
Eldridge Pope Dorchester
Bitter, Royal Oak, Taunton
Cider; Occasional guest beers
Friendly traditional village
pub 🍴 ⌁ ⟲ ➟ 🕮

East Harptree 5G1

11–2.30; 6–11

Castle of Comfort
B 3134
✆ West Harptree 221321
Butcombe Bitter; Courage Best
Bitter; Occasional guest beers
Stone freehouse on the
Mendips 🍴 Q ⌁ ⟲ ➟ ꜟ

East Lambrook 5F3

11.30–2.30 7–11

Rose & Crown
Off A303
✆ South Petherton 40433
Eldridge Pope Dorchester
Bitter; Ind Coope Burton Ale;
Tetley Bitter Ⓗ
Oak beamed pub with good
food 🍴 ⌁ ⟲ ➟ 🕮

East Lyng 5E3

10.30–2.30; 5.30–11

Rose & Crown
A361 ✆ Burrowbridge 235
Butcombe Bitter; Wessex Best
Bitter; Eldridge
Pope Royal Oak; Palmers IPA
Ⓗ

Excellent, friendly roadside
pub 🏠🍺♿🅿🐕🏕

Emborough   5G1

11–2.30; 7–11

Old Down Inn
A37 ℰ Stratton on the
Fosse 232398
**Draught Bass; Old Brewery
Oakhill Farmers Ale** Ⓗ
Occasional guest beers
Pub of character built in 1640
🏠♿🐕🍴🎵

Exford   4C2

10.30–2.30; 5.30–11

White Horse Hotel
B3224 ℰ 229
**Cotleigh Tawny Ale; Courage
Best Bitter** Ⓖ
Rambling hotel in picturesque
village. Beware of the parrot
🏠Q🍴♿🅿♿🍴🎵🏕🅿

Faulkland   5H1

10.30–2.30; 6–11

Tuckers Grave Inn
A366 ℰ 230
**Draught Bass; Whitbread
WCPA; Cheddar Valley
Cider** Ⓖ
The burial place of a 1747
suicide, a small farm cottage
that has doubled as an inn
for well over 200 years
🏠Q🅿🍴🏕

Frome   5H2

10.30–2.30; 6–11

Angel
King Street (off A361)
ℰ 62469
Open until 4 Wed lunch
**Courage Best Bitter,
Directors** Ⓗ
300 year old former posting
inn 🍴🅿🍺♿🍴🎵≈

Crown
Market Place ℰ 62156
Open until 4 Wed lunch
Draught Bass Ⓗ
Friendly market town local
🍴♿🍴≈

Sun
Catherine Street ℰ 73123
**Boddingtons Bitter; Courage
Best Bitter, Directors; Marston
Pedigree** Ⓗ **Regular guest
beers**
Comfortable busy locals pub
with large central chimney

Glastonbury   5F2

11–2.30; 6–11

Beckets
High Street (A39) ℰ 32928
**Wadworth Devizes Bitter, IPA,
6X, Farmers Glory (summer),
Old Timer (winter)** Ⓗ
Comfortable town centre pub
with 3 bars 🍺♿🍴

Try also: Mitre (Courage)

Hardington Mandeville   5F4

11–2.30 7–11

Mandeville Arms
High Street (off A30)
ℰ West Coker 2418
**Hardington Bitter, Somerset
Special; Usher Best Bitter** Ⓗ
Smart village pub former
home of Hardington Brewery
🏠🍺♿🐕

Haselbury Plucknett   5F4

11–2.30; 7–11

Haselbury Inn
(off A30) ℰ Crewkerne 72488
**Golden Hill Exmoor Ale;
Hancock's HB** Ⓗ
Plush roadside eating
establishment 🏠Q♿🐕

Henstridge   5H3

10.30–2.30; 5.30–11

Bird in Hand
(off A30) ℰ Stalbridge 62255
**Draught Bass; Hook Norton
Best Bitter** Ⓗ **Regular guest
beers**
Delightful village pub 🏠♿🐕

Highbridge   4E2

10.30–2.30; 5.30–11

Coopers Arms
Market Street (B3139)
**Eldridge Pope Royal Oak;
Palmers IPA** Ⓗ **Regular guest
beers**
Busy locals pub with friendly
welcome 🅿🍴🐕🏕≈

Holcombe   5G1

10.30–2.30; 6.30–11

Ring O' Roses
ℰ Stratton on the
Fosse 232448
**Courage Bitter; Wadworth 6X;
Thatchers Cider** Ⓗ
Popular local by village
football pitch 🏠🅿🍺♿🍴🎵

Holton   5G3

11–2.30; 7–11

Old Inn
(off B3149)
ℰ Wincanton 32002
Butcombe Bitter Ⓗ**; Smiles
Best Bitter** Ⓖ**; Wadworth
6X** Ⓗ**; Taunton Cider** Ⓖ
Occasional guest beers
Village pub, originally a
smithy. No food Sunday
🏠🍺♿🍴🎵🏕

Hungerford   4C2

11.30–2.30; 6–11

White Horse Inn
Washford Watchet (off A39)
ℰ Washford 40415
**Usher Best Bitter, Founder's
Ale; Bulmers Cider** Ⓗ
Former coaching inn; outdoor
play area, free-range eggs
🏠🅿🍺♿🍴🎵♿🏕

Ilchester   5F3

11–2.30; 6–11

Bull
Church Street ℰ 840318
Draught Bass Ⓗ
Very friendly locals pub near
Yeovilton Airbase 🍴♿🐕🍴

Knole   5E3

10.30–2.30; 6.30–11

Limekiln
A372 ℰ Long Sutton 242
**Draught Bass, Eldridge Pope
IPA; Palmers IPA** Ⓗ **Burrow
Hill Cider** Ⓖ
Charming old pub overlooking
Knole Hill 🏠🍺♿🐕

Langford Budville   4D3

12–2.30; 5–11

Martlett Inn
OS111228
ℰ Milverton 400262
**Draught Bass; Cotleigh Tawny
Bitter; Golden Hill Exmoor
Ale** Ⓗ
Fine old pub with plenty of
character. No food Sunday
🏠🍴 (summer) ♿🍴

Lovington   5G3

10.30–2.30; 6.30–11

Pilgrims Rest
(off B3153) ℰ Wheathill 310
Closed Mon lunch
**Butcombe Bitter; Wadworth
6X** Ⓗ**, Old Timer (winter)** Ⓖ
Smart roadside pub with good
food 🏠Q🍺♿🍴

Lower Knapp   4E3

11.30–2.30; 6–11

Rising Sun
Near A378 OS304257
ℰ North Curry 490436
Flowers IPA, Original Ⓗ
Cosy 16th century pub down
lane to moors
🏠🅿🍺♿ (not Mon) 🐕

Luxborough   4C2

11–2.30; 6–11

Royal Oak
OS984377 ℰ Washford 40319
**Eldridge Pope IPA; Flowers
IPA, Original; Golden Hill
Exmoor Ale** Ⓗ
Fine pub in lovely rural
setting. Known locally as the
'Blazing Stump' 🏠🅿🍺♿🐕🍴

Milborne Port   FG3

11–2.30; 6.30–11

Queens Head
A30 ℰ 250314
**Hook Norton Mild, Best Bitter;
Smiles Best Bitter; Wadworth
6X** Ⓗ **Regular guest beers**
Superb pub, good bar food and
restaurant. Piano 🍺♿🐕🍴

Milverton   4D3

10.30–2.30; 6–11

Globe
Fore Street (near A361)
✆ 400534
Usher Best Bitter; Taunton
Cider ⊞
Popular one-bar village local
🏠 🐾 🍴 🕭 🍷

Minehead 4C2
10.30–2.30; 5.30–11
Kildare Lodge
Townsend Road
Opens 11 and 6
Eldridge Pope IPA, Royal
Oak ⊞
Lutyens building; comfortable
lounge, smart restaurant
🏠 🎫 🐾 🍷 🍴

Old Ship Aground
The Harbour ✆ 2087
Opens 11 & 6
Usher Best Bitter; Founders
Ale ⊞
Pleasant quayside pub with
smart lounge. Good food
🏠 Q 🎫 (summer) 🐾 🕭 🕭 🍷 🍴 🐾 ᴧ

Over Stratton F54
11–2.30; 7–11
Royal Oak
(off A303)
✆ South Petherton 40906
Devenish Wessex Best Bitter;
Hook Norton Best Bitter;
Wadworth 6X ⊞ Occasional
guest beers
Large village pub of great
character, good food 🐾 🕭 🍴

Pitminster 4D3
10.30–2.30; 5.30–11
Queens Arms
(off B3170) OS219191
✆ Blagdon Hill 529
Cotleigh Tawny Bitter; Golden
Hill Exmoor Ale ⊞ Regular
guest beers
Friendly village local,
mentioned in Domesday Book,
complete with ghost. Live
piano music at weekends
🏠 🐾 🕭 🍴

Porlock 4B2
10.30–2.30; 5.30–11
Castle Hotel
High Street ✆ 862504
Draught Bass; Golden Hill
Exmoor Ale ⊞, Wadworths 6X
Occasional guest beers
Hotel in centre of village
🏠 🎫 🕭 🕭 🍷 ᴧ ᴧ

Queen Camel 5G3
10.30–2.30; 30–11
Mildmay Arms
A359
✆ Marston Magna 850456
Draught Bass; Hardington
Best Bitter; Marston Pedigree;
Oakhill Farmers Ale ⊞
Popular and crowded village
local 🏠 🕭 🕭 🍴 🍴

Rimpton FG3
10.30–2.30; 6.30–11
White Post Inn
Rimpton Hill (B3148)
✆ Marston Magna 850717
Butcombe Bitter; Wadworth
Devizes Bitter, 6X ⊞, Old
Timer (winter) ⒼRegular
guest beers
Often crowded pub; 1 bar in
Dorset, 1 in Somerset 🏠 🐾 🍷

Shepton Mallet 5G2
10–2.30; 6–11
Kings Arms
Leg Square ✆ 3781
Halls Harvest Bitter; Ind
Coope Burton Ale; Ruddle
County; Wadworth 6X ⊞
17th century pub of character
in north of town 🏠 🕭 🕭 🍷

Shurton 4D2
11–2.30; 7–11
Shurton Inn
OS204444
✆ Nether Stowey 732695
Usher Best Bitter; Rich Cider ⊞
Occasional guest beers
Friendly rural pub near
Caravan Club ground 🎫 🐾 🕭 🍷

Somerton 5E3
10.30–2.30 6–11
Globe
The Square ✆ 72474
Draught Bass ⊞
Smart old town pub, popular
with young people 🏠 🕭 🍷

South Petherton 5F3
10.30–2.30; 5.30–11
Brewers Arms
St James Street (off A303)
✆ 40294
Hardington Best Bitter,
Somerset Special Ⓖ
Busy locals pub with regular
folk evenings 🕭 🍴 🍴

Stoford 5G4
11–2.30; 6–11
Royal Oak
The Green (off A37)
✆ Yeovil 75071
Draught Bass; Hancocks HB ⊞
Small and friendly local on
village green 🏠 ᴧ ᴧ

Stogumber 4D2
11–2.30; 6–11
White Horse Inn
OS098373 ✆ 277
Cotleigh Tawny Bitter; Golden
Hill Exmoor Ale; Sheppys
Cider ⊞
Friendly pub by church,
landlord doubles as church
clockwinder 🏠 Q 🐾 🕭 🍴 🍴 🕭

Taunton 4D3
10.30–2.30; 5.30–11
Harp Inn
Shoreditch Road (B3170)
✆ 72367
Opens 11 & 6
Courage Best Bitter,
Directors ⊞
Cosy suburban pub on road to
racecourse 🏠 🐾 🕭 🍴 🍴

Try also: Westgate
(Whitbread)

Masons Arms
Magdalene Street ✆ 88916
Draught Bass; Golden Hill
Exmoor Ale; Miners Arms
Own Ale; Wadworth 6X ⊞
Regular guest beers
200 year old town centre pub.
Good food 🏠 🕭 ᴧ

Wood Street Inn
Wood Street ✆ 73011
Opens 11 & 6
Usher Best Bitter, Founders
Ale ⊞
Popular back-street local
🐾 🕭 🕭 🍴 🍴

Theale
11.30 (summer, 12 winter)–2.30; 6–11
Snooty Fox
(B3139) ✆ Wedmore 712220
Draught Bass; Butcombe
Bitter; Eldridge Pope IPA;
Miners Arms Own Ale
Occasional guest beers
Comfortable Georgian hotel,
live music weekend eves. No
food Mondays 🏠 🎫 🐾 🕭 🍷

Trudoxhill 5H2
12 (11.30 Sat)–2.30; 7–11
White Hart
(Near A361) ✆ Nunney 324
Bishops Best Bitter ⊞;
Butcombe Bitter Ⓖ; Marston
Pedigree ⊞; Thatchers Old
Barnie Cider Ⓖ Regular guest
beers
Welcoming inn with
restaurant 🏠 🕭 🍷

Watchet 4C2
10.30–2.30; 5.30–11
Anchor Inn
Anchor Street (off B3191)
✆ 31387
Whitbread West Country Pale
Ale Ⓖ; Bulmers Cider;
Taunton Cider ⊞
Characterful local in small
seaport 🏠 🕭 🕭 🍷 ᴧ ᴧ

Try also: Bell Inn (Bass)

Wedmore 5F2
11–2.30; 7–11
New Inn
Combe Batch (on B3139)
✆ 712099
Butcombe Bitter; Oakhill
Farmers Ale ⊞
Cosy pub on outskirts of
Saxon Borough. No food Sun
🎫 (if eating) 🐾 🕭 🍴 🍴

Wells   5G2

10.30–2.30; 6–11

Star Hotel
High Street ✆ 72283
**Draught Bass; Butcombe
Bitter; Wadworth 6X;** ⊞
Occasional guest beers
Comfortable coaching inn
with occasional live music
Q ⊞ ⊖ ➐

Westbury-sub-   5F1
Mendip

10.30–2.30; 6–11

Westbury Inn
A371 ✆ Wells 870223
**Archers Golden; Boddingtons
Bitter; Butcombe Bitter;
Flowers Original; Miners
Arms Own Ale; Bulmers
Traditional Cider** Occasional
guest beers
Cosy pub below the Mendips.
An ideal stop for refreshment
⊖ ➐ ♀

West Chinnock   5F4

11–2.30; 7–11

Muddled Man
(off A30) ✆ Chiselborough 235
Usher PA ⊞
Cosy village local near
Ham Hill Country Park
⚓ ✍ ⊖ ➐

West Coker   5F4

11–2.30; 6.30–11

Royal George
A30 ✆ 2334
**Hall & Woodhouse Badger
Best Bitter, Tanglefoot** ⊞
Cosy, friendly village
local with good food
⚓ ✍ ⊖ ➐

Try also: Castle (Usher)

West   5G2
Cranmore

11.30–2.30; 6.30–11

Strode Arms
Near A361 ✆ Cranmore 450
**Butcombe Bitter; Wadworth
Devizes Bitter, 6X** ⊞**; Wilkins
Cider** Ⓖ
Opposite village duck pond
⚓ ⊖ ➐ ♀

Williton   4D2

10.30–2.30; 5.30–11

Foresters Arms
Long Street (A39) ✆ 32508
**Draught Bass; Cotleigh Tawny
Ale** ⊞ Regular guest beers
17th century coaching inn
near West Somerset railway
station ⚓ ⊞ ⊞ ⊖ ➐ ♀ ♿ Å

Try also: Egremont Hotel
(Ushers)

Witham Friary   5H2

10–2.30; 6–11

Seymour Arms
OS745409
**Usher PA; Bulmer Cider;
Taunton Cider** Ⓖ
Delightful locals pub with
serving hatch
⚓ Q ⊞ (mornings) ✍ ♀

Wookey   5F2

11–2.30; 6.30–11

Burcott Inn
B3139 ✆ Wells 73874
Butcombe Bitter ⊞ Regular
guest beers
Perfect roadside pub
⚓ Q ⊞ ✍ ⊖ ➐ Å

Woolverton   5H1

11–2.30; 6.30–11

Red Lion
A36 ✆ Frome 830350

**Draught Bass; Wadworth IPA,
6X** ⊞
Popular roadside inn with
good food ⚓ ✍ ⊖ ➐

Wrantage   4E3

11–2.30; 6–11

Wheelwrights Arms
(A378)
✆ Hatch Beauchamp 480370
**Usher Best Bitter; Founders
Ale** ⊞**; Vickery Cider
(summer)** Ⓖ
Comfortable pub with good
facilities ⚓ ⊞ ✍ ⊞ ⊖ ➐ ♀

Yeovil   5G4

11–2.30; 5.30–11

Armoury
1 The Park ✆ 71047
Evenings opens 6.30
**Butcombe Bitter; Hall &
Woodhouse Badger Best
Bitter; Wadworth 6X, Old
Timer** ⊞
Busy young persons' pub with
good food at lunchtimes ✍ ⊖

Black Horse
Reckleford (A30) ✆ 23878
Evenings opens 6
Draught Bass ⊞
Good local pub near hospital
and cattlemarket ✍ ⊖ ♀

Glovers Arms
Reckleford (A30) ✆ 74223
**Courage Best Bitter,
Directors** ⊞
Oldest inn in town.
Comfortable lounge, busy bar
with darts and table skittles
✍ ⊖ ➐ ♀ ⚌

Hole in the Wall
Wine Street ✆ 75560
Evenings opens 6
**Courage Best Bitter,
Directors** ⊞
Friendly and cosy pub in town
centre ⊖ ➐

"YOU'RE A LITTLE **OLD** TO BE IN THIS PUB, AREN'T YOU?"

Abbots Bromley 23G7

10.30–2.30; 5.30–10.30 (11F, S)

Coach & Horses
High Street (B5014)
✆ Burton 840256
Ind Coope Burton Ale Ⓗ
Lively 16th century pub
🏠 🍴 🏠 🅱 🕐 ♪

Bagot Arms
Bagot Street (B5014)
✆ Burton 840371
Marston Pedigree Ⓗ, Owd
Rodger Ⓖ
Friendly, traditional village
pub with large bar 🏠 🍴 🕒 ♪ ♥

Alrewas 23G8

11–3; 6–11

George & Dragon
High Street (off A38)
✆ Burton 790202
Marston Pedigree Ⓗ
Pleasing village pub with
superb restaurant 🏠 🍴 🕒 ♪ ♥

Alstonefield 23G5

10.30–2.30; 6–11

George
OS132556 ✆ 205
Ind Coope Bitter, Burton Ale Ⓗ
Attractive 18th century inn
facing the village green.
Popular with walkers and
campers alike 🏠 🎯 🍴 🕒 ♥ ♪ ♣ 🅰

Alton 23G6

12–2.30 (11.30–3 summer); 6 (7 winter)–11

Talbot
Horse Road
✆ Oakamoor 702767
Ind Coope Bitter, Burton Ale Ⓖ
A timeless gem in scenic
Churnet Valley, close to Alton
Towers 🏠 🅰 Q 🕒 ♪ ♥ ♣

Anslow 23G7

10.30–2.30; 5.30–11

Bell Inn
Main Street (off B5017)
Marston Pedigree, Merrie
Monk Ⓗ
Friendly village pub with good
sized beer garden. Occasional
homemade lunches 🏠 Q 🍴 ♥

Try also: **Brickmaker Arms**
(Marston)

Bishops Offley 22E7

11.30–3; 7–11

Brown Jug
Off B5026 (3 miles W of
Eccleshall)
Draught Bass Ⓗ
Friendly rural local with
unusual sign 🏠 Q 🍴 ♥

Bradwell 23E6

12–3; 7–11

Cavalier
Riceyman Road (off A34)
Wem Pale Ale, Mild, Best
Bitter Ⓔ, Special Bitter Ⓗ

Good class estate pub repays a
visit. Busy bar with pool, large
comfortable lounge ♥

Brewood 23E8

11.30–3; 6–11

Bridge
High Green
Ansells Mild, Bitter Ⓗ
Village local next to
Shropshire Union Canal 🏠 🍴 ♥

Brocton 23F7

11–3; 6–11

Seven Stars
Cannock Road (A34)
Ansells Mild, Bitter; Tetley
Bitter Ⓗ
Wally's bar, Nigel's lounge!
Fun loving pub specialising in
sports, games and wind-ups
🍴 🕒 (Mon–Fri) ♥ ♣ 🅰

Brownhills 23F8

11–2.30; 6–10.30 (11 F, S)

Prince of Wales
Watling Street (A5) ✆ 372551
Open lunchtimes Thu–Sun
only
Ansells Mild, Bitter Ⓗ
Superb roadside pub to suit all
tastes ♥

Chase
Watling Street (A5)
Banks's Mild, Bitter Ⓔ
Lively one-room pub ♥

Try also: **White Horse**
(Banks's), **Railway Tavern**
(Ansells)

Burnhill Green 22E9

11–3 (June–Oct only); 7–11

Dartmouth Arms
OS787006 ✆ Ackleton 268
Ansells Bitter; Gibbs Mew
Wiltshire Bitter Ⓗ
Friendly country pub—well
worth finding 🏠 🕒 ♪ ♥

Burntwood 23F8

11.30–3; 6–11 (11 F, S)

Centurion
Chase Road
Ansells Mild, Bitter Ⓗ
Homely one-bar local 🎯 🍴

Try also: **Trident** (Marston)

Burton upon Trent 23H7

10.30–2.30; 5.30–11

Argyle Arms
Uxbridge Street/All Saints
Road Junction (off A5121)
✆ 68697
Morning opens 11
Draught Bass Ⓗ
Superb Victorian pub at the
centre of many local
community activities 🎯 🍴 ♥

Black Horse
72 Moor Street ✆ 34187
Sat eves opens 7

Marston Pedigree Ⓗ
Friendly local with cosy
lounge. Not far from Heritage
Brewery ♥ ≷

Burton Bridge Brewery

24, Bridge Street (A50)
✆ 36596
Opens 11 Mon–Sat
Burton Bridge XL Bitter;
Bridge Bitter; Porter; Festival
Ale; Old Expensive Ⓗ
Occasional guest beers
Truly traditional pub boasting
unique skittles alley (used by
local folk club on Fridays) Q ♪

Crown & Anchor

93 Wetmore Road (B5118)
Sat eves opens 7
Marston Pedigree, Owd
Rodger Ⓗ (winter)
Down-to-earth local on the
edge of industrial estate ♥

Roebuck

Station Street ✆ 68660
Ind Coope Bitter, Burton Ale Ⓗ
Small Victorian-style bar,
popular with brewery workers
♥ ≷

Try also: **Red Lion** (Marston)

Butt Lane 22E5

12–3; 7–11

Crown
67 Chapel Street (off A34)
✆ Kidsgrove 2107
Ansells Bitter; Tetley Bitter Ⓗ
Convivial 3-room local known
as the Corna Pin, 10 minutes
walk from the canal. Pool.
Good value food
🏠 🕒 ♪ (not Mon) ♥

Cannock 23F8

12–3; 7–11

Unicorn
Church Street ✆ 4331
Ansells Mild, Bitter Ⓗ
Small, friendly town local
🕒 ♪ ♥

Cauldon 23G6

10.30–2.30; 6–11

Yew Tree
Between A52 & A523
Draught Bass Ⓖ, Ind Coope
Bitter; M&B Mild; Winkles
Bitter Ⓗ
Superb country pub full of
antiques, including working
pianolas, polyphons and the
seats you sit on Q 🎯 🍴

Chase Town 23F8

11–3; 6–11

Crown
High Street
Banks's Mild, Bitter Ⓔ
Small, friendly pub ♥

Cheslyn Hay 23F8

12–2.30; 5.30–11

Mary Rose

Moon Lane ✆ 415114
**Ansells Mild, Bitter; Ind Coope
Burton Ale; Tetley Bitter** Ⓗ
Converted farmhouse with
Mary Rose memorabilia.
Excellent food ♨✿🕭➐🍴♿

Clayton 23E6

11.30–3; 5.30–11

Westbury Tavern
Westbury Road, Westbury
Park (off A519, near Jct 15
M6) ✆ 638766
**Ansells Mild, Bitter; Gibbs
Mew Wiltshire Bitter; Ind
Coope Burton Ale** Ⓗ
Large, deservedly popular new
pub, with pleasing contrast
between bar and lounge
✿🕭➐🍴♿

Draycott-in-the-Clay 23G7

10.30–2.30; 5.30–10.30 (11 F, S)

Swan
A515
**Ansells Mild; Ind Coope
Bitter** Ⓖ
Superb and unspoilt village
local ♨Q✿🍴♿ A

Eccleshall 23E7

11–3; 6–11

Bell
High Street (B5026)
Draught Bass Ⓗ
Popular pub with attractive
lounge fireplace. No food Sun
♨Q✿🕭➐🍴

Elford 23G8

12–2.30; 7–11

Crown
The Square
Draught Bass Ⓗ
Attractive village pub hidden
off main road. Houses former
courtroom. Skittle room at
back ♨Q🏠✿🕭➐🍴

Gnosall 22E7

11–3; 6–11

Boat
Wharf Road
✆ Stafford 822208
**Marston Burton Bitter,
Pedigree** Ⓗ
Popular pub on banks of
Shropshire Union Canal; bar
billiards ♨✿🕭➐🍴

Horns
High Street
**Draught Bass; Springfield
Bitter** Ⓗ
Village centre local. No meals
Sun Q🕭➐🍴

Great Chatwell 22E8

11–3; 7–11

Red Lion
Off A41 ✆ 270366
Wem Best Bitter Ⓗ
Relaxed rural pub with
traditional bar and genteel
lounge ♨Q🏠🕭🍴➐ A

Halfpenny Green 22E9

11–2.30; 6–10.30 (11 F, S)

Royal Oak
Six Ashes Road OS825920
Bank's Mild, Bitter Ⓔ
Popular old country local near
aerodrome 🏠✿🕭➐🍴♿ A

Handsacre 23G8

12–3; 6–11

Crown
The Green (off A513)
Draught Bass Ⓗ
Popular canalside pub with
comfortable lounge 🏠🍴

Haughton 23E7

11.30–3; 6–11

Bell
Newport Road (A518)
✆ Stafford 780301
**Courage Best Bitter,
Directors** Ⓗ
The acceptable face of the
Bass/Courage swap! ♨✿🕭➐

Hollington 23F6

11–3 (Sun only); 7–11

Star
OS059390 ✆ 250
**Aylesbury ABC Bitter; Ind
Cooper Bitter, Burton Ale;
Tetley Bitter** Ⓗ
One-room stone inn with
games area. Convivial
atmosphere and welcoming
hosts. Only 3 miles from Alton
Towers ♨Q✿🕭➐🍴

Hulme End 23G5

11–2.30; 6 (7 winter)–11

Manifold Valley Hotel
B5054 (off B5053) OS106593
✆ Hartington 537
**Darley Dark Mild, Thorne
Best Bitter; Ward Sheffield
Best Bitter; Thatchers
Farmhouse Scrumpy** Ⓗ
Good beer and excellent
home-cooked food make this
friendly pub well worth trying
♨Q✿🏠🕭➐🍴A

Hyde Lea 23E7

11–3; 7–11

Crown Inn
Burton Manor Road (off
A449) ✆ Stafford 54240
**Draught Bass; M&B
Springfield Bitter** Ⓗ
Popular village local
connected with Staffordshire
Regiment ♨✿🕭➐🍴

Kiddemore Green 23E8

11.30–3; 6–11

New Inn
OS859089
Ansells Mild, Bitter Ⓗ
Pleasant inn in Staffordshire
countryside ♨✿🕭

Kinver 15F2

11–2.30; 6–10.30 (11 F, S)

Cross
Dark Lane (off High Street)
Hansons Mild, Bitter Ⓔ
Local with smart lounge near
restored Tudor house ♨✿🕭🍴

Elm Tree
Enville Road (off A458)
Davenports Bitter Ⓗ
Pub at edge of village. Garden
former bowling green ♨✿🍴➐

Plough & Harrow (Steps)
High Street
**Batham Bitter, Delph Strong
Ale** Ⓗ
Split level local in centre of
village ➐➐🍴

Knighton 22E7

11–3; 6.30–11

Haberdashers Arms
OS753275
Banks's Mild, Bitter Ⓗ
Unspoilt country local selling
home-grown produce, ½ mile
from canal ♨Q✿🍴A

Knighton 22D6

11–3; 5.30–11

White Lion
B5026, at cross roads ¼ mile S
of village OS728398
**Marston Burton Bitter,
Pedigree** Ⓗ **Owd Rodger** Ⓖ
350 year-old country inn on
Shropshire border ♨Q✿🍴

Leek 23F5

10.30–2.30; 6–11

Britannia Inn
46 West Street
**Marston Mercian Mild,
Pedigree** Ⓗ
Thriving friendly street-corner
local with rare Marston
etched windows Q✿🍴

Flying Horse
Ashbourne Road (A523)
Winter eves opens 7
**Marston Mercian Mild,
Burton Bitter, Pedigree** Ⓗ
Smart, friendly local with
good atmosphere. Small
lounge ✿

Red Lion
7 Market Place
✆ 382025
Opens 11, closes 4 Wed lunch
**Burtonwood Dark Mild,
Bitter** Ⓗ
Formerly a Magistrates' Court,
now a town-centre hotel with
drinking corridor ♨🏠🏠🕭🍴

Sea Lion
36–38 Russell Street
Evenings opens 6.30
Banks's Mild, Bitter Ⓔ
Friendly 4-room pub with
extrovert landlady! ♨🏠

Lichfield 23G8

11–3; 5.30–11

Carpenters Arms
Christchurch Lane (A461)
Opens 12 & 7 weekdays
Banks's Mild, Bitter E
Convivial one-room local ▯

Duke of York
Greenhill ✆ 55171
Davenports Mild, Bitter H,
Weston Cider H & G
Occasional guest beers
Victorian lounge, beamed bar;
friendly and popular
▦▨▧🖪🟊♥▯≷

Prince of Wales
Bore Street ✆ 263657
**Ansells Mild; Ind Coope
Bitter** H
Friendly local ▯≷

Queens Head
Queens Street
**Marston Pedigree, Merrie
Monk** H
Popular, unspoilt pub with
small lounge ▯

Try also: Acorn (Ind Coope)

Longdon 23G8

11–2.30; 7–11

Swan With Two Necks
Brookend, Upper Longdon (off
A51) ✆ Armitage 490251
**Ansells Mild, Bitter; Ind Coope
Burton Ale** H
Friendly village local ▦🖪♥▯

Marchington 23G7

11–2.30; 7–11

Bulls Head
Off B5017, near Uttoxeter
Marston Pedigree H
Friendly village local.
Interesting poster collection
adorns bar walls ▦🖪🖪▯

Marston 23E8

12–3; 7–11

Fox
✆ Wheaton Aston 840729
**Holden Black Country Bitter;
Lloyds Best Bitter; Ruddle
County; Wadworth 6X;
Woods Special** H Occasional
guest beers
Enterprising country free
house. No food Sun
▦Q🖪🖪▯▵

Newcastle-under-Lyme 23E6

11–3; 5.30–11

Castle Mona
Victoria Street (off A34)
Opens 12 and 7
Wem Mild, Best Bitter E,
Special Bitter H
Friendly, welcoming locals'
pub in quiet corner of town.
Strong games fraternity ▯▵

Jolly Potters
9 Barracks Road ✆ 631736

Opens 12 & 7
Wem Mild, Best Bitter E
Special Bitter H
Welcoming 2-room pub
opposite Bus Station ▯▵

Victoria
62 King Street ✆ 615569
Opens 7 Sat eves
Draught Bass H
Bustling bar and comfortable
lounge just out of town.
Strong bar games fraternity ▯

Newtown 23F8

12–2.30; 6–11

Ivy House
Stafford Road
✆ Cannock 477607
**Draught Bass; M&B Highgate
Mild, Springfield Bitter** E
Old low-ceilinged pub on busy
main road. Childrens' garden
🖪🖪▯

Norbury 22E7

11–3; 6–11

Junction
Off A519 ✆ Woodseaves 288
Banks's Mild, Bitter E;
McEwan 80/- H
Superbly situated on former
canal junction. U-boat clock
on bar ▦🖪🖪🖪♥▯▵▵

Norton Canes 23F8

12–3; 7–11

Railway Tavern
Norton Green Lane
Ansells Mild, Bitter H
Small homely one-room pub ▯

Onecote 23F5

12–2.30; 7–11

Jervis Arms
B5063 (near A523) ✆ 206
**Marston Pedigree; McEwan
70/-; Ruddle County;
Theakston Best Bitter, Old
Peculier; Younger's No. 3** H
Occasional guest beers
Excellent country pub with
riverside beer garden. Noted
for its food—includes
vegetarian menu ▦🖪🖪♥

Outwoods 22E7

10.30–3; 6.30–11

Village Tavern
Off A518
Marston Burton Bitter H
Intimate, traditional village
local. Worth finding ▦Q🖪▯

Penkridge 23F8

11.30–3; 6–11

Cross Keys
Filance Lane OS926134
✆ 2826
**M&B Highgate Mild;
Springfield Bitter** E
Modernised pub by Staffs and
Worcs canal bridge No. 84.
Meals summer only 🖪🖪♥▵

Rugeley 23F8

11–3; 7–11

Albion
Albion Street (A51)
Banks's Mild, Bitter E
Basic bar and lounge ▯

Yorkshire Man
B5013
**Ruddles County; Samuel
Smith OBB** H Regular guest
beers
Lounge with high class decor
and area with restaurant-style
food service 🖪♥

Saverley Green 23F6

12–3; 7–11

Hunter
Off A50
✆ Blythe Bridge 392267
**Aylesbury ABC Bitter; Ind
Coope Burton Ale; Tetley
Bitter** H Occasional guest
beers
Occasional beer festivals
▦▨🖪🖪♥

Shenstone 23G8

11–3; 5.30–11

Railway
Main Street ✆ 480803
**Marston Burton Bitter,
Pedigree, Merrie Monk** H
Recently modernised village
pub; friendly atmosphere 🖪♥

Shraley Brook 22E5

12 (11 Sat)–3; 6.30–11

Rising Sun
Knowle Bank Road (off A52,
near M6 Junction 16)
✆ Stoke on Trent 720600
**Batham Bitter; Marston
Pedigree** H Thatchers Cider G
Regular guest beers
Friendly and very popular free
house. Regular live folk music
▦♥🖪🖪▵ (½ mile)

Spot Acre 23F6

12–3; 7–11

Spot Acre
B5066 ✆ Hilderstone 277
**Ansells Mild, Bitter; Ind Coope
Burton Ale** H
Large hostelry with restaurant
in Pullman carriages
▦♥🖪♥ (not Sun) ▯▵

Stafford 23F7

11–3; 6–11

Bird in Hand
Victoria Square ✆ 52198
**Courage Best Bitter,
Directors** H
Enterprising pub, rooms
include games, snug, lounge
and bar. Near St. Marys parish
church ♥🖪▯▵

Coach & Horses
4 Mill Bank (behind post
office) ✆ 3376

Draught Bass; M&B,
Springfield Bitter ⓗ
Straightforward town-centre
pub near Victoria Park ⓘ ≿

Cottage by the Brook
Peel Terrace (off Sandon
Road)
Ansells Mild; Aylesbury ABC
Bitter; Ind Coope Bitter,
Burton Ale ⓗ
Large pub catering for all
tastes. Variety of traditional
pub games ⌂ ℘ ☝ ⓘ

Garth Hotel
Wolverhampton Road (A449,
off M6 Exit 13) ✆ 56124
Banks's Mild, Bitter; Hansons
Black Country Bitter ⒠
Popular with drinkers and
diners. Lively bar, spacious,
comfortable lounge ℘ ▥ ☝ ⓘ

Holmcroft
Holmcroft Road (off A5013)
✆ 52634
Banks's Mild, Bitter; Hansons
Black Country Bitter ⒠
Busy estate pub, regular
organist in lounge ℘ ☝ ⓘ

Kings Arms
Peel Terrace ✆ 49872
Opens 10.30 & 7
Ansells Bitter ⓗ
Small, darts-oriented terraced
pub north of town centre ⓘ

Staffordshire Bull
Parkside ✆ 49839
Opens 11.30 weekday
mornings
Wem Mild, Best Bitter; Special
Bitter ⓗ
Comfortable one-roomed
estate pub ℘ ☝ (not Sun) ⓰

Try also: Crossbow (Ansells),
Eagle (Bass), Pheasant
(Ansells)

Standeford 24C5
11.30–3; 6–11

Harrows
A449 ✆ 790216
Ansells Mild, Bitter; Tetley
Bitter ⓗ
Comfortable friendly roadside
inn. Lounge in a jugular vein!
No meals weekends ⌂ ℘ ☝ ⓘ

Stanley 23F5
10.30–2.30; 7–11

Travellers Rest
Tompkin Road OS933523
Ansells Mild, Bitter; Ind Coope
Burton Ale; Tetley Bitter ⓗ
Very popular and comfortable
village pub
⌂ Q ℘ ☝ ❦ ⓘ ⚲ (½ mile)

Stoke on Trent 23E6
11–3; 5.30–11

Burslem:

Huntsman
13 Westport Road ✆ 84657
Evenings opens 7

Banks's Mild, Bitter;
Boddingtons Bitter; Marston
Pedigree ⓗ
Friendly bar. Large lounge,
popular with the young ☝ ⓘ ⓓ

Travellers Rest
239 Newcastle Street
✆ 810418
Lunchtimes opens 12
Ansells Mild; Ind Coope Bitter,
Burton Ale; Titanic Premium
Bitter, Xmas Ale; Coates
Cider ⓗ Occasional guest
beers
Popular, pleasant pub with
own brewery. Noted for good
food. Live music Mondays and
Tuesdays Q ℘ ☝ ❦ (not Sun) ⓘ
≿ (Longport)

Hanley:

Coachmakers Arms
65 Lichfield Street
Evenings opens 7
Draught Bass ⓗ
Good old-fashioned multi-
room pub near bus station
⌂ Q ⓘ

Globe Inn
Bucknall New Road (A52)
✆ 25539
Lunchtimes opens 12
Five Towns Dark Mild,
Bursley Bitter, Bennett Ale;
Robinson Old Tom ⓗ Regular
guest beers
Homely two-room local. Five
Towns brewery tap ⌂ ☝ ⓘ

Rose & Crown
Etruria Road (A53)
✆ 280503
Opens 12 & 7
Ansell's Mild, Bitter; Gibbs
Mew Wiltshire Bitter; Ind
Coope Burton Ale ⓗ
Occasional guest beers
Former Parkers Brewery
showpiece pub (see etched
windows). Regular live music.
Good value home-cooked food
(not Sun) ⌂ ℘ ☝ ⓘ ≿ (Etruria)

Tontine
20 Tontine Street ✆ 263890
Evening opens 7; closed Sun
lunch
Ansells Mild; Ind Coope
Burton Ale ⓗ
Busy town centre pub
opposite meat market.
Excellent value food ℘ ☝

Stoke:

Glebe
Glebe Street (next to Town
Hall) ✆ 45418
Banks's Mild, Bitter; Hansons
Black Country Bitter ⒠
Comfortable spacious lounge;
smaller basic bar with pool,
darts and table skittles ☝ ❦ ⓘ ≿

Jolly Potters
296 Hartshill Road, Hartshill
Evening opens 6
Draught Bass; M&B Mild ⓗ

Very popular pub of character
with four small rooms off
central passage Q ⓘ

White Lion
134 Honeywall, Penkhull
Opens 11.30 & 7
Ansells Bitter; Ind Coope
Burton Ale ⓗ
Comfortable one-room lounge;
pool table in separate games
area ℘ ☝ (Mon–Fri) ⓓ

Tunstall:

White Horse
143 Brownhills Road
Evening opens 7
Draught Bass; M&B
Springfield Bitter ⓗ
Old-fashioned basic pub at
lower end of town. Note
genuine "central heating"
⌂ Q ⓘ

Stone 23E7
11–3; 6–11

Pheasant
Old Road
Mornings opens 11.30
Draught Bass; M&B
Springfield Bitter ⓗ
Lively street corner former
Joules house ⌂ ℘ ⓘ ≿

Stone Inn
26 Radford Street
✆ 818269
Draught Bass ⓗ
Well-modernised pub sporting
Joules Brewery memorabilia ≿

Swindon 15F1
12–2.30; 6–10.30 (11 F, S)

Bush
High Street (off B4176)
OS864906
Hansons Mild, Bitter ⒠
Extended cottage, at heart of
village near Staffs and Worcs
Canal

Tamworth 23G8
10.30–2.30; 6–11

Bulls Head
Watling Street (A5) Two
Gates
Opens 7 winter eves
Marston Mercian Mild;
Pedigree ⓗ
Very friendly local on main
crossroads
Q ℘ ☝ ⓘ ≿ (Wilnecote)

Lamb Inn
Kettlebrook Road (A51)
✆ 66833
Draught Bass; M&B Mild ⓗ
Basic, friendly local next to
football ground Q ▧ ℘ ☝ ⓘ

Longwood
Lichfield Street (A5), Fazeley
✆ 284965
Banks's Mild, Bitter ⒠
Extensively modernised, large
estate pub
℘ ☝ ❦ (Fri & Sat only) ⓘ

Riftswood

Comberford Road (A513)
☎ 64480
Draught Bass; M&B Mild Ⓔ
Classically modernised with
conservatory overlooking
extensive garden ✿ ❤ ⌂ ❤ ❦

Tam o Shanter

Cedar Drive (off Comberford
Road A513) ☎ 62297
Home Mild, Bitter Ⓔ
Large estate pub serving the
only Home ales in the area ❤ ❦

Tweedale Arms

Victoria Road/Albert Road
☎ 62748
Draught Bass; M&B Mild Ⓗ
Bustling local opposite
Tamworth Station ≥

Tatenhill   23G7

11.30–2.30; 5.30–11
Horseshoe Inn

Main Street (1½ miles from
A38 at Branston)
☎ Burton 64913
Marston Pedigree Ⓗ, **Owd
Rodger** Ⓖ (winter)
Popular 18th century village
inn. Unspoilt beamed lounge
bar ✿ Q ❤ ❤ (not Sun/Mon)

Try also: **Red Lion** (Marston)

Trysull   22E9

11–2.30; 6–10.30 (11 F, S)
Plough

School Road OS851940
Banks's Mild, Bitter Ⓔ
Half-timbered 15th century
farmhouse featuring wattle
and daub panels ✿ ❤ ⌂ ❤ ❦

Uttoxeter   23G7

10.30–2.30; 6–10.30 (11 F, S)
Plough

Blounts Green, Stafford Road
(A518) ☎ 2381
Ind Coope Burton Ale Ⓗ
Comfortable 17th century pub
✿ Q ⌂

Roebuck

37 Dove Bank (A518) ☎ 5563
Opens 11.30 & 7
**Burton Bridge Bitter, Porter,
Old Expensive; Marston
Pedigree; Titanic Bitter;
Wilsons Original Bitter** Ⓗ & Ⓖ
Occasional guest beers
Interesting homely inn dating
back to 1608. Oak beamed
inglenook fireplace ✿ Q ❤ ☐ ❤

Try also: **Black Swan** (Bass)

Weston   23F7

11.30–3; 6–11
Coach & Horses

Pasturefields, Nr Great
Haywood (A51) ☎ 270324
**Banks's Mild, Bitter; Draught
Bass; Ind Coope Bitter; Lloyds
Best Bitter; Marston
Pedigree** Ⓗ Regular guest
beers

Comfortable, enterprising free
house with skittle alley
✿ ❤ ⌂ ❤ ❦ ⚿

Wetton   23G5

11–2.30; 6 (7 winter)–11
Ye Olde Royal Oak

OS108553
☎ Alstonefield 287
**Ruddle Rutland Bitter,
County; Theakston XB** Ⓗ
17th century country
freehouse with pub games,
including toe wrestling!
✿ Q ⊞ ❤ ☐ ⌂ ❤ ❦ ⚿

Wombourne   23E9

11–2.30; 6–10.30 (11 F, S)
Red Lion

Old Stourbridge Road
**Draught Bass; M&B Highgate
Mild; Springfield Bitter** Ⓔ;
Bulmers Cider Ⓖ
Old coaching inn, lying below
original main road ⌂ ❤ ⚿

Yarnfield   23E7

11–3; 6–11
Labour in Vain

Yarnfield Lane
☎ Stafford 760272
Draught Bass Ⓗ **M&B
Springfield Bitter** Ⓗ
Open-plan pub, popular with
Telecom students. Note see-
through panels to beer
engines ⌂ ❤ (Mon–Fri)

I SAID: 'ONE OF EDWIN'S FEW PLEASURES IS DROWNING THE PIPED MUSIC!'

AT the last count, there were exactly 57 card-carrying pub guides in the UK. Of these, 56 are compiled from paid-for advertising, recommendations from Rabbit's friends and relations, or salaried inspectors. Only one is surveyed by teams of independent volunteers who actually know and live in the areas they survey. This makes that particular guide the only one you can trust to give you unbiased and informed comment on pubs.

The guide has over 20,000 potential surveyors spread throughout Great Britain, which means that it is also the only one that is as useful and accurate in the North of England, the East of Scotland and the West of Wales as it is in the South of England. Each region is allocated a certain number of pubs on the basis of its population and area, combined with a factor for tourism – unlike most guides, which allocate pubs on the ease of access from their editors' London offices.

All the pubs in the guide are visited frequently during the year by the volunteers; it isn't too much of a chore, because they are people who actually like pubs ... and they have been known to take a drink now and then. The surveyors are of both sexes, all ages and all tastes, so the selection of pubs reflects the diversity which characterises our Great British pubs. This guide knows that all sorts of people go to all sorts of pubs in all sorts of moods, so it offers the widest possible range: pubs with family rooms for people who believe that having children and a social life shouldn't be incompatible; pubs where children and dogs are instantly impounded for Glaswegian misogynists who wish to enjoy a quiet drink without distractions; pubs with juke boxes and discos for ravers; pubs with nothing louder than the clack of dominoes and the murmur of friendly conversation; pubs where you can eat a 3-star, 5 course meal; pubs where a bar meal is a pork pie and a packet of crisps; pubs near stations; pubs near motorways; pubs that you'd need a compass and a large amount of luck to find at all!

Though readers' recommendations are always welcomed by the editor of this guide, they are all passed to the local volunteers and their decision is final. They assess a pub first and foremost on the quality of its beer. There is no great mystery to the keeping of good beer; what it does require is a bit of hard work and some tender loving care – qualities which also happen to be requisites of the ideal landlord and landlady as well. If they keep their beer in perfect condition, chances are that their pubs will be first-rate too.

Pubs in this particular guide won't be described as 'clean' – if they aren't they won't be included – and the surveyors won't go into 500 word rhapsodies about the noisettes de water buffalo or the termite mousseline, but if the food is good, they will tell you so. This guide works wonders in cramming all the facts you need to know about thousands of Great British pubs into a book that will still fit in your pocket without dislocating your shoulder. It tells you in simple, concise terms all a pub's facilities, its range of beers, its location, its points of interest and its atmosphere; in fact the kind of pub you can expect to find – and how to find it.

This guide is quite simply the best on the market, and it's the best-value too. The name of this paragon of virtues? Modesty forbids us to say, but here's a clue. . . . . You're looking at it!

Help keep real ale alive by joining CAMRA. Your voice helps encourage brewers big and small to brew cask beer and offer all beer drinkers a better choice. Send £9 for a year's membership or use the form on page 319.

Aldeburgh 19H6

11–2.30; 7–11
Albert Inn
Victoria Road
Adnams Mild (summer),
Bitter, Extra, Old ℍ
Formerly home of Flintnam
and Hall Brewery. Wide range
of pub games ⑤➤🍴🍽 Å

All pubs in Aldeburgh serve
real ale

Badingham 19H6

10.30–2.30 (2 winter); 6–11
White Horse Inn
A1120
Adnams Bitter, Extra
(summer), Old ℍ
Excellent country pub
catering for all tastes
🏚Q🌿⑤🍴🍽 Å

Bardwell 19E5

11–2.30; 5 (7 Sat)–11
Dun Cow
Upstreet, (off A143)
🕿 Stanton 50806
Greene King XX, IPA,
Abbot ℍ
Welcoming village local with
large plain bar and small
smart lounge 🌿🍴🍽

Try also: Six Bells (Free)

Barnby 19H4

10.30–2.30; 6.30–11
Swan Inn
Swan Lane (off A146) 🕿 646
Greene King IPA, Abbot;
Rayment BBA; Wethered
Bitter ℍ; James White Cider ⑤
Spacious country pub tucked
away behind main road.
Worth finding 🏚🌿⑤➤🍴 Å

Barton Mills 18D5

11–2.30; 7–11
Bell
Bell Lane (off A11)
🕿 Mildenhall 713625
Greene King XX, IPA,
Abbot ℍ
Popular community pub. Old
photos of village life in bar
🌿⑤➤🍴

Beccles 19H4

11–2.30; 7–11
Butchers Arms
London Road (A145)
🕿 712243
Flowers Original; Wethered
Bitter ℍ
Average brassy local 🌿⑤

Boxford 19E7

11–2.30; 5–11
Compasses
11 Stone Street 🕿 210468
Greene King IPA, Abbot ⑤
Typical centuries-old,
unaltered village pub with
friendly atmosphere and
service Q🌿🍽 Å

Bramfield 19H5

10.30–2; 6–11
Bell
The Street (A144)
Adnams Mild, Bitter ⑤
Down-to-earth pub with Ring
the Bull; crinkle crankle wall.
Near thatched church in
village 🏚🌿🍴 Å

Brandeston 19G6

11–2; 5.30 (6 Sat)–11
Queens Head
Queens Head
🕿 Earl Soham 307
Adnams Bitter, Old ℍ
Superbly run pub with large
children's play area. All food
home cooked. Deservedly
popular 🏚🛏🌿🞮⑤➤🍴 Å

Bredfield 19G7

11–3; 7–11
Castle
The Street (off A12)
🕿 Woodbridge 5927
Tolly Cobbold Bitter ℍ, Old
Strong ⑤
Comfortable lounge, good
value food 🏚🌿⑤➤

Brundish 19G5

11–2.30; 6–11
Crown Inn
🕿 Worlingworth 277
Adnams Mild (summer),
Bitter, Extra, Old ℍ
Local in rural setting
🏚🛏🌿⑤➤🍴 Å

Bungay 19H4

10.30–2.30; 6.30–11
Fleece
8 St. Mary's Street 🕿 2192
Adnams Bitter, Old ℍ
16th century coaching inn.
Active market town pub
🏚🛏🌿⑤➤🍴🍽 Å

Try also: Kings Head (Free)

Bury St. Edmunds 18E6

11–2.30; 5–11
Masons Arms
Whiting Street
Opens 6 Sat. eves
Greene King XX, IPA,
Abbot ℍ
Popular town centre pub
dating back 250 years
🌿⑤🍴🍽

Nutshell
The Traverse
Closes 4 pm Wed, Sat lunch;
winter eves opens 7
Greene King XX, IPA,
Abbot ℍ
Smallest pub in Britain. Full of
bric-a-brac Q🌿🞮≷

Suffolk Hotel
Buttermarket 🕿 3995
Eves opens 5.30 (7 Sat)
Adnams Bitter; Greene King
IPA, Abbot; Mauldon
Special ℍ Occasional guest
beers
Comfortable hotel bar in
market area Q🛏⑤➤🍴≷

Butley 19H7

11–2.30; 6–11
Oyster
Adnams Mild ℍ; Bitter, Extra
(summer), Old ⑤
Quaint old inn with folk
singing on Sundays 🏚Q🌿🍴

Buxhall 19F6

12–2.30; 7–11
Crown
Mill Road 🕿 Rattlesden 521
Greene King XX, IPA,
Abbot ℍ
Traditional 2-bar pub.
Specialises in home-cooked
food (not Sun)
🏚Q🛏🌿⑤➤ (not Sun) 🍴🍽 Å

Chelsworth 19E7

11–2.30; 6.30–11
Peacock
The Street (B1115)
🕿 Bildeston 740758
Adnams Bitter, Old; Greene
King IPA, Abbot; Mauldon
Bitter, Porter (winter) ℍ
Occasional guest beers
3-bar 14th century timbered
inn near River Brett
🏚Q🌿🛏⑤🍴🍽

Clare 18D7

11–2.30; 5–11
Globe
10 Callis Street
🕿 Sudbury 277551
Greene King IPA, Abbot ℍ
Friendly, beamed family pub
with restaurant 🏚🛏🌿⑤➤🍴🍽

Try also: Bell Hotel

Coddenham 19F6

11–2.30; 6–11
Dukes Head
High Street (B1078) 🕿 300
Tolly Cobbold Mild (summer),
Bitter, Original (summer), Old
Strong ⑤
Attractive village local
🏚🌿⑤🍴🍽

Try also: Henley Cross Keys

Debenham 19G6

10.30–2.30; 5.30–11
Red Lion
High Street 🕿 Ipswich 860113
Tolly Cobbold Bitter, Original,
Old Strong ℍ
15th century inn in unspoilt
village. Fine fireplace 🏚🌿⑤🍴🍽

East Bergholt 19F8

11–2.30; 6–11
Royal Oak (Dickey)
East End 🕿 Colchester 298221

Greene King IPA, Abbot ⧠
Friendly unspoilt village pub,
popular with campers during
summer ▲ Q ✿ ⅃ ▼ ♠ Å

Easton 19G6

11–2.30; 7–11
White Horse
Tolly Cobbold Mild, Bitter,
Original (summer), Old
Strong ⧠
Good pub, good food
▲ Q ⅃ ▼ ♠ Å

Edwardstone 19E7

11–2.30; 6.30–11
White Horse
Mill Green (2 miles off A1071)
☏ Boxford 211211
Greene King XX, IPA,
Abbot ⧠
Remote village pub; good
value meals Thu to Sun
▲ ✿ ⅃ ▼ ♠

Felixstowe 19G8

11–2.30; 5.30–11
Ferry Boat Inn
Felixstowe Ferry
☏ 284203
Eves opens 6
Tolly Cobbold Bitter, Original
Old Strong ⊡
Old-fashioned sailing haunt
on River Deben estuary
▲ Q ✿ ⅃ (not Sun)

Grosvenor
Ranelagh Road
☏ 284137
Tolly Cobbold Mild, Bitter, Old
Strong ⧠
Large, comfortable pub near
town centre. No food Sun
✿ ⅃ ▼ Å ≈

Framlingham 19G6

10.30–2.30; 5.30 (6 Sat)–11
Railway Inn
9 Station Road
☏ 723693
Adnams Bitter, Extra, Old ⧠;
James White Dry Cider ⧠
Popular pub with modern
lounge, simple public bar.
Strong sporting tradition
▲ Q ✿ ⅃ ♠ Å

Glemsford 18D7

11–2.30; 5–11
Angel
Egremont Street 281671
Greene King XX, IPA,
Abbot ⊡
This reputedly haunted pub is
the oldest house in Glemsford,
the home of Cardinal
Wolseys's secretary John
Cavendish Q ✿ ⅃
▼ (not Sun–Tues) ♠ &

Cock
27 Egremont Street (B1065)
☏ 280544
Opens 12 & 7
Greene King IPA; Mauldon
Bitter ⧠

A pleasant good-value
beamed pub and restaurant
Q ✿ ⅃ ▼ ♠

Try also: **Crown** (Greene
King), **Half Moon**

Great Glemham 19H6

11–2.30; 6.30–11
Crown Inn
3 Miles off A12
☏ Rendham 693
Adnams Bitter, Old; Greene
King XX, IPA, Abbot
Christmas Ale; Mauldon
Bitter ⧠ & ⊡ Occasional guest
beers
Homely country pub in
conservation area, close to
Heritage Coast. Superior
accommodation; home cooked
meals ▲ Q ✿ ⅃ ⊡ ♠ ⅃

Hadleigh 19F7

11–2.30; 5–11
George
52 High Street
☏ Ipswich 822151
Evenings opens 6
Greene King IPA, Abbot ⧠
Busy town pub. Good home
cooked food. Folk club first
Wed of month
▲ Q ✿ ⅃ ♠ (not Tue/Sun) ♦ &

White Hart
Bridge Street
☏ Ipswich 822206
Sat eves opens 6
Tolly Cobbold Bitter, Original ⧠ Old Strong ⊡
Good local with warm
welcome and pub games
▲ ✿ ⅃ ♠

Try also: **White Horse** (Free)

Haughley 19F6

11–2.30; 5.30–11
Railway Tavern
Station Road
☏ Stowmarket 673577
Adnams Old, Greene King XX,
IPA, Abbot; Mauldon Bitter ⧠
Occasional guest beers
Friendly 1-bar freehouse;
landlord breeds pedigree dogs
▲ Q ⊡ ✿ ⅃ ▼ ♠

White Horse
New Street (Old A45)
☏ Elmswell 40349
Eves opens 6.30
Greene King XX, IPA,
Abbot ⧠; Christmas Ale ⊡
16th century country pub
▲ ⊡ ✿ ⅃ ♠ (Thu–Sat) ♦ Å

Haverhill 18C7

11–2.30; 5–11
Queens Head
Queens Street ☏ 702026
Adnams Bitter; Courage Best
Bitter, Directors; Greene King
IPA; Mauldon Bitter, Porter ⧠
Cosy town centre pub with

dining room. Friendly
atmosphere, old Wards'
Brewery etched window
Q ⅃ ▼ ♠

Hundon 18D7

11–2.30; 7–11
Plough
Brockly Green OS722470
Charrington IPA; Mauldon
Bitter ⧠
Friendly country pub with
restaurant. Fine views
▲ Q ✿ ⅃ ▼ ♠

Icklingham 18D5

11–2.30; 5 (7 winter)–11
Plough Inn
The Street (A1101)
☏ Mildenhall 713370
Bateman XXXB; Greene King
XX, IPA, Abbot; Marston
Merrie Monk; Samuel Smith
OBB ⧠ Occasional guest beers
Old village flint-faced cottages
now a popular local. Games
room ▲ ✿ ⅃ ▼ ♠ ♦

Ipswich 19G7

11–2.30; 5–11
Arboretum
High Street ☏ 50711
Sat eves opens 7
Tolly Cobbold Mild, Bitter,
Original (summer), Old
Strong ⧠
Happy town local with fine
collection of plates ▲ ✿ ⅃ ▼ ♠

Great White Horse
Tavern Street ☏ 56558
Eves opens 5.30
Greene King IPA, Abbot ⧠
16th-century THF hotel
associated with Dickens and
Pickwick Papers. Quiet oasis
in busy town centre
Q ⊞ ⊡ ⅃ ▼ ≈

Greyhound
Henley Road
Adnams Bitter, Extra, Old ⧠
Popular, but not overcrowded
✿ ⅃ ▼ ♠

Station Hotel
Burrell Road ☏ 602664
Evening opens 5.30 (7 Sats)
Tolly Cobbold Mild, Bitter,
Original, Old Strong ⧠
Tasteful hotel opposite station
✿ ⊡ ⅃ ▼ ♠ ≈

Thrasher
Nacton Road (near A45)
☏ 73355
Evenings opens 6
Greene King XX, IPA,
Abbot ⧠, Christmas Ale ⊡
Active pub with many games,
near Ipswich Airport
✿ ⅃ ▼ (must book) ♦ & Å

Water Lily
100 St. Helens Street ☏ 57035
Evenings opens 7
Tolly Cobbold Mild, Bitter, Old
Strong ⊡

Enthusiastic pub games bar, quiet snug and large outdoor drinking area Q ✿ ⑤ ♀

Woolpack
Tuddenham Road
Lunchtime closes 2; eves opens 5.30
Tolly Cobbold Mild, Bitter, Original, Old Strong Ⓗ
Possibly the smallest bar in Ipwich. Mulled winter ale and hot toddies ▲ Q ✿ ♀

Try also: Airport Bar

Ixworth 19E5
11–2.30; 5.30 (6 Sat)–11
Pickerel
The Street
✆ Pakenham 30398
Greene King XX, IPA, Abbot Ⓗ
Old village coaching inn. Excellent seafood. Jazz every Friday Q ♫ ✿ ⑤ ♀ ♀

Try also: Crown (Greene King)

Lakenheath 18D5
11–2.30; 6–11
Plough
Mill Road (off B1112)
✆ Thetford 860285
Greene King XX, IPA, Abbot Ⓗ
Fine Victorian flint building in centre of bustling village. Pool room ✿ ⑤ ♀

Laxfield 19G5
10.30–2.30; 6–11
Lowhouse (Kings Head)
Gorams Mill Lane
✆ Ubbeston 395
Adnams Bitter, Old; Greene King Abbot; Mauldon Special Porter, Christmas Reserve; James White Dry Cider Ⓖ
600 year-old unspoilt alehouse, traditional country fayre and pets corner
▲ Q ⊞ ✿ ⑤ ♀ ♀ ⑤ Å

Lidgate 18D6
11–2.30; 7–11
Star
The Street (B1063)
✆ Ousden 275
Greene King IPA, Abbot Ⓗ
Centre of activity in attractive village, spit-roast beef a speciality. Bar billiards
▲ ✿ ⑤ ♀ ♀

Long Melford 18E7
11–2.30; 5–11
Crown Inn Hotel
Hall Street (A134)
✆ Sudbury 77666
Adnams Bitter, Old, Greene King IPA; Mauldon Bitter, Special Ⓗ Occasional guest beers
Family-run hotel with homely atmosphere and good value food ▲ Q ⊞ ✿ 🄴 ⑤ ♀ ♀

Swan
Hall Street (A134)
Sudbury 78740
Greene King XX, IPA, Abbot Ⓗ
Friendly local on main road; comfortable lounge
✿ 🄴 ⑤ ♀ ♀ ⑤

Lowestoft 19J4
10.30–2.30; 6–11
Prince Albert
Park Road ✆ 3424
Adnams Mild, Bitter 🄴**, Old** Ⓗ
Down-to-earth town pub in side street near lighthouse
Q ✿ ♀ Å

Hearts of Oak
Raglan Street (A12) ✆ 61125
Evenings opens 5.30
Flowers Original, Wethered Bitter Ⓗ
Pleasant lunchtime office workers' haven ⑤ ♀ ⑤ ≷

Triangle Tavern
St. Peter's Street (A12)
✆ 82711
Opens 11 and 7
Adnams Bitter, Old; Greene King IPA, Abbot; Marston Pedigree Ⓗ**; James White Cider** Ⓖ **Regular guest beers**
Town local with customers as varied as its beers Q ♀ ≷

Victoria Hotel
Kirkley Cliff (A12) ✆ 4433
Adnams Bitter Ⓖ
Plush bar with sea views
Q ⊞ 🄴 ⑤ ♀ ⑤

Middleton 19H6
10.30–2.30; 6–11
Bell
Middleton ✆ Westleton 286
Adnams Mild (summer), Bitter, Old Ⓖ
Friendly pub; listed building, 4 miles from coast ▲ ✿ ⑤ ♀ ♀ Å

Newbourne 19G7
11–2.30; 6–11
Fox
The Street
✆ Waldringfield 307
Tolly Cobbold Bitter, Old Strong Ⓖ
Popular pub in unusual smallholding village. Basic and friendly ▲ Q ♀ ♀

Orford 19H7
11–2; 6–11
Jolly Sailor
Quay Street ✆ 450243
Adnams Bitter, Old Ⓗ
16th century quayside inn, deserted by the sea in the 1700's ▲ 🄴 ✿ 🄴 ⑤ ♀ Å

Pakenham 18E6
11–2.30; 5–11
Fox
The Street ✆ 30347

Greene King XX, IPA, Abbot Ⓗ
Popular cosy village pub with inglenooks and dining room
✿ ⑤ ♀ ♀ ≷

Pin Mill 19G7
11–2.30; 5 (7 winter)–11
Butt & Oyster
Off B1456
✆ Woolverstone 224
Tolly Cobbold Mild, Bitter, Original, Old Strong Ⓗ **&** Ⓖ
Internationally known riverside inn. Unchanging and unchanged ▲ Q ⊞ ✿ ⑤ ♀ ♀

Risby 18D6
11–2.30; 6.30–11
Crown & Castle
South Street
✆ Bury St. Edmunds 810393
Greene King XX, IPA, Abbot Ⓗ
Comfortable village pub. 112 ft well in entrance hall. No food Sun ▲ ✿ ⑤ ♀ ♀

St. James South Elmham 19H5
10.30–2.30; 5.30–11
White Horse
OS320812 ✆ St. Cross 269
Adnams Mild (summer), Bitter, Old Ⓗ
Unspoilt family pub dating back to 14th century with a fine settle ▲ ⊞ ✿ 🄴 ⑤ ♀ ♀ Å

Shimpling 18E7
11–2.30; 5.30–11
Bush
✆ Cockfield Green 828257
Greene King XX, IPA, Abbot Ⓗ
Friendly village local
▲ Q ⊞ ✿ ⑤ ♀ ♀

Shottisham 19H7
11–3; 6.30–11
Sorrel Horse
Off B1083 ✆ 411617
Tolly Cobbold Mild, Bitter Ⓖ
Picturesque 500 year-old smuggler's inn ▲ Q ✿ ♀ ♀ Å

Snape 19H6
11–3; 5.30–11
Plough & Sail
The Maltings, Snape Bridge
✆ 413
Adnams Bitter, Extra, Old (winter) Ⓗ
Traditional pub and restaurant in Maltings complex ▲ Q ⊞ ✿ ⑤ ♀ ♀ Å

Somerleyton 19J4
11–2.30; 6–11
Duke's Head
Sluggs Lane (off B1074)
OS477972 ✆ 730281
Flowers Original; Wethered Bitter; Bulmer Cider Ⓗ
Occasional guest beers

Family pub with views of river and marsh ♨ Q 🎪 ♪ ⏰ ♪ Å ≷

Southwold 19J5

10.30–2.30; 6–11

Red Lion
2, South Green ✆ 722385
Adnams Bitter, Extra, Old (winter) ⒣
One bar pub with homely atmosphere Q 🎪 ♪ ⒣ ⏰ ♪ & Å

Southwold Arms
High Street ✆ 722099
Adnams Mild (summer) Bitter, Extra, Old (winter) ⒣
Comfortable pub with good locals bar and dining room
Q ♪ ⒣ ⏰ ♪ ♪ Å

All pubs in Southwold serve real ale

Spexhall 19H5

11–2.30; 7–11

Huntsman & Hounds
A144 ✆ Ilketshall 341
Adnams Bitter; Mauldon Bitter ⒣
Country local on main road
♨ ♪ ⏰ ♪ ♪ Å

Stansfield 18D7

12–2.30; 7–11

Compasses
High Street ✆ Hawkerdon 261
Greene King XX, IPA, Abbot ⒣
Fine country local with bar billiards ♨ ♪ ♪

Stanton 19E5

11–2.30; 7–11

Angel
The Street (off A143) ✆ 50119
Greene King XX, IPA, Abbot ⒣
1-bar local. Top quiz team and bar billiards ♨ ♪ ⏰ ♪

Stonham Aspal 19F6

10.30–2.30; 6–11

Ten Bells
A1120 ✆ 711601
Tolly Cobbold Mild, Bitter, Original ⒣
Friendly, busy roadside pub
♨ ♪ ⏰ ♪ ♪ Å

Stowupland 19F6

11–2.30; 6.30–11

Crown
Church Street (A1120)
Tolly Cobbold Mild, Bitter ⒣, **Old Strong** ⒢
Attractive old thatched country pub ♪ ♪

Stutton 19F8

11–2.30; 6.30–11

Kings Head
Manningtree Road ✆ 328344
Tolly Cobbold Mild, (summer) Bitter, Original ⒣, **Old Strong** ⒢
Village local. 400 year-old coaching inn ♨ Q 🎪 ♪ ⒣ ⏰ ♪ ♪

Sudbury 18E7

11–2.30; 6–11

Horn
North Street ✆ 73802
Greene King XX, IPA, Abbot ⒣
Busy local, venue of top darts players Q ♪ ♪

Waggon & Horses
Acton Square ✆ 73053
Greene King XX, IPA, Abbot ⒣
Back street local. Excellent value restaurant, keen pub games players in public
♪ ⏰ ♪

Thurston 19E6

12–2.30; 7–11

Black Fox
Barrells Road OS652939
✆ 30636
Adnams Bitter, Extra, Old; Greene King IPA, Abbot; Mauldon Bitter; Bulmers Cider ⒣
Basic beer house in quiet surroundings ♨ Q ♪ ♪

Walsham-le-Willows 19E5

11.30–2.30; 7–11

Six Bells
High Street ✆ 726
Greene King XX, IPA, Abbot ⒣
Beamed three-part public bar; small lounge
♨ ♪ ⒣ ⏰ (not Sat/Sun) ♪

Washbrook 19F7

11–2.30; 6–11

Brook
Back Lane ✆ Copdock 455
Tolly Cobbold Mild, Bitter, Original, Old Strong ⒣
Friendly village pub on Ipswich outskirts. Popular bar, comfortable lounge
♨ ♪ ⏰ ♪

West Row 18G5

11–2.30; 5 (7 winter)–11

Judes Ferry
Ferry Lane
✆ Mildenhall 712277
Greene King IPA, Abbot; Woodford Judes Tipple ⒣
Regular guest beers
Large historic house near

ancient crossing of River Lark. Moorings available
♨ 🎪 ♪ ⏰ ♪ Å

Wetheringsett 19G6

10.30–2.30; 5.30–11

Cat & Mouse
Pages Green
✆ Debenham 860765
Mauldon Special, Cat & Mouse Bitter; Flowers Original, Wethered Bitter; Whitbread Castle Eden ⒢
Welcoming, heavily beamed freehouse in pleasant rural surroundings
♨ Q 🎪 ♪ ⒣ ⏰ ♪ Å

Woodbridge 19G7

11–3; 5.30–11

Olde Bell & Steelyard
New Street (near Market Hill)
✆ 2933
Winter eves opens 6
Greene King IPA, Abbot ⒣
15th century oasis in Tolly country. Steelyard stands out over road. Vast range of games ♨ Q ♪ ⏰ ♪ ≷

Red Lion
Thoroughfare
✆ 2484
Evenings opens 6.30
Tolly Cobbold Mild, Bitter, Original, Old Strong ⒣
Listed building. Quiet lounge, lively bar with pool and darts
🎪 ♪ ⒣ ♪ ≷

Try also: **Seckford Arms** (Free), **Kings Head** (Tolly Cobbold)

Wrentham 19J5

10.30–2.30; 6–11

Horse & Groom
London Road (A12)
✆ 279
Adnams Mild, Bitter ⒣, **Old** ⒢
Good homely pub, best pub this side of heaven!!
♨ ♪ ⏰ ♪ &

Yoxford 19H6

10.30–2.30; 6–11

Blois Arms
High Street (A1120)
Adnams Mild, Bitter, Old ⒣
Friendly country pub. Good collection of old bottles ♪ ♪

How to Use the Guide

Facilities

♨	real fire	⏰	lunchtime meals
Q	quiet pub–no electronic music, TV or obtrusive games	♪	evening meals
		♪	public bar
🎪	indoor room for children	&	facilities for the disabled
♪	garden or other outdoor drinking area	Å	camping facilities close to the pub or part of the pub grounds
⬛	accommodation	≷	near British Rail station
		⊖	near Underground Station.

Abinger Common 7H4

11–2.30; 6–10.30 (11 F, S & summer)
Abinger Hatch
Abinger Lane (off A25)
Flowers Original; Hall &
Woodhouse Badger Best
Bitter; King & Barnes Sussex
Bitter; Wadworth 6X;
Whitbread Pompey Royal Ⓗ
Occasional guest beers
Popular country pub, stone
flags, large open fireplace
🚲⌂🅖🍺

Addlestone 7H3

10.30–2.30; 5.30–11
George Inn
109 Chertsey Road (A318)
Courage Best Bitter,
Directors Ⓗ
Picturesque listed building—
parts 400 years old ⌂🅖≷

Albury Heath 7H4

10.30–2.30; 5.30–10.30 (11 F, S & summer)
William IV
Little London (near A25)
OS066467 ✆ Shere 2685
Courage Best Bitter,
Directors Ⓗ
16th century rural beamed
pub; small restaurant 🚲Q⌂🍺

Ashford 7H2

11–2.30; 5.30–11
Ash Tree
Convent Road (B378)
Fuller London Pride, ESB Ⓗ
Roomy, smart, well-managed
pub ⌂🅖🍺

Betchworth 7J4

10.30–2.30; 5.30–10.30 (11 F, S & summer)
Red Lion
Old Road (off A25) ✆ 3336
Friary Meux Bitter; Ind Coope
Bitter, Burton Ale Ⓗ
Popular pub; good food (some
vegetarian). Cricket pitch and
squash court ⌂🅖🍺 (not Sun)

Blackbrook 10A5

11–2.30; 6–10.30 (11 F, S)
Plough
OS181467 Closes 11 summer
Thu
King & Barnes Sussex Mild,
Sussex Bitter, Old Ale,
Draught Festive Ⓗ
Country pub serving good
food. Collection of ties in
public bar—donations
welcome Q⌂🅖🍺🍺

Brockham 7J4

10.30–2.30; 6–10.30 (11 F, S & summer)
Spotted Cow
Middle Street, Strood Green
(off A25) ✆ Betchworth 2076
Friary Meux Bitter; Ind Coope
Burton Ale Ⓗ
Small, friendly modern pub on
the edge of award-winning
village ⌂🅖🍺🍺

Camberley 7G3

10.30–2.30; 5.30–11
Lamb
593 London Road (A30)
Morland Mild, Bitter, Best
Bitter Ⓗ
One bar split into games area
and 'lounge' with non-
smoking sections
🚲🅖 (not Sun) 🍺 (not Sun) 🚾
≷ (Blackwater)

Staff Hotel
191, London Road (A30)
Closes 10.30 (except Thu, Fri
and summer)
Friary Meux Bitter; Ind Coope
Burton Ale Ⓗ
Spacious saloon; public caters
for dart and pool players
🅖 (not Sun) 🍺≷

Caterham 10B5

11–2.30; 6–11
Royal Oak
68 High Street (B2030)
Draught Bass; Charrington
IPA; Fuller ESB (winter) Ⓗ
Small, friendly one-bar local
Q🅖🚾

Chertsey 7H3

10.30–2.30; 5.30–11
George
45 Guildford Street ✆ 62128
Opens 11
Courage Best Bitter,
Directors Ⓗ
Low-ceilinged 14th century
town pub. Public bar often
crowded 🚲Q⌂🅖🍺🍺

Vine
Bridge Road
Opens 11 & 6
Courage Best Bitter,
Directors Ⓗ
Convivial one-bar pub that
was once a school-house
🅖🚾

Chiddingfold 7G5

10.30–2.30; 5.30–10.30 (11 F, S & summer)
Winterton Arms
Petworth Road (A283)
Friary Meux Bitter; Ind Coope
Burton Ale Ⓗ
Attractive building;
magnificent water garden
🚲Q🅖⌂🅖🍺🚾

Chobham 7G3

10.30–2.30; 6–10.30 (11 F, S & summer)
Four Horseshoes
Burrowhill Green (B383)
Courage Best Bitter,
Directors Ⓗ
Attractive oak-beamed pub,
recently used by kings of
Greece and Spain. Public bar
used to be a mortuary—now
has pool and darts
🚲🚲🅖🅖 (not Sun)
🍺 (not Sun) 🍺

White Hart
High Street ✆ 7580

Courage Best Bitter, Directors Ⓗ

Courage Best Bitter,
Directors Ⓗ
Popular old pub, near village
cricket green. Don't mind the
grumpy landlord!
🚲🅖🍺 (not Mon)

Churt 7G4

11–2.30; 6–10.30 (11 F, S & summer)
Crossways
(A287)
Courage Best Bitter,
Directors Ⓗ
Friendly pub. Smart lounge,
busy public
🅖🅖 (not Sun) 🍺🚾Å (1 mile)

Claygate 7J3

10.30–2.30; 5.30–11
Griffin
Common Road
Watney Stag Bitter; Webster
Yorkshire Bitter Ⓗ
Comfortable pub outside
village. Good lunches
🅖🅖 (Mon-Fri) 🍺≷

Colnbrook 7H2

10.30–2.30; 5.30–11
Star & Garter
Park Street (B3378) ✆ 2157
Courage Best Bitter,
Directors Ⓗ
Cosy, friendly pub; attractive
brookside garden 🅖🅖🍺

Cranleigh 7H4

10.30–2.30; 6–10.30 (11 F, S & summer)
Leathern Bottle
Smithbrook (A281) ✆ 274117
King & Barnes Sussex Bitter,
Old Ale (winter), Draught
Festive Ⓗ
Traditional roadside pub. Bar
skittles and shove-ha' penny
🚲Q🅖🅖🍺 (not Wed) 🍺🚾

Dockenfield 7F4

10.30–2.30; 6–10.30 (11 F, S & summer)
Blue Bell
Batts Corner (off A325)
Ballard Best Bitter, Wassail;
Courage Best Bitter, Directors;
Fuller London Pride, ESB Ⓖ
Select cottage pub with large
children's garden 🚲Q🅖🅖🍺🚾

Dorking 7J4

10.30–2.30; 5.30–10.30 (11 F, S & summer)
Bush
10/11 South Street (A2003)
Evenings opens 6
Friary Meux Bitter; Ind Coope
Burton Ale Ⓗ
Friendly back street local.
Basic public, comfortable
lounge, and excellent food
🅖🚲🅖🍺🍺

Cricketers
81 South Street ✆ 889938
Sat evening opens 6
Fuller Chiswick Bitter, London
Pride, ESB Ⓗ
Popular one-bar, town centre
pub 🅖🅖 (weekdays)

Downside 7H3

10.30–2.30; 5.30–11

Plough
Plough Lane
**Courage Best Bitter, Directors;
John Smith's Bitter** H
Lively popular pub with
restaurant ♨Q♿🐕🍴♫

Eashing 7G4

10.30–2.30; 6–10.30 (11 F, S & summer)

Stag
Off A3
**Friary Meux Bitter; Ind Coope
Burton Ale** H
Traditional pub in riverside
setting. Liable to flooding
♨♿🍴&

East Molesey 7H3

11–2.30; 5.30–11

New Inn
50 Walton Road (B369)
**Courage Best Bitter,
Directors** H
Drink with the fish at this
popular, youthful pub
♨♿🐕🍴&

Egham 7H2

10.30–2.30; 5.30–11

Compasses
158 Thorpe Lea Road
**Truman Best Bitter, Sampson;
Webster Yorkshire Bitter** H
Pub hard to find, but well
worth the effort ⊞♨♿🐕&

Elstead 7G4

10.30–2.30; 5.30–10.30 (11 F, S & summer)

Star
Milford Road (B3001)
**Courage Best Bitter,
Directors** H
Village pub for all ages
♨♿🐕🍴⚓

Englefield Green 7G2

10.30–2.30; 5.30–11

Sun
Wick Lane, Bishopsgate
**Courage Best Bitter,
Directors** H
Excellent country pub near
Savill Garden
♨Q⊞♨♿🐕 (on request) &

Epsom 7J3

10.30–2.30; 5.30–10.30 (11 F, S)

Barley Mow
12 Pikes Hill (off Upper High
Street) ✆ 21044
Fuller London Pride, ESB H
Friendly backstreet local with
piano; aviary in garden ♨♿

Kings Arms
144 East Street (A24)
**Young Bitter, Special, Winter
Warmer** H
Popular, lively house away
from town centre ♨♿🍴

Ewell 7J3

10.30–2.30; 5.30–10.30 (11 F, S)

Green Man
71 High Street (off A24)
**Courage Best Bitter,
Directors** H
Comfortable, welcoming local
♨♿🐕🍴≥ (both)

Farncombe 7G4

10.30–2.30; 5.30–10.30 (11 F, S & summer)

Three Lions
Meadrow (A3100)
**Friary Meux Bitter; Ind Coope
Burton Ale; Taylor-Walker
Bitter** H
Known locally as "Scratchers".
Live rock music Thu and Sun
eves ♨♿🐕🍴≥

Farnham 7G4

10.30–2.30; 5.30–11

Plough
74 West Street ✆ 716332
**Gales HSB; Usher Best Bitter;
Webster Yorkshire Bitter** H
Thirties' rebuild of historic
town pub. Once had its own
brew house and dairy ♨♿

Queen's Head
9 The Borough (A287)
**Gales XXXD (summer); BBB;
XXXXX; HSB** H
Two diverse bars ♨Q♿🍴≥

Waverley Arms
Station Hill Road (B3001)
Opens 6 Sat evenings
**Courage Best Bitter,
Directors** H
Popular with diners; good
public bar with pool table
♨♿♿🐕🍴&≥

Frimley 7G3

10.30–2.30; 6–11

Railway Arms
78 High Street
Ind Coope Best, Burton Ale H
Old established village local;
darts in the public
♿ (not Sun) 🍴&≥

Godalming 7G4

10.30–2.30; 5.30–10.30 (11 F, S & summer)

Anchor
Ockford Road (A3100)
Opens 11 am
**Adnams Bitter; Eldridge Pope
Royal Oak; Fuller London
Pride; Hall & Woodhouse
Badger Best Bitter** H Regular
guest beers
Single large informal bar
♨♿≥

Inn on the Lake
Ockford Road (A3100)
**Flowers Original, Wethered
Bitter** H
Summer barbecues in scenic
grounds ⊞♨♿🐕🍴≥

Gomshall 7H4

10.30–2.30; 5.30–10.30 (11 F, S & summer)

Black Horse
A25 ✆ Shere 2242
**Young Bitter, Special, Winter
Warmer** H
Georgian pub with panelled
lounge; restaurant
♨Q♿⊞♿🍴≥

Guildford 7H4

10.30–2.30; 5.30–10.30 (11 F, S & summer)

Prince Albert
Stoke Road (A320)
Closes 10.30 pm Mon–Thu
summer
**Courage Best Bitter,
Directors** H
Good locals pub, near noted
fish and chip shop. Live music
Tue nights
♨♿🍴≥ (London Road)

Spread Eagle
Chertsey Street
**Courage Best Bitter,
Directors** H
Small popular local. Excellent
home cooked lunches ♨♿≥

Star
Quarry Street (off High Street)
Closes 10.30 Mon–Thu
summer
**Friary Meux Bitter; Ind Coope
Burton Ale** H
Oldest pub in Guildford;
rambling interior. Reputedly
haunted ⊞♿≥

Hersham 7H3

11–2.30; 5.30–11

Bricklayers Arms
Queens Road, Hersham (off
A317) ✆ Walton 220936
**Ruddle County; Watney
Combes Bitter; Webster
Yorkshire Bitter** H
Good food, parking difficult
♨♿🍴

Royal George
Hersham Road (off A244)
**Young Bitter, Special, Winter
Warmer** H
Pleasant and traditional pub
with mixed clientele ♨♿♿🐕

Hindhead 7G5

10.30–2.30; 5.30–11

**Devils Punchbowl
Hotel**
London Road (A3) ✆ 6565
**Ballards Best Bitter; Flowers
Original; Hall & Woodhouse
Badger Best Bitter; King &
Barnes Sussex Bitter, Draught
Festive; Young Bitter** H
Modern bar, cocktail lounge
and restaurant ⊞♨⊞♿🐕

Horley 10B5

10.30–2.30; 5.30–10.30 (11 F, S & summer Thu)

Olde Six Bells
Church Road (off A23)
**Draught Bass; Charrington
IPA** H
500 year-old beamed building
on 9th century wooden piles;
restaurant ♨♿🐕🍴

Leatherhead 7JB

10.30–2.30; 5.30–10.30 (11 F, S & summer)

Dukes Head
57 High Street ✆ 372076
Friary Meux Bitter; Ind Coope Burton Ale [H]
Friendly 1-bar pub in pedestrianised area
⌂Q✿◔◗≹

Long Ditton 7J3

10.30–2.30; 5.30–11

Masons Arms
Portsmouth Road (A307)
Courage Best Bitter, Directors [H]
Large one-bar pub with games ◔ (weekdays)

Plough & Harrow
64 Ditton Hill Road
Courage Best Bitter, Directors [H]
Two-bar pub with large garden at foot of Ditton Hill
⌂Q✿◔ (weekdays) ▮

Merstham 10B5

10.30–2.30; 5.30–10.30 (11 F, S & summer)

Railway Arms
London Road North (A23)
Charrington IPA [H]
Small 2-bar local by North Downs Way ◔▮≹

Mickleham 7J3

10.30–2.30; 5.30–10.30 (11 F, S & summer)

King William IV
Byttom Hill (off A24 south)
Friary Meux Bitter; Hall and Woodhouse Badger Best Bitter; Ind Coope Burton Ale [H] **Hancocks Cider** [G] **Occasional guest beers**
Unspoilt pub, on a rocky hillside; splendid garden
⌂Q✿◔▮

Mogador 10A5

11–2.30; 6–10.30 (11 F, S)

Sportsman
Off A217 OS241533
Courage Best Bitter, Directors [H]
Good atmosphere in this heathland pub; bar billiards
⌂Q✿◔

New Haw 7H3

11–2.30; 5.30 (6 Sat)–11

White Hart
New Haw Road (A318)
Courage Best Bitter, Directors [H]
Caters for local trade. Quiet saloon. Attractive canalside garden ✿◔◗ (May–Sept) ▮ ≹ (Byfleet & New Haw)

Oatlands Park 7H3

11–2.30; 5.30–11

Prince of Wales
Anderson Road
Adnams Bitter; Benskins Bitter; Boddingtons Bitter; Fuller London Pride; King & Barnes Draught Festive; Young Special [H] **Occasional guest beers**
Traditional decor, cosy atmosphere ⌂Q✿◔

Ockley 7H4

10.30–2.30; 6–10.30 (11 F, S & summer)

Kings Arms
Stane Street (A29)
Fuller ESB; Hall & Woodhouse Badger Best Bitter; King & Barnes Sussex Bitter; Ruddle Rutland Bitter [H]
Family-run establishment with restaurant ⌂✿⊞◔◗

Old Woking 7H3

10.30–2.30; 5.30–11

White Hart
150 High Street (B382)
Courage Best Bitter, Directors [H]
Busy public bar. Live jazz on Friday evenings ✿◔◗▮

Outwood 10B5

11–2.30; 6–10.30 (11 F, S & summer)

Bell
Outwood Road OS328457
Draught Bass; Charrington IPA; Fremlins Bitter; King & Barnes Sussex Bitter, Draught Festive; Pilgrim Progress [H] **Occasional guest beers**
Busy old, cosmopolitan pub beside Britains oldest working windmill (1666) ⌂✿◔◗

Oxted 10B5

10–2.30; 6–11

George
52 High Street (off A25)
Charrington IPA; Draught Bass [H]
14th century, 3-bar pub; darts and pool ✿◔ (not Sun) ▮♿

Pirbright 7G3

10.30–2.30; 5.30–11

White Hart
(A324) ✆ Brookwood 2366
Friary Meux Best Bitter; Ind Coope Burton Ale [H]
Inn facing village green; comfortable saloon; spartan, inexpensive public bar
⌂Q✿◔◗▮♿

Redhill 10A5

10.30–2.30; 5.30–10.30 (11 F, S & summer)

Home Cottage
3 Redstone Hill (A25)
Young Bitter, Special, Winter Warmer [H]
Popular pub which appeals to most tastes ⌂Q✿◔◗≹

Plough
11, Church Road, St Johns
Friary Meux Bitter; Ind Coope Bitter, Burton Ale; King and Barnes Old Ale [H]
Comfortable and popular one-bar pub with several eating and drinking areas
✿◔ (not Sun) ◗ (not Sun–Mon) ♿≹ (Earlswood)

Reigate 10A5

10.30–2.30; 5.30–10.30 (11 F, S & Summer)

Bulls Head
55 High Street (A25 Westbound)
Friary Meux Bitter; Ind Coope Bitter, Burton Ale [H]
Smart split-level town centre pub ⌂✿◔≹

Nutley Hall
Nutley Lane (off A25)
King & Barnes Sussex Mild (summer), Sussex Bitter, Old Ale, Draught Festive [H]
Busy, basic backstreet local
Q◔≹

Yew Tree
Reigate Hill (A217 near M25)
Courage Best Bitter, Directors [H]
Comfortable lounge with separate eating area. Public bar with bar billiards, pinball and model cars
✿◔◗ (Mon–Fri) ◗ (Thu–Sat) ▮♿

Rowledge 7F4

11–2.30; 6–10.30 (11 F, S & summer)

Hare & Hounds
2 The Square
Courage Best Bitter [H]
Welcoming village pub with small restaurant ✿◔◗♿

Shackleford 7G4

10.30–2.30; 5.30–10.30 (11 F, S & summer)

Cyder House
Peperharrow Road (off A3)
Courage Best Bitter; King & Barnes Sussex Bitter; Ringwood Best Bitter, Old Thumper; Young Special; Bulmer Cider [H] **Occasional guest beers**
Smart rural pub ⌂⊞✿◔◗▮♿

Shepperton 7H3

10.30–2.30; 5.30–11

Kings Head
Church Square (off B375)
Courage Best Bitter, Directors [H]
Old pub by church with parts dating from 14th century. Always busy ✿◔◗

South Godstone 10B5

11–2.30; 6–11

Fox & Hounds
Tilburstow Hill Road (off A22)
Friary Meux Bitter [H]

Friendly 14th century pub, has a resident ghost ♿ Q ℗ ⏚ ❜

Staines 7H2

10.30–2.30; 5.30–11

Jolly Farmer
The Hythe ✆ 52807
Courage Best Bitter, Directors Ⓗ
Traditional, friendly local near Staines Bridge Q ⏚ ♿

Three Tuns
63 London Road
Courage Best Bitter, Directors Ⓗ
Thriving town pub with cosy lounge Q ⊞ ℗ (summer) ⏚ ❜ ≷

Stanwell 7H2

10.30–2.30–5.30–11

Rising Sun
110 Oaks Road (opposite Heathrow cargo area)
✆ Ashford 44080
Friary Meux Bitter; Ind Coope Burton Ale Ⓗ
Pleasant local for airport workers. Good food ℗ ⏚ ❜

Stoke d'Abernon 7H3

10.30–2.30; 5.30–10.30 (11 F, S & summer)

Plough
Station Road (off A245)
Ruddle County; Watney Combes Bitter; Webster Yorkshire Bitter Ⓗ
Small cosy pub; conservatory at rear, overlooking garden
♿ ℗ ⏚ ≷ (Cobham)

Sunbury 7H2

10.30–2.30; 5.30–

Three Fishes
Green Street
Watney Combes Bitter, Stag Bitter; Webster Yorkshire Bitter Ⓗ
Small, mainly unspoilt 17th century pub ♿ ℗ ⏚ ❗

Tatsfield 10B4

10.30–2.30; 6–11

Old Ship
Ship Hill, Westmore Green
Charrington IPA Ⓗ
Pleasant pub with a relaxed atmosphere ♿ ℗ ⏚

The Sands 7G4

11–2.30; 6–10.30 (11 F, S & summer)

Barley Mow
Littleworth Road (off A31)
Courage Best Bitter, Directors Ⓗ
Uncomplicated rural pub with skittles, shove ha'penny and award-winning garden Q ℗ ❗

Thorpe 7G3

11–2.30; 5.30–11

Rose & Crown

Green Road (B589)
Courage Best Bitter, Directors Ⓗ
Pleasant, welcoming pub on edge of green ♿ Q ℗ ⏚ ❜ ❗ ♿

Walliswood 7H4

10.30–2.30; 6–10.30 (11 F, S)

Scarlett Arms
OS119382
King & Barnes Sussex Bitter, Old Ale, Draught Festive Ⓖ
Beautiful country pub which features immaculate floral displays in summer ♿ Q ℗

Walton-on-Thames 7H3

10.30–2.30; 5.30–11

Swan
Manor Road (off A3050)
Young Bitter, Special, Winter Warmer Ⓗ
Impressive and old multi-room pub next to the river with mixed clientele
♿ ⊞ ℗ ⏚ ❜ ❗ ♿

Walton-on-the-Hill 7J3

10.30–2.30; 5.30–10.30 (11 F, S)

Fox & Hounds
Walton Street
Charrington IPA Ⓗ
Formerly two cottages, this traditional pub has a friendly, old fashioned atmosphere
Q ⏚ ♿

Westcott 7H4

10.30–2.30; 6–10.30 (11 F, S & summer)

Cricketers
Guildford Road (A25)
Adnams Bitter; Hall & Woodhouse Badger Best Bitter; King & Barnes Sussex Bitter; Marston Pedigree; Theakston XB Ⓗ
Friendly one-bar free house, popular with locals and travellers alike
℗ ⏚ ❜ (not Mon)

Weston Green 7H3

10.30–2.30; 5.30–11

Alma Arms
Alma Road (off A309)
Courage Best Bitter, Directors Ⓗ
Enjoy the atmosphere of a typical country pub in the heart of suburbia
Q ℗ ⏚ ❗ ♿ ≷ (Esher)

Weybourne 7G4

11–2.30; 6–10.30 (11 F, S & summer)

Elm Tree
14 Weybourne Road (B3007)
Courage Best Bitter Ⓗ
Unsettling mock-Tudor exterior conceals a "proper" public bar and landlord to match ℗ ❗ ♿

Weybridge 7H3

10.30–2.30; 5.30–11

Lincoln Arms
Thames Street ✆ 42109
Adnams Bitter; Boddingtons Bitter; Fuller ESB; Tetley Bitter Ⓗ
Pub with pleasant farmhouse-style decor, overlooking river. Shove-ha'penny. No meals Sun Q ℗ ⏚ ❜

Woking 7H3

10.30–2.30; 5.30–11

Cricketers
Maybury Road (off A247/A320) ✆ 61409
Courage Best Bitter, Directors Ⓗ
Smart single bar with weekend disco; good lunchtime food ℗ ⏚ ❜

Star
Wych Hill OS992576 Opens 11 and 6 Sat eves
Friary Meux Bitter; Ind Coope Bitter, Burton Ale Ⓗ
Large, single bar and good value restaurant. ℗ ⊞ ⏚ ❜

Woodmansterne 10A4

10.30–2.30; 5.30–10.30 (11 F, S)

Woodman
Woodmansterne Street
Draught Bass, Charrington IPA Ⓗ
Basic village pub in same family since 1904 ℗ ⏚ ❗ ♿

Worplesdon 7G3

10.30–2.30; 5.30–11

Fox
Fox Corner (B380 off A322)
Courage Best Bitter, Directors Ⓗ
Comfortable friendly atmosphere. Children's garden ℗ ❗

Wrecclesham 7F4

10.30–2.30; 5.30–11

Cricketers
1 The Street (A325)
Opens 11 am
Courage Best Bitter, Directors Ⓗ
3-bar village pub with thriving darts team and folk club Monday night ♿ ℗ ⏚ ❜ ❗

Sandrock
Sandrock Hill Road, Upper Bourne (off B3384) Opens 12 and 6; 11 am Sat
Batham Bitter; Holden Black Country Bitter, Special Bitter; King & Barnes Sussex Bitter; Ma Pardoe Bitter; Bulmer Cider Ⓗ Regular guest beers
Bar billiards and shove ha'penny
♿ Q ℗ ⏚ (not Sun) ❜ ❗ ♿

Alfriston 10C8

10–2.30; 6–10.30 (11 F, S & summer)

Star Inn
High Street (B2108)
✆ 870495
Draught Bass; Hall &
Woodhouse Badger Best
Bitter Ⓗ
Intimate hotel bar in
picturesque village
🏚Q⊞🅷Ⓖ➐

Ardingly 10B6

11–2.30; 6–11

Avins Bridge
College Road (off B2029, near
college) ✆ 892393
King & Barnes Sussex Mild,
Sussex Bitter, Old Ale,
Festive Ⓗ
Comfortable pub in rural
setting Q🐾Ⓖ➐ (not Sun,Mon)

Arlington 10C8

10–2.30; 6–10.30

Old Oak Inn
Cane Heath (off A22)
OS558079 ✆ Polegate 2072
Flowers Original; Fremlins
Bitter; Hall & Woodhouse
Badger Best Bitter Ⓖ
Country inn and restaurant.
Summer barbeques
🏚Q🐾Ⓖ➐🅯

Arundel 7H6

10.30–2.30; 6–10.30 (11 F, S & summer)

General Abercrombie
Queen Street (off A27)
✆ 882347
Courage Directors; Eldridge
Pope Dorset Original IPA;
Gales HSB; Palmer IPA;
Young Bitter Ⓗ
Busy 16th century pub near
river 🏚🐾Ⓖ➐≥

Swan
High Street ✆ 88314
Hall & Woodhouse Badger
Best Bitter, Tanglefoot; Harvey
BB, XXXX, King & Barnes
Sussex Bitter; Young Special Ⓗ
Occasional guest beers
Large, popular pub near
castle. Busy food trade 🅷Ⓖ➐

Ashurst 7J6

11–2.30; 6–11

Fountain
Near Steyning (B2135)
Flowers Original, Wethered
Bitter; Samuel Whitbread,
Whitbread Strong Country
Bitter, Pompey Royal Ⓗ & Ⓖ
Country pub with duck pond
🏚Q🐾Ⓖ (not Sun)

Balls Cross 7G5

10.30–2.30; 6–10.30 (11 F, S & summer)

Stag Inn
Off A283 ✆ Kirdford 241
King & Barnes Sussex Mild,
Bitter, Old Ale, Festive Ⓗ
Lively 16th century pub

🏚Q⊞🐾Ⓖ (not Sun)
➐(Fri, Sat or by arr) ♿

Barcombe Mills 10B7

10.30–2.30; 6–10.30 (11 summer)

Anglers Rest
1 Mile W of A26 OS428150
✆ Barcombe 400270
Adnams Bitter; Fuller London
Pride; Harvey BB; Hook
Norton Old Hookey; Mole's
97 Ⓗ Regular guest beers
Free house near privately-
owned Barcombe Mills
station. Toad-in-the-hole
game
🐾Ⓖ➐ (not Sun; Mon summer
only) 🅯

Battle 10D7

10.30–3; 6–11

Chequers
Lower Lake (A2100) ✆ 2088
Flowers Original; Fremlins
Bitter Ⓗ Regular guest beers
Low-ceilinged 16th century
coaching inn. Restaurant
🏚🅷 (if eating) 🐾🅷Ⓖ➐♿≥

Bells Yew Green 10D6

10.30–2.30; 6–10.30 (11 F, S)

Brecknock Arms
Bayham Road (B2169)
Harvey XX, BB, XXXX Ⓗ
Two-bar village local opposite
the green 🏚Ⓖ🍴≥ (Frant)

Berwick Village 10C8

11–2.30; 6–10.30 (11 F, S & summer)

Cricketers Arms
Off A27 OS519053
✆ Alfriston 870469
Harvey XX, BB, XXXX Ⓖ
Traditional country cottage
pub, old Sussex game of toad-
in-the-hole
🏚Q🐾Ⓖ➐ (until 8.30 pm)

Bexhill 10B8

10.30–3; 6–11

Sportsman
Sackville Road (off A259)
✆ 214214
Adnams Bitter; Courage
Directors; King & Barnes
Festive; Websters Yorkshire
Bitter Ⓗ
Cheerful town pub 🐾Ⓖ➐≥

Traffers
19 Egerton Road ✆ 210240
Opens 11
Harvey BB; Young Special Ⓗ
Friendly bar opposite park,
near to seafront, no meals Sun
🐾Ⓖ➐≥ (Collington Halt)

Billinghurst 7H5

10.30–2.30; 6–10.30 (11 F, S summer)

Limeburners
B2133 near A272 Jct ✆ 2311
Friary Meux Bitter; Ind Coope

Burton Ale Ⓗ; Coates Medium
Cyder, Farmhouse Dry
Cyder Ⓖ
Attractive 400-year old oak-
beamed pub, popular with
campers 🏚🐾Ⓖ🅯

Ye Olde Six Bells
76 High Street
King & Barnes Sussex Mild,
Sussex Bitter, Old Ale,
Festive Ⓗ
Busy lunchtime pub
🏚🐾Ⓖ (not Sun)

Binsted 7G6

10.30–2.30; 6–10.30 (11 F, S & summer)

Black Horse
Binsted Lane (off A27/B2132)
OS980064 ✆ Yapton 551213
Gale XXXL, XXXD, BBB,
XXXXX, HSB Ⓖ
Fine views and food. Pool and
darts 🏚Q🐾🅷Ⓖ➐

Blackboys 10C7

10–2.30; 6–10.30 (11 F, S & summer)

Blackboys Inn
Lewes Road (B2192)
✆ Framfield 283
Harvey XX; BB; XXX Ⓗ
Large 600-year old country
pub, cosy saloon bars
🏚🐾Ⓖ🍴🍴

Bognor Regis 7G7

10–2.30; 6–10.30 (11 F, S & summer)

Terminus
26 Station Road ✆ 865674
Ind Coope Bitter, Burton Ale Ⓗ
Town centre pub, oak
panelled saloon; families
welcome. Extra lounge
upstairs Q⊞Ⓖ🍴➐≥

Unicorn
76 High Street ✆ 865536
Gales XXXL, BBB, XXXXX,
HSB Ⓗ
A London pub on the south
coast. Folk night Tues, no food
winter Suns ⊞Ⓖ➐≥

Bosham 7F7

10.30–2.30; 6–10.30 (11 F, S summer)

Berkeley Arms
Delling Lane (off A27)
✆ 573167
Ind Coope Bitter; Burton Ale Ⓗ
Friendly local in picturesque
village. King Canute's
daughter buried nearby
🏚🐾Ⓖ➐≥

Brede 10E7

10.30–3; 7–11

Red Lion
A28
Fremlins Bitter; Harvey BB;
Young Special Ⓗ
Village pub by church 🏚♿

Brighton 10B8

10–2.30; 5.30–11

Albion
28 Albion Hill ✆ 604439

Flowers Original; Wethered
Winter Royal; Whitbread
Strong Country Bitter;
Pompey Royal, Samuel
Whitbread; Bulmer Cider Ⓗ
Friendly popular local on steep
hill ✿ⓖ➔🍴

Coachmakers Arms
76 Trafalgar Street (off A23)
Opens 10.30
Raven Bitter, Best Bitter, Old
Master Ⓗ Occasional guest
beers
Street corner local ⓖ➔≹

Evening Star
55 Surrey Street ✆ 28931
Courage Best Bitter,
Directors Ⓗ
Compact one-bar local Q✿≹

Lamb & Flag
9 Cranbourne Street ✆ 26415
Opens 10.30
Charrington IPA Ⓗ
Popular town pub next to
main shopping centre ⓖ≹

Lord Nelson
36 Trafalgar Street (off A23)
Opens 10.30
Harvey XX (summer); PA, BB,
XXXX (winter); Merrydown
cider Ⓗ
Trafalgar ale (OG 1110+)
brewed anually for the pub on
Oct 21 ✿ⓖ🍴≹

Nobles Bar
20 New Road ✆ 682401
Ashford Old Gold; Everards
Tiger; Kentish Ales Royal
Sovereign; Taylor Landlord Ⓗ
Regular guest beers
Small cosy bar, popular with
theatre goers ⓖ

Queens Head
69–70 Queens Road ✆ 25284
Beckets Best Bitter, Special
Bitter; Gale HSB; Harvey BB;
Young Special Ⓗ Occasional
guest beers
One-bar house with ornate
mirror behind bar ⓖ➔≹

Robin Hood
3A Norfolk Place
Eldridge Pope Royal Oak; Gale
HSB; Hall & Woodhouse
Badger Best Bitter, Tanglefoot;
King & Barnes Sussex Bitter;
Young Special Ⓗ Regular
guest beers
Small, friendly, back street
pub, off Western Road ✿ⓖ

Sir Charles Napier
50 Southover Street
Evenings opens 6
Gales XXXL, BBB, XXXXX,
HSB; Bulmer Cider Ⓗ
Busy corner local
🍴 (until 8 pm)✿🍴

Bucks Green 7H5
11–2.30; 6–10.30 (11 F, S & summer)
Queens Head
A281 ✆ Rudgwick 2202
Hall & Woodhouse Badger

Best Bitter; King & Barnes
Sussex Bitter; Young Special Ⓗ
Occasional guest beers
Immaculate, oak-beamed pub,
motor cycles not welcome.
Restaurant
🏚Q🍴 (if dining) ✿ⓖ➔

Burwash 10D6
10–2.30; 6–10.30 (11 F, S & summer)
Bell
High Street (A265) ✆ 882304
Harvey XX, PA, BB, XXXX Ⓗ
Fine old village pub in Kipling
country ✿ⓖ➔🍴

Catsfield 10D7
10–3; 6–11
White Hart
The Green ✆ Ninfield 892427
Draught Bass; Charrington
IPA Ⓗ
Lively village pub 🏚🍴✿ⓖ➔

Chailey 10B7
11–2.30; 6–10.30 (11 F, S & summer)
Horns Lodge
South Chailey (A275)
Hall & Woodhouse Badger
Best Bitter; Harvey BB; King &
Barnes Festive Ⓗ
Friendly, popular free house
🏚🍴✿ⓖ➔

Chichester 7G7
10.30–2.30; 6–10.30 (11 F, S & summer)
Chequers
203 Oving Road ✆ 786427
Flowers Original; Whitbread
Strong Country Bitter; Samuel
Whitbread Ⓗ
Friendly local of character.
Games room, comfortable
lounge, busy public bar
🍴✿ⓖ🍴

Eastgate
4 The Hornet ✆ 774877
Gales BBB, XXXXX, HSB Ⓗ
Popular, comfortable town
local 🏚Q ⓖ🍴

George & Dragon
51 North Street ✆ 785660
Friary Meux Bitter; Ind Coope
Burton Ale Ⓗ
Popular local near Theatre.
Good value lunches
🏚🍴✿ (not Sun) 🍴

New Inn
34 Whyke Road ✆ 782238
Gales XXXD, BBB, HSB Ⓗ
Comfortable one-bar pub;
children's playground; folk
club Fri eve
✿ⓖ (not Sun) 🅰 (1 mile)

Chidham 7F7
10.30–2.30; 6–10.30 (11 F, S & summer)
Old House at Home
Cot Lane (off A27)
Draught Bass; Charrington
IPA; Hall & Woodhouse
Badger Best Bitter; Palmer
IPA Ⓗ Regular guest beers
Popular freehouse, near

harbour and sailing school.
Parking difficult 🏚✿ⓖ➔🍴& 🅰

Cocking 7G6
10.30–2.30; 6–10.30 (11 F, S & summer)
Potter & Vine
A286 ✆ Midhurst 3449
Flowers Original; Whitbread
Strong Country Bitter; Samuel
Whitbread Ⓗ
3 bar areas: quiet/drinking/
noisy 🏚🍴✿ⓖ➔ (not Sun) 🍴

Crawley 10A6
10.30–2.30; 6–10.30 (11 F, S & summer)
Swan
1 Horsham Road, West Green
Flowers Original; Whitbread
Strong Country Bitter;
Pompey Royal Ⓗ
Victorian pub with engraved
windows ✿ⓖ

White Hart
High Street ✆ 20033
Harvey XX, PA, BB,
XXXX Ⓗ
Comfortable pub in town
centre ⓖ🍴& ⊖

Crowborough 10C6
11–2.30; 6–10.30 (11 F, S)
Boars Head
Eridge Road (A26) ✆ 2412
Flowers Original; Fremlins
Bitter; Wethered Bitter Ⓗ & Ⓖ
Welcoming, picturesque old
country pub 🏚Q✿ⓖ➔

Cuckfield 10B6
10.30–2.30; 6–11
Wheatsheaf
Broad Street (A272)
Hall & Woodhouse Badger
Best Bitter; Harvey BB; Young
Special Ⓗ Occasional guest
beers
Comfortable free house with
heavy emphasis on food ✿ⓖ🍴

Danehill 10B6
11–2.30; 7–11
Coach & Horses
School Lane OS405285
King & Barnes Sussex Bitter Ⓗ
Regular guest beers
Traditional, friendly village
pub 🏚✿ⓖ➔🍴

Ditchling 10B7
10.30–2.30; 6–11
Bull
High Street (B2112)
Flowers Original; Whitbread
Strong Country Bitter,
Pompey Royal, Samuel
Whitbread Ⓗ
16th century village pub. Low
oak beams 🏚Q✿ⓖ➔

Sandrock Inn
High Street (B2112)
King & Barnes Festive; Usher
Best Bitter; Webster Yorkshire
Bitter Ⓗ
Friendly village local 🏚✿ⓖ🍴

Dragons Green 7H5

10.30–2.30; 6.30–10.30 (11 F, S & summer)

George & Dragon
Near A272 ☎ Coolham 230
**King & Barnes Sussex Bitter,
Old Ale, Festive** Ⓗ
Friendly old world country
local ▲ Q ⌖ ⌂ ➴ (Fri–Sun) ⛁

Easebourne 7G5

10.30–2.30; 6–10.30 (11 F, S)

Rother
Lutener Road (off A272/
A286) ☎ Midhurst 4024
**King & Barnes Sussex Mild,
(summer), Sussex Bitter, Old
Ale, Festive** Ⓗ **Bulmer Cider** Ⓖ
Victorian pub ▲ ⌖ Ⓗ ⌂ ➴ ♟

Eastbourne 10D8

10–2.30; 6–10.30 (11 F, S & summer)

Hurst Arms
Willingdon Road (A22)
Harvey BB, XXXX Ⓗ
Lively local with traditional
public bar ⌖ ♟

Marine
61 Seaside ☎ 20464
Opens 11
**King & Barnes Festive; Usher
Best Bitter; Webster Yorkshire
Bitter** Ⓗ
Great atmosphere; home
cooked meals (book in winter)
⛁ ⌖ ➴

**New Inn (Chef &
Brewer)**
Grange Road/South Street
Opens 10.30
**Truman Sampson; Usher Best
Bitter; Webster Yorkshire
Bitter** Ⓗ
Stylish comfortable bar and
good restaurant Q ⌖ ⌂ ➴ ≋

Prince Albert
9 High Street, Old Town
Opens 10.30
**Courage Best Bitter,
Directors** Ⓗ
Popular, friendly local. Classic
example of "Brewers Tudor."
Darts and pool
⌖ ⌂ (not Sun) ♟ ⛁

Terminus
153 Terminus Road ☎ 33964
**Harvey XX (summer), BB,
XXXX (winter)** Ⓗ
Busy lunch-time pub; pool
and darts ⛁ ⌂ ➴ ≋

East
Chiltington 10B7

10.30–2.30; 6.30–11

Jolly Sportsman
Chapel Lane (B21160)
OS37415
**Harveys XX, BB; King &
Barnes Sussex Bitter** Ⓗ
Occasional guest beers
Village hall, shop, and camp
site office as well as a pub.
Well off the beaten track ⌖ ▲

East Grinstead 10B6

11–2.30; 6–11

Rose & Crown
High Street (A22) ☎ 22176
**Friary Meux Best Bitter; Ind
Coope Burton Ale** Ⓗ
Pub in attractive conservation
area ▲ ⌂ ➴ ♟ ≋

Elsted 7F6

11–2.30; 6–10.30 (11 F, S)

Ballards Inn
OS815206 ☎ Midhurst 3662
Ballards Best Bitter, Wassail Ⓗ
Regular guest beers
Victorian inn. Ballards brewed
on the premises ▲ Ⓗ ⌖ ⌂ ➴ ♟

Emsworth 7F6

10.30–2.30; 6–10.30 (11 F, S & summer)

Sussex Brewery
36 Main Road, Hermitage
(A27) ☎ 371533
**Hall & Woodhouse Badger
Best Bitter; Hermitage Best,
Wyndam's Bitter, Best Bitter,
Lumley Old Ale; Marston
Pedigree** Ⓗ **Regular guest
beers**
2-bar pub brewery, piano
sing-songs Sunday evenings
▲ Q Ⓗ ⌖ ⌂ ➴ ♟

Eridge 10C6

10.30–2.30; 6–10.30 (11 F, S)

Huntsman
A26 next to station
**King & Barnes Sussex Bitter,
Old Ale, Draught Festive** Ⓗ
Small, friendly 3-bar pub
⌖ ⌂ ➴ ♟ ≋

Etchingham 10D6

10.30–3; 6–11

De Etchingham Arms
A265 ☎ 292
**Cotleigh Tawny Bitter; Harvey
BB; Ind Coope Burton Ale;
Wiltshire Old Devil; Bulmer
Cider** Ⓗ **Occasional guest
beers**
Friendly pub near Shire Horse
Centre Ⓗ (restaurant)
⌖ Ⓗ ⌂ ➴ ♟ ≋ ▲ ⛁

Falmer 10B7

11–2.30; 6–11 (winter may close early)

Swan Inn
Middle Street (A27/B2123)
**Fuller London Pride; Harvey
BB; King & Barnes Old Ale;
Young Bitter, Special** Ⓗ
Regular guest beers
Popular pub near University
▲ ⌖ ⌂ ➴ ≋

Firle 10C8

10–2.30; 6–10.30 (11 F, S & summer)

Ram
(Near A27) ☎ Glynde 222
Charrington IPA Ⓗ **Regular
guest beers**
Pretty village free house with
toad-in-the-hole game in tiny
lounge ⌖ ♟

Fletching 10B7

11–2.30; 6–10.30 (11 F, S & summer)

Griffin Inn
High Street (off A272)
**Hall & Woodhouse Badger
Best Bitter, Tanglefoot; Harvey
BB; King & Barnes Festive** Ⓗ
Smart oak-panelled saloon
bar, popular restaurant
▲ Ⓗ ⌖ ⌂ ➴ ♟ ▲

Graffham 7G6

11–2.30; 6–10.30 (11 F, S)

White Horse
OS931183 ☎ 331
**Ballards Best Bitter;
Whitbread Pompey Royal** Ⓗ
Hunting, shooting and fishing
a priority. Handy stop for
South Downs Way ▲ Q ⌖ ⌂ ➴

Hastings & St. 10E7
Leonards

11–3; 5.30–11

First In Last Out
14–15 High Street, Old Town
(off A259) ☎ 425079
Closed Mon lunch; evenings
opens 7 pm Fri, Sat, Mon; 6
pm Tue, Wed, Thu
**Kentish Ales Royal Sovereign;
St Clements Old Crofters,
Senlac Strong; Websters
Yorkshire Bitter** Ⓗ **Occasional
guest beers**
Small homebrew pub.
▲ ⌖ ⌂ ➴ ⛁ ▲ (½ mile)

Lord Nelson
The Bourne, Old Town (A259)
**Courage Best Bitter,
Directors** Ⓗ
Lively local, lots of character,
certainly different! ⌖ ♟

**Palace Bars (Pig in
Paradise)**
Seafront (A259)
☎ 439444
**Draught Bass; Charrington
IPA; Greene King Abbot Ale;
Kentish Ales, Canterbury
Ale** Ⓗ **Regular guest beers**
Friendly 2-bar pub, September
cultural festival! ▲ ⌂ ➴ ⛁ ≋

Prince Albert
28 Cornwallis Street (off
A259)
**Shepherd Neame Mild,
Bitter** Ⓗ **Stock Ale (winter)** Ⓖ
Corner pub near town centre
♟ ≋

Railway Hotel
Kings Road (opp. Warrior
Square Station), St Leonards
Fremlins Bitter Ⓗ
Small, cosy corner pub
▲ Q ≋

Town Crier
Queens Road (A259)
**Flowers Original; Fremlins
Bitter** Ⓗ
Modern pub near seafront
⌂ ▲ ≋

Haywards Heath   10B7

10.30–2.30; 6–11

Liverpool Arms Hotel
Clair Road ℰ 413710
Friary Meux Bitter; Ind Coope Bitter, Burton Ale Ⓗ
Small friendly local with rare brewery facade ⌂ⓖ🏵🍴≠

Horsham   7J5

11–2.30; 6–10.30 (11 F, S & summer)

Coot
Merryfield Drive (off A281)
Charrington IPA Ⓗ
Modern pub on outskirts of town; traditional games
Q🌣ⓖ🍴

Nelson
25 Trafalgar Road ℰ 4029
King & Barnes Sussex Bitter, Old Ale, Festive Ⓗ
Friendly street corner local
ⓖ≠

Stout House
Carfax ℰ 67777
King & Barnes Sussex Bitter, Old Ale, Festive Ⓗ
Old fashioned, friendly town centre pub ⌂ⓖ🍴≠

Hove   10A8

10–2.30; 6–11

Star of Brunswick
32 Brunswick Street East
Flowers Original; Whitbread Strong Country Bitter; Pompey Royal Ⓗ
Pleasant pub set in old mews.
Good bar snacks Qⓖ🍴

Hurstpierpoint   10A7

10.30–2.30; 6–11

Poacher
139 High Street ℰ 834893
Gales HSB; Usher Best Bitter; Webster Yorkshire Bitter Ⓗ
1-bar pub; saddlery a feature of the decor ⌂🌣ⓖ (not Sun) 🍴

Icklesham   11E7

11–3; 6–11

Queen's Head
(Off A259) ℰ 552
Cotleigh Tawny Bitter; Courage Directors; Greene King Abbot Ale; Hook Norton Best Bitter Ⓗ **Regular guest beers**
Comfortable old pub with old farm implements ⌂🌣ⓖ🍴

Ifield   10A6

10.30–2.30; 6–10.30 (11 F, S)

The Gate
Rusper Road ℰ Rusper 271
King & Barnes Sussex Bitter, Old Ale, Festive Ⓗ
Country pub, catering for all tastes 🌣ⓖ🍴🏵

Jevington   10C8

10.30–2.30; 6–10.30 (11 F, S & summer)

Eight Bells
High Street (B2109)
Courage Best Bitter, Directors Ⓗ
Friendly welcoming 600-year old pub, local produce on sale
🌣ⓖ🍴♿

Johns Cross   10D7

10.30–3; 6–11

Johns Cross Inn
(A21)
Flowers Original; Fremlins Bitter Ⓗ
Pleasant, weatherboarded inn
⌂🌣ⓖ🍴🏵⛺

Kingsfold   7H5

10.30–2.30; 6–10.30 (11 F, S & summer)

Dog & Duck
Durfold Hill
King & Barnes Sussex Bitter, Old Ale, Festive (summer) Ⓗ
15th century pub with split level bar ⌂🌣ⓖ🍴

Lewes   10B7

10–2.30; 6–11

Brewers Arms
91 High Street ℰ 477902
Adnams Bitter; Harvey BB; XXXX; Fuller London Pride, ESB; Young Bitter Ⓗ **Regular guest beers**
Excellent pub with old brewery signs, folk club Mons
🌣ⓖ🍴≠

Lansdown Arms
36 Lansdown Place ℰ 472807
Flowers Original, Wethered Bitter; Samuel Whitbread Ⓗ
Splendid, friendly 1-bar local
ⓖ≠

Lewes Arms
Mount Place ℰ 473152
Harvey BB, XXXX; King & Barnes Sussex Bitter, Festive Ⓗ
Fine small pub; attractive facade Qⓖ🍴≠

Lindfield   10B6

10.30–2.30; 6–11

Linden Tree
High Street (B2028) ℰ 2295
Harvey BB, XXXX, Marston Pedigree, Ringwood Fortyniner, Wadworth 6X, Young Special Ⓗ **Occasional guest beers**
Smart free house in picturesque village ⌂Q🌣ⓖ🍴

Snowdrop Inn
Snowdrop Lane OS354239
King & Barnes Sussex Bitter, Old Ale, Festive Ⓗ; **Bulmer Cider** Ⓖ
Converted farm cottages, well off beaten track. Friendly welcome Q🌣ⓖ🍴🏵

Littlehampton   7H7

10.30–2.30; 6–10.30 (11 F, S & summer, 12 Tue)

Arun View Inn
Wharf Road ℰ 722335

Flowers Original, Wethered Bitter; Samuel Whitbread Ⓗ
Riverside pub with mural in "Fishermen's" bar 🚗🔄ⓖ🍴🏵≠

Lower Beeding   7J5

11–2.30; 6–10.30 (11 F, S & summer)

The Crabtree
Brighton Road (A281) ℰ 257
King & Barnes Sussex Mild, Sussex Bitter, Old Ale, Festive Ⓗ
Busy pub in pleasant surroundings
⌂Q🌣ⓖ (not Sun)
🍴(not Mon/Tue) 🏵

Loxwood   7H5

10.30–2.30; 6–10.30 (11 F, S & summer)

Sir Rodger Tichbourne
Alfold Bars (B2133) ℰ 752377
King & Barnes Sussex Mild, Sussex Bitter Ⓗ, **Old Ale** Ⓖ, **Draught Festive** Ⓗ
Oak-beamed pub in rural setting ⌂🌣ⓖ (not Sun)
🍴(winter: Fri/Sat only) 🏵⛺

Mannings Heath   7J5

11–2.30; 6–10.30 (11 F, S & summer)

Dun Horse
Brighton Road (A281)
ℰ Horsham 65783
Flowers Original; Whitbread Strong Country Bitter, Pompey Royal Ⓗ
Pleasant busy pub with traditional games Q🌣ⓖ🍴🏵

Maplehurst   7J5

11–2.30; 6–10.30 (11 F, S & summer)

White Horse
Park Lane (off A272)
OS190245
Opens 12.30 pm winter lunchtimes
Ballards Best Bitter; Everards Tiger; King & Barnes Sussex Bitter, Old Ale; Merrydown Cider Ⓗ **Regular guest beers**
Old pub with panoramic view
⌂🌣ⓖ🍴 (until 9 pm)

Mark Cross   10C6

10.30–2.30; 6–10.30 (11 F, S)

Mark Cross Inn
(B2100) OS583313
Flowers Original; Fremlins Bitter; Whitbread Castle Eden Ale Ⓗ
Comfortable pub with restaurant ⌂🌣ⓖ🍴

Midhurst   7E5

10.30–2.30; 6–10.30 (11 F, S)

Crown
Edinburgh Square ℰ 3462
Gale HSB; Usher Best Bitter; Webster Yorkshire Bitter Ⓗ
Lively town pub. Spit-roast indoors ⌂🔄🌣ⓖ🍴

Wheatsheaf
Rumbolds Hill ☎ 3450
King & Barnes Sussex Mild,
Sussex Bitter, Old Ale,
Festive Ⓗ; Bulmers Cider Ⓖ
Cosy pub; good food ▩ᕼ🍴🍺

Newick 10B7

10–2.30; 6–10.30 (11 F, S & summer)

Royal Oak
Church Road (off A272)
Flowers Original; Whitbread
Strong Country Bitter,
Pompey Royal Ⓗ
Oak-beamed public bar with
wattle and daub panel ▩🅿ᕼ

Oving 7G7

11–2.30; 6–10.30 (11 F, S & summer)

Gribble Inn
Off A259 OS900050
Hall & Woodhouse Badger
Best Bitter; Harvey BB;
Ringwood Gribble Ale, Reg's
Tipple, Old Thumper; Bulmer
Cider Ⓗ Regular guest beers
Picturesque, thatched, 16th
century pub. Good food. Large
garden. Bar billiards
▩Q🅱🅿ᕼ🍺(not Sun/Mon) ᕼ

Pease Pottage 10A6

10.30–2.30; 6–11

Grapes
Off A23/M23
King & Barnes Sussex Bitter,
Old Ale, Festive Ⓗ
Friendly and popular village
pub near Crawley 🅿ᕼ🍴🍺ᕼ

Pett 11E7

11–3; 6–11

Royal Oak
Off A259 ☎ 2515
Fremlins Bitter; Harvey BB Ⓗ
Old pub with splendid fire-
place and good games ▩🅿🍺

Petworth 7G5

10.30–2.30; 6–10.30 (11 F, S & summer)

Red Lion
New Street ☎ 42181
Flowers Original, Wethered
Bitter; Whitbread Strong
Country Bitter Ⓗ
Sparse interior; wine bar and
restaurant upstairs
▩Q🅱🅿ᕼ🍺(not Sun/Mon) ᕼ

Pevensey Bay 10D8

11–2.30; 6–10.30 (11 F, S & summer)

Moorings
Seaville Drive
Courage Best Bitter, Directors;
Gale HSB; Marston Pedigree;
Merrydown Traditional
Draught Cider Ⓗ
Pub on the beach. Large
family room and very good
sea food
▩🅱🅿ᕼ🍺ᕼ▲ (1 mile)

Plumpton Green 10B7

10.30–2.30; 6–10.30 (11 summer)

Fountain Inn
Station Road ☎ 890294
Young Bitter, Special Ⓗ,
Winter Warmer Ⓖ
Cosmopolitan pub of real
character ▩ᕼ🚆

Portslade 10A8

10–2.30; 6–11

Blue Anchor
81–83 Station Road (A2038/
A259)
Flowers Original, Wethered
Winter Royal (Xmas);
Whitbread Strong Country
Bitter, Pompey Royal, Samuel
Whitbread Ⓗ
Saloon bar features unique
aerial photo of Brighton 🍺🚆

Pulborough 7H6

11–2.30; 6–10.30 (11 F, S & summer)

Oddfellows
99 Lower Street (A283)
Flowers Original; Whitbread
Strong Country Bitter Ⓗ
Popular 500 year old pub
with good food
▩Q🅿ᕼ🍺(not Sun)

Rogate 7F5

10.30–2.30; 6–10.30 (11 F, S)

Wyndham Arms
(A272) ☎ 315
Friary Meux Bitter; Ind Coope
Burton Ale Ⓗ
Excellent village pub ▩🅿ᕼ🍺🍴

Rotherfield 10C6

11–2.30; 6–10.30 (11 F, S)

Harvest Moon
Town Row (B2100) ☎ 2516
Charrington IPA; Harvey BB,
XXXX Ⓗ
Pleasant country pub next to
disused railway line ▩🅿ᕼ🍺🍴

Rushlake Green 10D7

12–2.30; 7–11

Horse & Groom
Harvey BB, XXXX; King &
Barnes Sussex Bitter Ⓗ
16th century country pub on
village green
🅱🅿ᕼ🍺(not Sun/Mon)

Rusper 7J4

11.30–2.30; 6–10.30 (11 F, S & summer)

Star
High Street ☎ 264
Wethered Bitter; Whitbread
Pompey Royal, Samuel
Whitbread Ⓗ
16th century coaching house
with traditional games
▩Q🅱🅿ᕼ

Rustington 7H7

11–2.30; 6–10.30 (11 F, S & summer)

Fletcher Arms
Station Road (off A280)
Friary Meux Bitter; Ind Coope
Burton Ale Ⓗ
Comfortable lounge, busy
public; pool and darts
▩🅿ᕼ🍺🍴ᕼ (Angmering)

Rye 11F7

11–3; 6–11

Standard Inn
The Mint (off A259) ☎ 3393
Fremlins Bitter; Young Special
Bitter Ⓗ Regular guest beers
Popular old pub in historic
town 🅱ᕼ🍺

Ypres Castle
Gun Garden (off A259)
Fremlins Bitter Ⓗ
Fine pub, behind castle 🅱🅿ᕼ

Seaford 10C8

10.30–2.30; 6–11

White Lion
74 Claremont Road (A259)
Charrington IPA; Harvey BB;
Young Special Ⓗ Regular
guest beers
Comfortable friendly bar;
games room 🅱🅿🅱ᕼ🍺🚆

Selsey 7G7

10.30–2.30; 6–10.30 (11 F, S & summer)

Lifeboat Inn
26 Albion Road ☎ 603501
Gales HSB; Usher Best Bitter;
Webster Yorkshire Bitter Ⓗ
Nautical public bar, good bar
food and restaurant, no food
Mon Q🅿ᕼ🍺ᕼ

Sharpthorne 10B6

11–2.30; 6–11

Bluebell Inn
Station Road ☎ 810264
Courage Best Bitter, Directors;
Everards Old Original; Fuller
ESB; Harvey BB; Young
Special Ⓗ Regular guest beers
Traditional pub with railway
connections
▩🅿🅱ᕼ🍺(not Mon)

Shoreham-by-Sea 10A8

10–2.30; 6–11

Red Lion
Upper Shoreham Road
Opens 11.30 am
Gale HSB; Usher Best Bitter;
Webster Yorkshire Bitter;
Bulmers Cider; Merrydown
Cider Ⓗ
Popular pub with no smoking
area ▩Q🅿ᕼ🍺🍴

Royal Sovereign
Middle Street ☎ 453518
Whitbread Strong Country
Bitter, Pompey Royal Ⓗ
Popular friendly local ᕼ🚆

Smock Alley 7H5

10.30–2.30; 6–10.30 (11 F, S & summer)

Five Bells
OS192070

King & Barnes Sussex Mild G,
**Sussex Bitter, Old Ale,
Draught Festive** H
Unspoilt, hard to find local
with a friendly welcome
⌂ ℘ ⟲ ❥

Southwick 10A8
10–2.30; 6–11

Romans Hotel
Manor Hall Road
Charrington IPA H
Friendly, welcoming local
℘ ⟲ ❢

Staplecross 10E7
10.30–3; 6–11

Cross Inn
B2165 ☎ 217
**Fremlins Bitter; Harvey BB;
Young Special** H
Old village pub with a warm
welcome ⌂ ▦ ⅋ Å

Stoughton 7F6
10.30–2.30; 6–10.30 (11 F, S & summer)

Hare & Hounds
(Off B2146) OS803115
Gales BBB, XXXXX, HSB H
Popular downland pub with
restaurant ⌂ ▦ ℘ ⟲ ❥ ❢

Sutton 7G6
11–2.30; 6–10.30 (11 F, S & summer)

White Horse
Off A285 OS978152 ☎ 221
**Arkell Kingsdown Ale;
Ballards Best Bitter; Harvey
BB, Elizabethan; King &
Barnes Sussex Mild, Bitter** H
Regular guest beers
Surprisingly large for a small
village, warm and
comfortable; restaurant
⌂ Q ▦ ℘ ⟲ ❥ ❢ Å

Telham 10E7
10.30–3; 6–11

Black Horse
Hastings Road (A2100)
☎ Battle 3109
**Flowers Original; Fremlins
Bitter; Wethered Bitter** G & H
Friendly pub with upstairs
games room ⌂ ℘ ⟲ ❢ Å Å

The Haven 7H5
10.30–2.30; 6–10.30 (11 F, S & summer)

Blue Ship
OS084305 ☎ Rudgwick 2709
**King & Barnes Sussex Bitter,
Old Ale, Festive** G
Timeless 16th century pub;
serving hatch in stable doors
⌂ Q ▦ ℘ ⟲ ❢ Å

Ticehurst 10D6
10–2.30; 6–10.30 (11 F, S & summer)

Duke of York
The Square (B2099)
Shepherd Neame Bitter H;
Biddenden Cider G Occasional
guest beers
Lively village local ℘ ⟲ ❥ ❢

Tillington 7G5
10.30–2.30; 6–10.30 (11 F, S)

Horseguards
Off A272 ☎ Petworth 42332
**Kings & Barnes Sussex Mild,
Sussex Bitter, Old Ale,
Festive** H
Village pub, near Petworth
Park; views of Rother Valley
⌂ Q ℘ ⟲ ❥ (not Tue) ❢

Turners Hill 10B6
11–2.30; 6–11

Red Lion
Lion Lane (off B2028)
**Harvey BB, XXXX; Bulmer
Cider** H
Very popular traditional
village local
⌂ ℘ ⟲ (not Tue/Sat/Sun)

Uckfield 10C7
10–2.30; 6–10.30 (11 F, S & summer)

Alma Arms
Framfield Road (B2102)
**Harvey XX, PA, BB,
XXXX** H
Excellent, well run traditional
local
Q ℘ ⟲ (not weekends) ❢ Å ⇌

Upper Beeding 10A7
11–2.30; 6–11

Bridge
High Street ☎ 812773
**King & Barnes Sussex Bitter,
Old Ale (winter), Draught
Festive** H
Basic village local, next to the
River Adur Q ℘ ⟲

Wadhurst 10D6
10–2.30; 6–10.30 (11 F, S)

Rock Robin Hotel
Station Road (B2099) ☎ 2313
**Flowers Original; Fremlins
Bitter; Harvey BB** H
Plush hotel bar reknowned for
its food ▦ ⟲ ❥ ⇌

West Ashling 7F6
10.30–2.30; 6–10.30 (11 F, S & summer)

Richmond Arms
Mill Road (¼ mile W of B2146)
OS805073 ☎ Bosham 575730
**Ballards Best Bitter, Wassail;
Boddingtons Bitter; King &
Barnes Draught Festive;
Marston Border Bitter;
Thwaites Bitter** H Regular
guest beers
Immensely popular;
imaginative lunches
⌂ Q ▦ ℘ ⟲ (not Sun) Å Å

Westbourne 7F6
10.30–2.30; 6–10.30 (11 F, S & summer)

Good Intent
North Street
**Friary Meux Bitter; Ind Coope
Burton Ale** H
Friendly local, oak-panelled
public. No meals Sundays
⌂ ℘ ⟲ ❢ Å

Westergate 7G6
10.30–2.30; 6–10.30 (11 F, S & summer)

Labour in Vain
Westergate Street (A29)
Ballards Best Bitter H,
Wassail G; **Harveys BB;
Young Bitter, Special** H
Village local, good value food;
bar billiards ⌂ Q ℘ ⟲ ❢ ❢ Å

West Wittering 7F7
10.30–2.30; 6–10.30 (11 F, S & summer)

Lamb
B2179 ☎ Birdham 511105
**Ballards Best Bitter; Friary
Meux Bitter; Ind
Coope Burton Ale** H Regular
guest beers
200-year old pub ⌂ Q ⟲ ❥

Wineham 10A7
10.30–2.30; 6–10.30 (11 F, S & summer)

Royal Oak
(Near B2166) OS236306
Whitbread Pompey Royal G
Traditional beamed country
pub; inglenook ⌂ Q ℘ Å

Withyham 10C6
10.30–2.30; 6–10.30 (11 F, S)

Dorset Arms
(B2110) OS496357
Harvey XX, BB, XXXX H
Fine old alehouse; restaurant
⌂ Q ℘ ⟲ ❥ ❢

Worthing 7J7
10–2.30; 6–10.30 (11 F, S & summer)

Chapmans Hotel
27 Railway Approach
☎ 30690
**Gale HSB; Hall & Woodhouse
Tanglefoot; Harvey BB; King
& Barnes Draught Festive;
Young Special** H Regular
guest beers
Popular free house, always
busy ℘ ▦ ⟲ ❥ ⇌

Cobden Arms
2 Cobden Road ☎ 36856
**Whitbread Strong Country
Bitter, Pompey Royal** H
Traditional local; original
Brickwoods sign Q ℘ ❢ ⇌

Seldon Arms
41 Lyndhurst Road
☎ 34854
Opens 11
**Harvey BB; Eldridge Pope
Royal Oak; King & Barnes
Sussex Bitter, Old Ale, Ruddle
County** H Regular guest beers
Busy free house close to town
hospital Q ⟲ ❥ ⇌

Vine Brewery
High Street, Tarring
**Hall & Woodhouse Badger
Best Bitter; Harvey BB; King &
Barnes Sussex Bitter** H
Regular guest beers
Splendid free house with
plans to start home brewing
Q ℘ ⟲

Barlow 33G8

11–3; 6–10.30

Black Horse
Barlow Lane
✆ Rowlands Gill 542808
Theakston Best Bitter, XB, Old Peculier Ⓗ
Cosy stonebuilt village pub
🏠🚭♿🍴🍺

Birtley 33H9

11–3; 6–10.30

Coach & Horses
Durham Road (A6127)
✆ Tyneside 4102756
Bass Extra Light, Draught Bass; Stones Best Bitter Ⓗ
Large pub and restaurant at northern end of town 🅿♿🍴🍺

Blackhall Mill 33G9

11–3; 6–10.30

Mill
River View (A694) OS120569
✆ Ebchester 562207
Darley Thorne Best Bitter; Drybrough's Eighty; McEwan 70/- Ⓗ
Large 3-roomed terraced free house by River Derwent ♿🍴🍺

Blaydon 33G8

11–3; 6–10.30

Black Bull
Bridge Street
✆ Tyneside 4142846
Cameron Lion Bitter, Strongarm; Everards Old Original Ⓗ
Photographs of Old Blaydon in lounge, regular music nights. A warm welcome assured
🏠🅿🍴🍺≈

Byker 33H8

11–3; 6–10.30

Free Trade Inn
Saint Lawrence Road (off A193) ✆ Tyneside 2655764
McEwan 80/-; Newcastle Exhibition; Younger No. 3 Ⓗ
Small one-room Victorian pub with unusual paintings and a large wall mirror 🏠🍴⊖

Glendale
Potts Street (off A193)
✆ Tyneside 2655174
Draught Bass; Stones Best Bitter Ⓗ
Recently altered, two-room friendly local 🍴 ⊖

Ship Inn
Stepney Bank (off A193)
✆ Tyneside 2324030
Whitbread Castle Eden Ⓗ
Basic two-room pub nestling in shadow of Byker Road Bridge and next to City Farm. Regular folk music evenings
♿🍴≈ Manors ⊖

Felling 33H8

11–3; 6–10.30

Wheatsheaf
Carlisle Street

✆ Tyneside 4386633
Big Lamp Bitter, ESB, Old Genie; Strathalbyn Beardmore Stout; Bland Cider Ⓗ
Revitalised back-street local with good atmosphere. Regular folk nights
🏠🍴 ⊖ Felling

Fencehouses 33H9

11–3; 6–10.30

Station Hotel
Morton Crescent (A1052)
✆ Durham 853363
Bass Extra light Ⓔ**; Stones Best Bitter** Ⓗ
Friendly roadside pub, plain comfortable lounge and locals bar with pool table 🅿🍴

Gateshead 33H8

11–3; 6–10.30

Five Wand Mill
201 Bensham Road (A692)
✆ Tyneside 4781147
Tetley Bitter Ⓗ
Large roadside urban pub with tasteful lounge and traditional bar 🍴

Queens Head
12 High Street (Bottle Bank) off A6127 near Tyne Bridge
✆ Tyneside 4783749
Mon–Fri evenings opens 5.30
Draught Bass Ⓗ
L-shaped bar with smaller lounge containing impressive temperance shield above fireplace ♿🍴 ⊖ Gateshead

Gosforth 33H8

11–3; 5.30–10.30

Gosforth Hotel
High Street (Great North Road) ✆ Tyneside 2856617
Jennings Bitter; Ruddle Best Bitter; Marston Pedigree; Tetley Bitter Ⓗ **Regular guest beers**
Popular meeting-place with two comfortable lounges
♿ ⊖ Regent Centre

Millstone
Haddricks Mill Road (A189)
✆ Tyneside 2856615
Draught Bass; Stones Best Bitter Ⓗ
Attracts a wide range of clientele. Two lounges and a proper public bar
♿🍴 ⊖ South Gosforth

Houghton-le-Spring 33H9

11–3; 6–10.30

Golden Lion
The Broadway ✆ 842460
Lorimer Best Scotch; Vaux Samson Ⓗ
Well-run town centre pub with three contrasting rooms
♿🍴🍺

Jarrow 33H8

11–3; 6–10.30

Royal Oak
Grange Road
✆ Tyneside 4898518
Closes 11 pm in summer
Samuel Smith OBB Ⓗ
Popular pub known locally as the long bar 🍴 (lunch) 🅿🍴 ⊖

Western
Western Road
✆ Tyneside 4896243
Cameron Strongarm; Everards Old Original Ⓗ
Community local with friendly atmosphere 🍴🍺

Kibblesworth 33G9

11–3; 6–10.30

Plough
✆ Tyneside 4102291
Draught Bass Ⓗ
Comfortable pub in former mining village ♿🍴 (not Sun) 🍺

Monkseaton 33H8

11–3; 6–10.30

Beacon
Earsdon Road (A192)
✆ Tyneside 2530353
Draught Bass; Stones Best Bitter Ⓗ
Large comfortable estate pub, plush lounge
🅿♿🍴 ⊖ W. Monkseaton

Newcastle 33H8

11–3; 5.30–10.30

Baltic Tavern
Broad Chare, Quayside
✆ Tyneside 2320214
Marston Pedigree; Theakston Old Peculier; Whitbread Castle Eden, Durham Ale Ⓗ
Interesting conversion of old pub and warehouse
♿ (not Sun)

Bridge Hotel
Castle Square (near High Level Bridge)
✆ Tyneside 2327780
Samuel Smith OBB; Theakston XB; Younger No. 3 Ⓗ **Regular guest beers**
Large former hotel near to Castle Keep. Good snob screens in bar. Folk music venue 🅿♿🍴≈ ⊖

Cooperage
32 The Close, Quayside
✆ Tyneside 2328286
Ind Coope Burton Ale; Marston Owd Rodger; Tetley Bitter; Theakston Old Peculier; Coates Cider Ⓗ
Regular guest beers
Former cooperage dating back to 14th century. Pricey high gravity beers ♿🍴≈ ⊖

Crown Posada
The Side, Quayside
✆ Tyneside 2321269
Belhaven 80/-; Samuel Smith OBB; Taylor Landlord Ⓗ
Regular guest beers
Tastefully preserved Victorian

bar. Exceptional stained glass windows Q

Darn Crook
Stowell Street
✆ Tyneside 2320339
Belhaven 80/-; Drybrough's Eighty Ⓗ
One-room lively city centre pub close to Gallowgate bus station and expanding "Chinatown" area
Ⓖ ⊖ St James

Forth
Pink Lane
Marston Pedigree; Tetley Bitter Ⓗ
City-centre pub handy for station 🍴⚏ ⊖

Haymarket
Percy Street
McEwan 80/-, Newcastle Exhibition; Younger's No. 3 Ⓗ
Interesting Victorian interior, popular pub for heavy music fans
🍴 ⊖ Haymarket

Newcastle Arms
Akenside Hill
✆ Tyneside 2326778
McEwan 80/-; Newcastle Exhibition; Younger's No. 3 Ⓗ
Panelled one-room pub directly beneath Tyne Bridge. Handy for Quayside Ⓖ

Old George Inn
Old George Yard (off Cloth Market) ✆ Tyneside 2323956
Draught Bass; Stones Best Bitter Ⓗ
Old former coaching inn steeped in history. Fine wood panelling, beams and impressive fireplace 🐾Ⓖ ⊖

Three Bulls Heads
Percy Street
✆ Tyneside 2326798
Draught Bass; Stones Best Bitter Ⓗ
Recently rebuilt to high standards with central bar and photographs of Old Newcastle 🍺Ⓖ ⊖

Trent House
Leazes Lane
✆ Tyneside 2617190
McEwan 80/-; Newcastle Exhibition; Younger's No. 3 Ⓗ
Drinking bar near University and Football Stadium 🍴Ⓖ🍴 ⊖

Villa Victoria
Westmorland Road
✆ Tyneside 2322460
Draught Bass; Stones Best Bitter Ⓗ
One room street corner local 🍴

North Hylton 33H9

11–3; 6–10.30
Shipwrights
Ferry Boat Lane
✆ Sunderland 495139
Vaux Samson, Lorimer Best Scotch Ⓗ

Riverside pub with good value snacks and restaurant
🍴🐾Ⓖ🍴

North Shields 33H8

11–3; 6–10.30
Berwick Arms
Coast Lane ✆ 572292
Draught Bass; Stones Best Bitter Ⓗ
Friendly and noisy 🍴

Chainlocker
New Quay ✆ 580147
McEwan 80/-; Newcastle Exhibition; Younger's No. 3 Ⓗ
Occasional guest beers
Small pub handy for ferry. Friendly atmosphere 🍺Ⓖ🍴🍴

Porthole
New Quay ✆ 576645
Marston Pedigree, Owd Rodger; McEwan 80/-; Ruddle Best Bitter; Younger's No. 3; Bland Cider Ⓗ **Regular guest beers**
Comfortable quayside bar with nautical theme
Q🍴🐾Ⓖ🍴🍴

Tynemouth Lodge Hotel
Tynemouth Road (A193)
✆ 577565
Belhaven 80/-; Jennings Bitter; Marston Pedigree; Samuel Smith OBB; Theakston Best Bitter; Wards Sheffield Best Bitter; Bland Cider Ⓗ
Popular pub, comfortable and friendly with jovial landlord
🍺QⒼ ⊖ (Tynemouth)

Wooden Doll
Hudson Street ✆ 573747
Matthew Brown Lion Mild, Bitter, John Peel; Theakston XB, Old Peculier; Younger's No. 3 Ⓗ **Regular guest beers**
Popular pub with superb view over mouth of Tyne. Art exhibitions held
🍺Ⓖ🍴 (to 8.30 pm) 🍴

Penshaw 33H9

11–3; 6–10.30
Bird in Hand
Station Road
✆ Durham 855022
Bass Extra Light; Stones Best Bitter Ⓗ
Refurbished local with locals bar and smart lounge 🐾🍴

Grey Horse
Old Penshaw
✆ Houghton 844882
Tetley Bitter Ⓗ
Popular pub on village green. Near Penshaw Monument
🍴 (lunchtimes) 🐾Ⓖ🚻

Ryhope 33J9

11–3; 6–10.30
Albion Inn
(A1018) The Green
✆ Sunderland 210293

Whitbread Durham Ale, Castle Eden; Bulmer Cider Ⓗ
Bright, friendly roadside inn
Ⓖ🍴

Ryton 33G8

Half Moon Inn
Village East
✆ Tyneside 4132755
Draught Bass Ⓗ
Welcoming friendly local in pleasant village 🐾🍴

Shieldfield 33H8

11–3; 6–10.30
Queens Arms
Shield Street/Simpson Terrace
✆ Tyneside 2324101
Matthew Brown Lion Mild, Bitter; Theakston Best Bitter, XB, Old Peculier Ⓗ
Dimly lit one-room refurbished pub
Ⓖ🍴 Manors ⊖

South Shields 33H8

11–3; 6–10.30
Adam & Eve
21 Frederick Street, Laygate
Samuel Smith OBB Ⓗ
Large Victorian pub 🍴

Beacon Inn
100 Greens Place ✆ 4562876
Vaux Samson; Wards Sheffield Best Bitter Ⓗ
Tastefully renovated pub overlooking River Tyne with welcoming atmosphere. Good value bar meals
🚻 (lunchtime) Ⓖ🍴🍴

Holborn Rose & Crown
East Holborn ✆ 4552379
McEwan 80/-; Newcastle Exhibition Ⓗ
Popular dockside pub, etched windows and ornate bar Ⓖ

Railway
Mill Dam ✆ Tyneside 4555227
Tetley Bitter Ⓗ **Regular guest beers**
Close to revitalised riverside area, just out of Market Square 🚻 (lunchtimes) 🍴

Stags Head
45 Fowler Street ✆ 4569174
Draught Bass; Stones Best Bitter Ⓗ
Compact terraced pub, tiled entrance lobby Ⓖ🍴

Sunderland: North 33J9

11–3; 6–10.30
Pilot Cutter
Harbour View, Roker
✆ 659371
Fri & Sat evening opens 5.30
Matthew Brown Mild, John Peel; Theakston Best Bitter, XB, Old Peculier; Bulmer Cider Ⓗ
Seafront hostelry with nautical theme. Views over river and sea from outside drinking area 🐾

Wolseley
40 Millum Terrace, Roker
☎ 672798
McEwan 80/- Ⓗ
Basic locals bar and friendly
bustling lounge ℘ⓒ➐❢

Sunderland: South   33J9

Borough
Vine Place ☎ 656316
**Darley Thorne Best Bitter;
Lorimer Best Scotch, 80/-;
Wards Sheffield Best Bitter;
Vaux Samson; Bulmer Cider** Ⓗ
Regular guest beers
Impressive Victorian-style
renovation with island bar,
bare floorboards and no keg
beers ⓒ (not Sun) ≩

Doxford Lad
Doxford Park Estate
☎ 280119
John Smith's Bitter Ⓗ
Popular modern estate pub
with large open plan interior.
Excellent bar meals ℘ⓒ&

Ivy House
Worcester Street ☎ 673399
**Darley Thorne Best Bitter;
Wards Sheffield Best Bitter** Ⓗ
Regular guest beers

Popular, well run pub, new
interior resembles a surplus
BBC set from I Claudius
ⓒ (not weekends) ❢

Rosedene
Queen Alexandra Road
☎ 284313
Wards Sheffield Best Bitter Ⓗ
Regular guest beers
Totally revamped to provide
three quality eating areas.
Extensive conservatory with
childrens play area ⌖℘ⓒ➐

Saltgrass
36 Ayres Quay, Deptford
☎ 657229
**Lorimer Best Scotch; Vaux
Samson; Wards Sheffield Best
Bitter** Ⓗ
Popular friendly dockside pub
⌂⌖ (lunchtimes) ℘ⓒ❢

Tynemouth   33H8

11–3; 6–10.30

Cumberland Arms
Front Street ☎ 571820
McEwan 80/- Ⓗ
Twin-decked, landlocked pub
with nautical atmosphere
❢& ⊖

Dolphin
King Edward Road ☎ 574342

**Marston Pedigree; Tetley
Bitter** Ⓗ
Mock-Tudor pub in residential
quarter ⌂Qⓒ❢ ⊖

Wallsend   33H8

11–3; 6–10.30

Rising Sun Hotel
Coast Road (off A1058)
☎ Tyneside 2623470
Stones Best Bitter Ⓗ
Large estate pub with noisy
bar and quieter lounge ❢

Washington   33H9

11–3; 6–10.30

Highwayman
Lambton Village Centre
☎ 4169471
**Cameron Strongarm; Everards
Old Original** Ⓗ
New estate pub in expanding
residential area ⓒ❢

Whitley Bay   33HB

11–3; 6–10.30

Victoria
Whitley Road
☎ Tyneside 2513753
Tetley Bitter; Theakston XB; Ⓗ
Regular guest beers
Large town centre pub
Q℘ⓒ❢ ⊖

Alcester 15H3

12–2.30; 5.30–11

Bell
Evesham Street A422 (A435)
☎ 762663
**Manns Mild; Wilsons
Original Bitter** H
Deceptively large market town
pub. Skittle alley
🏠 (lunch) 🍴 🕒 ➤ ❗

Ansty 16A4

11–2.30; 6–11

Sparrow Hall Hotel
Coombe Fields (off B4029
1 mile S of Ansty) OS410819
☎ Coventry 611817
**Draught Bass; Davenports
Bitter; Ruddle County** H
Plush country hotel and
restaurant. Occasional live
music 🏾 🍴 🖼 🕒 ➤

Atherstone 3H9

11–2.30; 6–11

Maid of the Mill
83 Coleshill Road (B4116)
☎ 3924
Davenports Mild, Bitter H
Small multi-roomed local with
games 🏾 🍴 ❗

Austrey 23H8

11–2.30; 6–11

Bird in Hand
Main Road
Marston Pedigree H, **Owd
Rodger** (winter) G
Splendid old village inn with
thatched roof 🏠 Q 🍴 ❗

Bedworth 16A3

11–2.30; 7 (6 summer)–11

Boat Inn
Black Horse Road (off B4113
Jct. 3 M6), Exhall
**Ansells Mild, Bitter; Ind Coope
Burton Ale; Tetley Bitter** H
A Heritage Inn, near canal
basin 🏠 🏾 🍴 🕒 (not Sat/Sun)

Bilton 16B4

11–2.30; 6–11

Black Horse
Main Street (A4071)
**Ansells Mild, Bitter; Ind Coope
Burton Ale** H
Basic bar with character;
large comfortable lounge 🍴 🕒 ❗

Birchmoor 23H8

11–2.30; 6–11

Gamecock
Cockspur Street
☎ Tamworth 895144
Draught Bass; M & B Mild H
Popular, friendly local Q 🍴 ❗

Brinklow 16B4

11–2.30; 6–11

Raven
Broad Street (A427)

**Ansells Mild, Bitter; Ind Coope
Burton Ale** H
Pleasant local at top of village.
Basic bar with bar billiards,
comfortable lounge. Sloping
garden with geese. Wide
variety of food 🍴 🕒 ➤ ❗

Bubbenhall 16A4

11–2.30; 6–11

Malt Shovel
Lower End (off A445)
☎ Coventry 301141
**Ansells Mild, Bitter; Tetley
Bitter** H
Village pub with plain bar and
comfortable lounge. Good
Italian and English food (not
Sun) 🏠 🍴 🕒 ➤ ❗

Bulkington 16A3

11–2.30; 7–11

Chequers
Chequer Street (off B4109)
**M & B Mild; Brew XI; Hansons
Black Country Bitter** H
Popular 18th century 3-room
pub 🏠 🕒 (not Sun)

All pubs in Bulkington sell
real ale

Chapel End 16A3

11–2.30; 6–11

Salutation Inn
Chancery Lane (off B4114)
OS326933
Banks's Mild, Bitter E
Hansons Black Country Bitter
Cosy village pub with
contrasting bar and lounge.
Popular for variety of pub
games 🏠 🍴 ❗

All pubs in Chapel End sell
real ale

Corley Moor 15J1

10.30–2.30; 6–11

Red Lion
Wall Hill Road OS277852
☎ Fillongley 40135
**Manns Bitter; Usher Founders
Ale; Wilsons Original Bitter** H
Pleasant large village pub
🏠 Q 🍴 🕒 ➤ (not Sun)

Ettington 15J4

10.30–2.30; 6–11

Chequers
Banbury Road (A422)
**Everards Old Original;
Marston Pedigree; M & B
Brew XI** H
Country free house, food
worth sampling 🍴 🕒 ➤ ❗

Fillongley 15J1

12–2.30; 7–11

Weavers Arms
Nuneaton Road, B4102
(1 mile E of village) ☎ 40399
**Draught Bass; M & B Mild,
Brew XI** H
Basic small, busy pub 🏠 Q 🍴 ❗

Five Ways 15J2

11–2.30; 6–11

Case Is Altered
Rowington Road (off A41)
OS225701
☎ Haseley Knob 206
**Ansells Mild, Bitter; Flowers
Original; Ind Coope Burton
Ale** G
Small rural local, run as two
separate pubs. Bar billiards
table takes 6d pieces! 🏠 Q 🏾 ❗

Grandborough 16B5

11–2.30; 7–11

Shoulder of Mutton
Sawbridge Road
Flowers IPA, Original H
Friendly village local. Cheese
skittles in games/family room.
Swings, climbing frame and
rabbit in large garden
Q 🏾 🍴 🕒 ❗

Harbury 16A5

11–2.30; 6–11

Gamecock
Chapel Street ☎ 612374
Manns IPA, Bitter H
Popular village local 🏠 🕒

Hartshill 16A3

11–2.30; 6–11

Anchor Inn
Mancetter Road (B4111)
OS335948
☎ Chapel End 394173
**Ansells Mild, Bitter; Everards
Old Original** H **Regular guest
beers**
Friendly, isolated canalside
pub with smart lounge and
busy bar 🏠 🏾 🍴 🕒 ➤ ❗

Henley in Arden 15H3

12–2.30; 7–11

Black Swan
High Street (A34) ☎ 2350
Davenports Bitter H
Popular pub in famous tourist
spot. No food Sun
🏠 Q 🕒 ➤ ❗ ⇌

Kenilworth 15J2

11–2.30; 6–11

Clarendon House
High Street (off A429)
☎ 57668
**Flowers IPA, Original; Hook
Norton Bitter; Samuel
Whitbread Strong** H
Welcoming lounge bar in a
small, smart hotel, noted for
good quality food Q 🏾 🍴 🕒 ➤

Virgins & Castle
High Street (off A429)
Davenports Mild, Bitter H
Small, medieval multi-roomed
pub in the old town. Named
from Elizabeth I's visit to the
castle nearby. No food Sun
🏠 Q 🏾 (weekends) 🍴 🕒 ➤ ❗ ⬥

Keresley End 15J2

11–2.30; 6–11
Golden Eagle
Howats Road, off Bennetts
Road ✆ Keresley 3066
**Banks's Mild, Bitter; Hansons
Black Country Bitter** Ⓔ
Large estate pub in colliery
village north of Coventry
🏚 🏠 👶 🍽

Kineton 15J4

10.30–2.30; 5.30 (6 Sat)–11
Red Lion
Bridge Street (B4086)
✆ 640240
**Draught Bass; M & B Mild,
Brew XI; Bulmers & Taunton
Cider** Ⓗ
Old coaching inn situated in
village where one of the Battle
of Edge Hill armies drank
🏚 🏠 🅿 Ⓔ 👶 🍽 🐕

Kingsbury 23G9

11–2.30; 6–11
Royal Oak
Tamworth Road (A51)
Marston Pedigree Ⓗ
Friendly village local with
comfortable lounge Q 🏕 🏠 🍽

White Swan
Tamworth Road (A51)
✆ Tamworth 872715
**Draught Bass; M & B Mild,
Springfield Bitter** Ⓗ
Easy reach of Kingsbury
Water Park Q 🏠 🐕 🍽 🍽

Lapworth 15H2

11–2.30; 5.30 (6 Sat)–11
Navigation
Old Warwick Road (B4439)
✆ 3337
**Draught Bass; M & B Mild,
Brew XI** Ⓗ
Country pub of character next
to canal 🏚 🏠 👶 🍽 🐕 ≥

Leamington Spa 16A5

11–2.30; 6–11
Newbold Comyn Arms
Newbold Terrace East
✆ 38810
**Marston Burton Bitter,
Pedigree** Ⓗ
Ex-farmhouse in the middle of
common land and golf course.
Large children's play area
🏚 🏠 👶 🐕 (not Sun) 🍽 🅰

Somerville Arms
Campion Terrace
**Ansells Mild, Bitter; Ind Coope
Burton Ale; Tetley Bitter** Ⓗ
Popular, friendly local; small
crowded lounge 🍽

Leek Wootton 15J3

11–2.30; 7–11
Anchor Inn
Warwick Road
**Draught Bass; M & B Brew
XI** Ⓗ

Plush lounge and locals bar in
an often busy village pub
🏚 🏠 👶 🍽

Long Itchington 16A5

11–2.30; 7–11
Green Man
Church Road
✆ Southam 2208
Davenports Bitter Ⓗ
Popular local village pub.
Beware low beams!!
🏚 Q 🏕 (lunch & early eve) 🐕 🍽

Harvesters
6 Church Road
✆ Southam 2698
**Hook Norton Best Bitter;
Ruddle Rutland Bitter,
County** Ⓗ **Occasional guest
beers**
Pleasant village free house
with quiet intimate restaurant
Q 🏕 👶 🐕 🍽 👶

Long Lawford 16B4

11–2.30; 7–11
Sheaf & Sickle
A428
Ansells Mild, Bitter Ⓗ
Small lounge; bright lively
bar. Pool room. Family room
in outbuilding, 2 gardens
🏕 🏠 👶 🍽

Try also: Country Inn (M & B)

Marston Jabbett 16A3

11–2.30; 6–11
Corner House
Bulkington Lane (B4112)
**Marston Burton Bitter, Merrie
Monk, Pedigree, Owd Rodger
(winter)** Ⓗ
Large, deservedly popular
pub. Many small rooms,
unusual pets in garden
🏚 Q 🏕 🏠 👶 (not Sun) 🍽

Try also: Chetwynd (Ansells)

Newbold on Avon 16B4

11–2.30; 6–11
Boat
Main Street (B4112)
**Davenports Mild, Bitter;
Weston Cider** Ⓗ
Cosy lounge at one end of
single room, cheese skittles at
other. Popular with canal
trade in season 🏚 🏕 🏠 👶 🐕

Newton Regis 23H8

11–2.30; 6–11
Queens Head
Main Road
✆ Tamworth 830271
Draught Bass Ⓗ
Busy pub, set in charming
village 🏠 👶 🐕

No-Mans Heath 23H8

11–2.30; 6–11
Four Counties
Ashby Road (A453)
Ind Coope Burton Ale Ⓗ
Popular and friendly; good
food 🏚 Q 🏠 👶 🐕

Nuneaton 16A3

11–2.30; 6–11
Griffin Inn
Coventry Road B4113,
Griff (near Bedworth)
OS358887
**Draught Bass; M & B Mild,
Brew XI** Ⓗ
Friendly and popular old
coaching inn;, games room.
Occasional live music
🏚 🏕 🏠 👶 🍽 👶 🅰

Prince of Wales
Arbury Road, Stockingford
(B4112, 1½ miles W of town
centre)
Opens 10.30
Flowers IPA, Original Ⓗ;
Whitbread Durham Mild Ⓔ
Single room with distinct bar
and lounge areas. Games pub
with pool, darts and doms
played seriously 🏚 🏠 👶

Railway Tavern
Bond Street
Opens 10.30 am
**Courage Directors; Marston
Pedigree** Ⓗ **Regular guest
beers**
Exterior painted in LMS livery.
Deceptively spacious multi-
roomed interior. Restaurant
(not Sun) 🏠 👶 🐕 ≥

Weavers Arms
7 Abbey Street
✆ 348271
Opens 10 am
Ansells Mild, Bitter Ⓗ
Popular town centre pub with
piano in large public. Quiet,
small lounge. Free and easy in
public on market days.
Summer-house in garden
🏠 👶 (not Sun) 🍽

Oxhill 16A6

10.30–2.30; 6–11
Peacock
Off A422
Draught Bass Ⓔ; **Donnington
BB** Ⓗ
Cosy village inn near Battle of
Edge Hill site 🏚 🏠 👶 🐕

Priors Marston 16B5

12–2.30; 7–11
Holly Bush
Holly Bush Lane
✆ Byfield 60934
**Marston Mercian Mild,
Burton Bitter, Pedigree** Ⓗ
Regular guest beers
Beautiful 15th century rural
pub 🏚 🏠 👶 🐕

Radford Semele 16A5

11–2.30; 7–11

White Lion
Southam Road (A425)
✆ Leamington Spa 20230
Davenports Bitter Ⓗ
Ancient thatched coaching
inn; now up-market village
pub with beamed bar, smart
lounge and restaurant ✿Ⓖ🍴🍺

Rugby 16B4

11–2.30; 6–11

Avon Mill
Newbold Road (A426)
M & B Mild, Brew XI Ⓔ
Large, tastefully modernised
pub. Swings in garden; cheese
skittles in bar, potted history
in lounge Q✿Ⓖ🍺

Half Moon
Lawford Road (A428)
Ansells Mild, Bitter; Ind Coope
Burton Ale Ⓗ
Popular and friendly terraced
town local Q

Raglan Arms
Dunchurch Road (A426)
Evening opens 7
Marston Burton Bitter,
Pedigree, Merrie Monk Ⓗ
Popular town pub opposite
famous school Q Ⓖ

Try also: Seven Stars (M & B);
William Webb Ellis (Banks's);
Merry Minstrel (Ansells)

Ryton-on-Dunsmore 16A4

11–2.30; 6–11

Blacksmiths Arms
High Street
✆ Coventry 301818
Draught Bass; M & B Mild,
Brew XI Ⓗ
Small, homely village pub
🔥Q✿Ⓖ🍺🍴

Shipston on Stour 15J4

10–2.30; 6–11

White Bear
The Square (off A34) ✆ 61558

WARMEST WELCOME

♦ A REAL FIRE PUB ♦

The 🔥 symbol denotes a pub
with a real solid fuel fire

Draught Bass; M & B
Springfield Bitter, Brew XI Ⓗ
Comfortable former coaching
inn 🔥✿🅿Ⓖ🍴🍺

Shrewley 15H3

10.30–2.30; 5.45–11

Durham Ox
Shrewley ✆ Claverdon 2283
M & B Mild, Brew XI Ⓗ
Country pub near railway and
canal; popular in summer
✿Ⓖ🍴🍺

Shustoke 23H9

12–2.30; 7–11

Griffin
B4114, near Coleshill
Everards Old Original;
Marston Pedigree; Theakston
Old Peculier Ⓗ Regular guest
beers
Fine old oak-beamed country
pub with inglenook fireplace
🔥Q✿Ⓖ

Southam 16A5

11.30–2.30; 6–11

Bowling Green
Coventry Street ✆ 2575
Davenports Mild, Bitter Ⓗ
Friendly and busy local ✿Ⓖ

Stratford upon Avon 15H3

Lamplighter
Rother Street ✆ 293071
Ansells Bitter; Courage
Directors; John Smith's Bitter;
Tetley Bitter Ⓗ Occasional
guest beers
Recent convert to real ale on
market square ✿Ⓖ🍺🚴

Old Tramway Inn
Shipston Road (A34)
✆ 297593
Davenports Bitter Ⓗ
Pub with large garden
backing onto old tramway
walk from town centre ✿Ⓖ

Shakespeare Hotel
Chapel Street ✆ 294771
Draught Bass; Courage
Directors; Davenports Bitter,
Hook Norton Best Bitter Ⓗ
Fine hotel in town centre.
Real ale in Froth & Elbow bar
🔥✿🅿Ⓖ🍺🚴

Squirrel
Drayton Avenue, Bishopton
✆ 297893
Ansells Mild, Bitter; Gibbs
Mew Wiltshire Bitter; Ind
Coope Burton Ale; Tetley
Bitter Ⓗ
Estate pub well worth a
15 min walk from town
centre. Good games facilities
✿Ⓖ🍺 (must book) 🍴🚴

Try also: Arden Hotel (Free);
Falcon Hotel (Free)

Stretton on Dunsmore 16A4

11–2.30; 6–11

Oak & Black Dog

Brookside
Manns Bitter; Usher Founders
Ale, Wilsons Original Bitter Ⓗ
Popular friendly lounge style
pub; games and dining area
Ⓖ🍺

Shoulder of Mutton

Off village green
Opens approximately 12 & 8
M & B Mild Ⓗ
Characterful, unspoilt old
regulars' pub. Small, rarely
used lounge, wood-panelled
snug, bar with fancy tiled floor
Q🍺

Studley 15H3

11–2.30; 5.30 (6 Sat)–11

Nags Head
Redditch Road ✆ 2405
Banks's Mild, Bitter Ⓔ;
Flowers Original Ⓗ
Popular, friendly pub, with
good value food Ⓖ (not Sun)

Warwick 15J3

10–2.30; 5.30–11

Racehorse
Stratford Road (A429)
✆ 491039
Opens at 11 & 6
Banks's Mild, Bitter; Hansons
Black Country Bitter Ⓔ
Large roadhouse on southern
edge of town, contrasting
bars. No food Sun 🔥✿Ⓖ🍺🍴

Zetland Arms
Church Street
Davenports Bitter Ⓗ
Busy town centre pub with
wood-panelled interior,
award-winning garden
✿🅿Ⓖ🍺

Wilmcote 15H3

11–2.30; 6–11

Masons Arms
Aston Cantlow Road
✆ Stratford 297416
Flowers IPA, Original Ⓗ
Stone house close to Mary
Arden's House and Stratford
Canal 🔥✿Ⓖ🍴🍺🚴

Try also: Swan House Hotel
(Free)

Help keep real ale alive by
joining CAMRA. Your voice
helps encourage brewers big
and small to brew cask beer
and offer all beer drinkers a
better choice. Send £9 for a
year's membership or use the
form on page 319.

Aldridge 24D6

10.30–2.30 (Sat only) 6–10.30 (11 F, S)

Lazy Hill Country Club (Pennard)
Walsall Wood Road (¾ mile from town centre)
Eves opens 7 pm–1 am (not Sun) no admittance after 10.30
Ansells Mild, Bitter Ⓗ
Despite name is a pub. Regular free 'n easy organ music Ⓔ🄖➐ (not Sun)

Bilston 24C6

12 (11 Sat)–2.30; 8–10.30 (11 F, S)

Trumpet
High Street ℰ 43723
Holden Black Country Bitter Ⓔ; Special Bitter Ⓗ
Popular one-room jazz centre. Live groups nightly and Sun lunch. Local caricatures and old film star photos Ⓖ (not weekends)

Birmingham

10.30–2.30; 5.30–10.30 (11 F, S)

Aston: 24E7

Bartons Arms
High Street ℰ 3590853
Opens 11 & 6
M & B Mild; Brew XI Ⓗ
Palatial tiled Victorian masterpiece. Jazz most nights Ⓐ🄖➐

Manor Tavern
61 Portland Street
Ansells Mild, Bitter Ⓗ
Small two-roomed back street pub close to the old brewery Ⓖ🄖≷ (Aston)

Camp Hill: 24E8

Brewer & Baker
58 Ravenhurst Street, 12 (off A41) ℰ 772 7839
Draught Bass; M&B Highgate Mild; Springfield Bitter; Brew XI Ⓗ
Friendly old pub. Collection of plates and jugs Ⓖ➐≷ (Bordesley)

Chelmsley Wood: 24E7

Greenwood
Helmswood Drive, 37
Opens 11 & 6
Ansells Mild, Bitter Ⓗ; Tetley Bitter Ⓗ
Lively, unpretentious local with downstairs lounge 🄖

City Centre: 24E7

Australian Bar
Hurst Street (off A38) ℰ 622 4256
Mornings opens 11
Davenports Mild, Bitter Ⓗ
Lovely old Victorian Gin Palace, rediscovered after renovation Ⓖ➐🄖≷

Fountain
Wrentham Street (off Bristol Street) ℰ 622 1452
Ansells Mild; Bitter Ⓗ
Old-fashioned corner local Ⓖ🄖

Gough Arms
Upper Gough Street, Lee Bank ℰ 643 0081
Courage Best Bitter, Directors Ⓗ
Small, friendly pub close to main GPO sorting office. Pool table in bar Ⓖ🄖≷ (New Street)

Holloway
89 Holloway Head, Lee Bank, 1
Opens 11.30 & 6
Davenports Mild, Bitter Ⓗ
Modern pub; basic bar; small but comfortable lounge Ⓖ🄖≷

Lamp Tavern
157 Barford Street, Highgate
Marston Pedigree Ⓗ Regular guest beers
Backstreet, one-room free house well worth finding ✍Ⓖ

Prince of Wales
Cambridge Street (near A456)
Mornings opens 11.30
Ansells Mild, Bitter; Ind Coope Burton Ale; Tetley Bitter Ⓗ
Popular local of character near Repertory Theatre 🄖

Roebuck
Hurst Street ℰ 622 4742
M & B Mild, Brew XI Ⓗ
Locals' pub near Hippodrome Theatre and markets area. Lively public bar, small quiet lounge Ⓖ🄖

Woodman
106 Albert Street, 5 ℰ 643 1959
Mornings opens 11; Sat eves opens 7
Ansells Mild, Bitter; Tetley Bitter Ⓗ; Coates Cider Ⓖ
2-bar tiled local, popular with postmen. Keen darts following 🄖≷

Try also: White Swan (Ansells), Queens Tavern (Courage)

Digbeth: 24D7

Old Wharf
81 Oxford Street ℰ 643 7339
Banks's Mild, Bitter; Hansons Black Country Bitter Ⓗ
Basic but friendly back street local. Busy bar with pool table Ⓖ🄖≷ (Moor Street)

Erdington: 24E7

Hare & Hounds
Marsh Hill, A4040 (outer ring road) ℰ 384 8047
Courage Best Bitter, Directors Ⓗ
Large two-roomed roadhouse with pleasant, comfortable lounge ✍Ⓖ🄖

Lad in the Lane
Bromford Lane, A4040 (outer ring road) ℰ 373 7739
Ansells Mild, Bitter; Ind Coope Burton Ale; Tetley Bitter Ⓗ
Reputed oldest pub in Brum. Old coaching inn thoughtfully decorated ✍Ⓖ

Gosta Green: 24E7

Old Union Mill
Holt Street/Heneage Street, 6 ℰ 359 1716
Mornings opens 11
Ansells Mild, Bitter; Gibbs Mew Wiltshire Bitter; Ind Coope Burton Ale; Tetley Bitter Ⓗ; Gaymers Cider Ⓖ
Comfortable 1930's pub near Holt's Brewery Ⓖ➐🄖

Sack of Potatoes
Draught Bass; M & B Mild, Springfield Bitter Ⓔ
Lively, Birmingham landmark, fondly remembered by generations of students Ⓖ🄖

Handsworth: 24D7

Red Lion
Soho Road, 21 (A41) ℰ 554 5169
Ansells Mild Ⓗ
Ornate Edwardian palace in a cosmopolitan area. Parking difficult. TV and pool table 🄖

Harborne: 24D8

Kings Arms
High Street ℰ 426 1048
Ansells Mild, Bitter; Tetley Bitter Ⓗ
Two-room pub at far end of village on corner of Outer Ring Road. Parking difficult Ⓖ🄖

Plough
High Street ℰ 427 4722
M & B Mild, Brew XI Ⓔ
Weston Cider Ⓖ
Basic pub at end of the village. Bowling green ✍Ⓖ🄖

Hockley: 24D7

St. Pauls Tavern
Ludgate Hill, 3
Opens 11; Sat eves opens 7
Draught Bass; M & B Mild, Springfield Bitter, Brew XI Ⓗ
Small friendly, corner of old Brum. Breakfasts served from 9 am Ⓖ➐🄖

Kings Heath: 24E8

Hare & Hounds
High Street (A435) ℰ 444 2081
Opens 11 & 6
Ansells Mild, Bitter; Gibbs Mew Wiltshire Bitter; Tetley Bitter Ⓗ
Young and trendy pub done out in Edwardian style Ⓖ🄖&

Moseley: 24E8

Prince of Wales
Alcester Road, 13 ☎ 449 4198
Opens 11 & 6
**Ansells Mild; Ind Coope
Burton Ale** Ⓗ
Busy 3 bars; interesting
mixture of students and local
clientele. Parking difficult ☙

Northfield: 24D8

Bell
Bristol Road South (A38)
☎ 478 1250
Opens 11; opens 6 Sat eves
Davenports Mild, Bitter Ⓗ
Comfortable, modern local.
Parking difficult ♿☙♨

Perry Barr: 24D7

Seventh Trap
Regina Drive,
Walsall Road, 42
**Banks's Mild, Bitter; Hansons
Black Country Bitter** Ⓔ
Barn-style, split-level lounge
with stained glass screens and
a clutter of antique knick-
knacks ♪♿ (Mon–Fri) ☙♿
≷ (Perry Barr)

Shard End: 25E7

Brook Meadow
Old Forest Way, 34
☎ 749 5656
**Banks's Mild, Bitter; Hansons
Black Country Bitter** Ⓔ
Modern estate pub;
comfortable "rural" lounge
♿ (Mon–Fri) ☙

Stetchford: 25E7

Cole Hall Farm
Cole Hall Lane, 33
Opens 11 & 6
**Banks's Mild, Bitter, Hansons
Black Country Bitter** Ⓔ
Converted Georgian
farmhouse ♪♿☙

Try also: Old Bill & Bull
(M & B)

Winson Green: 24D8

Bellefield
36–38 Winson Street (off
A457)
Opens 11.30 & 6
Davenports Mild, Bitter Ⓗ
Former Samuel White home
brew house. Ornate public bar
with striking ceiling, unique
green tiled snug 🚭♪☙

Try also: Bricklayer's Arms
(Davenports)

Yardley Wood: 25E8

Sherwood
Highfield Road
Opens 11
**Courage Best Bitter,
Directors** Ⓗ
Large 1930s roadhouse with
unusual lounge ♪☙♿≷

Blackheath 24C8

10.30–2.30; 6–10.30 (11 F, S)

Beech Tree Inn
111 Gorsty Hill Road (A4099)
☎ 559 2107
Opens 12 & 7
Holt Mild, Bitter, Entire Ⓗ
Popular, friendly 1930s local
🏠♿☙☙

Old Bush Revived
44 Powke Lane (B4100)
☎ 559 3202
Opens 11
Hansons Mild, Bitter Ⓔ
Popular, unspoilt 19th
century local 🚭♿☙☙≷

Bloxwich 24D6

11–2.30; 6–10.30 (11 F, S)

Royal Exchange
Stafford Road
**M & B Highgate Mild,
Springfield Bitter** Ⓔ
Former home-brew house ☙

Sneyd Inn
Vernon Way, Mossley Estate
(off A34)
Banks's Mild, Bitter Ⓔ
Basic one-room pub 🚭♪☙

Station
Station Street (off A34)
☎ 477004
Ansells Mild, Bitter Ⓗ
Bright, friendly local pub. Ask
for traditional beer ♪☙

Brierley Hill 24C8

11–2.30; 6–10.30 (11 F, S)

New Inn
Dudley Road (A461) ☎ 73792
**Wem Best Bitter, Special
Bitter** Ⓗ
Cosy, friendly local. Ex-
Simpkiss pub near town
centre 🏠☙

Roebuck
Amblecote Road ☎ 79137
Ansells Mild, Bitter Ⓗ; **Ind
Coope Burton Ale** Ⓗ
Popular Roadside local with
pool table ♿☙☙

Vine (Bull & Bladder)
Delph Road (off A461)
**Batham Mild, Bitter, Delph
Strong Ale** Ⓗ
Famous Black Country
brewery tap. Live jazz on
Mondays. Fresh seafood
🚭♪♿☙

Colley Gate 24C8

11–2.30; 6–10.30 (11 F, S)

Little White Lion
Windmill Hill (A458)
**Ansells Mild, Bitter; Batham
Bitter; Ind Coope Burton Ale;
Tetley Bitter** Ⓗ
Part of the enterprising
Little Brewery Co chain.
Serves Bear Steaks and
Desperate Dan Cow Pies
🏠♪♿☙☙

Round of Beef
Windmill Hill (A458)
**Banks's Mild, Bitter; Hansons
Black Country Bitter** Ⓔ
Friendly, popular local on
brow of hill. Live music
🚭♪♿☙

Coseley 24C7

11–2.30; 6–10.30 (11 F, S)

New Inn
Ward Street, Roseville (off
A4123)
Opens 12 (11 Sat) & 7
Holdens Mild, Bitter Ⓔ, **Special
Bitter** Ⓗ
Extended local, partly hidden
by chapel, nearby Coseley stop
on Birmingham Canal ♿☙≷

Old Bush
Skidmore Road, Daisy Bank
Holdens Mild, Bitter Ⓔ
Ex-home brew house,
reputedly haunted, affected by
subsidence. Pool room ♿☙≷

Coventry 25G8

11–2.30; 6–11

Biggin Hall Hotel
214 Binley Road (A427)
☎ 451046
**Marston Mercian Mild,
Burton Bitter, Pedigree, Owd
Rodger** Ⓗ
Plush wood panelled lounge.
Smart bar. Cable TV!? Not a
hotel 🏠🚭♪♿☙

Black Horse
Spon End (A4023)
**Draught Bass; M & B Mild,
Brew XI** Ⓗ
Popular old pub with panelled
lounge Q♿ (not Sun) ☙

Boat Inn
Shilton Lane, Walsgrave
(Nr M6)
**Draught Bass, M & B Mild,
Brew XI** Ⓗ
Small many roomed pub,
stood by canal arm, until it
was filled in. Part of lounge
was old brew-house ♪♿☙

Broomfield Tavern
14–16 Broomfield Place, Spon
End ☎ 28506
Evenings opens 7
**Ushers Founders Ale; Wilsons
Original Bitter; Bulmers
Cider** Ⓗ
Small pub with friendly
atmosphere, regular folk
music sessions ♪♿☙☙≷

Coombe Abbey Inn
Craven Street, Chapelfields
☎ 75743
**Draught Bass; M & B Mild,
Brew XI** Ⓗ
Popular pub with basic bar
and smart lounge. Regular
folk music sessions Q♪♿☙☙

Craven Arms
Craven Street, Chapelfields
Sat evenings opens 7
Flowers Original Ⓗ;

Whitbread Durham Mild Ⓔ
Regular guest beers
Friendly and lively street
corner local 🐾 ᴗ (not Sun)

Earlsdon Cottage
Warwick Street ☎ 74745
**Draught Bass; M & B Mild,
Highgate Mild, M & B Brew XI**
Large, popular pub. Music
most nights Q 🐾 ᵀ

Elastic Inn
Lower Ford Street ☎ 27039
**Ansells Mild, Bitter; Tetley
Bitter** Ⓗ
One-bar pub, near bus station

Greyhound
Much Park Street
Evenings opens 7
**Draught Bass; M & B Mild,
Brew XI** Ⓔ
Popular bar and comfortable
lounge ᴗ ᵀ

Malt Shovel
Spon End (A4023) ☎ 20204
**Ansells Mild, Bitter; Tetley
Bitter** Ⓗ
Ansells Heritage Inn in
medieval suburb. One bar, but
a number of drinking areas
🏠 🐾

Pitts Head
Far Gosford Street (A46)
☎ 22195
**Draught Bass, M & B Mild,
Brew XI** Ⓗ
One-time coaching inn now in
redevelopment area
🐾 ▣ ᴗ ➐ (Thu/Fri/Sat) ᵀ

Rising Sun
Spon Street ☎ 21814
**Draught Bass; M & B Mild,
Brew XI** Ⓗ
Comfortable, single-bar pub
with split levels and football
memorabilia 🐾 ᴗ

Waters (Dicks Bar)
High Street ☎ 26657
Opens 12 & 7
**Samuel Smith Tadcaster
Bitter, OBB** Ⓗ
Pleasant city centre wine bar,
real ale available only in Dicks
bar ᴗ

William IV
1059 Foleshill Road
☎ 686394
M & B, Brew XI Ⓔ
Smart pseudo-Regency pub
serving authentic Indian
meals (not Sun) 🐾 ᴗ ➐ ᵀ ♿

Cradley Heath   24C8
11–2.30; 6–10.30 (11 F, S)
Royal Oak (Laneys)
Bannister Street
Hansons Mild, Bitter Ⓔ
Friendly, small Black Country
boozer with many pictures of
Staffordshire Bull Terriers ᵀ ≷

Swan (Jaspers)
Providence Street
**Holdens Mild, Bitter, Special
Bitter, Old Ale** Ⓔ

Smart back street local with
speedway mementoes.
Comfortable family room
▣ 🐾 ᴗ ᵀ ≷

Darlaston   24C7
12–2.30 7–10.30 (11 F, S)
Green Dragon
55 Church Street
**M & B Highgate Mild,
Springfield Bitter** Ⓗ
Traditional workingman's
local. Quiet smokeroom, lively
bar ᵀ

Dudley   24C7
11–2.30; 6–10.30 (11 F, S)
British Oak
Salop Street
**Ansells Mild; Fox & Hounds
DDD; Ind Coope Burton Ale;
Tetley Bitter; Bulmers Cider** Ⓗ
Regular guest beers
Popular free house ᴗ ➐

Lamp Tavern
High Street (A459)
**Batham Mild, Bitter, Delph
Stronge Ale; Bulmers Cider** Ⓗ
Busy pub just off town centre.
Defunct brewery at rear 🏠 ᴗ ᵀ

Malt Shovel
Tower Street
Opens 7 Sat eves
Banks's Mild, Bitter Ⓔ
Smart town centre pub near
Castle and Zoo 🏠 Q 🐾 ᴗ ➐

Shakespeare
Stafford Street
Banks's Mild, Bitter Ⓔ
Unspoilt Black Country pub.
Tiny bar with scrubbed tables
and benches 🏠 ᵀ

Earlswood   25E9
11–2.30; 5.30–10.30 (11 F, S)
Bulls Head
Line Kiln Lane (off B4102)
OS122743 ☎ 728 2335
**Ansells Mild, Bitter; Ind Coope
Burton Ale** Ⓗ**; Coates Cider** Ⓖ
Smart lounge, basic bar.
Occasional live music. No food
Sun 🏠 🐾 ᴗ ᵀ

Halesowen   24C8
11–2.30; 5.30–10.30 (11 F, S)
Beehive
Hagley Road (off B4183)
Evenings opens 6
Hansons Mild, Bitter Ⓔ
Friendly bar, cosy lounge.
Disco at rear 🐾 ᴗ ᵀ

King Edward VII
Stourbridge Road (A458)
**Ansells Mild; Ind Coope
Burton Ale; Tetley Bitter** Ⓗ
Roadside local next to football
ground. Plush interior Q ᴗ ➐

Kingswinford   24B7
11–2.30; 6–10.30 (11 F, S)
Park Tavern
Barnett Lane (off A4101)

**Ansells Mild, Bitter; Batham
Bitter** Ⓗ
Busy local near Broadfield
House Glasss Museum 🐾 ᵀ

Try also: Old Court House
(Ansells)

Knowle   25F8
11–2.30; 5.30–10.30 (11 F, S)
Red Lion
Warwick Road (A41)
☎ 560 2461
**Ind Coope Burton Ale; Tetley
Bitter** Ⓗ
Traditional oak-beamed pub,
catering for all tastes. Opposite
village church 🏠 Q ᴗ ➐ ᵀ

Langley   24D7
11–2.30; 6–10.30 (11 F, S)
Brewery Inn
Station Road (B4182)
Holt Mild, Bitter, Entire Ⓗ
Canalside brewery tap near
Langley Maltings featuring
snob screens and Black
Country artefacts ᴗ ᵀ ≷

Try also: Crosswells (Holts)

Lower Gornal   24C7
11–2.30; 6–10.30 (11 F, S)
Old Bulls Head
Redhall Road (off B4175)
Holt Mild, Bitter, Entire Ⓗ
Victorian style local in front of
defunct Bradley's Brewery
🏠 ᴗ ᵀ

Red Cow
Grosvenor Road (off B4176)
Hansons Mild, Bitter Ⓔ
Unspoilt Black Country local ᵀ

Try also: Miners Arms
(Holdens)

Lye   24C8
11–2.30; 6–10.30 (11 F, S)
Castle
Balds Lane (off A458) ☎ 2799
**Wem Mild, Best Bitter, Special
Bitter** Ⓗ
Comfortable, friendly local
with bar billiards 🏠 🐾 ᴗ ➐ ᵀ

Shovel
Pedmore Road ☎ 3998
**Banks's Mild; Bathams Bitter;
Everards Tiger, Old Original;
Hook Norton Old Hookey** Ⓗ
Regular guest beers
Superb example of a Beer
Exhibition pub. Noted for
excellent range of food
🏠 ᴗ ᵀ ≷

Majors Green   25E8
11–2.30; 6–10.30 (11 F, S)
Drawbridge
Haslucks Green Road
☎ 434 5904
**Davenports Mild, Bitter;
Flowers Original; Westons
Cider** Ⓗ
New canalside pub, popular in
summer. No food Sun
🐾 ᴗ ➐ (until 8.15) ≷

Meer End 25F9

11.30–2.30; 6–10.30 (11 F, S)

Tipperary
(A4177 near Kenilworth)
✆ Berkswell 33224
**Davenport Mild, Bitter;
Flowers Original** H
Isolated country pub
dedicated to Harry Williams.
Try playing the piano
🍺🅿️🕒🕺🔥

Netherton 24C7

11–2.30; 6–10.30 (11 F, S)

Dry Dock
Windmill End (near A459)
**Ansells Mild; Ind Coope
Burton Ale, Lumphammer;
Tetley Bitter** H
Canalside pub that must be
seen to be believed. Beers
served from wooden Runcorn
boat. Desperate Dan Cow pies
a speciality 🅿️🕒🕺

**Old Swan
(Ma Pardoes)**
Halesowen Road (A459)
**Old Swan Bitter; Bulmers
Cider** H
Famous old home-brew house
recently extended into
adjacent premises 🍺

Oldbury 24D7

11–2.30; 6–10.30 (11 F, S)

Railway Inn
Bromford Road
M & B Mild, Brew XI E
Bright Victorian local on West
Bromwich boundary and close
to Birmingham Canal
🍺🛤 (Sandwell & Dudley)

White Swan
Church Street (A4034)
Banks's Mild, Bitter E
Friendly, Black Country
boozer near town centre
🍺🛤 (Sandwell & Dudley)

Old Hill 24C7

11–2.30; 6–10.30 (11 F, S)

Wharf
Station Road ✆ 559 2323
**Flowers Original; Hansons
Mild; Marston Pedigree,
Merrie Monk, Owd Rodger;
Whitbread Pompey Royal** H
Regular guest beers
Tastefully refurbished old
canalside pub with excellent
home-cooked food 🅿️🕒🕺🛤

Olton 25E8

12–2.30; 6–10.30 (11 F, S)

Lyndon Arms
Barn Lane ✆ 743 2179
Ansells Mild, Bitter H
Large 30's style pub to suit all
tastes. Excellent children's
playground 🎡🅿️🕒🍺

Pelsall 24D6

11.30–2.30; 6.30–10.30 (11 F, S)

Old Bush

Walsall Road (B4155)
✆ 682806
**Ansells Mild, Bitter; Holden
Special Bitter** H
Popular pub overlooking
common 🅿️🕒🕺🍺

Old House at Home
Norton Road (B4154)
Banks's Mild, Bitter E
Popular pub near common 🅿️🍺

Royal Oak
Norton Road ✆ 691811
Ansells Mild, Bitter H
Pleasant, friendly pub by side
of canal 🍺🕒🕺🍺

Pensnett 24C7

11–2.30; 6.30–10.30 (11 F, S)

Holly Bush
Bell Street (off A4101)
**Batham Mild, Bitter, Delph
Strong Ale** H
Modern, family estate pub 🍺

Quarry Bank 24C8

11–2.30; 6–10.30 (11 F, S)

Church Tavern
High Street (A4100)
Holt Mild, Bitter, Entire H
Cheerful, welcoming pub on
steep hill with Black Country
Society connections
🕒🍺🛤 (Cradley Heath)

Rushall 24D6

12–2.30; 6–10.30 (11 F, S)

Manor Arms
Park Road (off A461) ✆ 24491
**Draught Bass; M & B
Highgate Mild, Springfield
Bitter, Brew XI** E & H
Cosy canalside gem. Try the
hot pork sandwiches
🍺Q🅿️🕒🕺

Sedgley 24C7

11–2.30; 6–10.30 (11 F, S)

**Mount Pleasant
(Stump)**
Wolverhampton Road (A459)
Holt Mild, Bitter, Entire H
Small frontage belies lengthy
interior 🕒🍺

Try also: White Lion (Ansells)

Shirley 25E8

12–2 (Sat 11–3.30); 5.30 (Sat 7)–10 closed Mon

**Bernies Real Ale Off
Licence**
266 Cranmore Boulevard (off
A34)
**Batham Bitter; Everards Old
Original; Hook Norton Best
Bitter; Marston Pedigree;
Robinson Bitter; Somerset
Scrumpy Cider** H & E Regular
guest beers
Best choice for miles around,
always assured a welcome

Smethwick 24D7

10.30–2.30; 5.30–10.30 (11 F, S)

Bear Tavern

Bearwood Road, Bearwood
Opens 11 & 6
**Ansells Mild, Bitter; Tetley
Bitter** H
Large town pub with spacious
comfortable lounge 🕒 (Cold) 🍺

Waterloo
Waterloo Road ✆ 558 0198
M & B Mild, Brew XI H
Large Edwardian public house
featuring original tiled bar
🕒 (Mon–Fri) 🕺 (Thurs only) 🍺

Solihull 25E8

10.30–2.30; 6–10.30 (11 F, S)

Golden Lion
Warwick Road/Union Road
✆ 704 9969
**Courage Best Bitter,
Directors** H
Only pub in Solihull centre
with bar, snug, lounge, and
childrens play area
🅿️🕒🕺 (until 8.30) 🍺🛤

Stourbridge 24C8

11–2.30; 6–10.30 (11 F, S)

Bulls Head
High Street Wollaston (A461)
Opens 12 & 7
Davenports Mild, Bitter H
Pleasant 3-roomed pub with
panelled lounge 🕒🍺

Foresters Arms
Bridgnorth Road, Wollaston
A461
Opens 7
**Ansells Mild; Ind Coope
Burton Ale; Tetleys Bitter** H
Modernised, roadside pub;
good food, barbecues Q🅿️🕒🕺

Old Crispin Inn
Church Street ✆ 377581
**Cotleigh Tawny Bitter; Hook
Norton Best Bitter; Marston
Pedigree** H Occasional guest
beers
Modernised, extended pub just
off the Ring Road. Noted for
good food 🅿️🕒🕺🍺

Royal Exchange
Envile Street (A458)
Evenings opens 7
Batham Mild, Bitter H
Small, friendly local; bustling
bar, pool table in lounge 🅿️🕒🍺

Unicorn
Bridgnorth Road, Wollaston
(A458)
**M & B Springfield Bitter;
Marston Pedigree** H
Former home-brew house
with fine pewter collection
Q🅿️

Try also: Duke William
(Banks)

Sutton
Coldfield 25E6

10.30–2.30; 5.30–11

Blake Barn Inn
40 Shelley Drive, Four Oaks

Banks's Mild, Bitter; Hansons
Black Country Bitter E
Large open-plan pub with
mock barn decor. Particularly
popular with young people
🌳 ᗺ (not Sun) ᗱ
⇌ (Blake Street)

Duke
Duke Street ☎ 355 3479
Ansells Mild, Bitter; Gibbs
Mew Wiltshire Bitter; Ind
Coope Burton Ale; Tetley
Bitter H
Friendly, sidestreet local near
town centre
Q🌳🍴⇌ (Sutton Coldfield)

Gate
Mill Street ☎ 354 3365
Courage Best Bitter,
Directors H
Busy town centre pub; live
jazz Mon nights
🍴⇌ (Sutton Coldfield)

New Inns
Lichfield Road, Four Oaks
Mornings opens 11
Ansells Mild, Bitter; Tetley
Bitter H
Smart, unusually decorated,
with friendly atmosphere.
House beer brewed by Burton
Bridge Brewery. Bowling
green at rear
🌳ᗺ🍴⇌ (Butlers Lane)

Plough & Harrow
Slade Road, Roughley
(B4151)
Banks's Mild, Bitter; Hansons
Black Country Bitter E
Large suburban pub 🌳ᗺ🍴

Station
Station Street ☎ 355 3640
M & B Mild, Springfield Bitter,
Brew XI E
Victorian building in town
centre with pool and party
room 🌳ᗺ (not Sun) 🍴🍴ᗱ⇌

Three Tuns Hotel
High Street ☎ 355 2996
Ansells Mild, Bitter; Gibbs
Mew Wiltshire Bitter; Ind
Coope Burton Ale; Tetley
Bitter H
Old coaching inn with period
furnishing and photographs of
Old Sutton
🅰🌳ᗺ (Mon–Fri) 🍴⇌

Try also: Bitter End (Banks's)

Tipton   24C7
11–2.30; 6–10.30 (11 F, S)
Horseley Tavern
Horseley Heath (A461)
Hansons Mild, Bitter E
Traditional, unspoilt pub with
four rooms and cobbled
archway near Birmingham
Canal ᗺ (Dudley Port)

Old Court House
Lower Church Lane (B4163)
Flowers Original; Hansons
Mild; Marston Pedigree,
Merrie Monk H Regular guest
beers

Spartan one-roomed alehouse.
Also sells foreign bottled beers
🍴ᗺ (Dudley Port)

Try also: Crown & Cushion
(Holts)

Upper Gornal   24C7
11–2.30; 6–10.30 (11 F, S)
Old Mill
Windmill Street (off A459)
Holden Mild, Bitter, Special
Bitter E
Extended pub with Gornal
stone and mock Tudor
interior. Restaurant upstairs
ᗺ➤

Walsall   24D6
10.30–2.30; 5.30–10.30 (11 F, S)
Crown Inn (Funny
House)
6 Long Acre Street (off A34)
Opens 11.30 & 6.30
Ansells Mild; Tetley Bitter H
Lively two-roomed pub,
adorned with photos of
comedy legends. Note the
Beano till 🅰🍴⇌

Fountain
Lower Forster Street (off
A461)
Opens 12 & 7
M & B Highgate Mild,
Springfield Bitter E
Small, cosy back street local
ᗺ🍴⇌

Hamemakers Arms
Blue Lane West
Evenings opens 6
Banks's Mild, Bitter; Hanson's
Black Country Bitter E
Medium-sized 30's pub, handy
for town. Bright bar,
comfortable lounge
ᗺ (not Sun) 🍴⇌

Orange Tree
Hollyhedge Lane/
Wolverhampton Road (A454)
☎ 25119
Ansells Mild, Bitter; Tetley
Bitter H
Single L-shaped room,
entertainment Wed and Fri
eves ᗺ➤

Walsall Arms
Bank Street (off Pool Street)
Opens 12
Draught Bass; M & B
Highgate Mild H
Small, busy back street local
with skittle alley. Note the
Butlers Ales windows
ᗺ (not Sun) 🍴

Wheatsheaf
Birmingham Road (off A34)
Opens 11.30
Ansells Mild, Bitter; Ind Coope
Burton Ale H
Popular students pub, regular
live music upstairs 🌳ᗺ🍴

White Lion
Sandwell Street, Caldmore
Opens 12 & 6

Ansells Mild, Bitter; Ind Coope
Burton Ale H
Large, popular backstreet
local. Beware sloping floor in
bar. Separate pool room 🌳ᗺ🍴

Wednesbury   24D7
11–2.30; 6–10.30 (11 F, S)
Cottage Spring
106 Franchise Street (off
B4200)
Opens 12 & 7
Holden Black Country Mild,
Bitter, Special Bitter, Old
Ale H
Lively and popular local on
Darlaston border 🌳🍴

Horse & Jockey
Wood Green Road (A461),
½ mile Jct 9 of M6 ☎ 556 0464
Evenings opens 5.30
Ansells Mild, Bitter; Ind Coope
Burton Ale H
Fine wooden bar back and
tiled front in public, cocktail
bar and restaurant upstairs
(happy hour 5.30–7)
ᗺ➤🍴

Wednesfield   24C6
11–2.30; 6–10.30 (11 F, S)
Broadway
Lichfield Road (A4124)
Ansells Mild, Bitter; Holden
Black Country Bitter; Ind
Coope Burton Ale H
Multi-roomed pub with wood
panelling in lounge
🌳ᗺ (not Sun) 🍴

West
Bromwich   24D7
11–2.30; 6–10.30 (11 F, S)
George
Phoenix Street (B4149)
Hansons Mild, Bitter E
Compact, vibrant local in
industrial area near canal
🌳ᗺ

Nelson
New Street
M & B Mild, Brew XI H
Small local near bus station,
overlooking police HQ! ᗺ🍴

Try also: Railway (Wilsons)

Royal Oak
Newton Street (off A4041)
Opens 11.30
M & B Mild; Brew XI H
Small wedge-shaped pub in
cul-de-sac north of town
Q🌳🍴ᗱ

Willenhall   24D6
11–2.30; 6–10.30 (11 F, S)
Acorn
28 Walsall Road (A454)
Ansells Mild, Bitter; Holden
Special Bitter E Occasional
guest beers
Main road pub near Jct 10 of
M6. Comfortable lounge,
games room Q🌳ᗺ🍴

Robin Hood
54 The Crescent (A462)
Opens 12 & 6.30
Ansells Mild; Ind Coope
Burton Ale; Tetley Bitter H
Deservedly popular local 🏠 ✿

Tiger Inn
68 Stafford Street (off A454)
✆ 65356
Evenings opens 5.30
Wem Pale Ale; Mild; Best
Bitter; Special Bitter H;
Symonds Drystone Cider G
Town centre local with real
ale off-licence. Excellent pork
scratchings ⊞✿☾🍴

Wolverhampton
24C6

11–2.30; 6–10.30 (11 F, S)

British Queen
381 Dudley Road (A459),
Blakenhall ✆ 58188
Ansells Mild, Bitter H
Friendly old local at edge of
modern high rise estate and
industrial area 🏠🍴

Clarendon Hotel
Chapel Ash (A41) ✆ 20587
Banks's Mild, Bitter; Hansons
Black Country Bitter E
Popular Brewery tap. Various
rooms and corridor bar
⊞☾ (not Sun/Sat) 🍴

Combermere Arms
Chapel Ash (A41) ✆ 21880
Draught Bass; M & B
Highgate Mild H; Springfield
Bitter E; Bulmers Cider G
Charming little pub—like a
terraced house. Tree growing
in gents ✿🍴

Feathers
Molineux Street ✆ 26924
Banks's Mild; Bitter E;
Weston's Cider G

Small, friendly local next to
Polytechnic and football
ground ☾ (Mon–Fri) 🍴≷

Forge Hammer
Spring Road, Ettingshall
Opens 11.30 & 7
Hansons Mild, Bitter E
Basic local, full of character.
Pub games a major feature
🏠☾ (Mon–Fri) 🍴

**George & Dragon
(The Clog)**
104 Broad Lanes, Ladymoor
Banks's Mild, Bitter E
Lively and friendly pub with
antique shelving behind bar 🍴

Homestead
Lodge Road, Oxley
(off A449)
Ansells Mild, Bitter; Holdens
Black Country Bitter H
Pleasant suburban pub with
children's playground ✿☾🍴🍴

Lewisham Arms
Prosser Street (off A460), Park
Village
Banks's Mild, Bitter E
Gloriously unspoilt Victorian
alehouse with sense of
humour 🍴

Mitre
Lower Green, Tettenhall (off
A41)
Draught Bass; M & B
Highgate Mild; Springfield
Bitter E
Pleasant pub by village green
🏠✿☾ (Mon–Fri) 🍴

Newhampton
Riches Street (off A41)
Whitmore Reans
Courage Best Bitter, Directors
Bitter H
Bustling local focal point.
Regular Irish music ✿🍴

Parkfield Tavern
Parkfield Road (A4039)
Opens 12 & 7
Hansons Mild, Bitter E
Friendly and basic, unusual
darts alley at rear Q🍴

Posada
Lichfield Street ✆ 710738
Closes 10.30 F, S
Holt Mild, Bitter, Entire H
Very popular town-centre
hostelry; original bar fittings
and tiled front ☾ (Mon–Fri) ≷

Stile
Fawdry Street, Whitmore
Reans
Banks's Mild, Bitter E
Friendly 3-room, back street
local notable for L-shaped
bowling green and engraved
windows. Children welcome.
Unspoilt by renovation ✿🍴

Wheatsheaf
Market Street ✆ 24446
Closes 10.30 F, S
Banks's Mild, Bitter E
Busy town centre pub, table
service in lounge ✿⊞🍴≷

Winning Post
Gorsebrook Road (opposite
racecourse, off A449)
Wem Mild, Best Bitter, Special
Bitter E
Modern lounge only pub with
raised games area
☾ (not Sun) ♿

Woodsetton
24C7

11–2.30; 6–10.30 (11 F, S)

Brook
Bourne Street (off A457)
Banks's Mild, Bitter E
Unspoilt, split-level pub with
knee-high serving hatch.
Defunct Turley's Brewery at
rear ⊞✿🍴

Try also: **Park Inn** (Holdens)

THE MONOPOLIES COMMISSION
SAY THEY'VE NO OBJECTION
TO OUR TAKING OVER
PIDDLECROFT'S BREWERY—
WE ALREADY OWN IT

MEGALITHIC
INDUSTRIES

CHAIRMAN

Aldbourne 6C2

11–2.30; 7–10.30 (11 F, S)

Masons Arms
West Street (B4192)
Arkell BB, BBB ℍ
A rare, real village local. Small
and friendly ℘ⓒ♀

Amesbury 6B4

10.30–2.30; 6.30–10.30 (11 F, S & summer)

Antrobus Arms Hotel
Church Street (off A303)
✆ 23163
Draught Bass; Wadworth IPA,
6X ℍ
Old coaching inn well worth
finding after a visit to
Stonehenge ♙Q℘🅿ⓒ♀♿

Badbury 6B2

11–2.30; 6.30–10.30 (11 F, S & summer)

Bakers Arms
Off A345/M4
✆ Swindon 740313
Arkell BB, BBB, Kingsdown
Ale ℍ
Small, neat sideroad pub
♙℘ⓒ♀♀

Barford St Martin 6B5

10.30–2.30; 6–10.30 (11 F, S & summer)

Green Dragon
B3089, off A30 OS057314
✆ Salisbury 742242
Hall & Woodhouse Hectors
Bitter, Badger Best Bitter,
Tanglefoot ℍ
Ancient inn with beams and
oak panelled bar
♙℘🅿ⓒ♀ (not Mon) ♀

Beckhampton 6B3

11.30–2.30; 6–10.30 (11F, S & Summer)

Waggon & Horses
A4 ✆ Avebury 262
Wadworth IPA, 6X, Farmers
Glory, Old Timer ℍ
Attractive, old, thatched
coaching inn ♙℘ⓒ♀♀

Bishops Cannings 6A3

11–2.30; 6–10.30 (11 F, S & summer)

Crown Inn
off A361 ✆ Cannings 218
Wadworth IPA, 6X, Old
Timer ℍ
Fine, old, red-brick building in
pleasant surroundings. A
superb pub ♙℘ⓒ♀♀♿

Bowden Hill 15G9

11.30–2.30; 7–10.30 (11 F, S)

Bell Inn
OS926680 ✆ Lacock 308
Moles Bell Bitter, Moles Bitter;
Wadworth 6X ℍ Regular
guest beers
Small, friendly country free
house ♙Q℘♀♿

Rising Sun
32 Bowden Hill OS936680

✆ Lacock 363
Opens 11 closed Tue lunch
Bunce Best Bitter; Gibbs Mew
Salisbury Best; Moles Cask
Bitter ℍ Landlord's Choice ⓖ
Wadworth IPA, ⓖ 6X ℍ
Occasional guest beers
Hill top village pub with
superb views from large
terraced garden ♙Q℘ⓒ♀

Bradford-on-Avon 15F9

10.30–2.30; 6–11

Barge Inn
17, Frome Road (B3109)
✆ 3403
Opens 11.30
Usher PA (summer), Best
Bitter, Founders ℍ; Bulmer
Dry Cider ⓖ
Comfortable one bar inn next
to lock, large walled garden
℘🅿ⓒ (not Sun) ⇌

Bunch of Grapes
14 Silver Street (B3107)
Evenings opens 6.30
Draught Bass; Hook Norton
Best Bitter; Marston Pedigree;
Smiles Best Bitter ℍ
Busy town centre pub
ⓒ (not Sun) ♀⇌

Dog & Fox
Ashley Road (off A363)
Usher PA; Bulmer Cider;
Taunton Cider ⓖ
Country-style local on edge of
town ♙℘ⓒ♀

Bremhill 6A3

10.30–2.30; 6–10.30 (11 F, S)

Dumpost
Off A4 OS976727
Archer Best Bitter; Arkell BBB;
Wadworth 6X ℍ
Good value comfortable free
house with extensive views
♙Q℘♀

Broughton Gifford 15F9

11–2.30; 6–11

Bell
The Common (off B3107)
✆ North Trowbridge 782309
Wadworth IPA, 6X ℍ
Fine old village pub on edge of
local common ♙℘ⓒ♀♀

Burbage 6C3

10.30–2.30; 6–10.30 (11 F, S & summer)

Three Horseshoes
Stibb Green (A346)
Wadworth IPA, 6X, Old
Timer ℍ
Thatched pub near Savernake
Forest ♙℘ⓒ♀♀

Castle Combe 15F8

10.30–2.30; 6–10.30 (11 F, S)

White Hart
Off B4039 ✆ 782295
Eldridge Pope Royal Oak; Hall

& Woodhouse Badger Best
Bitter; Marston Pedigree;
Theakston Best Bitter ℍ
Regular guest beers
Very old pub of character;
excellent family room, garden
and good food ♙♿℘ⓒ♀

Charlton 15G8

12–2.30; 7–11 closed Sun eve & all day Mon

Horse & Groom
The Street (B 4040) ✆ 3904
Archers Village Bitter; Moles
Cask Bitter; Wadworth 6X ℍ
Restaurant/lounge with
homemade food including
vegetarian ♙Q℘ⓒ♀♀♿

Chicksgrove 6A5

12–2.30 (not Tue); 7–11

Compasses
Off A30 OS974295
✆ Fovant 318
Coopers Bitter; Halls Harvest
Bitter; Ind Coope Burton
Bitter; Wadworth 6X ℍ
Occasional guest beers
16th century bar below
cottage in peaceful
countryside ♙Q℘ⓒ♀

Chirton 6B3

10–2.30; 6–10.30 (11 F, S & summer)

Wiltshire Yeoman
Andover Road (A342) ✆ 665
Wadworth IPA, 6X, Farmers
Glory ℍ
Big and friendly roadhouse,
skittle alley ♙♿℘ⓒ♀♀⚲

Collingbourne Ducis 6C3

11–2.30; 6–10.30 (11 F, S & summer)

Shears
Off A338/A346 just outside
village ✆ 304
Bishops Best Bitter; Wadworth
IPA, 6X ℍ Occasional guest
beers
Picturesque, thatched, brick
and flint building. Animals
inhabit the car park ♙℘ⓒ♀

Corsley Heath 5H2

11–2.30; 6–11

Royal Oak
A362 ✆ Chapmanslade 238
Draught Bass; Wadworth IPA,
6X, Farmers Glory ℍ
Welcoming, spacious pub/
restaurant near Longleat
♙♿ⓒ♀♀

Dauntsey 15G8

10.30–2.30; 6–10.30 (11 F, S & summer)

Peterborough Arms
Dauntsey Lock (A420)
✆ Bradenstoke 890 409
Boddingtons Bitter; Daven-
ports Bitter; Eldridge Pope
Royal Oak; Wadworth 6X ℍ
Westons Cider; Blackthorn
Cider ⓖ Regular guest beers
Family pub to suit all tastes;
public with pool table and
darts ♙♿℘ⓒ♀♀⚲

Derry Hill 6A2

10.30–2.30; 6–10.30 (11 F, S)

Lansdowne Arms
A342 ☏ Calne 812422
Wadworth IPA, 6X, Farmers
Glory, Old Timer Ⓗ Taunton
Cider Ⓗ
Curious Victorian gothic
architecture opposite Golden
Gates of Bowood House.
Popular for food ♨ ✿ ᕀ ♥ 🍴

Devizes 6A3

10–2.30; 6–10.30 (11 F, S & summer)

Black Swan Hotel
Market Place ☏ 3259
Open until 4 Thu lunch
Wadworth IPA, 6X Ⓗ
Cosy L-shaped bar in 1737
coaching inn Q ✿🚻 ᕀ ♥

Hare & Hounds
Hare and Hounds Street
Opens 11 & 6.30
Wadworth IPA, 6X, Old
Timer Ⓗ
Friendly pub with a relaxed
atmosphere ♨ ✿ ᕀ (not Sun) 🍴

White Bear
Monday Market Street ☏ 2583
Open until 4 Thu lunch
Wadworth IPA, 6X Ⓗ
Quaint, low-ceilinged 1547
Tudor inn Q🚻 ᕀ ♥

Easton Royal 6C3

10.30–2.30; 6–10.30 (11 F, S & summer)

Bruce Arms
B3087
Whitbread Strong Country
Bitter Ⓖ
Unaltered and peaceful. Part
of a bygone age Q ✿ 🍴

Fonthill Gifford 5J3

10–2.30; 6 (6.30 summer)–10.30 (11 F, S & summer)

Beckford Arms
Off B3089 OS932312
☏ Tisbury 870385
Wadworth IPA, 6X, Old
Timer Ⓖ
Friendly unspoilt 17th
century inn ♨ ✿ 🚻 🍴

Giddeahall 15F8

11–2.30; 7–10.30 (11 F, S)

Crown Inn
A420 ☏ Chippenham 782229
Marstons Pedigree; Moles
Cask Bitter; Smiles Exhibition;
Wadworth 6X; Youngers
IPA Ⓗ
Roadside pub with split level
bars and restaurant ♨ ✿ ᕀ ♥

Great Cheverell 6A3

12–2.30; 7–10.30 (11 summer)

Bell Inn
Near B3098
☏ Lavington 3277
Marston Pedigree; Moles Cask
Bitter; Wadworth IPA, 6X Ⓗ
Bulmers Cider Ⓗ

Rustic village local with
friendly atmosphere
♨🚻 ✿ ᕀ 🍴

Heddington 6A3

10.30–2.30; 6–10.30 (11 F, S)

Ivy Inn
Off A4/B3102 OS000663
Wadworth IPA, 6X, Old
Timer Ⓖ
Fine thatched 15th century
village local ♨ Q🚻 ✿ 🍴

Hilcott 6B3

11–2.30; 6–10.30 (11 F, S & summer)

Prince of Wales
Off A342/345 OS107587
Wadworth IPA, 6X Ⓗ
Basic and off the beaten track
but well worth the effort to
find ✿ ᕀ

Little Bedwyn 6C3

11.30–2.30; 6–10.30 (11 F, S & summer)

Harrow
Off A4 ☏ Marlborough 870871
Harrow Inn Bitter; Hook
Norton Best Bitter; Marston
Pedigree Ⓗ Regular guest
beers
Well appointed pub in
pleasant canal-side village
♨ Q ✿ ᕀ ♥

Malmesbury 15G8

10.30–2.30; 6.30–10.30 (11 F, S & summer)

Red Bull
Sherston Road (B4040)
Archers Village Bitter;
Draught Bass Ⓗ
Popular, friendly pub with
good family facilities ♨🚻 ᕀ ♿

Manton 6B3

10–2.30; 6–10.30 (11 F, S & summer)

Up the Garden Path
Off A4 OS173685
Archer Best Bitter; Flowers
Original; Hook Norton Best
Bitter Ⓗ
Bright and cheerful little pub
with games room ♨ ✿ ᕀ ♥

Market Lavington 6A3

11–2.30; 6–10.30 (11 F, S & summer)

Volunteer
Church Street (B3098)
☏ Lavington 2342
Wadworth IPA, 6X, Ⓗ Old
Timer Ⓖ
Warm and friendly pub, bar
billiards ♨ Q ✿ ᕀ 🍴

Marlborough 6B3

10–2.30; 6–10.30 (11 F, S & summer)

Lamb
The Parade ☏ 52668
Opens 11
Wadworth IPA, 6X Ⓖ
Popular and full of character.
Occasional live music ✿ 🚻 ᕀ

Wellington Arms
High Street (A4) ☏ 52954
Evenings opens 6.30
Flowers Original; Whitbread
Strong Country Bitter Ⓗ
Single bar with an abundance
of ornaments ✿ ᕀ ♥

Nomansland 6C6

10.30–2.30; 6–10.30 (11 F, S & summer)

Lamb Inn
Near B3079/B3080
OS253173 ☏ Romsey 390246
Flowers Original; Whitbread
Strong Country Bitter Ⓗ
New Forest village cricket
green pub, favourite spot for
picnics ♨ ✿ ᕀ ♿ 🅰

Oare 6B3

11–2.30; 6–10.30 (11 F, S & summer)

White Hart
A345 ☏ Pewsey 2273
Wadworth IPA, 6X Ⓗ
Homely and comfortable
✿🚻 🍴 🅰

Porton 6B5

11.30–2.30; 6–10.30 (11 F, S & summer)

Porton Hotel
Off A338 ☏ Idmiston 610203
Draught Bass; Gibbs Mew
Wiltshire Bitter, Salisbury Best
Bitter, Bishops Tipple; Bulmer
Cider Ⓗ
Old Edwardian railway hotel
with a comfortable lounge
and bar games ♨ ✿ 🚻 ᕀ 🍴

Poulshot 6A3

10–2.30; 6.30–10.30 (11 F, S & summer)

Raven
Off A361 OS970601
☏ Seend 271
Wadworth IPA, 6X Ⓖ
Attractive half-timbered inn
♨ ᕀ ♥

Salisbury 6B5

10.30–2.30; 6–10.30 (11 F, S & summer)

Haunch of Venison
Minster Street ☏ 22024
Courage Best Bitter,
Directors Ⓗ
Friendly city pub with many
historic features. Look out for
the hand!
♨ Q ᕀ ♥ (not Sun winter) ⇌

Railway Tavern
South Western Road ☏ 28120
Gibbs Mew Wiltshire Bitter,
Premium Bitter, Salisbury Best
Bitter, Bishops Tipple Ⓗ
Occasional guest beers
Spacious and friendly town
pub ✿🚻 ᕀ 🍴 ⇌

The Boat House
Mill Stream Approach, Castle
Street ☏ 332963
Wadworth IPA, 6X Ⓗ Regular
guest beers
New pub by river Avon. Boats
for hire in summer ✿ ᕀ 🍴 ⇌

Old Mill Hotel
Harnham (off A3094)
☎ 27517
Closed Mon & Tue lunch
Wadworth 6X, Old Timer
(winter) Ⓗ Regular guest beers
Small friendly hotel bar by the
river. Views over water
meadows painted by
Constable ▲ ✿ ▣ Ⓖ ➐

Seend Cleeve 6A3

10–2.30; 6–10.30 (11 F, S & Summer)

Barge Inn
Near A361/A365
Wadworth IPA, 6X Ⓗ
Canalside pub, once the home
of the Wiltshire Giant Q ✿ ▮

Sells Green 6A3

11–2.30; 6–10.30 (11 F, S)

Three Magpies
A365 ☎ Seend 389
Wadworth IPA, 6X, Ⓗ Old
Timer (winter) Ⓖ Taunton
Cider Ⓖ
Roadside inn near Kennet and
Avon Canal ▲ ✿ Ⓖ ➐ ▮ ▲

Sherston 15F8

11–2.30; 6–10.30 (11 F, S)

Carpenters Arms
Easton Town (B4042)
Flowers Original; Whitbread
WCPA; Bulmers Extra Dry
Cider Ⓖ Regular guest beers
Unspoilt village locals pub
▲ Q ✿ Ⓖ ➐ ▮

South Wraxall 15F9

11–2.30; 6–

Longs Arms
Off B3109
☎ Bradford-on-Avon 4450
Wadworth IPA, 6X, Old Timer
(winter) Ⓗ; Bulmer Cider Ⓖ
Warm and inviting village
local ▲ ✿ Ⓖ ➐ (early eve) ▮

Staverton 15F9

11–2.30; 6.30–11

Old Bear
B3105
☎ North Trowbridge 782487
Draught Bass; Marston
Pedigree; Wadworth IPA,
6X Ⓗ
300-year-old roadside inn
▲ ✿ Ⓖ

Steeple Ashton 5J1

10.30–2.30; 6–10.30 (11 F, S)

Longs Arms
Off A350 ☎ Keevil 870245
Usher PA, Best Bitter,
Founders Ale; Taunton
Cider Ⓗ
Old coaching inn in a pretty
village. Bar once used as a
magistrates court ✿ Ⓖ ▮

Swindon 6B1

10.30–2.30; 5.30–10.30 (11 F, S & summer)

Bakers Arms

Emlyn Square ☎ 35199
Evenings Opens 7
Arkell BB, BBB Ⓗ
Cheerful locals' pub in railway
village ✿ Ⓖ ▮ ≋

Beehive
Prospect Hill ☎ 23187
Morrell Dark Mild, Varsity Ⓗ
Eccentric in both shape and
character. Good choice of
daily newspapers ▲ Ⓖ ➐

Duke of Wellington
27 Eastcott Hill ☎ 34180
Winter evenings opens 7
Arkell BB, BBB Ⓖ
Genuine, down to earth pub
just outside town centre ✿ ▮

Glue Pot
Emlyn Square ☎ 23935
John Devenish Bitter, Wessex
Best Bitter Ⓗ
Single bar pub near railway
museum ▣ Ⓖ (not Sat) ≋

Railway
Newport Street ☎ 38048
11–2.30 (3.30 Mon)
Archers Village Bitter, Best
Bitter, Special; Devenish
Wessex Best Bitter Ⓗ Regular
guest beers
Archer's only tied house in
Swindon Q ▣ ✿ ▣ Ⓖ ➐ ▮ ▲

Wheatsheaf
Newport Street ☎ 23188
Wadworth IPA, 6X, Old
Timer Ⓗ
Popular pub in Old Town
▲ Q ✿ Ⓖ ➐ (until 7.30) ▮

Trowbridge 5H1

10.30–2.30; 6.30–11.30 (11 F, S)

Lamb Inn
Mortimer Street ☎ 5947
Wadworth Devizes Bitter, 6X,
Old Timer Ⓗ
Pleasant lounge, public with
darts and music attracts
younger clientele ✿ Ⓖ ➐ ▮ ≋

Upper Chute 6C4

12–2.30; 7–10.30 (11 F, S & summer)

Cross Keys
3 Miles A342 OS299538
☎ Chute Standen 295
Draught Bass; Wadworth
6X Ⓗ Regular guest beers
300-year-old pub with well in
dining room ▲ Q ▣ ✿ Ⓖ ➐

Upper Minety 15G7

10.30–2.30; 6–10.30 (11 F, S summer)

Old Inn
St. Leonards OS009910
☎ Malmesbury 860292
Closed lunchtime Mon to Fri
Courage BA; Wadworth 6X,
Farmers Glory (summer) Old
Timer (winter) Ⓗ
Pleasant, comfortable village
inn, stone walls and beams.
▲ Q ▣ (summer only)
✿ Ⓖ (Sat & Sun) ➐ ▮ ▲

Urchfont 6A3

11–2.30; 6–10.30 (11 F, S & summer)

Lamb
The Street (off B3098)
Wadworth IPA, 6X Ⓗ, Old
Timer; Taunton Dry Cider Ⓖ
Village local with a skittle
alley ▲ Q ✿ ▮ ▲

Wanborough 6C2

10.30–2.30; 5.30–10.30 (11 F, S & summer)

Black Horse
Callas Hill (old B4507)
Arkell BB, BBB Ⓗ, Kingsdown
Ale Ⓖ
Genuine village local. Garden
with aviary, fine view &
childrens games
✿ Ⓖ (Mon–Sat) ▮ ▲

Warminster 5J2

10–2.30; 6–10.30 (11 summer)

Old Bell Hotel
42 Market Place ☎ 216611
Draught Bass; Wadworth
Devizes Bitter, 6X Ⓗ
Large 14th century coaching
inn in town centre ▣ ▣ Ⓖ ➐ ≋

Westbury 5J1

10–2.30; 6–10.30 (11 F, S & summer)

Crown Hotel
Market Place ☎ 822828
Opens 11 am
Wadworth 6X Ⓗ; Taunton
Cider Ⓖ
Bustling, small town local ✿ ▣ ▮

Ludlow Arms
Market Place ☎ 822612
Marston Pedigree; Smiles Best
Bitter; Wadworth 6X Ⓗ;
Thatchers Cider Ⓖ Regular
guest beers
Popular, well appointed town
local ✿ ▮

Whiteparish 6C5

10.30–2.30; 6–10.30 (11 F, S & summer)

Kings Head
On A27 OS245235 ☎ 287
Whitbread Strong Country
Bitter Ⓗ & Ⓖ
Unspoilt village pub ✿ ▲

Wilton 6B5

10–2.30; 6–10.30 (11 F, S & summer)

Bear
12, West Street (A30)
Hall & Woodhouse Badger
Best Bitter Ⓗ
A popular welcoming local
▲ ✿ ▮

Wroughton 6B2

11–2.30; 6.30–10.30 (11 F, S & summer)

Carters Rest
High Street (A361)
☎ Swindon 812288
Archers Best Bitter, Special;
Eldridge Pope Royal Oak;
Wiltshire Brewery Regency
Best Bitter, Old Devil Ⓗ
Regular guest beers
Popular, well-renovated
Victorian pub ✿ Ⓖ ➐ ▮

Ainderby Steeple
30C5

11–3; 6–11

Wellington Heifer
A684 ℰ Northallerton 5542
Tetley Bitter; Theakston Best Bitter ℍ
Conspicuous free house opposite the church ▲✎♿🎵

Ampleforth
30D6

10.30–2.30; 5.30–10.30 (11 F, S)

White Horse Inn
West End ℰ 378
Tetley Bitter ℍ
Cosy village pub, one main bar and dining room
▲✎🅿♿🎵

Askrigg
29H5

11–3; 7–11

Crown
Main Street (off A684)
ℰ Wensleydale 50298
McEwan 80/-; Younger's Scotch Bitter ℍ
Retains its character after modernisation ▲♿🍴

Atley Hill
30B4

12–3; 6–11

Arden Arms
B1263 OS286024
ℰ North Cowton 678
Theakston Best Bitter, XB, Old Peculier ℍ
Attractive, old unspoilt free house with two traditional rooms. Handy for North York Moors and Yorkshire Dales. Caravans welcome
▲Q✎🅿♿🍴

Austwick
29G6

11–3; 5.30–10.30 (11 F, S & summer)

Game Cock
ℰ Clapham 226
Thwaites Bitter ℍ
Snug little bar with separate dining room ▲Q✎🅿♿🍴

Barkston Ash
30D8

10.30–3; 6–10.30 (11 Thu, F, S)

Boot & Shoe
Off A162
Tetley Mild, Bitter ℍ
Comfortable lounge and busy bar ▲Q🍴

Beadlam
30E5

11–2.30; 6 (7 winter)–10.30 (11 F, S & summer)

White Horse Inn
A170, 3 miles E of Helmsley
OS654846 ℰ Helmsley 71270
Younger's Scotch Bitter, No. 3 ℍ
Roadside pub with lively public bar and extended lounge ▲✎♿🎵 (not Wed) Å

Bedale
30B5

10.30–3; 6–11

Old Black Swan

Market Place (A684) ℰ 22973
Open all day Tue
Theakston Best Bitter, XB, Old Peculier ℍ
Comfortable, friendly market town house. Games area ▲♿🎵

Bellerby
29J5

11–3; 5.30–11

Cross Keys
A6108 ℰ Wensleydale 22256
Marston Burton Bitter, Pedigree ℍ
Very welcoming village inn of character ▲🅿✎🅿🎵🍴

Bentham
29F6

11–3; 5.30–10.30 (11 F, S & summer)

Horse & Farrier
Main Street, High Bentham
(B6480) ℰ 61381
Open till 4 Wed lunchtime
Boddingtons Bitter; Tetley Bitter; Theakston Best Bitter, XB; Younger's No. 3 ℍ
Noisy, open-plan pub. Popular with young people ▲✎♿🎵

Punchbowl
B6480, Low Bentham
ℰ 61344
Mitchells Mild, Bitter ℍ
18th-century pub with rustic character. Angling in nearby river, if resident ▲🅿✎🅿🎵

Biggin
30D8

11–2.30; 7–11

Blacksmiths Arms
Off B1222
ℰ South Milford 682344
John Smiths Bitter; Tetley Bitter; Younger's Scotch Bitter, No. 3 ℍ
Comfortable inn with emphasis on food ▲Q✎♿🎵

Birstwith
30B7

11–3; 5.30 (6 winter)–11

Station Hotel
3 miles N of A59 OS245598
ℰ Harrogate 770254
Tetley Mild, Bitter ℍ
Former railway hotel, now with large lounge and small snug. Extensive array of porcelain and china, and several large dogs!
Q🅿✎♿🎵♿

Boroughbridge
30C7

11–3; 5.30–11

Three Horseshoes Hotel
Bridge Street ℰ 2314
Vaux Samson 🅴
Impressive hotel of real character, family run for 86 years. Distinct 1930s flavour; many interesting features.
Piano ▲Q🅿♿🎵🍴♿Å

Brearton
30C7

12–3; 7–11 (closed all day Mon)

Malt Shovel
Near Knaresborough (off B6165) OS322608

ℰ Harrogate 862929
Theakston Best Bitter, XB, Old Peculier; Wards Sheffield Best Bitter ℍ
16th century village pub, stone walls, oak beams. Friendly and popular. Good home-cooked food
▲Q✎♿🍴♿Å

Burniston
31G5

11–3; 5.30–10.30 (11 F, S & summer)

Oak Wheel
Coastal Road (A165)
ℰ Scarborough 870230
Cameron Lion Bitter ℍ
Low stone pub, busy, comfortable lounge
▲✎🅿♿🎵Å

Try also: Three Jolly Sailors

Cawood
30D8

10.30–3; 6–10.30 (11 Th, F, S)

Bay Horse
Sherburn Road (B1222)
ℰ 555
Tetley Mild, Bitter ℍ
Old cottage, now extended to bar, lounge and snug
▲🅿✎♿🎵

Chapel-le-Dale
29G6

11–3; 5.30–10.30 (11 F, S & summer)

Hill Inn
B6255 ℰ Ingleton 41256
Theakston Best Bitter, XB, Old Peculier ℍ
Isolated pub popular with hikers and cavers
▲✎🅿♿🎵🍴Å

Coxwold
30D6

10.30–3; 6–10.30 (11 F, S & summer)

Fauconberg Arms
ℰ 214
Tetley Bitter; Theakston Best Bitter; Younger's Scotch Bitter ℍ
Beautifully appointed old inn with lounge bar, oak room and restaurant. No food Mon
▲🅿✎♿🎵

Cridling Stubbs
26A3

12–3 (closed Mon, Sat); 7–11

Ancient Shepherd
Off A1, A19, M62(J33, 34)
ℰ Knottingley 83316
Taylor Best Bitter; Tetley Bitter ℍ
Daunting exterior belies welcoming mellow Victorian interior with flagstone floors
Q♿ (Tues–Fri)
🎵(Tues–Sat)♿♿

Dalton
30C6

11–3 (winter closed Mon, Tue) 6 (7 winter)–11

Jolly Farmers of Olden Times
Off A168 (4 miles S of Thirsk)
ℰ Thirsk 577359
Tetley Bitter; Webster

Yorkshire Bitter; Wilsons
Original Bitter Ⓗ Regular
guest beers
Beamed village pub; bar meals
and small dining room; games
room. Barbecues
🏠🍴♿🕐➐🅐

Danby 31E4

11–3; 7–10.30 (11 F, S)

Duke of Wellington
Dale End ✆ Whitby 60351
Cameron Strongarm Ⓗ
Stone-built 18th century pub
with several small rooms. No
food Dec–Jan 🏠🅱♿➐🍷≷

Darley 30B7

11.30–3; 6–11

Wellington Inn
Darley Head (B6451)
✆ Harrogate 780362
Taylor Landlord; Tetley Mild,
Bitter; Younger's Scotch
Bitter Ⓗ
Cosy country pub, delightful
Dales setting 🏠Q🍴♿🅐

Egton 31E4

11.30–3; 6–11

Wheatsheaf
Off A171 ✆ Whitby 85271
McEwan 80/- Ⓗ
Old village pub converted from
farm buildings in 18th
century
🏠🅱♿➐🍷🅐 (caravans)

Faceby 30D4

12–3; 7–11

Sutton Arms
Off A172 ✆ Stokesley 700382
Cameron Strongarm Ⓗ
Quaint, oak-beamed pub in
small village nestling into
Cleveland Hills 🏠🍷🅐

Fearby 30B6

11.30–3; 7–11

Kings Head
2 miles west of Masham, off
A6108 ✆ Ripon 89448
Matthew Brown Lion Mild
(summer); Theakston Best
Bitter, Old Peculier
(summer) Ⓗ
Small welcoming pub known
locally as "The Cross".
🏠Q🍴🅐

Fellbeck 30B7

11.30 (12 winter)–3; 6 (7winter)–11

Half Moon
B6265 OS200662
✆ Harrogate 711568
Taylor Landlord; Theakston
Best Bitter; Younger's Scotch
Bitter Ⓗ
Roadside inn near Brimham
Rocks. Traditional public bar
and large lounge. Pool
🏠🅱♿➐🍷🅐

Ferrensby 30C7

11–3; 5.30–11 (supper licence till 12)

General Tarleton
B6166 ✆ Copgrove 284
Old Mill Bitter, Tetley Bitter;
Theakston Best Bitter, XB, Old
Peculier; Wilsons Original
Bitter Ⓗ Occasional guest
beers
Popular 18th century village
pub. Lively clientele. New
restaurant in old granary,
music and dancing room
above—jazz Mon, rock Thurs
🏠🍴♿➐🍷

Filey 31H6

11–3; 5.30–10.30 (11 F, S & summer)

Grapes Inn
40 Queen Street
✆ Scarborough 514700
John Smith's Bitter Ⓗ
Friendly locals' pub with pool
room 🏠🅱🍷≷

Try also: Foords Hotel

Gargrave 29H7

11–3; 5.30–11 (10.30 winter)

Masons Arms
Marton Road (off A65) ✆ 304
Sat evenings opens 6
Whitbread Castle Eden Ⓗ
Smart, popular pub next to
the parish church. One large
partly-divided room
Q🍴♿➐🅐🍷🅐

Old Swan Inn
High Street (A65) ✆ 232
Whitbread Trophy, Castle
Eden Ⓗ
Coaching inn with Georgian
frontage. Four comfortable
rooms, darts. Traditional
home-cooking, singalong
Saturday night
🏠Q🅱🍴♿➐🍷🅐🅐≷

Grassington 29H7

11–3; 5.30–10.30 (11 F, S & summer)

Forresters Arms
20, Main Street ✆ 752349
Tetley Mild, Bitter Ⓗ
Last pub of character in
Grassington. Unaltered and
much favoured by locals.
Good food 🅱🍴♿🍷🅐

Great Edstone 31E6

11–2.30; 6–10.30 (11 F, S & summer)

Grey Horse Inn
2 miles SSE Kirkbymoorside
(off A170) OS706840
✆ Kirkbymoorside 32251
Matthew Brown, John Peel;
Theakston Best Bitter Ⓗ
Stone and pantile old inn; bar
with extended seating area
and separate restaurant
🏠🍴♿🍷🅐🅐

Harmby 30A5

11–3; 6–11

Pheasant
A684 ✆ Wensleydale 22223
Tetley Bitter Ⓗ
Popular rural inn at gateway
to Wensleydale 🏠🍷🅐

Harrogate 30C7

11–3; 5.30–11

Coach & Horses
16 West Park (A61) ✆ 68371
John Smith's Bitter Ⓗ
Welcoming town pub
overlooking The Stray. Pool
Q♿🍷≷

County
Devonshire Place (across
Stray from A59) ✆ 504024
Tetley Mild, Bitter Ⓗ
Large comfortable lounge,
popular with young. Basic
public bar. Games room, pool
🅱♿

Hales Bars
1 Crescent Road (opposite
Pump Room) ✆ 69861
Evening opens 5.45
Bass; Stones Best Bitter Ⓗ
Fascinating old pub. Gas
lights, mirrors, stuffed birds.
Comfortable and unique
Q♿🅐≷

Squinting Cat Inn
Whinney Lane, Pannal Ash
✆ 65650
Tetley Mild, Bitter Ⓗ
Popular stone-built 18th
century inn of great
character; sun trap patio,
summer barbecues
🏠🅱 (when eating) 🍴
♿ (not Sun)

Hawes 29G5

11–3; 5.30–11 (open all day Tues)

Board Hotel
Market Place (A684) ✆ 223
Marston Burton Bitter,
Pedigree, Owd Rodger Ⓗ
Unpretentious, friendly
market town hotel 🏠🍴🅱♿➐🍷

Hebden 29H7

11 (11.45 winter)–3; 5.30 (7 winter)–10.30 (11 F, S & summer)

Clarendon Hotel
✆ Grassington 752446
Taylor Best Bitter; Tetley Mild,
Bitter Ⓗ
Family run Dales pub. Open-
plan central fire. Separate
dining room. Popular with
walkers 🏠🍴🅱♿➐

Hubberholme 29H6

11–3; 6–10.30 (11 Fri & summer)

George Inn
OS926783 ✆ Kettlewell 223
Younger's Scotch Bitter,
IPA Ⓗ
Ancient hostelry in rural
surroundings of great beauty
and tranquility
🏠Q🅱🍴♿➐🅐

Huby 30D7

11–2.30 (closed winter); 6.30–10.30 (11 F, S & summer)

Queen of Trumps
Main Street
Tetley Mild, Bitter Ⓗ
Classic 2-room village local,

bar abuzz with darts and doms, deservedly popular 🏚♨️🍴

Hunmanby 31H6

11–3; 7–10.30; (11 F, S & summer)

Horseshoe Inn
Stonegate
☎ Scarborough 890419
Younger's Scotch Bitter, No. 3 Ⓗ
Busy village pub with a warm, friendly atmosphere 🏚🕓🍴🍽⇄

Hunton 30B5

11–3; 6–11

New Inn
Near A684 ☎ Bedale 50234
John Smith's Bitter; Tetley Bitter Ⓗ
Excellent village pub; dining room with a difference 🏚🎪♨️🕓🍴🍽Ⓐ

Hutton-le-Hole 31E5

10.30–2.30; 6–10.30 (11 F, S & summer)

Crown Inn
3 miles N Kirkbymoorside (off A170) OS705900
☎ Lastingham 343
Cameron Lion Bitter Ⓗ
Centre of open-plan village. Restaurant, caravan site. Merrills played in extended bar 🏚♨️🕓🍴Ⓐ

Hutton Rudby 30D4

12–3; 6–10.30 (11 F, S)

Kings Head
36 Northside
☎ Stokesley 700342
Cameron Strongarm Ⓗ
Small friendly local at top of village 🏚🎪♨️🍴👶

Ingleton 29F6

11–3; 5.30–10.30 (11 F, S & summer)

Craven Heifer
Main Street ☎ 41427
Thwaites Best Mild, Bitter Ⓗ
Four cottages amalgamated into two bars. Vault a haven for hikers and potholers 🏚🖼🕓🍴🍽

Kirkbymoorside 31E5

11–2.30; 5.30–10.30 (11 F, S & summer) open all day Wed

White Swan
Market Place ☎ 31041
John Smith's Bitter; Tetley Bitter Ⓗ
In centre of market town. Lively open-plan bar; pool room; occasional live music 🏚♨️🖼🕓🍴 (to 7.30) Ⓐ

Knaresborough 30C7

11–3 (4 Wed); 5.30–11

Cross Keys
17 Cheapside
☎ Harrogate 862163
Tetley Bitter Ⓗ

Busy pre-war town local with distinct Tetley touch. In town's historic core, near Castle ruins ♨️🕓🍴Ⓐ⇄

Groves
Market Place
☎ Harrogate 863022
Younger's Scotch Bitter, No. 3 Ⓗ
18th century stuccoed pub overlooking market square 🕓🍴⇄

Wellington Inn
23 Briggate
☎ Harrogate 862582
Samuel Smith OBB Ⓗ
Small two-roomed pub in old part of town. Cellar cut into Castle Rock sandstone 🏚♨️🕓🍴Ⓐ⇄

Lastingham 31E5

11–2.30; 6.30 (7.30 winter)–10.30 (11 F, S & summer)

Blacksmiths Arms
5 miles NE Kirkbymoorside (off A170) OS728905 ☎ 247
Tetley Mild, Bitter; Theakston Best Bitter, Old Peculier Ⓗ
18th century free house opposite church; bar has old cast iron kitchen range, darts in separate snug 🏚♨️🖼🕓🍴 (not winter Thurs)

Linton-in-Craven 29H7

11 (11.30 winter)–3; 6.30–10.30 (11 F, S & summer)

Fountaine Inn
☎ Grassington 210
Taylor Best Bitter, Landlord; Tetley Mild, Bitter; Theakston Best Bitter, XB, Old Peculier (summer) Ⓗ
Close to one of the oldest churches in England. Next to village green and stream. Idyllic setting 🏚🎪♨️🖼🕓🍴

Litton 29H6

11–3; 6–10.30 (11 F, S & summer)

Queens Arms
☎ Arncliffe 208
Younger's Scotch Bitter Ⓗ
17th century traditional Dales pub; much exposed stonework and beams 🏚Q🎪♨️🖼🕓🍴Ⓐ

Long Preston 29G7

11–3; 6 (5.30 Sat)–10.30 (11 F, S & summer)

Maypole Inn
A65 ☎ 219
Whitbread Trophy, Castle Eden Ⓗ
Welcoming village local. Good food in separate dining room 🏚♨️🖼🕓🍴👶⇄

Malton 31F6

11–2.30; 5.30–10.30 (11 F, S & summer) market day extension Tue, Fri, Sat

Blue Ball
14 Newbiggin ☎ 2236

Bass Special Bitter; Tetley Bitter Ⓗ **Occasional guest beers**
Rambling yet cosy old pub, full of character. Occasional live music Q🎪♨️🕓🍴⇄

Crown Hotel (Suddaby's)
12 Wheelgate ☎ 2038
Malton Double Chance Bitter, Pale Ale, Old Bob Ⓗ
Unpretentious bar in tidy hotel with brewery in old stables to rear 🏚🎪♨️🖼🕓⇄

Try also: Cross Keys; Spotted Cow

Marton-cum-Grafton 30C7

12–3 (closed Mon); 7–11

Shoulder of Mutton
3 miles S of Boroughbridge OS416634
☎ Boroughbridge 2246
Webster Yorkshire Bitter Ⓗ
Comfortable family-run pub in village centre. Intimate bar surrounding central servery 🏚♨️🕓🍴

Masham 30B6

11–3 (4 Wed); 6–11

King's Head Hotel
☎ Ripon 89295
Matthew Brown Lion Mild; Theakston Best Bitter, XB, Old Peculier Ⓗ
Friendly, comfortable country hotel. Lively, many local characters. Faces impressive market square 🏚Q🎪♨️🖼🕓🍴👶

Muker 29H5

11–3; 6–11

Farmers Arms
B6270 ☎ Richmond 86297
Theakston XB Ⓗ
Friendly, unspoilt pub in heart of beautiful Swaledale; stone-flagged bar 🏚Q🕓🍴Ⓐ

Newall 30B8

11–3; 6 (7 winter)–11

Spite
B6451 (1 mile N of Otley)
☎ Otley 463063
Webster Green Label Best, Yorkshire Bitter Ⓗ
Up-market stone pub, award-winning ploughman's lunches (booking advisable) 🏚Q♨️🕓 (not Mon, Sun)

Newton-on-Rawcliffe 31F5

10.30–2.30; 5.30–10.30 (11 F, S)

White Swan Hotel
OS813905 ☎ Pickering 72505
Tetley Bitter; Theakston Best Bitter Ⓗ
Grade II building overlooking village green. Cosy interior, book for food 🏚Q♨️🖼🕓🍴

Oswaldkirk 30D6

10.30–2.30; 6.30–10.30 (11 F, S)

Malt Shovel
(off B1363) ℰ Ampleforth 461
Samuel Smith OBB Ⓗ
Beautifully restored interior,
with interesting 17th century
staircase, warm and
welcoming, shove ha'penny
🏠🍴🅿♿🍺 (not Mon) 🍷

Pickhill 30C6

10.30–2.30; 5.30–11

Nags Head
Off A1 ℰ Thirsk 567391
**Tetley Bitter; Theakston Best
Bitter, XB; Younger's Scotch
Bitter** Ⓗ
Locals' public bar; lounge;
restaurant caters to a very
high standard 🏠♿🅿🍺🍷🍴

Port Mulgrave 31F4

10.30 (11.30 winter)–3; 6.30–11

Ship
Off A174 ℰ Whitby 840303
**Younger's Best Scotch,
No. 3** Ⓗ
Traditional stone-built pub
which served the ironstone
industry 🏠🅿♿🍺🍷🏕

Try also: **Badger Hounds**
Hinderwell (Tetley)

Rainton 30C6

11.30–2.30; 6.30–11

Bay Horse Inn
1 mile off A1 ℰ Thirsk 577307
**John Smith's Bitter, Tetley
Bitter, Younger's No. 3** Ⓗ
Small stone pub near village
green. Comfortable and
friendly, collections of
brassware and banknotes.
Pool room 🏠♿♿🍺

Reeth 29J5

11–3; 6–11

Buck
B6270 ℰ Richmond 84210
Webster Yorkshire Bitter Ⓗ
Imposing building overlooking
village green 🏠♿🅿♿🍺

Richmond 30B4

11–3; 6–11

Holly Hill
Sleagill OS172003 ℰ 2192
Theakston Best Bitter, XB Ⓗ
Occasional guest beers
Comfortable oak-beamed
lounge, pleasant bar ♿♿🍺🍷

Ripon 30C6

11–3 (4 Thu); 5.30–11

Black Bull Hotel
Old Market Place ℰ 2755
**Theakston Best Bitter, XB, Old
Peculier** Ⓗ
Historic coaching inn with
16th and 18th century
features. Large rambling bar,
popular with the young and
quieter lounge 🅿♿ (not Sun)

Lamb & Flag
High Skellgate ℰ 2895
Evening opens 6
**Darley Thorne Best Bitter;
Lorimer's Best Scotch; Vaux
Samson** Ⓗ
Old coaching house on steep
hill leading to Market Place.
Pool
🏠🅿♿♿ (Thu, Sat, Sun) 🍷

Turk's Head
Low Skellgate (A61) ℰ 4876
**Darley Thorne Best Bitter;
Lorimer's Best Scotch; Vaux
Samson** Ⓗ
Very old and friendly terraced
pub. Small snug and games
room, pool ♿

Wheatsheaf
Harrogate Road (A61) 1 mile
S of city centre ℰ Ripon 2410
Evening opens 6
**Darley Thorne Best Bitter;
Vaux Samson** Ⓗ
Intriguing old inn with very
long frontage but narrow
single span depth. Sunken
garden with peacocks
🏠Q🅿♿♿

Robin Hood's 31G4
Bay

10.30 (11.30 winter)–3; 6–11

Laurel
B1447 ℰ Whitby 880400
**Cameron Lion Bitter,
Strongarm; Tetley Bitter** Ⓗ
Occasional guest beers
Small, friendly corner local in
picturesque cliffside village
🅿♿♿🍷🏕

Rosedale 31E5
Abbey

11.30–2.30; 6.30–10.30 (11 F, S & summer)

Milburn Arms Hotel
Haygate Lane OS725960
ℰ Lastingham 312
**Cameron Lion Bitter; Tetley
Mild; Theakston Best Bitter,
XB; Younger's Scotch Bitter** Ⓗ
Welcoming old inn near
centre of village. Large bar
lounge. Family room.
Occasional live music
🏠🅿♿♿🍷🏕

Rufforth 30D8

11–3; 6–10.30 (11 F, S)

Tankard
Main Street ℰ 621
Samuel Smith OBB Ⓗ
Two 30's style rooms with
darts following
🏠♿♿♿ (not Mon)
🍷 (summer) 🍷🏕

Saxton 30D8

10.30–3; 6–10.30 (11 Th, F & S)

Greyhound
Main Street
Samuel Smith OBB Ⓗ
Unspoilt 3-roomed village
local 🏠Q♿

Scarborough 31G5

11–3; 5.30–10.30 (11 F, S & summer)

Cask
Cambridge Terrace, South Cliff
ℰ 360198
**Tetley Mild Bitter; Younger's
Scotch Bitter, IPA, No. 3** Ⓗ
Occasional guest beers
Popular pub offering variety of
live music
🅿♿Ⓗ (flatlets) ♿🍷🚆

Criterion Hotel
49 Castle Road ℰ 365626
Tetley Mild, Bitter Ⓗ
Bustling one-roomer with
much naval bric-a-brac 🚆

Crown Tavern
Scalby Road A170/A171
ℰ 363926
**Cameron Lion Bitter,
Strongarm** Ⓗ
Popular outskirts pub with
busy bar 🏠♿🍷🚆

Hole in the Wall
Vernon Road ℰ 373746
Opens 11.30 & 7
**Theakston Best Bitter, XB, Old
Peculier** Ⓗ Regular guest beers
Popular gem. Regular live
music and unusual pub games
♿🍷🚆

Leeds Arms
St Mary's Street ℰ 361699
Opens 11.30 & 7
Bass Ⓗ
Old town gem, nautical
atmosphere predominates 🏠

Plough Hotel
St Thomas Street ℰ 373621
**Cameron Lion Bitter,
Strongarm** Ⓗ
Busy town centre pub ♿🚆

Shakespeare Inn
St Helen's Square ℰ 363203
**Cameron Lion Bitter,
Strongarm** Ⓗ
Games oriented local next to
the old market 🍷🚆

Trafalgar Hotel
Trafalgar Street West
ℰ 372054
**Cameron Lion Bitter,
Strongarm** Ⓗ
Tidy pub just off town centre
with popular games oriented
bar 🍷🚆

Seamer 30D4

12–3 (closed Mon–Fri); 7–10.30 (11 F, S &
summer)

King's Head
Hilton Road (near Stokesley)
ℰ Middlesbrough 710397
**McEwan 80/-; Newcastle
Cask Exhibition; Younger
Scotch Bitter, No. 3** Ⓗ
Charming village free house
with long and fascinating
history 🏠🅿♿

Selby 30E9

10.30–3 (4.30 Mon); 6–10.30 (11 F, S)

New Inn
Gowthorpe (A19) ℰ 703429
Tetley Mild, Bitter Ⓗ
Busy town pub; wood
panelling, screens and leaded
lights ❢≷

Sinnington   31E5

11.30–2.30; 6 (7.30 winter)–10.30 (11 F, S & summer)

Fox & Hounds
3 miles E Kirkbymoorside (off
A170) OS744855
ℰ Kirkbymoorside 31577
Cameron Lion Bitter Ⓗ
Cosy two-room inn near
centre of unspoilt village. Pool
room. No food winter
🏚♨🖾ⓒ🍽❢

Skipton   29H8

11.3; 5.30–10.30 (11 F, S & summer)

Castle
2 Mill Bridge ℰ 2598
Evening opens 7
Tetley Mild, Bitter Ⓗ
Friendly town pub, mild is the
biggest seller; near Skipton
Castle ♨

Royal Shepherd
Canal Street ℰ 3178
**Chesters Best Bitter; Hartleys
XB; Whitbread Trophy, Castle
Eden** Ⓗ
Warm and welcoming, ale
quaffers' utopia. Much
Skipton bric-a-brac. Has a
happy cellar! 🏚♨ⓒ❢≷

Try also: Craven Hotel
(Thwaites)

Skipwith   30E8

10.30–3; 6–10.30 (11 F, S)

Hare & Hounds
The Green (off A163)
ℰ Bubwith 455
**Bass Light XXXXX; Stones
Best Bitter** Ⓗ
Cosy village local facing duck
pond. Pool and dominoes
🏚♨ⓒ❢

Sleights   31F4

11.30–3 (12–2.30 winter); 7–11

Salmon Leap
6, Coach Road
ℰ Whitby 810233
Cameron Lion Bitter Ⓗ,
Strongarm Ⓔ
Detached stone inn of some
character in scenic position
overlooking River Esk
♨🖾ⓒ❢❢♿Å≷

Snainton   31F6

11–3; 5.30–10.30 (11 F, S & summer)

Peacock Hotel
66 High Street (A170)
ℰ Scarborough 85257
**Cameron Lion Bitter,
Strongarm** Ⓗ
Village centre local. Recently
expanded with separate
garden and pool room
🏚🖾♨🖾ⓒ❢Å

South   30C5
Otterington

11–3 (closed Mon); 6–11

**Otterington
Shorthorn**
A167 ℰ Northallerton 3816
**Tetley Bitter; Younger's
Scotch Bitter** Ⓗ
Well-appointed rural inn.
Lounge bar; games room 🏚ⓒ❢

Staintondale   31G5

11–3; 5.30–10.30 (11 F, S & summer)

Shepherd's Arms
OS993981
ℰ Scarborough 870257
Cameron Lion Bitter Ⓗ
Solid country pub with superb
sea views 🏚Q🖾♨🖾ⓒ❢❢

Try also: Falcon Inn

Stapleton   30B4

11–3; 6–11

Bridge
ℰ Darlington 50106
**Lorimer Best Scotch; Vaux
Samson** Ⓗ
Substantial mock-timbered
inn with high-class restaurant
🏚Q♨ⓒ🍽 (Tues–Sat)

Starbotton   29H6

11.30–3; 6 (7 winter)–10.30 (11 F, summer)

Fox & Hounds
ℰ Kettlewell 269
**Theakston Best Bitter, XB, Old
Peculier; Younger's Scotch
Bitter** Ⓗ
Typical Dales pub, tastefully
enlarged 🏚Q🖾♨ⓒ❢Å

Summerbridge   30B7

11.45–3; 6–11

Flying Dutchman
B6165 ℰ Harrogate 780321
Samuel Smith OBB Ⓗ
Nidderdale village inn named
after racehorse. Brimham
Rocks nearby. Fishing tickets
Q♨🖾ⓒ❢❢Å

Sutton-in-   29H8
Craven

11–3; 5.30–10.30 (11 F, S & summer)

Kings Arms
High Street ℰ Crosshills 32332
Whitbread Castle Eden Ⓗ
Small friendly village local
🏚Q♨

Tadcaster   30D8

10.30–3; 5.30–11

Angel & White Horse
Bridge Street ℰ 835470
Sat evening opens 7
Samuel Smith OBB Ⓗ
Brewery tap in large Georgian
coaching inn with fine wood
panelling. View over brewery
yard to rear with stables and
shire horses ⓒ

Howden Arms
40, High Street ℰ 833804
Samuel Smith OBB Ⓗ
Compact and very busy one-
room pub. Children's play
facilities at rear ♨ⓒ❢

Thirsk   30C5

10.30–2.30; 6–11

Olde Three Tuns
15 Finkle Street (off Market
Square) ℰ 23291
Market day extension Monday
Tetley Bitter Ⓗ
Sympathetic restoration of a
very old building 🏚❢

Thornton-in-   29F6
Lonsdale

11–3; 5.30–10.30 (11 F, S & summer)

Marton Arms
ℰ Ingleton 41281
**Theakston Best Bitter, XB, Old
Peculier; Younger's Scotch
Bitter** Ⓗ
Whitewashed inn dated 1679
but reputedly older. Rambling
interior
🏚🖾♨ (with play area) 🖾ⓒ❢❢

Thornton-le-   30C5
Beans

11–2.30 (closed Tue); 6–11

Crosby
Near A168
ℰ Northallerton 2776
**Webster Yorkshire Bitter;
Wilsons Original Bitter** Ⓗ
Large, well-appointed village
pub 🏚🖾ⓒ❢Å

Tunstall   30B5

12–3 (closed Mon/Tue); 7–11

Bay Horse
Near A1 ℰ Richmond 818564
Samuel Smith OBB Ⓗ
17th century warm friendly
local. Quoits 🏚Q🖾♨🖾ⓒ❢Å

Ugthorpe   31F4

10.30–3; 6.30–11

Black Bull
Main Street (off A171)
ℰ Whitby 840286
**Cameron Strongarm; Tetley
Bitter; Theakston Best Bitter,
Old Peculier** Ⓗ Occasional
guest beers
Excellent village pub set in
row of cottages 🏚🖾♨ⓒ❢Å

Try also: Ellerby Hotel, Ellerby
(Cameron)

Welburn   31E6

10.30–2.30; 5–10.30

Crown & Cushion
Off A64
ℰ Whitwell-o-t-Hill 304
**Cameron Lion Bitter,
Strongarm** Ⓗ
Handsome popular old inn
with busy restaurant
🏚🖾♨🖾ⓒ❢Å

West Heslerton 31F6

10.30–2.30; 5.30–10.30 (11 F, S & summer)

Dawnay Arms

Church Street (off A64) 203

Cameron Lion Bitter; Younger's No. 3 [H]

Multi-roomed village local; also caters for passing trade

Whitby 31F4

10.30–3; 6–11

Fleece

Church Street 603649

Opens 11

Tetley Bitter [H]

1930's harbourside pub; recently renovated

Little Angel

Flowergate 602514

Tetley Bitter [H]

Street corner pub whose fabric contains much of historical interest

(not winter Sun)

Plough

Baxtergate 602388

Opens 11 & 7

Samuel Smith OBB, [H] & [E]

Busy town centre pub with several varied rooms

Wellington

Wellington Road 602899

Evening opens 6.30

Tetley Bitter [H]

Recently refurbished pub of great character, popular with both locals and visitors

Try also: Elsinore (Cameron); **Stakesby Arms** (Tetley)

Whixley 30C7

11–3; 5.30–11 (supper licence 12)

Anchor Inn

Green Hammerton 30432

John Smith's Bitter; Tetley Bitter [H]

Real village pub, revitalised and impressively renovated. Traditional furniture; beams and quarry tiles. Rustic brickwork is the main feature

Q

Wighill 30D8

12–2.45; 6–10.30 (11 F, S)

White Swan

Main Street

Stones Best Bitter; Theakston Best Bitter, XB, Old Peculier [H]

Old country local, friendly and popular, with many rooms of real character Q

Wombleton 30E6

11–2.30; 6 (7 winter)–10.30 (11 F, S & summer)

Plough Inn

3 miles SW Kirkbymoorside (off A170) OS669840

Kirkbymoorside 31356

Cameron Lion Bitter [H]

Regular guest beers

Friendly bar lounge with plush "best end". Popular with users of nearby windsports centre. No food Tues

York 30D8

11–3; 5.30–11

Bay Horse

Monkgate

Bass Light XXXXX; Stones Best Bitter [H]

Large city centre pub, with open-plan interior

Bootham Tavern

Bootham (A19) 31093

Tetley Bitter [H]

Compact and very busy 2-room local

Brown Cow

36, Hope Street 34010

Evening opens 6

Taylor Best Bitter, Landlord, Ram Tam [H]

Small pleasant local in estate. Games room with pool. Jukebox throughout

Crystal Palace

66, Holgate Road 25305

Samuel Smith OBB [H]

Comfortable pleasant lounge and lounge bar

Golden Ball

Cromwell Road, Bishophill

52211

Opens 11.45 & 7

John Smith's Bitter [H]

Street corner local with superb external glazed bricks and etched windows

John Bull

Layerthorpe 21593

Darley Thorne Best Bitter; Franklins Bitter; Malton Double Chance Bitter; Taylor Best Bitter, Landlord; Bulmer Cider [H] **Regular guest beers**

Very busy 2-room local, much 1930's memorabilia in front room. Regular live music

Red Lion

Merchantgate

John Smith's Bitter [H]

Tudor exterior. Smart lounge with public bar area. Darts (24 hrs notice)

Minster Inn

Marygate

Bass Light XXXXX; Bass; Stones Best Bitter [H]

Traditional 3-room layout. Close to ruins of St Marys Abbey

Spread Eagle

98, Walmgate 35868

Malton Double Chance Bitter; Marston Pedigree; Taylor Best Bitter, Landlord, Ram Tam; Bulmer Cider [H] **Regular guest beers**

Popular busy pub with several drinking areas

Swan

Bishopgate Street 55746

Tetley Bitter [H]

Traditional street-corner local. Dominoes

Wellington Inn

47, Alma Terrace (off A19)

Evening opens 6.30

Samuel Smith OBB [H]

Popular quiet pub in back street. Recently refurbished, retaining 3 separate rooms. Bar Billiards Q

York Arms

26, High Petergate 24508

Closes 10.30 F, S evening

Samuel Smith OBB [H]

3 comfortable lounges in shadow of York Minster

"LAGER? YES SIR! WHICH ONE?"
Krol
HEINKEL
Vilesburg

Arksey 26B4

11–3; 7–11

Plough
2 High Street
✆ Doncaster 874465
John Smith's Bitter ⊞
Locals pub hidden away
behind village church
✦ ᕱ ➔ (Fri-Sat)

Balby 26B4

11–3; 6–11

Spinney
The Spinney, Grenville Estate
(off A630)
Home Bitter ⒠
Large and busy post war pub;
games oriented bar ✦ ❶ ᕫ

Barnsley 23H2

11–3; 6–11

Manx
Sheffield Road
**Stones Best Bitter; Tetley
Bitter** ⊞
Deservedly popular town
centre pub ᕱ �

Pindar Oaks
280, Doncaster Road (A635,
1 mile from town centre)
✆ 281326
Opens 10.30
John Smith's Bitter ⊞
Comfortable local, regular
Wed quiz. Piranha fish in
lounge ᕱ ❶

Wheatsheaf
Dodworth Road, Townend
(A628)
Opens 12 & 7
Tetley Bitter ⊞
One of last traditional pubs in
town centre. ❶ �

Blackburn 23J3

10.30–3; 6–10.30 (11 F, S)

Crown
Blackburn Road (near M1 Jct
34)
Tetley Bitter ⊞
A real pub in every way.
Traditional pub games;
aviary, fishpond and childrens
games in garden
✦ ᕱ

Blacker Hill 23H2

10.30–3; 6–11

Royal Albert
Barnsley Road (off B6096)
✆ Barnsley 742193
**Ward Sheffield Best
Bitter** ⊞ & ⒠
Cosy, wood panelled snug
🎲 (upstairs) ᕱ ➔ ❶

Bolsterstone 23H3

11.30–3; 5.30–10.30 (11 F, S)

Castle
Stones Best Bitter ⒠
Popular local in picturesque
hilltop village. L-shaped
lounge, busy tap room
✦ ᕱ ❶ ᕫ

Brinsworth 23J3

10.30–3; 6–10.30 (11 F, S)

Waverley
Brinsworth Road, Catcliffe
✆ Rotherham 60906
**Stones Best Bitter; Webster
Yorkshire Bitter** ⊞
Newly built, enterprising free
house with excellent childrens
facilities. Ask for traditional
🎲 ✦ ᕱ (not Sat) ➔ ❶ ᕯ

Brookhouse 26B5

10.30–3; 6–10.30 (11 F, S)

Travellers
Stones Best Bitter ⒠
Modern pub in sleepy village.
Motorists' mecca ✦ ❶

Cadeby 26A4

10.30–3; 6–10.30 (11 F, S)

Cadeby Inn
Main Street
✆ Rotherham 864009
**Samuel Smith OBB; Tetley
Bitter** ⊞ Occasional guest
beers
Ex-farmhouse in quiet village.
Retains character and
atmosphere 🏚 Q ✦ ᕱ ➔ ❶

Chapeltown 23H3

11–3; 5.30–10.30 (11 F, S)

Thorncliffe
Warren Lane (off A6135)
Wards Sheffield Best Bitter ⒠
Comfortable local, snooker
room, collection of pottery
cows Q ✦

Crow Edge 23G2

11–3; 6–11

Victoria
Huddersfield Road (A616)
Tetley Bitter; Younger IPA ⊞
Welcoming moorland pub
with comfortable lounge and
a corridor bar

Darfield 23J2

12–3; 7–11

Cross Keys
Church Street (off A630)
Tetley Bitter ⊞ & ⒠
Excellent village pub near to
church; burial place of
Ebeneezer Eliot—the Corn
Law Rhymer ✦ ❶

Try also: **Bridge Inn** (John
Smith's)

Deepcar 23H3

11–3; 5.30–10.30 (11 F, S)

Royal Oak
Manchester Road (A616)
✆ Sheffield 882208
Tetley Mild, Bitter ⊞
Busy traditional village local
with central bar and two
distinct drinking areas.
Separate pool room ✦ ᕱ ➔

Doncaster 26B4

10.30–3; 6–11

**Corporation Brewery
Taps**

Cleveland Street ✆ 63715
Evenings opens 6.30 (7
winter)
Samuel Smith OBB ⊞
Friendly local, lively landlord.
Large concert room with
clubland atmosphere
ᕱ ❶ ᕫ �

Hallcross
Hallgate ✆ 27371
Opens 11
**Stocks Best Bitter, Select, Old
Horizontal; Bulmers Cider** ⊞
Busy home-brew house, fine
mirrors and woodwork
✦ ᕱ ᕫ �

Masons Arms
Market Place
Opens 11 closes 4 pm Tue
lunch
Tetley Bitter ⊞
200 year old former home-
brew house. Many photos of
old Donny Q ✦ ❶

Three Horseshoes
Town End A19/A638 1 mile
north of town centre ✆ 23571
Wards Sheffield Best Bitter ⒠
Traditional pub by River Don;
functions room ✦ 🎲 ᕱ ❶ ᕫ

St Leger Tavern
8 Silver Street ✆ 65446
Evenings opens 6.30
Shipstone Bitter ⊞
Compact racing-oriented town
centre pub 🎲 ❶ ᕫ �

Vine
Kelham Street, Balby Bridge
(A18/A630) 1 mile from
centre
Opens 11
Darley Thorne Best Bitter ⊞
Former street corner local,
survivor of planners' blitz ❶

Try also: **Old Castle** (Home)
White Swan (Wards)

Edenthorpe 26B4

10.30–3; 6–11

Ridge Wood
Thorne Road (A18)
Samuel Smith OBB ⊞
Popular post war-pub. Garden
always full in summer 🏚 ✦ ᕱ ❶

Elsecar 23H2

11.30–3; 7–11

Market
Wentworth Road (off B6097)
Stones Best Bitter ⊞ & ⒠
Multi-room local in model
mining village built by Earl
Fitzwilliam Q ❶ �

Finningley 26C4

10.30–3; 6–11

Harvey Arms
Finningley (off A614)
✆ Doncaster 770200
Bass ⊞
Unspoilt tap room, large busy
lounge; vegetarian menu
🏚 ✦ ᕱ ➔ ❶ ᕫ ᕯ

Greenhill 23H4

12–3; 5.30–10.30 (11 F, S)

White Hart
27 Greenhill Main Road
Tetley Bitter H
2-room friendly local. Large,
comfortable lounge on two
levels. Busy tap room ℗ⓖ¶☕

Try also: White Swan
(Whitbread)

Grenoside 23H3

11–3; 5.30–10.30 (11 F, S)

Cow & Calf
88 Skew Hill Lane (off A61)
Samuel Smith OBB E
Converted 17th century farm
buildings with four cosy
drinking areas. Tuck shop for
children in summer. Farm
animals Q❀℗ⓖ¶

Hatfield 26C4
Woodhouse

10.30–3; 6–11

Green Tree
Bearswood Green (A18/A614)
☎ Doncaster 840305
Darley Dark, Thorne Best
Bitter H
Very welcoming 17th century
posting house; emphasis on
food ♨℗ⓖ✦¶

**Robin Hood & Little
John**
Main Street (A614)
Stones Best Bitter E
Friendly, comfortable village
local. Very busy at weekends
℗ⓖ¶

Higham 23H2

11–3; 6–11

Hermit
Higham Common Road (off
A628)
Tetley Bitter H
Lively local ℗ⓖ

High Green 23H3

11.30–3; 7–10.30 (11 F, S)

Olde Cart & Horses
2 Wortley Road
Tetley Bitter H
Cosy village local with three
rooms and central bar.
Brassware collection ℗¶

Ingbirchworth 23H2

11–3; 6–11

Fountain Inn
Wellthorpe Lane (off A629)
☎ Barnsley 763125
Tetley Mild, Bitter H
Ancient farmhouse now a
Tetley Family Inn known
locally as the Rag & Louse
♨❀℗ⓖ✦¶

Kilnhurst 26A4

11–3; 6–10.30 (11 F, S)

Terrace

Hooton Road (B6090)
Stones Best Bitter E
Friendly miners' local near
river ♨℗ⓖ

Kiveton Park 26A5

10.30–3; 6–10.30 (11 F, S)

Forge
Wales Road (B6059)
Home Bitter E
Modern local in a mining
village. Pool table in front.
Games room and large lounge
at rear ¶⇄

Low Barugh 23H2

11.30–3; 6–11

Millers Inn
Dearnehall Road (B6428)
☎ Barnsley 382888
Stones Best Bitter; Tetley
Bitter H
Comfortable two-bar riverside
pub. No food Sunday ℗ⓖ✦¶

Maltby 26B5

11.30–3; 6–10.30 (11 F, S)

Toll Bar
Rotherham Road (A631)
Stones Best Bitter E
Popular and friendly street-
corner local with lively public
bar ¶

Millhouse 23G2
Green

11–3; 6–11

Blacksmiths Arms
Manchester Road (A628)
☎ Barnsley 762211
Stones Best Bitter H
Busy village pub. Taproom
and comfortable lounge ¶

Mosborough 23J4

11–3; 5.30–10.30 (11 F, S)

British Oak
High Street (A616)
Mosborough Moor
☎ Sheffield 486442
Shipstone Bitter E
Comfortable lounge and
traditional games room.
Locals pub despite main road
site ℗¶

Try also: Queen (Wards)

Newington 26B4

11–3; 6–11

Ship
Misson Road (off A614)
Home Bitter E
Comfortable and popular
country pub close to the River
Idle ¶

Oughtibridge 23H3

11–3; 5.30–10.30 (11 F, S)

Travellers Rest
Langsett Road South (A616)
☎ 2221
Samuel Smith OBB H
3-room local. Friendly service
with pool and darts ⓖ✦¶

Oxspring 23H2

12–3; 7–11

Travellers
Four Lane Ends (A629)
Wards Sheffield Best Bitter E
Windswept pub overlooking
moors ♨Q

Penistone 23H2

11–3; 6–11

Cubley Hall
Mortimer Road, Cubley
Darley Thorne Best Bitter;
Tetley Mild, Bitter H
Former country house. Fine
mosaic floors and plasterwork
❀℗ⓖ✦

Rotherham 23J3

10.30–3; 6–10.30 (11 F, S)

Bridge
Greasbrough Road ☎ 363683
Stones Best Bitter E
Many-roomed pub next to the
famous chapel on the bridge.
Old photos and maps of the
town ⓖ¶

Butchers Arms
Midland Road (A629)
Tetley Bitter H
Small and cosy 2-room pub
near football ground. Pie and
peas in supper room ⓖ⇄

Clifton
105 Clifton Lane ☎ 372497
Stones Best Bitter E
2-room pub near Clifton Park;
drawings of old Rotherham ¶

Turners Arms
53 Psalters Lane (off A6109)
Wards Sheffield Best Bitter E
Pleasant 3-room local with
photos of old Rotherham.
Known as the "Green Bricks"
℗ⓖ¶⇄

Woodman
115 Midland Road (off A629)
Stones Best Bitter H
Solid, old but friendly pub
with several games teams.
Snooker table upstairs
℗ⓖ (Mon–Fri) ¶⇄

Sheffield: 23H3
Central

11–3; 5.30–10.30 (11 F, S)

Globe
Howard Street ☎ 23688
Evenings opens 6
Stones Best Bitter E
Popular with students and
locals, 3 rooms of different
character, opposite
Polytechnic Q¶⇄

Grapes
80/82 Trippett Lane ☎ 20230
Evenings opens 7
Tetley Bitter H
A "Heritage pub" catering for
all tastes. Victorian tiles in
bar. Regular live music. Quiz
night Tuesdays ℗ⓖ¶☕

Lord Nelson
166/8, Arundel Street
✆ 22650
Sat evening opens 7.30
Stones Best Bitter Ⓗ
Small basic 2-roomed local
near town centre Ⓖ🍴≷

Manchester
108 Nursery Street ✆ 22420
Sat evenings opens 6.30
Wards Sheffield Best Bitter Ⓔ
Friendly 3-room local. Pool
table and active games teams
Ⓖ🍴&≷

Matilda Tavern
100 Matilda Street ✆ 20733
Opens 11.30 & 7
Wards Sheffield Best Bitter Ⓔ
Warm comfortable 2-room
local, popular with all ages.
History of Queen Matilda
written up outside the pub on
the green tiles 🍴&≷

Moseley's Arms
81/83 West Bar ✆ 21591
Stones Best Bitter Ⓔ
Friendly many-roomed town
centre local. Snooker in
upstairs room 🍴&

Red Deer
18 Pitt Street (off West Street)
Tetley Mild, Bitter Ⓗ
Small one-room town centre
pub. Traditional and friendly.
Quiz night Sundays. Selection
of prints and paintings usually
on sale 🏛🌿Ⓖ

Red House
168 Solly Street ✆ 27926
Wards Sheffield Best Bitter Ⓗ
Friendly traditional local, two
comfortable rooms, one with
dartboard and central bar
area. Folk music some nights
QⒼ

Sportsman
24 Cambridge Street ✆ 26957
Tetley Bitter Ⓔ
Smart city centre pub with a
warm welcome for all QⒼ🍷

Washington
79 Fitzwilliam Street
✆ 754937
**Tetley Mild, Falstaff Best,
Bitter** Ⓗ
Friendly two-room local with
teapot collection QⒼ🍴

Sheffield: East

Cocked Hat
75 Worksop Road, Attercliffe
**Marston Burton Bitter;
Pedigree** Ⓗ
In the Attercliffe
environmental corridor,
attractively renovated in
Victorian style. Excellent food
🌿Ⓖ (Mon-Fri)

Cross Keys
400 Handsworth Road (A57),
Handsworth
Opens 11.30
Stones Best Bitter Ⓔ

Popular pub in corner of
parish church graveyard.
Superb example of an unspoilt
warm and friendly village
local 🏛🍴

Excelsior Inn
1 Carbrook Street
Wards Sheffield Best Bitter Ⓔ
Busy local with organ music
at weekends. Rear garden a
recent and welcome addition
🌿Ⓖ (Mon-Fri)

Sheffield: North

Golden Perch
2/4 Earsham Street,
Burngreave
**Darley Thorne Best Bitter;
Marston Mercian Mild,
Pedigree; Taylor Landlord;
Vaux Samson; Wards Sheffield
Best Bitter** Ⓗ
Spartan local with bar
billiards in lounge and
"no smoking" taproom
🏛🌿🍴&

Meadow
110 Meadow Street ✆ 25491
Wards Sheffield Best Bitter Ⓔ
Old established pub serving
local community. Fairly large
lounge with games area off
and cosy snug. Ⓖ🍴&

Pitsmoor Hotel
448 Pitsmoor Road ✆ 23962
Sat evening opens 6.45
Tetley Bitter Ⓗ
Cosy 2-room traditional local.
Owl collection in lounge 🌿🍴

Sheffield Arms
107 Upwell Street,
Grimesthorpe
Stones Best Bitter Ⓔ
Popular 2-room local with
busy tap room. Snooker table
🍴

Sheffield: South

Byron House
16 Nether Edge Road (off
A621)
Opens 11.30
Bass; Stones Best Bitter Ⓔ
Busy, friendly 2-room
suburban local. Large
comfortable lounge,
traditional taproom Q🌿🍴

Horse & Groom
426, Blackstock Road
Gleadless Valley ✆ 397283
Opens 12 & 7
Tetley Bitter Ⓗ
Mid-sixties estate pub. Open-
plan lounge and bar. Local
clientele. Pool table 🌿Ⓖ🍴&

Nailmakers Arms
Backmoor Road, Norton
✆ 550092
Opens 11.30
**Younger Scotch Bitter,
No. 3** Ⓗ
Possibly Sheffield's oldest pub
dating back to 1646. Stone

fronted and modern inside
with darts and pool area
🌿Ⓖ🍴&

Sheldon Hotel
27 Hill Street ✆ 21707
Opens 11.30 & 7
Stones Best Bitter Ⓗ
Traditional local near Bramall
Lane football ground. Large
public bar, quiet lounge 🌿🍴&

Sheffield: West

Banner Cross Hotel
971 Ecclesall Road (A625)
✆ 661479
Opens 11.30
Tetley Bitter Ⓗ
Busy, 2-room friendly pub;
separate snooker room and
bar upstairs
🌿Ⓖ🍷 (until 7 pm) 🍴&

Crown Inn
2 Walkley Bank Road,
Walkley ✆ 335523
Tetley Bitter Ⓗ
Tap room with snooker table,
lounge decorated with nautical
theme. Friendly pub
🌿Ⓖ🍷 (5.30–7.30) 🍴&

Devonshire Arms
118 Ecclesall Road (A625)
Wards Sheffield Best Bitter Ⓔ
Quiet locals pub opposite
Wards Brewery. Friendly
welcome. Green tiled exterior,
bay windows with etched
glass Ⓖ&

Firwood Cottage
279 Whitehouse Lane,
Walkley
Opens 12 & 6
Tetley Bitter Ⓗ
Pleasant local. Comfortable
and well furnished. Well
worth finding 🌿Ⓖ🍴&

Noah's Ark
94 Crookes ✆ 663300
**Whitbread Trophy, Castle
Eden Ale** Ⓗ
Excellent local, popular with
all ages 🌿Ⓖ🍷 (5.30–7) 🍴

Pomona
255 Ecclesall Road (A625)
Home Bitter Ⓔ
Modern pub with
conservatory. Busy tap room,
games playing a large part.
Plush and warm lounge, large
local following 📺🌿Ⓖ🍴&

Star & Garter
82 Winter Street ✆ 20694
Tetley Bitter Ⓗ
2-room local close to
University. Popular with all
ages. Snooker in taproom Ⓖ🍴

Sprotborough 26B4

11–3; 6–11

Ivanhoe
Melton Road
✆ Doncaster 853130
Samuel Smith OBB Ⓗ & Ⓔ
Large pub near village cricket

pitch and play area. Snooker table ✿⌒❶ (Thu-Sun) 🕭

Stainborough 23H2

11.30–3; 7–11

Strafford Arms
Park Drive
John Smith's Bitter Ⓗ
Country pub of character.
Traditional Yorkshire range in
open bar ♨✿⌒

Stainforth 26B3

11–3; 6.30–10.30 (11 F, S)

Harvester
Thorne Road
☎ Doncaster 841660
John Smith's Bitter Ⓗ
Pleasant, comfortable well-
established estate pub; in
typical John Smith's style.
Games in bar
⌒ (not Sun) ❶🕭❖⇌

Try also: Peacock (Sam Smith)

Swinton 26A4

11.20–3; 6.20–10.30 (11 F, S)

Sportsmans
149 Fitzwilliam Street
☎ Rotherham 582537
Stones Best Bitter Ⓔ
Popular sports-oriented local
✿⌒❶🕭❖

Thorne 26C3

10.30–3; 6–11

Thornensians R.U.F.C.
Church Balk (off A614)
12–2 Fri; 7 (4 Sat in rugby
season)–11
Darley Thorne Best Bitter Ⓔ
Non-affiliated rugby club.
Large club room and small
lounge. Snooker and pool

Thorne High Levels 26C3

10.30–3; 6–11

Black Bull
Scunthorpe Road (A18)
☎ Thorne 812744
Stones Best Bitter Ⓔ
Excellent roadside inn, well-
appointed lounge bar and
restaurant ✿⌒❶⚑

Thorpe Hesley 23J3

10.30–3; 6.30–10.30 (11 F, S)

Horse & Tiger
Brook Hill
Tetley Bitter Ⓗ
Friendly locals' pub with
unique name ✿

Thorpe Salvin 26B5

10.30–3; 6–10.30 (11 F, S)

Olde Parish Oven
Worksop Road OS522811
☎ Worksop 770685
Phone for lunchtime opening
Youngers Scotch Bitter,
No. 3 Ⓗ

Modern pub with a traditional
village atmosphere. Caters for
everyone ⚑⌒❶

Thrybergh 26A4

10.30–3; 6.30–10.30 (11 F, S)

Reresby Arms
Vale Road (off A630)
☎ Rotherham 850335
Home Bitter Ⓔ
Estate pub, friendly local
trade. C&W Tues evenings
✿⌒❶🕭❖

Thurlstone 23H2

11–3; 6–11

Huntsman
Manchester Road (A628)
Marston Pedigree, Owd
Rodger; Stones Best Bitter;
Theakston XB; Thurlstone
Bitter Ⓗ Regular guest beers
Roadside pub in ancient
weavers' village. Only regular
outlet for Thurlstone beers

Tickhill 26B4

11–3; 6–11

Buttercross
Northgate (A60)
Clarks Traditional Bitter;
Whitbread Durham Ale,
Castle Eden Ale Ⓗ
Cosy village inn. Lively at
weekends ♨✿❖

Ulley 26A5

10.30–3; 6 (7 winter)–10.30 (11 F, S)

Royal Oak
Turnshaw Lane (off A618)
Samuel Smith OBB Ⓔ
Welcoming and deservedly
popular inn set in attractive
village. Excellent value food
✿⌒ (not Sun) ❶ (Mon-Fri) ❖

Wath-upon-Dearne 26A4

10.30–3; 7–10.30 (11 F, S)

New Inn
West Street
John Smith's Bitter Ⓗ
Two room inn; an oasis in a
beer desert ⌒🕭❖

Wentworth 23J3

10.30–3; 6–10.30 (11 F, S)

George & Dragon
Main Street (B6090)
☎ Barnsley 742440
Taylor Best Bitter, Landlord;
Tetley Bitter Ⓗ Occasional
guest beers
300 year old village inn with
excellent reputation for food.
Many interesting landmarks
nearby ♨✿⌒❶ (Thu-Sat)

Rockingham Arms
Main Street (B6090)
☎ Barnsley 742075
Youngers Scotch Bitter, IPA,
No.3 Ⓗ

Welcoming, cosy village pub,
folk, jazz and C&W concerts in
barn ♨Q✿⚑⌒

Whiston 23J3

11.30–3; 6–10.30 (11F, S)

Sitwell Arms
Pleasley Road (A618)
☎ Rotherham 377007
Tetley Bitter Ⓔ & Ⓗ
Attractively set inn with
farmhouse-style interior.
Cavalier restaurant ✿⌒❶🕭❖

Wombwell 23J2

11–3; 7–11

Railway
37 Station Road (off A663)
Tetley Bitter Ⓗ
Former station waiting rooms
🕭

Try also: Wat Tyler (Free)

Woodhouse 23J3

11–3; 5.30–10.30 (11 F, S)

Junction
Station Road (off A57)
Tetley Bitter Ⓗ
Popular estate pub.
Comfortable lounge. Large
public bar with pool, darts, TV
✿❖⇌

Woodlands 26B4

10.30–3; 6–11

Woodlands Hotel (Swinger)
Great North Road (A638)
☎ Doncaster 723207
Tetley Bitter Ⓗ
Caters for all tastes; taproom
an eye opener! ♨✿⚑🕭

Worsbrough 23H2

11–3; 6–11

Edmunds Arms
Worsbrough village (off A61)
☎ Barnsley 206865
Samuel Smith OBB Ⓗ
Splendid country village inn
opposite church. Near
Country Park
✿⌒❶ (Thu, Fri, Sat)

The ♨ symbol denotes a pub
with a real solid fuel fire

Aberford 30C8
11–3; 5.30–10.30 (11 Th, F, S)
Arabian Horse
Main Street (off A1)
Tetley Mild, Bitter; Younger Scotch Bitter, No. 3 H
Once on the A1—now on the village green. Worth a visit for the fireplaces ♨ ♪ ♀

Addingham 30A8
11.30–3; 5.30–11
Swan
106 Main Street ☎ 830375
Bass Light XXXXX, Bass; Stones Best Bitter H
Old village coaching inn, reputedly haunted. Full of character. Unused room at back was a mortuary!
♨ Q ❷ ⏰ (Mon-Fri) ♀

Bardsey 30C8
11–3; 5.30.–10.30 (11 Th, F, S)
Bingley Arms
Church Lane (off A58)
☎ Collingham Bridge 72462
Tetley Mild, Bitter H
Reputed to be Englands oldest inn—superb setting.
Restaurant ♨ ♪ ⏰ ♪ ♀

Barwick in Elmet 30C8
11.30–3; 6–10.30 (11 Th, F, S)
New Inn
Main Street
John Smith's Bitter H
Delightful, cosy village pub.
Unusual small bar Q ♪ ♀

Batley 23H1
11–3; 5.30 (7 Sat & winter)–11
Rose of York
466, Bradford Road (A652)
Boddington Mild, Bitter H
Tasteless tie and beermat collection. Live music Tuesday and Thursday nights. Summer patio barbeques
♪ ⏰ (not Sun) ➷

Bingley 30B8
11–3; 5.30–10.30 (11 F, S)
Granby
Dubb Lane (off A650)
Bass Light XXXXX; Stones Best Bitter H
Lively end of terrace local ➷

Birstall 23G1
11.30–3; 7–11
Black Bull
Kirkgate, Whitechapel (off A652)
Whitbread Durham Ale, Trophy, Castle Eden H
Last trial held 1839 in former court house. Tucked away behind 350 year old church
⏰ (not Sun)

Bradford 30B9
11–3; 5.30–10.30 (11 F, S)
Brewery Arms
Louisa Street, Idle ☎ 614910
Midnight licence for diners
Trough Bitter, Wild Boar Bitter H
Plush brewery tap. Odd-shaped bar downstairs.
Restaurant ♪ ⏰ ➷

Brown Cow
Little Horton Lane (A6177)
Opens 12 & 7
Samuel Smith OBB H
Cosy lounge and thriving basic tap 'oil ♀

Crown
1033, Great Horton Road (A647)
Tetley Mild, Bitter H
Thriving pub at top of Horton Bank Q ♪ ⏰ ♀

Fighting Cock
Preston Street (off B6145)
Boddingtons Bitter; Bass; Old Mill Traditional Bitter; Taylor Landlord; Tetley Bitter H
Regular guest beers
Small basic back street beer drinkers mecca overlooking old mill ruins ♨ ⏰

Flagship
Kirkgate ☎ 721783
Opens 7 Mon-Thu & Sat eves.
Closed Sun lunch
Trough Bitter, Wild Boar Bitter H
Traditional interior behind modern facade ⏰ ➷

Lancaster
154, Westgate (B6144)
☎ 723259
Evenings opens 6 Mon-Thu
Webster Green Label Best, Yorkshire Bitter; Wilsons Original Bitter H
Splendid little 2-room pub, good value meals
⏰ ➷ ➷ (Forster Sq)

Metropole
144, Sunbridge Road
Opens 12 & 7 (5.30 Fri)
Boddingtons Mild, Bitter; Whitbread Trophy H
Large many roomed family run pub. Three gents loos! ♨ ⏰

Oakleigh
Oak Avenue (off A650)
Opens 12 & 6 Mon-Fri, 12 & 7 Sat
Marston Pedigree; Old Mill Traditional Bitter; Taylor Best Bitter, Landlord; Theakston Best Bitter; Thwaites Bitter H
Regular guest beers
Good bar in Victorian ex-hotel, excellent garden
Q ♪ ⏰ (not Sun)

Rams Revenge
Ivegate
Clark's Traditional Bitter; Taylor Best Bitter, Landlord;
Tetley Bitter H **Regular guest beers**
Bare floorboards. Loo is up stairway to heaven! ⏰ ➷

Red Lion
589, Thornton Road (B6145)
Sat evening opens 6
Samuel Smith Tadcaster Bitter, OBB H
Thriving tap room. Well patronised, cosmopolitan lounge area ♪ ⏰ ♀

Ring o' Bells
18, Bolton Road
Sat evening opens 7
Tetley Mild, Bitter H
Splendid glass and woodwork in this popular pub. Good value food ⏰ ➷ (Forster Sq)

Robin Hood
513, Otley Road, Undercliffe (A658) ☎ 633528
Sat evenings opens 7
Tetley Mild, Bitter H
Fine Melbourne windows
♪ ⏰ ♪ ♀

Royal Oak
32, Sticker Lane (A6177)
Taylor Golden Best; Tetley Mild, Bitter; Younger No. 3 H
Popular, friendly pub. Use supermarket car park ♪ ⏰ ♀ ♿

Shoulder of Mutton
Kirkgate ☎ 726038
Samuel Smith Tadcaster Bitter, OBB H
18th century pub. Award winning beer garden ♪ ⏰ ➷

Watmough Arms
94, Lumb Lane ☎ 724717
Sat evenings opens 6.30
Trough Bitter, Wild Boar Bitter H
Modernised pub in business area

Westgate Hill
Westgate Hill Street (A650)
Opens 12 & 7
Webster Green Label Best, Yorkshire Bitter H
Out of town pleasant pub

Westleigh
30, Easby Road (A647)
☎ 727089
Opens 11.30
McEwan 80/-; Younger Scotch, No. 3 H
Comfortable small hotel often busy with students ❷ ♪ ♨ ⏰ ♪

White Hart
44, Victoria Road, Eccleshill
Sat evenings opens 6.30
Whitbread Trophy, Castle Eden H
Modernised smart village corner local. Can be noisy
♪ ⏰ (Mon-Fri)

Wild Boar
863, Bolton Road (off A6177)
☎ 733648
Trough Bitter, Wild Boar Bitter H

Refurbished local with cooking range in lounge
🅰♿⏱🍴🍺

Yates Wine Lodge
Ivegate
Evenings opens 7
McEwan 80/-; Tetley Bitter; Webster Green Label Best; Wilsons Original Bitter; Younger No. 3 H
Modern but traditional, excellent lively atmosphere
♿🍴🍺

Bramhope 30B8
11–3; 5.30–10.30 (11 Th, F, S)

Fox & Hounds
Church Hill
Tetley Mild, Bitter H
18th century pub in commuter village. Comfortable smart lounge with eyecatching fireplaces
🅰♿⏱🍴

Brighouse 23G1
11.30–3; 5–11

Black Horse
6 Westgate, Clifton (near A643) ✆ 713862
Sat evening opens 6
Whitbread Castle Eden Ale H
Busy pub/hotel with noted restaurant 🅰🎲♿⏱🍴🍺

Dusty Miller
290 Halifax Road, Hove Edge (A644)
Sat evening opens 7
Tetley Mild, Bitter H
Popular roadhouse. Small lounge, large games room
♿⏱ (Mon–Fri)

Red Rooster
123 Elland Road, Brookfoot (A6025)
Boddington Bitter; Marston Pedigree; Old Mill Traditional Bitter; Tetley Bitter; Thatchers Cider H Regular guest beers
Simple, no-frills pub 🅰🍴

Burley in Wharfedale 30B8
12 (11 Sat)–3; 5.30–10.30 (11 F, S)

White Horse
Main Street (A65)
Tetley Mild, Bitter
Small village pub. Very popular 🅰≈

Castleford 23J1
11–3.30; 6–11

Eagle
Leeds Road (A6032)
Tetley Bitter H
Friendly corner local, small lounge, lively tap room 🍺≈

Rock Hotel
Rock Hill, Glasshoughton (off A639)
Darley Mild, Thorne Best Bitter H
Well-modernised traditional local; folk music Weds 🅰🍺

Cleckheaton 30B9
11–3; 5.30 (7 Sat)–11

Rose & Crown
Westgate (A643) ✆ 872785
Tetley Mild, Bitter H
Games in lounge-like public; young and locals in open-plan lounge. Near bus station, chip shop and methodist chapel! 🍺

Crossroads 29H8
12–3; 7–11

Quarry House Inn
Bingley Road
✆ Haworth 42239
Supper licence till midnight
Bass Light XXXXX, Bass; Stones Best Bitter, Special Bitter H
Converted farmhouse, high above Keighley; worth seeking out. Excellent food
🅰🎲♿⏱🍴🅰

Denholme Gate 30A9
11.30–3; 5.30–10.30 (11 F, S)

Brown Cow
Thornton Road (A644/B6145)
Tetley Mild, Bitter H
Real family pub. Distinct railwayana theme 🎲♿⏱🍴🍺🅰

Dewsbury 23H1
11–3; 5.30–11

Alma Inn
Combs Hill, Thornhill (B6117)
Opens 12 noon
Matthew Brown Lion Mild, Lion Bitter, John Peel; Theakston Best Bitter, Old Peculier H
Village pub near 15th century church and site of 1893 mine disaster—recorded in bar display ♿⏱ (Mon–Fri)

Woodman Inn
Hartley Street, Batley Carr (off A652) ✆ 463825
Sat evenings opens 7
Tetley Mild, Bitter H
Pleasant thriving local behind Technical College. Strong darts team, pool
♿⏱ (Mon–Fri) 🍺

Drighlington 30B9
11–3; 5.30 (7 Sat)–10.30 (11 Th, F, S)

Painters Arms
35 Bradford Road (A650)
Boddingtons Bitter H
Welcoming, busy pub ♿🍺🍺

Durkar 23H1
11–3; 7–11

New Inn
Denby Dale Road East (off A636 near M1 exit 39)
Tetley Mild, Bitter H
Popular village inn, pleasant lounge ♿⏱

Elland 23G1
11.30–3; 5–11

Druids Arms

2/4 Spring Lane, Greetland (off B6113) ✆ 72465
Closed Mon lunch, evenings opens 7
Bass Light XXXXX, Old Mill Traditional Bitter; Stones Best Bitter H
Comfortable local. Look for sign on main road 🅰♿⏱🍺

Rawsons Arms
502 Elland Road (A6025)
✆ 78648
Sat evening opens 7
Webster Green Label Best, Yorkshire Bitter H
Comfortable pub, surrounded by products of local pipeworks ♿⏱🍺 (Fri–Sat) 🅰

Farnley Tyas 23G2
11.30–3; 5.30 (6 Sat)–11

Golden Cock
The Village (off A629)
✆ Huddersfield 661979
Bass Light XXXXX; Stones Best Bitter H
Wellies at bar, minks in restaurant sum up this fine house. Near Elizabethan Woodsome Hall. Childrens playground 🅰🎲♿⏱🍺

Featherstone 23J1
11–3.30; 6–11

White House
Pontefract Road, Purston (A645)
Samuel Smith OBB H
Pleasant white-washed pub with stylish L-shaped lounge ♿🍺

Garforth 30C9
11–3; 5.30–10.30 (11 Th, F, S)

Gaping Goose
Selby Road (A63)
Tetley Mild, Bitter H
Pleasant, friendly and popular pub with fine brassware Q

Gildersome 30B9
11–3; 5.30–10.30 (11 Th, F, S)

New Inn
Church Street (B6126)
✆ Morley 534821
Samuel Smith OBB H
Pleasant local, games, garden and own air raid siren! ♿🍺🍺

Golcar 23G1
11.30–3; 6–11

Walkers Arms (Ben Idles)
Parkwood Road, off Leymoor Road
Bass Mild XXXX, Light XXXXX; Stones Best Bitter H
End of lane hosterly in hillside weaving community 🅰♿

Gomersal 23G1
11–3; 5.30–11

California
92, Oxford Road (A651)

Matthew Brown John Peel;
Theakston Best Bitter, XB, Old
Peculier Ⓗ
Innovative childrens playground. Landlord messes
around with cars but not his
beers! ▲ ✦ Ⓖ (not Sun)

Goose Eye 29J8

11.30–3; 8–11 closed Mon

**Goose Eye Hotel
Mint Bar**
Laycock OS029406
☎ Keighley 605807
**Goose Eye Bitter, Wharfedale
Bitter, Pommies Revenge;
Thwaites Best Mild, Bitter** Ⓗ
Converted mill next to
brewery. Restaurant. Look at
or through window into cellar
▲ Ⓔ Ⓖ ➤

Halifax 23G1

11.30–3; 5–11

Duke of York
West Street, Stone Chair, Shelf
(A644) ☎ 202056
Evenings opens 6 (7 F, S)
**Whitbread Trophy, Castle
Eden Ale** Ⓗ
Attractive, ancient inn ✦ Ⓔ Ⓖ

Lewins
24/26 Bull Green ☎ 52043
**Bass Light XXXXX, Bass;
Stones Best Bitter** Ⓗ
Busy town-centre pub ▲ Ⓖ ☕ ➤

Ring o' Bells
3 Upper Kirkgate
**Whitbread Trophy, Castle
Eden Ale** Ⓗ
Haunted ancient hostelry next
to parish church ✦ Ⓖ ☕ ≷

Shears Inn
Paris Gates, Boys Lane (off
A629)
Opens 12 & 7 (7.30 winter)
**Taylor Best Bitter; Younger
Scotch Bitter, No. 3** Ⓗ Regular
guest beers
Popular pub by Hebble Brook,
dwarfed by mills ▲ ✦ Ⓖ ≷

Sportsman Inn
Lee Lane, Shibden (off A647)
OS093272 ☎ 67000
12–2.30 & 6–11 Mon–Fri,
12–3 & 7–11 Sat (supper
licence to 12 F, S)
**Old Mill Traditional Bitter;
Ruddle County; Tetley Mild,
Bitter; Theakston Old
Peculier** Ⓗ Regular guest beers
Popular hilltop pub, squash,
sauna, and ski-slope
Ⓔ (lunchtime) ✦ Ⓖ

West End Hotel
216, Parkinson Lane
**Whitbread Trophy, Castle
Eden Ale** Ⓗ
Comfortable local. Games
room, large lounge
▲ Ⓔ (Sun lunch) ✦ Ⓖ

William IV
247 King Cross Road (off
A58)

Sat evenings opens 7
Tetley Falstaff Best, Bitter Ⓗ
Popular pub in local shopping
street, split-level bar ✦ Ⓖ

Woodcock
213 Gibbet Street
**Bass; Boddington Bitter;
Marston Pedigree; Old Mill
Traditional Bitter; Taylor
Landlord; Thatcher Cider** Ⓗ
Regular guest beers
No-frills local Ⓖ ☕

Haworth 30A8

11–3; 5.30–11

Fleece
Main Street ☎ 42172
Taylor Bitter Ale, Landlord Ⓗ
Bustling 3-room historic
alehouse. Packed in summer.
Pool ▲ Ⓔ Ⓖ ➤ (Mon–Fri)
≷ (Worth Valley Rly.)

Hebden Bridge 23F1

11.30–3; 5–11

Cross Inn
46 Towngate, Heptonstall
☎ 843833
Evenings opens 7
**Taylor Golden Best, Best
Bitter** Ⓗ
Welcoming pub in historic
hilltop village. Parking
difficult ✦ Ⓔ Ⓖ ➤ ☕ ▲

**Nutclough House
Hotel**
Keighley Road (A6033)
☎ 842910
Evenings opens 7. Supper
licence
**Old Mill Bullion; Thwaites
Bitter** Ⓗ
3-room hotel
Ⓔ (to 9 pm) ✦ Ⓔ Ⓖ ➤ ≷

Railway
12 New Road (A646)
☎ 844088
Tetley Mild, Bitter Ⓗ
Friendly traditional local by
canal marina ▲ ✦ Ⓖ ➤ ☕ ≷

Shoulder of Mutton
New Road (B6138)
☎ Halifax 883165
Evenings opens 7
**Hartley XB; Whitbread Castle
Eden Ale** Ⓗ
Small village local. Next to
Mytholmroyd Station
✦ Ⓖ ➤ ☕ ▲ ≷

Heckmondwike 23G1

11.30–2; 7–11

Royal
111, High Street (A638)
Tetley Mild, Bitter Ⓗ
Epitome of convivial urban
local, save for flowered tiles in
gents

Hemsworth 23J2

11–3.30; 6–11

Kinsley Hotel

Wakefield Road, Kinsley
(B6273)
Boddingtons Bitter Ⓗ
Vast Edwardian pub in mining
area, community atmosphere
☕

Holmfirth 23G2

11.30–3; 5.30–11

Elephant & Castle
Hollowgate (off A635)
Summer evenings opens 6
**Bass Light XXXXX; Stones
Best Bitter** Ⓗ
Former coaching inn now
famed for proximity to
"Nora's" ▲

Farmers Arms
Liphill Bank Road, Burnlee
(off A635) ☎ 683713
Closed Mon lunch. Evenings
opens 6 (winter Sat 5)
**Marston Pedigree; Stones Best
Bitter; Taylor Best Bitter;
Tetley Mild, Bitter** Ⓗ
Occasional guest beers
No longer just a local, out of
the way pub welcomes
everyone. Parking difficult but
don't let it put you off ▲ Ⓖ ➤

Rose & Crown ('Nook)
Victoria Square (off A635)
Sat evening opens 7
**Samuel Smith OBB; Stones
Best Bitter; Taylor Landlord;
Tetley Mild, Bitter, Younger
No. 3** Ⓗ Regular guest beers
Basic non-tourist boozer near
beck. Lacks trappings, bar
provides succour, should be
visited ▲ Ⓖ

Horbury 23H1

11–3, 7–11

Old Halfway House
Westfield Road (B6128)
Tetley Mild, Bitter Ⓗ
Suburban stone-built inn,
attractive lounge, childrens'
playground ✦ Ⓖ (not Sun) ☕

Horsforth 30B8

11–3; 5.30–10.30 (11 F, S)

Black Bull
The Green, Town Street (off
A6120)
Tetley Mild, Bitter Ⓗ
Many rooms, beer garden
with playground. Always
busy ✦ Ⓖ ☕

Huddersfield 23G1

11.30–3; 5–11

College Arms
Queensgate (ring road)
☎ 21410
**Wilsons Original Mild, Bitter;
Webster Yorkshire Bitter** Ⓗ
Inexpensive pub on edge of
town centre, close to
Polytechnic Ⓖ ➤ (5–7) ≷

Grey Horse
Halifax Road, Birchencliffe
(A629 off M62)

Bass Mild XXXX, Light
XXXXX, Bass; Stones Best
Bitter ⊞
Re-modelled pub in select
area. Jazz Monday, C&W
Tuesday ♨🅿♿

Marsh House
Westbourne Road, Marsh
(A641)
Tetley Mild, Bitter ⊞
Altered urban local retaining
domino parlour and pool
room ♥

Shoulder of Mutton
Neale Road, Lockwood (near
A616)
Closed Mon–Fri lunch;
evenings opens 7
Taylor Landlord; Tetley Mild,
Bitter; Theakston XB;
Thwaites Bitter ⊞ Regular
guest beers
Popular multi-roomed pub
with upstairs games room—a
place for everybody! 🍴♥

Ilkley 30A8

11–3; 5.30–10.30 (11 F, S)

Wharfe Cottage
Leeds Road (A65)
Taylor Best Bitter, Landlord;
Tetley Mild, Bitter; Younger
Scotch ⊞
Smart small pub on edge of
town. Very popular
♨🍴♿🍲 (summer) ⇌

Keighley 29J8

11–3; 5.30–11

Albert Hotel
Bridge Street ✆ 602306
Evenings opens 6.30
Taylor Golden Best, Best
Bitter, Ram Tam ⊞
Spacious Victorian pub. Pool
room; mixed, friendly clientele
⇌

Boltmakers Arms
117, East Parade
Sat evening opens 6.30
Taylor Golden Best, Best
Bitter, Landlord ⊞
Towns smallest pub. One split-
level room, popular local ⇌

Cricketers Arms
Coney Lane ✆ 669912
Taylor Golden Best, Best
Bitter ⊞
Cosy local sandwiched
between mills near town
centre ♿♨♥

Eastwood Tavern
37, Bradford Road
Opens 11.30 & 6
Taylor Golden Best, Best
Bitter, Landlord (summer),
Ram Tam ⊞
Pleasant pub. Room for pool
and darts ♨⇌

Vine Tavern
Hope Place, Greengates Road
Opens 11.30 & 7
Taylor Golden Best, Best
Bitter ⊞

Neat and tidy locals pub off
Halifax road. ½ mile from
Keighley centre ♥

Volunteers Arms
Lawkholme Lane ✆ 600173
Taylor Golden Best, Best
Bitter, Landlord (summer),
Ram Tam, Porter
(occasionally) ⊞
Tucked-away little gem with
upstairs pool room 🎱♥⇌

Worth Valley Inn
1, Wesley Place, Ingrow
Evenings opens 7
Whitbread Trophy, Castle
Eden ⊞
Handy for Worth Valley
railway. One mile from centre
on Halifax road. Small and
cosy
♿♥⇌ (Ingrow West–WVR)

Kirkburton 23G2

11.30–3; 7–11

Woodman
Thunderbridge Lane,
Thunderbridge (off A629)
Taylor Best Bitter; Tetley Mild,
Bitter; Younger Scotch
Bitter ⊞
2-bar country pub in wooded
valley 🍴⇌ (Stocksmoor)

Ledsham 30C9

11–3; 5.30–10.30 (11 Th, F, S)

Chequers
Claypit Lane (off A1)
✆ South Milford 683135
Closed all day Sun
Theakston Best Bitter, XB;
Younger Scotch Bitter,
No. 3 ⊞
Classic rambling country pub
in historic village. Restaurant
♨Q🎱🍴♿🍲

Leeds 30B8

11–3; 5.30–10.30 (11 F, S)

Adelphi
Hunslet Road,
Leeds Bridge, 10
Sat evening opens 7
Tetley Mild, Bitter ⊞
Surely the most elaborate
brewery tap in Britain ♿🍴⇌

Albion
Armley Road, 12 (off A647)
Tetley Mild, Bitter ⊞
Beautifully restored
traditional pub. CAMRA's pub
preservation award winner
♨♿♥

Brown Hare
388 Harehills Lane, 9 (A146)
near Lupton Avenue Jct
Samuel Smith OBB ⊞
Comfortable and popular
modern pub. Tadcaster Bitter
has CO_2 blanket pressure ♿♥♿

Cardigan Arms
364 Kirkstall Road, Burley, 4
(A65)
Tetley Mild, Bitter ⊞

Lots of rooms, and Victorian
glass and woodwork ♿♥

City of Mabgate
Mabgate, 2
Sat evenings opens 7
Whitbread Trophy, Castle
Eden Ale ⊞
Pleasant Victorian pub. Fine
tiles and glasswork ♨🍴♿♥

Duck & Drake
Kirkgate, 2 (nr parish church)
Bass Mild XXXX, Bass;
Boddingtons Bitter; Marston
Pedigree; Old Mill Traditional
Bitter, Bullion ⊞ Regular guest
beers
Unpretentious real ale mecca.
Live music some eves ♨♿🍴⇌

Gardeners Arms
Beza Street, Hunslet, 10 (nr
M1)
Sat Evenings opens 7
Tetley Mild, Bitter ⊞
Simple unspoilt village pub
surrounded by factories.
Heritage Inn 🍴♥

Garden Gate
Waterloo Road, Hunslet, 10
(pedestrian precinct off A61)
Tetley Mild, Bitter ⊞
Victorian gem—etched glass,
tiles and beautiful woodwork
♨♥

Golden Lion
Beeston Road, 11
Boddingtons Mild, Bitter ⊞
Basic pub catering for varied
clientele, discos at weekends
♿♥

Grove
Back Row, Holbeck, 11 (off
A653)
John Smith's Bitter ⊞
Bustling and friendly pub,
folk music some evenings
♨♿⇌

Mulberry
152 Hunslet Road, 10 (A61)
✆ 457621
Sat evenings opens 7
Marston Pedigree; Old Mill
Traditional Bitter; Stones Best
Bitter; Taylor Landlord, Ram
Tam; Younger No. 3 ⊞
Occasional guest beers
Prize-winning 1-bar, 2-level
free house, parking difficult ♿

Mustard Pot
Stainbeck Lane, Chapel
Allerton, 7 (off A61)
Evenings opens 6
Mansfield 4XXXX Bitter ⊞
Tasteful conversion of 18th
century house. One room but
contrasting areas 🍴♿

Nelson
Armley Road, Armley, 12
(A647)
Younger Scotch Bitter,
No. 3 ⊞
Smart pub, former HQ of Sam
Ledgard, Leeds bus pioneer ♿♥

Old Unicorn
Stocks Hill, Town Street,
Bramley, 13 (A657)
**Tetley Mild, Bitter; Younger
No. 3** H
Comfortable and friendly
200 year old free house,
opposite shopping centre
℘ & ❢

Old Vic
17 Whitecote Hill, Bramley,
13 (A657) ℰ Pudsey 561207
Evenings opens 6.30
**Taylor Golden Best, Landlord;
Tetley Mild, Bitter** H
Occasional guest beers
Comfortably furnished and
spacious. Restaurant & ➐

Park
Hyde Park Road, 6
**Bass Light XXXXX; Stones
Best Bitter** H
Always busy, contrasting
crowds in lounge and tap
℘ & ❢

Pig & Whistle
Woodhouse Lane, Merrion
Centre, 2
**Cameron Lion Bitter,
Strongarm; Everards Old
Original** H
Smart 1-bar pub at the foot of
an office block ℘ &

Skinners Arms
Sheepscar Street North, 7
Tetley Mild, Bitter H
Busy suburban pub with
prizewinning cellar ❢

Town Hall Tavern
Westgate, 1
**Tetley Mild, Bitter; Whitbread
Castle Eden Ale** H
Pleasant furnished popular
pub & ≷

Victoria
Great George Street (behind
Town Hall)
Tetley Mild, Bitter H
Busy city centre pub with
splendid Victorian interior.
Live jazz Sunday evenings & ≷

Whitelocks
Turks Head Yard, Briggate,
ℰ 453950
Closes 10.30 F, S. Sat
evenings opens 5.30
**Younger Scotch Bitter, IPA,
No. 3** H
Nothing much changes in this
superb Edwardian luncheon
bar ⌂ Q ℘ & ➐ (until 7.30) ≷

Linthwaite 23G1

11.30–3; 5–11

George (Alma)
4 Edge Hill, Gillroyd Lane (off
A62)
**Bass Mild XXXX, Light
XXXXX; Stones Best Bitter** H
Etched windows, old photos,
cosy atmosphere. Sop suppers
every Thursday

Sair
Lane Top, Hoyle Ing
Evenings opens 7–11; Sat
lunch opens 12 noon
**Linfit Bitter, Special, English
Guineas, Old Eli, Leadboiler,
Enochs Hammer** H
Home brew pub on steep hill
in winter, short climb in
summer! Overlooking Colne
Valley. Folk club Tues
⌂ ⊞ ℘ ❢ ⏚

Liversedge 23G1

11–3; 5.30–11

Rising Sun
Norristhorpe Lane (off A62)
Evenings opens 7
Tetley Mild, Bitter H
Urban local, overlooking
industrial Spen Valley ℘ ❢

Lofthouse 30C9

11–3; 5.30–10.30 (11 Th, F, S)

Gardeners Arms
383, Leeds Road (A61)
Tetley Bitter H
Friendly out of town local, fine
Melbourne Brewery windows.
Large lounge, small public ℘ ❢

Luddendenfoot 23F1

11.30–3; 5–11

Coach & Horses
Burnley Road (A646)
ℰ Halifax 884102
Evenings opens 7
**Matthew Brown Lion Mild;
Theakston Best Bitter, XB, Old
Peculier** H
Roomy, comfortable, with lots
of brassware ℘ & ➐ (summer)

Middlestown 23H1

12–3; 7–11

Little Bull
New Road (A642)
Tetley Bitter H
Delightful old village inn, low
ceilings

Mirfield 23G1

11–3; 5.30–11

Flower Pot
Calder Road, Lower Hopton
(off A644)
Evenings opens 7.30
**Tetley Mild, Falstaff Best,
Bitter** H
1807 pub attitudes and plan
probably unchanged since.
Commemorative tablet to
local builder in tap room; to
landlord by the bar Q ℘ ❢ ⅋ ≷

Pear Tree
259, Huddersfield Road,
Battyeford (A644) ℰ 493079
**Webster Dark Mild, Green
Label Best, Yorkshire Bitter;
Wilsons Original Bitter** H
River/canalside house,
expanding food trade, wide
clientele. Near moorings and
clubhouse ⌂ ⊞ ℘ & ➐ ❢

Newmillerdam 23H1

11–3; 7–11

Fox & Hounds
Barnsley Road (A61)
Whitbread Trophy H
Attractive coaching inn in
picturesque village ⊞ ℘ & ➐

Normanton 23J1

11–3; 5.30–11

Lee Brigg Hotel
Lee Brigg, Altofts
Darley Thorne Best Bitter H
Cheerful 2-room local
community pub ❢

Talbot
Talbot Street (off A655)
Tetley Mild, Bitter H
Large Victorian local retains
much original character. Bar,
snug, lounge and pool room
❢ ≷

Norwood Green 23G1

11.30–3; 5–11

Pear Tree Inn
Station Road (½ Ml N.W. A58/
A641)
Evenings opens 7
Tetley Mild, Bitter H
Modernised village local.
Children's play area ⌂ Q ℘ &

Ossett 23H1

11–3; 5.30–11

Boons' End
Low Mill Road, off Healey
Road (near River Calder)
**Clark's HB, Bitter,
Hammerhead; Taylor
Landlord; Tetley Bitter;
Bulmer Cider** H **Regular guest
beers**
Ordinary old pub with added
Victoriana in industrial/rural
setting. Frequent live music;
games room & ➐ ❢

Commercial
Dewsbury Road
Stones Best Bitter H
Thriving roadside pub with
strong local following ℘ ❢

George
Bank Street
Tetley Mild, Bitter H
Old town-centre inn; cosy
lounge, basic tap
℘ & (not Sun) ❢

Park Tavern
Park Square, off Station Road
(B6128)
**Boddingtons Bitter; Oldham
Mild** H
Locals pub. Cheerful lounge
and games room in quiet
backwater

Otley 30B8

11–3 (4 Mon & Fri); 5.30–10.30 (11 Th, F, S &
summer)

Bay Horse

Market Place (off A660)
Tetley Mild, Bitter Ⓗ
Small traditional gem,
opposite the old market place
Ⓖ🍸

Junction
Bondgate/Charles Street
(A660)
**Taylor Best Bitter, Landlord;
Tetley Mild, Bitter; Theakston
XB, Old Peculier** Ⓗ Occasional
guest beers
Lively pub, attracting young
people. Always busy ♨Ⓖ

Ripponden 23F1
11.30–3; 5.30–11
Bridge Inn
Priest Lane (off A58 next to
church) ✆ Halifax 822595
**Taylor Best Bitter; Tetley
Falstaff; Younger Scotch
Bitter** Ⓗ
Comfortable, genuine, old
world inn ♨Q🍴Ⓖ🍸

Roberttown 23G1
11–3; 6.30–11
New Inn
Child Lane (off A62)
✆ Heckmondwike 402069
Supper licence
**Webster Green Label Best,
Pennine Bitter** Ⓗ
Village pub noted for
traditional meals, especially
Sunday lunch. Coffee any time
Q🍴Ⓖ🍸♿

Shipley 30B8
11–3; 5.30 (7 Sat)–10.30 (11 F, S)
Oddfellows Hall
Otley Road (A6038)
John Smith's Bitter Ⓗ
Friendly mid-19th century
local Ⓖ (not Sun) 🍸≥

Silsden 30A8
11–3; 7–11
Bridge
Keighley Road
John Smith's Bitter Ⓗ
Totally unspoilt pub next to
Leeds—Liverpool Canal. Long-
standing landlord ♨🍴▲

Sowerby Bridge 23F1
11.30–3; 5–11
Ash Tree
Wharf Street (A58)
✆ Halifax 831654
Evenings opens 7 (Mon–Thu),
6 (F, S)
**Old Mill Traditional Bitter;
Bullion; Stones Best Bitter;
Taylor Best Bitter, Landlord** Ⓗ
Roadside pub/restaurant, fine
Indonesian cuisine
♨Q🍴Ⓖ🍸≥

Moorings
No. 1 Warehouse, Canal Basin
(off A58) ✆ Halifax 833940
Evenings opens 6.30
**Clark's Bitter; Younger Scotch
Bitter, IPA, No. 3** Ⓗ Regular
guest beers

Converted canalside
warehouse. Imaginative bar
food 🏠🍴Ⓖ🍸≥

William IV
80, Wharf Street (A58)
Winter evenings opens 6.30
(7 F, S)
**Matthew Brown Lion Mild,
John Peel Special; Theakston
Best Bitter** Ⓗ
Terrace pub with four small
rooms Ⓖ≥

Stanningley 30B9
11–3; 5.30–10.30 (11 F, S)
Fleece
116 Town Street (B6157)
**Taylor Best Bitter, Landlord,
Ram Tam; Tetley Mild, Bitter;
Whitbread Castle Eden Ale** Ⓗ
Regular guest beers
Busy friendly, main road pub
Ⓖ🍸

Sun
153 Town Street (B6157)
Sat evening opens 6.30
summer closes 11 Mon–Sat
Tetley Mild, Bitter Ⓗ
Several rooms each with
different appeal 🍴Ⓖ🍸

Thurstonland 23G2
11.30–3; 7–11
Rose & Crown
The Village (off A616)
**Bass Light XXXXX; Stones
Best Bitter** Ⓗ
Unspoilt rural village pub
close to the cows ♨Q🍴🍸♿

Todmorden 23F1
12.30–3; 5–11
Masons Arms
1, Bacup Road (A681) ✆ 2180
Sat evening opens 7
**Taylor Golden Best; Tetley
Falstaff, Bitter; Thwaites Best
Mild** Ⓗ
Intimate local next to railway
viaduct and canal ♨Ⓖ🍸

Staff of Life
550, Burnley Road (A646)
✆ 2929
Evenings opens 7
**Moorhouse's Premium Bitter;
Taylor Best Bitter, Landlord,
Ram Tam; Theakston XB, Old
Peculier** Ⓗ Regular guest beers
Cottage-style, tiny freehouse
in dramatic gorge ♨🍴Ⓖ🍸▲

Wakefield 23H1
11–3; 5.30–11
Albion
Stanley Road (off A642)
Samuel Smith OBB Ⓗ
1930s estate pub catering for
local community ♨🍴🍸

Blue Light
Green Lane (off Batley Road)
Alverthorpe
Tetley Mild, Bitter Ⓗ
Smart lounge, basic tap room;
typical suburban local 🍴🍸

Cock Inn
Batley Road, Alverthorpe
Stones Best Bitter Ⓗ
Cheerful thriving 1930s local
🍸

Jockey
Northgate
Tetley Mild, Bitter Ⓗ
Spacious town centre pub
caters for all types
Ⓖ (not Sun) 🍸≥

Kings Arms
Heath Village (near A655)
**Tetley Mild, Bitter; Theakston
Best Bitter** Ⓗ
Piece of history in beautifully
conserved village. Gas lights,
wood panelling ♨Q🍴🍸

Redoubt
Horbury Road (A642)
Tetley Mild, Bitter Ⓗ
Well-preserved Yorkshire local
(Heritage Inn). 4 small rooms
and plenty of atmosphere 🍸≥

York Street Hotel
Lower York Street (off Marsh
Way ring road)
Bass; Stones Best Bitter Ⓗ
Smart open-plan lounge.
Handy for sports centre
Ⓖ (not Sun)

Wentbridge 26A3
11–3; 7–11
Blue Bell
Moor Lane (B6474, near A1)
✆ Pontefract 620697
**Taylor Best Bitter; Tetley
Bitter** Ⓗ
17th century coaching inn, in
picturesque village 🏠🍴Ⓖ🍸

Wragby 23J1
11–3, 6–11
Spread Eagle
Doncaster Road (A638)
Samuel Smith OBB Ⓗ
Homely 400 year old country
inn near Nostell Priory. Tiny
unspoilt tap room ♨🍴🍸

Yeadon 30B8
11–3; 5.30–10.30 (11 Th, F, S)
Oddfellows (The Rag)
The Green, Kirk Lane
Tetley Mild, Bitter Ⓗ
Pleasant and popular old style
village pub. Piano ♨Q🍸

WARMEST WELCOME

♦ A REAL FIRE PUB ♦

The ♨ symbol denotes a pub
with a real solid fuel fire

THE Thatcher government has made much of its belief in the merits of small businesses and free competition; is this reality, or just pork pie in the sky?

Here is a way that Mags, Norm and the rest of the gang could give us proof that they mean what they say . . . and that they aren't just whistling the same old tune to hide the fact that the tills are alive with the sound of the giant companies' donations to Tory party funds. A change to the West German system of excise duty (Biersteuer) would give small businesses in the brewing industry a tremendous boost – without costing the government a penny in lost revenue.

The system by which excise duty is levied hurts small brewers financially and is a disincentive to brewing properly conditioned beers. British duty is levied on the original gravity of the beer – at the point when brewing begins, in other words – and every day that the beer spends conditioning from then on is another day's damage to the brewery's cash-flow. In Germany and in most of Europe, duty is levied on the 'factory gate' system – as the product leaves the brewery – so there is no financial penalty for allowing the beer to condition and mature for as long as is necessary.

The Germans tax beer in three basic quality bands. Einfach (simple or plain) beer is the weakest category, ordinary beer (vollbier) in bottles for supermarket and other off-sales outlets. Second is Schank (on draught) beer, including slightly stronger pilsners and export beers intended for sale in pubs and restaurants. Thirdly there is Stark (strong) beer, usually festival or special seasonal beers like Spring Bocks or Oktoberfest Beers.

In addition, and this is where the real benefit to Britain's small breweries would come, duty is levied at different rates depending on the annual production of the brewery. The smaller the brewery, the lower the base excise rate that it pays – only 12DM per hectolitre for a brewery producing less than 2000 hectolitres a year, compared to a duty rate of 15DM for those with an annual production of more than 120,000 hectolitres. This base figure is multiplied by a percentage rating for each of the three quality bands: 50% for Einfach, 75% for Schank and 150% for Stark beer.

Though the overall level of duty is far lower in West Germany, just over 4p per litre on average, the principles apply whatever the level.

If adopted in Britain, the German system of excise duty would encourage the brewing of properly conditioned beers and lagers and would give a welcome and much-needed lift to small brewing companies. It might even lead to the preservation or creation of some jobs, and that's something we can all drink to.

We would like to see our governments, whatever their political complexion, stop using excise duty to kick our small breweries and their customers in the teeth and give them and us an even break for a change – we may be drinkers, but that doesn't mean we're suckers . . .

TO CELEBRATE GETTING A JOB WITH THE EEC, RODNEY'S DRINKING A METRE OF LAGER

*B*rewery takeovers and mergers continue to make headlines, and no brewing company, from the largest to the smallest is currently safe from the predators. In all the financial wheeling and dealing, it is easy to lose sight of the basic facts of life about takeovers: they mean less competition and less choice for the customers; they also mean unemployment for some, or even all, of the victim's employees.

In the 1986 Good Beer Guide, I described the model approach of George Bateman, who treats his responsibilities to the communities his brewery serves as seriously as the profit to be made from selling beer to them – an increasing rarity in the hard-nosed world of modern business. By a cruel irony, my article was scarcely written when George Bateman's own brewery was threatened with takeover and closure by the wish of the other half of his family to sell their shares in the company. Since then, George and his immediate family have faced a long, lonely and arduous fight to try and save their brewery from the clutches of several would-be predators.

George Bateman was a guest speaker at CAMRA's 1986 AGM, where he told us of his continuing struggle to keep Bateman's alive. In a business (never mind brewing) world apparently gone mad, George Bateman's care and compassion for his customers, tenants and employees is a beacon that does not deserve to be extinguished – there is an alternative to the fight for profits at any human cost. George's speech to CAMRA earned him a richly deserved standing ovation. It merits a wider audience, and an edited version of it appears below.

Neil Hanson

When Neil Hanson discussed with me, many months ago, my thoughts on 'saving the locals' for the 1986 Good Beer Guide, little did I think at that time that, I would be more involved with the pages on takeovers of breweries. When the problem that we were having with the rest of our family became public, he did give me the opportunity to change it. I said 'it's as appropriate today as it was then,' and I still stand by it.

I and my family have had 14 very hard and terrible months. We were given the opportunity to take the other family's 60% holding in our brewery. My old briefcase and I, we've carpet bagged from town to town and throughout the City, we've been to merchant bankers, institutions, trade unions, banks – God knows where we haven't been. We've talked to tenant groups, and all varieties of people; and we have received support from children offering a collecting tin through to tenants taking shares in the brewery – which is the sort of thing that we have really dreamed of. Not being the 'Grand Owners' by ourselves of a brewery but, if you like, running a co-operative.

I am a believer in the tied house system, so long as that tie is by an understanding brewer who has a handclasp rather than a stranglehold. I hope I always have been, and always will be philanthropic, but our brewery has been run in a philanthropic manner in order to ensure that we do not increase the dole queue. If someone had worked for us for 30 or 40 years there was no way that they were going to land on the scrap heap just for the sake of a few more pounds in the bank. I want to make that totally clear.

Now as far as the support is concerned, it's been overwhelming, absolutely overwhelming. The problem for us and CAMRA has been that, unlike the Matthew Brown or Davenports campaigns against takeovers, this has not been the straightforward 'save Bateman's' campaign. This has been a struggle between the desires of one part of a family and of another and that makes it much more difficult.

As time has gone on the figure that it was thought we would have to produce has gradually receded from our grasp rather like poor old Tantalus in

Hades. Sometimes in the early hours of the morning, having argued and argued as to whether this scheme or that scheme was viable, we decided 'well, that's it, we've fought a good fight and we can go no further'. Then I have got up in the morning and said '... one more idea, just one more please, let's have a go at it ...' and then for some reason the figure's increased or it just couldn't be done.

What we've got today, what we're all up against is merger-mania – and I haven't made up the word myself. I've been reading a book on merger-mania and in the preface the author says how interested he is in businesses and the people in businesses. He then writes 150 pages and never mentions a single *person* again. He mentions 'leverage' and 'arbitrage' and 'arbitrageurs' and 'dawn raids' and 'bear hugs' and God knows what but none of it mentions a single person. It's how to make a quick buck out of buying in Sydney and selling in Perth because the times are four hours different.

I wonder whether we ought not to have some sort of organisation called the Campaign for Real People, because people are being left out of all this discussion far, far too much. There's manipulation of money and, having manipulated the money, then the assets have got to 'sweat' – that's the great idea now. Even Sir John Harvey-Jones, the chairman of ICI, has complained that he is now expected by the institutions to show ever improving quarterly figures, he can't look at the long term view and this makes life extraordinarily difficult.

One really good thing has come out of this – the support and love that has enveloped our family over the last eight to ten months has really been something quite extraordinary. In our village of Wainfleet the love that abounds throughout and envelops us is ... well ... it's a word that in Wainfleet we weren't accustomed to using until just a few months ago.

George Bateman

Pubs that do not open Sundays are marked ★

Clwyd

Abergele 21H4

11–3; 5.30–11

Gwindy
Market Street (A548)
Open all day Mon & 3rd Wed
in month
**Marston Mercian Mild,
Burton Bitter, Pedigree** Ⓗ
Popular local with old-style
lounge Q ⚲ ᗐ

Harp
Market Street (A548)
Higsons Mild, Bitter Ⓗ
Small, friendly pub. Cosy
inglenook round old kitchen
range ⌂ ⚲ ᗐ

Acrefair 22A6

11.30–3; 7–11

Hampden Arms
Llangollen Road (A539)
Banks's Mild, Bitter Ⓔ
A local drinkers haunt ♉

Bersham 22B6

11–3; 5.30–11

Black Lion
Bersham Road (B5099)
Hydes Best Mild, Bitter Ⓔ
Village local near Heritage
Trail and Museum
⌂ ⚲ ᗐ (not Sun) ♉♈

Brymbo 22B5

11.30–3; 7–11

Black Lion
Railway Road (off B5101)
**Burtonwood Dark Mild,
Bitter** Ⓗ
Comfortable local near steel
works ⚲ ♉

Buckley 22A5

11–3; 5.30–11

White Lion
Mold Road (A549)
**Greenall Whitley Local Mild,
Bitter** Ⓗ
Friendly local with several
rooms 🎦 ⚲ ᗐ (not Sun) ♉ ᗷ

Bwlchgwyn 22A5

11–3; 5.30–11

Kings Head
Bwlchgwyn (A525)
✆ Wrexham 755961
Hydes Mild, Bitter Ⓔ
Friendly village pub, good
view near Welsh Hills
⌂ Q ⚲ 🎦 ᗐ ♉♈

Bylchau 21H5

11.30 (12 winter)–3; 6 (6.30 winter)–10.30 (11 F,
S & summer)

Sportsmans Arms
Bryntrillyn (A543)
Closed Winter Mon, Tue, Wed
Lees GB Mild, Bitter Ⓗ

Friendly pub reputedly the
highest in Wales: 1,500 feet
above sea level ⌂ 🎦 ⚲ ᗐ ♉♈ ⛰

Caerwys 21J5

12–3.30, 7–10.30 (11 F, S)

Travellers Inn
Pen-y-Cefn near Caerwys
(A55) OS112757 ✆ 720251
**Marston Border Mild, Bitter,
Pedigree** Ⓗ
Pleasant pub catering for
tourists and locals alike
⌂ 🎦 ⚲ ᗐ (cottage) ᗐ ♉♈ ⛰

Chirk 22B6

10.30–3; 6–11

Bridge Inn
Chirk Bank (A5) ✆ 773213
Banks's Mild, Bitter Ⓔ
Known locally as "The Trap".
Very close to impressive
viaducts and aqueducts
🎦 ᗐ ♉♈ ⛰ ᗷ

Connah's Quay 22A4

11.30–3; 5.30–11

**Sir Gawain & the
Green Knight**
Golftyn Lane
Samuel Smith OBB Ⓗ
Tastefully converted former
farmhouse ⌂ ⚲ ᗐ (not Mon)

Cymau 22B5

11.30–3; 7–11

Olde Talbot
Off A541 OS297562
Hydes Mild, Bitter Ⓔ
Good dominoes pub. Fine
views 🎦 ⚲ ᗐ ♉

Denbigh 21J5

11–3; 5.30–11

Eagles Inn
Back Road (near Town Square
off A543) ✆ 3203
Ansells Mild, Tetley Bitter Ⓗ
Town centre pub with
nightclub. Good value snacks
⌂ ᗐ

Masons Arms
Rhyl Road (A525) ✆ 2463
**Ind Coope Burton Ale; Tetley
Bitter** Ⓗ
One-bar pub near old station;
pool and juke box ⌂ ⛰

Dyserth 21J4

11–3; 5.30–11

Red Lion
Waterfall Road (opposite
Dyserth waterfalls) ✆ 570404
**Greenall Whitley Local
Bitter** Ⓗ
Village local near popular
beauty spot
Q ⚲ 🎦 ᗐ ♉ (summer)

Ffynnongroew 22A4

12–3; 7–11

Garth Mill

Garth Lane (A528 between
Gronant and Mostyn)
McEwan 70/- Ⓗ
Left off A548 to Penyffordd.
First left up Garth Lane for
400 yds. Leave your car in the
park and cross river by foot-
bridge or ford river in car
⌂ Q ⚲

Flint 22A4

11.30–3.30; 5.30–10.30 (11 F, S)

Cross Foxes
18 Church Street (A5119)
✆ 4221
**Greenall Whitley Local Mild,
Bitter, Original Bitter** Ⓗ
Town centre pub with locals'
bar, comfortable lounge and
pool room ⌂ 🎦 ᗐ ♉ ᗷ

Flint
Mountain 22A4

11.30–3.30; 5.30–10.30 (11 F, S)

Coach & Horses
Northop Road (A5119)
OS239705 ✆ Flint 61371
**Greenall Whitley Local Mild,
Bitter, Original Bitter** Ⓗ
Popular village local ⚲ ᗐ ♉

Froncysyllte 22A6

11–3; 5.30–11

Britannia
A5
**Marston Border Mild, Bitter,
Pedigree** Ⓗ
Excellent local near canal and
Pontcysyllte Aqueduct. Large
goat ⌂ Q ⚲ ᗐ ♉

Graig-fechan 21J6

11–3; 5.30–11

Three Pigeons Inn
B5429 ✆ Ruthin 3178
Ind Coope Bitter Ⓖ
Remote country local.
Magnificent views. Difficult to
find ⌂ Q 🎦 ⚲ ♉ ᗷ ⛰

Greenfield 22A4

11.30–3.30; 5.30–10.30 (11 F, S)

Packet House
Mostyn Road (A548)
OS196777
✆ Holywell 714774
**Greenall Whitley Local Mild,
Bitter** Ⓗ
Comfortable lounge, locals'
bar with pool and darts. Near
Greenfield Valley Heritage
Park ⚲ ᗐ ♉♈

Gresford 22B5

11–3; 5.30–11

Yew Tree
High Street ✆ 2566
**Marston Border Mild, Bitter,
Burton Bitter, Pedigree** Ⓗ
Pleasant village pub named

after ancient yew tree in
church grounds. No meals
Sun ✦

Try also: Griffin Inn (Greenall)

Gronant   21J4

12–3; 7 (6.30 S)–11

Bells
Mostyn Road (A548)
✆ Prestatyn 3770
McEwan 70/-, 80/- (summer);
Younger No 3 ℍ
Surrounded by fields, popular
for its food as well as its ale
✦

Gwernymynydd
                             22A5

11.30–3; 5.30–11

Owain Glyndwr
Glyndwr Road (off A494, turn
at Rainbow Garage)
OS217612 ✆ Mold 2913
Burtonwood Dark Mild,
Bitter ℍ
Friendly country pub on
hillside near America! Great
view towards Dee Estuary
✦

Halkyn   22A4

11.30–3; 6 (7 winter)–11

Britannia Inn
Pentre Road (off A55)
OS211711 ✆ 780272
Lees GB Mild, Bitter ℍ,
Moonraker (winter) Ⓖ
500-year old inn; comfortable
lounge and bar; pool room
✦

Hanmer   22C6

11.30–3; 5.30–11

Hanmer Arms
Off A539 OS455399 ✆ 532
Tetley Mild, Bitter ℍ
Coaching inn in scenic village
near Hanmer Mere
✦

Holywell   22A4

11.30–3.30; 5.30–10.30 (11 F, S)

Volunteer Arms
1 Brynford Street ✆711735
Burtonwood Bitter ℍ
Unspoilt small town pub. A
gem; full of characters; three
rooms plus pool room ▮

Try also: Boar's Head
(Wilsons)

Llanddulas   21H4

12–3; 5.30–11

Valentine
Mill Street (B5443)
Draught Bass; M & B Mild ℍ
Friendly pub with a good local
atmosphere

Try also: Dulas Arms (Lees)

Llanfair
Talhaiarn   21H5

12 (11 summer)–3; 6.30 (5.30 summer)–11

Swan
Off A548 OS927702
Marston Mercian Mild,
Burton Bitter, Pedigree ℍ
Occasional guest beers
Friendly village pub. Pool,
darts ✦

Llangollen   22A6

11–3; 5.30–11

Bridge End
Abbey Road (A539)
Robinson Best Mild
(summer) Ⓔ, Best Bitter ℍ
Food-oriented hotel twixt
river, canal and railway
✦ ⇌ (Llangollen Rwy)

Cambrian Hotel
Berwyn Street (A5)
Opens 12 & 7
Younger Scotch ℍ
Tiny rooms in old guest house
✦ ⇌ (Llangollen Rwy)

Llansannan   21H5

12–3; 5.30–11

Saracens Head
A544
Robinson Best Mild, Best
Bitter Ⓔ
Popular local with character
✦

Try also: *Red Lion (Lees)

Lloc   21J4

11.30–3.30; 5.30–10.30 (11 F, S)

Rock Inn
St. Asaph Road (A55)
OS145766
✆ Holywell 710049
Burtonwood Dark Mild,
Bitter ℍ
Popular with locals and
travellers alike
✦ (not Tue) ▮

Marchwiel   22B6

11.30–3; 5.30–11

Red Lion
✆ Ruabon 262317
Marston Border Mild, Bitter,
Pedigree ℍ
Popular roadside pub near
caravan site ✦

Meliden   21J4

11–3; 5.30–10.30 (11 F, S & summer)

Star
Ffordd Talargoch (A5118)
Marston Mercian Mild,
Burton Bitter, Pedigree ℍ
Small village local ✦

Try also: Melyd Arms Hotel
(Marston)

Minera   22A5

11.30–3; 6–11

City Arms
Wern Road (B5426)
OS275512
Minera Bitter, Winter
Warmer; Tetley Mild, Bitter ℍ

Popular, comfortable home-
brew pub on Minera
Mountain. Restaurant and bar
meals ✦

Mold   22A5

11.30–3; 6.30–11

Queens Head
Chester Road (A541)
Burtonwood Dark Mild,
Bitter ℍ
Popular with locals and
tourists ✦

Ruthin Castle
75/77 New Street (A494)
✆ 2748
Whitbread Castle Eden ℍ
Cosy three-roomed local ✦

Mostyn   21J4

11.30–3.30; 6.30–10.30 (11 F, S)

Lletty Hotel
Coast Road (A548) ✆ 560292
Burtonwood Dark Mild,
Bitter ℍ
Old smugglers' retreat, now a
popular local handy for
travellers ✦

Old Colwyn   21G4

11.30–3; 6–11

Sun Inn
Abergele Road (A55)
Marston Burton Bitter,
Pedigree ℍ
Popular local in traditional
style; pool table, darts ✦

Try also: Red Lion
(Whitbread)

Pentre
Broughton   22B5

11–3; 5.30–11

Cross Foxes
High Street (B5433)
OS303533
Burtonwood Dark Mild,
Bitter ℍ
Typical example of an old
Welsh pub ✦

Pen-y-Mynydd   22B5

12–3; 7–11

White Lion
A5119 (off A550) OS306637
Marston Border Bitter ℍ
Friendly, old-fashioned local
✦

Rhosesmor   22A4

12–3; 5.30–11

Red Lion
Village Road (B5123, off
A541) OS213681
✆ Halkyn 780570
Burtonwood Dark Mild,
Bitter ℍ
Unspoilt two-bar pub, worth
finding, a gem
✦ (lunch) ✦

Rhyl   21H4

11–3; 5.30–11

Galley
Vale Road (A525) ☎ 53432
**Marston Mercian Mild,
Burton Bitter** Ⓗ
Friendly, lively local ⛿

Liverpool Arms
Wellington Road (A548)
**Draught Bass; M & B Mild,
Brew XI** Ⓗ
Small lively regulars' pub ⚲⇄

Load of Mischief
143 High Street ☎ 53141
**Burtonwood Dark Mild,
Bitter** Ⓗ
Large, friendly town pub with
pool table and darts ⛿⇄

Rossett 22B5

11.30–3; 5.30–11

Butcher's Arms
Chester Road (A483)
OS368574 ☎ 570233
**Burtonwood Dark Mild,
Bitter** Ⓗ
Basic, friendly locals' pub. Ex-
Caergwrle Brewery; landlord
has the old sign. Great Sunday
lunch ▲Q⚲⇥⛿

Ruabon 22B6

12–3; 7–11

Great Western Inn
Pont Adam (off A483)
☎ 821005
Burtonwood Bitter Ⓗ
Tucked away local ⛿⇄

Ruthin 21J5

11–3; 5.30–11

Park Place Hotel
Clwyd Street ☎ 2764
**Marston Mercian Mild,
Burton Bitter, Pedigree** Ⓗ
Friendly hotel on outskirts of
town centre ▣⚲⇥⛿

Wine Vaults
St. Peters Square ☎ 2067
**Robinson Best Mild, Best
Bitter** Ⓔ**, Old Tom** Ⓖ
Town centre hotel, popular
with locals ▣▣⛿

St. Asaph 21J4

11–3; 5.30–11

Swan Inn
The Roe ☎ 582284
**Marston Mercian Mild,
Burton Bitter** Ⓗ
The locals' local; the beer tells
you why ⚲

Try also: Red Lion (Allied)

Summerhill 22B5

11–3; 5.30–11

Crown Inn
Top Road OS309538
Hydes Mild, Bitter Ⓔ
Friendly pub ⚲⚲⇥⛿

Treuddyn 22A5

11.30–3; 5.30–11

Farmer's Arms

Fford-y-Llan (off A5104)
OS252581
**Burtonwood Dark Mild,
Bitter** Ⓗ
Stone-built friendly local;
bagatelle ▲Q⚲⛿

Wrexham 22B5

11.30–3; 5.30–11

Nags Head
Mount Street ☎ 2611677
**Marston Border Bitter,
Pedigree, Merrie Monk, Owd
Rodger** Ⓗ
Historic pub with typical
border decor in the shadow of
the closed Border Brewery ⚲⛿

Oak Tree Inn
Ruabon Road (A5152)
☎ 261540
Opens 12 noon
Marston Border Mild Ⓔ**,
Burton Bitter, Pedigree, Owd
Rodger** Ⓗ
Friendly oasis. Two
contrasting rooms; strong
community involvement ⚲⛿⇄

Seven Stars
Chester Street ☎ 263753
Opens 6.30 S eves
Whitbread Castle Eden Ⓗ
Fine Victorian exterior,
comfortable, thoughtfully
modernised interior; friendly
service ⚲⛿⇄

Turf Hotel
Mold Road (A541) ☎ 261484
**Marston Burton Bitter,
Pedigree** Ⓗ**, Owd Rodger** Ⓖ
Comfortable, well-run two
roomed pub; almost part of
the Wrexham FC ground!
⚲▣⚲⛿⇄

Aberaeron 13F3

11–3; 5.30–11

Royal Oak★
North Road (A487) ☎ 570233
Felinfoel Double Dragon Ⓗ
Small welcoming local ⚲⇥⛿

Aberporth 12E4

11–3; 5.30–11

Headland Hotel★
Off B4333 ☎ 810501
Welsh Brewers HB Ⓗ
Popular hotel with a splendid
view of the bay ⚲▣⚲⇥▲

Aberystwyth 13G2

10.30–2.30; 5.30–11

Nags Head★
Bridge Street ☎ 4725
Banks's Mild, Bitter Ⓔ
Cosy town centre local
▣⚲▣⛿⇄

Pier★
Pier Street ☎ 615126
Banks's Mild, Bitter Ⓔ
A friendly pub just off the
promenade ▣⚲⛿⇄

Plough★
Mill Street ☎ 615767
Banks's Mild, Bitter Ⓔ
Comfortable friendly local
▣⚲⇥⇄

Weston Vaults★
Northgate Street ☎ 617641
Banks's Mild, Bitter Ⓔ
Comfortable pub on busy
street corner ▣⚲⇥⇄

Ammanford 13G6

11.30–4; 6–11

Old Cross
Quay Street ☎ 2657
Buckley Mild, Best BitterⒽ
Busy pub on the towns
crossroads with a large locals
bar ⚲⇥ (bookable) ⛿⇄

Borth 13G1

11–3; 5.30–11

Friendship★
B4353
Burtonwood Best Bitter Ⓗ
Friendly pub in main street of
rather run down resort ▲⛿⇄

Broadhaven 12B6

11.30–3; 5.30–11

Royal Hotel
Trafalgar Terrace ☎ 249
**Draught Bass; Welsh Brewers
BB** Ⓗ
Spartan bar in a hotel tucked
away from seafront ▣▣⚲⇥⛿

Burry Port 13F7

11–3; 5.30–11

Pemberton Arms
Colbey Road (A484) ☎ 2129
Buckley Mild, Best Bitter Ⓗ
Excellent, well run suburban
local ⚲▣⚲⇥⛿

Burton Ferry 12C7

11–3; 5.30–11

Jolly Sailor
Off A477 ☎ Neyland 600378
Ansells Bitter Ⓗ
Popular riverside pub
▲⚲⚲⇥⛿

Bynea 13F7

11–3; 5.30–10.30 (11 F, S & summer)

Lewis Arms
90 Yspitty Road (A484)
☎ Llanelli 2878
**Felinfoel Mild, Bitter, Double
Dragon** Ⓗ
Friendly popular local. Right
by Loughor Estuary ⚲⇥⛿⇄

Capel Bangor 13G2

11–3; 5.30–11

Tynllidart Arms★
A44
Usher Best Bitter Ⓗ
Small traditional village local
▲⛿

Cardigan 12D4

11–3; 5.30–11 (open all day Mon, S)

Lamb★
Finch Square
Buckley Best Bitter Ⓗ
Pleasant, old-fashioned local
by the bus station Q♿

Carmarthen 13F6
11–10.30 (11 F, S & summer)
closed 3–5.30 Tue, F

Harp
Lammas Street ✆ 7110
Buckley Mild, Best Bitter Ⓗ
Small basic town pub ♿♿≥

Queens
Queen Street ✆ 31800
**Draught Bass; Welsh Brewers
Dark** Ⓗ
Smart, friendly pub near the
Castle remains ♿♿≥

Cenarth 12E4
11–3; 5.30–11

Three Horseshoes★
A484
✆ Newcastle Emlyn 710217
**Buckley Mild; Flowers IPA,
Original** Ⓗ Regular guest
beers
Large friendly hostelry
♿♿♿♿♿

White Hart★
A484
✆ Newcastle Emlyn 710305
**Buckley Best Bitter; Courage
Best Bitter, Directors** Ⓗ
Occasional guest beers
Bright, attractive pub in
popular tourist village
♿♿♿♿♿

Cilgerran 12D4
11–3; 5.30–11

Pendre
High Street
✆ Cardigan 614223
**Ansells Bitter; Felinfoel
Double Dragon; Ind Coope
Burton Ale (summer)** Ⓗ
Friendly 14th century pub
♿♿♿♿♿

Cosheston 12C7
12–3; 5.30–11

Brewery Inn
Off A477 ✆ Pembroke 686678
**Courage Directors; Welsh
Brewers BB** Ⓗ
Impeccably kept, flower-
bedecked pub. Excellent food
♿Q♿♿

Cresswell Quay 12C7
11–3; 5.30–11

Cresselly Arms
Off B4075 ✆ Carew 210
**Welsh Brewers Worthington
M** Ⓖ
Unspoilt rural pub by a
beautiful creek ♿Q♿♿

Croesgoch 12B5
11–3; 5.30–11

Artramont Arms
A487 ✆ 309

**Felinfoel Double Dragon; Ind
Coope Burton Ale** Ⓗ
Quiet lounge in popular local.
Games room with pool table
♿♿♿♿♿♿

Cross Inn 13F3
11–3; 5.30–11

Rhos Yr Hafod★
B4577/B4337 ✆ Nebo 644
**Flowers IPA; Welsh Brewers
HB** Ⓗ
Excellent rural inn.
Restaurant and games room
♿Q♿♿♿

Cwmbach 13F7
12–3; 6–10.30 (11 F, S & summer)

Farriers Arms
B4308 ✆ Llanelli 4256
**Felinfoel Double Dragon;
Marston Pedigree** Ⓗ Regular
guest beers
Popular, attractive country
pub just outside Llanelli ♿♿

Cwmmawr 13F6
11–3; 5.30–11

Gwendraeth Arms
Gwendraeth Road (B4310)
Felinfoel Mild, Bitter Ⓗ,
Double Dragon Ⓖ
Comfortable old local ♿♿

Dreen Hill 12B6
11–3; 6–11

Masons Arms
Dale Road (B4327)
OS922143
**Draught Bass; Welsh Brewers
BB** Ⓖ Occasional guest beers
Small, homely front parlour
bar ♿Q♿♿♿♿

Fishguard 12C5
11–3; 5.30–11 (open all day Thu)

Fishguard Arms
24 Main Street
**Marston Pedigree; Welsh
Brewers BB; Bulmer Cider** Ⓖ
Regular guest beers
Small, old-fashioned cosy local
♿Q♿

Garnant 13G6
11.30–4; 6–11

Lamb & Flag
Cwmamman Road
Buckley Best Bitter Ⓖ
Outstanding local;
exceptionally well kept and
unchanged for half a century
♿♿

Goginan 13G2
11–3; 5.30–11

Druid Inn★
A44 ✆ Capel Bangor 650
**Usher Best Bitter, Founders
Ale** Ⓗ
Friendly village local in
popular walking area
♿Q♿♿♿

Haverfordwest 12C6
11–3; 5.30–11 (open all day Sat)

Bristol Trader Inn
Quay Street ✆ 2122
Open all day Mon, Tue in
summer
**Ind Coope Burton Ale;
Pembrokeshires Own Ales
Benfro Bitter** Ⓗ
14th century riverside inn
♿♿♿♿≥

Mainbrace Hotel
23 Hill Street ✆ 5084
**Ind Coope Burton Ale;
Pembrokeshires Own Ales
Benfro Bitter** Ⓗ
A friendly popular hotel
♿♿♿♿♿♿

Pembroke Yeoman
11 Hill Street ✆ 2500
Ansells Bitter Ⓗ
Smart, popular, comfortable
pub ♿♿♿♿

Try also: **Hotel Mariners** (Ind
Coope)

Jameston 12C7
11–3; 5.30–11

Swan Lake
A4139 ✆ Manorbier 262
**Courage Best Bitter, Directors;
Ind Coope Burton Ale; Welsh
Brewers BB** Ⓗ
Very inviting pub with
welcoming host
♿Q♿♿♿♿≥

Lampeter 13G4
11–3; 5.30–11 (open alt. Mon & Tue)

Kings Head★
14 Bridge Street ✆ 422598
Buckley Best Bitter Ⓗ
Comfortable, pleasant local in
the town centre ♿♿♿♿

Lamphey 12C7
11–2.30; 5.30–11

Dial Inn
The Ridgeway ✆ 672426
**Draught Bass; Crown SBB;
Welsh Brewers Dark** Ⓗ
Unusual pub with squash
court ♿Q♿♿♿♿

Laugharne 12E6
11–3; 5.30–10.30 (11 F, S & summer)

Corporation Inn
Gosport Street (A4066)
Buckley Best Bitter Ⓗ
Cosy main road pub Q♿♿♿

Little Haven 12B6
11–3; 5.30–11

St. Brides Inn
Off B4341 ✆ Broad Haven 266
Welsh Brewers BB Ⓗ
Plush, quiet village pub
♿Q♿♿♿

Llanboidy 12D6
11–3; 5.30–11

Lamb
OS216233 ✆ 243

Buckley Best Bitter G
Splendid welcoming
traditional Welsh village inn
🏠🎱🛏🌣🍴🍷

Llanddewi Brefi 13G4

11–3; 5.30–11

Foelallt Arms★
B4343 ✆ Tregaron 306
Ansells Bitter; Ind Coope
Burton Ale
Large popular local on the
main square 🏠🌣🎱🛏🌣🍴🍷

Llanddowror 12D6

11–3; 5.30–11

Coopers Arms
A477 ✆ St. Clears 230793
Buckley Best Bitter H
Cosy, friendly pub on major
holiday route 🏠🎱🛏🌣🍴🍷

Llandeilo 13G6

11–3; 5.30–11 (open all day market day)

White Horse
Rhosmaen Street (A483)
✆ 822424
Draught Bass, Welsh Brewers
BB H
Lively popular old pub with its
own courtyard
🏠🎱🌣🛏 (not Sun) 🍴🍷≈

Llandissilio 12D6

11–3; 5.30–11

Bush
B478 ✆ Clynderwen 626
Crown SBB G
Very comfortable pub with
excellent food 🏠Q🎱🛏🌣

Llandovery 13H5

11–3; 5.30–11 (open all day F, fairdays & all Tue)

White Swan
47 High Street (A40) ✆ 20816
Hook Norton Best Bitter;
Marston Pedigree; Wadworth
6X G Regular guest beers
Excellent small free house on
the edge of town
🏠🎱🌣🛏🍴🍷🅰≈

Llanelli 13F7

11–3; 5–10.30 (11 F, S & summer)

Clarence
42 Murray Street
Open all day. S
Draught Bass; Welsh Brewers
Dark, BB H
Friendly town centre pub 🛏🍷

Marshfield Tap
Station Road ✆ 4504
Buckley Best Bitter H
Pleasant corner pub 🛏🍷≈

Llangadog 13G5

11–3; 5.30–11

Castle Hotel
Queens Square ✆ 777377
Marston Pedigree H
Occasional guest beers

Popular, welcoming village
local 🏠🎱🛏🌣🍴🍷🅰

Llangeitho 13G3

11–3; 5.30–11

Three Horseshoes★
B4342 ✆ 244
Marston Pedigree H
Pleasant village local 🏠🌣🛏🍴

Llanilar 13G2

11–3; 5.30–11

Falcon★
A485 ✆ 633
Usher Best Bitter H
Quiet pub in out-of-the-way
village 🏠🛏🍴

Llanwnen 13F4

11–3; 5.30–11

Fish & Anchor★
B4337—1 mile N of village
✆ Cwrt Newydd 233
Draught Bass; Buckley Best
Bitter H
Welcoming rural pub with a
reputation for food and a large
whisky selection 🏠🎱🌣🛏🍴🅰

Llanybydder 13F4

11–3; 5.30–11

Tan-y-Graig
B4337 ✆ 480542
Felinfoel Bitter G
Small village local with
character 🏠🍴

Llanychaer 12C5

11–3; 5.30–11

Bridge End
B4313
Draught Bass; Courage
Directors; Marston Pedigree G
Regular guest beers
Enterprising village pub in the
foothills of the Preseli
Mountains 🏠🎱🌣🛏🍴🍷

Meinciau 13F6

11–3; 5.30–10.30 (11 F, S & summer)

Black Horse
B4309
Buckley Mild; Felinfoel
Bitter G
Outstandingly friendly local in
predominantly Welsh
speaking village 🌣🍴

Narberth 12D6

11–3; 5.30–11

Barley Mow
Water Street B60145
Crown SBB H Regular guest
beers
Lively cheerful meeting place
for locals 🏠🛏🍷

Newcastle Emlyn 12E5

11–3; 6–11 (open all day F, fairdays & bank holidays)

Pelican Inn
Sycamore Street ✆ 710606

Felinfoel Double Dragon; Ind
Coope Burton Ale;
Pembrokeshires Own Ale
Benfro Bitter H
Comfortable free house. Car
park through archway
🏠🌣🛏🍴🍷

Newgale 12B6

11.30–3; 7–11

Duke of Edinburgh
A487 ✆ St. Davids 720586
Usher Best Bitter, Founders
Ale H
Quiet lounge very
comfortable. Cowboy saloon-
type bar 🎱🛏🌣🍴🍷🅰

Newport 12C5

11–3; 5.30–11

Llwyngwair Arms
East Street (A478) ✆ 820267
Welsh Brewers BB H; Draught
Bass (summer); Courage
Directors (summer) G
Friendly and welcoming free
house. Fine town centre local
🏠Q🌣🛏🌣🍴🍷

Newquay 13E3

11–3; 5.30–11

Black Lion★
Off B4342 ✆ 560209
Usher Best Bitter, Founders
Ale H
Hotel bar with superb view of
the harbour 🏠🎱🌣🛏🌣🍴🍷

Sea Horse★
Uplands Square (B4342)
✆ 560226
Buckley Mild, Best Bitter H
Friendly, welcoming pub
popular with locals and
visitors 🌣🍴🍷

Nolton Haven 12B6

11–3; 6.30–11

Mariners Inn
Off A487 OS859186
✆ Camrose 710469
Draught Bass; Felinfoel
Double Dragon H Occasional
guest beers
Popular inn with a spacious
bar and large games room
🏠🌣🛏🌣🍴🍷🅰

Pentregat 13E4

11–3; 5.30–11

New Inn★
A487 ✆ Llangranog 285
Usher Best Bitter H
Comfortable pub on main
holiday route 🌣🛏🍴🍷

Pisgah 13G2

12–3; 6–11

Halfway Inn★
A4120 ✆ Capel Bangor 631
Range changes daily. Choice
of 4–8 ales, cider &
perry G & H
Isolated but lively pub in
scenic setting. Customers can
serve themselves from the
cask 🏠Q🎱🌣🛏🍴🍷

Pontargothi 13F6

11–3; 5.30–11

Cothi Bridge Hotel
A40 ℰ Nantgaredig 251
**Courage Best Bitter,
Directors** Ⓗ
Pleasant hotel in idyllic
riverside setting 🏠🅿️🌳Ⓗ�Ⓖ➤

Pontarllechau 13G5

11–3; 5.30–11

Three Horseshoes
A4069 OS728245
Marston Pedigree Ⓗ
Isolated free house 🏠Ⓖ➤🍴

Pontfaen 12C5

11–3; 5.30–11 (11.30 summer)

Dyffryn Arms
Off B4313 OS026341
ℰ Puncheston 305
**Draught Bass; Ind Coope
Burton Ale** Ⓖ
Remote traditional rural pub
with a warm welcome
🏠Ⓠ🌳🍴

Rhydowen 13F4

11–3; 5.30–11

Alltyrodyn Arms★
A415 ℰ Pontshaen 363
**Buckley Best Bitter; Marston
Pedigree** Ⓗ **Regular guest
beers**
Friendly welcoming
traditional inn 🏠🅴🌳Ⓖ➤🍴🏕️

Rosebush 12C5

11–3; 5.30–11

New Inn
B4313/B4329
ℰ Maenclochog 614
Supper licence to 12 S, 1 am
Wed, Thu, F
**Draught Bass; Felinfoel
Double Dragon** Ⓗ **Occasional
guest beers**
Remote pub in picturesque
setting with its own
swimming pool
🏠🅴🌳🅿️Ⓖ➤🍴🏕️

St. Davids 12A5

11–3; 5.30–11

Saint Nons Hotel
A487 OS752253 ℰ 720239
**Draught Bass; Welsh Brewers
BB** Ⓗ
Friendly pub/hotel. Good
accommodation and
restaurant 🏠🌳Ⓟ🅖➤

Solva 12B5

11.30–3; 6.30–11

Ship Inn
St. Davids Road (A487)
ℰ St. Davids 721247
Welsh Brewers BB Ⓗ
Small quiet pub in attractive
coastal village 🏠Ⓠ🅖➤🍴

Talybont 13G1

11–3; 5.30–11

White Lion★
A487 ℰ 245
Banks's Mild, Bitter Ⓔ
Attractive, welcoming pub
facing the village green
🏠🌳🅿️Ⓖ➤🍴

Tegryn 12D5

11–3; 5.30–11

Butchers Arms
Off A478 OS228333
ℰ Llwyndrain 680
Buckleys BB Ⓗ
Splendid pub, worth finding
🏠Ⓠ🅴🌳🅿️Ⓖ➤🍴🏕️

Templeton 12D6

11–3; 5.30–11

Boars Head
A478 ℰ Narberth 860286
Usher Best Bitter Ⓗ
Attractively decorated low-
beamed pub with good food
Ⓠ🌳Ⓖ➤🍴🅖

Tenby 12D7

11–3; 5.30–11

Lamb Inn
High Street ℰ 2154
**Courage Best Bitter, Directors;
Welsh Brewers Dark, BB,
HB** Ⓗ
Popular pub with a friendly
welcome 🌳Ⓖ➤🍴➤

Try also: White Hart
(Felinfoel)

Trer-ddol 13G1

11–3; 5.30–11

Wildfowler★
A487 ℰ Talybont 333
Draught Bass Ⓗ
Unusual-looking pub on the
main road catering for locals
and tourists 🏠🅴🌳Ⓖ➤🍴

Whitland 12D6

11–3; 5.30–11

Fishers
A40 ℰ 240371
Felinfoel Bitter Ⓗ
Welcoming town pub,
attractive interior
🏠🅴🌳🅿️Ⓖ➤🍴🏕️➤

Wolfs Castle 12C5

11–3; 6–11

Wolfe Inn
A40 ℰ Treffgarne 662
Felinfoel Double Dragon Ⓗ
Immaculate inn besides busy
main road 🏠🅴🌳🅿️Ⓖ
➤(Tue–Sat) 🍴

Mid Glamorgan

**General opening hours:
11.30–4; 6–11**

Aberaman 14A7

Rock Inn
167 Cardiff Road (A4224)
ℰ Aberdare 872906

**Draught Bass; Felinfoel
Double Dragon; Ind Coope
Burton Ale** Ⓗ
Small and friendly 🌳🅿️Ⓖ🍴

Temple Bar Vaults
Cardiff Road (A4224)
ℰ Aberdare 876137
**Courage Best Bitter; Samuel
Smith OBB; Younger IPA** Ⓗ
Homely local. Bar library and
unobtrusive games room 🏠Ⓠ🍴

Abercanaid 14A7

Colliers Arms
Nightingale Street (off A470)
Flowers IPA Ⓗ
Comfortable, bustling village
local 🍴➤ (Pentrebach)

Aberdare 13J7

Glandover Arms
Gadlys Road (A4059)
ℰ 872923
Ansells BitterⒽ; **Ind Coope
Burton Ale** Ⓔ
Comfortable local near town
centre 🌳Ⓖ➤

Whitcombe Hotel
Whitcombe Street ℰ 872817
Welsh Brewers PA Ⓗ
Side street local near main
shopping centre 🍴

Aberkenfig 13H8

Swan
128 Bridgend Road
(off A4063)
**Brain Bitter; Flowers
Original** Ⓗ
Pleasant and comfortable
village pub 🏠🌳Ⓖ🍴

Try also: Colliers Arms (Brain)

Bridgend 13J8

Kings Head
Nolton Street ℰ 3820
**Draught Bass; Welsh Brewers
BB** Ⓗ
Plush, decorative town centre
pub Ⓖ➤

Victoria Hotel
Adare Street ℰ 59802
**Courage Best Bitter,
Directors** Ⓗ
Comfortable town centre pub
Ⓖ➤

Bryncethin 13J8

Masons Arms
A4061
ℰ Aberkenfig 720253
**Draught Bass; Brain Dark,
Bitter; Welsh Brewers BB** Ⓗ
Bar full of atmosphere, plush
lounge 🌳Ⓖ➤🍴🅖

Caerphilly 14B8

Boar's Head
Market Street (A469)
ℰ 882497
Brain Dark, Bitter, SA Ⓗ
Large old inn opposite the

Castle. Smart lounge, small
public. No food Sun ᏸ♦▮≠

Try also: Courthouse
(Courage); **Masons Arms**
(Whitbread)

Cefn Cribwr   13H8

Farmers Arms
Cefn Road (B4281)
☎ Kenfig Hill 740443
Draught Bass Ⓗ
Village local. Mining
memorabilia in bar
▥🄳🗷ᏸ♦▮Ᏸ

Coychurch   13J8

White Horse Inn
Off A473 ☎ Bridgend 2583
Brain Dark, Bitter, SA Ⓗ
Popular, friendly village local
🗷ᏸ▮

Creigiau   14A8

Creigiau Inn
Off A4119
☎ Pentyrch 890768
Flowers IPA Ⓗ
Large single-bar local with
mock Tudor beams ▮

Try also: Caesars Arms
(Whitbread)

Draethen   14B8

Hollybush
Off A468 OS220874
☎ Machen 440216
Ansells Dark Bitter Ⓗ
Country inn with restaurant
▥Q🗷ᏸ▮

Efail Castellau   14A8

Lamb & Flag
Off Llantrisant Common
(off B4595) OS051856
Flowers IPA, Original Ⓗ
Friendly, unspoilt pub in
attractive countryside ▥🗷▮

Hengoed   14B7

Junction
King's Hill (off A469)
☎ 814499
Flowers Original Ⓗ
Smart, friendly local near
famous viaduct. No food Sun
ᏸ♦▮≠

Hirwaun   13J7

Glancynon Inn
Off A4059 OS960055
**Felinfoel Double Dragon;
Fuller London Pride, ESB** Ⓗ
Occasional guest beers
Popular and comfortable, bar
has large games area.
Beware—no pub sign ▥ᏸ▮

Kenfig   13H8

Prince of Wales
Ton Kenfig (off B4283)
☎ Kenfig Hill 740356
Draught Bass; Marston

Pedigree; **Sam Powells Best
Bitter, Samson Strong Ale** Ⓖ;
Welsh Brewers BB Ⓗ& Ⓖ
Occasional guest beers
Historic pub linked to ancient
city buried under sand dunes
▥Q🗷ᏸ▮Ᏸ▲

Laleston   13H8

Mackworth Arms
High Street ☎ Bridgend 3714
Flowers IPA, Original Ⓗ
Plush, comfortable, attractive
pub ▥ᏸ♦

Llangeinor   13J8

Llangeinor Arms
Off A4093 OS925879
☎ Pontycymmer 870268
Opens 12 & 7
**Draught Bass; Welsh Brewers
BB** Ⓗ
Isolated hilltop pub.
Restaurant. Superb views
▥ᏸ♦▮

Llangynwyd   13H8

Old House (Hen Dy)
Off A4063 ☎ Maesteg 733310
Flowers IPA, Original Ⓗ
Old pub with "Mari Llwyd"
tradition ▥Q🗷ᏸ▮▮

Try also: Corner House
(Courage)

Llantrisant   14A8

Cross Keys
High Street (B4595)
Flowers IPA, Original Ⓗ
Popular local. Mid-week jazz
and folk. Wide selection of
good value meals ▥ᏸ♦▮

Wheatsheaf
High Street (B4595)
Draught Bass Ⓗ
Friendly traditional local.
Small public bar with two
adjoining rooms ▮

Llantwit Fardre   14A8

Bush
A473 ☎ 203958
Crown SBB Ⓗ
Small popular, one-bar pub
Q▮

Maesteg   13H8

King Alfred
Commercial Street ☎ 739090
Flowers IPA Ⓗ
Busy town centre local ᏸᏰ

Merthyr Tydfil   14A6

Anchor
High Street ☎ 3840
Draught Bass Ⓗ
Popular town centre local.
Busy bar. Pool room ▮≠

Mwyndy   14A8

Castell Mynach

Cardiff Road (A4119) near
M4 Jct. 34
**Draught Bass; Welsh Brewers
PA, HB** Ⓗ
Smart, comfortable, popular
with all types. Good food
QᏸÀ (Mon–Fri)

Nantyffyllon   13H8

Elder Bush
High Street
Brain Dark, Bitter, SA Ⓗ
Valley local ▮Ᏸ

Nantymoel   13J7

Nant-y-Moel
Commercial Street
Welsh Brewers HB Ⓗ
Valley local. Large lively bar,
comfortable lounge ▮

Ogmore   13H9

Pelican
B4524
☎ Southerndown 880049
**Courage Best Bitter,
Directors** Ⓗ
Comfortable pub and
restaurant overlooking
Ogmore Castle ruins 🗷ᏸ♦

Ogmore by Sea   13H9

Sealawns
B4524
☎ Southerndown 880311
**Draught Bass; Welsh Brewers
BB** Ⓗ
Comfortable bar in seaside
hotel. Magnificent coastal
views 🗷🄳ᏸ♦▮

Penderyn   13J7

Lamb
A4059
**Felinfoel Double Dragon;
Fuller London Pride** Ⓗ
Village local opposite stock
market ▥▮

Red Lion
Off 4059 OS945089
Open noon or later
**Brain Dark; Everard Tiger;
Fuller ESB; Marston Owd
Rodger; Robinson Best Bitter;
Wadworth 6X** Ⓖ **Regular
guest beers**
Superb hilltop pub with
splendid views ▥Q🗷▮

Pontyclun   14A8

Owain Arms
Coedcae Lane (off A473)
☎ Llantrisant 222012
**Brain Dark, SA; Welsh
Brewers HB** Ⓗ **Regular guest
beers**
Friendly bar in motel 🄳🄳ᏸ♦

Pontypridd   14A7

Greyhound
The Broadway (A4058)
Draught Bass Ⓗ
Small popular pub opposite
station ▮≠

Llanover Arms
Bridge Street (Jct. of A470)
Brain Dark, Bitter Ⓔ
Popular old inn near famous
bridge and park 🏠⮮

Try also: **Malsters** (Whitbread)

Porth 14A7

Black Crown
The Square ☎ 682013
**Flowers IPA, Original; Samuel
Whitbread** Ⓗ
Comfortable open-plan pub in
town centre Ⓖ🍴(not Fri)⮮

Porthcawl 13H8

Jolly Sailor
Church Street, Newton
Brain Dark, Bitter, SA Ⓗ
Village pub with nautical
flavour ♨🐾🏠♿

Rock
John Street ☎ 2380
**Draught Bass, Welsh Brewers
BB** Ⓗ
Town centre pub. Basic bar,
comfortable lounge
🔧🐾🍴♿

Quakers Yard 14A7

Glan Taff Inn
Off A470 ☎ Treharris 410822
Opens 12 & 7
Courage Directors Ⓗ
Victorian inn above Bargoed-
Taff river. Restaurant
Q🐾Ⓖ(Mon–Fri)
🍴(Wed–Sat) 🏠

Rhymney 14B6

Farmers Arms
Off A469 ☎ 840257
Flowers IPA Ⓗ
Traditional pub 🐾Ⓖ🍴🏠⮮

Rudry 14B8

Griffin Inn
Off A468 OS187875
☎ Caerphilly 883396
Brain Bitter Ⓗ; **Marston
Pedigree** Ⓖ
Country inn with restaurant,
in attractive area. Part of
small motel Q🔧🐾Ⓖ🍴🏠

Try also: **Maenllwyd** (Free)

Taffs Well 14B8

Anchor Hotel
Cardiff Road (off A470, near
M4 exit 33) ☎ 810104
Evening opens 7
Flowers IPA, Original Ⓗ
Comfortable and
contemporary 🐾Ⓖ🍴⮮

Taffs Well Inn
Cardiff Road (A4054)
**Ansells Dark, Bitter; Ind
Coope Burton Ale** Ⓗ
Comfortable open-plan pub
with lively atmosphere 🐾Ⓖ⮮

Tonyrefail 14A8

Ely Hotel
Haverford Road (off A4119)
Brain Bitter Ⓗ
Large free house with split-
level bar 🏠

Tirphil 14B7

Dynevor Arms
A469 ☎ Bargoed 834219
Welsh Brewers PA Ⓗ
Small village pub 🏠⮮

Treforest 14A8

Otley Arms
Forest Road (A473)
☎ Pontypridd 402033
Draught Bass Ⓗ; **Brain
Dark** Ⓔ, **SA; Crown SBB;
Welsh Brewers HB** Ⓗ; **Farmers
Tipple Cider** Ⓖ
Bustling Polytechnic local
Ⓖ🏠⮮

Try also: **Forest** (Whitbread)

Treorchy 13J7

Prince of Wales
High Street (A4058)
Flowers IPA, Original Ⓗ
Friendly town local Ⓖ🏠⮮

Tyle Garw 14A8

Boars Head
Coed Cae Lane (off A473)
OS029819
**Crown SBB; Welsh Brewers
HB** Ⓗ
Small plain, unspoilt local,
quiet and friendly; forest
walks opposite 🐾🏠

Ynyswen 13J7

Crown Hotel
Ynyswen Road (A4061)
**Draught Bass; Brain SA;
Welsh Brewers BB** Ⓗ
Regular guest beers
Friendly and popular local
♨🏠⮮ (Treorchy)

Ystrad Mynach 14B7

Olde Royal Oak
Commercial Street (A469)
☎ Hengoed 814196
Draught Bass Ⓗ
Comfortable pub on
crossroads. No food Sun
Q Ⓖ🏠⮮

South Glamorgan

Aberthin 14A8

11–3.30; 6–11

Hare & Hounds
A4222 ☎ Cowbridge 4892
**Draught Bass; Welsh Brewers
PA, HB** Ⓖ
Superb traditional village
local, friendly and well worth
visiting ♨Q🔧🐾

Barry 14B9

11.30–3.30; 5.30–11

Glenbrook Inn
Dobbins Road, Palmerston
(off A4231) ☎ 746696
**Brain Dark, Bitter, SA; Welsh
Brewers HB** Ⓗ
Attractive estate pub. Bar
billiards 🐾Ⓖ🏠

Three Bells
Coldbrook Road, Cadoxton
☎ 736039
Evening opens 6
**Flowers IPA, Original; Samuel
Whitbread Strong Ale** Ⓗ
Popular, cheerful old village
pub ♨🔧Ⓖ🏠⮮ (Cadoxton)

Bonvilston 14A8

11.30–3.30; 5.30–11

Red Lion
A48 ☎ 208
Brain Dark, Bitter, SA Ⓗ
Cosy, stone-walled, village
pub
♨🐾Ⓖ (not winter Sun)

Cardiff 14B8

11–3; 5.30–10.30

Albert
St. Mary Street ☎ 383032
Brain Dark, Bitter, SA Ⓗ & Ⓔ
Busy city centre pub. The
brewery tap Ⓖ🏠⮮

Apollo Hotel
36 Cathedral Road (A4119)
☎ 42167
**Courage Best Bitter,
Directors** Ⓗ
Lounge bar close to S4C
studios, Sophia Gardens and
national sports centre for
Wales
🐾📺Ⓖ (not Sat) 🍴(not Sun)

Brownhills Hotel
Saunders Road (near station
car-park) ☎ 33413
Brain Dark, Bitter Ⓗ & Ⓔ
Comfortable hotel bar,
formerly the Merchant Navy
Hotel 🔧📺Ⓖ (Mon—Fri) ⮮

Butchers Arms
High Street, Llandaff
(off A4119) ☎ 561898
**Draught Bass; Welsh Brewers
HB** Ⓗ
Popular pub near Llandaff
Cathedral. Small bar, pleasant
lounge QⒼ (Mon—Fri) 🏠

Butchers Arms
Hoel-y-Felin, Rhiwbina
☎ 693526
**Ansells Dark, Bitter; Ind
Coope Burton Ale** Ⓔ
Busy pub in quiet residential
area. Video juke-box popular
with younger clientele
🐾Ⓖ🏠⮮ (Rhiwbina)

Coach House
Station Terrace, Ely ☎ 555573
Closed Sat lunchtime
Younger Scotch, IPA Ⓗ
Friendly and attractive lounge

*W*ales: *South Glamorgan* 260

bar with restaurant near Ely
Bridge. IPA sold as Coach
House Special ♨ ♿ ⚓

Conway
Conway Road, Pontcanna (off
A4119)
Flowers IPA, Original Ⓗ
Stylish street corner pub near
Llandaff Fields ♿ 🍴

Crown
37 Bute Street ℰ 463945
**Ansells Dark, Bitter; Ind
Coope Burton Ale** Ⓔ
Excellent, unspoilt city centre
pub ♿ ⚓ ≷

Fox & Hounds
Old Church Road,
Whitchurch
Brain Dark, Bitter, SA Ⓗ
Popular, bustling, suburban
local ♿🍴≷ (Whitchurch &
Rhiwbina)

Fox & Hounds
Chapel Row, St. Mellons
Brain Dark, Bitter, SA Ⓗ
Old village inn, now
comfortable suburban pub
♿♿

Gower
Gwennyth Street, Cathays
Brain Dark, Bitter, SA Ⓗ
Large, busy, backstreet pub.
Snooker table in bar ♿🍴

Inn on the River
76 Taff Embankment,
Grangetown
Brain Dark, Bitter, SA Ⓗ
Large pub with variety of bars.
Live music Tue to Sat eves,
Sun lunch time. Excellent
service ♿♿≷ (Grangetown)

Insole Arms
Harvey Street, Canton
Brain Dark, Bitter, SA Ⓗ
Busy, friendly local. Cards,
darts in bar; smart lounge ♿🍴

Kings Castle
Cowbridge Road East, Canton
**Flowers IPA, Original; Samuel
Whitbread Strong Ale** Ⓗ
Popular Art Nouveau style
pub ♿ (not Sun)

Packet
92 Bute Sreet, Butetown
Brain Dark, Bitter, SA Ⓗ
Superbly modernised
dockland pub near Industrial
and Maritime Museum
♿♿≷ (Bute Road)

Pantmawr
Off Tyla Teg, Pantmawr Estate
**Draught Bass; Welsh Brewers
HB** Ⓗ
Popular suburban pub,
difficult to find but worth the
effort Q♿♿ (Mon–Fri)

Plough Inn
Merthyr Road, Whitchurch
Brain Dark, Bitter, SA Ⓗ
Busy, friendly many-roomed
local ♿♿≷ (Whitchurch)

Royal Oak
Broadway, Roath ℰ 491953
Brain Dark, Bitter Ⓗ; SA Ⓖ
Basic street corner boozer
with live rock music ♿🍴

Three Horseshoes
Merthyr Road, near Gabalfa
Interchange ℰ625703
Brain Dark, Bitter, SA Ⓗ
Friendly local. Good food
♿♿ (Mon–Fri) 🍴

Westgate
Cowbridge Road East
Brain Dark, Bitter, SA Ⓗ
Prominent multi-room corner
pub. Handy for city centre and
Sophia Gardens ♿🍴

Cowbridge   14A8
11.30–3.30; 5.30–11

Bear Hotel
High Street ℰ 4814
**Brain Dark, Bitter, SA; Welsh
Brewers HB** Ⓗ Regular guest
beers
Well-appointed hotel in
attractive small town
Q♿♿♿🍴

Try also: Duke of Wellington
(Brain)

Dinas Powis   14B9
11.30–3.30; 5.30–11

Star
Station Road (off A4055)
Brain Dark, Bitter, SA Ⓗ
Spacious village pub of
character ♨♿♿≷

East Aberthaw   14A9
11.30–3.30; 5.30 (6 Sat)–11

Blue Anchor
B4265
**Brain Dark; Flowers IPA;
Marston Pedigree; Robinson
Best Bitter; Theakston Old
Peculier; Wadworth 6x** Ⓗ
Regular guest beers
14th century smuggler's inn
with six interconnecting
rooms ♨Q♿♿🍴

Llancadle   14A9
11.30–3.30; 6–11

Green Dragon
ℰ St. Athan 750367
**Courage Best Bitter,
Directors** Ⓗ Regular guest
beers
Cheerful and friendly thatched
village pub ♨Q♿♿ (not Mon)
♿ (Tue–Sat) 🍴

Llancarfan   14A9
11.30–3.30 (3 winter); 6 (6.30 winter)–11

Fox & Hounds
Off A48 ℰ Bonvilston 297
**Brain Dark, Bitter; Felinfoel
Double Dragon; Wadworth
6X** Ⓗ Regular guest beers
Popular 16th century village
pub with restaurant. Evening
meals must be booked
♿♿ (not Sun)

Marcross   13J9
11.30–3.30; 5.30–11

Horseshoe Inn
Off B4265 ℰ Wick 387
**Brain Dark; Buckley Best
Bitter; Felinfoel Double
Dragon; Marston Pedigree** Ⓗ
Regular guest beers
Superb village local, friendly,
welcoming atmosphere
♨♿♿🍴♿

Moulton   14A9
11.30–3.30; 5.30–11

Three Horseshoes
Of A4226 ℰ Rhoose 710428
Brain Dark, Bitter Ⓗ & Ⓔ,
SA Ⓔ; **Welsh Brewers HB** Ⓗ
Surprisingly large,
multiroomed pub in a tiny
village ♨♿♿♿ (not Sun) 🍴

Penarth   14B9
11.30–3.30; 5.30–11

Albion
Glebe Street ℰ 708361
Brain Dark, Bitter, SA Ⓗ
Friendly street-corner local
with lively bar. Darts 🍴≷

St. Fagans
Glebe Street ℰ 706139
**Courage Best Bitter,
Directors** Ⓗ
Town centre pub with lounge
and disco ≷

Peterston-   14A8
Super-Ely
11.30–3.30; 6–11

Three Horseshoes
Off A48 ℰ760388
Brain Dark, Bitter, SA Ⓗ
Friendly, traditional pub in
small village ♨♿♿🍴♿

Treoes   13J9
11.30–3.30; 5.30–11

Star
Off A48 ℰ Bridgend 58458
Crown SBB, Star Special Ⓗ
Comfortable village local
♨♿♿⚓

West Glamorgan

Bishopston   13G8
11.30–3.30; 5.30–10.30 (11 F, S)

Beaufort
Kittle (B4436)
Draught Bass Ⓔ
Interesting 3-level pub ♿♿🍴♿

Plough & Harrow
Murton (off B4436) ℰ 4459
**Draught Bass; Brain SA;
Usher BB** Ⓗ; **Founders** Ⓖ;
**Webster Yorkshire Bitter,
Welsh Dark** Ⓗ
Large 1-bar village local ♿♿

Valley Hotel
Bishopston Road (off B4436)
Welsh Brewers Dark, BB Ⓗ

Attractive pub overlooking Bishopston Valley ⚲🕭🍷🍴🏕

Try also: Joiners (Free)

Briton Ferry 13H7

Rose & Crown
Bethel Street (off A474)
☎ 812915
Courage Best Bitter, Directors H **Regular guest beers**
Smart popular open-plan pub with nightly live music 🕭🍷

Cheriton 13F7

11.30–3.30; 6–10.30 (11 F, S)

Brittania
Near Llanrhidian, on Oldwalls/Llanmadoc Road
☎ Llangenith 624
Draught Bass E
Pleasant rural pub in depths of Gower. Good restaurant
⚲🕭🍷🍴🏕

Clydach 13G7

11.30–4; 6–10.30 (11 F, S)

Old Glais Inn
Birchgrove Road (B4291)
Usher Best Bitter H
Comfortable pub on the edge of town ⚲🕭

Cwmgwrach 13H7

11.30–4; 6–10.30 (11 F, S)

Dunraven
High Street (off A465)
Flowers IPA H
Friendly local 🍷

Dunvant 13G7

11.30–3.30; 5.30–10.30 (11 F, S)

Found Out
Killan Road (off B4296)
Flowers IPA, Original H
Friendly estate pub up the hill from the Square 🍷

Gorseinon 13G7

11.30–4; 6–10.30 (11 F, S)

Tafarn-y-Trap
Swansea Road (A4067)
Buckley Mild, Best Bitter E
Well-appointed pub ⚲🕭🍷

Gowerton 13G7

11.30–4; 6–10.30 (11 F, S)

Berthllwyd
B4295 between Gowerton & Penclawod ☎ 873454
Opens noon
Buckley Best Bitter; Courage Directors; Felinfoel Double Dragon H
Extensive, well-appointed pub. Fine food selection. Overlooks Loughor Estuary ⚲🕭🍷

Commercial
Station Road (B4295)
Open all day Tuesday
Buckley Mild, Best Bitter H

Busy public bar with pool table. Comfortable lounge ⚲🍷🍴

Try also: Welcome To Gower (Buckley)

Killay 13G8

11.30–3.30; 5.30–10.30 (11 F, S)

Railway Inn
Gower Road (A4118)
Draught Bass; Welsh Brewers PA, Dark H
Former station house. Pleasant walk through Clyne Valley to Swansea Bay starts from car park ⚲🍷

Llanrhidian 13F8

11.30–3.30; 5.30–10.30 (11 F, S)

Greyhound
Oldwalls/Llangenith Road
Draught Bass; Welsh Brewers HB H **range may vary**
Pleasant pub in heart of Gower 🍴🕭🍷🍴

North Gower Hotel
B4295/B4271
☎ Gower 390042
Buckley Best Bitter H
Large country house with large beer garden overlooking Loughor Estuary ⚲🍴🕭🍷

Welcome to Town
Off B4295
Opens 12 & 6
Marston Pedigree G
Delightful unspoilt inn on village green Q⚲🍷

Mumbles 13G8

11.30–3.30; 5.30–10.30 (11 F, S)

Oystercatcher
Oystermouth Road (B4433)
Usher BB, Founders H
Comfortable pub near waterfront

Waterloo
Oystermouth Road (B4433)
Draught Bass H
Friendly local pub near waterfront

White Rose
Newton Road ☎ 66182
Draught Bass; Welsh Brewers Dark E
Bustling bar with comfortable lounge, near waterfront ⚲🍷

Neath 13H7

11.30–4; 6–10.30 (11 F, S)

Three Cranes
Wind Street
Courage Best Bitter, Directors H
Pleasant pub in shopping area 🕭🍷

Welsh Bard
1 Commercial Street ☎ 2882
Opens all day Wed & 1st & 3rd Fri of month
Buckley Mild, Best Bitter H
Friendly pub under railway arches 🕭🍷🍴♿

Windsor Castle
Windsor Road
Ansells Bitter H
Basic bar. Lively lounge 🕭🍷🏕

Morriston 13G7

11.30–3.30; 5.30–10.30 (11 F, S)

Lamb & Flag
Morriston Cross (A48/A4067)
☎ 71663
Courage Best Bitter, Directors H
Large oak-panelled lounge 🕭🍷

Penclawdd 13F7

11.30–3.30; 5.30–10.30 (11 F, S)

Royal Oak
B4298 ☎ 782
Welsh Brewers Dark E
Pleasant estuary pub overlooking marshes ⚲🕭🍷🍴🏕

Penllergaer 13G7

11.30–4; 6–10.30 (11 F, S)

Old Inn
A48 (off M4 exit 47)
Buckley Mild, Best Bitter H
Large roadside pub 🍷

Pontardawe 13G7

11.30–4; 6–10.30 (11 F, S)

Ivy Bush Hotel
High Street (A4067)
Draught Bass E
Friendly old fashioned pub with folk club on Fridays 🍷

Pontardulais 13G7

11.30–4; 6–10.30 (11 F, S)

Farmers Arms
St. Teilo Street (A48)
☎ 882451
Draught Bass; Welsh Brewers Dark H
Friendly pub with live bands most weekends ⚲🕭🍷🍴

Wheatsheaf
St. Teilo Street (A48)
Felinfoel Mild, Bitter H
Homely, traditional, locals' pub 🍷

Pontneddfechan 13J7

11.30–4; 6–10.30 (11 F, S)

Angel
B4242 OS899076
☎ Glynneath 721142
Flowers IPA, Original H
Pleasantly situated pub near waterfalls ⚲🕭🍷🍴

Port Talbot 13H8

11.30–4; 6–11

St. Oswalds
Station Road
Crown SBB; St. Oswalds Special H
Comfortable bar with restaurant 🕭🍷♿

Rhyd-y-Pandy 13G7

11.30–4; 6–10.30 (11 F, S)

Masons Arms
OS668020 ☎ Clydach 842535
Courage Directors Ⓗ
Pleasant rural pub near
Morriston ⌂ ⌀ ☾ ➐

Skewen 13G7

11.30–4; 6–10.30 (11 F, S)
Crown
216 New Road
Brain Dark, MA Ⓗ
Only outlet for MA, a brewery
mix of SA and Dark. Ask for
"Light" ☻

Swansea 13G7

11.30–3.30; 5.30–10.30 (11 F, S)
Adam & Eve
207 High Street ☎ 55913
Brain Dark, Bitter, Ⓗ
Traditional, 3-room pub with
plenty of atmosphere ☻ ⇌

Adelphi Hotel
Wind Street
**Draught Bass, Welsh Brewers
Dark** Ⓗ
Friendly locals pub ☻ ⇌

Bryn-y-Mor
Bryn-y-Mor Road ☎ 466650
**Ansells Dark, Bitter; Ind
Coope Burton Ale** Ⓔ
Regulars bar. Pub games,
pool, bar billiards. Live music
Sunday evenings ⌀ ☾ ☻

Builders
Oxford Street ☎ 476189
Buckley Mild, Best Bitter Ⓗ
Smart, split-level pub near
football ground ☾

Lockett Inn
Waunarlwydd Road (A4216)
Buckley Mild, Best Bitter Ⓗ
Spacious bar, comfortable
lounge ⌂ ☻

Duke
Wind Street ☎ 54567
Welsh Brewers Dark, BB Ⓗ
Victorian city bar, popular
with business men and
dockers ☻ ⇌

Glamorgan
Oystermouth Road
Draught Bass Ⓗ
Pleasant, seafront pub ☾ ➐

Quadrant Gate
Nelson Street
**Usher BB, Founders; Webster
Yorkshire Bitter** Ⓗ
Smart pub very close to
Quadrant shopping centre ☾

Rhyddings
Brynmill
**Ansells Dark, Bitter; Ind
Coope Burton Ale** Ⓔ
Large bar with comfortable
lounge. Near Singleton Park
East entrance ⌀ ☻

Star
Carmarthen Road, Fforestfach
(A48)
Buckley Mild, Best Bitter Ⓔ
Popular local serving nearby
industrial estate ☻

Three Crosses 13G7

11.30–3.30; 5.30–10.30 (11 F, S)
Joiners
Joiners Road
☎ Gowerton 873479
**Usher Best Bitter; Webster
Yorkshire Bitter** Ⓗ
Gower village pub ⌀ ☾ ➐

Gwent

Abergavenny 14C6

10.30–3 (10–4 Tues); 6–11
Hen & Chicken
Flannel Street ☎ 3613
Draught Bass Ⓗ
Small, friendly, old-fashioned
pub in town centre Q ☻

Station Hotel
Brecon Road (A40)
Brain SA; Davenports Bitter Ⓗ
Occasional guest beers
Friendly local. Wood-burning
stoves ⌂ ⌂ ☾ ➐ (not Sun) ☻

Blackrock 14B6

12–4.30; 7–11
Old Drum & Monkey
Off A465 ☎ Gilwern 830542
Draught Bass Ⓗ **Regular guest
beers**
Open-plan interior with bar
and restaurant
⌂ ☾ ➐ (not Mon)

Brynmawr 14B6

11.30–3; 6.30–11
Hobby Horse
30 Greenland Road ☎ 310996
Flowers IPA Ⓗ
Smart little pub with
restaurant ⌀ ☾ ➐ (not Sun)

Caerleon 14C7

11–3; 5.30–11
Hanbury Arms
Caerleon Road ☎ 420292
Draught Bass Ⓗ
Historic pub on banks of the
River Usk ⌂ ⌀ ☾ ➐ ☻

Rising Sun Inn
Ponthir Road ☎ 420534
**Brain SA; Felinfoel Double
Dragon** Ⓗ **Regular guest beers**
Small, comfortable free house
⌂ ⌂ ☾ ➐ ☻

Caldicot 14D8

11–3; 6–11
Castle
Church Road ☎ 420509
**Flowers IPA; Samuel
Whitbread Strong Ale** Ⓗ
Pleasant pub with dining
room at entrance to Caldicot
Castle ⌀ ☾ ➐ ☻

Chepstow 14D7

11–3; 5.30–11
Bridge Inn
25 Bridge Street (A48)
Opens evening 6

**Usher Best Bitter, Founders
Ale** Ⓗ
Old pub on bank of River Wye.
Restaurant ⌂ Q ⌂ ☾ ➐ ☻

Coach & Horses
Welsh Street ☎ 2626
**Brain SA; Marston Pedigree;
Theakston Best Bitter; Usher
Best Bitter, Founders Ale** Ⓗ
Lively free house. No food
weekends ⌂ ☾ ➐

Cross Keys 14B7

12–4.30; 7–11
Eagle
High Street ☎ 270643
**Draught Bass; Welsh Brewers
PA** Ⓗ
Friendly local off main valley
road ☻

Cwmbran 14C7

11–3; 6–11
Blinkin' Owl
Henllys Way, Coed Eva
Brain Dark, Bitter, SA Ⓗ
Modern estate pub ⌀ ☾ ☻

Llandegveth 14C7

11–3; 6–11
Farmers Arms
Off A4042
OS336957 ☎ Tredunnock 244
Brain Dark, Bitter Ⓗ
Friendly country pub with
well in lounge Q ⌀ ☾ ➐ ☻

**Llanfihangel
Crucorney** 14C6

11–3; 6–11
Skirrid Inn
Off A465 ☎ Crucorney 258
**Robinson Best Bitter;
Wadworth 6X** Ⓗ
Reputedly Wales' oldest pub.
Dates from 1110 ⌂ Q ⌂ ☾ ➐ ☻

Llangybi 14C7

11–3; 6–11
White Hart
B4596 ☎ Tredunnock 258
**Marston Pedigree; Theakston
Best Bitter** Ⓗ **Regular guest
beers**
Friendly historic coaching inn,
two original 12th century
fireplaces ⌂ Q ⌀ ☾ ➐ ☻

Llanhennock 14C7

11–3; 6–11
Wheatsheaf
Off B4596
**Draught Bass; Samuel Smith
OBB; Welsh Brewers BB** Ⓗ
Friendly country pub, busy in
summer ⌂ ⌀ ☻

Llanishen 14D7

11–3; 6.30–11
Carpenters Arms
B4293 ☎ Trelleck 860405
**Butcombe Bitter; Courage
Directors; Hook Norton Best
Bitter; Robinson Best Bitter** Ⓖ

Pleasant roadside pub.
Paintings by local artist on
sale 🍺📷🌜➤

Llanwenarth 14B6

11–3; 6–11

Llanwenarth Arms
Brecon Road (A40)
𝄐 Abergavenny 810550
**Robinson Best Bitter;
Wadworth 6X** Ⓗ
Pleasant hotel. Beautiful view
over River Usk Q🍴🌜📷🌜➤

Marshfield 14B8

12–3; 7–11

Port o' Call
𝄐 Castleton 680204
**Courage Best Bitter,
Directors** Ⓗ
Solitary pub with a
welcoming atmosphere.
Three-tier lounge. Excellent
bar meals 🌜🌜➤🍷

Mathern 14D7

11–3; 7–11

Millers Arms
Off A48 𝄐 Chepstow 2133
Flowers IPA Ⓗ
Comfortable, friendly village
local 🍺Q🍴🌜🌜➤🍷⛺

Monmouth 14D6

10.30–3 (4 Mon & Fri); 6–11

Punch House
Agincourt Square 𝄐 3855
**Draught Bass; Wadworth 6X;
Welsh Brewers BB** Ⓗ
Large pub, renowned for its
restaurant meals 🌜➤

Queens Head
St. James Street 𝄐 2767
Opens 11
**Brain SA; Flowers Original;
Monmouth 1035, Piston
Bitter** Ⓗ
17th century hotel. Large
comfortable lounge, small bar
with pool table 📷🌜➤🍷

Newport 14C8

11–3; 5.30–11

Globe
Chepstow Road, Maindee
Courage Best Bitter Ⓗ
Small local in shopping area
Q🌜🍷

Lamb
Bridge Street
**Courage Best Bitter,
Directors** Ⓗ
Perennially popular town pub.
Lively atmosphere ⇄

Lyceum Tavern
110 Malpas Road 𝄐 858636
**Courage Best Bitter,
Directors** Ⓗ
Popular local. Thursday
evening folk club 🌜🍷

Orange Tree
25 St. Michaels Street,
Pillgwenlly 𝄐 58569

Brain SA Ⓗ **Regular guest
beers**
Basic local with varied
clientele 🌜🍷

Prince of Wales
Cardiff Road (A48)
**Draught Bass; Welsh Brewers
BB** Ⓗ
Distinctly nautical, akin to
drinking on a cross-Channel
ferry 🌜🍷

Pullman
Spytty Road
**Usher Best Bitter, Founders
Ale** Ⓗ
Cross between a station and
Kew Gardens tea rooms. Only
pub containing a level
crossing gate? 🌜🌜➤🍷

Riverside Tavern
Clarence Place 𝄐 67499
**Courage Best Bitter,
Directors** Ⓗ
New pub under office block,
popular with young 🌜🌜⇄

Royal Albert Grill
164 Commercial Street
𝄐 64261
**Draught Bass, Welsh Brewers
BB** Ⓗ
Berni Inn. Real ale in Victoria
Bar only 🌜➤🍷

Talisman Inn
59 Commercial Street
Courage Best Bitter Ⓗ
A pub in a passage! Small
frontage belies interior 🌜🍷

Pant-yr-Esk 14B7

11.30–4.30; 7–11

Pant-yr-Esk Inn
Pant-yr-Esk Road, West End,
Abercarn OS202956
Crown SBB Ⓗ
The proverbial gem: the pub
that time forgot! Q🍷

Penallt 14D6

11–3; 6–11

Boat
Lone Lane (off A466)
𝄐 Monmouth 2615
**Archers Village Bitter;
Butcombe Bitter; Hook Norton
Best Bitter; Smiles Best Bitter;
Theakston Old Peculier;
Wadworth 6X** Ⓖ **Regular
guest beers**
Friendly pub on River Wye.
Access by footbridge from car
park. Folk on Tues, jazz on
Thurs 🍺🌜🌜➤

Pontnewynydd 14C7

12–4; 7–11

Forge Hammer
Hanbury Road (off A4043)
𝄐 55727
**Courage Best Bitter,
Directors** Ⓗ
Popular local 🌜➤🍷

Pontypool 14C7

11.30–4; 7–11

George Hotel
Commercial Street 𝄐 4734
**Courage Best Bitter,
Directors** Ⓗ
Popular Victorian-style one-
room town centre pub 🌜➤🍴

Wellington Inn
Tranch Road (above High
Street off A472) 𝄐 53477
Opens 12
Usher Best Bitter Ⓗ
Cosy 3-room pub in 600 year
old building; known as the
"Sally", live music Wed
evenings Q🌜🍷

Raglan 14C6

11–3; 7–11

Crown Inn
Usk Road
Flowers IPA Ⓗ
Comfortable local in centre of
village 🌜🌜➤

Try also: Ship (Davenport)

Rhiwderin 14C8

11–3; 5.30–11

Rhiwderin Inn
Caerphilly Road (A468)
**Draught Bass; Welsh Brewers
HB, BB** Ⓗ
Popular, busy local 🌜🌜🍷

Rogerstone 14B8

11.30–3; 6–11

Tredegar Arms
Old Road (A467)
**Courage Best Bitter,
Directors** Ⓗ
Busy, comfortable pub on old
main valleys road
🌜🍷 (Mon–Fri) 🍷

St. Bride's Wentlooge 14C8

11–3; 6–11

Church House Inn
𝄐 Castleton 680807
Brain Dark, Bitter, SA Ⓗ
Popular country pub on
coastal plain 🌜🌜➤ (not Sun) 🍷

Sebastopol 14C7

11–3; 6–11

Open Hearth
Wern Road (off A4051)
𝄐 Pontypool 3752
**Boddingtons Bitter; Courage
Best Bitter; Davenports Bitter;
Felinfoel Double Dragon;
Marston Pedigree; Theakston
XB** Ⓗ **Regular guest beers**
Busy local by Brecon and
Monmouthshire Canal.
Restaurant Q🌜🌜🍷

Shirenewton 14D7

11–3; 5.30–11

Tredegar Arms
The Square 𝄐 274
**Smiles Best Bitter; Usher Best
Bitter, Founders Ale;
Wadworths 6X** Ⓗ
Friendly village local 🌜➤🍷

Try also: Carpenters Arms
(Free)

Tintern 14D7

11–3; 6–11

Cherry Tree
Devauden Road (off A466)
Winter evening opens 7
**Welsh Brewers PA; Bulmer
Cider** G
Small, unspoilt local in fine
walking area ▲ Q ✿ ¶

Rose & Crown
A466 ✆ 254
Courage Best Bitter H
Comfortable pub near River
Wye in beautiful, historic
village. Real ale in lounge only
▲ ▣ ☾ ¶ ¶

Tredegar 14B6

12–4.30; 7–11

Cambrian
The Circle
Draught Bass H**; Brain Bitter,
SA; Ind Coope Burton Ale** E
Busy pub in town centre ▲

Trelleck 14D7

11–3; 6–11

Lion
B4293 ✆ 860322
Draught Bass; Crown SBB H
Friendly village local. Good
value bar food ▲ ✿ ▣ ☾ ¶ ¶ Å

Usk 14C7

11–3; 7–11

Kings Head
Old Market Street ✆ 2963
Opens 5.30
Brain SA; Flowers IPA H
Large comfortable pub.
Impressive fire in lounge
▲ ▣ ☾ ¶ ¶

Royal Hotel
New Market Street ✆ 2931
**Draught Bass; Felinfoel
Double Dragon; Welsh
Brewers PA** H
Comfortable pub, Victorian-
style surroundings ▲ ☾ ¶ ¶

Abersoch 20D7

11–3; 5.30–10.30 (11 summer F, S)

St. Tudwal's Hotel★
✆ 2539
Robinson Best Mild E**, Best
Bitter, Old Tom** G
Strong local custom; smart
lounge ▲ ⊞ ✿ ▣ ☾ ¶ ¶ Å

Bangor 21F5

11–3; 5.30–10.30 (11 summer F, S)

Bulkeley Arms
Caernarfon Road (A4087)
**Marston Burton Bitter,
Pedigree** H
1-room workingmen's local
¶ ≷

Union
Garth Road (off A5) ✆ 2462
**Burtonwood Dark Mild,
Bitter** H
Tiny rooms crowded with
bric-a-brac, backing onto bay
near the pier ✿ ▣ ¶

Beaumaris 21F4

11–3.30; 6–10.30 (11 summer F, S)

Olde Bull's Head
Castle Street ✆ 810329
Draught Bass H
Historic inn dating from 1472
▲ Q ▣ ☾ ¶

Bethesda 21F5

11–3; 5.30–10.30 (11 summer F, S)

Victoria Hotel
High Street (A5) ✆ 600481
**Greenall Whitley Local Mild,
Bitter** H
Tiny two-room pub in former
slating village; boxing photos
a feature in the bar ⊞ ▣ ¶

Betws-y-Coed 21G6

11 (12 winter Mon–Fri)–3; 5.30–10.30 (11 F, S & summer)

Pont-y-Pair Hotel
A5 ✆ 407
**Younger Scotch Bitter, IPA,
No 3** H
Small hotel, handy base for
visitors; lounge, pool room,
wide range of bar food
▲ ⊞ ✿ ▣ ☾ ¶

Bodedern 20D4

11–3.30; 6–10.30 (11 summer F, S)

Crown Hotel
B5109 ✆ Valley 740734
Burtonwood Bitter H
Comfortable, popular village
pub. Good grub ▲ ⊞ ✿ ▣ ☾ ¶ ¶

Bontnewydd 21E5

11–3; 5.30–10.30 (11 summer F, S)

Newborough Arms
A487 ✆ Caernarfon 3126
Ansells Mild; Tetley Bitter H
Popular, comfortable local.
Good selection of food
▲ ✿ ☾ ¶ ¶ Å

Caernarfon 21E5

11–3; 5.30–10.30

Hole in the Wall
Wall Street
Closes 11 F, S in summer
Marston Pedigree
Noisy, basic bar ¶

Palace Vaults
Castle Ditch
**Marston Mercian Mild,
Burton Bitter** H
Busy, basic pub opposite
Castle ▲ ☾ ¶ ≷

Clynnog Fawr 20E6

11–3; 6–10.30 (11 summer F, S)

St. Beuno★
A499 ✆ 212
Ansells Mild; Draught Bass H

Comfortable, spacious inn
dating back to AD616! Low-
cost accommodation in 12
person bunkhouse
▲ ⊞ ✿ ▣ ☾ ¶ ¶ Å

Conway 21G4

11–3; 5.30–10.30 (11 F, S)

Albion Vaults
Upper Castle Street
**Inc Coope Bitter; Tetley Mild,
Bitter** H
Working man's bar. Lounge
with pool & small, quiet snug
▲ ☾ ¶

Corris 21G9

11–3; 6–10.30 (11 summer F, S)

Slater's Arms
Lower Corris (off A487)
Banks's Mild, Bitter H
Friendly local in former
slating village ¶

Criccieth 21E7

11–3; 6–10.30 (11 summer F, S)

Prince of Wales★
High Street (A497)
Whitbread Trophy H
Popular with tourists and
locals ▲ ☾ ¶ ¶ Å ≷

Deganwy 21G4

11–3; 5.30–10.30 (11 F, S & summer)

Farmer's Arms
Pentwyn Road ✆ 83197
**Ansells Mild; Ind Coope Bitter,
Burton Ale** H
Busy pub, decorated with
farming implements
⊞ ☾ ¶ ¶ ≷

Dolgellau 21G8

10.30–3 (4 F); 6–10.30 (11 F, S)

Stag
Bridge Street
**Burtonwood Dark, Mild,
Bitter** H
Popular local with cheerful
atmosphere and a warm
welcome ▲ ⊞ ✿ ¶ Å

Dolwyddelan 21G6

11–3 (12–2.30 winter); 6–10.30 (11 F, S & summer)

Gwydyr
A470 ✆ 209
Banks's Bitter H
Cosy bar and good
atmosphere in this village pub
▲ ✿ ▣ ☾ ¶ ¶ Å ≷

Dwygyfylchi 21G4

11–3; 5.30–10.30

Fairy Glen
Sychnant Pass
✆ Penmaenmawr 3316
Marston Pedigree
Clean, pleasant pub in fine
setting ✿ ☾ ¶

Fairbourne 21F8

10.30–3; 6–10.30 (11 F, S)

Fairbourne Hotel
Off A493

Draught Bass; McEwan 70/-
Ⓗ
Large, well-appointed hotel,
good base for touring
🏠🏥 (summer) 🅿🏦🕒🍴🅰🚲

Gaerwen 21E5

11–3.30; 6–10.30 (11 summer F, S)

Dinam Arms
½ mile off A5 OS485709
☎ 287
Burtonwood Dark Mild,
Bitter Ⓗ
Pleasant little local 🏠🍴

Harlech 21F7

10.30–3; 6–10.30 (11 summer F, S)

Castle Hotel
Castle Square ☎ 780529
Whitbread Castle Eden Ⓗ
Large pub facing castle
🏥🅿🏦 (summer) 🍴🚲

Holyhead 20D4

11–3.30; 6–10.30 (11 summer F, S)

Boston
London Road ☎ 2449
Ansells Mild; Ind Coope
Bitter Ⓗ
Busy, open-plan local 🍴🚲

Llanbedrog 20D7

11–3; 5.30–10.30 (11 summer, F, S)

Ship★
Bryn-y-Gro (B4413) ☎ 270
Burtonwood Dark Mild,
Bitter Ⓗ
Pleasant old pub 🏠🅿🕒🍴🍴🅰🅱

Llanbedr-y-Cennin 21G5

11.30–3; 6–10.30 (11 F, S & summer)

Old Bull Inn
Off B5106 ☎ Dolgarrog 508
Lees GB Mild, Bitter Ⓗ
16th century inn; excellent
food 🏠🏥🅿🏦🕒🍴🅰

Llandudno 21G4

11–3; 5.30–11

Kings Arms
Mostyn Street ☎ 75882
Opens winter eves 7–10.30
Ansells Mild; Minera Bitter;
Tetley Bitter; Coates Cider Ⓗ
Friendly barmaids and real
floorboards! Central for shops
& beach. One-room pub with
alcove for meals
Q🏦🅿 (summer) 🕒
🍴 (summer) 🅱🚲

Washington Hotel
Clarence Road
(off Promenade)
Ansells Mild, Bitter; Ind Coope
Bitter Ⓗ
Comfortable pub, home of
Lloyd & Trouncer. Pool and
darts 🅿🕒

Try also: Albert (Greenall);
Links (Lees); Snowdon Hotel
(Bass)

Llanfaethlu 20D4

11–3.30; 6–10.30 (11 F, S summer)

Black Lion
A5025 ☎ 730209
Burtonwood Bitter Ⓗ
Friendly old pub. Beware keg
mild on hand-pump 🏠🅿🍴

Llanfrothen 21F7

11–3; 6–10.30 (11 summer F, S)

Bron Danw Arms
A4085
Draught Bass; M & B Mild,
Brew XI Ⓗ
Magnificent view of Snowdon
🏠🏥🅿🕒🍴🍴🅰

Llanwnda 20E6

11.30–3; 6–10.30 (11 summer, F, S)

Mount Pleasant
A487
Draught Bass; M & B Mild Ⓗ
Comfortable lounge with oak
beams 🏠🏥🅿🕒🍴🍴🅰

Marianglas 21E4

11–3.30; 6–10.30 (11 summer F, S)

Parciau Arms
B5110 ☎ Tynygongl 853766
Banks's Bitter; Draught Bass;
Marston Pedigree; Younger
No 3 Ⓗ
Cosy, welcoming hostelry
with good food 🏠🏥🅿🕒🍴🍴

Morfa Nefyn 20D7

11–3; 6–10.30 (11 summer F, S)

Bryn Cynan★
☎ Nefyn 720879
Ind Coope Bitter; Tetley
Walker Bitter Ⓗ
3-bar village pub busy with
locals and tourists 🏠🅿🕒🍴🅰🍴

Nant Peris 21F5

12–2; 6 (6.30 winter)–10.30 (11 summer F, S)

Vaynol Arms
A4086
Robinson Best Mild, Bitter Ⓔ
Timeless village pub 'twixt
mountains and slate quarries.
Haunt of climbers. Campers'
breakfast available 🏠🕒🍴🍴🅰

Nefyn 20D7

11–3; 5.30–10.30 (11 summer F, S)

Sportsman★
Stryd Fawr (B4417)
Ind Coope Bitter, Burton Ale Ⓗ
Friendly pub with small
lounge 🏠🕒🅰

Newborough 20E5

11 (12 winter)–3.30; 6 (6.30 winter)–10.30
(11 summer F, S)

White Lion
A4080 ☎ 236
Marston Mercian Mild,
Burton Bitter Ⓗ
Friendly village pub
🏠🅿🍴 (summer) 🍴

Penmaenmawr 21G4

11.30–3; 7–10.30 (11 F, S & summer)

Red Gables Hotel

Bangor Road (A55) ☎ 623722
Webster Yorkshire Bitter;
Wilsons Original Mild,
Bitter Ⓗ
Comfortable olde-world
lounge, snooker room and
conservatory with splendid
sea views. No food Mon
🏠🏥🅿🏦🕒🍴🚲

Penrhyndeudraeth 21F7

10.30–3; 6–10.30 (11 summer F, S)

Royal Oak
High Street ☎ 770501
Burtonwood Dark Mild,
Bitter Ⓗ
Good welcome. Food summer
only 🏠🏥🅿🕒🍴🍴🅰

Penrhynside 21G4

12 (11 summer)–3; 7 (5.30 F, S & summer)–10.30
(11 summer F, S)

Cross Keys
Pendre Road
Banks's Bitter; Ind Coope
Bitter; Tetley Bitter; Coates'
Old English Cider Ⓗ
Small, friendly, unspoilt local
🅿🕒🍴🅰

Port Dinorwic 21E5

11–3; 5.30–10.30 (11 summer F, S)

Gardd Fôn
Beach Road (off A487)
Burtonwood Bitter Ⓗ
Small pub by Menai Straits 🍴

Pwllheli 20D7

11–3; 5.30–10.30 (11 summer F, S)

Penlan Fawr★
Penlan Street
Ind Coope Bitter Ⓗ
Old pub, popular with the
young 🏠🏥🅿🕒🅰🚲

Red Wharf Bay 21E4

11–3.30; 6–10.30 (11 summer F, S)

Ship
☎ Tynygongl 852568
Bank's Bitter
Welcoming free house near
the beach 🏠🏥🅿🕒🍴

Try also: Min-y-Don
(Burtonwood)

Tal-y-Cafn 21G5

12–3; 6–10.30

Tal-y-Cafn Hotel
Llanrwst Road
Greenall Whitney Local Bitter
Popular pub 🏦 (summer) 🕒🚲

Talysarn 21E6

11–3; 5.30–10.30 (11 summer F, S)

Nantlle Vale
B4418 ☎ Penygroes 310
Marston Mercian Mild,
Pedigree, Merrie Monk Ⓗ
Friendly pub. Comfortable,
cheap accommodation
🏥🅿🏦🕒🍴🍴

Trawsfynydd 21F7

10.30–3; 6–10.30 (11 summer F, S)

White Lion
Off A470 ℰ 277
**Burtonwood Dark Mild,
Bitter** Ⓗ
Unspoilt village pub
🏚🚷🅿Ⓖ◖🔴

Powys

Abercrave 13H6

12–4; 6–11

Copper Beech
Off A4067 ℰ 730269
**Courage Best Bitter; Felinfoel
Double Dragon; Tetley
Bitter** Ⓗ **Regular guest beers**
Friendly village pub near the
famous Dan-Yr-Ogof caves
🏚🚷🅿Ⓖ◖

Brecon 14A5

11–3; 5.30–11 (open all day Tue, F)

Boars Head
Watergate ℰ 2856
**Brain SA; Courage Best Bitter;
Felinfoel Double Dragon;
Fuller ESB; Smiles Exhibition;
Samuel Whitbread Strong
Ale** Ⓗ **Regular guest beers**
Lively, enterprising town
centre pub ◖🔴◖

Gremlin Hotel
The Watton (A40) ℰ 3829
**Draught Bass; Everards Old
Original; Robinson Best Bitter;
Younger Scotch Bitter** Ⓗ
Occasional guest beers
Comfortable welcoming pub
🏚🚷🅿Ⓖ◖🔴

Caersws 13J2

10.30–2.30; 6–11

Red Lion
Main Street ℰ 606
Tetley Bitter Ⓗ
Village local with a welcome
for tourists Ⓖ◖🔴≋

Crickhowell 14B6

10.30–3; 6–11

Beaufort Street
(A40) ℰ 810402
Davenports Bitter Ⓗ
Hotel bar with welcoming
atmosphere 🚷🏚🅿

Bridge End
New Road (A4077) ℰ 810338
Morning opens 12
**Draught Bass; Brain Bitter,
SA; Robinson Best Bitter** Ⓗ
16th century pub overlooking
the river 🏚🚷Ⓖ🅰

Erwood 14A4

10.30–3; 6–11

Erwood Inn
A470 ℰ 218
Flowers IPA Ⓗ; **Wadworth
6X** Ⓖ
Friendly village local near the
River Wye 🏚🚷🅿Ⓖ◖🔴🅰

Garthmyl 22A9

11–2.30; 6–11

Nags Head
A483 ℰ Berriew 287
Ind Coope Bitter Ⓗ
18th century coaching inn.
Good food at an affordable
price 🏚🚷🅿Ⓖ◖🔴🅰

Glasbury 14B4

11–3; 6–11

Maesllwch Arms
Off A438 ℰ 226
Felinfoel Double Dragon Ⓗ
Regular guest beers
Specialises in holidays for
families and outdoor activity
groups 🏚🚷🅿Ⓖ◖🔴🅰

Try also; Harp (Free)

Guilsfield 22A8

11–3; 5.30–11

Oak Inn
Off B4392 ℰ Welshpool 3391
**Wem Pale Ale, Mild, Best
Bitter** Ⓔ, **Special Bitter** Ⓗ
Large oak-beamed pub. No
food weekends 🚷Ⓖ🔴

Llandinam 14A1

11–2.30; 6–11

Lion Hotel
A470 ℰ Caersws 233
Draught Bass Ⓗ
Comfortable village local
🏚Q🚷Ⓖ🔴🍴

Llandrindod 14A3
Wells

11.30–3; 6–11

Llanerch
Waterloo Road (over railway
foot bridge) ℰ 2086
**Draught Bass; Flowers IPA;
Robinson Best Bitter** Ⓗ
16th century coaching inn
🏚🚷🅿Ⓖ◖🔴≋

Llanfair 21J9
Caereinion

11–3; 5.30–11

Wynstay Arms
Watergate Street ℰ 810203
Ansells Mild; Tetley Bitter Ⓗ
Imposing corner pub with
restaurant 🏚🚷🅿Ⓖ◖🔴🍴

Llanfyllin 21J8

11–3; 5.30–11

Cain Valley Hotel
High Street ℰ 366
**Draught Bass; Ind Coope
Bitter; Marston Burton Bitter,
Pedigree** Ⓗ
Superb 17th century coaching
inn 🏚🚷🅿Ⓖ◖🔴🍴

Llangurig 13J2

10.30–2.30; 5.30–11

Blue Bell
A44 ℰ 254
**Banks's Mild (summer),
Bitter** Ⓔ; **Sam Powells Bitter** Ⓗ

16th century fishing inn
🏚🚷🏚Ⓖ◖🔴🍴

Llangynidr 14B6

11–3; 6–11

Coach & Horses
Cwm Crawnon Road (B4558)
ℰ Bwlch 730245
**Draught Bass; Welsh Brewers
HB** Ⓗ **Regular guest beers**
Spacious old pub. Local HQ for
official Monster Raving Loony
Party 🚷Ⓖ🔴

Llanhamlach 14A5

11–3; 6–11

Old Ford
A40 ℰ Llanfrynach 220
Wem Best Bitter Ⓗ; **Bulmer
Cider** Ⓔ **Occasional guest
beers**
Roadside pub with a beautiful
view over the Usk Valley.
Amazing collection of bottled
beers 🏚🚷🅿Ⓖ◖🔴🅰

Llanidloes 13J2

10.30–2.30; 5.30–11 (all day S)

Angel Hotel
High Street ℰ 2381
Wem Mild, Best Bitter Ⓗ
Old pennies mounted in top of
bar in lounge Ⓖ◖🔴🍴&

Mount Inn
China Street ℰ 2247
**Welsh Brewers Dark, Light
Mild** Ⓗ
Boasts a fascinating old cast-
iron stove 🏚🚷🚷🔴

Llanrhaedr- 21J5
Ym-Mochnant

11–3; 5.30–11

Plough
B4580
Draught Bass Ⓖ
Unspoilt small locals pub with
cast-iron stove 🏚Q🔴

Llansantffraid- 22A7
Ym-Mechain

11.30 (12 winter)–3; 6.30–11

Sun Hotel
A495 ℰ 214
**Marston Border Exhibition,
Burton Bitter, Pedigree** Ⓗ;
Owd Rodger (winter) Ⓖ
Food a speciality 🚷🚷🅿Ⓖ◖🔴🍴🅰

Llanwrtyd 13H4
Wells

11–3; 6–11

Neuadd Arms
A483 ℰ 236
**Felinfoel Double Dragon;
Welsh Brewers BB** Ⓗ
Occasional guest beers
Large, comfortable friendly
hotel 🏚🚷🚷🅿Ⓖ◖🔴🍴≋

Machynlleth 21G9

10.30–2.30 (4 Wed); 5.30–10.30 (11 F, S &
summer)

Dyfi Forester
Doll Street ✆ 2004
Banks's Mild, Bitter Ⓔ;
Hansons Black Country Bitter;
Marston Pedigree; Sam Powell
Bitter (summer) Ⓗ
Enterprising free house
🏠🍴🅿🌳🕒🚻🍴≷

Try also: **Skinners Arms**
(Burtonwood)

Red Lion
Maengwyn Street ✆ 2675
Banks's Mild, Bitter Ⓔ
Friendly local opposite the
Post Office 🍴🅿🏠🍴≷

Montgomery   22A9

10.30–2.30; 6–11

Crown
Castle Street ✆ 533
Wem Pale Ale, Best Bitter Ⓔ
Bustling old pub 🏠🍴🛏

Newtown   14A1

10.30–2.30; 5.30–11

Bear Hotel
Broad Street ✆ 26964
Open all day Tue
Sam Powell Bitter Ⓗ
Town centre hotel with lively
public bar 🏠🕒🚻🍴≷

Try also: **Black Boy** (Welsh
Brewers)

Pheasant
Market Street ✆ 25966
Open all day Tue
Burtonwood Best Bitter Ⓗ
Friendly old market pub
🏠🅿🕒🍴≷

Wagon & Horses
Lower Canal Road ✆ 25790
Marston Border Exhibition,
Pedigree Ⓗ
Old homely pub by canal
basin 🅿🕒🚻🍴

Pant Mawr   13H2

10.30–2.30; 6.30–11

Glansevern Arms

A44 ✆ Llangurig 240
Draught Bass Ⓗ
Comfortable isolated hotel.
Must book for food 🏠🅿🍴🏠🕒🍴

Penybont   14B3

11–3; 6–11

Severn Arms Hotel
A44 ✆ 224
Draught Bass Ⓗ
Hotel with traditional bar and
fishing rights 🏠🍴🅿🏠🕒🚻🍴≷

Pontrobert   21J8

11.30–2.30; 6.30–11

Royal Oak
Off A495 ✆ Meifod 474
Marston Pedigree Ⓗ
Comfortable, well-appointed
country pub with adventure
playground 🏠🍴🅿🕒🚻🍴

Presteigne   14C3

11–3; 6–11

Royal Oak
High Street ✆ 267510
Draught Bass Ⓗ
Busy local. Sunday lunch a
speciality Q🅿🕒🍴🚻

Rhayader   13J3

11–3; 5.30–11

Cwmdauddwr Arms
West Street ✆ 810763
Marston Pedigree Ⓗ Regular
guest beers
16th century locals inn
🏠🍴🅿🕒🚻🍴🛏

Triangle Inn
Cwmdauddwr (off Bridge
Street) ✆ 810537
Evening opens 6
Draught Bass; Flowers IPA Ⓗ
Inn overlooking River Wye
🏠🅿🕒🚻🍴🛏

Sarn   14B1

11–2.30; 6–11

Sarn Inn
A489 ✆ Kerry 601
Burtonwood Best Bitter Ⓔ

Well kept country pub
🍴🅿🕒🚻🍴🛏

Talgarth   14B5

11–3; 6–11 (all day F & 2nd & 4th Sat in month)

Tower Hotel
The Square ✆ 711253
Flowers IPA, Original; Samuel
Whitbread Strong Ale Ⓗ
Large, popular town centre
hotel 🏠🏠🕒🚻🍴

Talybont on   14B5
Usk

11–3; 6–11 (all day Thu & last Sat in month)

Star
B4558 ✆ 635
Everard Old Original; Fuller
London Pride; Marston Owd
Rodger; Smiles Exhibition;
Tates Traditional Bitter Ⓗ
Regular guest beers
Friendly village pub full of
character. Vegetarian dishes
on menu
🏠🅿🕒🍴🚻🛏

Trecastle   13J5

11 (12 winter)–3; 5.30–11

Three Horseshoes
A40 ✆ Sennybridge 432
Everards Tiger; Hook Norton
Best Bitter; Wadworth 6X Ⓗ
Regular guest beers
Comfortable old coaching inn
🏠🍴🅿🏠🕒🍴

Welshpool   22A8

11–3; 5.30–11

Mermaid
High Street ✆ 2027
Open all day Mon
Banks's Mild, Bitter Ⓔ
Friendly town centre pub
🕒🚻🍴≷

Pheasant
High Street ✆ 3104
Marston Pedigree Ⓗ; Woods
Special Bitter Ⓔ
Friendly old pub with good
restaurant 🏠🅿🕒🚻🍴≷

THIS
PUB'S
AUTHORITY
ON FOOTBALL
WEATHER
POLITICS, ETC

KenPyne

General opening hours: 11–2.30; 5–11. Sunday 12.30–2.30; 6.30–11
N.B. Not all Scottish pubs open Sundays.

Borders

Capercleuch 35G6

Tibbie Shiels Inn
St. Mary's Loch
(A708 2 miles S)
12.30–11 Sun
**Lorimer & Clark 80/- (winter);
70/- (summer)** Ⓐ
Marvellous, remote lochside
inn on the Southern Upland
Way Q🏠🍴🅱️🕐🍷🍽️👶

Carlops 35F5

Allan Ramsay
A702 ☎ West Linton 60258
11–11 (1 am F, S); 12.30–11 (Sun)
**Belhaven 80/-; Theakston
Best Bitter** Ⓗ Occasional guest
beers
Friendly country inn. Unusual
bartop inset with old pennies.
Food all day 🏠🍴🅱️🕐🍷🍽️👶

Coldstream 35J6

Besom Inn
Main Street (A697)
McEwan 70/-; Younger No 3
Ⓐ
Robust wee local of timeless
character 🏠🍷

Commercial
30–32 High Street (A697)
11–11 Sat
Belhaven 70/-, 80/- Ⓗ
Convivial main street drinking
shop 🍷

Newcastle Arms
High Street (A697)
11–11; 12.30–11 Sun
Arrols 70/- Ⓔ
Bustling Borders bar,
bedecked with model motors
🅱️🍴🅱️🕐

Duns 35H5

Black Bull
Black Bull Street
☎ 83379
11–11; 12.30–11 Sun
Tennent Heriot 80/- Ⓗ
Cheery wee two-bar hotel,
soon to be home-brew house
🅱️🍴🅱️🕐🍷🍽️👶

Hawick 35G7

Queen's Head
High Street ☎ 72057
11–3; 5–11; 11–4.30; 6.30–11 Sat
McEwan 80/- Ⓐ
Thriving town centre bar
where rugby is spoken
fluently 🍷

Kelso 35H6

Black Swan Hotel
Horse Market ☎ 24563
11–11 (midnight F, S); 12.30–11 Sun
Tennent Heriot 80/- Ⓗ

Basic, friendly bar popular
with locals 🅱️🍴🅱️🕐🍷🍽️👶

Red Lion
Crawford Street ☎ 24817
11–11; 12.45 am F, midnight S; open Sun
Arrols 70/- Ⓗ
Fine interior. Long bar divided
by screen in middle 🏠🕐🍷

White Swan
9 Woodmarket ☎ 24216
11–11; open Sun
Arrols 70/- Ⓗ
Thriving low-ceilinged local's
bar approached through close
🏠🅱️🍷

Stow 35G6

Manorhead Hotel
168 Main Street (A7) ☎ 201
Open all day, 7 days
**Lorimer & Clark 70/-, 80/-,
Caledonian Strong Ale** Ⓗ
Excellent, steady local with a
warm welcome for visitors.
Meals available all day and
highly recommended
🏠🍴🅱️🕐🍷

Town Yetholm 35H6

Plough Hotel
Main Street ☎ 215
11–11 (midnight [11 winter] F, S); 12.30–11 Sun
Arrols 70/- Ⓗ
Cosy, welcoming howff in
deepest Borders arcadia, near
England 🏠🍴🕐🍷🍽️

West Linton 35F5

Linton Hotel
Main Street ☎ 60228
11–12 Fri–Sun
**Tennent 80/-, Broughton
Special Bitter** Ⓗ
Couthy village local 🏠🍴🕐🍷🍽️

Yarrow 35G6

Gordon Arms Hotel
A708 ☎ 222
11–11 Sat; 12.30–11 Sun
Broughton Greenmantle Ale Ⓗ
Isolated, small, cosy bar at
remote crossroads 🏠🅱️👶

Central

Aberfoyle 34D4

Altskeith Hotel
Lochard Road, 3 miles W
☎ Kinlochard 266
11–12 Sat
**Broughton Greenmantle
Ale** Ⓗ; **McEwan 80/-** Ⓐ
Beautifully situated on banks
of Loch Ard. Boat hire and
fishing 🏠🍴🅱️🕐🍷🍽️👶

Alloa 35F4

Crams Bar
Candleriggs
6 am–8 am; 11–11 (midnight F, S); open Sun

Maclay 80/- Ⓐ
Small homely pub, worth a
visit 🍷

Thistle Bar
1 Junction Place
11–midnight Thu, F, S; open Sun
Maclay 80/- Ⓐ
Popular lounge and bar.
Maclay's brewery tap 🍷

Alva 35F4

No. 5 Inn
Brook Street
11–11 Thu; 11–am F; 11–midnight Sat
Maclay 80/- Ⓐ
Friendly, traditional coaching
inn where Burns rested for
refreshment in 1787 🍷

Bridge of Allan 35E4

Queens Hotel
Henderson Street
☎ Stirling 833268
11–1 am; 12.30–1 Sun
Ind Coope Burton Ale Ⓗ;
Younger IPA, No 3 Ⓐ
Renowned for its IPA; bar
suppers till midnight. Beer
garden 🅱️🍴🅱️🕐🍷👶🚻

Westerton Arms
Henderson Street
11–midnight; Sun closes midnight
**Arrols 70/-; Ind Coope Burton
Ale** Ⓗ; **McEwan 80/-** Ⓐ;
**Theakston Best Bitter, Old
Peculier** Ⓗ
Open-plan bar with copper
pots and old guns
🏠🍴🕐🍷👶🚻

Callander 34E4

Bridgend House
Bridgend ☎ 30130
11–11 (1 am F, S)
**Broughton Greenmantle Ale;
Strathalbyn Original** Ⓗ
Friendly, country hotel on the
banks of the River Teith
🏠🅱️🍴🅱️🕐🍷🍽️👶

Dunblane 35E4

Sheriffmuir Inn
Sheriffmuir ☎ 823285
11–11 Mon–Sun
Maclay 80/- Ⓗ
Picturesque country pub
overlooking Sheriffmuir Battle
site 🏠🍴🅱️🍴🅱️🕐🍷👶

Falkirk 35F5

Burns Bar
Vicar Street ☎ 21397
11–11
**Broughton Greenmantle Ale,
Special Ale, Merlin's Ale;
Theakston Best Bitter, XB** Ⓐ
Occasional guest beers
Broughton Brewery's own
outlet 🕐🍷🚻

Crossbow
Union Road, Camelon
✆ 24414
11–11.45; open Sun
Tennent Heriot 80/- Ⓗ
Uninspiring modern exterior
conceals friendly and well
kept interior Ⓒ🍴&

Grangemouth 35F5

Oxgang House
Oxgang Road ✆ 473131
Opens 11.30
McEwan 80/- Ⓔ
Very popular, with smart
modern lounge bar
⊞ (lunchtime) Ⓐ Ⓒ🍴

Stirling 35E4

Barnton Bar & Bistro
Barnton Street ✆ 61698
11–11
Maclay 80/- Ⓐ
Popular town centre bistro;
fine set of mirrors, unusual
phone box ⊞ Ⓒ🍴🎵≷

Birds & Bees
Easter Cornton Road
Closes midnight Thu; 11–midnight F, S; open Sun
Harviestoun 80/-; McEwan
80/-; Maclay 80/- Ⓐ
Open-plan bar decorated with
metal birds and bees. French
restaurant, petanque played
outside 🍴Ⓒ🍴&

Wallace
Airthrey Road, Causewayhead
11–midnight; open Sun
Belhaven 70/-, 80/- Ⓐ
Excellent pub, colourful
characters abound Ⓒ🍴🍴

Dumfries & Galloway

Annan 35F8

Blue Bell
High Street (A75) ✆2385
Open Sun
McEwan 70/-; Younger
No 3 Ⓐ; Theakston Best
Bitter Ⓗ
Lively ex-State Brewery pub
Q🍴≷

Canonbie 35G8

Riverside Inn
A7 ✆ 295
Theakston Best Bitter Ⓗ
Pleasant country inn with
good food Q🍴⊞Ⓒ🍴

Dumfries 35F8

Ship Inn
97 St. Michaels Street
Open Sun
McEwan 70/-, 80/- Ⓐ
A real collectors item: fine
Toby jugs Q🍴

Tam o' Shanter
117 Queensberry Street
McEwan 80/-; Younger No 3
Homely pub near town centre
Q🍴≷

Somewhere Else
Station Hotel, Lovers Lane
✆ 52881
Closes midnight Sat; Open Sun
Tennent Heriot 80/- Ⓗ
Modern disco style pub, very
noisy! Ⓒ🍴≷

Eastriggs 35G8

Graham Arms
West end of village (A75)
✆ 244
Open Sun
Greenall Whitley Bitter Ⓗ
Friendly comfortable 2-room
inn ⊞🍴Ⓒ🍴🍴Å

Gretna 35G8

Solway Lodge Hotel
Annan Road ✆ 37655
Theakston Best Bitter Ⓗ
Comfortable lounge bar with
restaurant ⊞🍴Ⓒ🍴&Å

Lockerbie 35F8

Kings Arms
High Street ✆ 2410
Open Sun
McEwan 80/- Ⓐ
17th century town centre
coaching inn ⊞Ⓒ🍴🍴Å≷

Moffat 35F7

Star Hotel
High Street ✆ 20156
Open Sun
Marston Pedigree Ⓗ
Friendly hotel near War
Memorial ⊞Ⓒ🍴🍴Å

New Abbey 35F8

Criffel Inn
B710 ✆ 244
Younger No 3 Ⓗ
Owner a traction engine
enthusiast. Real ale in public
bar Q⊞🍴Ⓒ🍴🍴

Newton Stewart 34D8

Creebridge House
Minnigaff
Opens 12; closed 2.30–6 winter; open Sun
Broughton Greenmantle;
Theakston Best Bitter, Old
Peculier Ⓗ
Comfortable hotel close to
town centre. Good food
🍴⊞🍴Ⓒ🍴&Å

Stranraer 34C8

Golden Cross
Younger No 3 Ⓐ
Popular main street local 🍴

Fife

Aberdour 35G4

Aberdour Hotel
High Street (A92) ✆ 860325
11–11 Sat; 12.30–11 Sun
Belhaven 70/-; 80/- Ⓗ

Pleasant bar with stables in
yard of old coaching inn
🍴⊞Ⓒ🍴🍴≷

Carnock 35F4

Old Inn
6 Main Street ✆ 850381
11–11 F, S; open Sun
Maclay 80/- Ⓐ
Pleasant friendly village pub
with good, reasonably-priced
lunches Ⓒ🍴

Dunfermline 35F4

Old Inn
Kirkgate (opp. Abbey)
✆ 736652
11–11; open Sun
McEwan 80/-; Younger No
3 Ⓐ
Oldest pub in city. Fine gantry,
wide range of malt whiskies
Ⓒ🍴≷

Elie 35G4

Ship Inn
Toft
11–11 (midnight Thu, F, S); open Sun
Belhaven 80/- Ⓗ
Quaint waterfront bar with
strong nautical features
🍴Q⊞🍴🍴Å

Freuchie 35G4

Albert Tavern
Main Street (off A914)
✆ Falkland 57719
11.30–2.30; 5–11.30
(12 Thu–Sat)
Lorimer & Clark 80/- Ⓗ
Cosy country pub with fine
mirrors ⊞Ⓒ🍴🍴

Hillend 35F4

Hillend Tavern
37 Main Street (A92)
✆ 415391
11–11 F, S; open Sun
Drybrough Eighty Ⓐ
Comfortable 1-room village
pub with nautical antiques
🍴Ⓒ🍴

Inverkeithing 35F4

Volunteer
61 High Street ✆ 412834
11–11; open Sun
Maclay 70/- Ⓐ
Town centre local with good
atmosphere. Occasional live
music in basic bar 🍴≷

Kettlebridge 35G4

Kettlebridge Inn
A92 ✆ Ladybank 30232
11.30–2.30; 4–11; 12.30–11 Sun
Maclay 60/-, 70/-, 80/- Ⓗ
Small, friendly public bar;
darts room and lounge
Q Ⓒ🍴🍴

Kirkcaldy 35G4

Novar Bar
17 Nicol Street ✆ 260545

11–11 F, S; open Sun
McEwan 80/-; Younger No 3 Ⓐ
Fine 60s pub on site of old Novar Ⓖ🍴⇌

Largoward 35G4

Staghead Hotel
A915/B940 OS465073
✆ Peat Inn 205
11–11 Mon & Wed; closed Tue am; 11–12 Thu, S; 11–1 am F; 12.30–11 Sun
Ind Coope Burton Ale Ⓗ
Occasional guest beers
Basic public bar, comfortable lounge. Good food
🏨Q🅿🚼Ⓖ🍴⇌Å

Limekilns 35F5

Ship Inn
Halketts Hall ✆ 872247
Belhaven 70/-; 80/-; Lorimer & Clark 70/- Ⓗ
Large bar with separate games area overlooking River Forth
Ⓖ

Lochgelly 35F4

Central Bar
59 Main Street ✆ 780394
11–11 F, S; open Sun
Belhaven 60/- Ⓐ
Basic, many-roomed pub in mining town 🍴⇌

Lower Largo 35G4

Railway Inn
3 Station Wynd (off A915)
11–1 am; open Sun
Tennent 80/- Ⓗ
Low-roofed, quaint hostelry. Nautical charts a decorative feature Q🚼🅿Ⓖ🍴Å⇌

Try also: Crusoe Hotel (Ind Coope/Arrol)

St. Andrews 35H3

Russell Hotel
26 The Scores ✆ 73447
Opens 12; open Sun
Broughton Greenmantle Ale Ⓗ
Well furnished bar. Supports trivial pursuit league
🏨Q🚼Ⓖ🍴Å

Victoria Cafe
St. Mary's Place ✆ 76964
Maclay 80/- Ⓐ
Spacious, high-ceilinged continental cafe of faded elegance Q🅿🍴Å

Grampian

Aberdeen 37J8

Albyn
1 Queens Cross ✆ 322594
Ind Coope Burton Ale Ⓗ
Dizzy, popular night spot, good for rhythm and Burton!
Q🅿Ⓖ🍴

Carriages
101 Crown Street ✆ 595440
11–11; open Sun

Whitbread Castle Eden, Durham Ale Ⓗ
Comfortable lounge with up-market pretensions. Good value food Q🚼Ⓖ🍴⇌

Dobbies Ale House
22 Guild Street
11–11; 12–4 Sun
McEwan 80/-; Newcastle Exhibition; Younger No 3 Ⓐ
Unusual outlet which can turn a "straight" man to a "jug" 🚼Ⓖ🍴⇌

Gordon Motel
Wellington Road (A956)
✆ 873012
11–11 Mon–F; open Sun
Arrols 70/-; Ind Coope Burton Ale Ⓗ
Large hotel on south side of town, friendly pleasant service
🏨Q🅿🚼Ⓖ🍴🍴

Grill
213 Union Street
11–10.30
McEwan 80/- Ⓐ
Splendidly preserved wood-panelled bar with famed service 🍴🍴⇌

Kirkgate Bar
18 Upper Kirkgate ✆ 640515
11–11; open Sun
Devanha XXX; Ind Coope Burton Ale Ⓗ
Basic, friendly local, very popular with students Q Ⓖ🍴⇌

Old Frigate
57 Netherkirkgate ✆ 640505
11–11; 12.30–2.30 Sun
Lorimer & Clark 80/- Ⓗ; **Younger No 3** Ⓐ
Earthy local. Large range of malts and randy but well-trained "cat"! 🍴⇌

Pittodrie Bar
339 King Sreet ✆ 636920
11–11; open Sun
Tennent Heriot 80/- Ⓗ
Working class pub. Island bar, fine old mirrors 🍴

Prince of Wales
7 St. Nicholas Lane ✆ 640597
11–11; open Sun
Lorimer & Clark 80/-; Tennent Heriot 80/-; Theakston Best Bitter, Old Peculier Ⓗ; **Younger No 3** Ⓐ
Regular guest beers
Welcome as ever—marvellous bar Q Ⓖ🍴⇌

Tilted Wig
Castle Street
11–11; open Sun
Alice Ale; Devanha XXX; Dryborough Eighty Ⓐ
Bar with unusual legal theme and witty comments on wall
Ⓖ⇌

Yardarm
40 Regent Quay ✆ 590548
11–11
McEwan 80/-; Younger No 3 Ⓐ
Popular harbourside bar
Q Ⓖ⇌

Alford 37J8

Forbes Arms Hotel
✆ 2108
11–11; 11.30–2.30; 5–10.30 Sun
Devanha XB Ⓗ
Good food and fishing
🚼🅿Ⓖ🍴🍴

Banchory 37H9

Scott Skinners Restaurant
North Deeside Road ✆ 4393
11–12 S; closes midnight Mon–F; open Sun (all day in summer)
Drybrough Eighty Ⓗ
Small, cosy bar on east side of Banchory 🏨🚼Ⓖ🍴

Tor-na-Coille
Inchmarlo Road ✆ 2242
Open Sun
Devanha XB Ⓗ
Large hotel on edge of town. Expansive gardens and excellent sports facilities nearby 🏨Q🚼🚼Ⓖ🍴

Elgin 37G7

Braelossie Hotel
2 Sheriffmill Road ✆7181
McEwan 80/- Ⓐ
Imposing family-run hotel on outskirts of town Q🚼🅿🚼Ⓖ🍴

Laichmoray Hotel
Maisondeau Road ✆ 7832
5–11.45 F, S
McEwan 80/- Ⓐ
Comfortable, 2-star hotel, ½ mile from town centre
Q🚼🚼Ⓖ🍴⇌

Elrick 37H8

Broadstraik Inn
A944 ✆ Aberdeen 743217
11–11 S; open Sun
Younger No 3 Ⓗ
Real ale in public bar of old style country pub 🏨Q🚼Ⓖ🍴🍴

Findhorn 37F7

Crown & Anchor
Findhorn ✆ 30243
11–11 (11.45 F, S); open Sun
Devanha XB, XXX; Heriot 80/-; Maclay 80/-; Westons Cider Ⓗ Regular guest beers
Situated very close to Findhorn Bay—a must. Free boat hire for residents. Peat fires 🏨Q🅿🚼Ⓖ🍴🍴Å

Forres 37F7

Red Lion Hotel
Tolbooth Street ✆ 72716
11–11 (11.45 F, S); open Sun
McEwan 80/- Ⓗ; **Younger No 3** Ⓐ
Town centre pub locally known as "The Red Beastie". Fine wood-panelled lounge and popular, no-frills public. Darts 🚼🍴

Royal Hotel
Tyler Road ✆ 72617

11–11 lounge only
Younger No 3 Ⓐ
100 year-old hotel on
outskirts of town. Do not miss
visiting the quite magnificent
gents loo! Pool room
🍴🏠📶🕭ᴴ⛄≋

Fraserburgh   37J7

Crown Bar
45 Broad Street/125 Shore
Street ✆ 24941
11–11; open Sun
Ind Coope Burton Ale Ⓗ
Traditional long bar, couthie
service. Tattie pies a speciality
🍴

Hopeman   37F7

Station Hotel
36 Harbour Street ✆ 830258
11–11 F, S
Devanha Pale Eighty Ⓗ
Popular village pub near
beach; pool and darts
🏠🍴🕭🍽⛄

Inverurie   37H8

Thainstone House
A96 1½ miles S ✆ 21643
11–11 S; 12.30–11 Sun
Tennent Heriot 80/- Ⓗ
Imposing country house with
excellent summer day facilities
🏛Q🏠🕭🍽

Kincardine   37H9
o'Neil

Gordon Arms
A93 ✆ 236
11–midnight daily
Devanha Pale Eighty Ⓗ
Excellent hospitality in a
friendly atmosphere on main
Deeside road 🏛Q🏠🍴🕭🍽🍺

Lossiemouth   37G7

Clifton Bar
Clifton Road ✆ 2100
5–11.45 F, S
**McEwan 80/-; Younger
No 3** Ⓐ **Regular guest beers**
Busy pub near to seafront.
Pool and darts in public bar
🍴🍺

Huntly House
Stotfield Road ✆2085
11–11 (11.45 F, S)
McEwan 80/- Ⓗ
Tudor-style family hotel with
tastefully extended lounge.
Magnificent view of Moray
Firth and Sutherland Hills
Q🏠🍴🕭🍽🍺

Stonehaven   37J9

Heugh Hotel
Westfield Road ✆ 62379
Open Sun
Tennent Heriot 80/- Ⓐ
Imposing Baronial style hotel
Q🏠🍴🕭🍽🍺🍺

Marine Hotel
9–10 Shore Head ✆ 62155

11–11 Mon–Sat; open Sun
**Devanha XB; McEwan 80/-;
Tennent Heriot 80/-** Ⓗ
Popular pub beside
picturesque harbour. Wood-
panelled bar and games room
🏛🏠🍴🕭🍽

Highland

Borve, Isle of Lewis

Borve House
Off A857 ✆ 223
11–11 June–August
Borve House Ale Ⓗ; **ES** Ⓖ
Friendly, though remote bar
serving crofting community.
Gaelic spoken Q🍴⛄🍽

Bower   37F4

Bower Inn
Off B876 OS239624
✆ Gillock 292
Younger No 3 Ⓐ
Tastefully renovated barn,
popular with all age groups
🏛Q🍴🕭🍽

Cawdor   37E7

CawdorTavern
The Lane (B9090) ✆ 316
Arrols 70/-; Younger No 3 Ⓗ
Old coaching house tastefully
restored with warm, friendly
atmosphere 🏛Q🍴🕭🍽🍺

Conon Bridge   36D7

Drouthy Duck
High Street (A862) ✆ 61806
11–11 (1 am F, 11.45 S)
McEwan 80/- Ⓐ
Lively traditional lounge
bar—said to be haunted 🍴🕭🍺

Dores   36E8

Dores Inn
B862 ✆ 203
Alice Ale Ⓗ
Traditional village pub on the
banks of Loch Ness—a few
pints and they say you see the
monster! 🏠🍴🕭🍽🍺

Fortrose   36E7

Royal Hotel
High Street (A832) ✆ 20236
Younger No 3 Ⓐ
Popular hotel bar just off the
Cathedral (ruins of) Square.
Real Ale Festival in August
Q🍴🕭🍽🍺

Fort William   34C2

Nevis Bank Hotel
Belford Road (off A82) ✆ 5721
11–11; 12.30–11 Sun
**McEwan 80/-; Younger
No 3** Ⓐ
Busy hotel with Ceilidh bar at
rear 🏠🍴🕭🍽⛄≋

Gairloch   36B6

Old Inn

The Harbour (A832) ✆ 2006
11–11 Mon–Sun (Thu–Sun winter); 11–1 am F;
11–10.30 S
Tennent 80/- Ⓐ
Busy, friendly local hotel with
horse brasses in lounge bar
and superb views of lochs and
mountains 🏠🍴🕭🍽🍺⛄

Inverness   36E7

Clachnaharry Inn
High Street (A862) ✆ 239806
11–11 (midnight Thu, F, S)
**McEwan 80/-; Younger
No 3** Ⓐ
Traditional old coaching inn
with magnificent views across
the Beauly Firth. At the head
of the Caledonian Canal
🏠🍴⛄

Fluke Inn
Culcabock Road ✆ 220957
Younger No 3 Ⓐ
Very noisy, lively bar near the
hospital and army barracks
🕭🍺

Glenmhor Hotel
10 Ness Bank ✆ 234308
Ind Coope Burton Ale Ⓗ
Pleasant traditional stable bar
and smart Italian bistro.
Magnificent view across River
Ness to Cathedral
🏠🍴🕭🍽🍺≋

Haugh Bar
41 Haugh Road ✆ 232631
Younger No 3 Ⓐ
Popular "folk singers" bar
close to town centre 🍺≋

Innes Bar
61 Innes Street ✆ 232387
11–11 Thu, F, S
Younger No 3 Ⓐ
Popular pool bar close to the
harbour and town centre
🕭🍺

Kingsmills Hotel
Culcabock Road ✆ 237166
Alice Ale Ⓗ; **McEwan 80/-;
Younger No 3** Ⓐ
Very comfortable hotel beside
the golf course on the edge of
town Q🍴🕭🍽🍺

Lochardil Hotel
Stratherrick Road ✆ 235995
Younger No 3 Ⓐ
Splendid lounge bar in what
was a grand town house. Now
a popular weddings hotel with
special grounds and sunken
garden 🏛🏠🍴🕭🍽

Muirtown Motel
Clachnaharry Road ✆ 234860
11–11 (1 am Thu, F, 11.45 S) Mon–Sun
Younger No 3 Ⓐ
Popular meeting place by the
first step of locks at the east
end of the Caledonian Canal
🍴🕭🍽

Phoenix Bar
106 Academy Street
✆ 233685
11–11 (midnight Thu, F, S)

McEwan 70/-; Younger
No 3 Ⓐ
Unspoilt traditional horseshoe
bar with sawdust on floor.
Folk music in lounge
Q Ⓖ ✽ Ⓑ ⟨ symbols ⟩

Raigmore Motel
Perth Road ✆ 221546
Ind Coope Burton Ale Ⓗ
Modern busy bar near the
main hospital Ⓑ Ⓖ

Nairn 37E7

Invernairn Hotel
Thurlow Road (A96) ✆ 52039
Younger No 3 Ⓐ
Traditional lounge bar with
some no smoking tables. Live
jazz Mondays Ⓐ Q Ⓑ ✽ Ⓑ Ⓖ ➐

Struy 36D8

Struy Inn
B831, 10 miles SW of Muir of
Ord OSNH4040 ✆ 219
11–11 summer Mon–Sun
Alice Ale Ⓗ
Small friendly locals' bar of
late Victorian origins
Ⓐ Q Ⓑ ✽ Ⓑ Ⓖ ➐ ⟨ symbols ⟩

Thurso 37F3

Station Bar
Princes Street
Evening closed 10; closed Sun
McEwan 80/-; Younger
No 3 Ⓐ
Friendly traditional Scottish
bars, adorned with large old
brewery mirrors Ⓐ ⟨symbols⟩ ≈

Lothian

Balerno 35F5

Grey Horse Inn
Main Street (off A70)
Closed Sun
Belhaven 60/-, 80/- Ⓗ
Traditionally-run, wood-
panelled village local with
some fine mirrors Q ⟨symbol⟩

Marchbank Hotel
Marchbank Road (off A70)
✆ 449 3970
Opens 12 & 6; open Sun
Lorimer & Clark 70/-, 80/- Ⓗ
Wood-panelled bar with
restaurant in splendid hotel
set in fine grounds
Ⓐ Ⓑ ✽ Ⓑ Ⓖ ➐

Dalkeith 35G5

Justinlees Inn
Dalhousie Road, Eskbank Toll
✆ 663 2166
Opens 11.30; open Sun
Ind Coope Burton Ale Ⓗ;
Younger No 3 Ⓐ
Pleasant triangular pub at
busy roundabout. Restaurant
Ⓐ Q Ⓖ ➐

Dirleton 35H4

Castle Inn

Off A198 ✆ 221
Open all day Sun
McEwan 80/- Ⓐ
Friendly, well run wee gem
with superb mirrors, in idyllic
setting. Tall founts. Pool,
darts, doms Ⓐ Q Ⓑ Ⓖ ⟨symbol⟩

East Linton 35H5

Crown
Bridge Street (off A1)
✆ 860335
Belhaven 80/- Ⓐ
Friendly "L"-shaped bar with
lounge off Ⓑ Ⓖ ⟨symbol⟩

Edinburgh 35G5

Athletic Arms (Gravediggers)
1–3 Angle Park Terrace
✆ 337 3822
Closes 10.30; closed Sun
McEwan 80/ Ⓐ
This pub exists solely to sell its
legendary beer to the thirsty
masses who pack the plain bar
and doms rooms every night
Q ⟨symbol⟩

Bannermans
53/57 Niddry Street (on
Cowgate) ✆ 556 3254
11–12 (1 am F, S); open Sun
Arrol's 70/-; Ind Coope
Burton Ale; Lorimer & Clark
70/- Ⓗ
Spacious stone-vaulted bar—
no plastic in sight. Folk music
Sun, Mon & Tue. Sunday
breakfasts Q Ⓖ ✽ ≈ (Waverley)

Blue Blazer
2 Spittal Street ✆ 229 6850
11–11; closed Sun
McEwan 70/-, 80/- Ⓐ
City centre locals' pub with
breweriana adorning the
walls. Tall founts ⟨symbol⟩

Cavern
7 Bernard Street, Leith
✆ 554 7515
6 am–11 pm; open Sun
McEwan 80/- Ⓐ
Enterprising, basic local,
popular with dock workers.
Surprising menu & wine list
Ⓖ ➐ ⟨symbol⟩

Clark's Bar
142 Dundas Street
✆ 556 1067
11–10.30; closed Sun
Younger IPA Ⓐ
Boisterous but well-kept
public bar ⟨symbol⟩

Coppers
19 Cockburn Street
✆ 225 1441
11–11 (midnight F, S); closed Sun
Arrols 70/; Ind Coope Burton
Ale; Lorimer & Clark 70/-,
80/- Ⓗ
Small, friendly pub with good
atmosphere Ⓖ ➐ ≈

Corstorphine Inn
Corstorphine High Street
✆ 334 1019
11–11 (11.45 Thu, F, S); open Sun

McEwan 80/- Ⓐ
Welcoming village local with
wood panelling and skittle
alley. Marred by TV, juke box
and bandit Ⓖ (not Sun) ⟨symbol⟩

Covenanter Tavern
150 High Street ✆ 225 6145
11–11 F, S
Maclay 70/-, 80/- Ⓐ
Small, popular lounge in
historic street Q ≋

Cramond Inn
Cramond Glebe Road
✆ 336 2035
Lorimer & Clark 80/- Ⓐ
Long established inn on Forth
Estuary Q ✽ Ⓖ ➐

Fiddlers Arms
9/11 Grassmarket
✆ 229 2665
11–11; open Sun
McEwan 70/-, 80/- Ⓐ
Mellow enclave of conviviality
with mature ceiling, rare
McLennan and Urquhart
mirror and magnificent founts
Ⓖ ⟨symbol⟩

Green Mantle
133 Nicolson Street
✆ 667 3749
11–11 (1 am Thu, F; 11.45 S); open Sun
Arrols 70/-; Broughton
Greenmantle Ale; Ind Coope
Burton Ale; Lorimer & Clark
70/-, 80/- Ⓗ
Small, thriving local in the
city's Southside, friendly
atmosphere Ⓖ ⟨symbol⟩

Kay & Company
39 Jamaica Street ✆ 225 1858
11–11; closed Sun
Belhaven 70/-, 80/-; Lorimer
& Clark 80/- Ⓗ; McEwan 80/-;
Younger No 3 Ⓐ
Small, worthwhile bar tucked
away in the New Town Ⓐ Q

Kilderkin
125 Constitution Street, Leith
✆ 554 3268
11–11 (12 Thu, F, S); closed Sun
Maclay 70/-, 80/- Ⓐ
Smart, spacious, modern
comfortable lounge which
deserves to be busier. ¾ snooker
table Ⓖ ➐

Laurie's Bar
105 Lauriston Place
✆ 229 3256
11–1 am; open Sun
McEwan 80/- Ⓐ
Tollcross tenement lounge,
busy with locals and Heart of
Midlothian afficionados. Tall
founts

Leslie's Bar
45 Ratcliffe Terrace
✆ 667 5957
11–11; open Sun
Lorimer & Clark 70/-, 80/-;
Younger No 3 Ⓐ
Outstanding Victorian pub
with carved snob screens,
superb ceiling and panelling
Ⓐ Ⓖ ➐

Liberton Inn
Kirk Brae/Kirkgate
11.45–10.45; open Sun
McEwan 70/-, 80/- Ⓐ
Fascinating three-bar inn with exceptionally fine '30s saloon
Q♪

Malt Shovel
13 Cockburn Street
☎ 225 6843
11–12.30 (11 S); open Sun
Lorimer & Clark Caledonian Strong Ale Ⓗ; Maclay 70/- Ⓐ; Marston Pedigree Ⓗ; McEwan 80/- Ⓐ; Theakston XB Ⓗ
Regular guest beers
Thriving city centre lounge bar with regular jazz music ⓒ♪≥

H.P. Mather's Bar
Queensferry Street, West End
11–11 (11.45 Thu, F, S); 12.30–2.30 pm Sun
McEwan 80/- Ⓐ
Sadly lacking the leadership of previous years, this traditional 1-room local is still worth a visit ♥≥ (Haymarket)

Olde Golf Tavern
Bruntsfield Links ☎ 229 3796
11–midnight (11.45 S); opens 7.30 pm Sun
Belhaven 60/-, 80/- Ⓐ
Large, popular lounge with unique Reid founts in fine old building Qⓒ (restaurant)

Olde Inn
22/25 Main Street, Davidsons Mains (off A90) ☎ 336 2437
11–11 (summer & winter F, S)
Belhaven 70/-; Drybrough's Eighty; Strathalbyn Beardmore Stout Ⓐ
Village local in city suburb ⚲ⓒ♥

Rutherford's
3 Drummond Street
11–11; open Sun
Broughton Greenmantle Ale; McEwan 80/- Ⓐ
Genuine and robust with fine façade outside and colourful clientele inside. Tall founts Q♥≥

Starbank Inn
64 Laverockbank Road, Newhaven ☎ 552 4141
11–11 (11.30 Thu, F, S); open Sun
Belhaven 70/-, 80/-; Maclay 70/-, 80/-; Taylor Best Bitter, Landlord, Porter (winter), Ram Tam (summer) Ⓗ
Excellent lounge overlooking Firth of Forth. A museum of breweriana. Recommended restaurant Qⓒ♪

Windsor Buffet
45 Elm Row, Leith Walk
☎ 556 4195
Open till 11.45 Thu, F (11.30 S); open Sun
McEwan 80/- Ⓐ
Attractive late Victorian bar with leaded glass windows and seating in alcoves. Tall founts ⓒ (not Sun) ≥

Howgate   35G5

Old Howgate Inn

Off A703 ☎ Penicuik 74244
Open Sun
Belhaven 80/-; Broughton Greenmantle Ale; McEwan 80/-; Theakston Best Bitter Ⓗ
Cosy low-ceilinged coaching inn with fine restaurant specialising in Danish cuisine
⚲Qⓒ♪

Kirkliston   35F5

Newliston Arms
Main Street ☎ 333 3328
11–11; 12.30–11 Sun
Lorimer & Clark 70/-, 80/- Ⓐ
Boisterous local with wood-panelled ceiling ⚲ⓒ♥

Linlithgow   35F5

Four Marys
67 High Street ☎ 842171
Opens noon
Belhaven 70/-, 80/- Ⓗ
Occasional guest beers
Tasteful winebar/bistro; parts date back to 1580, reflects town's history ⓒ♪≥

Red Lion
50 High Street
11–11 Thu, F, S
McEwan 80/- Ⓐ
Small, friendly bar, popular for pool and darts ♥≥

Penicuik   35G5

Carnethy Inn
John Street (A703)
☎ Penicuik 76838
11–11 am Thu, F; 11–11.30 pm S; open Sun
Belhaven 70/-; Drybrough Eighty Ⓐ
Large tiled bar dominated by pool table, very popular with locals. Enormous disco-style lounge ⓒ♪ (must book) ♥⚃

South Queensferry   35F5

Moorings
24–26 Hopetoun Road (B924)
☎ 331 2638
11–11; open Sun
Maclay 80/- Ⓐ
Modern wood-panelled pub with nautical theme and fine views of the Forth Bridges. Tall founts ⚃ⓒ⚃

Airdrie   34E5

Tudor Hotel (Elizabethan Lounge)
39 Alexander Street (A89)
☎ 64144
Closed Mon, Tue; open 6–11 Wed–Sun
Ind Coope Burton Ale Ⓗ
Small lounge with stained glass and wood panelling
⚃ⓒ♪⚃≥

Ardrossan   34C6

High Tide Hotel

23 Parkhouse Road (A78)
☎ 61527
11–midnight (11 Mon, Tue winter)
McEwan 80/- Ⓐ
Modern hotel, lively public with pool and darts, large lounge, live music weekends
⚃ (if dining) ⚲⚃ⓒ♪♥⚃
≥ (South Beach)

Ayr   34D6

Isle of Skye Bar
5/7 Kyle Street, off High Street (A79) ☎ 265339
Open all day Mon–S; open Sun
McEwan 80/- Ⓐ
One of the few remaining traditional town centre pubs. Folk music. Beware of "bright" 80/- from adjacent fount ♥≥

Old Racecourse Hotel
2 Victoria Park, off Racecourse Road (A719) ☎ 262873
11–3; 5–1 am Mon–S; 12–1 am Sun
Belhaven 80/- Ⓗ
Comfortable lounge in free-standing sandstone hotel
Q⚃⚃ⓒ♪≥

Balloch   34D5

Balloch Hotel
Balloch Road ☎ 52579
11–11; 12.30–11 Sun
Arrols 70/- Ⓗ
Beautiful waterside location close to Loch Lomond
⚲⚃⚲ⓒ♪♥⚃Å≥ (Central)

Bearsden   34D5

Burnbrae Hotel (Brae Bar)
Milngavie Road
☎ 041 942 5951
Thu open till midnight; F 11–midnight; S 11–11.45; Sun 12.30–11
McEwan 70/-, 80/-; Younger No 3; Strathalbyn Original, II Ⓐ
Beer in bar at rear of large modern hotel. Restaurant
⚃ⓒ♪

Beith   35D5

Eglinton Inn
48 Eglinton Street (B7049)
☎ 2736
Open all day S; closes midnight
McEwan 80/- Ⓐ
Popular modernised town pub in attractive street ⓒ♥

Biggar   35F6

Fleming Arms
Main Street (A702)
Open Sun
McEwan 80/- Ⓐ
Friendly, basic local in pleasant market town. Tall founts ⚲♥

Hartree Country House Hotel
1 mile off A702 ☎ 20215
11–midnight
Broughton Greenmantle Ale Ⓗ
Baronial-style hotel with peacocks in spacious grounds
⚲⚃ⓒ♪

Bishopton 34D5

Golf Inn
28/30 Greenock Road ℰ 2303
Closed Mon; open Sun
Belhaven 80/-; Broughton
Greenmantle Ale; Strathalbyn
Porter Ⓐ Regular guest beers
Real ale stalwart with well
stocked off-licence. 19th
century coaching inn Q🍴

Blackwaterfoot 34B6
Isle of Arran

Kinloch Hotel
ℰ 286
12–12.30 am; 12.30–midnight Sun
Younger No 3Ⓐ
Basic modern bar in large hotel
🏨🎨ᕋ🍴🍷⚲

Blantyre 34E5

Carrigans
360 Main Street, High
Blantyre ℰ823441
11–11
Maclay 80/-; Strathalbyn
Beardmore Stout Ⓐ
Traditional Scottish public bar
and tastefully modernised
lounge 🍷ᕋ

Bridge of 34D5
Weir

Wylies Tavern
Main Road ℰ 613228
Tennent Heriot 80/- Ⓐ
Popular village local 🍷

Brodick, 34C6
Isle of Arran

Ormidale Hotel
Knowe Road ℰ 2293
*12–2.30, 4.30–12 Mon–F; 12–midnight S;
12.30–midnight Sun*
McEwan 70/- Ⓐ
Splendid sandstone edifice on
outskirts with unusual sun
lounge and children's play
area. Tall founts 🏨🎨🏊‍♂️ᕋ🍴🍷

Caldercruix 34E5

Railway Tavern
67 Main Street (off A89)
11–11 F, S
Belhaven 60/-, 70/- Ⓐ
Magnificent Robert Younger's
mirror is centrepiece of this
vibrant public bar 🎨🍷

Cambuslang 34E5

Sefton
40 Main Street ℰ3463
11–11
Belhaven 60/- Ⓐ
Fine Art Deco interior in one of
the few pubs of genuine
architectural merit in Glasgow
area 🍷🚆

Castlecary 35E5

Castlecary House
Off A80 ℰ Banknock 840233

11–11
Belhaven 80/-; Broughton
Greenmantle Ale; Harviestoun
Ale; Maclay 70/-; Theakston
Best Bitter, Old Peculier Ⓗ
Busy village pub with mixed
clientele 🏨ᕋ🍴🍷ᕋ⚲

Catacol Bay, 34C6
Isle of Arran

Catacol Bay Hotel
ℰ 231
11–1 am; 12.30–midnight Sun
McEwan 70/- Ⓗ
Pleasant hotel on coast road
with view of Kintyre
🏨Q🎨🏊‍♂️ᕋ🍴🍷

Clydebank 34D5

Chandlers
2 Kilbowie Road
ℰ 041 952 8190
7.30 am–11 pm Mon–F; 11–11 Sat; open Sun
Strathalbyn II Ⓗ
Are these Britain's longest
opening hours? Food noon–
9 pm
ᕋ🍴🍷⚲🚆 (Central)

Cumbernauld 35E5

Spur Hotel
Main Street, The Village
11–11
Drybrough's Eighty Ⓐ
Warm, friendly pub hosted by
ex-footballer. Real ale in bar
only 🎨ᕋ🍷

Dalry 34D6

Greenbank Inn
97 New Street (A737) ℰ 2202
Open all day F, S; open Sun
McEwan 80/- Ⓐ
Plain public bar and small
comfortable lounge. Darts and
separate pool room. Has its
own golf club 🍷🚆

Dreghorn 34D6

Dreghorn Inn
39 Main Street (off A71)
ℰ Irvine 211557
11–11 (11.30 Thur–S); open Sun
Younger No 3 Ⓐ
Modernised 1-bar village local.
Quite noisy, but friendly

Dumbarton 34D5

Stags Head
116 Glasgow Road ℰ 32642
11–11 (midnight Thu–S); open Sun
Drybrough's Eighty Ⓐ
Only oasis for the sons of The
Rock 🍷🚆 (East)

Eaglesham 34D5

Swan Inn
23 Poldon Street
Open all day S; open Sun
McEwan 80/- Ⓐ
Busy local pub with regular
clientele 🏨

Eglington Arms
Gilmour Street ℰ 2631

Open till midnight Thu–S; 12–11 Sun
McEwan 80/-; Younger
No 3 Ⓐ
Popular village hotel on the
borders of Renfrewshire. Real
ale in lounge only 🎨ᕋ🍷

Try also: Cross Keys
(Greenmantle)

Fenwick 34D6

King's Arms
89 Main Road (off A77) ℰ 276
Closes 11.30; open all day F, S; open Sun
Younger No 3 Ⓐ
Busy rural local with bar and
snug. Unusual half-timbered
exterior with old wooden
porch 🚪 (snug) ᕋ🍷

Gatehead 34D6

Cochrane Inn
42/47 Main Road (A759)
ℰ Kilmarnock 29899
11–11.45 S; closes midnight Mon–F; open Sun
Maclay 60/- Ⓐ
Deservedly popular village
local. Cheery bar, two small
lounges, darts and pool room,
dominoes 🍷

Giffnock 34D5

Macdonald Hotel
(Sportsman Bar)
Eastwood Toll ℰ 041 638 2225
11–11 F, S; open Sun
Younger No 3 Ⓐ
Corner bar of Thistle Hotel.
Separate entrance, games
room 🎨ᕋ🍴🍷🚆 (White Craigs)

Glasgow 34E5

Allison Arms
720–722 Pollokshaws Road,
Pollokshields
11–11; open Sun
Belhaven 80/- Ⓐ
Basic, friendly bar, popular
with locals 🍷🚆 (Queens Park)

Athena Greek Taverna
780 Pollokshaws Road,
Strathbungo ℰ 494 0858
Belhaven 80/-; Lorimer &
Clark 80/- Ⓗ; Strathalbyn II Ⓐ;
Ward Sheffield Bitter Ⓗ
Quality and value for money in
unique little pub. Cafe licence
allows accompanied children
until 8 pm
ᕋ🍴🍷🚆 (Queens Park)

Babbity Bowster
16–18 Blackfriars Street
ℰ 552 5055
12–midnight; open Sun
Maclay 70/-, 80/- Ⓐ
Neo-trendy bar in revitalised
merchant city
🏨Qᕋ🍴🍷🚆 (High Street)

Bon Accord
153 North Street (off M8)
ℰ 248 4427
11–11 (midnight Thu, F, 11.45 S); open Sun
Belhaven 60/-, 80/-; Ind Coope
Burton Ale Ⓗ; Maclay 70/-,
80/- Ⓐ; Marston Pedigree;

Strathalbyn Beardmore ⊞
Regular guest beers
Popular bar with 14 plus beers
usually available
☉♥¶≷ (Charing X)
⊖ (St. Georges X)

Doublet
74 Park Road ✆ 334 1982
11–11; open Sun
Belhaven 80/-; McEwan 80/-;
Younger No. 3 Ⓐ
Rustic cottage interior bar with
upstairs lounge
¶ ⊖ (Kelvin Bridge)

Gables
6 Baillieston Road ✆ 778 9655
11–11; open Sun
Lorimer & Clark 80/- ⊞
Friendly bar on eastern
outskirts of city, with stained
glass windows ¶

Hayfield
148 Old Dalmarnock Road
✆ 554 7452
11–11
Belhaven 70/-; Drybrough's
Eighty Ⓐ
Popular, East-End two-bar
pub. Good cheap grub ☉¶

Mitre
12 Brunswick Street
✆ 552 3764
11–11; closed Sun
Belhaven 80/-; Ind Coope
Burton Ale ⊞
Victorian gem in city centre.
Choice selection of malt
whiskies
☉♥¶≷ (Argyle Street)
⊖ (St. Enoch)

Orwells
70 Elderslie Street ✆ 221 4439
11–11; open Sun
Belhaven 80/- ⊞
Beer superb despite depressing
pub name ☉≷ (Charing X)

Partick Tavern
165 Dumbarton Road
✆ 339 7571
11–11; 6.30–11 Sun
Ind Coope Burton Ale ⊞
Modernised large bar and
lounge ☉ (until 7 pm) ¶
⊖ (Kelvin Hall)

Quaich
52 Coustonholm Road
✆632 9003
11–11; open Sun
Belhaven 80/- Ⓐ
Quaint method of dispense
involves a handpump
☉¶≷ (Pollokshaws East)

Rams Head
1971 Maryhill Road
✆ 946 0251
11–11
Younger No 3 Ⓐ
Basic bar, comfortable
lounge—colourful characters
in both ☉ (Mon–Fri) ¶&

Tolbooth
11 Saltmarket ✆ 552 4149
Lorimer & Clark Caledonian
Strong Ale; Strathalbyn
Original, II, Beardmore Stout Ⓐ

Old Glasgow pub with superbly
restored Victorian features
♨☉♥¶
≷ (Argyle Street/High Street)

Tron
72/74 Bedford Street (off
Eglinton Street) ✆ 429 1583
Strathalbyn Original, II,
Beardmore Porter Ⓐ
Cosy lounge, often with live
music, basic bar with darts, set
in an urban wasteland that
was once The Gorbals. Keen
prices ¶& ⊖ (Bridge Street)

Ubiquitous Chip
12 Ashton Lane (off Byres
Road) ✆334 5007
11–11; open Sun
Belhaven 80/- Ⓐ
Above illustrious dining salon,
light-hearted clientele
♨Q☉ ⊖ (Hillhead)

Gourock 34D5

Cardwell
49 Cardwell Road (A78 at
Greenock side of town)
✆31281
11–11; open Sun
Drybrough's Eighty Ⓐ
Views out to Gourock Pier.
Smart appearance
☉¶&≷ (Fort Matilda)

Spinnaker Hotel
121 Albert Road (A78 S. of
town) ✆33107
Open till 11.45 F; 11–4; 5–11.45 S: open Sun
Belhaven 80/- Ⓐ; **Bulmer**
Cider
Popular hotel on sea front
⊞ (till 8 pm) ♪⊠☉♥ (5–7)

Hamilton 34E5

George
18 Campbell Street
11–11; 6.30–11 Sun
Maclay 60/-, 70/-, 80/- ⊞
Modern lounge ☉≷ (Central)

Helensburgh 34D5

Royal Bar
8 West Clyde Street (A814)
✆ 5033
11–11 (12 Thu,F, 11.45 S); open Sun
McEwan 80/-; Younger
No 3 Ⓐ
Wood-panelled pub with
nautical overtones. Fine
gantry ☉¶≷

Houston 34D5

Fox & Hounds
Main Street (B789)
✆ Bridge of Weir 612448
11–11 (12.30–2.30, 6.30–11 Sun)
Dryborough's Eighty;
Strathalbyn Original Ⓐ
Hunt theme pub. Pleasant
atmosphere attracts people
from near and far. Restaurant
⊞☉♥¶

Try also: Cross Keys
(Belhaven); **Houston Inn**
(McEwan)

Inverbeg 34D4

Inverbeg Inn
Near Luss (A82)
✆ Luss 686678
11–11; 12.30–11 Sun
Strathalbyn II ⊞
Popular hotel near bonnie
banks of Loch Lomond
♨⊠☉♥¶Å

Inverkip 34C5

Langhouse Hotel
Langhouse Road (leads to
hotel ½ mile behind village)
✆Wemyss Bay 521211
Open Sun
Belhaven 80/- ⊞
Country house hotel with
friendly atmosphere. Beautiful
grounds and views over Firth
of Clyde Q⊞♪⊠☉♥Å≷

Irvine 34D6

Crown Inn
162 High Street ✆79715
11–11 (12 Thu, F, 11.45 S); open Sun
Younger No 3 Ⓐ
Modernised town centre pub.
Single bar well divided by
screens and alcoves. Pool and
darts ⊞☉&≷

Johnstone 34D5

Coanes
26 High Street
Open Sun
Broughton Merlin's Ale;
McEwan 80/-; Younger
No 3 Ⓐ
Friendly pub with varied
clientele and jovial staff
☉¶&≷

Lynnhurst Hotel
Park Road ✆ 24331
Opens 10; open Sun
McEwan 80/-; Younger
No 3 Ⓐ
Residential hotel with full
facilities ⊞☉♥

Kilbarchan 34D5

Trust Inn
6 Low Barholm ✆2401
11–11 Thu–S; open Sun
Ind Coope Burton Ale ⊞
Friendly olde world pub with
atmosphere to match. Trivial
pursuit and cribbage ☉♥

Kilmarnock 34D6

Gordon's Lounge
Fowlds Street (A71) ✆ 42122
11–11; closed Sun
Belhaven 80/- ⊞
Town centre lounge with
restaurant. Converted from a
grain store ☉♥≷

Hillhead Tavern
Hill Street (A735) ✆24308
11–11 F, S; closes 10.30 Mon–Thu; closed Sun
Maclay 60/- Ⓐ
Lively modern local. Separate

lounge and pool room.
Dominoes ♟❓

Try also: Kay Park Tavern
(Maclay)

Kilmun 34C5

Coylet Hotel
Loch Eck (A815) OS144885
✆ 322
Open till midnight F, S; 12.30–2.30, 5–midnight Sun

McEwan 80/-; Youngers
No 3 Ⓐ
Country hotel in idyllic setting
♨⛏🅟⚲❓❤⚑

Largs 34C5

Clachan
Bath Street (B7025, off A78)
11–11 (midnight F, S); open Sun
Broughton Greenmantle Ale,
Merlin's Ale Ⓐ; McEwan 80/-
Ⓗ; Younger No 3 Ⓐ
Cheery sidestreet, 1-bar pub
just behind seafront. Vast
whisky selection. Good
lunches ⚲≋

Linwood 34D5

Venture
Bridge Street (off A761)
✆ Johnstone 22496
11–11 F, S; open Sun
Arrols 70/- Ⓗ
Nautical theme in lounge,
large selection of malt
whiskies in public bar
⚲ (not Sun) ❓❤

Loans 34D6

Dallam Tower Hotel
Old Loans Road, near Troon
(off A759, ½ mile E of
crossroads) OS349321
✆ 312511
Closes midnight Mon–Sun; open all day Sun
Broughton Greenmantle Ale;
Lorimer & Clark 80/- Ⓗ;
Strathalbyn Beardmore
Stout Ⓐ; Bland's Farmhouse
Cider Ⓗ Regular guest beers
Hillside hotel has even wider
Clyde views due to new
lounge extension. Excellent
food Q🅗♨⛏⚲❤

Lochranza, 34B6
Isle of Arran

Lochranza Hotel
Shore Road ✆ 223
11–1 am; 12.30–11 am Sun
McEwan 70/-, 80/- Ⓗ
Attractive hotel with view of
Loch Ranza. Popular with
yachtsmen
🍺Q🅗 (until 8 pm) ♨⛏⚲❤❓⚑

Muirkirk 34E6

Central Bar
22 Main Street (A70) ✆ 231
11–midnight; open Sun
Maclay 60/- Ⓗ
Local in remote former mining
village. "Cellar" is above

bar—no pressure required!
Darts, dominoes ❓

Oban 34B3

Lorn Hotel
Stevenson Street
11–11
McEwan 80/- Ⓗ
Attractive old building with a
feel for tradition ⛏⚲❓≋

Oban Bar
1 Stafford Street
11–11
McEwan 80/-; Younger
No 3 Ⓐ
Popular local with coat of
arms and marble fireplace ❓≋

Ochiltree 34D6

Commercial Inn
1 Mill Street (A70) ✆ 432
Closes midnight F, S; open Sun
Maclay 60/- Ⓐ
Busy local in mining area
conservation village. Pool
room 🍺❓

Paisley 34D5

Argyll Bar
16 Old Sneddon Street
✆ 889 2996
McEwan 80/- Ⓗ
Fine collection of historic
photos of Paisley
❓⚲≋ (Gilmour Street)

Barpoint
42 Wellmeadow Street, 1½
miles from town centre
✆ 889 5188
11–11 F, S
Belhaven 80/- Ⓗ
Busy, friendly lounge.
Occasional live music; chess,
backgammon, dominoes and
daily papers at bar. Excellent
meals ♨⚲❤

Buddies
23 Broomlands Street
✆ 889 5314
11–11; open Sun
Belhaven 80/- Ⓗ
Fine corner shop-type pub.
Friendly staff; library and
chess club ⚲❤❓

Corkers
51 Causeyside Street
✆ 887 4409
11–11
Tennent 80/- Ⓐ
Very busy lounge approx
½ mile from town centre ⚲

Stag's Head
9–11 Renfrew Road
✆ 889 6667
11–11; open Sun
Drybrough's Eighty Ⓐ
Large comfortable lounge,
popular with the young ❓≋

Wee Howff
52 High Street ½ mile from
town ✆ 889 2095
11–11; open Sun

Arrols 70/-; Ind Coope Burton
Ale Ⓗ
Traditional Scottish bar.
Friendly staff

Try also: Finlays

Plains 34E5

Gordons/Star
Main Street (A89)
✆ Caldercruix 842126
11–11
Maclay 60/- Ⓗ
Plain, unpretentious pub with
no frills (but the occasional
thrill) in old mining village ❓⛏

Prestwick 34D6

Butler's House
132 Main Street (A79)
✆77566
11–midnight Mon–Sun
Ind Coope Burton Ale Ⓗ
Modern town centre hotel
with three bars. Real ale in
"Overdraught" bar
🅗♨⛏⚲❓≋

Parkstone Hotel
2 Ardayre Road ✆ 77286
Belhaven 80/- Ⓗ
Modernised lounge bar in sea
front hotel 🅗♨⛏⚲❤≋

Renfrew 34D5

Ferry Inn
Ferry Road ✆ 886 2104
11–11; open Sun
Belhaven 80/- Ⓗ
Basic 200 year-old pub, next
to Renfrew Ferry 🍺❓

Pickwicks
7 Meadowside Street
✆ 886 6552
Lorimer & Clark 80/- Ⓗ
Circular bar with TV lounge
off. Popular with darts players
⚲❓

Rhu 34D4

Ardencaple Hotel
Shore Road (A814)
✆ 820200
11–11 (11.45 Thu, F, S); 12.30–11 Sun
Arrol's 70/- Ⓗ
Prominent hotel, old-
fashioned bar and smart
lounge 🍺🅗♨⛏⚲❤❓

Saltcoats 34C6

Windy Ha'
31 Bradshaw Street
(off A738) ✆ 63688
11–11 (midnight Thu–S); open Sun
McEwan 80/- Ⓗ
Deservedly popular street-
corner pub. Traditional island
bar, snug. Below average
prices. Pool, darts, doms ❓≋

Stewarton 34D6

Millhouse Hotel
8 Dean Street (B769) ✆ 82255
11–11.30 (2 am F, 1 am S, Sun)

Younger No 3 Ⓐ
Small hotel on Glasgow road.
Small bar, larger lounge with
function suite. 🏠🅿♿⊙⚐

Troon 34D6

Anchorage Hotel
149 Templehill (B749)
☎ 311044
11–12 (1 am F, S); 12.30–11 Sun
Belhaven 60/-, 80/- Ⓗ
Catamaran-shaped bar in
harbourside hotel. Darts, pool
room, disco 🏠🅱⊙⚐

Lookout
Troon Marina, Harbour Road
(B749) ☎ 311523
11–11 S; 12.30–3.30, 6.30–11 Sun
Broughton Greenmantle Ale Ⓐ
1st-floor modern bar and
restaurant in marina building.
Pool ♿⊙⚐ (restaurant)

Twechar 34E5

Quarry Inn
Main Street OS700755
11–11; open Sun
Maclay 60/-, 70/- Ⓗ Regular
guest beers
Superb village pub with oak-
panelled walls and pot-bellied
stoves in the bar 🏠⚐

Uddingston 34E5

Rowan Tree
Old Mill Road
Maclay 70/-, 80/- Ⓐ
Superb pub rescued by caring
tenant. Restoration of coal
fires symbolises renaissance
🏠⊙⚐⚐♿

Whiting Bay, 34C6 Isle of Arran

Cameronia Hotel
Whiting Bay ☎ 254
11–1 am; (12.30–3; 6.30–12 Sun)
Broughton Greenmantle Ale Ⓗ
Extensive views, good bar
food, folk music Saturday
nights 🏠Q🏠🅿🅱⊙⚐⚐🛏

Tayside

Almondbank 35F3

Almondbank Inn
Main Street (off A85)
☎ 242
11–11.30 F, S; open Sun
Broughton Greenmantle Ale Ⓗ
Modernised village pub with
excellent bar lunches (booking
advised) 🏠♿⊙⚐

Arbroath 35H3

St. Thomas Bar
17 James Street
☎ 72466
Open Sun
Maclay 80/- Ⓐ
Extremely friendly local near
the Abbey ⚐🅱🛏♿

Bankfoot 35F3

Hunter's Lodge
Main Street (off A9)
☎ 325
11–11 F, S, Sun & summer
Broughton Greenmantle Ale Ⓗ
Comfortable roadhouse with
chalet accommodation and
good food 🏠🅱⊙⚐⚐♿

Bridge of 35F3 Earn

Cyprus Inn
Back Street (off M90, exit 9)
11–11 S & summer; open Sun
Belhaven 80/-; Broughton
Greenmantle Ale Ⓗ; Younger
No 3 Ⓐ
200 year-old inn with ales in
cosy lounge to rear. Orders
can be made in basic public
bar 🏠⊙⚐

Broughty Ferry 35G3

Fisherman's Tavern
12 Fort Street (near Lifeboat
Station) ☎ Dundee 75941
11–2.30 (4 summer); 4.45–11 Mon–Thu;
11–midnight F, S; open Sun
Broughton Greenmantle Ale;
McEwan 80/-; Maclay 80/-;
Theakston Best Bitter Ⓗ;
Younger No 3 Ⓐ Regular
guest beers
Splendid, deservedly popular
traditional pub Q⊙⚐⚐🅱🛏

Carnoustie 35H3

Glencoe Hotel
Esplanade ☎ 53273
Maclay 80/- Ⓐ
Comfortable international
golfing hotel Q🏠🅱⊙⚐🛏

Crieff 35E3

Oakbank Inn
Turret Bridge
☎ 2420
Closes 11.45 F, S; open Sun
Arrol's 70/- Ⓗ
Modern comfortable pub with
600 year-old tree in garden
♿⊙🅱🛏

Dundee 35G3

Balmore
47 Dura Street
☎ 453992
11–11; open Sun
McEwan 80/- Ⓐ
Local with fine Victorian
interior. Scottish music on
accordion at weekends. 🅱

Blue Mountains
21 Old Hawkhill
Closes midnight Thu–S; closed Sun
Broughton Greenmantle Ale,
Merlin; McEwan 70/- Ⓐ
Recently reopened after many
years; features such as high
bar and gas lighting skilfully
recapture former atmosphere
🏠⊙🅱♿

Count De Beers (Off Licence)
264 Perth Road
☎66441
10–10; closed Sun
Regular guest beers
Unsurpassed range of draught
and bottled beers

Shakespeare Bar
267–271 Hilltown ☎ 21454
11–11; Mon, Tue; 11–11.45 Thu–S; open Sun
Belhaven 60/-, 80/- Ⓐ
Regular guest beers
Popular pub, good community
spirit. CAMRA stronghold 🅱

Speedwell Bar (Mennies)
165 Perth Road ☎ 67783
Closes 11.30 F; 11–11.30 S
Belhaven 80/-; Ind Coope
Burton Ale Ⓗ; McEwan 80/-;
Younger No 3 Ⓐ
Fine interior and mixed
clientele Q🅱

Monifieth 35H3

Panmure Hotel
Princes Street
11–midnight; Sun 12.30–midnight
McEwan 80/- Ⓐ
Conveniently situated for
visitors, beside caravan site
and golf courses 🏠♿🅱⊙🅱🛏🛏

Montrose 35H2

Salutation Inn
71 Bridge Street (A92)
11–11
Younger No 3 Ⓐ
Comfortable, well furnished
local Q🅱🛏🛏

Perth 35F3

Lamplight Lounge Bar
Union Lane, off Kinoull Street
11–11 S; 7–11 Sun
Drybroughs Eighty Ⓗ
Spacious lounge tucked away
in side street basement ♿⊙

Olde St. Johnstoun Tavern
103 South Street ☎ 37208
11–11; closed Sun
McEwan 80/- Ⓐ
Popular and friendly town
centre pub. Good value bar
lunches ⊙🅱

Ship Inn
31 High Street/Skinnergate
11–11 F, S; closed Sun
Arrol's 70/; Ⓗ
Friendly, old-world pub just
off High Street ⊙⚐🅱

Scone 35F3

Scone Arms
Perth Road (A94)
☎ 51341
11–11
McEwan 80/- Ⓐ
Scottish decor. Traditional
music weekends—Ceilidhs
🏠 (if eating) ⊙⚐🅱🛏

General opening hours: 10.30 am–10.45 pm (summer);
12 noon–10 pm (10.45 F, S) (winter). Sunday: 12–1.30; 8–10.
Children with an adult are admitted 12–2.30 for a cooked meal,
with landlord's permission

Ballasalla   20B3

Whitestone Inn
Okell Mild, Bitter Ⓗ
Comfortable, historic inn at
village centre
🅰Q☺🍽♿⚥ (IMR)

Castletown   20B3

**Castle Arms (Glue
Pot)**
Quayside
Okell Bitter Ⓗ
Quayside local opposite castle
entrance Q🍽

Union Hotel
The Square ☎ 823214
Castletown Bitter Ⓗ
H.Q. of Castletown Ale
Drinkers' Society 🍽

Victoria Hotel
Malew Street ☎ 823529
Castletown Bitter Ⓗ
Basic local, undiscovered by
tourists 🅰Q🍽

Crosby   20B2

Crosby Hotel
Main Road
Okell Mild, Bitter Ⓗ
Strong TT theme with photos
and racing bike 🅰☺🍽♿

Douglas   20C3

Bridge Inn
North Quay ☎ 75268
Castletown Bitter Ⓗ
Quayside pub; good range of
cooked meals
🅰☺🍽♿⚥ (IMR)

Bushy's Bar
Zhivago's, Victoria Street
Closed lunchtimes
Old Bushy Tail Ⓗ
Bar serving home-brew ale
🅰☺

Clarendon
North Quay
Okell Mild, Bitter Ⓗ
Busy haunt of off-duty
transport personnel 🅰🍽

Manor
Willaston Estate ☎ 76957
Castletown Bitter Ⓗ
Former manor house with
comfortable panelled lounge
🅰Q🍽♿

Queen's Hotel
Queen's Promenade ☎ 75543
Okell Mild ,Bitter Ⓗ
Seafront pub which can be
reached by horse tram from
town centre 🅰♨🅿☺🍽

Waterloo
Strand Street ☎ 76833
Okell Mild, Bitter Ⓗ

Small town centre pub in
pedestrian shopping street 🍽

Wheatsheaf
Ridgeway Street ☎ 73144
Okell Mild, Bitter Ⓗ
Large and lively town pub
🅰🅿☺⚥ (IMR)

Woodbourne
Alexander Drive ☎ 21766
Okell Mild, Bitter Ⓗ
Splendid Edwardian pub Q☺🍽

Glenmaye   20B2

Waterfall Hotel
☎ Peel 2238
Castletown Bitter Ⓗ
Pub near well-known beauty
spot. Up-market meals ♨☺🍽🍽

Kirk Michael   20B2

Mitre
Castletown Bitter Ⓗ
Reputed to be the oldest Manx
pub ☺🅰

Laxey   20C2

Mines Tavern
Electric Railway Station
Okell Mild, Bitter Ⓗ
Picturesquely situated pub
with railway and mining
relics ♨☺⚥ (MER)

New Inn
New Road
Okell Bitter Ⓗ
Well-kept village local
🅰☺⚥ (MER)

Queen's Hotel
New Road
Castletown Bitter Ⓗ
Comfortable pub supporting
motor cycle racing

Maughold   20C2

Glen Mona Hotel
Main Road, Glen Mona
Okell Mild, Bitter Ⓗ
Suitable halt for road and rail
travellers between Laxey and
Ramsey 🅰♨🅿☺🍽🅰⚥ (MER)

Peel   20B2

Central Hotel
Castle Street
Castletown Mild, Bitter Ⓗ
Small, backstreet local 🅰☺🍽♿

Creek Inn
Station Place ☎ 2216
Okell Mild, Bitter Ⓗ
Modernised pub near harbour
🅰☺🍽🍽

Whitehouse
Tynwald Road ☎ 2252

Okell Mild, Bitter Ⓗ
Deceptively large pub with
cosy lounge 🅰☺🍽

Port Erin   20A3

Station Hotel
Station Road ☎ 832236
Okell Bitter Ⓗ
Ideal place of refreshment for
steam railway travellers
🅰🅿 (summer) ☺⚥ (IMR)

Port St Mary   20A3

Bay View Hotel
Bay View Road ☎ 832234
Okell Bitter Ⓗ
Children admitted to pool
room at landlord's discretion.
Summer haunt of yachtsmen
from nearby busy harbour
🅰🅿♨🅿☺🍽

Station Hotel
Station Road ☎ 832249
Castletown Bitter Ⓗ
By steam railway station
🅰🅿 (summer) ☺🍽⚥ (IMR)

Ramsey   20C1

Bridge Inn
Bowring Road ☎ 3248
Okell Bitter Ⓗ
Attractive lounge with
nautical flavour. Panoramic
photos in bar 🍽

Plough
Parliament Street
Okell Bitter Ⓗ
Unspoilt town pub 🅰🍽

Royal George
Castletown Bitter Ⓗ
Large central pub with mock
Tudor lounge 🅰☺🍽

St John's   20B2

**Central Hotel
(Farmers Arms)**
Castletown Bitter Ⓗ
Village pub near Tynwald Hill;
busy on Market Day (Fri) 🅰☺🍽

Sulby   20C1

Ginger Hall
Castletown Bitter Ⓗ
Unspoilt Victorian pub with
fine brass handpumps 🅰🍽🅰

Union Mills   20B2

Railway Inn
Castletown Mild, Bitter Ⓖ
Small, basic freehouse. T.T.
Race viewpoint. Access by
back road only during races
Q🍽

General opening hours: 11.30 am–11 pm Mon–Sat, closed Sunday

Antrim 36B2

Paul's Bar
16 Castle Street (A6) ✆ 63122
Herald Old Faithful Ⓔ
Modern town pub near
shopping centre ⓎⒶ≋

Belfast 36B2

Botanic Inn
23 Malone Road (off B23)
✆ 660460
Hilden Ale Ⓔ
Busy pub near Queen's
University ⌂ⒼⓎ≋ (Botanic)

Duke of York
11 Commercial Court (off
Donegall Street) ✆ 241062
Generally closes 8 pm
Hilden Ale Ⓗ
Popular lunchtime hostelry on
North side of City centre Ⓖ

Harper's Bar (Forum Hotel)
Great Victoria Street
✆ 245161
Hilden Ale Ⓗ
Popular bar in Belfast's main
City centre hotel Ⓖ≋ (Botanic)

Kings Head
Lisburn Road (A1) opposite
Kings Hall ✆ 667805

Hilden Ale, Special Reserve Ⓗ
Plush establishment with
impressive lounges, pleasant
public bar and restaurant.
Opposite Exhibition Centre
⌂ⒼⓎⓎ≋ (Balmoral)

Linen Hall
9 Clarence Street ✆ 248458
Hilden Ale, Special Reserve Ⓗ
Friendly Edwardian-style bar
near City Hall. Live music
often in rear lounge. Good
lunchtime food ⒼⓎ≋ (Botanic)

Carrickfergus 36C2

Dobbins Inn Hotel
Main Street (off A2) ✆ 63905
Hilden Ale Ⓗ
Popular hotel near Castle. Bar
with naval regalia ⌂ⒼⓎⓎ≋

Glengormley 36B2

Crown & Shamrock
585 Antrim Road (A6, near
M2). approx 2 miles NW of
town centre
Herald Ale Ⓗ
Traditional Irish country pub
⌂☙Ⓟ

Hillsborough 36B2

Hillside Bar

21 Main Street
✆ 682765
Opens 12 noon
Hilden Ale Ⓗ
Comfortable country town bar
⌂☙ⒼⓎⒶ

Plough Inn
3 The Square
✆ 682985
Hilden Special Reserve Ⓔ
Recently modernised pub at
top of Main Street ⌂ⒼⓎ

Killinchy 36C2

Balloo House
1 Comber Road (A22)
✆ 541210
Hilden Ale, Special Reserve Ⓗ;
Bulmer Cider Ⓔ
Rambling pub with
restaurant, close to Strangford
Lough ⌂☙ⒼⓎⓎ

Lisburn 36B2

Down Royal Inn
Ballinderry Road (B104)
1¾ miles from town centre
✆ 82870
Down Royal Export, Gold Cup Ⓗ
Modern split-level roadhouse.
Brewery seen through glass
mural behind bar ☙ⒼⓎ

Channel Islands

10–1 am (midnight Sat & winter); Sun 12–2; 8–midnight

St Anne
5J8

Coronation Inn
36 High Street ✆ 2630
Randall Draught Bitter Ⓖ
Friendly local 🅰🍴

Guernsey

10.30 am–11 pm; closed Sun

Castel
5F7

Rockmount Hotel
Cobo Bay ✆ 57188
Randall Mild Ⓖ
Popular hotel, pleasant views
of bay. Pool, darts and shove-
ha'penny 🅰♿🍴🅻🍺🍴

St. Andrews

Hangmans Inn
Bailiff's Cross ✆ 38809
Closed 2–4.30 (not Sat)
Guernsey LBA, Draught
Bitter Ⓗ
Pleasant local, rumoured to be
haunted. Darts, bar billiards 🍴

Last Post
Les Buttes ✆ 36353
Randall Mild, Draught
Bitter Ⓔ
Busy pub, with comfortable
lounge. Darts, pool 🅰🍴♿🍺🍴

St Martins
5G8

Captains Hotel
La Fosse ✆ 38990
Closed 2–4.45
Guernsey LBA, Draught
Bitter Ⓗ
Attractive hotel. Darts, shove-
ha'penny ♿🅻🍴 (summer) 🍴

Greenacres Hotel
Les Hubits ✆ 35711
Guernsey Draught Bitter Ⓗ
Pleasant country hotel,
swimming pool. Good food
Q♿♿🅻🍺🍴

L'Auberge Divette
Jerbourg (below Doyle
Monument)
Guernsey LBA, Draught
Bitter Ⓗ
Popular country pub, good
food, marvellous views
🅰♿♿🍺🍴

St Peter Port
5G7

Couture Inn
La Couture ✆ 25322
Closed 2–4.30 (not Sat)
Guernsey LBA Ⓗ
Popular local with good
atmosphere 🅰🍴

Crown (Ship & Crown)
North Esplanade (opposite
Crown Pier) ✆ 21368

Guernsey Draught Bitter Ⓗ
Busy 1-bar pub overlooking
marina. Good food ♿🍴

Golden Lion
Market Street ✆ 26862
Guernsey LBA, Draught
Bitter Ⓗ
Historic 1-bar pub opposite
market. Cosy and very busy
🅰♿

**Kosy Korner (Albion
House)**
Church Square ✆ 23518
Guernsey Draught Bitter Ⓖ
Busy pub overlooking
harbour, cellar in the roof!
Restaurant. Bar billiards ♿🍴

Prince of Wales
Smith Street ✆ 20166
Closed 2–5
Randall Mild Ⓗ
Fine historic pub. Darts in
unique "coal hole" bar.
Handy for police station! Q♿🍴

Rohais Inn
Rohais ✆ 20060
Closed 2–4.30 (not Sat)
Guernsey LBA Ⓖ
Friendly local on outskirts 🍴

Salerie Inn
Salerie Corner ✆ 24484
Closed 2–5 (not Sat)
Guernsey LBA Ⓖ
Small but cosy pub
overlooking "North Beach"
development 🍴

Victoria Arms
Victoria Road ✆ 25049
Closed 2–5
Guernsey LBA Ⓖ
Busy local. Pool, darts ♿🅻🍴

St Sampsons
5G7

Pony Inn
Petites Capelles Road ✆ 44374
Guernsey LBA, Draught
Bitter Ⓗ
Large, friendly pub. Near
Oatlands Craft Centre. Live
music some evenings ♿♿🍺🍴

Vale
5G7

Trafalgar Inn (Parrot)
Trafalgar Road, Northside
Closed 2–3 (not Sat)
Guernsey LBA, Draught
Bitter Ⓖ
Basic, sociable local. Darts,
shove-ha'penny, and
magnificent St Bernard Q🍴

Herm
5G7

10.30 am–11 pm; closed Sun

Mermaid Tavern
✆ Guernsey 710170
Guernsey Draught Bitter Ⓗ
Popular with yachtsmen, day-
trippers and fishermen. Sun-
trap garden 🅰♿♿♿🍺🍴Ⓐ

Jersey

9 am–11 pm; 11–1, 4.30–11 Sun

Grouville
5J9

Pembroke
Coast Road ✆ 55756
Draught Bass Ⓗ
Friendly pub near golf course.
Darts, pool, bar billiards. No
food Sun 🅰♿♿♿🍺🍴

St Brelade
5H9

La Pulente Hotel
La Pulente ✆ 41760
Draught Bass Ⓗ
Cheerful, friendly pub at south
end of island's longest beach.
No food Sun 🅰Q♿♿🍺🍴

Old Smugglers Inn
Ouaisne Bay ✆ 41510
Opens 11
Draught Bass Ⓗ
Picturesque inn by beautiful
bay. No food Sun 🅰Q♿🍺🍴

St Helier
5H9

Esplanade
The Esplanade ✆ 22925
Opens 10
Draught Bass Ⓗ
Locals pub. Bar billiards, pool,
darts. No food Sun ♿♿🍺🍴

Lamplighter
Mulcaster Street ✆ 23119
Draught Bass; Bulmer Cider Ⓗ
Warm, gas-lit pub near old
town church. Darts, doms,
crib, cards. Well worth a visit
Q♿ (not Sun)

Pierson Hotel
Royal Square ✆ 22726
Draught Bass Ⓗ
Historic town pub, occasional
live music ♿ (not Sun)

St Martin
5J9

Castle Green Hotel
Gorey ✆ 53103
Draught Bass Ⓖ
Comfortable pub with fine
views. Bar billiards, darts 🅰🍴

The 🅰 symbol denotes a pub
with a real solid fuel fire

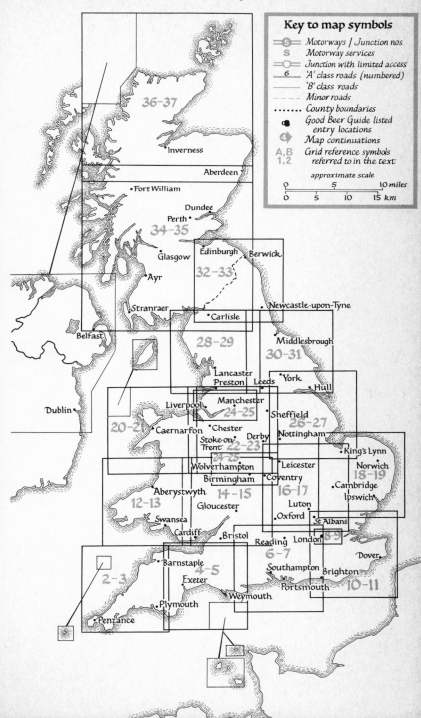

The Good Beer Guide
Map Section

Key to map symbols

⎓5⎓	*Motorways / Junction nos.*
S	*Motorway services*
⎓○⎓	*Junction with limited access*
6	*'A' class roads (numbered)*
——	*'B' class roads*
- - -	*Minor roads*
....	*County boundaries*
●	*Good Beer Guide listed entry locations*
➔	*Map continuations*
A,B 1,2	*Grid reference symbols referred to in the text*

approximate scale

```
0          5          10 miles
0     5      10     15 km
```

36-37

• Inverness

Aberdeen

• Fort William

Dundee
Perth •
34-35

Glasgow   Edinburgh   Berwick
             32-33
Ayr

Stranraer   Newcastle-upon-Tyne

                • Carlisle
Belfast   28-29
                          Middlesbrough
                          30-31

Dublin •   Lancaster •York
                Preston Leeds   • Hull

                Liverpool Manchester
         20-21   24-25
              • Caernarfon • Chester   Sheffield
                                           26-27
                       Stoke-on- Derby Nottingham
                       Trent
                       22-23
                       24-25
                                            • King's Lynn
               Wolverhampton   18-19 Norwich
               Birmingham   • Leicester
       12-13   Coventry   • Cambridge
         Aberystwyth 14-15   16-17   Ipswich
              Gloucester   Luton
         Swansea   Oxford   St Albans
              Cardiff   • Bristol   8-9
                         Reading London
                              6-7   Dover •
                  • Barnstaple   Southampton Brighton
       2-3   Exeter   Portsmouth 10-11
                              Weymouth
              • Plymouth
         • Penzance

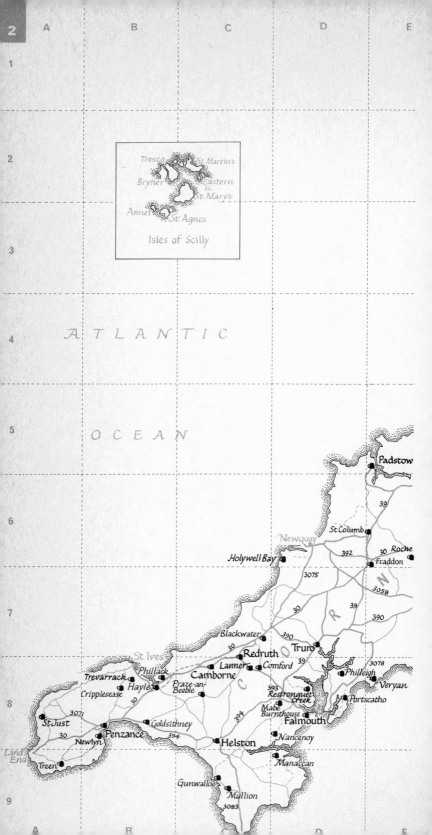

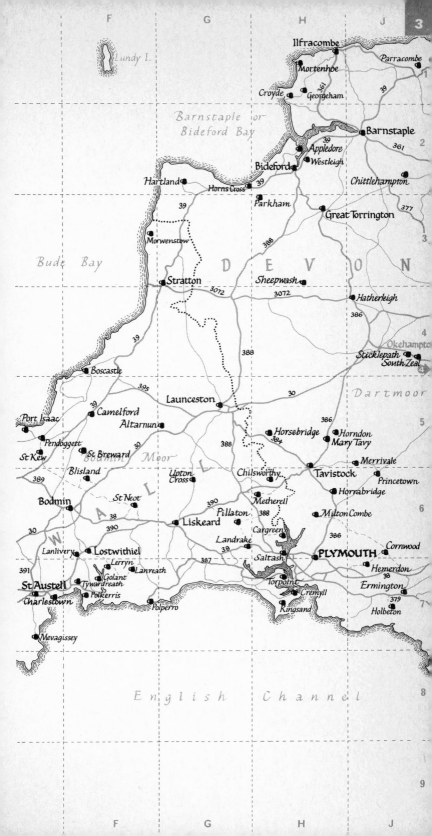

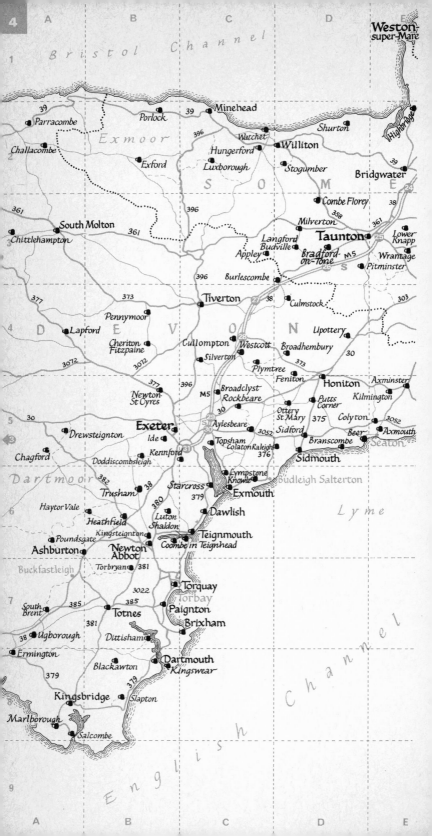

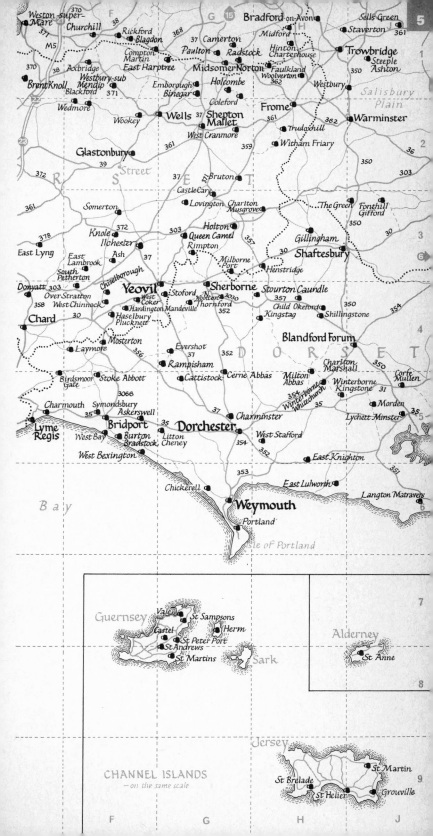

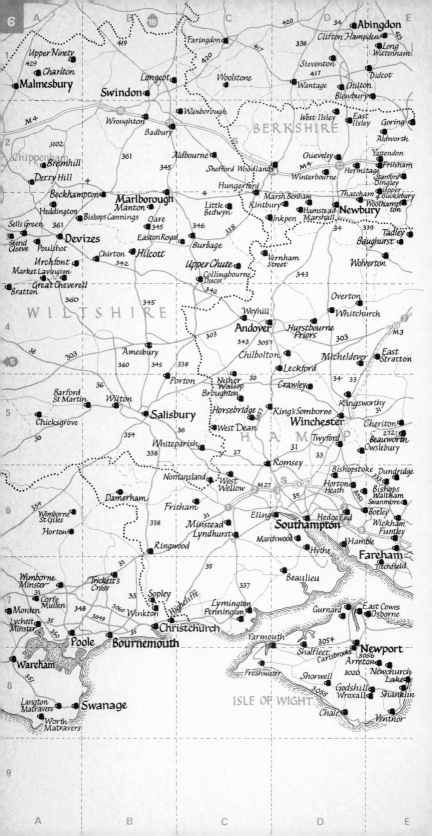

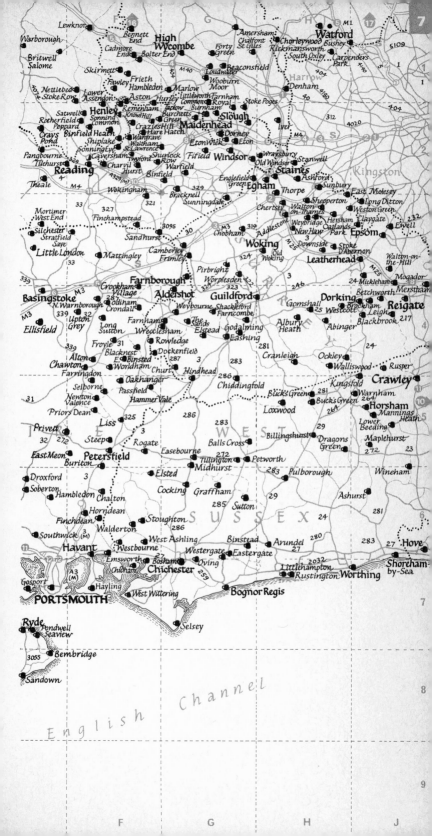

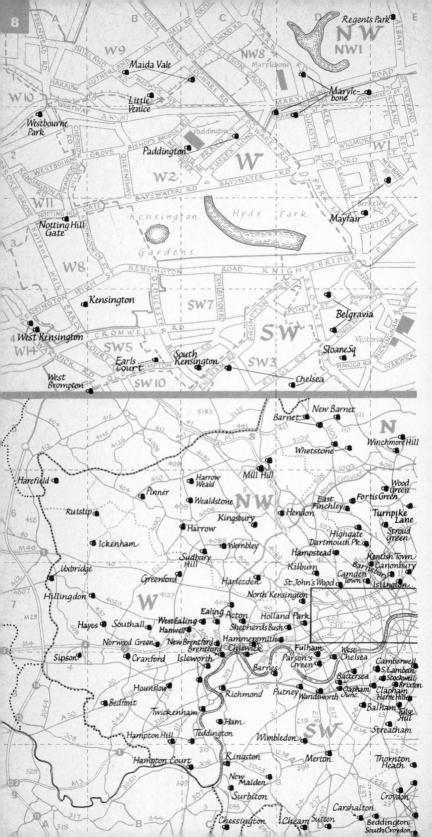

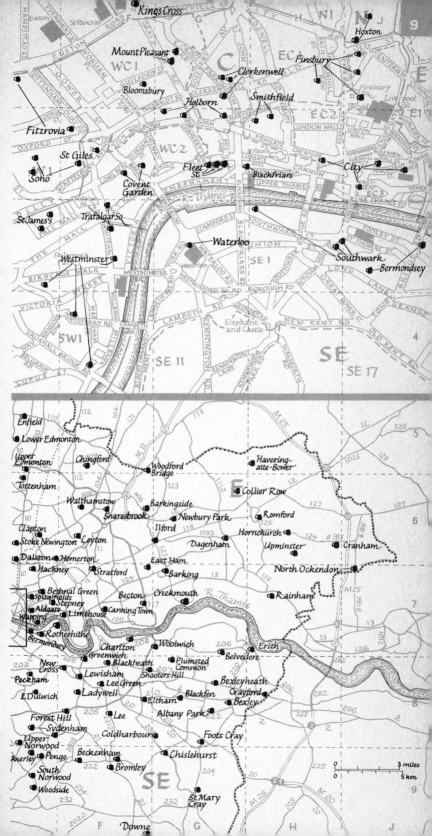

9

Kings Cross
Euston · St Pancras

Hoxton

Mount Pleasant

WC1

Finsbury

EC1

Clerkenwell

Bloomsbury

Smithfield

Holborn

EC2

London Wall

Fitzrovia

WC2

City

St Giles

Fleet St

EC3

Soho

Blackfriars

Covent Garden

St James's

Trafalgar Sq

Waterloo

Southwark

Westminster

SE1

Bermondsey

WESTMINSTER

Elephant and Castle

SW1

SE11

SE17

SE

Enfield

Lower Edmonton

Upper Edmonton

Chingford

Woodford Bridge

Havering-atte-Bower

Tottenham

Collier Row

Walthamstow

Barkingside

Romford

Snaresbrook

Newbury Park

Clapton

Ilford

Hornchurch

Stoke Newington

Leyton

Upminster

Cranham

Dalston

Homerton

Dagenham

Hackney

Stratford

East Ham

North Ockendon

Bethnal Green

Barking

Spitalfields

Becton

Creekmouth

Stepney

Rainham

Aldgate

Limehouse

Canning Town

Wapping

Rotherhithe

Bermondsey

Charlton

Woolwich

Erith

New Cross

Greenwich

Belvedere

Peckham

Blackheath

Plumsted Common

Lewisham

Shooters Hill

Bexleyheath

E Dulwich

Lee Green

Crayford

Ladywell

Eltham

Blackfen

Bexley

Forest Hill

Lee

Albany Park

Sydenham

Coldharbour

Upper Norwood

Foots Cray

Anerley

Penge

Beckenham

Chislehurst

South Norwood

Bromley

Woodside

SE

St Mary Cray

3 miles

5 km

Downe

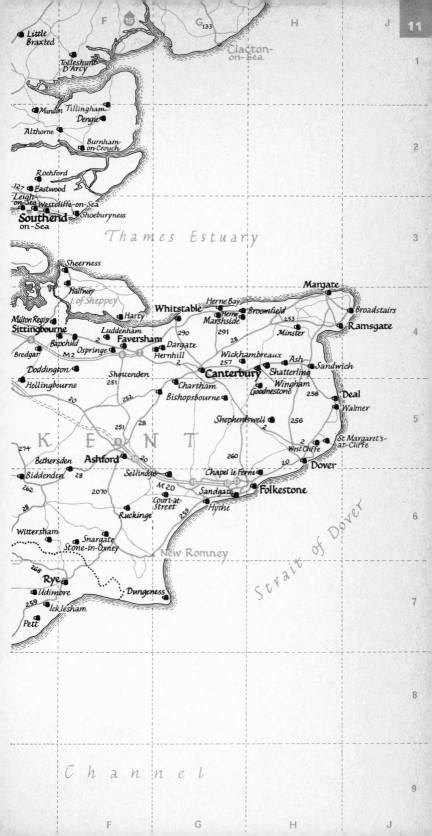

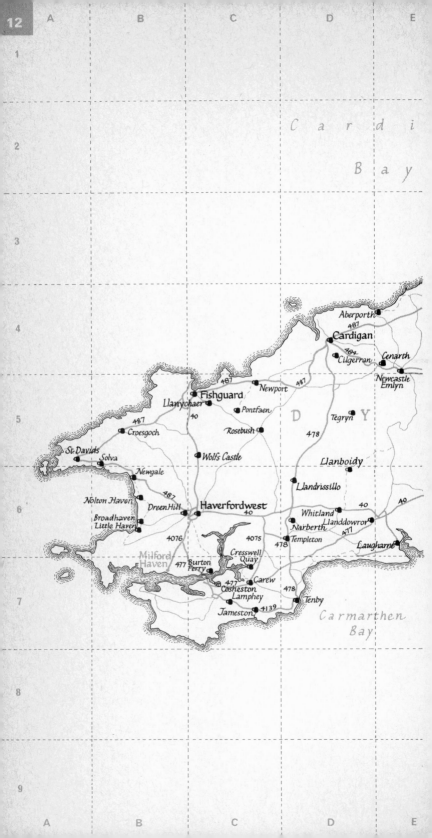

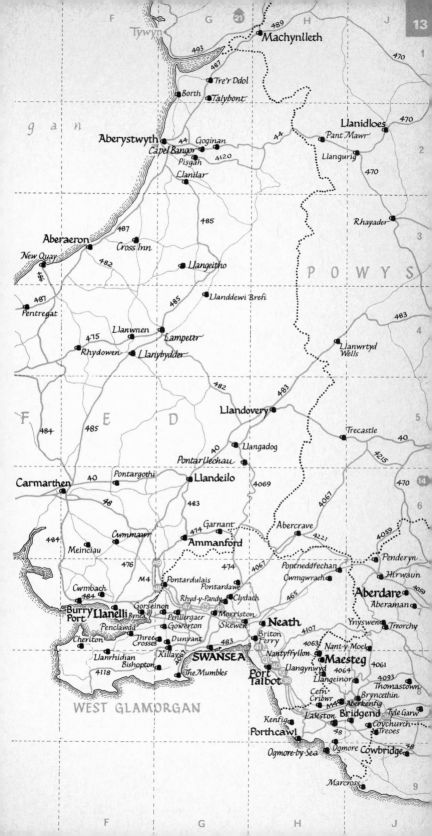

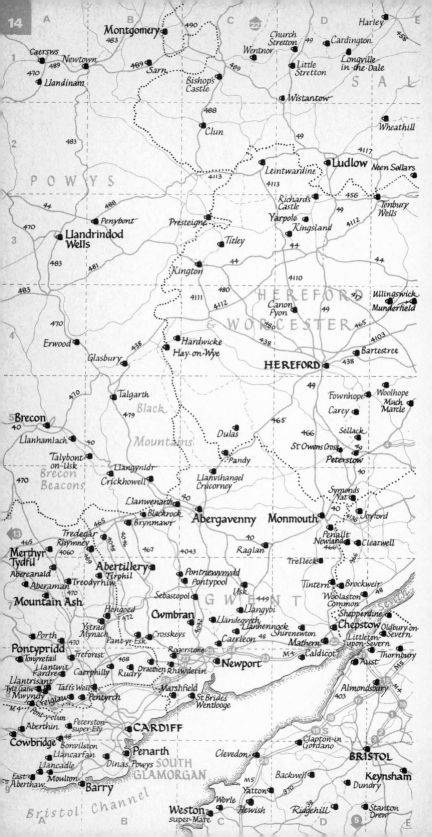

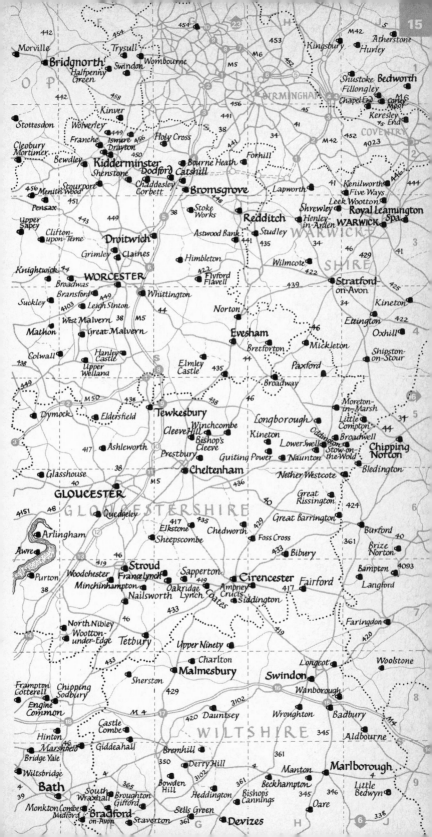

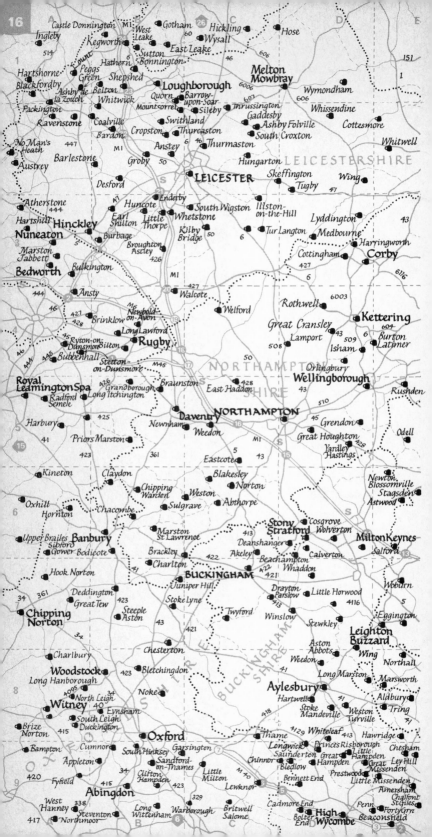

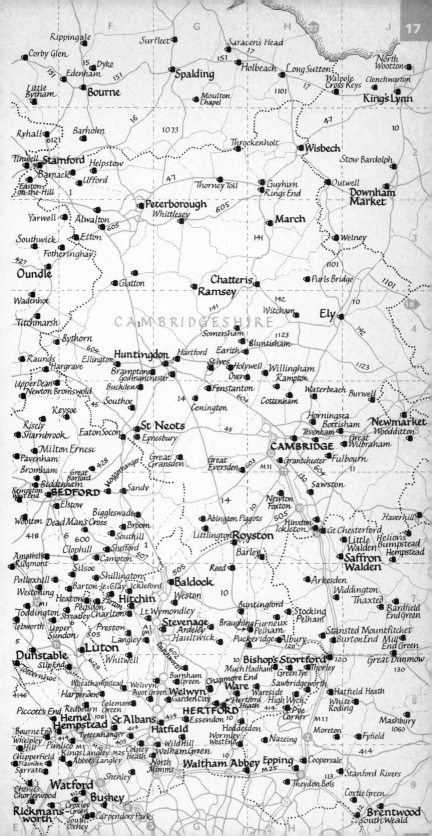

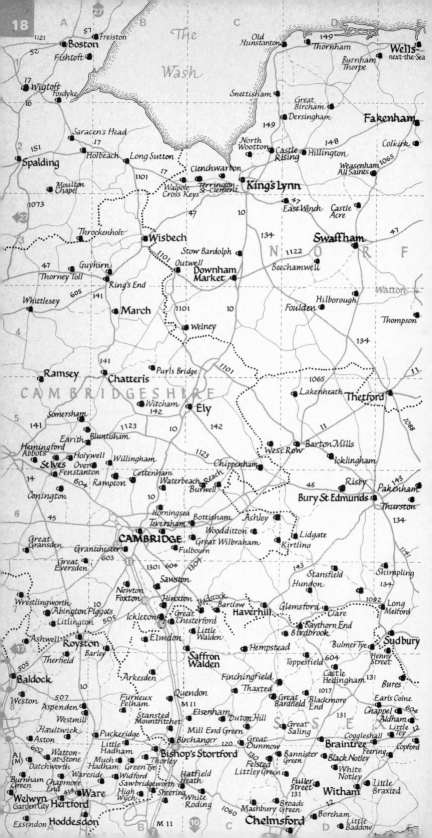

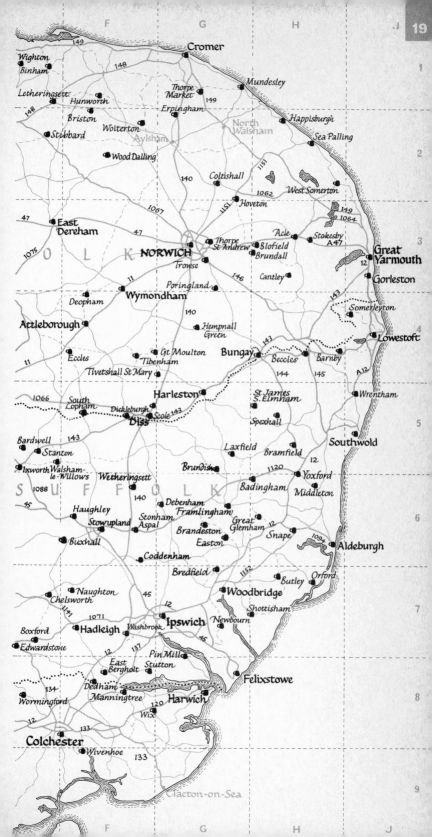

ISLE OF
MAN

A 10

A17
A14   A 13
A3   Sulby   **Ramsey**
Kirk Michael   Maughold
                        A18
            A14   A2

Peel   A3   A 4   Laxey
        St John's   A18
Glenmaye   A1   A2
A27   Crosby
                 Union
                  Mills   **Douglas**

        A 4   A 5 Santon
Port Erin A5   Ballasalla
     Port   Castletown
   St Mary

                        S025
                    Llanfaethlu
                              Anglesey
            Holyhead   *Bodedern*
                          5
                        4080

                              Caernarfon

                                Newborough

                              Llanwnda

                        Bay

                    Clynnog-fawr 499
                                      487

                        Nefyn
                    Morfa
                    Nefyn   497
                          499   497
                              Pwllheli
                        Llanbedrog
                  Abersoch

                        Cardigan

                        Bay

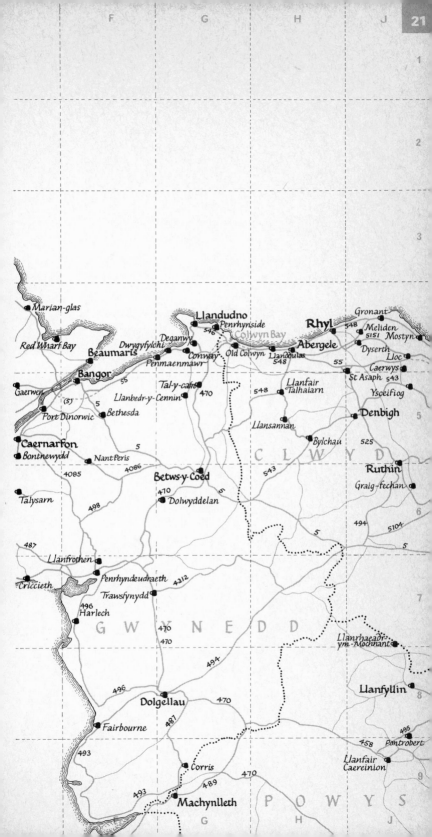

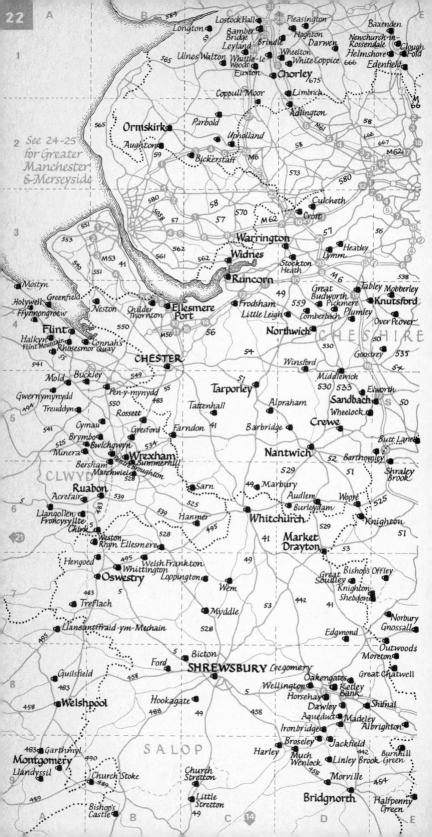

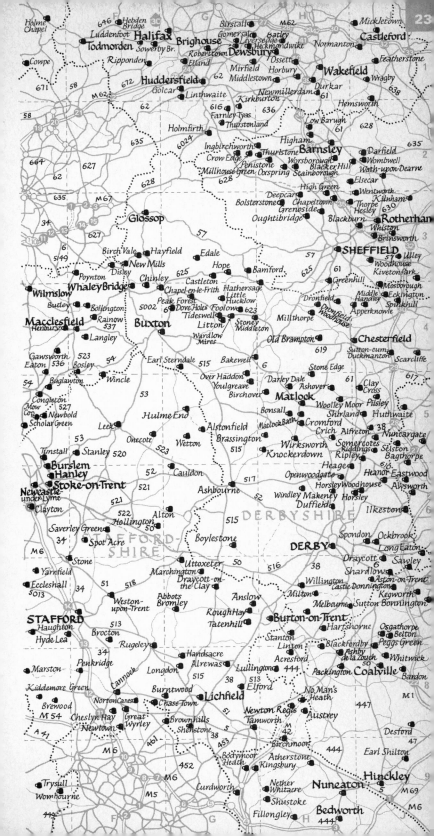

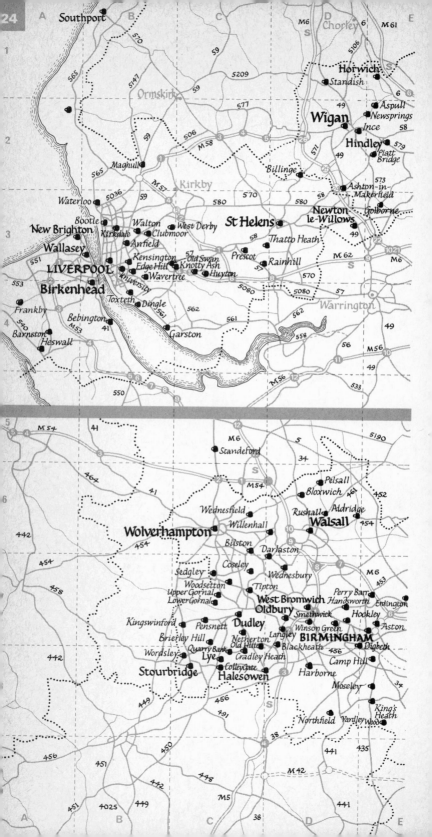

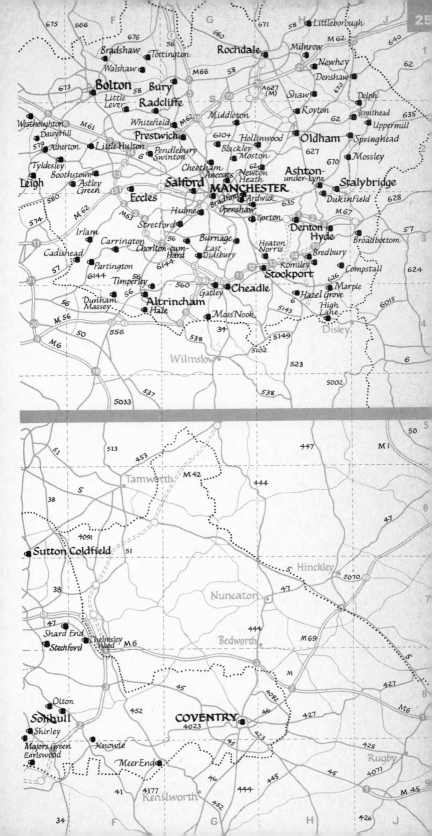

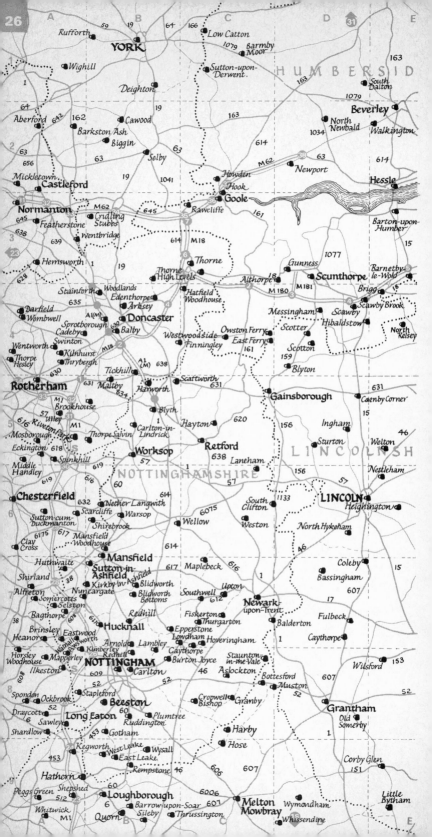

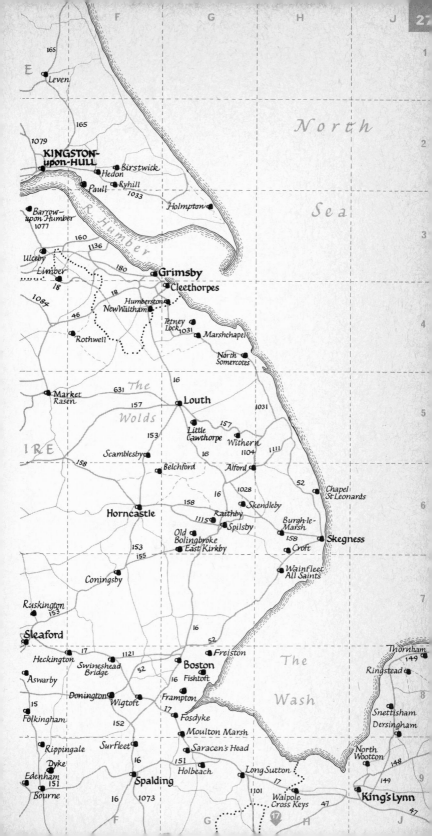

E

F   G   H   J

165

Leven

North

1

165

1079

KINGSTON-
upon-HULL

Birstwick

Hedon   Ryhill

Paull   1033

Holmpton

Sea

Barrow-
upon Humber
1077

R. Humber

2

160

1136

Ulceby

Limber   180

18   **Grimsby**

1084   **Cleethorpes**

Humberston

46   NewWaltham

Rothwell

Tetney
Lock   1031

Marshchapel

North
Somercotes

3

The   16

Market
Rasen   631

157   **Louth**

Wolds

153

Little
Cawthorpe

157

Scamblesby   16   Withern

IRE   158   1104   1111

Belchford   Alford

16   1028

158   Skendleby

52   Chapel
St Leonards

Horncastle   1115   Raithby

Old   Spilsby

Bolingbroke   Burgh-le-
Marsh

East Kirkby   158

153   Croft

155

Coningsby   Wainfleet
All Saints

1031

4

5

6

7

Ruskington

153

Sleaford

16

Heckington   17   1121

Swineshead   52

Aswarby   Bridge

Donington   16

Wigtoft   17

15

Folkingham

152

Rippingale   Surfleet   16

Dyke   151

Edenham   151

Bourne   16   **Spalding**   1073

Freiston

52

Boston

Fishtoft

Frampton

Fosdyke

Moulton Marsh

Saracen's
Head

Holbeach

Long Sutton   17

1101   Walpole
Cross Keys   47

The

Wash

Thornham
149

Ringstead

Snettisham

Dersingham

North
Wootton   148

149

King's Lynn   47

8

9

17

F   G   H   J

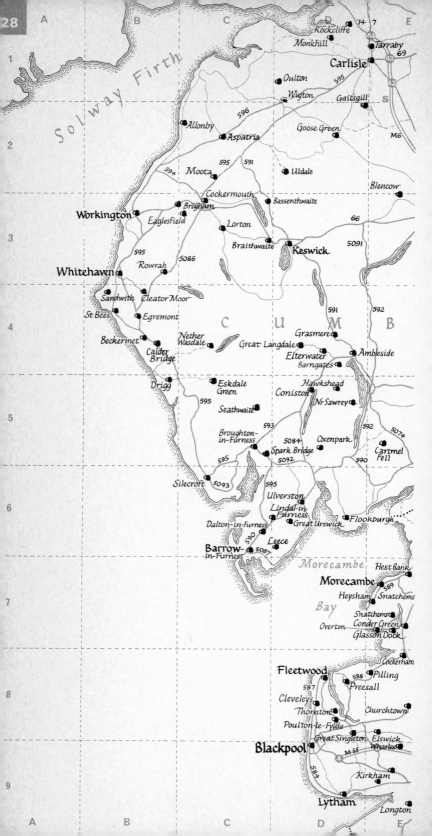

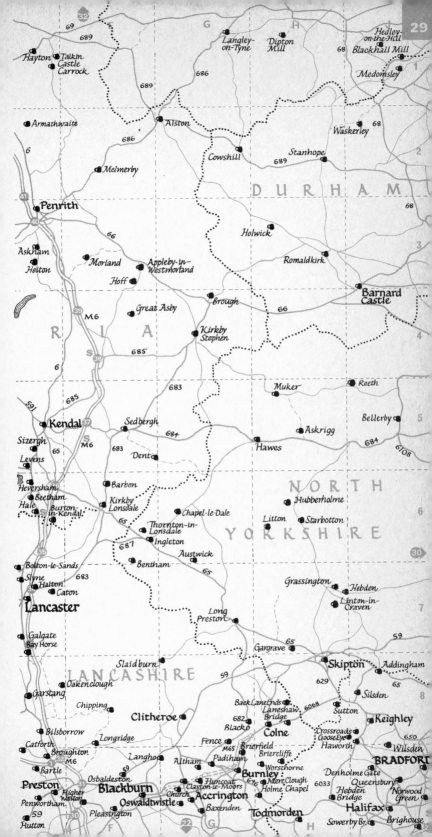

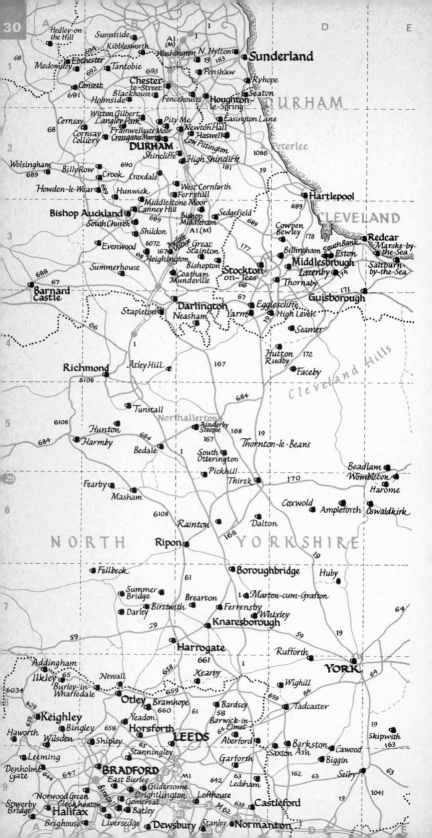

F   G   H   J

1

North

2

Sea

3

Brotton

Port Mulgrave

174

Ugthorpe

Whitby

Danby

171

Sleights

4

Egton
Bridge

Robin Hood's
Bay

North York Moors

Rosedale Abbey

169

Staintondale

Burniston

5

Lastingham

Hutton-
le-Hole

Newton on
Rawcliffe

171

Sinnington

170

64

Scarborough

Kirkbymoorside

Great Edstone

Snainton

64

165

Filey

7

169

64

West Heslerton

Hunmanby

6

Malton

Welburn

Flamborough

64

Langtoft

Rudston

Bridlington

Sledmere

Kilham

166

The Wolds

166

Little Driffield

166

7

166

Stamford Bridge

Low Catton

Skerne

1079

Barmby Moor

164

165

Sutton-on
Derwent

H U M B E R S I D E

163

South Dalton

Leven

8

1079

1035

Arnold

163

North Newbald

Beverley

Aldborough

1174

165

614

Walkington

Howden

M62

Newport

63

1033

Hedon

9

Hook

Hessle

**KINGSTON
upon HULL**

Burstwick

Goole

Paull

27

EDINBURGH
Leith
Musselburgh
198
Dunbar
90
8
Tranent
Haddington
1
71
68
6093
1
70
720
68
1107
7
Dalkeith
68
702
6094
6112
701
Penicuik
7
Durts
701
703
6105
Lauder
697
Peebles
6105
697
72
Galashiels
Coldstream
72
7
6105
6089
698
Melrose
68
Kelso
6091
699
Selkirk
699
Jedburgh
708
7
698
Hawick
68
6088
7
S C O T L A N D
Chevi
(SEE PAGE 35)
68
N O R T H
Falstone
Langholm
Stannersburn
7
74
Gretna
8
75
6071
Twice Brewed
Haltwhistle
69
7
Langley-
69
on-Tyne
Rockcliffe
M6
689
Monkhill
Tarraby
Hayton
Talkin
Castle
Carrock
Carlisle
43
69
686
Allendale
C U M B R I A
595
689
Wigton
M6
Gaitsgill
6
Alston
596
595
29

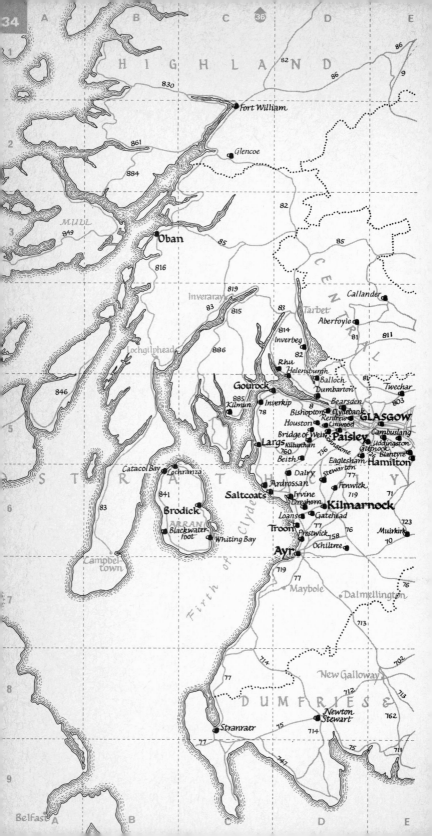

A | B | C | 36 | D | E

1

HIGHLAND
830
86
82
86
9

Fort William

2
861
884
Glencoe

82

3
MULL
849
Oban
85
85
CENTRAL
816
819
Callander
Inveraray
83
815
Tarbet
Aberfoyle
811
4
814
Inverbeg
81
886
82
Rhu
81
Helensburgh
Balloch
Twechar
Gourock
Dumbarton
803
Lochgilphead
885
Bearsden
Kilmun
Inverkip
8
Bishopton
Clydebank
846
78
Renfrew
GLASGOW
Houston
Linwood
Cambuslang
Bridge of Weir
Paisley
Uddingston
Largs
Kilbarchan
736
Gifnock
Blantyre
760
Johnstone
Hamilton
Beith
Eaglesham
Catacol Bay
Lochranza
Dalry
stewarton
77
841
Ardrossan
Fenwick
83
Saltcoats
Irvine
719
Brodick
Dreghorn
Kilmarnock
ARRAN
Loans
Gatehead
723
Blackwater-
Troon
77
Muirkirk
foot
Whiting Bay
Prestwick
158
76
71
Campbel
Ayr
Ochiltree
10
town
719
77
7
Maybole
Dalmellington
76
713
714
702
New Galloway
8
77
712
713
DUMFRIES &
Newton
762
Stewart
Stranraer
75
714
75
711
9
77
747

Belfast A | B | C | D | E

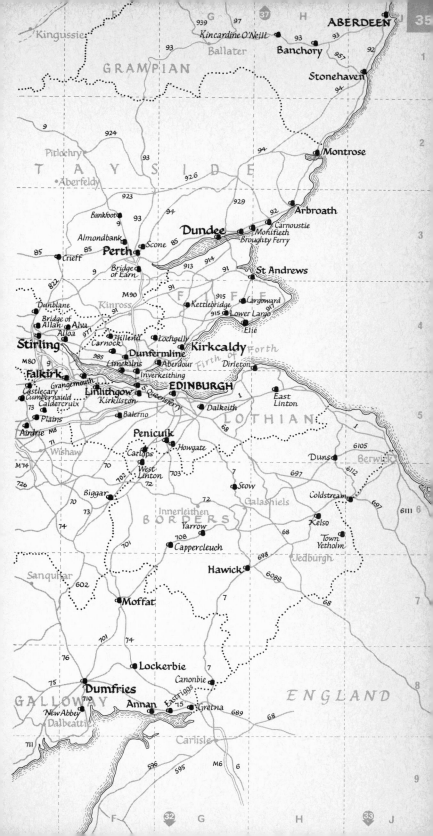

F   G   J

1

ORKNEY
ISLANDS

2

North

3

836

Thurso

836   *882* • *Bower*

897   *Wick*

Sea

4

895

9

5

9

6

Tain

Lossiemouth   *Banff*

Findhorn *Hopeman*   **Fraserburgh**

Cromarty   *981*   *952*

Nairn *96* **Elgin**   *96*   *98*   *92*

Forres   *950*

939   *95*   *97*   *Turriff*

Cawdor   *940*   *941*   *948*

                                        96   *975*

9   Grantown-   *941* *97*   *92*

on-Spey   G R A M P I A N   *Inverurie*   *92*

                                        Alford   *96*   *947*

• *Aviemore*   *939*   *944* *Elvick*   **ABERDEEN**

                                                980   *93*

                        97   *93* *Kincardine O'Neill*

Ballater   **Banchory**   *92*

                                                        957

                        85   *94*   **Stonehaven**

G   H   J

Know Your Landlord! 318

AS a fairly frequent pub-goer for most of my life, I am convinced that the secret of obtaining a good quality pint of beer lies with the landlord, landlady or cellarman of the particular establishment. In the good old days, one had to have a vocation to become a licensee and business thrived on the output of consistently good quality products. Customers, too, were more discerning in their tastes, perhaps because of the lack of misleading advertising. True, there were few temperature-controlled cellars then, which often led to warm beers, but nonetheless, a good landlord overcame that problem by a little extra endeavour.

The introduction of filtered and pasteurised keg beers was seen by the big breweries as a profitable way out of the problem and, backed by mass media misleading advertising, they were able to employ as licensees, any Tom, Dick or Harry who possessed enough loot as a down-payment on the rent of the premises or whose wife possessed a rudimentary knowledge of cookery. Suddenly it became fashionable to own a pub and, with the boost of mass national advertising, earn pots of money with little or no effort involved. The customer was conned into acceptance of an inferior product.

In the early 1970's CAMRA proved conclusively that there was a demand for good, wholesome real ale, instead of gassy, tasteless keg beers. Small independent brewers suddenly found a new lease of life and, through their small family-type estates, were able to produce and serve a genuine good quality product,

and still do, though some licensees still need to be taught the simple art of cellarmanship. The big national brewers, noting the developments, reversed their policies and overnight, flooded their estates with real ale with little or no regard to training licensees in cellarmanship. If the beer went 'off' it was still sold to the customer, who naturally thought little of this so-called 'real ale' and reverted to bland but consistent keg beer. The big brewers conveniently refer to this experience as 'lack of public demand for real ale' and use it as an excuse to continue with their profitable keg-lager promotion.

Far too many licensees these days do not have the 'vocation' I mentioned; others, with proper training, would probably be acceptable. There are also the 'cowboys' who purvey infinite varieties of real ales under the 'free-house' banner at quite exorbitant prices.

Nobody can possibly argue that keg beers are better for one's health than traditional real ale. Provided real ale is properly brewed there is no good reason, except the licensee, why it should not be served up in prime condition to the customer.

A good landlord likes to sell a good quality product to his customer even if he has to put in a little extra effort in the process. He will not add 'wastage' beer or water to the barrel, nor will he allow beer pipes to go uncleaned for weeks or months. There are good landlords about but, sadly, not enough. I hope this Guide will lead you to discover some more worthy holders of the title .... 'licensee'.

Jim Scanlon
CAMRA Chairman

O K. You've read the Good Beer Guide from cover to cover (well almost, the back one's just over the page). You've tried a few of the recommendations. You may even have tried a pint or two. So . . . are you going to join CAMRA, or are we going to have to come round and fit you up with a concrete swimsuit?

Fighting

If you believe in the value of freedom of choice, traditional British pubs and traditional British beer, there's only one thing to do – join the organisation that's fighting to preserve them – CAMRA. We have a full-time staff of only seven people – every other one of our 20,000 plus members is a volunteer, which means that the maximum amount of our income is spent where it matters – campaigning for real ale and real pubs.

Generous

Your £9 membership brings you generous discounts on a wide range of products and books, including this one – the best-selling Good Beer Guide. You also receive a monthly copy of our newspaper 'What's Brewing', a member's handbook and the chance to join in all CAMRA's many activities – socials, sport, foreign travel, brewery visits, beer exhibitions, conferences, etc.

Falling Standards

Above all, though, your subscription enables us to carry on the Campaign on your behalf – fighting *against* brewery and pub closures, falling standards and rising prices; fighting *for* British beer and British pubs.

Don't leave it to others, fill in the form below, send us £9 and we'll not only enrol you as a member . . . we'll let you keep your kneecaps as well!

Full membership £9 Joint husband/wife membership £9 Life membership £90
I/We wish to become members of CAMRA Ltd.. I/We agree to abide by the memorandum and articles of association of the company.
I/We enclose a cheque/p.o. for £9/£90.

Name(s)
Address
Signature(s)

Product (specify colour where appropriate)	Quantity	Price	Amount
Traditional Mirror		£21.50	
Real Beer Mirror		£17.50	
CAMRA Ties: Blue, Brown or Maroon		£4.20	
CAMRA Tea Towels		£1.75	
CAMRA Bar Towels		£1.50	

All the above prices include p&p

£ _____

Send to CAMRA Ltd. 34 Alma Road, St Albans, Herts. AL1 3BW. Make cheques payable to CAMRA Ltd and allow 3 weeks for delivery.
In addition to the products listed, CAMRA HQ carries a large stock of local beer guides, publications and products. SAE to CAMRA, 34 Alma Road, St Albans, Herts, AL1 3BW, for an up-to-date list.

Name	
Address	
Post Code	

New Pub Submission

Pub Name	
Address	
Reason	
Please supply your name and address above	